Essentials of
Organization Theory and Design

Essentials of Organization Theory and Design

Richard L. Daft
Vanderbilt University

SOUTH-WESTERN College Publishing

An International Thomson Publishing Company

Publishing Team Director: John Szilagyi
Developmental Editor: Esther Craig
Production Editor: Kelly Keeler
Production House: DPS Associates, Inc.
Cover Design: Paul Neff
Marketing Manager: Steve Scoble

1 2 3 4 5 WST 1 0 9 8 7

Printed in the United States of America

ISBN: 0-538-87927-0

Library of Congress Cataloging-in-Publication Data

Daft, Richard L.
    Essentials of organization theory and design / by Richard Daft.
        p.   cm.
    Includes index.
    ISBN 0-538-87927-0
    1. Organization.   2. Organizational effectiveness.   I. Title.
HD31.D132   1997
658.1--dc21   97-11016
                                             CIP

International Thomson Publishing

South-Western College Publishing is an ITP Company. The ITP trademark is used under license.

Contents

Preface

The world of organizations is changing rapidly, and so is the teaching of organization theory. Many instructors are teaching courses in organization theory and organization design that do not require a full text with all teaching materials and ancillary support. Students can use a shorter text to learn organization design essentials within the context of a course in which the instructor provides outside cases, readings, and videos. This essentials book offers instructors greater flexibility in selecting their own cases, experiential exercises, or other readings to supplement the text fundamentals. This is a valuable alternative to a full-service textbook because it allows instructors to tailor their courses to meet a variety of teaching objectives.

The purpose of this essentials textbook is to include key, recent, and relevant concepts and models with contemporary examples to provide an accurate and concise view of organization theory and design. The examples interwoven through the text illustrate how companies are coping with today's turbulent, competitive, international environment. Significant trends in organization design, such as empowerment of employees, reengineering, horizontal structures, breaking down barriers within and between organizations, new technologies, and changing corporate cultures are thoroughly covered. In addition, many recent ideas are brought together in the final two chapters. Chapter 14 describes recent approaches toward interorganizational collaborations and evolving corporate ecosystems. Chapter 15 integrates materials from previous chapters and describes organizational efforts to move toward the emerging phenomenon called the learning organization.

Although this text focuses on the essential elements of organization theory and design, it also provides learning aids for the students. Each chapter begins with a series of questions for students to keep in mind as they read the chapter. Frequent exhibits help students visualize material and relationships among concepts. Each chapter closes with a brief summary of key issues and a list of review questions. Overall, this text provides the essentials needed to provide a solid organization theory foundation.

I want to thank Rick Leyh for suggesting this text and providing the motivation for it. In addition, Esther Craig, Developmental Editor, did a great job of pulling together all the things needed to produce this book.

As always, I want to give special thanks to my editorial associate, Pat Lane. Pat provided enormous help in identifying and pulling together the true essentials of organization theory and design needed for this text. Pat also skillfully drafted materials on a variety of cases and topics, and did an outstanding job with the copyedited manuscripts and page proofs.

Richard Daft
Nashville, TN

part one

Introduction to Organizations

1

chapter one
Organizations and
Organization Theory

1

chapter one

Organizations and Organization Theory

While reading this chapter, think about your answers to the following questions:

- What is an organization and why are organizations important to society?

- What are some of the common challenges faced by managers of today's organizations?

- What are the specific structural and contextual dimensions that define organization design?

- When an organization shifts from a modern to a postmodern organization paradigm, what types of changes are involved?

Twenty years ago, owning stock in IBM was like owning a gold mine. The overwhelming success of the IBM PC sent the company's already high profits soaring, and IBM was ranked as the world's largest company in terms of stock market value. Big Blue, as the company was known, was creating jobs around the world; its workforce ultimately swelling to 407,000.

A decade later, those who had invested their lives—or their money—in a company they thought could never fail watched long-cherished dreams go down the drain. The company went from earning a $6 billion profit to reporting a whopping $5 billion loss two years later. IBM stock lost more than $75 billion in value, an amount equal to the gross domestic product of Sweden. IBM went from literally being at the top of the world to fighting for its life, and everyone associated with the once-great company suffered. Yet, on the eve of the 21st century, IBM has shifted into growth mode again, with some hot-selling new products, growing profits, and rebounding share prices. The shifting fortunes of IBM represent a classic story of organizational decline and renewal.

The introduction of the System/360 line of mainframe computers in the mid-1960s sealed IBM's leadership in the computer industry. Yet many believe this marked the beginning of IBM's decline as well. Retired IBM executive Malcolm Robinson, who rose to a senior post in IBM Europe, said, "The scale of the [System/360 project] created a complexity in the business that almost couldn't be handled. It was chaos for awhile. So an organization had to be created to bring things under control and make sure that kind of breakdown never happened again. And that really may have been what made the bureaucracy take off."[1]

Many mistakes made by IBM executives were caused by too many people and too many meetings. Decisions that should have been made quickly in response to changes in the computer market were delayed or ignored because of the cumbersome management system that demanded everything be done "the IBM way." The company choked on the bureaucratic culture and lost the vision and flexibility to adapt to changes in the industry.

IBM was late getting into the personal computer market, choosing to steer what company leaders in the 1970s thought was a safe course—preserving the company's mainframe profits. By the time IBM decided to enter the personal computer game in earnest, the death knell was already starting to toll on profits from mainframes. And although the IBM PC was an instant success, the PC war was already lost. The company failed to take advantage of new technologies and opportunities for collaboration with fledgling companies such as Microsoft. In addition, executives refused to accept that the values and policies of the past—the caution, the obsessive training of employees, a focus on following rather than anticipating customer needs, and a guarantee of lifetime employment—were no longer effective in the fast-paced, rapidly changing world in which the company was operating. When chairman John Akers resigned in 1993, the media had a field day, further tarnishing IBM's once-shining image.

IBM's current chairman and CEO, Louis V. Gerstner, Jr., stepped into this mess with the determination to bring back the shine by creating a culture in which IBM people waste fewer opportunities, minimize bureaucracy, and put the good of the company ahead of their separate divisions. In his first year on the job, he revamped IBM's finances, brought in outsiders to head up several critical divisions, and dramatically altered financial incentives for top executives, basing about 75 percent of their variable pay on the overall performance of the company. Today, sweaters, chinos, and loafers have replaced starched white shirts and suits in many IBM offices, an outward symbol that the company's stiff bureaucratic culture has given way to a more relaxed, adaptable one. Gerstner, known for his sometimes lightning-quick decisions, dismantled a top-management committee that often stifled action and began talking to employees and customers directly through e-mail.

IBM suffered by missing opportunities and delaying action; Gerstner wants to make sure the same thing doesn't happen in the new networking era. He's pulling together resources from all over the giant company and focusing them on the goal of bringing customers all sorts of network computing services. Gerstner envisions a future in which major corporations will buy computing power and applications software the way they buy electric service, never even knowing or caring where the computer that does the work is located. Can his wide-ranging vision once again put IBM at the top of the computer world? Or has that world been altered so dramatically that IBM can never catch up? One thing is certain—Lou Gerstner isn't afraid of change: "If the organization doesn't work right one way, we'll change it."[2] As Gerstner continues his efforts to lead the biggest corporate transformation of all time, the world will be watching.[3]

Welcome to the real world of organization theory. IBM managers were deeply involved in organization theory each day of their working lives, but they never realized it. Company managers didn't fully understand how the organization related to the environment or how it should function internally. Familiarity with organization theory can help current IBM managers analyze and diagnose what is happening to the company and the changes needed to turn the company around. Organization theory gives us the tools to explain what happened to IBM. Organization theory also helps us understand what may happen in the future so we can manage our organizations more effectively.

ORGANIZATION THEORY IN ACTION

Topics

Each of the topics to be covered in this book is illustrated in the IBM case. Consider, for example, IBM's failure to respond to or control such elements as customers, suppliers, and competitors in the fast-paced external environment; its inability to coordinate departments and design control systems that promoted efficiency; slow decision making, such as delaying action on exploiting the potential of new technology; handling the problem of large size; the absence of a forceful top management team that allowed IBM to drift further and further into chaos; and an outmoded corporate culture that strangled change efforts. These are the subjects with which organization theory is concerned. Organization theory can also help Lou Gerstner find the right organizational structure and strategy to revitalize the giant company.

Of course, organization theory is not limited to IBM. Every organization, every manager in every organization, is involved in organization theory. Johnsonville Foods, a Sheboygan, Wisconsin sausage maker, turned a floundering family business into a dynamic fast-growing company by reorganizing into self-managed teams. Hewlett-Packard Company—which was suffering from some of the same problems as IBM in the 1980s—went through a major, highly successful reorganization using concepts based in organization theory. By the mid-1990s, HP was one of the fastest growing companies in the computer industry. Eastman Kodak Company is undergoing a similar structural transformation, as leaders struggle to turn an organization characterized by rigid bureaucracy, indecisive management, and demoralized workers into one marked by teamwork, focus on the customer, and willingness to take risks.[4]

Organization theory draws lessons from these organizations and makes those lessons available to students and managers. The story of IBM's decline is important because it demonstrates that even large, successful organizations are vulnerable, that lessons are not learned automatically, and that organizations are only as strong as their decision makers. The stories of Johnsonville Foods, Hewlett-Packard, Eastman Kodak, and IBM also illustrate that organizations are not static; they continuously adapt to shifts in the external environment. Today, many companies are facing the need to transform themselves into dramatically different organizations because of new challenges in the environment.

Current Challenges

Research into hundreds of organizations provides the knowledge base to make IBM and other organizations more effective. For example, challenges facing organizations on the eve of the 21st century are quite different from those of the 1970s and 1980s, and thus the concept of organizations and organization theory is evolving. For one thing, the world is changing more rapidly than ever before. In a recent survey, coping with rapid change emerged as the most common problem for managers and organizations today.[5] Some specific challenges IBM and other organizations face are global competition, the need for organizational renewal, finding strategic advantage, managing changing employee relationships, supporting diversity, and maintaining high standards of ethics and social responsibility.

Global Competition.   Every company, large and small, faces international competition on its home turf at the same time it confronts the need to be competitive in international markets. After Japan's economic bubble burst in the early 1990s, many American managers thought Japanese companies were no longer a threat. However, Japanese leaders are quietly rebuilding their recession-battered companies, once again gaining a competitive edge in speed, quality, and efficiency.[6] Today's managers also deal with increasing global interdependence, with products, services, capital, and human resources crossing borders at a dizzying pace. It's difficult to tell these days which country a product actually comes from—your Mercury Tracer may have come from Mexico, and a neighbor's Nissan may have been built in Tennessee. A Gap polo shirt may be made from cloth cut in the U.S. but sewn by workers in Honduras. Eat an all-American Whopper and you've just purchased from a British company.[7] At the McDonald's in Cracow, the burgers come from a Polish plant, partly owned by Chicago-based OSI Industries, the onions come from Fresno, California, the buns from a production and distribution center near Moscow, and the potatoes from a plant in Aldrup, Germany.[8] In the face of this growing interdependence, companies such as IBM and Ford are working to globalize their management structures.

Organizational Renewal. Companies throughout the United States and Canada face the formidable task of reinventing themselves due to dramatic economic and social changes that have forever altered the playing field and the rules for business success. Never before have so many companies across an array of industries simultaneously faced such a challenge. The patterns of behavior and attitude that were once successful no longer work, yet new patterns are just emerging. As one management scholar put it, "Most managers today have the feeling that they are flying the airplane at the same time they are building it."[9]

One of the hottest trends in recent years is called *reengineering,* a radical redesign of business processes that can lead to big results—and usually big layoffs. Organization structures are flatter, with middle management being eliminated and teams of employees empowered to make decisions. The concept of teamwork is a fundamental change in the way work is organized, as companies recognize that the best way to meet the challenges of higher quality, faster service, and total customer satisfaction is through an aligned and coordinated effort by motivated workers. At the Frito-Lay plant in Lubbock, Texas, team members handle everything from potato processing to equipment maintenance. In addition, the team has the authority to select new hires, determine crew scheduling, and discipline team members who aren't pulling their load.[10] Teamwork and empowerment of employees are key elements in companies that are shifting to what has been called the learning organization, an organization in which everyone is engaged in identifying and solving problems, enabling the organization to continuously experiment, improve, and increase its capability. Changing employee behaviors and attitudes is key to the continuous organizational renewal needed in today's rapidly changing world.[11]

Strategic Advantage. What still matters most for an organization to remain successful is producing results for customers—having a product or service that people want and getting it to them quickly at a competitive price.[12] Canadian and U.S. companies have made dramatic improvements in product and service quality over the past two decades. Although quality and cost are still important, the distinguishing competitive issue today is how fast products and services can be delivered to customers. In his efforts to revitalize IBM, one of Lou Gerstner's top priorities is getting products to market faster than competitors. The giant electronics operation of 3M in Austin, Texas, cut its product development time from two years to about two months. Through aggressive use of new information technology, GTE Telephone Operations managers reduced the time it takes to complete a customer order from four days to less than two hours.

Information technology facilitates communication and group formation in whatever way is needed to accomplish tasks or projects. Technology dramatically flattens organization structures, so that there may be hundreds of far-flung sites, such as stores or offices, all transmitting information to a single headquarters.[13] New information technology also empowers employees, giving them access to complete information, which enables them to get the job done in less time than if they had to solicit information from superiors or colleagues.

Employee Relationships. The demand for speed and advances in information technology also play a role in another challenge facing today's workers and organizations. As companies become more flexible, employees become more flexible as well. At IBM's Cranford, New Jersey, sales office, 600 sales representatives do most of their work on the road or from home via modem. Gone are the fancy offices and chats around the water cooler. "This isn't about importance, about epaulets," says manager Duke Mitchell. "It's about what you get done."[14] At the start of 1996, 9.2 million Americans were defined as telecommuters, and the number is predicted to triple within the next 15 to 20 years.[15]

Working one's way up the career ladder has become a thing of the past as work is being repackaged to meet new economic realities. Managers spend more time moving along a horizontal ladder than a vertical one, as strong project managers become increasingly important in flatter organizations. There is no longer a single career path, but various paths: the entrepreneurial path, the small business path, temporary and contract work, and a multitude of freelancing opportunities.[16] Careers may be defined less by companies than by professions as more people become permanent freelancers or contract workers. In this shifting work environment, organizations are finding new ways to motivate and reward workers, provide needed coordination and information flow, and direct and control activities to meet organizational goals.

Diversity. Diversity is a fact of life that no organization can afford to ignore. The workforce—as well as the customer base—is changing in terms of age, gender, race, national origin, sexual orientation, and physical ability. Estimates are that by the year 2000 only 15 percent of new entrants to the workforce will be white males.[17] Recent studies also project that in the 21st century Asian Americans, African Americans, and Hispanics will make up 85 percent of U.S. population growth and constitute about 30 percent of the total workforce.[18] The growing diversity of the workforce brings a variety of challenges, such as maintaining a strong corporate culture while supporting diversity, balancing work and family concerns, and coping with the conflict brought about by varying cultural styles. For example, Service Merchandise, in Nashville, Tennessee, wisely hired about a dozen Hispanic workers to answer calls from Spanish-speaking customers. But the company became embroiled in a serious employee-rights controversy by dictating that the workers could use their native language only while on the phone with customers or in the break room for lunch.[19]

People from diverse ethnic and cultural backgrounds offer varying styles, and organizations must learn to welcome and incorporate this diversity into the upper ranks. For example, recent research has indicated that women's style of doing business may hold important lessons for success in the emerging world of the 21st century. Yet the glass ceiling persists, keeping women from reaching positions of top leadership.[20]

Ethics and Social Responsibility. Ethics and social responsibility have become hot topics in corporate America. Companies of all sizes are rushing to adopt codes of ethics, and most are also developing other policies and structures that encourage ethical conduct. Organizations get into trouble when they fail to pay attention to ethical issues in the blind pursuit of making money. For example, under pressure from CEO Dan Gill to maintain Bausch & Lomb's double-digit sales and earnings growth, managers resorted to inflating revenues by faking sales, shipping products that customers never ordered, and accepting cash and third-party checks that may have indirectly helped launder drug money. After the juggling act at B&L's Hong Kong division began to unravel, a full-scale investigation was launched and the widespread corruption ultimately led to the company's financial downfall.[21]

More companies are recognizing the benefits of contributing to the community. St. Paul Companies, a major insurance company that tops the list of *Business Ethics'* one hundred most socially responsible companies, gave $2.5 million for a new Science Museum of Minnesota and provides numerous employee programs, such as an on-site daycare facility, which leaders believe attracts better workers. Campbell's Soup Company has for more than two decades sponsored the Camden Summer Program, which provides educational, recreational, and employment opportunities to young people.[22] The public is tired of unethical and socially irresponsible business practices, and organizations will increasingly face the challenge of maintaining high standards in this area.

PURPOSE OF THIS CHAPTER

The purpose of this chapter is to explore the nature of organizations and organization theory today. Organization theory has developed from the systematic study of organizations by scholars. Concepts are obtained from living, ongoing organizations. Organization theory can be very practical, as illustrated in the IBM case. It helps people understand, diagnose, and respond to emerging organizational needs and problems.

The next section begins with a formal definition of organization and then explores introductory concepts for describing and analyzing organizations. The following section discusses the scope and nature of organization theory more fully and looks at some of the changes occurring in today's organizations. The chapter closes with a brief overview of the important themes to be covered in this book.

WHAT IS AN ORGANIZATION?

Organizations are hard to see. We see outcroppings, such as a tall building or a computer workstation or a friendly employee; but the whole organization is vague and abstract, and may be scattered among several locations. We know organizations are there because they touch us every day. Indeed, they are so common we take them for granted. We hardly notice that we are born in a hospital, have our birth records registered in a government agency, are educated in schools and universities, are raised on food produced on corporate farms, are treated by doctors engaged in a joint practice, buy a house built by a construction company and sold by a real estate agency, borrow money from a bank, turn to police and fire departments when trouble erupts, use moving companies to change residences, receive an array of benefits from government agencies, spend forty hours a week working in an organization, and are even laid to rest by an undertaker.[23]

Definition

Organizations as diverse as a church, a hospital, and the International Business Machines Corporation have characteristics in common. The definition used in this book to describe organizations is as follows: **organizations** (1) are social entities that (2) are goal directed, (3) are designed as deliberately structured and coordinated activity systems, and that (4) are linked to the external environment.

The key element of an organization is not a building or a set of policies and procedures; organizations are made up of people and their relationships with one another. An organization exists when people interact with one another to perform essential functions that help attain goals. Recent trends in management recognize the importance of human resources, with most new approaches designed to empower employees with greater opportunities to learn and contribute as they work together toward common goals. Managers deliberately structure and coordinate organizational resources to achieve the organization's purpose. However, even though work may be structured into separate departments or sets of activities, most organizations today are striving for greater horizontal coordination of work activities, often using teams of employees from different functional areas to work together on projects. Boundaries between departments as well as those between organizations are becoming more flexible and diffuse as companies face the need to respond to changes in the external environment more rapidly. An organization cannot exist without interacting with customers, suppliers, competitors, and other elements of the external environment. Today, some companies are even cooperating with their competitors, sharing information and technology to their mutual advantage.

Importance of Organizations

Organizations are all around us and shape our lives in many ways. But what contributions do organizations make? Why are they important? Exhibit 1.1 lists seven reasons organizations are important to you and to society. First, organizations bring together resources to accomplish specific goals. Consider the 1996 Summer Olympics. After Atlanta won the bid to host the games, the Atlanta Committee for the Olympic Games (ACOG) had to pull together $1.7 billion, thousands of staff members and volunteers, security and sanitation services, venues for the various activities, computer technology and broadcasting services, and many other types of resources, all directed toward the goal of presenting the Olympics without any city or state support.[24]

Organizations also produce goods and services that customers want at a competitive price. Companies look for innovative ways to produce and distribute goods and services more efficiently. One way is through the use of modern manufacturing technology and new information technology. Redesigning organizational structures and management practices can also contribute to increased efficiency. Organizations create a drive for innovation rather than a reliance on standard products and outmoded ways of doing things. The trend toward the learning organization reflects the desire to improve in all areas. Computer-aided design and manufacturing and new information technology also help promote innovation.

1. Bring together resources to achieve desired goals and outcomes
2. Produce goods and services efficiently
3. Facilitate innovation
4. Use modern manufacturing and computer-based technology
5. Adapt to and influence a changing environment
6. Create value for owners, customers, and employees
7. Accommodate ongoing challenges of diversity, ethics, career patterns, and the motivation and coordination of employees

Exhibit 1.1

Importance of Organizations

Organizations adapt to and influence a rapidly changing environment. Some large companies have entire departments charged with monitoring the external environment and finding ways to adapt to or influence that environment. One of the most significant changes in the external environment today is globalization. In an effort to influence the environment, for example, Coca-Cola entered into a joint venture with Romania's largest bottler of soft drinks, Ci-Co S.A., to be more competitive with Pepsi in newly opened Eastern European markets.[25]

Through all of these activities, organizations create value for their owners, customers, and employees. Managers need to understand which parts of the operation create value and which parts do not—a company can be profitable only when the value it creates is greater than the cost of resources. McDonald's made a thorough study of how to use its core competencies to create better value for customers. The study resulted in the introduction of Extra Value Meals and the decision to open restaurants in different locations, such as inside Wal-Mart and Sears stores.[26] Finally, organizations have to cope with and accommodate today's challenges of workforce diversity, growing concerns over ethics and social responsibility, and changing career patterns, as well as find effective ways to motivate employees to work together to accomplish organizational goals.

Organizations shape our lives, and well-informed managers can shape organizations. A systematic study and understanding of organization theory enables managers to design organizations to function more effectively.

DIMENSIONS OF ORGANIZATION DESIGN

One important step for understanding organizations is to look at dimensions that describe specific organizational design traits. These dimensions describe organizations much the same way that personality and physical traits describe people.

Organizational dimensions fall into two types: structural and contextual, which are illustrated in Exhibit 1.2. **Structural dimensions** provide labels to describe the internal characteristics of an organization. They create a basis for

Exhibit 1.2

Interacting Contextual and Structural Dimensions of Organization Design

measuring and comparing organizations. **Contextual dimensions** characterize the whole organization, including its size, technology, environment, and goals. They describe the organizational setting that influences and shapes the structural dimensions. Contextual dimensions can be confusing because they represent both the organization and the environment. Contextual dimensions can be envisioned as a set of overlapping elements that underlie an organization's structure and work processes. To understand and evaluate organizations, one must examine both structural and contextual dimensions.[27] These dimensions of organization design interact with one another and can be adjusted to accomplish the purposes listed earlier in Exhibit 1.1.

Structural Dimensions

1. *Formalization* pertains to the amount of written documentation in the organization. Documentation includes procedures, job descriptions, regulations, and policy manuals. These written documents describe behavior and activities. Formalization is often measured by simply counting the number of pages of documentation within the organization. Large state universities, for example, tend to be high on formalization because they have several volumes of written rules for such things as registration, dropping and adding classes, student associations, dormitory governance, and financial assistance. A small, family-owned business, in contrast, may have almost no written rules and would be considered informal.
2. *Specialization* is the degree to which organizational tasks are subdivided into separate jobs. If specialization is extensive, each employee performs only a narrow range of tasks. If specialization is low, employees perform a wide range of tasks in their jobs. Specialization is sometimes referred to as the *division of labor.*
3. *Standardization* is the extent to which similar work activities are performed in a uniform manner. In a highly standardized organization like McDonald's, work content is described in detail, and similar work is performed the same way at all locations.
4. *Hierarchy of authority* describes who reports to whom and the span of control for each manager. The hierarchy is depicted by the vertical lines on an organization chart, as illustrated in Exhibit 1.3. The hierarchy is related to *span of control* (the number of employees reporting to a supervisor). When spans of control are narrow, the hierarchy tends to be tall. When spans of control are wide, the hierarchy of authority will be shorter.
5. *Complexity* refers to the number of activities or subsystems within the organization. Complexity can be measured along three dimensions: vertical, horizontal, and spatial. Vertical complexity is the number of levels in the hierarchy. Horizontal complexity is the number of job titles or departments existing horizontally across the organization. Spatial complexity is the number of geographical locations. The organization in Exhibit 1.3 has a vertical complexity of five levels. The horizontal complexity can be calculated as either thirty-four job titles or seven major departments. Spatial complexity is low because the organization is located in one place.
6. *Centralization* refers to the hierarchical level that has authority to make a decision. When decision making is kept at the top level, the organization is centralized. When decisions are delegated to lower organizational levels, it is decentralized. Organizational decisions that might be centralized or

Exhibit 1.3

Organization Chart Illustrating the Hierarchy of Authority and the Structural Complexity for a Community Job Training Program

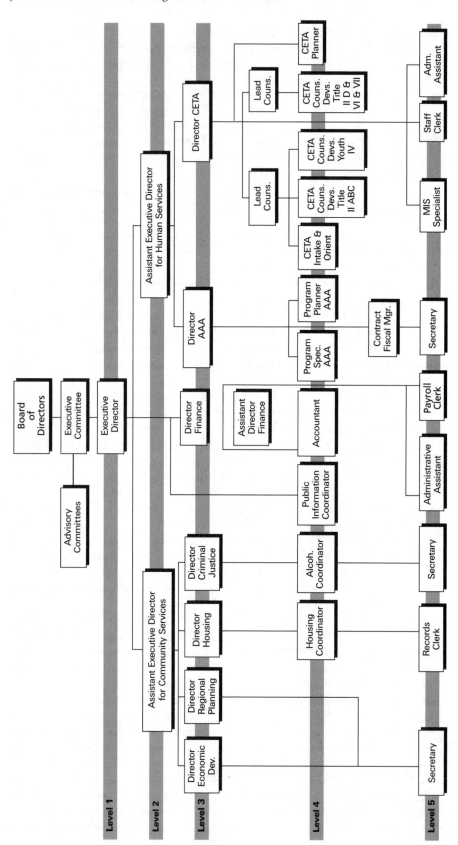

decentralized include purchasing equipment, establishing goals, choosing suppliers, setting prices, hiring employees, and deciding marketing territories.

7. *Professionalism* is the level of formal education and training of employees. Professionalism is considered high when employees require long periods of training to hold jobs in the organization. Professionalism is generally measured as the average number of years of education of employees, which could be as high as twenty in a medical practice and less than ten in a construction company.

8. *Personnel ratios* refer to the deployment of people to various functions and departments. Personnel ratios include the administrative ratio, the clerical ratio, the professional staff ratio, and the ratio of indirect to direct labor employees. A personnel ratio is measured by dividing the number of employees in a classification by the total number of organizational employees.

Contextual Dimensions

1. *Size* is the organization's magnitude as reflected in the number of people in the organization. It can be measured for the organization as a whole or for specific components, such as a plant or division. Since organizations are social systems, size is typically measured by the count of employees. Other measures such as total sales or total assets also reflect magnitude, but they do not indicate the size of the human part of the social system.

2. *Organizational technology* is the nature of the production subsystem, and it includes the actions and techniques used to change organizational inputs into outputs. An assembly line, a college classroom, and an oil refinery are technologies, although they differ from one another.

3. The *environment* includes all elements outside the boundary of the organization. Key elements include the industry, government, customers, suppliers, and the financial community. Environmental elements that affect an organization the most are often other organizations.

4. The organization's *goals and strategy* define the purpose and competitive techniques that set it apart from other organizations. Goals are often written down as an enduring statement of company intent. A strategy is the plan of action that describes resource allocation and activities for dealing with the environment and for reaching the organization's goals. Goals and strategies define the scope of operations and the relationship with employees, clients, and competitors.

5. An organization's *culture* is the underlying set of key values, beliefs, understandings, and norms shared by employees. These underlying values may pertain to ethical behavior, commitment to employees, efficiency, or customer service, and they provide the glue to hold organization members together. An organization's culture is unwritten but can be observed in its stories, slogans, ceremonies, dress, and office layout.

The thirteen contextual and structural dimensions discussed here are interdependent. For example, large organization size, a routine technology, and a stable environment all tend to create an organization that has greater formalization, specialization, and centralization. More detailed relationships among the thirteen dimensions are explored in later chapters of this book. These dimensions provide a basis for the measurement and analysis of characteristics that cannot be seen by the casual observer, and they reveal significant information about an organization.

WHAT IS ORGANIZATION THEORY?

Organization theory is not a collection of facts; it is a way of thinking about organizations. Organization theory is a way to see and analyze organizations more accurately and deeply than one otherwise could. The way to see and think about organizations is based upon patterns and regularities in organizational design and behavior. Organization scholars search for these regularities, define them, measure them, and make them available to the rest of us. The facts from the research are not as important as the general patterns and insights into organizational functioning.

History

You may recall from an earlier management course that the modern era of management theory began early in this century with the classical management perspective, which included both scientific management and administrative principles approaches. **Scientific management,** pioneered by Frederick Taylor, claimed decisions about organization and job design should be based on precise, scientific procedures after careful study of individual situations. **Administrative principles** focused more on the total organization and grew from the insights of practitioners. For example, Henry Fayol proposed fourteen principles of management, such as "each subordinate receives orders from only one superior" (unity of command) and "similar activities in an organization should be grouped together under one manager" (unity of direction).[28] Scientific management and administrative principles were closed systems approaches that did not anticipate the uncertain environment and rapid changes facing today's companies.

Following classical management theory, other academic approaches emerged. The Hawthorne studies showed that positive treatment of employees increased motivation and productivity and laid the groundwork for subsequent work on leadership, motivation, and human resource management. The work of sociologists on bureaucracy, beginning with Weber, appeared in the 1950s and 1960s and helped establish the notions of bureaucracy that will be discussed in Chapter 5. Later organizations came to be characterized as rational, problem-solving, decision-making systems.[29]

Scientific management, administrative principles, and bureaucratic approaches to organizing seemed to work well into the 1950s and 1960s. Now we see that success during this period occurred because the economies of Europe and Japan had been shattered by World War II, so North American companies had the playing field to themselves. Organizations became horrendously overmanaged, with bloated administrative ratios and professional staff ratios that would sink many organizations in the 1970s and 1980s. International competition from Europe and Japan provided the rude awakening. For example, Xerox discovered it was using 1.3 overhead workers for every direct worker, while its Japanese affiliate needed only 0.6 overhead workers. By the 1980s, North American companies had to find a better way. AT&T cut 30,000 managers during the 1980s. The merger of Chevron and Gulf led to the dismissal of 18,000 employees, many of whom were managers. GE laid off 50,000 salaried employees.[30]

The 1980s produced new corporate cultures that valued lean staff, flexibility, rapid response to the customer, motivated employees, caring for customers, and quality products. The world was changing fast because corporate boundaries were altered by waves of merger activity, much of it international, and increased international competition.

Today, the world—and thus the world of business—is undergoing a change more profound and far-reaching than any experienced since the dawn of the modern age and the scientific revolution about 500 years ago. Just as civilization was altered irrevocably in the transition from the Agrarian to the Industrial Age, emerging events will change the ways in which we interact with one another in our personal and professional lives. Old organization forms and management methods are inadequate to cope with the new problems in the emerging postmodern world.[31] The net effect of the evolving business environment and the evolving study of organization theory is a new, more flexible approach to management and the use of contingency theory to describe and convey organizational concepts.

The Postmodern Organization Paradigm

The challenges produced by today's rapidly changing environment—global competitiveness, diversity, ethical issues, rapid advances in technology and communications, a shift away from an exploitative to an ecologically sensitive approach to the natural environment, and the growing expectation of workers for meaningful work and opportunities for personal and professional growth—require dramatically different responses from people and organizations. A recent book argued that most business schools are not preparing students for the postmodern world but rather are stuck in the old way of doing things, essentially offering degrees in "Bureaucratic" Administration rather than Business Administration.[32] Yet it is the managers of tomorrow who will have to design and orchestrate new responses to a dramatically new world.

Significant changes are already occurring in organizations in response to changes in the society at large. These are reflected in Exhibit 1.4 as a shift from the modern to the postmodern organization paradigm.[33]

A **paradigm** is a shared mind-set that represents a fundamental way of thinking, perceiving, and understanding the world. Our beliefs and understandings direct our behavior. In today's fast-paced society, a number of shifts in ways of

Contextual variables	Modern	Postmodern
Environment	Stable	Turbulent
Form of capital	Money, buildings, machines	Information
Technology	Routine	Nonroutine
Size	Large	Small to moderate
Goals	Growth, efficiency	Learning, effectiveness
Culture	Employees taken for granted	Employees empowered

Organizational outcomes	Modern	Postmodern
Structure	Rigid & centralized, distinct boundaries	Flexible & decentralized, diffuse boundaries
Leadership	Autocratic	Servant leadership
Communication	Formal, written	Informal, oral
Control	Bureaucratic	Decentralized, self-control
Planning & decision-making	Managers	Everyone
Guiding principles	Patriarchal	Egalitarian

Exhibit 1.4
Modern vs. Postmodern Organization Paradigms

thinking and understanding are occurring and these in turn are associated with shifts in understanding and behavior taking place in organizations.

Before the Industrial Revolution, most organizations were related to agriculture or craft work. Communication was primarily face-to-face. Organizations were small, with simple structures and fuzzy boundaries, and were generally not interested in growing larger. In the modern, industrial age, however, a new organization paradigm emerged. Growth became a primary criterion for success. Organizations became large and complex, and boundaries between functional departments and between organizations were distinct. Environments were relatively stable, and technologies tended to be mass-production manufacturing processes. The primary forms of capital in the modern age were money, buildings, and machines. Internal structures became more complex, vertical, and bureaucratic. Leadership was based on solid management principles and tended to be autocratic, while communication was primarily through formal, written documents, such as memos, letters, and reports. Managers did all the planning and "thought work," while employees did the manual labor in exchange for wages and other compensation.

In the postmodern world of today, the environment is anything *but* stable, and the postmodern organization recognizes the chaotic, unpredictable nature of the world. In a world characterized by rapid change, complexity, and surprise, managers can't measure, predict, or control in traditional ways the unfolding drama inside or outside the organization. To cope with this chaos, organizations need a newer paradigm, in which they tend toward moderate size, with flexible, decentralized structures that emphasize horizontal cooperation. In addition, boundaries between organizations again become more diffuse, as even competitors learn to cooperate to meet turbulent environmental conditions. The primary form of capital in the postmodern organization is not money or machines, but *information,* and methods of motivation provide workers more intrinsic satisfaction from their jobs. Workers are often empowered to make decisions once reserved for managers, and emphasis on a clear and powerful vision or mission helps to ensure that decisions are made to achieve the organization's overriding purpose. Sound management is still important in postmodern organizations; however, leadership qualities are often quite different. "Servant" leadership takes center stage, as managers serve employees who in turn serve customers. In addition, informal leaders frequently emerge for limited periods of time in response to specific problems and then fade back into organizational teams as new conditions require other leaders with different skills and capabilities. Qualities traditionally considered egalitarian—equality, empowerment, horizontal relationships, and consensus building—are particularly important in the postmodern organization.

Contingency

Despite the changes in the environment, organizations are not all alike. A great many problems occur when all organizations are treated as similar, which was the case with both the administrative principles and bureaucratic approaches that tried to design all organizations alike. The organization charts and financial systems that work in the retail division of a conglomerate will not be appropriate in the manufacturing division.

Contingency means that one thing depends upon other things, and for organizations to be effective, there must be a "goodness of fit" between their structures and the conditions in their external environments.[34] What works in one setting may not work in another setting. There is not one best way. Contingency theory means "it depends." The terms in Exhibit 1.4, for example, illustrate contingency theory. Some organizations may experience a stable environment, use a routine technology, and desire efficiency. In this situation, a management approach that uses bureaucratic control procedures, a functional structure, and formal communication would be appropriate. Likewise, free-flowing management processes work best in an uncertain environment with a nonroutine technology. The correct management approach is contingent upon the organization's situation.

FRAMEWORK FOR THE BOOK

What topic areas are relevant to organization theory and design? How does a course in management or organizational behavior differ from a course in organization theory? The answer is related to the concept called level of analysis.

Levels of Analysis

In systems theory, each system is composed of subsystems. Systems are nested within systems, and one **level of analysis** has to be chosen as the primary focus. Four levels of analysis normally characterize organizations, as illustrated in Exhibit 1.5. The individual human being is the basic building block of organizations. The human being is to the organization what a cell is to a biological system. The next higher system level is the group or department. These are collections of individuals who work together to perform group tasks. The next level of analysis is the organization itself. An organization is a collection of groups or departments that combine into the total organization. Organizations themselves can be grouped together into the next higher level of analysis, which is the interorganizational set and community. The interorganizational set is the group of organizations a single organization interacts with. Other organizations in the community also make up an important part of an organization's environment.

Organization theory focuses on the organizational level of analysis but with concern for groups and the environment. To explain the organization, one should

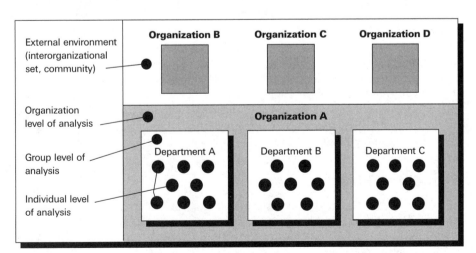

Exhibit 1.5

Levels of Analysis in Organizations

Source: Based on Andrew H. Van de Ven and Diane L. Ferry, *Measuring and Assessing Performance* (New York: Wiley, 1980), p. 8; and Richard L. Daft and Richard M. Steers, *Organizations: A Micro/Macro Approach* (Glenview, Ill.: Scott, Foresman, 1986), p. 8.

look not only at its characteristics but also at the characteristics of the environment and of the departments and groups that make up the organization. The focus of this book is to help you understand organizations by examining their specific characteristics, the nature and relationships among groups and departments that make up the organization, and the collection of organizations that make up the environment.

Are individuals included in organization theory? Organization theory does consider the behavior of individuals, but in the aggregate. People are important, but they are not the primary focus of analysis. Organization theory is distinct from organizational behavior. **Organizational behavior** is the micro approach to organizations because it focuses on the individuals within organizations as the relevant units of analysis. Organizational behavior examines concepts such as motivation, leadership style, and personality and is concerned with cognitive and emotional differences among people within organizations. **Organization theory** is a macro examination of organizations because it analyzes the whole organization as a unit. Organization theory is concerned with people aggregated into departments and organizations and with the differences in structure and behavior of the organization level of analysis. Organization theory is the sociology of organizations, while organizational behavior is the psychology of organizations.

A new approach to organization studies is called meso theory. Most organizational research and many management courses specialize in either organizational behavior or organization theory. Meso means "in between," and **meso theory** concerns the integration of both micro and macro levels of analysis. Individuals and groups affect the organization and the organization in return influences individuals and groups. To thrive in organizations, managers and employees need to simultaneously understand multiple levels. For example, research may show that employee diversity enhances innovation. To facilitate innovation, managers need to understand how structure and context (organization theory) are related to interactions among diverse employees (organizational behavior) to foster innovation, because both macro and micro variables account for innovations.[35]

For its part, organization theory is directly relevant to top- and middle-management concerns and partly relevant to lower management. Top managers are responsible for the entire organization and must set goals, develop strategy, interpret the external environment, and decide organization structure and design. Middle management is concerned with major departments, such as marketing or research, and must decide how the department relates to the rest of the organization. Middle managers must design their departments to fit work-unit technology and deal with issues of power and politics, intergroup conflict, and information and control systems, each of which is part of organization theory. Organization theory is only partly concerned with lower management because this level of supervision is concerned with employees who operate machines, type letters, teach classes, and sell goods. Organization theory is concerned with the big picture of the organization and its major departments.

Plan of the Book

The topics within the field of organization theory are interrelated. Chapters are presented so that major ideas unfold in logical sequence. The framework that guides the organization of the book is shown in Exhibit 1.6. Part I introduces the basic idea of organizations as social systems and the nature of organization theory. This discussion provides the groundwork for Part II, which is about top management goals and effectiveness, and the external environment. Organizations are

Exhibit 1.6
Framework for the Book

Part I Introduction to Organizations	**Chapter 1**	Organizations and Organization Theory

Part II The Open System	**Chapter 2**	Strategic Management and Organizational Effectiveness
	Chapter 3	The External Environment

Part III Organization Structure and Design	**Chapter 4**	Manufacturing, Service, and Advanced Information Technologies
	Chapter 5	Organization Size and Life Cycle
	Chapter 6	Fundamentals of Organization Structure
	Chapter 7	Contemporary Designs for Global Competition

Part IV Organization Design Process	**Chapter 8**	Innovation and Change
	Chapter 9	Information Technology and Organizational Control
	Chapter 10	Organizational Culture and Ethical Values
	Chapter 11	Decision-Making Processes
	Chapter 12	Power and Politics
	Chapter 13	Interdepartmental Relations and Conflict

Part V Strategy and Structure for the Future	**Chapter 14**	Interorganizational Relationships
	Chapter 15	Toward the Learning Organization

linked to the environment and they exist for a purpose. The nature of the environment and the achievement of that purpose are the topics of Part II. Part III describes how to design the organization's structure. Organization design is related to such factors as organizational technology and size. This section includes a chapter that explains how to design organization charts and reporting relationships for divisional, functional, and matrix structures. It concludes with a chapter on new team-based and international designs.

Part IV looks at dynamic processes inside the organization. Chapters 8 and 9 describe how structure can be designed to influence internal systems for innovation and change and for information and control. Chapters 10–13 explore the management of interdepartmental conflict, decision making, power and politics, and organizational leadership and culture. Part V considers organizational issues of the future, which include the burgeoning network of relationships among organizations and the newly emerging learning organization.

SUMMARY OF KEY ISSUES

One important idea in this chapter is that organizations are social systems that interact with the external environment. Change has replaced stability as a key trait in today's organizations. Some of the specific challenges managers and organizations face include global competition, the need for organizational renewal, getting products and services to customers fast at competitive prices, adapting to changing career patterns, coping with diversity, and maintaining high ethical standards. These challenges are leading to changes in organization structures and management methods. The trend is away from highly structured bureaucratic approaches toward looser, more flexible management systems that empower employees to make decisions and provide more intrinsic job satisfaction. Teamwork, consensus-building, and horizontal collaboration are increasingly important.

The focus of analysis for organization theory is not individual people but the organization itself. Relevant concepts include the dimensions of organization structure and context. The dimensions of formalization, specialization, standardization, hierarchy of authority, complexity, centralization, professionalism, personnel ratios, size, organizational technology, environment, goals and strategy, and culture provide labels for measuring and analyzing organizations. These dimensions vary widely from organization to organization. Subsequent chapters provide frameworks for analyzing organizations with these concepts.

Most concepts in organization theory pertain to the top- and middle-management levels of the organization. This book is concerned more with the topics of those levels than with the operational level topics of supervision and motivation of employees, which are discussed in courses on organizational behavior.

Discussion Questions

1. What is the definition of *organization*? Briefly explain each part of the definition.
2. What is the difference between formalization, specialization, and standardization? Do you think an organization high on one of these three dimensions would also be high on the other two? Discuss.

3. Discuss ways in which your own life has been affected by the shift from the modern to the postmodern age.
4. What does *contingency* mean? What are the implications of contingency theories for managers?
5. What levels of analysis are typically studied in organization theory? How would these contrast with the level of analysis studied in a course in psychology? Sociology? Political science?
6. Early management theorists believed that organizations should strive to be logical and rational, with a place for everything and everything in its place. Discuss the pros and cons of this approach for today's organizations.

Notes

1. Carol J. Loomis, "Dinosaurs?" *Fortune,* 3 May 1993, 36–42.

2. Stratford Sherman, "Is He Too Cautious to Save IBM?" *Fortune,* 3 October 1994, 78–90.

3. The analysis of IBM was based on Paul Carroll, *Big Blues: The Unmaking of IBM* (New York: Crown Publishers, 1993); Brent Schlender, "Big Blue is Betting on Big Iron Again," *Fortune,* 29 April 1996, 102–12; Sherman, "Is He Too Cautious to Save IBM?"; Ira Sager, "The View From IBM," *Business Week,* 30 October 1995, 142–52; John Greenwald, "A Blue Chip Case of Blues," *Time,* 16 May 1994, 71–72; David Kirkpatrick, "First: With New PCs and a New Attitude, IBM is Back," *Fortune,* 11 November 1996, 28–29; Judith H. Dobrzynski, "Rethinking IBM," *Business Week,* 4 October 1993, 86–97; Michael W. Miller and Laurence Hooper, "Akers Quits at IBM under Heavy Pressure; Dividend Is Slashed," *The Wall Street Journal,* 27 January 1993, A1, A6; John W. Verity, "IBM: A Bull's-Eye and a Long Shot," *Business Week,* 13 December 1993, 88–89; and G. Pascal Zachary and Stephen Kreider Yoder, "Computer Industry Divides into Camps of Winners and Losers," *The Wall Street Journal,* 27 January 1993, A1, A4.

4. John A. Byrne, "Management Meccas," *Business Week,* 18 September 1995, 122–34; Catherine Arnst, "Now HP Stands for Hot Products," *Business Week,* 14 June 1993, 36; Ronald E. Yates, "Fisher Exposes Kodak to Motorola Experience," *Chicago Tribune,* 14 April 1996, Section 5, p. 1, 2.

5. Eileen Davis, "What's On American Managers' Minds?" *Management Review,* April 1995, 14–20.

6. Ronald Henkoff, "New Management Secrets from Japan—Really," *Fortune,* 27 November 1995, 135–46.

7. Richard L. Daft, *Management,* 3d ed. (Fort Worth, Texas: The Dryden Press, 1994), 80; James L. Gibson, John M. Ivancevich, and James H. Donnelly, Jr., *Organizations,* 8th ed. (Burr Ridge, Illinois: Irwin, 1994), 54–55.

8. Karen Lowry Miller, with Bill Javetski, Peggy Simpson, and Tim Smart, "Europe: The Push East," *Business Week,* 7 November 1994, 48–49; Andrew E. Serwer, "McDonald's Conquers the World," *Fortune,* 17 October 1994, 103–16.

9. Nicholas Imparato and Oren Harari, "When New Worlds Stir," *Management Review,* October 1994, 22–28.

10. Patricia Booth, "Embracing the Team Concept," *Canadian Business Review,* Autumn, 1994, 10–13; Jeffrey Pfeffer, "Producing Sustainable Competitive Advantage Through the Effective Management of People," *Academy of Management Executive,* 1995, Vol. 9, No. 1, 55–72; Wendy Zellner, "Team Player: No More Same Ol'–Same Ol'," *Business Week,* 17 October 1994, 95–96.

11. Christopher A. Bartlett and Sumantra Ghoshal, "Rebuilding Behavioral Context: Turn Process Reengineering into People Rejuvenation," *Sloan Management Review,* Fall 1995, 11–23.

12. Byrne, "Management Meccas."

13. Walter Kiechel III, "How We Will Work in the Year 2000," *Fortune,* 17 May 1993, 38–52.

14. Keith H. Hammonds, Kevin Kelly, and Karen Thurston, "The New World of Work," *Business Week,* 17 October 1994, 76–87.

15. Patricia Galagan, "Signs of the Times," *Training and Development,* February 1996, 32–36.

16. William Bridges, "A Nation of Owners," *Inc.–The State of Small Business 1995,* 16 May 1995, 89–91; Arno Penzias, "New Paths to Success," *Fortune,* 12 June 1995, 90–94; John P. Kotter, *The New Rules: How to Succeed in Today's Post-Corporate World,* (New York: The Free Press, 1994) and Judith H. Dobrzynski, "New Secret of Success: Getting Off the Ladder," an interview with John P. Kotter, *The New York Times,* 19 March 1995, F14.

17. Genevieve Capowski, "Managing Diversity," *Management Review,* June 1996, 13–19.

18. Octave V. Baker, "Meeting the Challenge of Managing Cultural Diversity," in *Managing in the Age of Change: Essential Skills to Manage Today's Diverse Workforce,* edited by Roger A. Ritvo, Anne H. Litwin, and Lee Butler, (Burr Ridge, IL: Irwin, 1995).

19. Bonna M. de la Cruz, "Language Battle Flares in the Office," *The Tennessean,* 5 June 1996, A1, A2.

20. Joline Godfrey, "Been There, Doing That," *Inc.,* March 1996, 21–22; Paula Dwyer, Marsha Johnston, and Karen Lowry Miller, "Out of the Typing Pool, Into Career Limbo," *Business Week,* 15 April 1996, 92–94.

21. Mark Maremont, "Blind Ambition," *Business Week,* 23 October 1995, 78–92.

22. Dale Kurschner, "The 100 Best Corporate Citizens," *Business Ethics,* May/June 1995, 24–35.

23. Howard Aldrich, *Organizations and Environments* (Englewood Cliffs, N.J.: Prentice-Hall, 1979), 3.

24. David Greising, "The Virtual Olympics," *Business Week,* 29 April 1996, 64–66.

25. Nathaniel C. Nash, "Coke's Great Romanian Adventure," *The New York Times,* 26 February 1995.

26. Michael A. Hitt, R. Duane Ireland, and Robert E. Hoskisson, *Strategic Management: Competitiveness and Globalization* (St. Paul, Minn.: West, 1995), 238.

27. The following discussion was heavily influenced by Richard H. Hall, *Organizations: Structures,* *Processes, and Outcomes* (Englewood Cliffs, N.J.: Prentice-Hall, 1991); D. S. Pugh, "The Measurement of Organization Structures: Does Context Determine Form?" *Organizational Dynamics* I (Spring 1973): 19–34; and D. S. Pugh, D. J. Hickson, C. R. Hinings, and C. Turner, "Dimensions of Organization Structure," *Administrative Science Quarterly* 13 (1968): 65–91.

28. Richard L. Daft, *Management,* 3d ed. (Chicago: Dryden, 1994).

29. Richard L. Daft and Arie Y. Lewin, "Can Organization Studies Begin to Break Out of the Normal Science Strait-jacket? An Editorial Essay," *Organization Science* 1 (1990): 1–9.

30. Amanda Bennett, *The Death of the Organization Man* (New York: William Morrow, 1990).

31. Ian I. Mitroff, Richard O. Mason, and Christine M. Pearson, "Radical Surgery: What Will Tomorrow's Organizations Look Like?", *Academy of Management Executive,* 1994, Vol. 8, No. 2, 11–21; Nicholas Imparato and Oren Harari, "When New Worlds Stir," *Management Review,* October 1994, 22–28; and William Bergquist, *The Postmodern Organization: Mastering the Art of Irreversible Change,* (San Francisco: Jossey-Bass Publishers, 1993).

32. David M. Boje and Robert F. Dennehy, *Managing in the Postmodern World: America's Revolution Against Exploitation,* 2d ed., (Dubuque, Iowa: Kendall/Hunt Publishing Company, 1994).

33. This discussion is based on Bergquist, *The Postmodern Organization,* 1993, and Richard L. Daft, *Organization Theory and Design,* 5th ed., (Minneapolis/St. Paul: West Publishing Company, 1995), 13–14 and 22–23.

34. Johannes M. Pennings, "Structural Contingency Theory: A Reappraisal," *Research in Organizational Behavior* 14 (1992): 267–309.

35. Robert House, Denise M. Rousseau, and Melissa Thomas-Hunt, "The Meso Paradigm: A Framework for the Integration of Micro and Macro Organizational Behavior," *Research in Organizational Behavior,* Vol. 17, 1995, 71–114.

2

chapter two

Strategic Management and Organizational Effectiveness

While reading this chapter, think about your answers to the following questions:

- What is the difference between official goals (the mission) and operative goals?

- What are five types of operative goals found in organizations?

- What organizational characteristics are associated with a low-cost leadership strategy, a differentiation strategy, and a focus strategy?

- How can managers develop internal organizational characteristics in the areas of strategic orientation, top management, organization design, and corporate culture that contribute to organizational excellence?

- What are the various approaches to measuring organizational effectiveness?

An **organizational goal** is a desired state of affairs that the organization attempts to reach.[1] A goal represents a result or end point toward which organizational efforts are directed. For example, to achieve its mission of becoming number one in PC and workstation market share by 1996, Compaq Computer's goals included developing new, competitively priced computers for all markets, better distribution of products, including outlets such as Wal-Mart, money-saving manufacturing systems, and alliances with other computer-related companies, such as Microsoft.

PURPOSE OF THIS CHAPTER

Top managers give direction to organizations. They set goals and develop the strategies for their organization to attain those goals. The purpose of this chapter is to help you understand the types of goals organizations pursue and some of the competitive strategies managers develop to reach those goals. We will examine characteristics common to successful organizations and discuss how managers help their organizations achieve excellence. The chapter also describes the most popular approaches to measuring the effectiveness of organizational efforts. To manage organizations well, managers need a clear sense of how to measure effectiveness.

TOP MANAGEMENT STRATEGIC DIRECTION

An organization is created and designed to achieve some end, which is decided by the chief executive officer and/or the top management team. Organization structure and design is an outcome of this purpose. Indeed, *the primary responsibility of top management is to determine an organization's goals, strategy, and design, therein adapting the organization to a changing environment.*[2] Middle managers do much the same thing for major departments within the guidelines provided by top management. The relationships through which top managers provide direction and then design are illustrated in Exhibit 2.1.

The direction setting process typically begins with an assessment of the opportunities and threats in the external environment, including the amount of change, uncertainty, and resource availability, which will be discussed in more detail in Chapter 3. Top management also assesses internal strengths and weaknesses to define the company's distinctive competence compared with other firms in the industry.[3] The assessment of internal environment often includes an evaluation of each department and is shaped by past performance and the leadership style of the CEO and top management team. The next step is to define the overall mission and official goals based upon the correct fit between external opportunities and internal strengths. Specific operational goals or strategies can then be formulated to define how the organization is to accomplish its overall mission.

In Exhibit 2.1, organization design reflects the way goals and strategies are implemented. Organization design is the administration and execution of the strategic plan. *This is the role of organization theory.* Organization direction is achieved through decisions about structural form, information technology and

Exhibit 2.1 *Top Management Role in Organization Direction, Design, and Effectiveness*

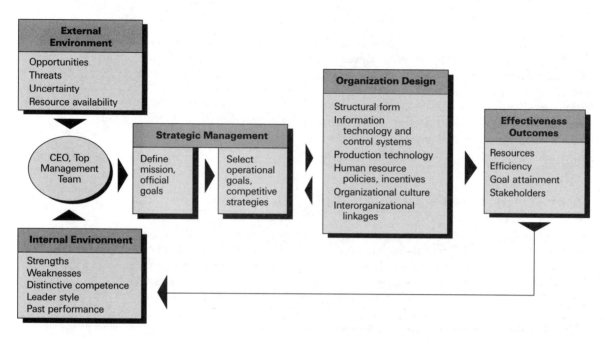

Source: Adapted from Arie Y. Lewin and Carroll U. Stephens, "Individual Properties of the CEO as Determinants of Organization Design," unpublished manuscript, Duke University, 1990, and Arie Y. Lewin and Carroll U. Stephens, "CEO Attributes as Determinants of Organization Design: An Integrated Model," *Organization Studies* 15, No. 2 (1994), 83–212.

control systems, the type of production technology, human resource policies, culture, and linkages to other organizations. Changes in structure, technology, human resource policies, culture, and interorganization linkages will be discussed in subsequent chapters. Also note the arrow in Exhibit 2.1 running from Organization Design back to Strategic Management. This means that strategies often are made within the current structure of the organization, so that current design constrains, or puts limits on, goals and strategy. More often than not, however, the new goals and strategy are selected based on environmental needs, and then the top management team attempts to redesign the organization to achieve those ends.

Finally, Exhibit 2.1 illustrates how managers evaluate the effectiveness of organizational efforts—that is, the extent to which the organization realizes its goals. This chart reflects the most popular ways of measuring performance. It is important to note here that performance measurements feed back into the internal environment, so that past performance of the organization is assessed by top management in setting new goals and strategies for the future.

The role of top management is important because managers can interpret the environment differently and develop different goals. An interesting example occurred in New York City, where the crime rate plunged farther and faster than anywhere else in the nation after former Police Commissioner William Bratton issued a clear, simple goal: "Cut crime." Top managers before Bratton had started with the premise that law-breaking was caused by factors in the external environment that were beyond the control of the police department. Thus, cops reacted to crime rather than actually trying to reduce crime. Bratton, however, believed his department could impact the environment and dramatically cut the crime rate by managing resources more effectively. He devised strategies that target specific criminal behaviors, and invested resources in cracking down on minor offenders, believing this created a more orderly environment, thereby reducing serious crimes as well. Using new information technology, crime data were computerized and collected daily so Bratton and his staff could immediately spot trends and problems. So long as precinct commanders demonstrated results, they were given unprecedented autonomy to run their station houses and deploy resources as they saw fit. Bratton's strategies led to a 39 percent decline in the murder rate and a reduction in overall crime of more than 15 percent.[4] Top management choices about goals, strategies, and organization design can have a tremendous impact on organizational effectiveness.

Remember that goals and strategy are not fixed or taken for granted. Top managers and middle managers must select goals for their respective units, and the ability to make these choices largely determines firm success. Organization design is used to implement goals and strategy and also determines organizational success. We will now discuss further the concept of organizational goals and strategy, and in the latter part of this chapter, we will discuss various ways to evaluate organizational effectiveness.

ORGANIZATIONAL GOALS

Many types of goals exist in an organization, and each type performs a different function. One major distinction is between the officially stated goals, or mission, of the organization and the operative goals the organization actually pursues.

Mission

The overall goal for an organization is often called the **mission**—the organization's reason for existence. The mission describes the organization's vision, its shared values and beliefs, and its reason for being. It can have a powerful impact on an organization.[5] The mission is sometimes called the **official goals**, which are the formally stated definition of business scope and outcomes the organization is trying to achieve. Official goal statements typically define business operations and may focus on values, markets, and customers that distinguish the organization. Whether called a mission statement or official goals, the organization's general statement of its purpose and philosophy often is written down in a policy manual or the annual report. The mission statement for Hallmark is shown in Exhibit 2.2. Note how the overall mission, values, and goals are all defined.

Operative Goals

Operative goals designate the ends sought through the actual operating procedures of the organization and explain what the organization is actually trying to do.[6] Operative goals describe specific measurable outcomes and are often concerned with the short run. Operative versus official goals represent actual versus stated goals. Operative goals typically pertain to the primary tasks an organization must perform.[7] Specific goals for each primary task provide direction for the day-to-day decisions and activities within departments.

THIS IS HALLMARK

We believe:

That our *products and services* must enrich people's lives
and enhance their relationships.

That *creativity and quality*—in our concepts, products and
services—are essential to our success.

That the *people* of Hallmark are our company's most valuable
resource.

That distinguished *financial performance* is a must, not as an
end in itself, but as a means to accomplish our broader
mission.

That our *private ownership* must be preserved.

The values that guide us are:

Excellence in all we do.

Ethical and moral conduct at all times and in all our
relationships.

Innovation in all areas of our business as a means of
attaining and sustaining leadership.

Corporate social responsibility to Kansas City and to each
community in which we operate.

*These beliefs and values guide our business strategies, our
corporate behavior, and our relationships with
suppliers, customers, communities, and each other.*

Source: Patricia Jones and Larry Kahaner, *Say It and Live It: 50 Corporate Mission
Statements That Hit the Mark* (New York: Currency Doubleday, 1995).

Overall Performance. Profitability reflects the overall performance of for-
profit organizations. Profitability may be expressed in terms of net income,
earnings per share, or return on investment. Other overall goals are growth and
output volume. Growth pertains to increases in sales or profits over time.
Volume pertains to total sales or the amount of products or services delivered.
At Pier 1 Imports, beating last year's Christmas sales numbers by 5 percent is
a chainwide goal set by CEO Clark Johnson. Some stores then set even higher
performance goals, as did Paula Hankins and Eva Goldyn, managers of Pier 1's
smallest Nashville, Tennessee, store. Meeting the goal of a 36 percent increase
in Christmas season sales became a storewide obsession.[8]

Not-for-profit organizations such as labor unions do not have goals of
profitability, but they do have goals that attempt to specify the delivery of
services to members within specified budget expense levels. Growth and volume goals also may be indicators of overall performance in not-for-profit
organizations.

Resources. Resource goals pertain to the acquisition of needed material and financial resources from the environment. They may involve obtaining financing for the construction of new plants, finding less expensive sources for raw materials, or hiring top-quality college graduates.

Market. Market goals relate to the market share or market standing desired by the organization. Market goals are the responsibility of marketing, sales, and advertising departments. PepsiCo's Frito Lay division controls more than half of the market share for salty snacks. The division has the operative goal of having the largest market share in a specific industry.[9]

Employee Development. Employee development pertains to the training, promotion, safety, and growth of employees. It includes both managers and workers. At Franciscan Health System in Tacoma, Washington, a top goal is to "create an organizational environment that values, empowers, enriches, and supports those with whom we work." The goal includes supporting educational activities for employees, providing change management seminars and retraining, developing reward and recognition systems, and encouraging diversity. These activities improve employee morale and help workers continue to learn and grow.[10]

Innovation. Innovation goals pertain to internal flexibility and readiness to adapt to unexpected changes in the environment. Innovation goals are often defined with respect to the development of specific new services, products, or production processes. For example, 3M has a goal of generating enough new products so that 30 percent of sales come from products introduced within the past four years.[11]

Productivity. Productivity goals concern the amount of output achieved from available resources. They typically describe the amount of resource inputs required to reach desired outputs and are thus stated in terms of "cost for a unit of production," "units produced per employee," or "resource cost per employee." For example, Rubbermaid has a productivity goal of increasing the number of units produced per worker per day. Total output increased from three hundred units per worker per day in 1952 to five hundred units in 1980 and 750 in 1988. Another productivity goal was to reduce the number of sales representatives and to increase the workforce by only 50 percent while doubling sales. The resulting increases in productivity have produced fresh profits for Rubbermaid.[12]

Successful organizations use a carefully-balanced set of operative goals. For example, while achieving profitability is important, some of today's best companies recognize that a single-minded focus on bottom-line profits may not be the best way to achieve high performance.

Purposes of Goals

Both official goals and operative goals are important for the organization, but they serve very different purposes. Official goals provide legitimacy, while operative goals provide employee direction, decision guidelines, and criteria of performance. These purposes are summarized in Exhibit 2.3.

Exhibit 2.3
*Goal Type and
Purpose*

Type of Goals	Purpose of Goals
Official goals, mission:	Legitimacy
Operative goals:	Employee direction and motivation
	Decision guidelines
	Standard of performance

Legitimacy.   A mission statement (or official goals) communicates legitimacy to external and internal stakeholders. The mission describes the purpose of the organization so people know what it stands for and accept its existence. Moreover, employees join and become committed to an organization when they identify with the organization's stated goals.

Most top managers want their company to look good to other companies in their environment. Managers want customers, competitors, suppliers, and the local community to look upon them in a favorable light. The dynamics of a company's interaction with the organizational environment often depend as much on cultural norms, symbols, and beliefs as on technological or material factors, and the concept of organizational legitimacy plays a critical role.[13] The mission statement is a powerful first step in communicating legitimacy to external and internal stakeholders and creating a positive impression.

Fortune magazine reflects the corporate concern for legitimacy with ratings of the reputations of corporations in each of 37 industries. Mirage Resorts, which runs gambling casinos, popped into the number 2 spot based largely on its strong commitment to high-quality service—employees are empowered to do whatever it takes to keep guests smiling. And the company's treatment of its workers keeps them smiling too; with turnover in the hotel-casino game at about 43 percent per year, Mirage's 12 percent turnover rate is the envy of the industry. Mirage's mission and goal statements help communicate the company's commitment to its workers and emphasis on total customer satisfaction. As another example, telephone companies in the U.S. have been criticized for offering sexually explicit dial-up message services. Public sentiment has caused many companies to shut them down and develop mission and goal statements that communicate legitimacy and social responsibility. A similar situation in Norway led to the cancellation of quite lucrative dial-up services offered by a national tabloid newspaper. Managers determined that these services were detrimental to their image of corporate responsibility and their goal of serving as a major national news medium.[14]

Employee Direction and Motivation.   Goals give a sense of direction to organization participants. The stated end toward which an organization is striving, and strategies for how to get there, tell employees what they are working for. Goals help motivate participants, especially if participants help select the goals. At 3M, for example, the overall goal that "30 percent of sales should come from products developed in the past four years" is widely accepted and pursued by employees. All employees work toward innovation.

Decision Guidelines.   The goals of an organization also act as guidelines for employee decision making. Organizational goals are a set of constraints on individual behavior and decisions.[15] They help define the correct decisions concerning organization structure, innovation, employee welfare, and growth. When Owens-Illinois, a glass container manufacturer, established the goal of reducing volume to improve profits, internal decisions were redirected. Owens-Illinois had been running marginal plants just to maintain volume. The new goal of increased profits provided decision guidelines that led to the closing of these marginal plants.

Criteria of Performance. Goals provide a standard for assessment. The level of organizational performance, whether in terms of profits, units produced, or number of complaints, needs a basis for evaluation. Is a profit of 10 percent on sales good enough? The answer lies in goals. Goals reflect past experience and describe the desired state for the future. If the profit goal is 8 percent, then a 10 percent return is excellent. When Owens-Illinois shifted from volume to profit goals, profits increased by 30 percent. This occurred during the period when two competitors reported profit declines of 61 percent and 76 percent. Profit thus replaced production volume as the criterion of performance.[16]

Summary of Organizational Goals

Official goals and mission statements describe a value system for the organization, while operative goals represent the primary tasks of the organization. Official goals legitimize the organization, while operative goals are more explicit and well defined. For example, when Datapoint Corporation was trying to achieve greater efficiency in customer service, managers adopted the operative goals of schedule, cost, and quality. Manufacturing was expected to "deliver a product to the customer on time, deliver it at minimal cost, and deliver a good quality product."[17] These operative goals provided direction to employees and helped attain the overall company goal of continuing to have consecutive quarterly increases in net revenues, net earnings, and shipments.

ORGANIZATIONAL STRATEGIES

A **strategy** is a plan for interacting with the competitive environment to achieve organizational goals. Some managers think of goals and strategies as interchangeable, but for our purposes, goals define where the organization wants to go and strategies define how it will get there. For example, a goal may be to achieve 15 percent annual sales growth; strategies to reach that goal might include aggressive advertising to attract new customers, motivating salespeople to increase the average size of customer purchases, and acquiring other businesses that produce similar products. Strategies can include any number of techniques to achieve the goal. The Porter model of competitive strategies provides one framework for competitive action. Managers try to develop strategies that will be congruent with the external environment.

Porter's Competitive Strategies

Michael E. Porter studied a number of businesses and introduced a framework describing three competitive strategies.[18] These strategies and the organizational characteristics associated with each are summarized in Exhibit 2.4.

1. Low-Cost Leadership. The **low-cost leadership** strategy tries to increase market share by emphasizing low cost compared to competitors. With a low-cost leadership strategy, the organization aggressively seeks efficient facilities, pursues cost reductions, and uses tight controls to produce products more efficiently than its competitors.

This strategy is concerned primarily with stability rather than taking risks or seeking new opportunities for innovation and growth. A low-cost position means the company can undercut competitor's prices and still offer comparable quality and earn a reasonable profit. Compaq Computer used a low-cost leadership strategy to reach its goal of being the world's Number 1 PC supplier. Compaq has been cutting costs better than anyone in the industry and is therefore able to supply price-busting products that are creating huge demand from consumers.[19] Being the low-cost producer can help a company defend against current competitors because customers cannot find lower prices elsewhere. In addition, if substitute products or potential new competitors enter the picture, the low-cost producer is in a better position to prevent loss of market share.

2. Differentiation. In a **differentiation** strategy, organizations attempt to distinguish their products or services from others in the industry. An organization may use advertising, distinctive product features, exceptional service, or new technology to achieve a product perceived as unique. This strategy usually targets customers who are not particularly concerned with price, so it can be quite profitable. Mercedes-Benz automobiles, Maytag appliances, and Tylenol are the products of companies that have benefited from a differentiation strategy.

Exhibit 2.4

Organizational Characteristics for Porter's Competitive Strategies

Strategy	Organizational Characteristics for Porter's Competitive Strategies
Low-cost Leadership	Strong central authority; tight cost control Standard operating procedures Easy-to-use manufacturing technologies Highly efficient procurement and distribution systems Close supervision; limited employee empowerment Frequent, detailed control reports
Differentiation	Acts in an organic, loosely-knit way, with strong coordination among departments Creative flair, thinks "out-of-the-box" Strong capability in basic research Strong marketing abilities Rewards employee innovation Corporate reputation for quality or technological leadership
Focus	Combination of above policies directed at specific strategic target Values and rewards flexibility and customer intimacy Measures cost of providing service and maintaining customer loyalty Pushes empowerment to employees with customer contact

Source: Based on Michael E. Porter, *Competitive Strategy: Techniques for Analyzing Industries and Competitors* (New York: The Free Press, 1980); Michael Treacy and Fred Wiersema, "How Market Leaders Keep Their Edge," *Fortune,* 6 February 1995, 88–98; and Michael A. Hitt, R. Duane Ireland, and Robert E. Hoskisson, *Strategic Management* (St. Paul, Minn.: West Publishing, 1995), 100–113.

A differentiation strategy can reduce rivalry with competitors and fight off the threat of substitute products because customers are loyal to the company's brand. However, companies must remember that successful differentiation strategies require a number of costly activities, such as product research and design and extensive advertising. Companies that pursue a differentiation strategy need strong marketing abilities and creative employees who are given the time and resources to seek innovations.

3. *Focus.* With Porter's third strategy, the **focus strategy,** the organization concentrates on a specific regional market or buyer group. The company will try to achieve either a low-cost advantage or a differentiation advantage within a narrowly defined market. One example of focus strategy is Enterprise Rent-a-Car, which has made its mark by focusing on a market where the major companies like Hertz and Avis don't even compete—the low-budget insurance replacement market. Customers whose cars have been wrecked or stolen have one less thing to worry about when Enterprise delivers a rental car right to their driveway. Enterprise has been able to grow rapidly by using a focus strategy.[20]

Strategies for Organizational Excellence

Managers not only develop strategies for interacting with the external environment, they also want to build internal organizational characteristics that contribute to long-lasting company success. As we saw in Chapter 1, today's competitive organizations exhibit a number of shifts in thinking in response to changes in society. Successful organizations remain flexible to adapt quickly to a chaotic international environment. Another shift is a concern for empowering employees and a stronger interest in corporate values and culture. One recent book, *Built to Last: Successful Habits of Visionary Companies,* examines companies that have remained successful over long time periods and argues that there are certain "timeless fundamentals" that help companies achieve and sustain long-term organizational excellence.[21] Other publications, such as *Reengineering the Corporation* about corporate redesign, and *Control Your Destiny or Someone Else Will* about Jack Welch's revolution at General Electric, have also added new understanding about organizational excellence.[22] Some of the major ideas from these publications are summarized in Exhibit 2.5. They are organized into four categories: strategic orientation, top management, organization design, and corporate culture.

Strategic Orientation. Three characteristics identified in corporate research pertain to an organization's strategic orientation: being *close to the customer,* providing a *fast response,* and having a *clear business focus and goals.*

Excellent organizations are customer-driven. Organizations are increasingly looking at customers as their most important stakeholders, and a dominant value in successful organizations is satisfying customer needs.[23] Today's top managers often call customers directly to learn their needs. For example, the president of Pepsi Cola North America makes a point of calling at least four customers directly per day.[24]

A fast response means successful companies respond quickly to problems and opportunities. They lead rather than follow. They take chances. They make continuous improvement a way of life and often achieve their greatest accomplishments through constant experimentation and improvement. A classic

Exhibit 2.5 *Factors Associated with Organization Excellence*

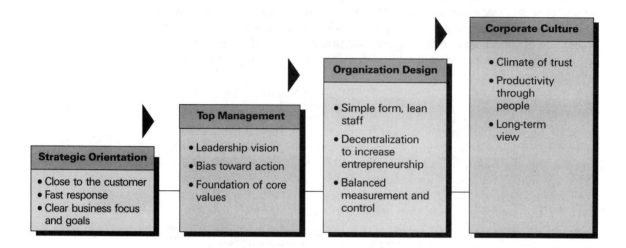

example is 3M. The company encourages employees to try just about anything and gives them 15 percent of their time to do it.[25]

Moreover, to sustain excellence, companies need to have a clear focus and goals. They know that to be successful, they should do what they do best. At Gerber, for example, the motto is "Babies are our business . . . our only business." Eastman Kodak, which thrived for decades in its camera and film business, suffered disastrous results when managers lost sight of the core business and moved into pharmaceutical and consumer health products.[26] As part of his ongoing transformation of the company, CEO George Fisher is selling off these product lines to refocus Kodak on its core imaging business.

Top Management.   Management techniques and processes are another dimension of excellent organizations. Three factors are unique to managers who are part of a highly successful company: *leadership vision, a bias toward action*, and *promoting a foundation of core values*.

To achieve and maintain excellence, an organization needs a special kind of leadership vision that provides leadership of the organization, not just leadership within the organization. Leaders must provide a vision of what the organization can be and what it stands for; they give employees a sense of direction, shared purpose, and meaning that persists despite changes in product line or manager turnover. When asked to name the most important decisions contributing to Hewlett-Packard's immense growth, David Packard speaks entirely in terms of organizational characteristics, such as creating an environment that encourages creativity, rather than in terms of technological breakthroughs.[27]

Managers and employees in excellent organizations are also oriented toward action—they don't talk problems to death before making decisions or creating solutions. Successful companies "do it, try it, fix it." The decision philosophy at PepsiCo, for example, is "Ready, Fire, Aim."[28]

Yet decisions are not based on thin air; top managers support and promote a core ideology that permeates organizational life and guides all decision making. The best companies, like Johnson & Johnson, Wal-Mart, and 3M, are guided by values and a sense of purpose that go beyond just making money. For example, the well-known Johnson & Johnson Credo, a code of ethics that tells employees what to care about and in what order, puts profits dead last—yet the company has never lost money since going public in 1944.[29] At McDonald's, no exceptions are made to the core values of quality, service, cleanliness, and value; yet in other areas, employees are free to experiment, to be flexible, and to take risks in ways that can help the company reach its goals.

Organization Design. Excellent organizations are characterized by three design attributes: *simple form and lean staff, decentralization to increase entrepreneurship,* and *a balance between financial and nonfinancial measures of performance.*

Simple form and lean staff means that the underlying form and systems of excellent organizations are elegantly simple and few personnel are in staff positions. There is little bureaucracy. Large companies are divided into small divisions for simplicity and adaptability.

Organization structure is decentralized to encourage innovation and change. Creativity and innovation by employees at all levels are encouraged and rewarded. Technical people are located near marketing people so they can lunch together. Organizational units are kept small to create a sense of belonging and shared problem solving.

In addition, successful organizations measure more than the bottom line, recognizing that excellence depends upon a diverse set of competencies and values.[30] Balancing financial and nonfinancial measures provides a better picture of the company's performance and also helps managers align all employees toward key strategic goals.[31] Organizations such as Mobil Corporation's Americas Marketing and Refining division gauge progress by a constellation of measures, including key strategic performance areas like customer satisfaction, employee performance, innovation/change, and community/environmental issues. One study found that companies that carefully track these "soft" competencies along with "hard" data, like financial performance and operating efficiency, were more successful over the long term.[32]

Corporate Culture. Companies throughout the United States and Canada are discovering that employee commitment is a vital component of organization success. Excellent companies manage to harness employee energy and enthusiasm. They do so by creating a *climate of trust,* encouraging *productivity through people*, and taking a *long-term view.*

A climate of trust is necessary so that employees can deal openly and honestly with one another. Collaboration across departments requires trust. Managers and workers must trust one another to work together in joint problem solving. At Ford Motor Company, where workers were historically suspicious of management, a new climate of trust has led to increased productivity and reduced costs.[33]

Productivity through people simply means that everyone must participate. Rank-and-file workers are considered the root of quality and productivity. People are empowered to participate in production, marketing, and new product improvements. Conflicting ideas are encouraged rather than suppressed. The ability to move ahead through consensus preserves the sense of trust, increases motivation, and facilitates both innovation and efficiency.

Another lesson from successful companies is the importance of taking a long-term view. Organizational excellence is not built in a day. Successful companies realize they must invest in training employees and commit to employees for the long term. Career paths are designed to give employees broad backgrounds rather than rapid upward mobility.

The ideas summarized in Exhibit 2.5 are important, but they may not always translate into short-term success. Some research suggests that organizations that have these characteristics often go through periods of lower performance.[34] But a preponderance of these characteristics can help organizations adapt and evolve as the environment changes and thus sustain a long-term commitment to excellence.

ORGANIZATIONAL EFFECTIVENESS

Understanding organizational goals and strategies is the first step toward understanding organizational effectiveness. Organizational goals represent the reason for an organization's existence and the outcomes it seeks to achieve. The next few sections of the chapter explore the topic of effectiveness and how effectiveness is measured in organizations.

Goals were defined earlier as the desired future state of the organization. Organizational **effectiveness** is the degree to which an organization realizes its goals.[35] Effectiveness is a broad concept. It implicitly takes into consideration a range of variables at both the organizational and departmental levels. Effectiveness evaluates the extent to which multiple goals—whether official or operative—are attained.

Efficiency is a more limited concept that pertains to the internal workings of the organization. Organizational efficiency is the amount of resources used to produce a unit of output.[36] It can be measured as the ratio of inputs to outputs. If one organization can achieve a given production level with fewer resources than another organization, it would be described as more efficient.[37]

Sometimes efficiency leads to effectiveness. In other organizations, efficiency and effectiveness are not related. An organization may be highly efficient but fail to achieve its goals because it makes a product for which there is no demand. Likewise, an organization may achieve its profit goals but be inefficient.

Overall effectiveness is difficult to measure in organizations. Organizations are large, diverse, and fragmented. They perform many activities simultaneously. They pursue multiple goals. And they generate many outcomes, some intended and some unintended.[38] However, when managers tie performance measurement to strategy execution, it can be a valuable tool for helping organizations reach their goals.[39]

Traditionally, the measurement of effectiveness has focused on different parts of the organization. Organizations bring resources in from the environment, and those resources are transformed into outputs delivered back into the environment, as shown in Exhibit 2.6. The **goal approach** to organizational effectiveness is concerned with the output side and whether the organization achieves its goals in terms of desired levels of output.[40] The **system resource approach** assesses effectiveness by observing the beginning of the process and evaluating whether the organization effectively obtains resources necessary for high performance. The **internal process approach** looks at internal activities and assesses effectiveness by indicators of internal health and efficiency.

These traditional approaches to organizational effectiveness all have something to offer, but each one tells only part of the story. In addition, a more recent **stakeholder approach** acknowledges that each organization has many

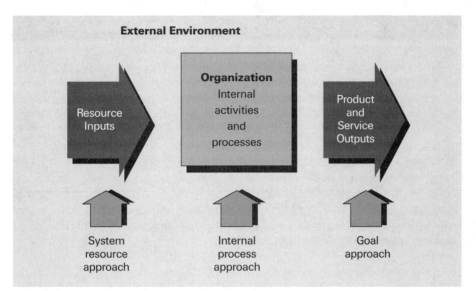

constituencies that have a stake in its outcomes. The stakeholder approach integrates several indicators of effectiveness in a single framework by focusing on stakeholders inside and outside the organization.

Goal Approach

The goal approach to effectiveness consists of identifying an organization's output goals and assessing how well the organization has attained those goals.[41] This is a logical approach because organizations do try to attain certain levels of output, profit, or client satisfaction. The goal approach measures progress toward attainment of those goals.

Indicators. The important goals to consider are operative goals. Efforts to measure effectiveness have been more productive using operative goals than using official goals.[42] Official goals tend to be abstract and difficult to measure. Operative goals reflect activities the organization is actually performing.

One example of multiple goals is from a survey of U.S. business corporations.[43] Their reported goals are shown in Exhibit 2.7. Twelve goals were listed as being important to these companies. These twelve goals represent outcomes that cannot be achieved simultaneously. They illustrate the array of outcomes organizations attempt to achieve.

Usefulness. The goal approach is used in business organizations because output goals can be readily measured. Business firms typically evaluate performance in terms of profitability, growth, market share, and return on investment. However, identifying operative goals and measuring performance of an organization are not always easy. Two problems that must be resolved are the issues of multiple goals and subjective indicators of goal attainment.

Since organizations have multiple and conflicting goals, effectiveness often cannot be assessed by a single indicator. High achievement on one goal may mean low achievement on another. Moreover, there are department goals as well as overall performance goals. The full assessment of effectiveness should take into consideration several goals simultaneously.

Exhibit 2.7
Reported Goals of U.S. Corporations

Goal	% Corporations
Profitability	89
Growth	82
Market share	66
Social responsibility	65
Employee welfare	62
Product quality and service	60
Research and development	54
Diversification	51
Efficiency	50
Financial stability	49
Resource conservation	39
Management development	35

Source: Adapted from Y. K. Shetty, "New Look at Corporate Goals," *California Management Review* 22, No. 2 (1979), 71–79.

The other issue to resolve with the goal approach is how to identify operative goals for an organization and how to measure goal attainment. For business organizations, there are often objective indicators for certain goals. The stated objectives of top management and such measures as profit or growth are available in published reports. Some goals cannot be measured objectively. For example, in business organizations, subjective assessment is needed for such outcomes as employee welfare or social responsibility. Many not-for-profit organizations and some businesses rely heavily on subjective assessment of goals. Someone has to go into the organization and learn what the actual goals are. Since goals reflect the values of top management, the best informants are members of the top management coalition.[44] These managers can report on the actual goals of the organization. Once goals are identified, subjective perceptions of goal achievement can be obtained if quantitative indicators are not available. Top managers rely on information from customers, competitors, suppliers, and employees, as well as on their own intuition, when considering these goals.[45]

The goal approach seems to be the most logical way to assess organizational effectiveness. Effectiveness is defined as the ability of an organization to attain its goals. However, the actual measurement of effectiveness is a complex problem. Organizations have many goals, so there is no single indicator of effectiveness. Some goals are subjective and must be identified by managers within the organization. The assessment of organizational effectiveness using the goal approach requires that the evaluator be aware of these issues and allow for them in the evaluation of effectiveness.

System Resource Approach

The system resource approach looks at the input side of the transformation process shown in Exhibit 2.6. It assumes organizations must be successful in obtaining resource inputs and in maintaining the organizational system to be effective. Organizations must obtain scarce and valued resources from other organizations. From a systems view, organizational effectiveness is defined as the ability of the organization, in either absolute or relative terms, to exploit its environment in the acquisition of scarce and valued resources.

Indicators. Obtaining resources to maintain the organization system is the criterion by which organizational effectiveness is assessed. In a broad sense, indicators of system resource effectiveness encompass the following dimensions:

1. Bargaining position—the ability of the organization to exploit its environment in the acquisition of scarce and valued resources
2. Ability of the system's decision makers to perceive and correctly interpret the real properties of the external environment
3. Maintenance of internal day-to-day organizational activities
4. Ability of the organization to respond to changes in the environment.[46]

Usefulness. The system resource approach is valuable when other indicators of performance are difficult to obtain. In many not-for-profit and social welfare organizations, for example, it is hard to measure output goals or internal efficiency. George Mason University recently received a lot of attention for increasing its academic reputation. The indicators used to evaluate George Mason's effectiveness were its ability to obtain scarce and valued resources. At one time, its faculty was considered second-rate, but George Mason has since been able to hire top professors to fill endowed chairs in several departments. Another indicator is the ability to obtain gifts of money. In four years, George Mason went from an endowment of less than $1 million and no professorships to an endowment of $20 million and twenty-nine professorships. Another scarce and valued resource is students. George Mason was able to increase the diversity of its student body and attract students with higher scholastic aptitude test scores. The ability to attract better students and faculty, plus winning large gifts from businesses and foundations, are used by George Mason administrators to indicate effective performance.[47]

Although the system resource approach is valuable when other measures of effectiveness are not available, it does have shortcomings. Often the ability to acquire resources seems less important than the utilization of those resources. For example, a college football program that recruits many star players would not be considered effective if the program did not develop the players to produce a winning team. This approach is most valuable when measures of goal attainment cannot be obtained.

Internal Process Approach

In the internal process approach, effectiveness is measured as internal organizational health and efficiency. An effective organization has a smooth, well-oiled internal process. Employees are happy and satisfied. Departmental activities mesh with one another to ensure high productivity. This approach does not consider the external environment. The important element in effectiveness is what the organization does with the resources it has, as reflected in internal health and efficiency.

Indicators. The best-known proponents of a process model are from the human relations approach to organizations. Such writers as Chris Argyris, Warren G. Bennis, Rensis Likert, and Richard Beckhard have all worked extensively with human resources in organizations and emphasize the connection between human resources and effectiveness.[48] Writers on corporate culture and organizational excellence have stressed the importance of internal processes. Results from a recent study of nearly two hundred secondary schools showed that both human resources and employee-oriented processes were important in explaining and promoting effectiveness in those organizations.[49]

Indicators of an effective organization as seen from an internal process approach are:

1. Strong corporate culture and positive work climate
2. Team spirit, group loyalty, and teamwork
3. Confidence, trust, and communication between workers and management
4. Decision making near sources of information, regardless of where those sources are on the organizational chart
5. Undistorted horizontal and vertical communication; sharing of relevant facts and feelings
6. Rewards to managers for performance, growth, and development of subordinates and for creating an effective working group
7. Interaction between the organization and its parts, with conflict that occurs over projects resolved in the interest of the organization.[50]

A second indicator of internal process effectiveness is the measurement of economic efficiency. William Evan developed a method that uses quantitative measures of efficiency.[51] The first step is to identify the financial cost of inputs (I), transformation (T), and outputs (O). Next, the three variables can be combined in ratios to evaluate various aspects of organizational performance. The most popular assessment of efficiency is O/I. For an automaker, this would be the number of cars produced per employee. For a hospital, the O/I ratio is the number of patients per annual budget. For a university, it is the number of students graduated divided by the resource inputs. The O/I ratio indicates overall financial efficiency for an organization.

Usefulness. The internal process approach is important because the efficient use of resources and harmonious internal functioning are ways to measure effectiveness. As discussed in Chapter 1, a significant recent trend in management is the empowerment of human resources as a source of competitive advantage. Most managers believe participative management approaches and positive corporate culture are important components of effectiveness.

The financial approach to efficiency is useful for measuring the performance of departments concerned with efficiency, such as manufacturing. For example, the manufacturing efficiency of Chrysler enabled it to become the low-cost producer in the automobile industry. The assembly line was reorganized, and the number of robots was increased from 300 to 1,242. The payoff in productivity was an increase from 4,500 to 8,000 cars and trucks a day, while the number of worker-hours to build a vehicle shrank from 175 to 102.[52]

The internal process approach does have shortcomings. Total output and the organization's relationship with the external environment are not evaluated. Also, evaluations of internal health and functioning are often subjective, because many aspects of inputs and internal processes are not quantifiable. Managers should be aware that efficiency alone represents a limited view of organizational effectiveness.

Stakeholder Approach

A **stakeholder** is any group within or outside an organization that has a stake in the organization's performance. Creditors, suppliers, employees, and owners are all stakeholders. In the stakeholder approach (also called the constituency approach), the satisfaction of such groups can be assessed as an indicator of the organization's performance.[53] Each stakeholder will have a different criterion of effectiveness because it has a different interest in the organization. Each stakeholder group has to be surveyed to learn whether the organization performs well from its viewpoint.

Indicators. The initial work on evaluating effectiveness on the basis of stakeholders included ninety-seven small businesses in Texas. Seven stakeholder groups relevant to those businesses were surveyed to determine the perception of effectiveness from each viewpoint.[54] Each stakeholder and its criterion of effectiveness are:

Stakeholder	Effectiveness Criteria
1. Owners	Financial return
2. Employees	Worker satisfaction, pay, supervision
3. Customers	Quality of goods and services
4. Creditors	Creditworthiness
5. Community	Contribution to community affairs
6. Suppliers	Satisfactory transactions
7. Government	Obedience to laws, regulations

The survey of stakeholders showed that a small business found it difficult to simultaneously fulfill the demands of all groups. One business may have high employee satisfaction, but the satisfaction of other groups may be lower. Nevertheless, measuring all seven stakeholders provides a more accurate view of effectiveness than any single measure. Evaluating how organizations perform across each group offers an overall assessment of effectiveness.

Usefulness. The stakeholder approach is gaining in popularity, based on the view that effectiveness is a complex, multidimensional concept that has no single measure.[55] Recent research has shown that the assessment of multiple stakeholder groups is an accurate reflection of effectiveness, especially with respect to organizational adaptability.[56] Moreover, research shows that firms really do care about their reputational status and do attempt to shape stakeholders' assessments of their performance.[57] If an organization performs poorly according to several interest groups, it is probably not meeting its effectiveness goals. However, satisfying some stakeholders may alienate others. For example, at Safeway, Inc., stock prices soared after CEO Steve Burd began aggressively cutting costs and improving service. Yet, while shareholders and customers were satisfied, suppliers began complaining that the drastic cost-cutting often meant transferring more expenses to vendors.[58]

The strength of the stakeholder approach is that it takes a broad view of effectiveness and examines factors in the environment as well as within the organization. The stakeholder approach includes the community's notion of social responsibility, which was not formally measured in traditional approaches. The stakeholder approach also handles several criteria simultaneously—inputs, internal processing, outputs—and acknowledges that there is no single measure of effectiveness. The well-being of employees is just as important as attaining the owner's goals.

SUMMARY OF KEY ISSUES

This chapter discussed organizational goals and the strategies top managers use to help organizations achieve those goals. Goals specify the mission or purpose of an organization and its desired future state; strategies define how the organization will reach its goals. The chapter also discussed the most popular approaches to measuring effectiveness, that is, how well the organization realizes its purpose and attains its desired future state.

Organizations exist for a purpose; top managers define a specific mission or task to be accomplished. The mission, or official goals, makes explicit the purpose and direction of an organization. Official and operative goals are a key element in organizations because they meet these needs—establishing legitimacy with external groups and setting standards of performance for participants.

Managers must develop strategies that describe the actions required to achieve goals. They attempt to develop strategies that are compatible with the external environment. Porter's model of competitive strategies provides one framework for competitive action. In addition, managers can develop a number of internal organization characteristics that contribute to organizational excellence.

Today's most successful companies remain flexible to adapt quickly to a chaotic international environment. This chapter examined characteristics of strategic orientation, top management, organization design, and corporate culture that are usually found in excellent companies.

Assessing organizational effectiveness is complex and reflects the complexity of organizations as a topic of study. No easy, simple, guaranteed measure will provide an unequivocal assessment of performance. Organizations must perform diverse activities well—from obtaining resource inputs to delivering outputs—to be successful. Traditional approaches used output goals, resource acquisition, or internal health and efficiency as the criteria of effectiveness. Contemporary approaches consider multiple criteria simultaneously. One recent approach assesses organization effectiveness by surveying constituencies that have a stake in organizational performance. No approach is suitable for every organization, but each offers some advantage that the others may lack.

From the point of view of managers, the goal approach to effectiveness and measures of internal efficiency are useful when measures are available. The attainment of output and profit goals reflects the purpose of the organization, and efficiency reflects the cost of attaining those goals. Other factors such as top management preferences, the extent to which goals are measurable, and the scarcity of environmental resources may influence the use of effectiveness criteria. In not-for-profit organizations, where internal processes and output criteria often are not quantifiable, stakeholder satisfaction or resource acquisition may be the only available indicators of effectiveness.

From the point of view of people outside the organization, such as academic investigators or government researchers, the stakeholder approach to organizational effectiveness may be preferable. The stakeholder approach evaluates the organization's contribution to various stakeholders, including owners, employees, customers, and the community.

Discussion Questions

1. Discuss the role of top management in setting organizational direction.
2. How do operative market goals differ from resource and productivity goals?
3. Compare the twelve qualities associated with organizational excellence with the internal process and goal approaches to *measuring effectiveness.* Which approach would seem to best measure excellence in a company?
4. What is the difference between a goal and a strategy?
5. Discuss the difference between a low-cost leadership and a differentiation strategy described in Porter's model of competitive strategies. Identify a company you are familiar with that illustrates each strategy and explain why.
6. Do you believe mission statements and official goal statements provide an organization with genuine legitimacy in the external environment? Discuss.
7. Suppose you have been asked to evaluate the effectiveness of the police department in a medium-sized community. Where would you begin, and how would you proceed? What effectiveness approach would you prefer?
8. What are the advantages and disadvantages of the system resource approach versus the goal approach for measuring organizational effectiveness?
9. A noted organization theorist once said, "Organizational effectiveness can be whatever top management defines it to be." Discuss.

Notes

1. Amitai Etzioni, *Modern Organizations* (Englewood Cliffs, N.J.: Prentice-Hall, 1964), 6.

2. John P. Kotter, "What Effective General Managers Really Do," *Harvard Business Review* (November–December 1982): 156–67; Henry Mintzberg, *The Nature of Managerial Work* (New York: Harper & Row, 1973).

3. Charles C. Snow and Lawrence G. Hrebiniak, "Strategy, Distinctive Competence, and Organizational Performance," *Administrative Science Quarterly* 25 (1980): 317–35.

4. Elizabeth Lesly, "A Safer New York," *Business Week,* 11 December 1995, 81–84; and Eric Pooley, "One Good Apple," *Time,* 15 January 1996, 54–56.

5. David L. Calfee, "Get Your Mission Statement Working!" *Management Review,* January 1993, 54–57; John A. Pearce II and Fred David, "Corporate Mission Statements: The Bottom Line," *Academy of Management Executive* 1 (1987): 109–16; Fred R. David, "How Companies Define Their Mission," *Long-Range Planning* 22 (1989): 90–97.

6. Charles Perrow, "The Analysis of Goals in Complex Organizations," *American Sociological Review* 26 (1961): 854–66.

7. Johannes U. Stoelwinder and Martin P. Charns, "The Task Field Model of Organization Analysis and Design," *Human Relations* 34 (1981): 743–62; Anthony Raia, *Managing by Objectives* (Glenview, Ill.: Scott, Foresman, 1974).

8. Kevin Helliker, "Pressure at Pier 1: Beating Sales Numbers of Year Earlier Is a Storewide Obsession," *The Wall Street Journal,* 7 December 1995, B1, B2.

9. Myron Magnet, "Let's Go For Growth," *Fortune,* 7 March 1994, 60–72; Patricia Sellers, "Pepsi Keeps on Going after No. 1," *Fortune,* 11 March 1991, 64.

10. William W. Arnold, "Lessons of Value-Driven Leadership," *Healthcare Executive,* July/August 1995, 12–15.

11. Rahul Jacob, "Corporate Reputations," *Fortune,* 6 March 1995, 54–57.

12. Alex Taylor III, "Why the Bounce at Rubbermaid," *Fortune,* 13 April 1987, 77–78.

13. Mark C. Suchman, "Managing Legitimacy: Strategic and Institutional Approaches," *Academy of Management Review,* Vol. 20, No. 3, 1995, 571–610.

14. Edward A. Robinson, "America's Most Admired Companies," *Fortune,* 3 March 1997, 68–75; Anne B. Fisher, "Corporate Reputations," *Fortune,* 4 March 1996, 90–98; Ken Friedman, Norwegian School of Management, Oslo, Norway, personal communication.

15. James D. Thompson, *Organizations in Action* (New York: McGraw-Hill, 1967), 83–98.

16. "Owens-Illinois: Giving up Market Share to Improve Profits," *Business Week,* 11 May 1981, 81–82.

17. Richard Crone, Bruce Snow, and Ricky Waclawcayk, "Datapoint Corporation," unpublished manuscript, Texas A&M University, 1981.

18. Michael E. Porter, *Competitive Strategy: Techniques for Analyzing Industries and Competitors* (New York: Free Press, 1980).

19. Peter Burrows, "Compaq Stretches for the Crown," *Business Week,* 11 July 1994, 140–42.

20. Greg Burns, "It Only Hertz When Enterprise Laughs," *Business Week,* 12 December 1994, 44.

21. James C. Collins and Jerry I. Porras, *Built to Last: Successful Habits of Visionary Companies,* (New York: HarperBusiness, 1994).

22. Michael Hammer and James Champy, *Reengineering the Corporation* (New York, HarperCollins, 1993); Noel M. Tichy and Stratford Sherman, *Control Your Destiny or Someone Else Will* (New York: Currency Doubleday, 1993).

23. Oren Harari, "You're Not in Business to Make a Profit," *Management Review,* July 1992, 53–55.

24. Sellers, "Pepsi Keeps on Going after No. 1."

25. James C. Collins, "Building Companies to Last," *Inc.—The State of Small Business 1995,* 16 May 1995, 83–85.

26. Kenneth Labich, "Why Companies Fail," *Fortune,* 14 November 1994, 52–68.

27. James C. Collins and Jerry I. Porras, "Building a Visionary Company," *California Management Review,* Vol. 37, No. 2, Winter 1995, 80–100.

28. Amy Dunkin, "Pepsi's Marketing Magic: Why Nobody Does It Better," *Business Week,* 10 February 1986, 52–57.

29. James C. Collins, "Building Companies to Last"; Brian O'Reilly, "J&J Is on a Roll," *Fortune,* 26 December 1994, 178–91.

30. James V. Koch and Richard J. Cebula, "In Search of Excellent Management," *Journal of Management Studies,* Vol. 31, No. 5, September 1994, 681–99.

31. Robert S. Kaplan and David P. Norton, "Using the Balanced Scorecard as a Strategic Management System," *Harvard Business Review,* January–February, 1996, 75–85.

32. Brian McWilliams, "The Measure of Success," *Across the Board,* February 1996, 16–20; and John H. Lingle and William A. Schiemann, "From Balanced Scorecard to Strategic Gauges: Is Measurement Worth It?" *Management Review,* March 1996, 56–61.

33. Neil Templin, "A Decisive Response to Crisis Brought Ford Enhanced Productivity," *The Wall Street Journal,* 15 December 1992, A1, A8.

34. Michael A. Hitt and R. Duane Ireland, "Peters and Waterman Revisited: The Unended Quest for Excellence," *Academy of Management Executive* 1 (1987): 91–98.

35. Etzioni, *Modern Organizations,* 8.

36. Etzioni, *Modern Organizations,* 8; Gary D. Sandefur, "Efficiency in Social Service Organizations," *Administration and Society* 14 (1983): 449–68.

37. Richard M. Steers, *Organizational Effectiveness: A Behavioral View* (Santa Monica, Calif.: Goodyear, 1977), 51.

38. Karl E. Weick and Richard L. Daft, "The Effectiveness of Interpretation Systems," in Kim S. Cameron and David A. Whetten, eds. *Organizational Effectiveness: A Comparison of Multiple Models* (New York: Academic Press, 1982).

39. Robert S. Kaplan and David P. Norton, "Using the Balanced Scorecard as a Strategic Management System," *Harvard Business Review,* January–February 1996, 75–85; Craig Eric Schneider, Douglas G. Shaw, and Richard W. Beatty, "Performance Measurement and Management: A Tool for Strategy Execution," *Human Resource Management* 30 (Fall 1991): 279–301.

40. Steven Strasser, J. D. Eveland, Gaylord Cummins, O. Lynn Deniston, and John H. Romani, "Conceptualizing the Goal and Systems Models of Organizational Effectiveness—Implications for Comparative Evaluation Research," *Journal of Management Studies* 18 (1981): 321–40.

41. James L. Price, "The Study of Organizational Effectiveness," *Sociological Quarterly* 13 (1972): 3–15.

42. Richard H. Hall and John P. Clark, "An Ineffective Effectiveness Study and Some Suggestions for Future Research," *Sociological Quarterly* 21 (1980): 119–34; Price, "Study of Organizational Effectiveness"; Perrow, "Analysis of Goals."

43. George W. England, "Organizational Goals and Expected Behaviors in American Managers," *Academy of Management Journal* 10 (1967): 107–17.

44. Johannes M. Pennings and Paul S. Goodman, "Toward a Workable Framework," in Paul S. Goodman, Johannes M. Pennings, et al., *New Perspectives on Organizational Effectiveness* (San Francisco: Jossey-Bass, 1979), 152.

45. David L. Blenkhorn and Brian Gaber, "The Use of 'Warm Fuzzies' to Assess Organizational Effectiveness," *Journal of General Management,* Vol. 21, No. 2, Winter 1995, 40–51.

46. J. Barton Cunningham, "A Systems-Resource Approach for Evaluating Organizational Effectiveness," *Human Relations* 31 (1978): 631–56; Ephraim Yuchtman and Stanley E. Seashore, "A System Resource Approach to Organizational Effectiveness," *Administrative Science Quarterly* 12 (1967): 377–95.

47. David Shribeman, "University in Virginia Creates a Niche, Aims to Reach Top Ranks," *The Wall Street Journal,* 30 September 1985, 1, 9.

48. Chris Argyris, *Integrating the Individual and the Organization* (New York: Wiley, 1964); Warren G. Bennis, *Changing Organizations* (New York: McGraw-Hill, 1966); Rensis Likert, *The Human Organization* (New York: McGraw-Hill, 1967); Richard Beckhard, *Organization Development Strategies and Models* (Reading, Mass.: Addison-Wesley, 1969).

49. Cheri Ostroff and Neal Schmitt, "Configurations of Organizational Effectiveness and Efficiency," *Academy of Management Journal* 36 (1993): 1345–61;

Peter J. Frost, Larry F. Moore, Meryl Reise Louis, Craig C. Lundburg, and Joanne Martin, *Organizational Culture* (Beverly Hills, Calif.: Sage, 1985).

50. J. Barton Cunningham, "Approaches to the Evaluation of Organizational Effectiveness," *Academy of Management Review* 2 (1977): 463–74; Beckhard, *Organization Development.*

51. William M. Evan, "Organization Theory and Organizational Effectiveness: An Exploratory Analysis," *Organization and Administrative Sciences* 7 (1976): 15–28.

52. Alex Taylor III, "Lee Iacocca's Production Whiz," *Fortune,* 22 June 1987, 36–44.

53. Anne S. Tusi, "A Multiple-Constituency Model of Effectiveness: An Empirical Examination at the Human Resource Subunit Level," *Administrative Science Quarterly* 35 (1990): 458, 483; Charles Fombrun and Mark Shanley, "What's in a Name? Reputation Building and Corporate Strategy," *Academy of Management Journal* 33 (1990): 233–58; Terry Connolly, Edward J. Conlon, and Stuart Jay Deutsch, "Organizational Effectiveness: A Multiple-Constituency Approach," *Academy of Management Review* 5 (1980): 211–17.

54. Frank Friedlander and Hal Pickle, "Components of Effectiveness in Small Organizations," *Administrative Science Quarterly* 13 (1968): 289–304.

55. Kim S. Cameron, "The Effectiveness of Ineffectiveness," in Barry M. Staw and L. L. Cummings, eds., *Research in Organizational Behavior* (Greenwich, Conn.: JAI Press, 1984), 235–86; Rosabeth Moss Kanter and Derick Brinkerhoff, "Organizational Performance: Recent Developments in Measurement," *Annual Review of Sociology* 7 (1981): 321–49.

56. Tusi, "A Multiple-Constituency Model of Effectiveness."

57. Fombrun and Shanley, "What's in a Name?"

58. Russell Mitchell, "Safeway's Low-Fat Diet," *Business Week,* 18 October 1993, 60–61.

3

chapter three

The External Environment

While reading this chapter, think about your answers to the following questions:

- What is the difference between the general environment and the task environment, and what are the specific dimensions of each?

- How do the simple-complex and stable-unstable dimensions of the environment influence an organization?

- How do organizations adapt to highly uncertain environments?

- What are some techniques managers can use to influence or control the external environment?

A T&T once ruled the long-distance telephone market, but after a lawsuit in the mid-1980s paved the way for MCI, Sprint, and other carriers, AT&T rapidly lost 30 percent of market share. Today, government deregulation is sparking more upheaval in the telecommunications industry, clearing the way for local phone companies to compete in the long-distance market while AT&T, MCI, and Sprint will be able to offer local as well as long-distance services. The merger of MCI with British Telecommunications will offer even greater competitive challenges to the once-supreme AT&T.[1]

AT&T was surprised by the external environment in the mid-1980s, and managers are working overtime to ensure that the same thing doesn't happen again. AT&T managers know they are operating in a highly competitive and rapidly changing industry, and they search for ways to interpret, influence, and adapt to the environment. Similar turbulence and uncertainty face major European telecommunications companies such as British Telecommunications, France Telecom, and Deutsche Telekom AG, as countries in the European Union prepare to open their phone markets to full competition by 1998.

The problem of a changing environment is not unique to telecommunications firms. Companies in all industries confront difficulties because of changes in the environment. Apple Computer is struggling to survive in an industry that has become dominated by PC clones based on Intel and Microsoft technology.[2] Small retailers have long suffered threats from huge discount stores, such as Wal-Mart. But even the mighty Wal-Mart is vulnerable to changes in the environment. Small retailers are challenging some of the giant chain's competitive tactics in court, claiming it is violating antitrust laws, and stubborn New Englanders have slowed the expansion of Wal-Mart into that region largely with zoning requirements and legal arguments that it will have a detrimental impact on the local environment.[3]

Firms that attempt to grow through mergers and acquisitions have run into brick walls in the form of tough regulations in many states. For other firms, new technology such as digital communications, microrobots from Japan, or Nucor's highly efficient thin-slab steel casting poses major threats. Also, firms in all industries agree that international competition worries everyone. The list could go on and on. The external environment is the source of important threats facing major corporations today.[4]

PURPOSE OF THIS CHAPTER

The purpose of this chapter is to develop a framework for assessing environments and how organizations can respond to them. First, we will identify the organizational domain and the sectors that influence the organization. Then, we will explore two major environmental forces on the organization—the need for information and the need for resources. Organizations respond to these forces through structural design, planning systems, imitation, and attempts to change and control elements in the environment.

THE ENVIRONMENTAL DOMAIN

In a broad sense, the environment is infinite and includes everything outside the organization. However, the analysis presented here considers only the aspects of the environment to which the organization is sensitive and must respond to survive. Thus, **organizational environment** is defined as all elements that exist outside the boundary of the organization and have the potential to affect all or part of the organization.

The environment of an organization can be understood by analyzing its domain within external sectors. An organization's **domain** is the chosen environmental field of action. It is the territory an organization stakes out for itself with respect to products, services, and markets served. Domain defines the organization's niche and defines those external sectors with which the organization will interact to accomplish its goals. For example, the domain of AT&T brings it into contact with customers, competitors, suppliers, and government rules and regulations.

The environment comprises several **sectors** or subdivisions of the external environment that contain similar elements. Ten sectors can be analyzed for each organization: industry, raw materials, human resources, financial resources, market, technology, economic conditions, government, sociocultural, and international. The sectors and a hypothetical organizational domain are illustrated in Exhibit 3.1. For most companies, the sectors in Exhibit 3.1 can be further subdivided into the task environment and general environment.

Task Environment

The **task environment** includes sectors with which the organization interacts directly and that have a direct impact on the organization's ability to achieve its goals. The task environment typically includes the industry, raw materials, and market sectors, and perhaps the human resources and international sectors.

For example, in the *industry sector*, brand name products are fighting it out with lower-cost store brands. Procter & Gamble cut prices on Joy dishwashing liquid, Era detergent, and Luvs disposable diapers to compete with discount brands of similar products. Other companies decided if they couldn't beat store brands, they might as well join them. RJR Nabisco, for example, has announced plans to test-market lower-priced private label cookies and crackers in some stores. An interesting example in the *raw materials sector* concerns the beverage can industry. Steelmakers owned the beverage can market until the mid-1960s, when Reynolds Aluminum Company launched a huge aluminum recycling program to gain a cheaper source of raw materials and make aluminum cans price-competitive with steel.[5]

General Environment

The **general environment** includes those sectors that may not have a direct impact on the daily operations of a firm but will indirectly influence it. The general environment often includes the government, sociocultural, economic conditions, technology, and financial resources sectors. These sectors affect all organizations eventually. For example, in the *sociocultural sector*, a growing concern for environmental protection and animal welfare is impacting numerous companies. Companies such as Aveda and John Paul Mitchell include in

Exhibit 3.1
An Organization's Environment

(a) Competitors, industry size and competitiveness, related industries

(b) Suppliers, manufacturers, real estate, services

(c) Labor market, employment agencies, universities, training schools, employees in other companies, unionization

(d) Stock markets, banks, savings and loans, private investors

(e) Customers, clients, potential users of products and services

(f) Techniques of production, science, research centers, automation, new materials

(g) Recession, unemployment rate, inflation rate, rate of investment, economics, growth

(h) City, state, federal laws and regulations, taxes, services, court system, political processes

(i) Age, values, beliefs, education, religion, work ethic, consumer and green movements

(j) Competition from and acquisition by foreign firms, entry into overseas markets, foreign customs, regulations, exchange rate

their marketing campaigns a commitment to environmental protection and "cruelty free" products, while Procter & Gamble and Gillette have both been targeted for boycott because of their continued use of animal testing.[6]

General *economic conditions* also affect the way a company does business. To remain competitive in an era of low inflation, furniture maker Ethan Allen needed to keep its prices low. To make a healthy profit without raising prices, the company turned to making simpler furniture designs and increasing its technological efficiency.[7]

International Context

The *international sector* can directly affect many organizations, and it has become extremely important in the last few years. In addition, all domestic sectors can be affected by international events. Despite the significance of international events for today's organizations, many students fail to appreciate the importance of international events and still think domestically. Think again. Even if you stay in your hometown, your company may be purchased tomorrow by the British, Canadians, Japanese, or Germans. The Japanese alone own more than one thousand U.S. companies, including steel mills, rubber and tire factories, automobile assembly plants, and auto parts suppliers. Nationwide, more than 350,000 Americans work for Japanese companies. People employed by Pillsbury, Shell Oil, Firestone, and CBS Records are working for foreign bosses.[8]

The impact of the international sector has grown rapidly with advances in technology and communications. Ideas, capital investments, business strategies, products, and services flow freely and rapidly around the world. One small company, Montague Corporation, designs unique folding mountain bikes in Cambridge, Massachusetts, makes them in Taiwan, and sells most of them in Europe. Design changes are sent back and forth across three continents, sometimes on a daily basis. U.S.-based Coca-Cola, Canada's Northern Telecom, Switzerland's Nestlé, and France's Carrefour, the retailer that invented the "hypermarket" concept, all get a large percentage of their sales from outside their home countries.[9] In this global environment, it is no surprise that foreign-born people with international experience have been appointed to run such U.S. companies as Coca-Cola, Ford, Gerber, NCR, and Heinz. Consider the following predictions:[10]

- One analyst believes that in the 21st century, most of the economic activity in the world will take place in Asia and the Pacific Basin.[11] Already, nine of the world's ten largest banks are Japanese, sharply affecting the financial resources sector.
- The North American Free Trade Agreement is spurring many companies, including small businesses, to move into Canada and Mexico, affecting the market and human resources sectors.
- Japan, United Germany, and the European Union of 1992 may spawn large, powerful companies that compete easily with U.S. firms. These companies could reshape the industry and market sectors as we now know them.
- Newly industrialized countries such as Korea, Taiwan, Singapore, and Spain produce huge volumes of low-cost, high quality commodities that will have an impact on the competitiveness of many industries, markets, and raw materials in North America.
- Eastern Europe, Russia, and China are all shifting toward market economies that also will affect markets, raw materials, industry competition, and worldwide economic conditions.
- Hundreds of partnerships are taking place between North American firms and firms in all parts of the world, facilitating the exchange of technology and production capability, thereby redefining the technology, raw materials, and industry sectors.
- Many companies in the United States build twin plants—one in Texas and one in Mexico. The Mexican plants provide component assembly, and that helps combat Mexico's high unemployment. Called maquiladoras, these plants reshape the human resources and raw materials sectors.

- All of these international connections are spawning new state and federal regulations, thereby affecting the government sector, and beliefs and values are becoming shared worldwide, shaping the sociocultural sector.

What kind of chaos does global competition create for organizations? Consider this. By making and designing more of their automobiles in the United States, Japanese auto firms are intensifying their challenge to Detroit. Honda, Nissan, Toyota, Mazda, Mitsubishi, Subaru, and Isuzu have all shifted manufacturing to the United States, and they already own a 30 percent share of the U.S. car market. In addition, the United States is sinking like a rock in the consumer electronics industry. In the 1990s, production in Japan grew three times and production in Europe grew nearly two times faster than in the United States. Zenith is the only remaining U.S. maker of television sets, and it will soon be producing all of its televisions in Mexico, while foreign-owned companies such as Sony and Thomson (once General Electric) produce TVs in the United States. AT&T, once the world's largest telecommunications company, loses that status with the merger of MCI and British Telecommunications, and the Number 3 U.S. long distance company, Sprint, is already 20 percent owned by French and German phone companies.[12]

Yet, there is also a positive side. When companies think globally, the whole world is their marketplace, and there is evidence that U.S. companies are becoming more competitive on a worldwide scale. The Global 1000, a ranking of the world's one thousand most valuable corporations compiled by Geneva-based Morgan Stanley Capital International, found that U.S. corporations have gained a lead over Japanese and European rivals.[13] And for the first time in the nine-year history of the Global 1000, a U.S. company, General Electric, topped the list. GE has put together a portfolio of products and services, such as power-generating equipment, jet engines, and financial services, that fit the needs of emerging-market nations investing heavily in infrastructure. Today, GE's international sales equal 40 percent of the company's total revenues and are expected to reach the half-way mark soon.[14]

GE has been able to outmaneuver less flexible global competitors, but the international environment is ever-changing and companies must be poised for rapid response. Every organization faces environmental uncertainty domestically as well as globally. In the following section, we will discuss in greater detail how companies cope with and respond to this uncertainty.

ENVIRONMENTAL UNCERTAINTY

How does the environment influence an organization? The patterns and events occurring across environmental sectors can be described along several dimensions, such as whether the environment is stable or unstable, homogeneous or heterogeneous, concentrated or dispersed, simple or complex; the extent of turbulence; and the amount of resources available to support the organization.[15] These dimensions boil down to two essential ways the environment influences organizations: (1) the need for information about the environment and (2) the need for resources from the environment. The environmental conditions of complexity and change create a greater need to gather information and to respond based on that information. The organization also is concerned with scarce material and financial resources and with the need to ensure availability of resources.

Each sector can be analyzed relative to these three analytical categories. The remainder of this section will discuss the information perspective, which is concerned with the uncertainty that environmental complexity and change creates for the organization. Later in the chapter, we will discuss how organizations control the environment to acquire needed resources.

Organizations must cope with and manage uncertainty to be effective. **Uncertainty** means that decision makers do not have sufficient information about environmental factors, and they have a difficult time predicting external changes. Uncertainty increases the risk of failure for organizational responses and makes it difficult to compute costs and probabilities associated with decision alternatives.[16] Characteristics of the environmental domain that influence uncertainty are the extent to which the external domain is simple or complex and the extent to which events are stable or unstable.[17]

Simple-Complex Dimension

The **simple-complex dimension** concerns environmental complexity, which refers to heterogeneity, or the number and dissimilarity of external elements relevant to an organization's operations. In a complex environment, many diverse external elements interact with and influence the organization. In a simple environment, as few as three or four similar external elements influence the organization.

Telecommunications firms such as AT&T have a complex environment, as do universities. Universities span a large number of technologies and are a focal point for cultural and value changes. Government regulatory and granting agencies interact with a university, and so do a variety of professional and scientific associations, alumni, parents, foundations, legislators, community residents, international agencies, donors, corporations, and athletic teams. A large number of external elements thus make up the organization's domain, creating a complex environment. On the other hand, a family-owned hardware store in a suburban community is in a simple environment. The only external elements of any real importance are a few competitors, suppliers, and customers. Government regulation is minimal, and cultural change has little impact. Human resources are not a problem because the store is run by family members or part-time help.

Stable-Unstable Dimension

The **stable-unstable dimension** refers to whether elements in the environment are dynamic. An environmental domain is stable if it remains the same over a period of months or years. Under unstable conditions, environmental elements shift abruptly. Instability may occur when competitors react with aggressive moves and counter-moves regarding advertising and new products. For example, aggressive advertising and introduction of new services creates instability for long-distance companies like AT&T. In one year alone, the three major U.S. long-distance carriers pumped over $1 billion into advertising.[18] Sometimes specific, unpredictable events—such as reports of syringes in cans of Pepsi or glass shards in Gerber's baby foods, the poisoning of Tylenol, or Union Carbide's gas leak in Bhopal, India—create unstable conditions.

Although environments are becoming more unstable for most organizations today, an example of a traditionally stable environment is a public utility.[19] In the rural Midwest, demand and supply factors for a public utility are stable. A gradual increase in demand may occur, which is easily predicted over time. Toy companies, by contrast, have an unstable environment. Hot new toys are difficult to predict, a problem compounded by the fact that toys are subject to fad buying. Coleco Industries, makers of the once-famous Cabbage Patch Kids, and Worlds of Wonder, creators of Teddy Ruxpin, went bankrupt because of the unstable nature of the toy environment. Their once-winning creations were replaced by Bandai's Mighty Morphin Power Rangers or Playmate Toys' Teenage Mutant Ninja Turtles.[20]

Framework

The simple-complex and stable-unstable dimensions are combined into a framework for assessing environmental uncertainty in Exhibit 3.2. In the *simple, stable* environment, uncertainty is low. There are only a few external elements to

Exhibit 3.2 *Framework for Assessing Environmental Uncertainty*

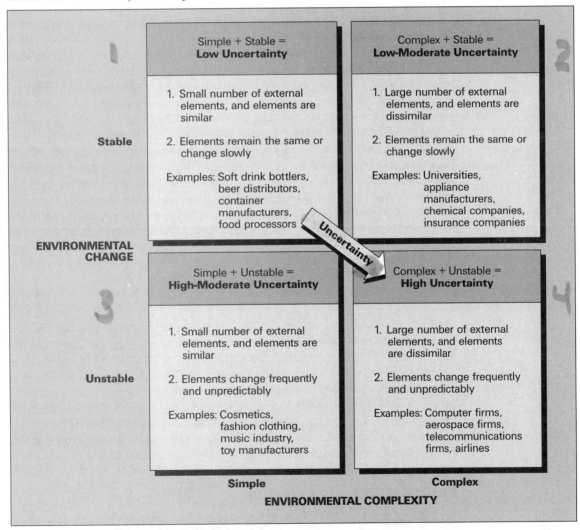

Source: Adapted and reprinted from "Characteristics of Perceived Environments and Perceived Environmental Uncertainty" by Robert B. Duncan, published in *Administrative Science Quarterly* 17 (1972): 313–27, by permission of *The Administrative Science Quarterly*. Copyright © 1972 by Cornell University.

contend with, and they tend to remain stable. The *complex, stable* environment represents somewhat greater uncertainty. A large number of elements have to be scanned, analyzed, and acted upon for the organization to perform well. External elements do not change rapidly or unexpectedly in this environment.

Even greater uncertainty is felt in the *simple, unstable* environment.[21] Rapid change creates uncertainty for managers. Even though the organization has few external elements, those elements are hard to predict, and they react unexpectedly to organizational initiatives. The greatest uncertainty for an organization occurs in the *complex, unstable* environment. A large number of elements impinge on the organization, and they shift frequently or react strongly to organizational initiatives. When several sectors change simultaneously, the environment becomes turbulent.[22]

A beer distributor functions in a simple, stable environment. Demand for beer changes only gradually. The distributor has an established delivery route, and supplies of beer arrive on schedule. State universities, appliance manufacturers, and insurance companies are in somewhat stable, complex environments. A large number of external elements are present, and although they change, changes are gradual and predictable.

Toy manufacturers are in simple, unstable environments. Organizations that design, make, and sell toys, as well as those that are involved in the clothing or music industry, face shifting supply and demand. Mattel is currently trying to regain ground in the toy business with an ambitious push into designing and marketing toys for boys.[23]

The computer industry and the airline industry face complex, unstable environments. Many external sectors are changing simultaneously. In the case of airlines, in just a few years they were confronted with deregulation, the growth of regional airlines, surges in fuel costs, price cuts from competitors such as Southwest Airlines, shifting customer demand, an air-traffic controller shortage, overcrowded airports, and a reduction of scheduled flights.[24] A recent series of major air traffic disasters has further contributed to the complex, unstable environment for the industry.

ADAPTING TO ENVIRONMENTAL UNCERTAINTY

Once you see how environments differ with respect to change and complexity, the next question is, "How do organizations adapt to each level of environmental uncertainty?" Environmental uncertainty represents an important contingency for organization structure and internal behaviors. An organization in a certain environment will be managed and controlled differently from an organization in an uncertain environment with respect to positions and departments, organizational differentiation and integration, control processes, institutional imitation, and future planning and forecasting. Organizations need to have the right fit between internal structure and the external environment.

Positions and Departments

As the complexity in the external environment increases, so does the number of positions and departments within the organization, which in turn increases internal complexity. This relationship is part of being an open system. Each sector in the external environment requires an employee or department to deal with it. The human resources department deals with unemployed people who want to work for the company. The marketing department finds customers. Procurement employees obtain raw materials from hundreds of suppliers. The finance group deals with bankers. The legal department works with the courts and government agencies.

Buffering and Boundary Spanning

The traditional approach to coping with environmental uncertainty was to establish buffer departments. The **buffering role** is to absorb uncertainty from the environment.[25] The technical core performs the primary production activity of an organization. Buffer departments surround the technical core and exchange materials, resources, and money between the environment and the organization. They help the technical core function efficiently. The purchasing department buffers the technical core by stockpiling supplies and raw materials. The human resources department buffers the technical core by handling the uncertainty associated with finding, hiring, and training production employees.

A newer approach some organizations are trying is to drop the buffers and expose the technical core to the uncertain environment. These organizations no longer create buffers because they believe being well connected to customers and suppliers is more important than internal efficiency. For example, John Deere has assembly-line workers visiting local farms to determine and respond to customer concerns. Whirlpool pays hundreds of customers to test computer-simulated products and features.[26] Opening up the organization to the environment makes it more fluid and adaptable.

Boundary-spanning roles link and coordinate an organization with key elements in the external environment. Boundary spanning is primarily concerned with the exchange of information to (1) detect and bring into the organization information about changes in the environment and (2) send information into the environment that presents the organization in a favorable light.[27]

To detect important information, boundary personnel scan the environment. For example, a market research department scans and monitors trends in consumer tastes. Boundary spanners in engineering and research and development (R&D) departments scan new technological developments, innovations, and raw materials. Boundary spanners prevent the organization from stagnating by keeping top managers informed about environmental changes. Often, the greater the uncertainty in the environment, the greater the importance of boundary spanners.[28]

Today, with global trade barriers falling and competition becoming more fierce, one of the fastest-growing areas of boundary spanning is competitive intelligence. Companies, large and small, are setting up competitive intelligence departments or hiring outside specialists to gather information on competitors. Competitive intelligence gives top executives a systematic way to collect and analyze public information about rivals and use it to make better decisions.[29] Using techniques that range from Internet surfing to digging through trash cans, intelligence professionals dig up information on competitors' new products, manufacturing costs, or training methods and share it with top leaders. For example, NutraSweet's competitive intelligence department helped the company delay a costly advertising campaign when it learned that a rival sweetener from Johnson & Johnson was at least five years away from FDA approval.[30] In today's uncertain environment, competitive intelligence is a trend that is likely to increase.

The boundary task of sending information into the environment to represent the organization is used to influence other people's perception of the organization. In the marketing department, advertising and sales people represent the organization to customers. Purchasers may call on suppliers and describe purchasing needs. The legal department informs lobbyists and elected officials about the organization's needs or views on political matters.

Differentiation and Integration

Another response to environmental uncertainty is the amount of differentiation and integration among departments. Organization **differentiation** is "the differences in cognitive and emotional orientations among managers in different functional departments, and the difference in formal structure among these departments."[31] When the external environment is complex and rapidly changing, organizational departments become highly specialized to handle the uncertainty in their external sector. Success in each sector requires special expertise and behavior. Employees in a research and development department thus have unique attitudes, values, goals, and education that distinguish them from employees in manufacturing or sales departments.

A study by Paul Lawrence and Jay Lorsch examined three organizational departments—manufacturing, research, and sales—in ten corporations.[32] This study found that each department evolved toward a different orientation and structure to deal with specialized parts of the external environment. The market, scientific, and manufacturing subenvironments identified by Lawrence and Lorsch are illustrated in Exhibit 3.3. Each department interacted with different external groups. The differences that evolved among departments within the organizations are shown in Exhibit 3.4. To work effectively with the scientific sub-environment, R&D had a goal of quality work, a long-time horizon (up to five years), an informal structure, and task-oriented employees. Sales was at the opposite extreme. It had a goal of customer satisfaction, was oriented toward the short term (two weeks or so), had a very formal structure, and was socially oriented.

Exhibit 3.3 *Organizational Departments Differentiate to Meet Needs of Subenvironments*

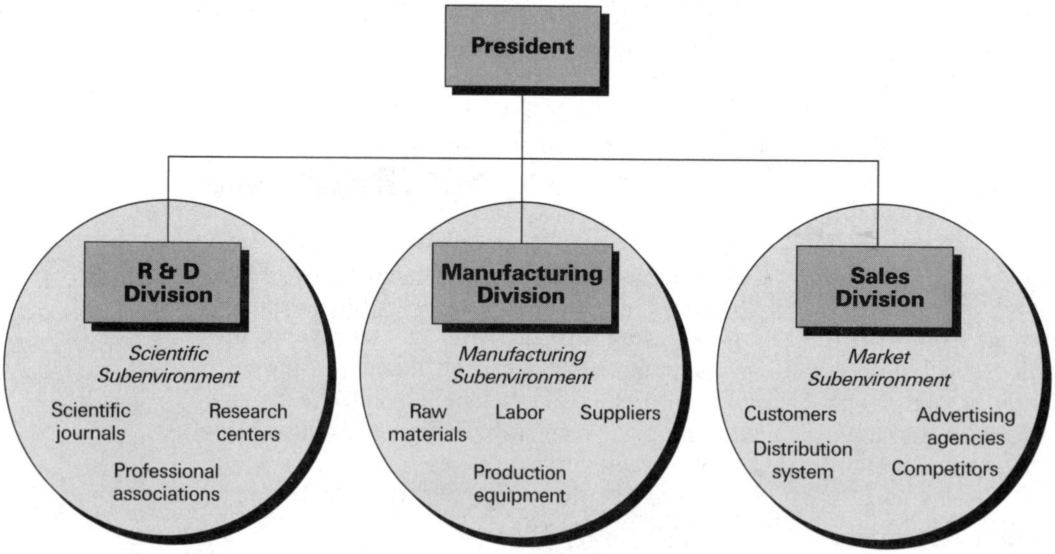

Exhibit 3.4
Differences in Goals and Orientations among Organizational Departments

Characteristic	R&D Department	Manufacturing Department	Sales Department
Goals	New developments, quality	Efficient production	Customer satisfaction
Time horizon	Long	Short	Short
Interpersonal orientation	Mostly task	Task	Social
Formality of structure	Low	High	High

Source: Based on Paul R. Lawrence and Jay W. Lorsch, *Organization and Environment* (Homewood, Ill.: Irwin, 1969), 23–29.

One outcome of high differentiation is that coordination between departments becomes difficult. More time and resources must be devoted to achieving coordination when attitudes, goals, and work orientation differ so widely. **Integration** is the quality of collaboration between departments.[33] Formal integrators are often required to coordinate departments. When the environment is highly uncertain, frequent changes require more information processing to achieve coordination, so integrators become a necessary addition to the organization structure. Sometimes integrators are called liaison personnel, brand managers, or coordinators. As illustrated in Exhibit 3.5, organizations with highly uncertain environments and a highly differentiated structure assign about 22 percent of management personnel to integration activities, such as serving on committees, on task forces, or in liaison roles.[34] In organizations characterized by very simple, stable environments, almost no managers are assigned to integration roles. Exhibit 3.5 shows that, as environmental uncertainty increases, so does differentiation between departments; hence, the organization must assign a larger percentage of managers to coordinating roles.

Lawrence and Lorsch's research concluded that organizations perform better when the levels of differentiation and integration match the level of uncertainty in the environment. Organizations that performed well in uncertain environments had high levels of both differentiation and integration, while those performing well in less uncertain environments had lower levels of differentiation and integration.

Organic Versus Mechanistic Management Processes

Another response to environmental uncertainty is the amount of formal structure and control imposed on employees. Tom Burns and G. M. Stalker observed

Exhibit 3.5
Environmental Uncertainty and Organizational Integrators

	Plastics	Industry Foods	Container
Environmental uncertainty	High	Moderate	Low
Departmental differentiation	High	Moderate	Low
Percent management in integrating roles	22%	17%	0%

Source: Based on Jay W. Lorsch and Paul R. Lawrence, "Environmental Factors and Organizational Integration," *Organization Planning: Cases and Concepts* (Homewood, Ill.: Irwin and Dorsey, 1972), 45.

twenty industrial firms in England and discovered that external environment was related to internal management structure.[35] When the external environment was stable, the internal organization was characterized by rules, procedures, and a clear hierarchy of authority. Organizations were formalized. They were also centralized, with most decisions made at the top. Burns and Stalker called this a **mechanistic** organization system.

In rapidly changing environments, the internal organization was much looser, free-flowing, and adaptive. Rules and regulations often were not written down or, if written down, were ignored. People had to find their own way through the system to figure out what to do. The hierarchy of authority was not clear. Decision-making authority was decentralized. Burns and Stalker used the term **organic** to characterize this type of management structure.

Exhibit 3.6 summarizes the differences in organic and mechanistic systems. As environmental uncertainty increases, organizations tend to become more organic, which means decentralizing authority and responsibility to lower levels, encouraging employees to take care of problems by working directly with one another, encouraging teamwork, and taking an informal approach to assigning tasks and responsibility. Thus, the organization is more fluid and is able to adapt continually to changes in the external environment.[36]

Institutional Imitation

An emerging view, called the **institutional perspective**, argues that under high uncertainty, organizations mimic or imitate other organizations in the same institutional environment. The institutional environment includes other similar organizations in the industry that deal with similar customers, suppliers, and regulatory agencies.[37] One example is the current trend toward mergers in some industries, such as banking. The trend began when a few banks merged to combine their capabilities and become more competitive. Others followed suit and eventually small, locally-owned banks became a thing of the past. Today, the entertainment industry is also merging, with Disney and ABC Television, Westinghouse and CBS Television, and Time Warner and Turner Broadcasting System all joining the merger trend to compete in this rapidly changing industry.

Managers in an organization experiencing great uncertainty assume that other organizations face similar uncertainty. These managers will copy the

Exhibit 3.6
Mechanistic and Organic Organization Forms

Mechanistic	Organic
1. Tasks are broken down into specialized, separate parts.	1. Employees contribute to the common task of the department.
2. Tasks are rigidly defined.	2. Tasks are adjusted and redefined through employee teamwork.
3. There is a strict hierarchy of authority and control, and there are many rules.	3. There is less hierarchy of authority and control, and there are few rules.
4. Knowledge and control of tasks are centralized at the top of organization.	4. Knowledge and control of tasks are located anywhere in the organization.
5. Communication is vertical.	5. Communication is horizontal.

Source: Adapted from Gerald Zaltman, Robert Duncan, and Jonny Holbek, *Innovations and Organizations* (New York: Wiley, 1973), 131.

structure, management techniques, and strategies of other firms that appear successful. Such mimicking serves to reduce uncertainty for managers, but it also means that organizations within an industry will tend to look alike over time. For example, all retail department stores will tend to operate in a similar way, as will airlines, banks, and drug companies.

In general, corporations do not want to be criticized by shareholders for being too different. As a result, if a successful company in an industry establishes a formal intelligence department, other firms are likely to do likewise.

Organizations experience fads and fashions just as people do. In addition to the establishment of intelligence departments and the trend toward mergers, other recent fads include downsizing to eliminate excess personnel, MBWA (management by wandering around), and "intrapraneuring" (promoting change from within). The institutional perspective will be discussed in greater detail in Chapter 14.

Planning and Forecasting

The final organizational response to uncertainty is to increase planning and environmental forecasting. When the environment is stable, the organization can concentrate on current operational problems and day-to-day efficiency. Long-range planning and forecasting are not needed because environmental demands in the future will be the same as they are today.

With increasing environmental uncertainty, planning and forecasting become necessary.[38] Planning can soften the adverse impact of external shifting. Organizations that have unstable environments often establish a separate planning department. In an unpredictable environment, planners scan environmental elements and analyze potential moves and countermoves by other organizations. Planning can be extensive and may forecast various scenarios for environmental contingencies. As time passes, plans are updated through replanning. However, planning does not substitute for other actions, such as boundary spanning. Indeed, under conditions of extraordinarily high uncertainty, planning may not be helpful because the future is so difficult to predict.

FRAMEWORK FOR ORGANIZATIONAL RESPONSES TO UNCERTAINTY

The ways environmental uncertainty influences organizational characteristics are summarized in Exhibit 3.7. The change and complexity dimensions are combined and illustrate four levels of uncertainty. The low uncertainty environment is simple and stable. Organizations in this environment have few departments and a mechanistic structure. In a low-moderate uncertainty environment, more departments are needed along with more integrating roles to coordinate the departments. Some planning and imitation may occur. Environments that are high-moderate uncertainty are unstable but simple. Organization structure is organic and decentralized. Planning is emphasized and managers are quick to imitate successful attributes of competitors. The high uncertainty environment is both complex and unstable and is the most difficult environment from a management perspective. Organizations are large and have many departments, but they are also organic. A large number of management personnel are assigned to coordination and integration, and the organization uses boundary spanning, imitation, planning, and forecasting.

Exhibit 3.7 *Contingency Framework for Environmental Uncertainty and Organizational Responses*

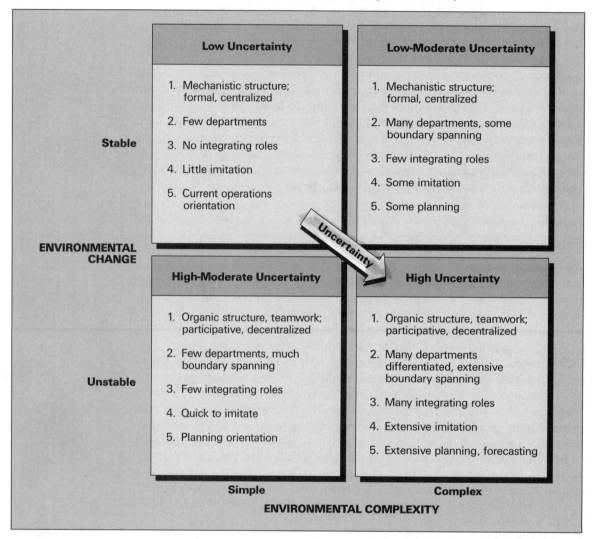

RESOURCE DEPENDENCE

Thus far, this chapter has described several ways in which organizations adapt to the lack of information and to the uncertainty caused by environmental change and complexity. Now, we turn to the third characteristic of the organization-environment relationship that affects organizations, which is the need for material and financial resources. The environment is the source of scarce and valued resources essential to organizational survival. Research in this area is called the resource dependence perspective. **Resource dependence** means that organizations depend on the environment but strive to acquire control over resources to minimize their dependence.[39] Organizations are vulnerable if vital resources are controlled by other organizations, so they try to be as independent as possible. However, when costs and risks are high, companies also team up to reduce resource dependence and the possibility of bankruptcy.

In today's volatile environment, companies are collaborating as never before to share scarce resources and be more competitive. However, formal relationships with other organizations present a dilemma to managers. North American organizations seek to reduce vulnerability with respect to resources by developing links with other organizations, but they also like to maximize their own autonomy and independence. Organizational linkages require coordination,[40] and they reduce the freedom of each organization to make decisions without concern for the needs and goals of other organizations. Interorganizational relationships thus represent a trade-off between resources and autonomy. To maintain autonomy, organizations that already have abundant resources will tend not to establish new linkages. Organizations that need resources will give up independence to acquire those resources.

Dependence on shared resources gives power to other organizations. Once an organization relies on others for valued resources, those other organizations can influence managerial decision making. When a large company like DuPont, Motorola, or Xerox forges a partnership with a supplier for parts, both sides benefit, but each loses a small amount of autonomy. For example, some of these large companies are now putting strong pressure on vendors to lower costs, and the vendors have few alternatives but to go along.[41] In much the same way, dependence on shared resources gives advertisers power over print and electronic media companies. For example, as newspapers face increasingly tough financial times, they are less likely to run stories that are critical of advertisers. Though newspapers insist advertisers don't get special treatment, some editors admit there is growing talk around the country of the need for "advertiser-friendly" newspapers.[42]

CONTROLLING ENVIRONMENTAL RESOURCES

In response to the need for resources, organizations try to maintain a balance between linkages with other organizations and their own independence. Organizations maintain this balance through attempts to modify, manipulate, or control other organizations.[43] To survive, the focal organization often tries to reach out and change or control elements in the environment. Two strategies can be adopted to manage resources in the external environment: (1) establish favorable linkages with key elements in the environment and (2) shape the environmental domain.[44] Techniques to accomplish each of these strategies are summarized in Exhibit 3.8. As a general rule, when organizations sense that valued resources are scarce, they will use the strategies in Exhibit 3.8 rather than go it alone. Notice how dissimilar these strategies are from the responses to environmental change and complexity described in Exhibit 3.7. The dissimilarity reflects the difference between responding to the need for information rather than to the need for resources.

Establishing Interorganizational Linkages

Ownership. Companies use ownership to establish linkages when they buy a part of or a controlling interest in another company. This gives the company access to technology, products, or other resources it doesn't currently have. The communications industry has become particularly complex, and many companies have been teaming up worldwide.

Exhibit 3.8
*Organization
Strategies for
Controlling the
External
Environment*

Establishing Interorganizational Linkages	Controlling the Environmental Domain
1. Ownership	1. Change of domain
2. Contracts, joint ventures	2. Political activity, regulation
3. Cooptation, interlocking directorates	3. Trade associations
4. Executive recruitment	4. Illegitimate activities
5. Advertising, public relations	

A greater degree of ownership and control is obtained through acquisition or merger. An *acquisition* involves the purchase of one organization by another so that the buyer assumes control. A *merger* is the unification of two or more organizations into a single unit.[45] In the world of computer software, Novell and Digital Research merged in an $80 million deal. Acquisition occurred when Philip Morris Company purchased Kraft Foods and when Maytag bought Magic Chef.[46] These forms of ownership reduce uncertainty in an area important to the acquiring company.

Formal Strategic Alliances. When there is a high level of complementarity between the business lines, geographical positions, or skills of two companies, the firms often go the route of a strategic alliance rather than ownership through merger or acquisition.[47] Such alliances are formed through contracts and joint ventures.

Contracts and joint ventures reduce uncertainty through a legal and binding relationship with another firm. Contracts come in the form of *license agreements* that involve the purchase of the right to use an asset (such as a new technology) for a specific time and *supplier arrangements* that contract for the sale of one firm's output to another. Contracts can provide long-term security by tying customers and suppliers to specific amounts and prices. For example, McDonald's contracts for an entire crop of russet potatoes to be certain of its supply of french fries. McDonald's also gains influence over suppliers through these contracts and has changed the way farmers grow potatoes and the profit margins they earn, which is consistent with the resource dependence perspective.[48] *Joint ventures* result in the creation of a new organization that is formally independent of the parents, although the parents will have some control.[49] In a joint venture, organizations share the risk and cost associated with large projects or innovations, such as when Pratt & Whitney joined a consortium to develop a new engine or Tenneco created a joint venture with other oil companies to drill for oil in Africa.

Cooptation, Interlocking Directorates. **Cooptation** occurs when leaders from important sectors in the environment are made part of an organization. It takes place, for example, when influential customers or suppliers are appointed to the board of directors, such as when the senior executive of a bank sits on the board of a manufacturing company. As a board member, the banker may become psychologically coopted into the interests of the manufacturing firm. Community leaders also can be appointed to a company's board of directors or to other organizational committees or task forces. These influential people are thus introduced to the needs of the company and are more likely to include the company's interests in their decision making.

An **interlocking directorate** is a formal linkage that occurs when a member of the board of directors of one company sits on the board of directors of another company. The individual is a communications link between companies and can influence policies and decisions. When one individual is the link between two companies, this is typically referred to as a **direct interlock**. An **indirect interlock** occurs when a director of Company A and a director of Company B are both directors of Company C. They have access to one another but do not have direct influence over their respective companies.[50] Recent research shows that, as a firm's financial fortunes decline, direct interlocks with financial institutions increase. Financial uncertainty facing an industry also has been associated with greater indirect interlocks between competing companies.[51]

Executive Recruitment. Transferring or exchanging executives also offers a method of establishing favorable linkages with external organizations. For example, each year the aerospace industry hires retired generals and executives from the Department of Defense. These generals have personal friends in the department, so the aerospace companies obtain better information about technical specifications, prices, and dates for new weapon systems. They can learn the needs of the defense department and are able to present their case for defense contracts in a more effective way. Companies without personal contacts find it nearly impossible to get a defense contract. Having channels of influence and communication between organizations serves to reduce financial uncertainty and dependence for an organization.

Advertising and Public Relations. A traditional way of establishing favorable relationships is through advertising. Organizations spend large amounts of money to influence the taste of consumers. Advertising is especially important in highly competitive consumer industries and in industries that experience variable demand. Because of the declining demand for health care, hospitals have begun to advertise through billboards, newspapers, and broadcast commercials to promote special services and bonuses, such as steak dinners and champagne. Dow Chemical used skillful advertising to create a new image on college campuses. It invested $50 million over five years in its "Dow lets you do great things" advertising campaign, the success of which has enabled Dow to hire excellent college graduates, an important resource.[52]

Public relations is similar to advertising, except that stories often are free and aimed at public opinion. Public relations people cast an organization in a favorable light in speeches, in press reports, and on television. Public relations attempts to shape the company's image in the minds of customers, suppliers, and government officials. For example, in an effort to survive in this anti-smoking era, tobacco companies have launched an aggressive public relations campaign touting smokers' rights and freedom of choice.[53]

Summary. Organizations can use a variety of techniques to establish favorable linkages that ensure the availability of scarce resources. Linkages provide control over vulnerable environmental elements. Strategic alliances, interlocking directorates, and outright ownership provide mechanisms to reduce resource dependency on the environment. American companies like IBM, Apple, AT&T, and Motorola have been quick in recent years to turn rivalry into partnership. The other major strategy companies can use to manage resource dependency is to control or redefine the external environmental domain.

Controlling the Environmental Domain

In addition to establishing favorable linkages to obtain resources, organizations often try to change the environment. There are four techniques for influencing or changing a firm's environmental domain.

Change of Domain. The ten sectors described earlier in this chapter are not fixed. The organization decides which business it is in, the market to enter, and the suppliers, banks, employees, and location to use, and this domain can be changed.[54] An organization can seek new environmental relationships and drop old ones. An organization may try to find a domain where there is little competition, no government regulation, abundant suppliers, affluent customers, and barriers to keep competitors out.

Acquisition and divestment are two techniques for altering the domain. Rockwell International felt vulnerable with 63 percent of its revenues coming from the federal government; thus, it acquired Allen Bradley to move into factory automation—a new domain that was not dependent on the government. Robert Mercer, CEO of Goodyear Tire & Rubber Company, changed Goodyear's domain to get the company away from the cutthroat competition in tires. He did this by reallocating resources into nontire lines of businesses, such as auto parts, aerospace products, and plastics. Goodyear also acquired an oil and gas company. Entering these new domains has taken the pressure off the tire business and enabled Goodyear to prosper. When British conglomerate Grand Metropolitan acquired Pillsbury, it also sold Bennigans, Steak & Ale, and Bumble Bee fish-canning operations, thereby redefining its domain in the food-processing industry.

Political Activity, Regulation. Political activity includes techniques to influence government legislation and regulation. For example, General Motors used political activity to successfully settle a battle with the U.S. Transportation Department over the safety of some of its pickup trucks. The settlement requires that GM spend $51 million on safety programs over a five-year period, but saved the company the cost of a $1 billion recall.[55]

In one technique, organizations pay lobbyists to express their views to members of federal and state legislatures. In the telecommunications industry, the Baby Bells hired powerful lobbyists to influence a sweeping new telecommunications bill giving local phone companies access to new markets.[56] Many CEOs, however, believe they should do their own lobbying. CEOs have easier access than lobbyists and can be especially effective when they do the politicking. Political activity is so important that "informal lobbyist" is an unwritten part of almost any CEO's job description.[57]

Political strategy can be used to erect regulatory barriers against new competitors or to squash unfavorable legislation. Corporations also try to influence the appointment to agencies of people who are sympathetic to their needs. The value of political activity is illustrated by Bethlehem Steel's effort to roll back foreign steel imports by 15 percent. Assuming domestic consumption remained the same, the average price for steel would have increased about $50 a ton, and the increase in tons for Bethlehem would have meant a quarter of a billion dollars of new business.

Trade Associations. Much of the work to influence the external environment is accomplished jointly with other organizations that have similar interests. Most manufacturing companies are part of the National Association of Manufacturers and also belong to associations in their specific industry. By pooling resources, these organizations can pay people to carry out activities such as lobbying legislators, influencing new regulations, developing public relations campaigns, and making campaign contributions.

Illegitimate Activities. Illegitimate activities represent the final technique companies sometimes use to control their environmental domain. Certain conditions, such as low profits, pressure from senior managers, or scarce environmental resources, may lead managers to adopt behaviors not considered legitimate.[58] Many well-known companies have been found guilty of behavior considered unlawful. Example behaviors include payoffs to foreign governments, illegal political contributions, promotional gifts, and wire tapping. In the defense industry, the intense competition for declining contracts for major weapon systems led some companies to do almost anything to get an edge, including schemes to peddle inside information and to pay off officials.[59] One study found that companies in industries with low demand, shortages, and strikes were more likely to be convicted for illegal activities, implying that illegal acts are an attempt to cope with resource scarcity.[60] In another study, social movement organizations such as Earth First! and the AIDS Coalition to Unleash Power (ActUp) were found to have acted in ways considered illegitimate or even illegal to bolster their visibility and reputation.[61]

Organization-Environment Integrative Framework

The relationships illustrated in Exhibit 3.9 summarize the two major themes about organization-environment relationships discussed in this chapter. One theme is that the amount of complexity and change in an organization's domain influences the need for information and hence the uncertainty felt within an organization. Greater information uncertainty is resolved through greater structural flexibility, the assignment of additional departments and boundary roles, and imitation. When uncertainty is low, management structures can be more mechanistic, and the number of departments and boundary roles can be fewer. The second theme pertains to the scarcity of material and financial resources. The more dependent an organization is on other organizations for those resources, the more important it is to either establish favorable linkages with those organizations or control entry into the domain. If dependence on external resources is low, the organization can maintain autonomy and does not need to establish linkages or control the external domain.

SUMMARY OF KEY ISSUES

The external environment has an overwhelming impact on management uncertainty and organization functioning. Organizations are open social systems. Most are involved with hundreds of external elements. The change and complexity in environmental domains have major implications for organizational design and action. Most organizational decisions, activities, and outcomes can be traced to stimuli in the external environment.

Organizational environments differ in terms of uncertainty and resource dependence. Organizational uncertainty is the result of the stable-unstable and

Exhibit 3.9 *Relationship Between Environmental Characteristics and Organizational Actions*

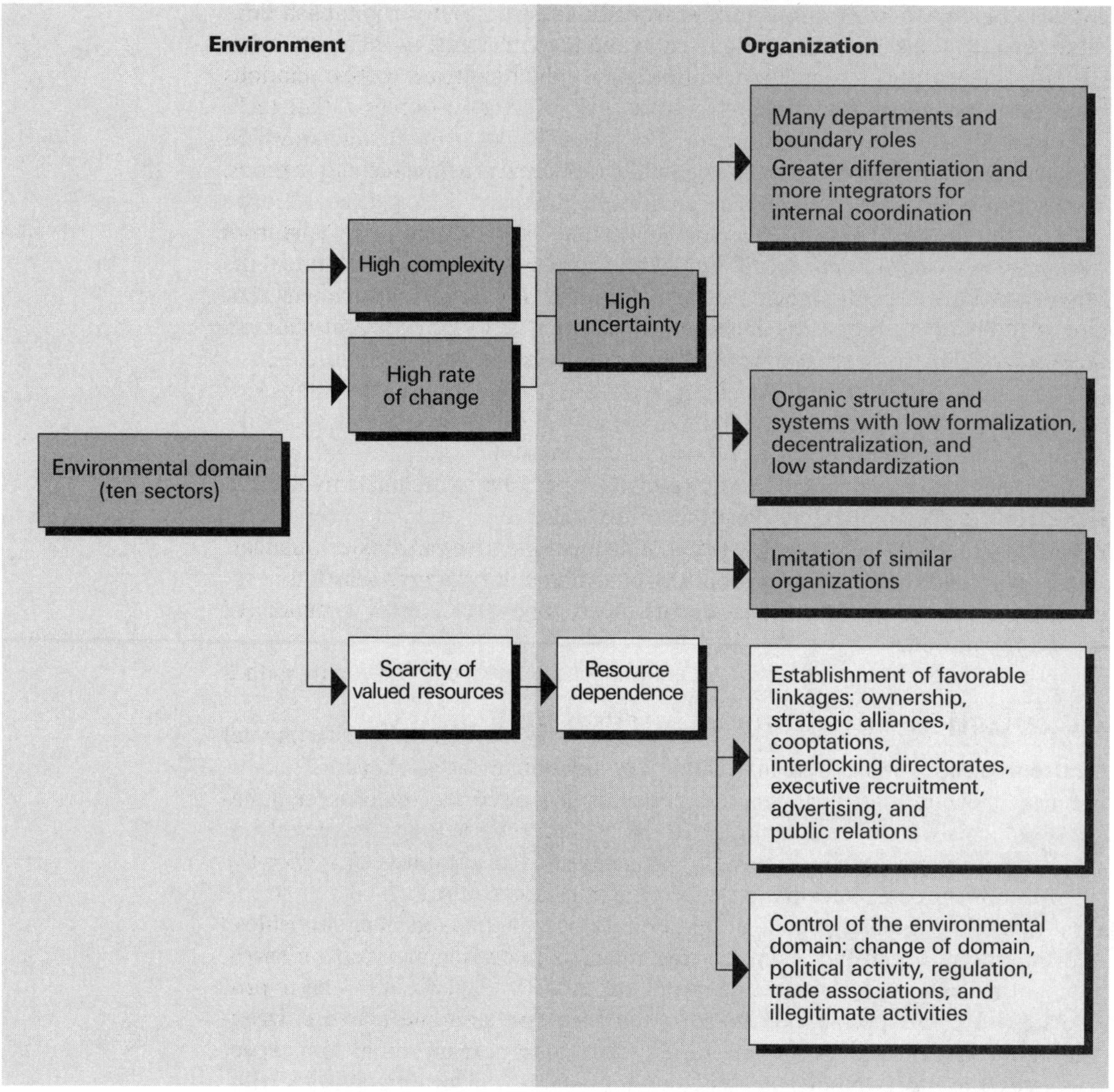

simple-complex dimensions of the environment. Resource dependence is the result of scarcity of the material and financial resources needed by the organization.

Organization design takes on a logical perspective when the environment is considered. Organizations try to survive and achieve efficiencies in a world characterized by uncertainty and scarcity. Specific departments and functions are created to deal with uncertainties. The organization can be conceptualized as a technical core and departments that buffer environmental uncertainty. Boundary-spanning roles provide information about the environment.

The concepts in this chapter provide specific frameworks for understanding how the environment influences the structure and functioning of an organization. Environmental complexity and change, for example, have specific impact on internal complexity and adaptability. Under great uncertainty, more resources are allocated to departments that will plan, deal with specific environmental elements, and integrate diverse internal activities. Moreover, when risk is great or resources are scarce, the organization can establish linkages through the acquisition of ownership and through strategic alliances, interlocking directorates, executive recruitment, or advertising and public relations that will minimize risk and maintain a supply of scarce resources. Other techniques for controlling the environment include a change of the domain in which the organization operates, political activity, participation in trade associations, and perhaps illegitimate activities.

Two important themes in this chapter are that organizations can learn from and adapt to the environment and that organizations can change and control the environment. These strategies are especially true for large organizations that command many resources. Such organizations can adapt when necessary but can also neutralize or change problematic areas in the environment.

Discussion Questions

1. Define *organizational environment*. Is it appropriate to include only the elements that actually interact with the organization?
2. What is environmental uncertainty? Which has the greatest impact on uncertainty—environmental complexity or environmental change? Why?
3. Why does environmental complexity lead to organizational complexity? Explain.
4. Is changing the organization's domain a feasible strategy for coping with a threatening environment? Explain.
5. Describe differentiation and integration. In what type of environmental uncertainty will differentiation and integration be greatest? Least?
6. Under what environmental conditions is organizational planning emphasized? Is planning an appropriate response to a turbulent environment?
7. What is an organic organization? A mechanistic organization? How does the environment influence organic and mechanistic structures?
8. Why do organizations become involved in interorganizational relationships? Do these relationships affect an organizations's dependency? Performance?
9. Assume you have been asked to calculate the ratio of staff employees to production employees in two organizations—one in a simple, stable environment and one in a complex, shifting environment. How would you expect these ratios to differ? Why?

Notes

1. John Keller, Leslie Cauley, and Douglas Lavin, "AT&T Job Cutbacks Are Just the First Shot in Global Telecom War," *The Wall Street Journal Europe*, 5–6 January 1996, A1; Jaclyn Fierman, "When Genteel Rivals Become Mortal Enemies," *Fortune*, 15 May 1995, 90–100; John Greenwald, "MCI's New Extension," *Time*, 18 November 1996, 103.

2. Brent Schlender, "Paradise Lost: Apple's Quest for Life after Death," *Fortune*, 19 February 1996, 64–74.

3. Wendy Zellner, "Not Everyone Loves Wal-Mart's Low Price," *Business Week*, 12 October 1992, 36–38;

Suzanne Alexander, "Feisty Yankees Resist Wal-Mart's Drive to Set Up Shops in New England Towns," *The Wall Street Journal*, 16 September 1993, B1, B6.

4. Alan Deutschman, "What 25-Year Olds Want," *Fortune*, 27 August 1990, 42–50; Dean Foust and Tim Smart, "The Merger Parade Runs into a Brick Wall," *Business Week,* 14 May 1990; Michael Schroeder and Walecia Konrad, "Nucor: Rolling Right into Steel's Big Time," *Business Week*, 19 November 1990, 76–81.

5. Jonathan Berry, Zachary Schiller, Richard A. Melcher, and Mark Maremont, "Attack of the Fighting Brands," *Business Week*, 2 May 1994, 125; Dana Milbank, "Aluminum Producers, Aggressive and Agile, Outfight Steelmakers," *The Wall Street Journal*, 1 July 1992, A1.

6. Barbara Carton, "Gillette Faces Wrath of Children in Testing on Rats and Rabbits," *The Wall Street Journal*, 5 September 1995, A1.

7. Lucinda Harper and Fred R. Bleakley, "An Era of Low Inflation Changes the Calculus for Buyers and Sellers," *The Wall Street Journal*, 14 January 1994, A1, A3.

8. Andrew Kupfer, "How American Industry Stacks Up," *Fortune*, 9 March 1992, 36–46.

9. Alan Farnham, "Global—or Just Globaloney?" *Fortune*, 27 June 1994, 97–100; William C. Symonds, Brian Bremner, Stewart Toy, and Karen Lowry Miller, "The Globetrotters Take Over," *Business Week*, 8 July 1996, 46–48; Carla Rapoport, "Nestlé's Brand Building Machine," *Fortune,* 19 September 1994, 147–56; and "Execs with Global Vision," *USA Today*, International Edition, 9 February 1996, 12B.

10. Tom Peters, "Prometheus Barely Unbound," *Academy of Management Executive* 4 (1990): 70–84.

11. Clifford C. Hebard, "Managing Effectively in Asia," *Training & Development*, April 1996, 35–39.

12. Kupfer, "How American Industry Stacks Up"; Greenwald, "MCI's New Extension."

13. Symonds, et. al., "The Globetrotters Take Over."

14. Tim Smart, "GE's Welch: 'Fighting Like Hell to Be No. 1'," *Business Week*, 8 July 1996, 48.

15. Allen C. Bluedorn, "Pilgrim's Progress: Trends and Convergence in Research on Organizational Size and Environment," *Journal of Management* 19 (1993): 163–91; Howard E. Aldrich, *Organizations and Environments* (Englewood Cliffs, N.J.: Prentice-Hall, 1979); Fred E. Emery and Eric L. Trist, "The Casual Texture of Organizational Environments," *Human Relations* 18 (1965): 21–32.

16. Christine S. Koberg and Gerardo R. Ungson, "The Effects of Environmental Uncertainty and Dependence on Organizational Structure and Performance: A Comparative Study," *Journal of Management* 13 (1987): 725–37; Frances J. Milliken, "Three Types of Perceived Uncertainty about the Environment: State, Effect, and Response Uncertainty," *Academy of Management Review* 12 (1987): 133–43.

17. Robert B. Duncan, "Characteristics of Organizational Environment and Perceived Environmental Uncertainty," *Administrative Science Quarterly* 17 (1972): 313–27; Gregory G. Dess and Donald W. Beard, "Dimensions of Organizational Task Environments," *Administrative Science Quarterly* 29 (1984): 52–73; Ray Jurkovich, "A Core Typology of Organizational Environments," *Administrative Science Quarterly* 19 (1974): 380–94.

18. Jaclyn Fierman, "When Genteel Rivals Become Mortal Enemies."

19. J.A. Litterer, *The Analysis of Organizations*, 2d ed. (New York: Wiley, 1973), 335.

20. Joseph Pereira, "Toy Industry Finds It Harder and Harder to Pick the Winners," *The Wall Street Journal*, 21 December 1993, A1, A5.

21. Rosalie L. Tung, "Dimensions of Organizational Environments: An Exploratory Study of Their Impact on Organizational Structure," *Academy of Management Journal* 22 (1979): 672–93.

22. Joseph E. McCann and John Selsky, "Hyperturbulence and the Emergence of Type 5 Environments," *Academy of Management Review* 9 (1984): 460–70.

23. Eric Schine with Gary McWilliams, "Mattel: Looking for a Few Good Boy Toys," *Business Week*, 17 February 1992 , 116–18.

24. Judith Valente and Asra Q. Nomani, "Surge in Oil Price has Airlines Struggling, Some Just to Hang On," *The Wall Street Journal*, 10 August 1990, A1, A4.

25. James D. Thompson, *Organizations in Action* (New York: McGraw-Hill, 1967), 20–21.

26. Sally Solo, "Whirlpool: How to Listen to Consumers," *Fortune*, 11 January 1993, 77–79.

27. David B. Jemison, "The Importance of Boundary Spanning Roles in Strategic Decision Making," *Journal of Management Studies* 21 (1984): 131–52; Mohamed Ibrahim Ahmad At-Twaijri and John R. Montanari, "The Impact of Context and Choice on the Boundary-Spanning Process: An Empirical Extension," *Human Relations* 40 (1987): 783–98.

28. Robert C. Schwab, Gerardo R. Ungson, and Warren B. Brown, "Redefining the Boundary-Spanning Environment Relationship," *Journal of Management* 11 (1985): 75–86.

29. Ken Western, "Ethical Spying," *Business Ethics*, September/October 1995, 22–23; Stan Crock, Geoffrey Smith, Joseph Weber, Richard A. Melcher, and Linda Himelstein, "They Snoop to Conquer," *Business Week*, 28 October 1996, 172–76; Kenneth A. Sawka, "Demystifying Business Intelligence," *Management Review*, October 1996, 47–51.

30. Crock, et. al., "They Snoop to Conquer."

31. Jay W. Lorsch, "Introduction to the Structural Design of Organizations," in Gene W. Dalton, Paul R. Lawrence, and Jay W. Lorsch, eds., *Organizational Structure and Design* (Homewood, Ill.: Irwin and Dorsey, 1970), 5.

32. Paul R. Lawrence and Jay W. Lorsch, *Organization and Environment* (Homewood, Ill.: Irwin, 1969).

33. Lorsch, "Introduction to the Structural Design of Organizations," 7.

34. Jay W. Lorsch and Paul R. Lawrence, "Environmental Factors and Organizational Integration," in J. W. Lorsch and Paul R. Lawrence, eds., *Organizational Planning: Cases and Concepts* (Homewood, Ill.: Irwin and Dorsey, 1972), 45.

35. Tom Burns and G. M. Stalker, *The Management of Innovation* (London: Tavistock, 1961).

36. John A. Courtright, Gail T. Fairhurst, and L. Edna Rogers, "Interaction Patterns in Organic and Mechanistic Systems," *Academy of Management Journal* 32 (1989): 773–802.

37. Paul J. DiMaggio and Walter W. Powell, "The Iron Cage Revisited: Institutional Isomorphism and Collective Rationality in Organizational Fields," *American Sociological Review* 48 (1983): 147–60; Richard H. Hall, *Organizations: Structures, Processes, and Outcomes* (Englewood Cliffs, N.J.: Prentice-Hall, 1987); Christine Oliver, "Strategic Responses to Institutional Processes," *Academy of Management Review* 16 (1991): 145–79.

38. Thomas C. Powell, "Organizational Alignment as Competitive Advantage," *Strategic Management Journal* 13 (1992): 119–34, Mansour Javidan, "The Impact of Environmental Uncertainty on Long-Range Planning Practices of the U.S. Savings and Loan Industry," *Strategic Management Journal* 5 (1984): 381–92; Tung, "Dimensions of Organizational Environments," 672–93; Thompson, *Organizations in Action*.

39. David Ulrich and Jay B. Barney, "Perspectives in Organizations: Resource Dependence, Efficiency, and Population," *Academy of Management Review* 9 (1984): 471–81; Jeffrey Pfeffer and Gerald Salancik, *The External Control of Organizations: A Resource Dependent Perspective* (New York: Harper & Row, 1978).

40. Andrew H. Van de Ven and Gordon Walker, "The Dynamics of Interorganizational Coordination," *Administrative Science Quarterly* (1984): 598–621; Huseyin Leblebici and Gerald R. Salancik, "Stability in Interorganizational Exchanges: Rulemaking Processes of the Chicago Board of Trade," *Administrative Science Quarterly* 27 (1982): 227–42.

41. Kevin Kelly and Zachary Schiller with James B. Treece, "Cut Costs or Else: Companies Lay Down the Law to Suppliers," *Business Week*, 22 March 1993, 28–29.

42. G. Pascal Zachary, "Many Journalists See a Growing Reluctance to Criticize Advertisers," *The Wall Street Journal*, 6 February 1992, A1, A9.

43. Judith A. Babcock, *Organizational Responses to Resource Scarcity and Munificence: Adaptation and Modification in Colleges within a University* (Ph.D. diss., Pennsylvania State University, 1981).

44. Peter Smith Ring and Andrew H. Van de Ven, "Developmental Processes of Corporative Interorganizational Relationships," *Academy of Management Review* 19 (1994): 90–118; Jeffrey Pfeffer, "Beyond Management and the Worker: The Institutional Function of Management," *Academy of Management Review* 1 (April 1976): 36–46; John P. Kotter, "Managing External Dependence," *Academy of Management Review* 4 (1979): 87–92.

45. Bryan Borys and David B. Jemison, "Hybrid Arrangements as Strategic Alliances: Theoretical Issues in Organizational Combinations," *Academy of Management Review* 14 (1989): 234–49.

46. Brian Bremmer with Kathy Rebello, Zachary Schiller, and Joseph Weber, "The Age of Consolidation," *Business Week*, 14 October 1991, 86–94.

47. Julie Cohen Mason, "Strategic Alliances: Partnering for Success," *Management Review* (May 1993): 10–15.

48. John F. Love, *McDonald's: Behind the Arches* (New York: Bantam Books, 1986).

49. Borys and Jemison, "Hybrid Arrangements as Strategic Alliances."

50. Donald Palmer, "Broken Ties: Interlocking Directorates and Intercorporate Coordination," *Administrative Science Quarterly* 28 (1983): 40–55; F. David Shoorman, Max H. Bazerman, and Robert S. Atkin, "Interlocking Directorates: A Strategy for Reducing Environmental Uncertainty," *Academy of Management Review* 6 (1981): 243–51; Ronald S. Burt, *Toward a Structural Theory of Action* (New York: Academic Press, 1982).

51. James R. Lang and Daniel E. Lockhart, "Increased Environmental Uncertainty and Changes in Board Linkage Patterns," *Academy of Management Journal* 33 (1990): 106–28; Mark S. Mizruchi and Linda Brewster Stearns, "A Longitudinal Study of the Formation of Interlocking Directorates," *Administrative Science Quarterly* 33 (1988): 194–210.

52. "Dow Chemical: From Napalm to Nice Guy," *Fortune*, 12 May 1986, 75.

53. Linda Himelstein, Laura Zinn, Maria Mallory, John Carey, Richard S. Dunham, and Joan O'C. Hamilton, "Tobacco: Does It Have a Future?" *Business Week*, 4 July 1994, 24–29.

54. Kotter, "Managing External Dependence."

55. Daniel Pearl and Gabriella Stern, "How GM Managed to Wring Pickup Pact and Keep on Truckin'," *The Wall Street Journal*, 5 December 1994, A1.

56. Rick Wartzman and John Harwood, "For the Baby Bells, Government Lobbying is Hardly Child's Play," *The Wall Street Journal*, 15 March 1994, A1.

57. David B. Yoffie, "How an Industry Builds Political Advantage," *Harvard Business Review* (May–June 1988): 82–89; Jeffrey H. Birnbaum, "Chief Executives Head to Washington to Ply the Lobbyist's Trade," *The Wall Street Journal*, 19 March 1990, A1, A16.

58. Anthony J. Daboub, Abdul M. A. Rasheed, Richard L. Priem, and David A. Gray, "Top Management Team Characteristics and Corporate Illegal Activity," *Academy of Management Review*, Vol. 20, No. 1, 1995, 138–70.

59. Stewart Toy, "The Defense Scandal," *Business Week*, 4 July 1988, 28–30.

60. Barry M. Staw and Eugene Szwajkowski, "The Scarcity-Munificence Component of Organizational Environments and the Commission of Illegal Acts," *Administrative Science Quarterly* 20 (1975): 345–54.

61. Kimberly D. Elsbach and Robert I. Sutton, "Acquiring Organizational Legitimacy through Illegitimate Actions: A Marriage of Institutional and Impression Management Theories," *Academy of Management Journal* 35 (1992): 699–738.

part three

Organization Structure and Design

3

chapter four

Manufacturing, Service, and Advanced Information Technologies

chapter five

Organization Size and Life Cycle

chapter six

Fundamentals of Organization Structure

chapter seven

Contemporary Designs for Global Competition

4

chapter four

Manufacturing, Service, and Advanced Information Technologies

While reading this chapter, think about your answers to the following questions:

- How is an organization's technology related to its structure and management systems?

- What are the major differences between manufacturing and service technologies and how are these differences reflected in organizational structure and systems?

- How can structure be designed to accommodate department technologies and interdependence between departments?

- How does the adoption of advanced information technology influence management processes, organization design, and workplace culture?

Technology is the tools, techniques, and actions used to transform organizational inputs into outputs.[1] Technology is an organization's production process and includes machinery and work procedures.

Organizational technology begins with raw materials of some type (for example, unfinished steel castings in a valve manufacturing plant). Employees take action on the raw material to make a change in it (they machine steel castings), which transforms the raw material into the output of the organization (control valves ready for shipment to oil refineries). For Federal Express, the production technology includes the equipment and procedures for delivering overnight mail.

Exhibit 4.1 features an example of production technology for a manufacturing plant. Note how the technology consists of raw material inputs, a transformation process that changes and adds value to these items, and the ultimate product or service output that is sold to consumers in the environment. In today's large, complex organizations, it can be hard to pinpoint technology. Technology can be partly assessed by examining the raw materials flowing into the organization,[2] the variability of work activities,[3] the degree to which the production process is mechanized,[4] the extent to which one task depends upon another in the workflow,[5] or the number of new product outputs.[6]

Recall from Chapter 3 that organizations have a technical core that reflects the organization's primary purpose. The technical core contains the transformation process that represents the organization's technology. As today's organizations try to become more flexible in a changing environment, new technology may influence organizational structure, but decisions about organizational structure may also shape or limit technology. Thus, the interaction between core technology and structure leads to a patterned relationship in many organizations.[7]

Exhibit 4.1
Transformation Process for a Manufacturing Company

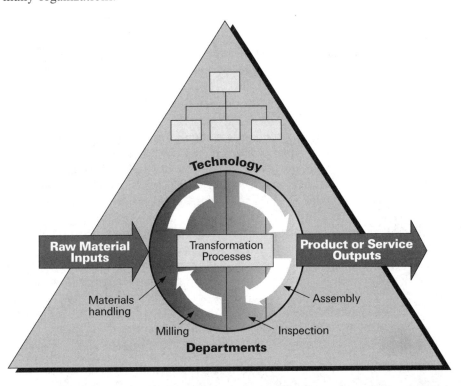

In today's large, complex organizations, many departments exist and each may employ a different technology for its own function. Thus, research and development transforms ideas into new product proposals, and marketing transforms inventory into sales, each using a different technology. Moreover, the administrative technology used by managers to run the organization represents yet another technology. Computers and advanced information technology have impact on the administrative arena.

PURPOSE OF THIS CHAPTER

In this chapter, we will explore the nature of organizational technologies and the relationship between technology and organization structure. Chapter 3 described how the environment influences organization design. The question addressed in this chapter is, "How should the organization structure be designed to accommodate and facilitate the production process?" Form usually follows function, so the form of the organization's structure should be tailored to fit the needs of the production technology.

The remainder of the chapter will unfold as follows. First, we will examine how the technology for the organization as a whole influences organization structure and design. This discussion will include both manufacturing and service technologies and will introduce new concepts about computer-integrated manufacturing. Next, we will examine differences in department technologies and how the technologies influence the design and management of organizational subunits. Third, we will explore how interdependence—flow of materials and information—among departments affects structure. Finally, we will examine how new computer-based information technologies are influencing organization design by their impact on administration and management of the organization.

ORGANIZATION-LEVEL TECHNOLOGY

Organization-level technologies are of two types—manufacturing and service. Manufacturing technologies include traditional manufacturing processes and new computer-based manufacturing systems.

Manufacturing Firms

Woodward's Study. The first and most influential study of manufacturing technology was conducted by Joan Woodward, a British industrial sociologist. Her research began as a field study of management principles in south Essex. The prevailing management wisdom at the time (1950s) was contained in what was known as universal principles of management. These principles were "one best way" prescriptions that effective organizations were expected to adopt. Woodward surveyed one hundred manufacturing firms firsthand to learn how they were organized.[8] She and her research team visited each firm, interviewed managers, examined company records, and observed the manufacturing operations. Her data included a wide range of structural characteristics (span of control, levels of management) and dimensions of management style (written versus verbal communications, use of rewards) and the type of manufacturing process. Data were also obtained that reflected commercial success of the firms.

Woodward developed a scale and organized the firms according to technical complexity of the manufacturing process. **Technical complexity** represents the extent of mechanization of the manufacturing process. High technical complexity means most of the work is performed by machines. Low technical complexity means workers play a larger role in the production process. Woodward's scale of technical complexity originally had ten categories, as summarized in Exhibit 4.2. These categories were further consolidated into three basic technology groups:

- *Group I: Small-Batch and Unit Production.* These firms tend to be job shop operations that manufacture and assemble small orders to meet specific needs of customers. Custom work is the norm. **Small-batch production** relies heavily on the human operator; it is thus not highly mechanized. Examples include many types of made-to-order manufactured products, such as specialized construction equipment, custom electronic equipment, and custom clothing.
- *Group II: Large-Batch and Mass Production.* **Large-batch production** is a manufacturing process characterized by long production runs of standardized parts. Output often goes into inventory from which orders are filled, because customers do not have special needs. Examples include most assembly lines, such as for automobiles or trailer homes.
- *Group III: Continuous Process Production.* In **continuous process production** the entire process is mechanized. There is no starting or stopping. This

Exhibit 4.2 *Woodward's Classification of 100 British Firms According to their Systems of Production*

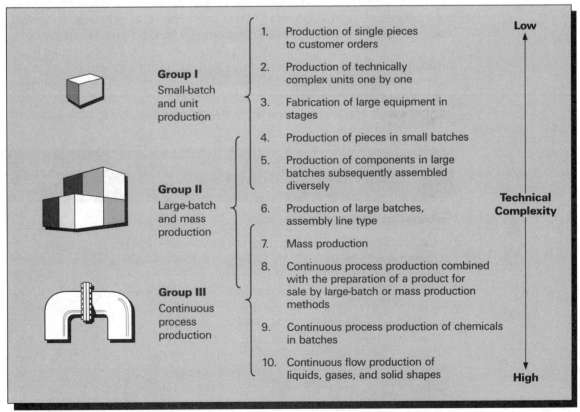

Source: Adapted from Woodward, *Management and Technology* (London: Her Majesty's Stationery Office, 1958). Used with permission of Her Britannic Majesty's Stationery Office.

represents mechanization and standardization one step beyond those in an assembly line. Automated machines control the continuous process, and outcomes are highly predictable. Examples would include chemical plants, oil refineries, liquor producers, and nuclear power plants.

Using this classification of technology, Woodward's data made sense. A few of her key findings are given in Exhibit 4.3. The number of management levels and the manager/total personnel ratio, for example, show definite increases as technical complexity increases from unit production to continuous process. This indicated that greater management intensity is needed to manage complex technology. Direct/indirect labor ratio decreases with technical complexity because more indirect workers are required to support and maintain complex machinery. Other characteristics, such as span of control, formalized procedures, and centralization, are high for mass production technology but low for other technologies because the work is standardized. Unit production and continuous process technologies require highly skilled workers to run the machines and verbal communication to adapt to changing conditions. Mass production is standardized and routinized, so few exceptions occur, little verbal communication is needed, and employees are less skilled.

Overall, the management systems in both unit production and continuous process technology are characterized as organic. They are more free-flowing and adaptive, with fewer procedures and less standardization. Mass production, however, is mechanistic, with standardized jobs and formalized procedures. Woodward's discovery about technology thus provided substantial new insight into the causes of organization structure. In Joan Woodward's own words, "Different technologies impose different kinds of demands on individuals and organizations, and those demands have to be met through an appropriate structure."[9]

Strategy, Technology, and Performance. Another portion of Woodward's study examined the success of the firms along dimensions such as profitability, market share, stock price, and reputation. As indicated in Chapter 2, the measurement of effectiveness is not simple or precise, but Woodward was able to rank firms on a

Exhibit 4.3

Relationship between Technical Complexity and Structural Characteristics

Structural Characteristic	Technology		
	Unit Production	Mass Production	Continuous Process
Number of management levels	3	4	6
Supervisor span of control	23	48	15
Direct/indirect labor ratio	9:1	4:1	1:1
Manager/total personnel ratio	Low	Medium	High
Workers' skill level	High	Low	High
Formalized procedures	Low	High	Low
Centralization	Low	High	Low
Amount of verbal communication	High	Low	High
Amount of written communication	Low	High	Low
Overall structure	Organic	Mechanistic	Organic

Source: Joan Woodward, *Industrial Organization: Theory and Practice* (London: Oxford University Press, 1965). Used with permission.

scale of commercial success according to whether they displayed above-average, average, or below-average performance on strategic objectives.

Woodward compared the structure-technology relationship against commercial success and discovered that successful firms tended to be those that had complementary structures and technologies. Many of the organizational characteristics of the successful firms were near the average of their technology category, as shown in Exhibit 4.3. Below-average firms tended to depart from the structural characteristics for their technology type. Another conclusion was that structural characteristics could be interpreted as clustering into organic and mechanistic management systems. Successful small-batch and continuous process organizations had organic structures, and successful mass production organizations had mechanistic structures. Subsequent research has replicated her findings.[10]

What this illustrates for today's companies is that strategy, structure, and technology need to be aligned, especially when competitive conditions change. Several researchers have argued that the strength of Japanese firms in many industries can be credited to a close alignment among strategy, structure, and technology,[11] as shown in Exhibit 4.4. Some insurance companies in the U.S. are currently realigning strategy, structure, and technology because of increased competition in the insurance business. Companies such as Geico and USAA are growing rapidly through the use of direct mail and phone solicitation, avoiding the costs associated with doing business through independent insurance agents. Agency-based companies like State Farm and Allstate have had to put new emphasis on a low-cost strategy and are adopting efficiency-oriented information technology to cut costs and more effectively serve customers.

Failing to adopt appropriate new technologies to support strategy, or adopting a new technology and failing to realign strategy to match it, can lead to poor performance. Today's increased global competition means more volatile markets, shorter product life cycles, and more sophisticated and knowledgeable consumers; flexibility to meet these new demands has become a strategic imperative for many companies.[12] Manufacturing companies can adopt new technologies to support the strategy of flexibility. However, organization structures and management processes must also be realigned, as a highly mechanistic structure hampers flexibility and prevents the company from reaping the benefits of the new technology.[13]

Exhibit 4.4

Co-alignment of Strategy, Technology, and Structure

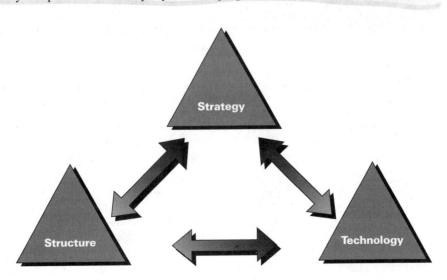

Computer-Integrated Manufacturing

In the years since Woodward's research, new developments have occurred in manufacturing technology. New manufacturing technologies include robots, numerically controlled machine tools, and computerized software for product design, engineering analysis, and remote control of machinery. The ultimate technology is called **computer-integrated manufacturing** (CIM).[14] Also called *advanced manufacturing technology, agile manufacturing, the factory of the future, smart factories,* or *flexible manufacturing systems,* CIM links together manufacturing components that previously stood alone. Thus, robots, machines, product design, and engineering analysis are coordinated by a single computer. The result has already revolutionized the shop floor, enabling large factories to deliver a wide range of custom-made products at low mass production costs.[15]

Computer-integrated manufacturing also enables small companies to go toe-to-toe with large factories and low-cost foreign competitors. For example, Techknits, Inc., a small manufacturer located in New York City, competes successfully against low-cost sweater-makers in the Far East by using $8 million worth of computerized looms and other machinery. The work of designing sweaters, which once took two days, can now be accomplished in two hours. Looms operate round-the-clock and crank out 60,000 sweaters a week, enabling Techknits to fill customer orders faster than foreign competitors.[16]

Computer-integrated manufacturing is typically the result of three subcomponents.

- Computer-aided design (CAD). Computers are used to assist in the drafting, design, and engineering of new parts. Designers guide their computer to draw specified configurations on the screen, including dimensions and component details. Hundreds of design alternatives can be explored, as can scaled-up or scaled-down versions of the original.[17]
- Computer-aided manufacturing (CAM). Computer-controlled machines in materials handling, fabrication, production, and assembly greatly increase the speed at which items can be manufactured. CAM also permits a production line to shift rapidly from producing one product to any variety of other products by changing the instruction tapes or software in the computer. CAM enables the production line to quickly honor customer requests for changes in product design and product mix.[18]
- Administrative automation. The computerized accounting, inventory control, billing, and shop-floor tracking systems allow managers to use computers to monitor and control the manufacturing process.

The combination of CAD, CAM, and administrative automation components represents the highest level of computer-integrated manufacturing. A new product can be designed on the computer, and a prototype can be produced untouched by human hands. The ideal factory can switch quickly from one product to another, working fast and with precision, without paperwork or record-keeping to bog down the system.[19]

A company can adopt CAD in its engineering design department and/or CAM in its production area and make substantial improvements in efficiency and quality. However, when all three components are brought together in a truly advanced plant, the results are breathtaking. Companies such as Xerox, Westinghouse, Texas Instruments, Hewlett-Packard, and Boeing are leading the way. Boeing's new 777, the largest twin-engine plane ever built, has been called the first "paperless" jetliner. The company designed the plane with eight IBM mainframe computers supporting 2,200 workstations that eventually handled 3,500 billion bits of information. The digital design system reduced the possibility of human error and cut engineering changes and reworking of ill-fitting components by more than 50 percent over previous plane projects.[20]

This ultra-advanced system is not achieved piecemeal. CIM reaches its ultimate level to improve quality, customer service, and cost-cutting when all parts are used interdependently. The integration of CIM and flexible work processes is changing the face of manufacturing. The wave of the manufacturing future is mass customization, whereby factories are able to mass-produce products designed to exact customer specification. Levi Strauss recently began offering "made-to-order" jeans. A salesclerk enters a customer's measurements into a computer that creates a unique digital pattern. The pattern is then sent by modem to the factory, where robotic cutters and other advanced sewing and finishing equipment produce thousands of pairs of jeans, each tailored to a specific customer.[21] Some U.S. business leaders envision a time in the near future when even cars can be custom-made in as little as three days.[22]

Performance. The awesome advantage of CIM is that products of different sizes, types, and customer requirements freely intermingle on the assembly line. Bar codes imprinted on a part enable machines to make instantaneous changes—such as putting a larger screw in a different location—without slowing the production line.

A manufacturer can turn out an infinite variety of products in unlimited batch sizes, as illustrated in Exhibit 4.5. In traditional manufacturing systems studied by Woodward, choices were limited to the diagonal. Small batch manufacturing allowed for high product flexibility and custom orders, but because of the craftsmanship involved in custom-making products, batch size was necessarily small. Mass production could have large batch size, but offered limited product flexibility. Continuous process could produce a single standard product in unlimited quantities. Computer-integrated manufacturing allows plants to break free of this diagonal and to increase both batch size and product flexibility at the same time. When taken to its ultimate level, CIM allows for mass customization, with each individual product tailored to customer specification. This high-level use of CIM has been referred to as "computer-aided craftsmanship" because computers tailor each product to meet a customer's exact needs.[23]

Studies suggest that with CIM, machine utilization is more efficient, labor productivity increases, scrap rates decrease, and product variety and customer satisfaction increase.[24] Many United States manufacturing companies are reinventing the factory using CIM and associated management systems to increase productivity.

Structural Implications. Research into the relationship between CIM and organizational characteristics is beginning to emerge, and the patterns are summarized in Exhibit 4.6. Compared with traditional mass production technologies, CIM has a narrow span of control, few hierarchical levels, adaptive tasks, low specialization, decentralization, and the overall environment is characterized as organic and self-regulative. Employees need the skills to participate in teams, training is broad (so workers are not overly specialized) and frequent (so workers are up-to-date). Expertise tends to be cognitive so workers can process abstract ideas and solve problems. Interorganizational relationships in CIM firms are characterized by changing demand from customers—which is easily

Exhibit 4.5 *Relationship of Computer-Integrated Manufacturing Technology to Traditional Technologies*

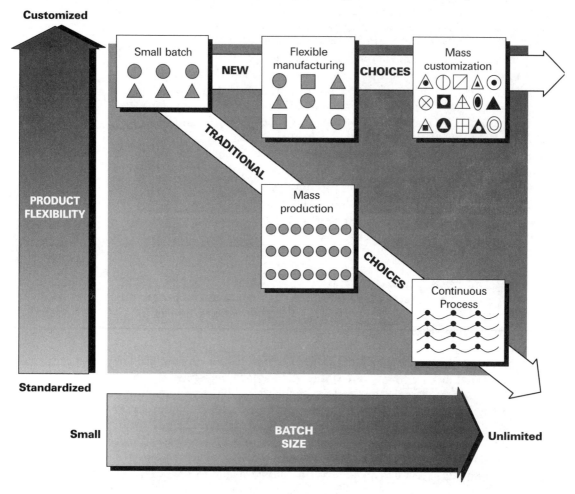

Source: Based on Jack Meredith, "The Strategic Advantages of New Manufacturing Technologies for Small Firms," *Strategic Management Journal* 8 (1987): 249–58; Paul Adler, "Managing Flexible Automation," *California Management Review* (Spring 1988): 34–56; and Otis Port, "Custom-Made Direct from the Plant," *Business Week/21st Century Capitalism,* 18 November 1994, *158–59.*

handled with the new technology—and close relationships with a few suppliers that provide top-quality raw materials.[25]

Computer-integrated manufacturing can help companies be more competitive when managers implement new structures and processes that empower workers and support a learning environment.[26]

The other major change occurring in the technology of organizations is a growing service sector. Service technologies are different from manufacturing technologies and, in turn, require a specific organization structure.

Service Firms

The United States and Canada are rapidly becoming service-oriented economies. In the U.S., services now generate 74 percent of gross domestic product and account for 79 percent of all jobs. In addition, the Bureau of Labor Statistics expects services to account for all net job growth in the next decade.[27]

Exhibit 4.6

Comparison of Organizational Characteristics Associated with Mass Production and Computer-Integrated Manufacturing

Characteristic	Mass Production	CIM
Structure		
Span of control	Wide	Narrow
Hierarchical levels	Many	Few
Tasks	Routine, repetitive	Adaptive, craftlike
Specialization	High	Low
Decision making	Centralized	Decentralized
Overall	Bureaucratic, mechanistic	Self-regulation, organic
Human Resources		
Interactions	Stand alone	Teamwork
Training	Narrow, one time	Broad, frequent
Expertise	Manual, technical	Cognitive, social
		Solve problems
Interorganizational		
Customer demand	Stable	Changing
Suppliers	Many, arm's length	Few, close relations

Source: Based on Patricia L. Nemetz and Louis W. Fry, "Flexible Manufacturing Organizations: Implications for Strategy Formulation and Organization Design," *Academy of Management Review* 13 (1988): 627–38; Paul S. Adler, "Managing Flexible Automation," *California Management Review* (Spring 1988): 34–56; Jeremy Main, "Manufacturing the Right Way," *Fortune*, 21 May 1990, 54–64.

Definition. Recent studies of service organizations focused on the unique dimensions of service technologies. **Service technologies** are defined based on the five elements in Exhibit 4.7. The first major difference is *simultaneous production and consumption*, which means a customer and an employee interact to provide the service. A client meets with a doctor or attorney, for example, and students and teachers come together in the classroom. This also means that customers tend to receive *customized output* and that *customers participate* in the production process. In manufacturing, by contrast, goods are produced at one time and inventoried for sale and consumption at another time; outputs tend to be standardized, and the production process tends to be removed and buffered from customers.

Another major difference is *intangible output* in a service firm. A service is abstract and often consists of information or knowledge in contrast with the tangible physical products made by manufacturing firms. This typically means service firms are *labor intensive*, with many employees needed to meet the needs of customers, while manufacturing firms tend to be capital intensive, relying on mass production, continuous process, and CIM technologies.[28]

The characteristics in Exhibit 4.7 are prototypical, or the standard case, but exceptions arise. Some service firms try to take on characteristics of manufacturers, and vice versa. Some firms end up in the middle—such as fast-food outlets, banks, and stockbrokers, which provide both a product and a service. These firms do not actually make a product, they provide it as a service, but a tangible product is part of the transaction. In addition, in today's competitive environment, manufacturers are placing a greater emphasis on service as well, which is one reason for the increased use of the CIM technology we have just discussed. Thus, manufacturers are shifting to organization structures and processes that

Exhibit 4.7 *Examples of Service Technology versus Manufacturing Technology*

Prototypical Service Technology

1. Simultaneous production and consumption
2. Customized output
3. Customer participation
4. Intangible output
5. Labor intensive

Prototypical Manufacturing Technology

1. Goods inventoried for later consumption
2. Standardized output
3. Technical core buffered from customer
4. Tangible output
5. Capital intensive

Service	Product and Service	Product
Airlines	Fast-food outlets	Soft drink companies
Hotels	Banks	Steel companies
Consultants	Cosmetics	Automobile manufacturers
Teachers	Real estate	Mining corporations
Health clinics	Stockbrokers	Food processing plants
Law firms	Retail stores	

Source: Based on David E. Bowen, Caren Siehl, and Benjamin Schneider, "A Framework for Analyzing Customer Service Orientations in Manufacturing," *Academy of Management Review* 14 (1989): 75–95.

have generally been characteristic of service firms.[29] The important point is that all organizations can be classified along a continuum that includes both manufacturing and service characteristics, as illustrated in Exhibit 4.7.

Structure. The feature of service technologies with a distinct influence on organizational structure and control systems is the need for technical core employees to be close to the customer.[30] The differences between service and product organizations necessitated by customer contact are summarized in Exhibit 4.8.

The impact of customer contact on organization structure is reflected in the use of boundary roles and structural disaggregation.[31] Boundary roles are used extensively in manufacturing firms to handle customers and to reduce disruptions for the technical core. They are used less in service firms because a service is intangible and cannot be passed along by boundary spanners, so service customers must interact directly with technical employees, such as doctors or brokers.

A service firm deals in information and intangible outputs and does not need to be large. Its greatest economies are achieved through disaggregation into small units that can be located close to customers. Stockbrokers, doctors' clinics, fast-food franchises, consulting firms, and banks disperse their facilities into regional and local offices. Some fast-food chains, such as Taco Bell, are taking this a step further, selling chicken tacos and bean burritos anywhere people gather—airports, supermarkets, college campuses, or street corners.

Manufacturing firms, on the other hand, tend to aggregate operations in a single area that has raw materials and an available work force. A large manufacturing firm can take advantage of economies derived from expensive machinery and long production runs.

Structure	Service	Product
1. Separate boundary roles	Few	Many
2. Geographical dispersion	Much	Little
3. Decision making	Decentralized	Centralized
4. Formalization	Lower	Higher
Human Resources		
1. Employee skill level	Higher	Lower
2. Skill emphasis	Interpersonal	Technical

Exhibit 4.8
Configuration and Structural Characteristics of Service Organizations versus Product Organizations

Service technology also influences internal organization characteristics used to direct and control the organization. For one thing, the skills of technical core employees need to be higher. These employees need enough knowledge and awareness to handle customer problems rather than just enough to perform a single, mechanical task. Some service organizations give their employees the knowledge and freedom to make decisions and do whatever is needed to satisfy customers, while others, such as McDonald's, have set rules and procedures for customer service. Yet in all cases, service employees need social and interpersonal skills as well as technical skills.[32] Because of higher skills and structural dispersion, decision making often tends to be decentralized in service firms, and formalization tends to be low. Many Taco Bell outlets operate with no manager on the premises. Self-directed teams manage inventory, schedule work, order supplies, and train new employees.

Understanding the nature of service technology helps managers align strategy, structure, and management processes that may be quite different from those for a product-based or traditional manufacturing technology.

Now let's turn to another perspective on technology, that of production activities within specific organizational departments. Departments often have characteristics similar to those of service technology, providing services to other departments within the organization.

DEPARTMENTAL TECHNOLOGY

This section shifts to the department level of analysis for departments not necessarily within the technical core. Each department in an organization has a production process that consists of a distinct technology. General Motors has departments for engineering, R&D, human resources, advertising, quality control, finance, and dozens of other functions. This section analyzes the nature of departmental technology and its relationship with departmental structure.

The framework that has had the greatest impact on the understanding of departmental technologies was developed by Charles Perrow.[33] Perrow's model has been useful for a broad range of technologies, which made it ideal for research into departmental activities.

Variety

Perrow specified two dimensions of departmental activities that were relevant to organization structure and process. The first is the number of exceptions in the work. This refers to task **variety**, which is the frequency of unexpected and novel events that occur in the conversion process. When individuals encounter a large number of unexpected situations, with frequent problems, variety is considered high. When there are few problems, and when day-to-day job requirements are repetitious, technology contains little variety. Variety in departments can range from repeating a single act, such as on an assembly line, to working on a series of unrelated problems or projects.

Analyzability

The second dimension of technology concerns the **analyzability** of work activities. When the conversion process is analyzable, the work can be reduced to mechanical steps and participants can follow an objective, computational procedure to solve problems. Problem solution may involve the use of standard procedures, such as instructions and manuals, or technical knowledge, such as that in a textbook or handbook. On the other hand, some work is not analyzable. When problems arise, it is difficult to identify the correct solution. There is no store of techniques or procedures to tell a person exactly what to do. The cause of or solution to a problem is not clear, so employees rely on accumulated experience, intuition, and judgment. The final solution to a problem is often the result of wisdom and experience and not the result of standard procedures. The brewmaster department at Heineken Brewery has an unanalyzable technology. Brewmasters taste each batch of product to identify the mix of ingredients and to see whether it fits within acceptable flavor limits. These quality control tasks require years of experience and practice. Standard procedures will not tell a person how to do such tasks.

Framework

The two dimensions of technology and examples of departmental activities on Perrow's framework are shown in Exhibit 4.9. The dimensions of variety and analyzability form the basis for four major categories of technology: routine, craft, engineering, and nonroutine.

Routine technologies are characterized by little task variety and the use of objective, computational procedures. The tasks are formalized and standardized. Examples include an automobile assembly line and a bank teller department.

Craft technologies are characterized by a fairly stable stream of activities, but the conversion process is not analyzable or well understood. Tasks require extensive training and experience because employees respond to intangible factors on the basis of wisdom, intuition, and experience. Although advances in machine technologies seem to have reduced the number of craft technologies in organizations, a few craft technologies remain. For example, steel furnace engineers continue to mix steel based on intuition and experience, and pattern makers at apparel firms still convert designers' rough sketches into saleable garments.

Engineering technologies tend to be complex because there is substantial variety in the tasks performed. However, the various activities are usually handled on the basis of established formulas, procedures, and techniques. Employees normally refer to a well-developed body of knowledge to handle problems. Engineering and accounting tasks usually fall in this category.

Nonroutine technologies have high task variety, and the conversion process is not analyzable or well understood. In nonroutine technology, a great deal of effort is devoted to analyzing problems and activities. Several equally acceptable options typically can be found. Experience and technical knowledge are used to

Exhibit 4.9 *Framework for Department Technologies*

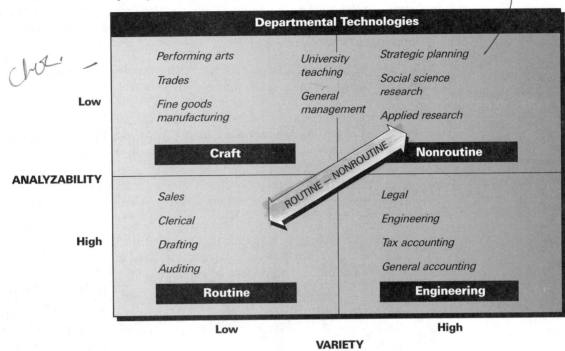

Source: Adapted with permission from Richard Daft and Norman Macintosh, "A New Approach to Design and Use of Management Information," *California Management Review* 21 (1978): 82–92. Copyright © 1978 by the Regents of the University of California. Reprinted by permission of the Regents.

solve problems and perform the work. Basic research, strategic planning, and other work that involves new projects and unexpected problems are nonroutine.

Exhibit 4.9 also illustrates that variety and analyzability can be combined into a single dimension of technology. This dimension is called *routine versus nonroutine technology*, and it is the diagonal line in Exhibit 4.9. The analyzability and variety dimensions are often correlated in departments, meaning that technologies high in variety tend to be low in analyzability, and technologies low in variety tend to be analyzable. Departments can be evaluated, along a single dimension of routine versus nonroutine that combines both analyzability and variety, which is a useful shorthand measure for analyzing departmental technology.

The following questions show how departmental technology can be analyzed for determining its placement on Perrow's technology framework in Exhibit 4.9.[34] Employees normally circle a number from one to seven in response to each question.

Variety
1. To what extent would you say your work is routine?
2. Does most everyone in this unit do about the same job in the same way most of the time?
3. Are unit members performing repetitive activities in doing their jobs?

Analyzability
1. To what extent is there a clearly known way to do the major types of work you normally encounter?

2. To what extent is there an understandable sequence of steps that can be followed in doing your work?
3. To do your work, to what extent can you actually rely on established procedures and practices?

If answers to the above questions indicated high scores for analyzability and low scores for variety, the department would have a routine technology. If the opposite occurs, the technology would be nonroutine. Low variety and low analyzability indicate a craft technology, and high variety and high analyzability indicate an engineering technology. As a practical matter, most departments fit somewhere along the diagonal and can be most easily characterized as routine or nonroutine.

DEPARTMENT DESIGN

Once the nature of a department's technology has been identified, then the appropriate structure can be determined. Department technology tends to be associated with a cluster of departmental characteristics, such as the skill level of employees, formalization, and pattern of communication. Definite patterns do exist in the relationship between work unit technology and structural characteristics, which are associated with departmental performance.[35] Key relationships between technology and other dimensions of departments are described in this section and are summarized in Exhibit 4.10.

1. *Organic versus Mechanistic.* The single most persistent pattern is that routine technologies are associated with a mechanistic structure and processes and nonroutine technologies with an organic structure and processes. Formal rules and centralized management apply to routine units. When work is nonroutine, department administration is more organic and free-flowing. In the R&D lab at Datapoint Corporation, employees wear T-shirts and sandals, may wear beards, and ride to work on motorcycles. In the production department, employees wear more traditional dress, including shoes, shirts, and short haircuts, which reflects the more structured nature of the work.[36]
2. *Formalization.* Routine technology is characterized by standardization and division of labor into small tasks that are governed by formal rules and procedures. For nonroutine tasks, the structure is less formal and less standardized. When variety is high, as in a research department, fewer activities are covered by formal procedures.[37]
3. *Decentralization.* In routine technologies, most decision making about task activities is centralized to management.[38] In engineering technologies, employees with technical training tend to acquire moderate decision authority because technical knowledge is important to task accomplishment. Production employees who have long experience obtain decision authority in craft technologies because they know how to respond to problems. Decentralization to employees is greatest in nonroutine settings, where many decisions are made by employees.
4. *Worker Skill Level.* Work staff in routine technologies typically require little education or experience, which is congruent with repetitious work activities. In work units with greater variety, staff are more skilled and often have formal training in technical schools or universities. Training for craft activities, which are less analyzable, is more likely to be through job experience. Nonroutine activities require both formal education and job experience.[39]

Exhibit 4.10 *Relationship of Department Technology to Structural and Management Characteristics*

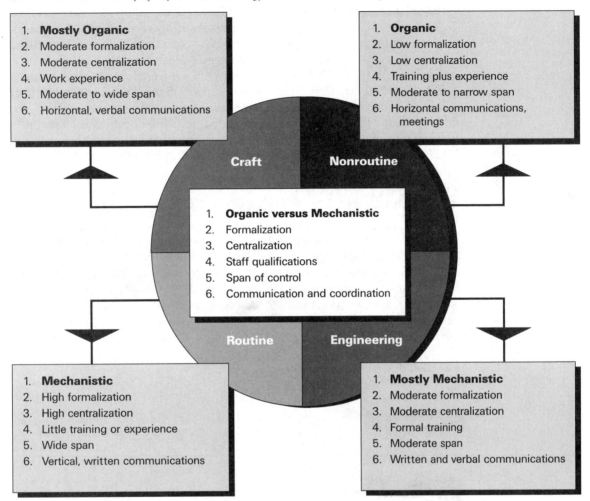

5. *Span of Control.* Span of control is the number of employees who report to a single manager or supervisor. This characteristic is normally influenced by departmental technology. The more complex and nonroutine the task, the more problems arise in which the supervisor becomes involved. Although the span of control may be influenced by other factors, such as skill level of employees, it typically should be smaller for complex tasks because on such tasks the supervisor and subordinate must interact frequently.[40]

6. *Communication and Coordination.* Communication activity and frequency increase as task variety increases.[41] Frequent problems require more information sharing to solve problems and ensure proper completion of activities. The direction of communication is typically horizontal in nonroutine work units and vertical in routine work units.[42] The form of communication varies by task analyzability.[43] When tasks are highly analyzable, statistical and written forms of communication (memos, reports, rules, and procedures) are frequent. When tasks are less analyzable, information typically is conveyed face-to-face, over the telephone, or in group meetings.

Two important points are reflected in Exhibit 4.10. First, departments do differ from one another and can be categorized according to their workflow technology.[44] Second, structural and management processes differ based on departmental technology. Managers should design their departments so that requirements based on technology can be met. Design problems are most visible when the design is clearly inconsistent with technology. Studies have found that when structures and communication characteristics did not reflect technology, departments tended to be less effective.[45] Employees could not communicate with the frequency needed to solve problems. Sometimes employees had to deviate from misplaced rules to behave as needed to fit the technology.

WORKFLOW INTERDEPENDENCE AMONG DEPARTMENTS

So far, this chapter has explored how organization and department technologies influence structural design. The final characteristic of technology that influences structure is called interdependence. **Interdependence** means the extent to which departments depend upon each other for resources or materials to accomplish their tasks. Low interdependence means that departments can do their work independently of each other and have little need for interaction, consultation, or exchange of materials. High interdependence means departments must constantly exchange resources.

Types

James Thompson defined three types of interdependence that influence organization structure.[46] These interdependencies are illustrated in Exhibit 4.11 and are discussed in the following sections.

Pooled. **Pooled interdependence** is the lowest form of interdependence among departments. In this form, work does not flow between units. Each department is part of the organization and contributes to the common good of the organization, but works independently. McDonald's restaurants or branch banks are examples of pooled interdependence. An outlet in Chicago need not interact with an outlet in Urbana. The connection between branches is that they share financial resources from a common pool, and the success of each branch contributes to the success of the organization.

Thompson proposed that pooled interdependence would exist in firms with what he called a mediating technology. A **mediating technology** provides products or services that mediate or link clients from the external environment and, in so doing, allows each department to work independently. Banks, brokerage firms, and real estate offices all mediate between buyers and sellers, but the offices work independently within the organization.

The management implications associated with pooled interdependence are quite simple. Thompson argued that managers should use rules and procedures to standardize activities across departments. Each department should use the same procedures and financial statements so the outcomes of all departments can be measured and pooled. Very little day-to-day coordination is required among units.

Exhibit 4.11
Thompson's
Classification of
Interdependence and
Management
Implications

Form of Interdependence	Demands on Horizontal Communication, Decision Making	Type of Coordination Required	Priority for Locating Units Close Together
Pooled (bank)	Low communication	Standardization, rules, procedures	Low
Sequential (assembly line)	Medium communication	Plans, schedules, feedback	Medium
Reciprocal (hospital)	High communication	Mutual adjustment, cross-departmental meetings, teamwork	High

Sequential. When interdependence is of serial form, with parts produced in one department becoming inputs to another department, then it is called **sequential interdependence**. The first department must perform correctly for the second department to perform correctly. This is a higher level of interdependence than pooled, because departments exchange resources and depend upon others to perform well.

Sequential interdependence occurs in what Thompson called **long-linked technology**, which "refers to the combination in one organization of successive stages of production; each stage of production uses as its inputs the production of the preceding stage and produces inputs for the following stage."[47] Large organizations that use assembly line production, such as in the automobile industry, use long-linked technologies and are characterized by sequential interdependence.

The management requirements of sequential interdependence are more demanding than for pooled interdependence. Coordination among the linked plants or departments is required. Since the interdependence implies a one-way flow of materials, extensive planning and scheduling are generally needed. Plant B needs to know what to expect from Plant A so both can perform effectively. Some day-to-day communication among plants is also needed to handle unexpected problems and exceptions that arise.

Reciprocal. The highest level of interdependence is **reciprocal interdependence**. This exists when the output of operation A is the input to operation B, and the output of operation B is the input back again to operation A. The outputs of departments influence those departments in reciprocal fashion.

Reciprocal interdependence tends to occur in organizations with what Thompson called **intensive technologies,** which provide a variety of products or services in combination to a client. Hospitals are an excellent example because they provide coordinated services to patients. A patient may move back and forth between X-ray, surgery, and physical therapy as needed to be cured. A firm developing new products is another example. Intense coordination is needed between design, engineering, manufacturing, and marketing to combine all their resources to suit the customer's product need.

Management requirements are greatest in the case of reciprocal interdependence. The structure must allow for frequent horizontal communication and adjustment. Extensive planning is required in hospitals, for example, but plans will not anticipate or solve all problems. Daily interaction and mutual adjustment among departments are required. Managers from several departments are jointly involved in face-to-face coordination, teamwork, and decision making. Reciprocal interdependence is the most complex interdependence for organizations to handle.

Structural Priority

As indicated in Exhibit 4.11, since decision making, communication, and coordination problems are greatest for reciprocal interdependence, reciprocal interdependence should receive first priority in organization structure.

New product development is one area of reciprocal interdependence that is of growing concern to managers as companies face increasing pressure to get new products to market fast. Many firms are revamping the design-manufacturing relationship by closely integrating computer-aided design (CAD) and computer-aided manufacturing (CAM) technologies discussed earlier in this chapter.[48]

Activities that are reciprocally interdependent should be grouped close together in the organization so managers have easy access to one another for mutual adjustment. These units should report to the same person on the organization chart and should be physically close so the time and effort for coordination can be minimized. Poor coordination will result in poor performance for the organization. If the reciprocally interdependent units cannot be located close together, the organization should design mechanisms for coordination, such as daily meetings between departments or an electronic mail network to facilitate communication. The next priority is given to sequential interdependencies, and finally to pooled interdependencies.

This strategy of organizing keeps the communication channels short where coordination is most critical to organizational success. For example, Boise Cascade Corporation experienced poor service to customers because customer service reps located in New York City were not coordinating with production planners in Oregon plants. Customers couldn't get delivery as needed. Boise was reorganized, and the two groups were consolidated under one roof, reporting to the same supervisor at division headquarters. Now customer needs are met because customer service reps work with production planning to schedule customer orders.

Structural Implications

Most organizations experience various levels of interdependence, and structure can be designed to fit these needs, as illustrated in Exhibit 4.12.[49] In a manufacturing firm, new product development entails reciprocal interdependence among the design, engineering, purchasing, manufacturing, and sales departments. Perhaps a cross-departmental team could be formed to handle the back-and-forth flow of information and resources. Once a product is designed, its actual manufacture would be sequential interdependence, with a flow of goods from one department to another, such as between purchasing, inventory, production control, manufacturing, and assembly. The actual ordering and delivery of products is pooled interdependence, with warehouses working independently. Customers could place an order with the nearest facility, which would not require coordination among warehouses, except in unusual cases such as a stock outage.

When consultants analyzed NCR to learn why new products were so slow being developed, they followed the path from initial idea to implementation. The problem was that the development, production, and marketing of products took place in separate divisions, and communication across the three interdependent groups was difficult. NCR broke up its traditional organization structure and created several stand-alone units of about 500 people, each with its own development, production, and marketing people. This enabled new products to be introduced in record time.

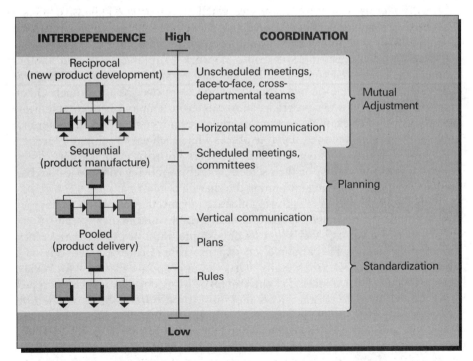

Exhibit 4.12

Primary Means to Achieve Coordination for Different Levels of Task Interdependence in a Manufacturing Firm

Source: Adapted from Andrew H. Van de Ven, Andre Delbecq, and Richard Koenig, "Determinants of Communication Modes within Organizations," *American Sociological Review* 41 (1976): 330.

ADVANCED INFORMATION TECHNOLOGY

Organizations have rapidly moved from the computer age to the information age, brought about by the microprocessor revolution. A typical microprocessor contains semiconductor chips that can execute tens of thousands of calculations in the blink of an eye, all in a space no larger than a fingernail. This revolution enabled the emergence of computer-integrated manufacturing (CIM) systems described earlier in this chapter.

Microprocessors also enabled the disaggregation of large centralized computers into personal computers and workstations scattered around the organization, each having enormous computing power. Moreover, the solitary machines have become networks of interacting computers that greatly magnify their power and impact. Indeed, the impact of advanced information technologies on the administrative side of organizations is just as significant as that of CIM technologies on manufacturing. New corporate structures have combined with advanced information technology to increase productivity in many corporations.[50]

Those aspects of **advanced information technology** (AIT) most significant for administration are executive information systems, groupware, and workflow automation. An **executive information system** is the use of computer technology to support the information needs of senior managers. For example, the CEO of Duracell was able to use his personal computer to compare the performance of work forces in the United States and overseas. His computer produced a crisp table in color showing differences in productivity. Digging for more data, he discovered that overseas salespeople were spending too much time calling on small stores, prompting a decision to service small stores in less expensive ways.[51] Executive information systems have the capacity for supporting nonroutine decisions, such as company strategy and competitive responses.

Groupware enables employees on a network to interact with one another through their personal computers. The simplest form of groupware is *electronic mail,* which allows one-on-one communication from one PC to another. Other, more complex groupware programs allow numerous employees to communicate simultaneously. For example, a team of employees might sit around a conference table or even remain in their separate offices while each uses a computer terminal through which the comments of other members are registered. All participants may view the same display on their screens, thereby removing communication barriers in group meetings and facilitating the sharing of information.[52]

Workflow automation is a growing niche in advanced information technology. Workflow software enables computer networks to automatically send documents, such as invoices, check requests, or customer inquiries, to the correct location for processing. For example, an expense report can be filled out on a computer which checks the details, alerts the appropriate manager for review, then prints the check and notifies the employee by electronic mail where to pick it up. Workflow automation allows the entire procedure to be completed via computer without a single employee ever having to handle a paper document. Workflow automation also enables small companies to handle paperwork jobs that only firms with large numbers of employees could do in the past.

For management, the rapid advancements in information technology call for new decisions on how it should be used in the organization. AIT makes the organization and the external environment more transparent to top managers. Should they use this power to centralize and tightly control the organization, or should they provide employees with the information needed to act autonomously? AIT can give employees all kinds of data about their customers, market, service, and efficiency. Some organizations use the new technology to simply reinforce rigid hierarchies, centralize decision making, and routinize work. For the most part, however, successful organizations are using this technology to decentralize, and its impact is being felt on management processes, organization design, and workplace culture.

Management Implications

Advanced information technology enables managers to be better connected with the organization, the environment, and each other. Specific improvements in management processes are:

1. *Broader Participation in Decision Making.* Communication among managers takes time and effort, and AIT greatly reduces this effort, especially when managers are physically separated. For example, a product developer sent an electronic message asking for suggestions for a new product feature. He received more than 150 messages from every corner of the organization, almost all from people he did not know.[53] Moreover, research shows that AIT increases contact between the top of the organization and the bottom. Lower-level managers can communicate directly with the CEO, and a vice president can communicate directly with a project engineer. At Mrs. Fields, Inc., the world's largest retailer of cookies, branch employees use electronic mail to communicate directly to CEO Debbi Fields their opinions about products, competitors, and customer reactions. "On-line" at Wright-Patterson Air Force Base in Ohio, enlisted personnel can send messages directly to colonels, a level of communication that would have been unheard of five years ago.[54]

2. *Faster Decision Making.* AIT uses less of the organization's time for decision-related meetings.[55] The technology also reduces the time required to authorize organizational actions. Messages are handled fewer times, and interested parties can communicate directly. For example, Xerox dramatically reduced meeting time with its new computer system. Prior to a presentation, papers are no longer sent back and forth. Each unit submits a plan electronically five days in advance, which each top executive reads before the meeting. The meeting itself is short because time is spent on substantive issues.

3. *Better Organizational Intelligence, Including More Rapid Identification of Problems and Opportunities.*[56] With AIT, organizational activities become visible to managers. For example, sales and market research data are now available from grocery store checkout scanners. Organizations can purchase access to hundreds of databases about industry, financial, and demographic patterns in their environments. AIT enables the accumulation and widespread communication of a larger volume as well as a larger range of information. For example, at MTV Networks, groupware became a new weapon for the affiliate sales force. When MTV was battling against rival Turner Broadcasting System's Cartoon Channel, trying to get operators to carry MTV's Comedy Central instead, salespeople encountered unexpectedly strong resistance. A saleswoman in Chicago discovered a cable system in her area had been offered a special two-year rock-bottom price by the Cartoon Channel. She shared this intelligence on the computer network so other

salespeople could research pricing in their own areas. Ultimately, MTV's top managers were able to counterattack by offering their own special pricing and terms, helping to close several deals that appeared lost.[57]

Organization Design

The impact of advanced information technology on the administrative structure of organizations is now being felt. Specific outcomes are:

1. *Flatter Organization Structure.* AIT has been enabling the lean structures many organizations are adopting. One organization in London that used information technology to empower employees rather than maintain a rigid hierarchy reduced the structure from thirteen to four layers. Hercules, a chemical company, adopted a combination of electronic messaging and groupware, after which the number of management levels between the president and plant foreman was reduced from a dozen to about seven, yet decision speed and effectiveness improved. New information technology has enabled Aetna Life and Casualty Company's sales force to replace its old hierarchy of supervisors and agents with small work teams.[58]

2. *Greater Centralization or Decentralization.* Depending on manager choices, AIT can either centralize or decentralize the organization. Managers who want to centralize can use the technology to acquire more information and make more decisions, often with greater responsiveness than previously. Likewise, managers can decentralize information to employees and increase participation and autonomy.[59] Management philosophy and corporate culture have substantial bearing on how AIT influences decision making, but enlightened companies seem to use it to empower employees whenever possible. For example, at the Chesebrough-Ponds, Inc. plant in Jefferson City, Missouri, line workers routinely tap the company's computer network to track shipments, schedule their own workloads, order production increases, and perform other functions that used to be the province of management.

3. *Improved Coordination.* Perhaps one of the great outcomes of AIT is the ability to connect managers even when offices or stores are scattered worldwide. At Chase Manhattan Bank, groupware links fifty-two hundred bankers throughout the world. The new technology enables managers to communicate with one another and be aware of organization activities and outcomes. It can help to break down barriers and create a sense of team and organizational identity that was not previously available, especially when people work at different locations.[60]

4. *Fewer Narrow Tasks.* Fewer administrative tasks under AIT will be subject to narrowly defined policies and job descriptions. Companies using AIT will closely resemble professional service firms. Remaining administrative and clerical tasks will provide intellectual engagement and more challenging work.[61]

5. *Larger Professional Staff Ratio.* The implementation of sophisticated information systems means that employees have to be highly trained and professional to both operate and maintain such systems. For the most part, unskilled employees will be replaced by the new technology, such as when the North American Banking Group installed a customer service information system that shifted the staff mix from 30 percent professionals to 60 percent professionals. Many clerical personnel were replaced by AIT. Fewer employees

were needed to type letters, file memos, and fill out forms. Middle- and upper-level managers can use the new technology to type their own memos and send them instantly through electronic mail.

Workplace Culture

All these changes in management processes and organization design also mean changes in office life. Corporate culture often changes with the introduction of advanced information technology. Depending on the approach of management, this can lead to a sense of empowerment when employees are given increased access to information previously available only to their bosses, or to a loss of privacy for employees whose bosses now keep tabs on their every move. Relationships among workers are also affected when managers decide who within the organization should have access to what information and who should communicate with whom. It is important to remember that advanced information technology affects not just the structure of an organization but the people within it.

SUMMARY OF KEY ISSUES

This chapter reviewed several frameworks and key research findings on the topic of organizational technology. The potential importance of technology as a factor in organizational structure was discovered during the 1960s. During the 1970s and 1980s, a flurry of research activity was undertaken to understand more precisely the relationship of technology to other characteristics of organizations.

Five ideas in the technology literature stand out. The first is Woodward's research into manufacturing technology. Woodward went into organizations and collected practical data on technology characteristics, organization structure, and management systems. She found clear relationships between technology and structure in high-performing organizations. Her findings are so clear that managers can analyze their own organizations on the same dimensions of technology and structure. In addition, technology and structure can be co-aligned with organizational strategy to meet changing needs and provide new competitive advantages.

The second important idea is that service technologies differ in a systematic way from manufacturing technologies. Service technologies are characterized by intangible outcomes and direct client involvement in the production process. Service firms do not have the fixed, machine-based technologies that appear in manufacturing organizations; hence, organization design often differs also.

The third significant idea is Perrow's framework applied to department technologies. Understanding the variety and analyzability of a technology tells one about the management style, structure, and process that should characterize that department. Routine technologies are characterized by mechanistic structure and nonroutine technologies by organic structure. Applying the wrong management system to a department will result in dissatisfaction and reduced efficiency.

The fourth important idea is interdependence among departments. The extent to which departments depend on each other for materials, information, or other resources determines the amount of coordination required between them. As interdependence increases, demands on the organization for coordination increase. Organization design must allow for the correct amount of communication and coordination to handle interdependence across departments.

The fifth important idea is that new technologies—computer-integrated manufacturing and advanced information technologies—are being adopted by organizations and having impact on organization design. For the most part, the impact is positive, with shifts toward more organic structures both on the shop floor and in the management hierarchy. These technologies replace routine jobs, give employees more autonomy, produce more challenging jobs, encourage teamwork, and let the organization be more flexible and responsive. The new technologies are enriching jobs to the point where organizations are happier places to work.

Discussion Questions

1. Where would your university or college department be located on Perrow's technology framework? Look for the underlying variety and analyzability characteristics when making your assessment. Would a department devoted exclusively to teaching be put in a different quadrant from a department devoted exclusively to research?

2. Explain Thompson's levels of interdependence. Identify an example of each level of interdependence in the university or college setting. What kinds of coordination mechanisms should administration develop to handle each level of interdependence?

3. Describe Woodward's classification of organizational technologies. Explain why each of the three technology groups is related differently to organization structure and management processes.

4. What relationships did Woodward discover between supervisor span of control and technological complexity?

5. How does computer-integrated manufacturing differ from other manufacturing technologies? What is the primary advantage of CIM?

6. What is a service technology? Are different types of service technologies likely to be associated with different structures? Explain.

7. Edna Peterson is a colonel in the air force in charge of the finance section of an air base in New Mexico. Financial work in the military involves large amounts of routine matters and paperwork, and Peterson gradually developed a philosophy of management that was fairly mechanistic. She believed that all important decisions should be made by administrators, that elaborate rules and procedures should be developed and followed, and that subordinates should have little discretion and should be tightly controlled. The finance section is about to introduce advanced information technology that will take over most paperwork. Based on what you know about AIT, what advice would you give Edna Peterson?

8. A top executive claimed that top-level management is a craft technology because the work contains intangibles, such as handling personnel, interpreting the environment, and coping with unusual situations that have to be learned through experience. If this is true, is it appropriate to teach management in a business school? Does teaching management from a textbook assume that the manager's job is analyzable, and hence that formal training rather than experience is most important?

9. In which quadrant of Perrow's framework would a mass production technology be placed? Where would small-batch and continuous process technologies be placed? Why? Would Perrow's framework lead to the same recommendation about organic versus mechanistic structures that Woodward made?

Notes

1. Charles Perrow, "A Framework for the Comparative Analysis of Organizations," *American Sociological Review* 32 (1967): 194–208; Denise M. Rousseau, "Assessment of Technology in Organizations: Closed versus Open Systems Approaches," *Academy of Management Review* 4 (1979): 531–42.

2. Linda Argote, "Input Uncertainty and Organizational Coordination in Hospital Emergency Units," *Administrative Science Quarterly* 27 (1982): 420–34; Charles Perrow, *Organizational Analysis: A Sociological Approach* (Belmont, Calif.: Wadsworth, 1970); William Rushing, "Hardness of Material as Related to the Division of Labor in Manufacturing Industries," *Administrative Science Quarterly* 13 (1968): 229–45.

3. Lawrence B. Mohr, "Organizational Technology and Organization Structure," *Administrative Science Quarterly* 16 (1971): 444–59; David Hickson, Derek Pugh, and Diana Pheysey, "Operations Technology and Organization Structure: An Empirical Reappraisal," *Administrative Science Quarterly* 14 (1969): 378–97.

4. Joan Woodward, *Industrial Organization: Theory and Practice* (London: Oxford University Press, 1965); Joan Woodward, *Management and Technology* (London: Her Majesty's Stationery Office, 1958).

5. Hickson, Pugh, and Pheysey, "Operations Technology and Organization Structure"; James D. Thompson, *Organizations in Action* (New York: McGraw-Hill, 1967).

6. Edward Harvey, "Technology and the Structure of Organizations," *American Sociological Review* 33 (1968): 241–59.

7. Wanda J. Orlikowski, "The Duality of Technology: Rethinking the Concept of Technology in Organizations," *Organization Science* 3 (1992): 398–427.

8. Based on Woodward, *Industrial Organization* and *Management and Technology*.

9. Woodward, *Industrial Organization*, vi.

10. William L. Zwerman, *New Perspectives on Organizational Theory* (Westport, Conn.: Greenwood, 1970); Harvey, "Technology and the Structure of Organizations," 241–59.

11. Dean M. Schroeder, Steven W. Congden, and C. Gopinath, "Linking Competitive Strategy and Manufacturing Process Technology," *Journal of Management Studies* 32:2, March 1995, 163–89.

12. Fernando F. Suarez, Michael A. Cusumano, and Charles H. Fine, "An Empirical Study of Flexibility in Manufacturing," *Sloan Management Review*, Fall 1995, 25–32.

13. Raymond F. Zammuto and Edward J. O'Connor, "Gaining Advanced Manufacturing Technologies' Benefits: The Roles of Organization Design and Culture," *Academy of Management Review*, Vol. 17, No. 4, 1992, 701–28; and Dean M. Schroeder, Steven W. Congden, and C. Gopinath, "Linking Competitive Strategy and Manufacturing Process Technology."

14. Jack R. Meredith, "The Strategic Advantages of the Factory of the Future," *California Management Review* 29 (Spring 1987): 27–41; Jack Meredith, "The Strategic Advantages of the New Manufacturing Technologies for Small Firms," *Strategic Management Journal* 8 (1987): 249–58; Althea Jones and Terry Webb, "Introducing Computer Integrated Manufacturing," *Journal of General Management* 12 (Summer 1987): 60–74.

15. Raymond F. Zammuto and Edward J. O'Conner, "Gaining Advanced Manufacturing Technologies' Benefits: The Roles of Organization Design and Culture," *Academy of Management Review* 17 (1992): 701–28.

16. John S. DeMott, "Small Factories' Big Lessons," *Nation's Business,* April 1995, 29–30.

17. Paul S. Adler, "Managing Flexible Automation," *California Management Review* (Spring 1988): 34–56.

18. Bela Gold, "Computerization in Domestic and International Manufacturing," *California Management Review* (Winter 1989): 129–43.

19. Graham Dudley and John Hassard, "Design Issues in the Development of Computer Integrated Manufacturing (CIM)," *Journal of General Management* 16 (1990): 43–53.

20. John Holusha, "Can Boeing's New Baby Fly Financially?" *The New York Times*, 27 March 1994, Section 3, 1, 6.

21. Joel D. Goldhar and David Lei, "Variety is Free: Manufacturing in the Twenty-First Century," *Academy of Management Executive*, Vol. 9, No. 4, 1995, 73–86.

22. Len Estrin, "The Dawn of Manufacturing," *Enterprise*, April 1994, 31–35; Otis Port, "The Responsive Factory," *Business Week/ Enterprise* 1993, 48–52.

23. Joel D. Goldhar and David Lei, "Variety is Free: Manufacturing in the Twenty-First Century," *Academy of Management Executive*, Vol. 9, No. 4, 1995, 73–86.

24. Meredith, "Strategic Advantages of the Factory of the Future."

25. Patricia L. Nemetz and Louis W. Fry, "Flexible Manufacturing Organizations: Implementations for Strategy Formulation and Organization Design," *Academy of Management Review* 13 (1988): 627–38; Paul S. Adler, "Managing Flexible Automation," *California Management Review* (Spring 1988): 34–56; Jeremy Main, "Manufacturing the Right Way," *Fortune*, 21 May 1990, 54–64; Frank M. Hull and Paul D. Collins, "High-Technology Batch Production Systems: Woodward's Missing Type," *Academy of Management Journal* 30 (1987): 786–97.

26. Len Estrin, "The Dawn of Manufacturing," *Enterprise*, April 1994, 31–35; and Goldhar and Lei, "Variety is Free."

27. Ronald Henkoff, "Service Is Everybody's Business," *Fortune*, 27 June 1994, 48–60; and Ronald Henkoff, "Finding, Training, and Keeping the Best Service Workers," *Fortune*, 3 October 1994, 110–22.

28. David E. Bowen, Caren Siehl, and Benjamin Schneider, "A Framework for Analyzing Customer Service Orientations in Manufacturing," *Academy of Management Review* 14 (1989): 79–95; Peter K. Mills and Newton Margulies, "Toward a Core Typology of Service Organizations," *Academy of Management Review* 5 (1980): 255–65; Peter K. Mills and Dennis J. Moberg, "Perspectives on the Technology of Service Operations," *Academy of Management Review* 7 (1982): 467–78; G. Lynn Shostack, "Breaking Free from Product Marketing," *Journal of Marketing* (April 1977): 73–80.

29. Ronald Henkoff, "Service Is Everybody's Business," *Fortune*, 27 June 1994, 48–60.

30. Richard B. Chase and David A. Tansik, "The Customer Contact Model for Organization Design," *Management Science* 29 (1983): 1037–50.

31. *Ibid.*

32. David E. Bowen and Edward E. Lawler III, "The Empowerment of Service Workers: What, Why, How, and When," *Sloan Management Review* (Spring 1992): 31–39; Gregory B. Northcraft and Richard B. Chase, "Managing Service Demand at the Point of Delivery," *Academy of Management Review* 10 (1985): 66–75; Roger W. Schmenner, "How Can Service Businesses Survive and Prosper?" *Sloan Management Review* 27 (Spring 1986): 21–32.

33. Perrow, "Framework for Comparative Analysis" and *Organizational Analysis*.

34. Michael Withey, Richard L. Daft, and William C. Cooper, "Measures of Perrow's Work Unit Technology: An Empirical Assessment and a New Scale," *Academy of Management Journal* 25 (1983): 45–63.

35. Christopher Gresov, "Exploring Fit and Misfit with Multiple Contingencies," *Administrative Science Quarterly* 34 (1989): 431–53; and Dale L. Goodhue and Ronald L. Thompson, "Task-Technology Fit and Individual Performances," *MIS Quarterly*, June 1995, 213–36.

36. Richard Cone, Bruce Snow, and Ricky Waclawcayk, *Datapoint Corporation* (Unpublished manuscript, Texas A&M University, 1981).

37. Gresov, "Exploring Fit and Misfit with Multiple Contingencies"; Charles A. Glisson, "Dependence of Technological Routinization on Structural Variables in Human Service Organizations," *Administrative Science Quarterly* 23 (1978): 383–95; Jerald Hage and Michael Aiken, "Routine Technology, Social Structure and Organizational Goals," *Administrative Science Quarterly* 14 (1969): 368–79.

38. Gresov, "Exploring Fit and Misfit with Multiple Contingencies"; A. J. Grimes and S. M. Kline, "The Technological Imperative: The Relative Impact of Task Unit, Model Technology, and Hierarchy on Structure," *Academy of Management Journal* 16 (1973): 583–97; Lawrence G. Hrebiniak, "Job Technologies, Supervision and Work Group Structure," *Administrative Science Quarterly* 19 (1974): 395–410; Jeffrey Pfeffer, *Organizational Design* (Arlington Heights, Ill.: AHM, 1978), ch. 1.

39. Patrick E. Connor, *Organizations: Theory and Design* (Chicago: Science Research Associates, 1980); Richard L. Daft and Norman B. Macintosh, "A Tentative Exploration into Amount and Equivocality of Information Processing in Organizational Work Units," *Administrative Science Quarterly* 26 (1981): 207–24.

40. Paul D. Collins and Frank Hull, "Technology and Span of Control: Woodward Revisited," *Journal of Management Studies* 23 (1986): 143–64; Gerald D. Bell, "The Influence of Technological Components of Work upon Management Control," *Academy of Management Journal* 8 (1965): 127–32; Peter M. Blau and Richard A. Schoenherr, *The Structure of Organizations* (New York: Basic Books, 1971).

41. W. Alan Randolph, "Matching Technology and the Design of Organization Units," *California Management Review* 22–23 (1980–1981): 39–48; Daft and Macintosh, "Tentative Exploration into Amount and Equivocality of Information Processing"; Michael L. Tushman, "Work Characteristics and Subunit Communication Structure: A Contingency Analysis," *Administrative Science Quarterly* 24 (1979): 82–98.

42. Andrew H. Van de Ven and Diane L. Ferry, *Measuring and Assessing Organizations* (New York: Wiley, 1980); Randolph, "Matching Technology and the Design of Organization Units."

43. Richard L. Daft and Robert H. Lengel, "Information Richness: A New Approach to Managerial Behavior and Organization Design," in Barry Staw and Larry L. Cummings, eds., *Research in Organizational Behavior*, Vol. 6 (Greenwich, Conn.: JAI Press, 1984), 191–233; Richard L. Daft and Norman B. Macintosh, "A New Approach into Design and Use of Management Information," *California Management Review* 21 (1978): 82–92; Daft and Macintosh, "Tentative Exploration in Amount and Equivocality of Information Processing"; W. Alan Randolph, "Organizational Technology and the Media and Purpose Dimensions of Organizational Communication," *Journal of Business Research* 6 (1978): 237–59; Linda Argote, "Input Uncertainty and Organizational Coordination in Hospital Emergency Units," *Administrative Science Quarterly* 27 (1982): 420–34; Andrew H. Van de Ven and Andre Delbecq, "A Task Contingent Model of Work Unit Structure," *Administrative Science Quarterly* 19 (1974): 183–97.

44. Peggy Leatt and Rodney Schneck, "Criteria for Grouping Nursing Subunits in Hospitals," *Academy of Management Journal* 27 (1984): 150–65.

45. Gresov, "Exploring Fit and Misfit with Multiple Contingencies"; Michael L. Tushman, "Technological Communication in R&D Laboratories: The Impact of Project Work Characteristics," *Academy of Management Journal* 21 (1978): 624–45; Robert T. Keller, "Technology-Information Processing Fit and the Performance of R&D Project Groups: A Test of Contingency Theory," *Academy of Management Journal* 37:1, 1994, 167–79.

46. James Thompson, *Organizations in Action* (New York: McGraw-Hill, 1967).

47. *Ibid.*, 40.

48. Paul S. Adler, "Interdepartmental Interdependence and Coordination: The Case of the Design/ Manufacturing Interface," *Organization Science*, Vol. 6, No. 2, March–April 1995, 147–67.

49. Christopher Gresov, "Effects of Dependence and Tasks on Unit Design and Efficiency," *Organization Studies* 11 (1990): 503–29; Andrew H. Van de Ven, Andre Delbecq, and Richard Koenig, "Determinants of Coordination Modes within Organizations," *American Sociological Review* 41 (1976): 322–38; Linda Argote, "Input Uncertainty and Organizational Coordination in Hospital Emergency Units"; Jack K. Ito and Richard B. Peterson, "Effects of Task Difficulty and Interdependence on Information Processing Systems," *Academy of Management Journal* 29 (1986): 139–49; Joseph I. C. Cheng, "Interdependence and Coordination in Organizations: A Role-System Analysis," *Academy of Management Journal* 26 (1983): 156–62.

50. Howard Gleckman with John Carey, Russell Mitchell, Tim Smart, and Chris Roush, "The Technology Payoff," *Business Week*, 14 June 1993, 57–68; Michele Liu, Héléné Denis, Harvey Kolodny, and Benjt Stymne, "Organization and Design for Technological Change," *Human Relations* 43 (January 1990): 7–22; George P. Huber, "A Theory of the Effects of Advanced Information Technologies on Organizational Design, Intelligence, and Decision Making," *Academy of Management Review* 14 (1990): 47–71.

51. Jeremy Main, "At Last, Software CEOs Can Use," *Fortune*, 13 March 1989, 77–82.

52. Richard C. Huseman and Edward W. Miles, "Organizational Communication in the Information Age: Implementations of Computer-Based Systems," *Journal of Management* 14 (1988).

53. Huber, "A Theory of the Effects of Advanced Information Technologies"; Lee Sproull and Sara Keisler, "Reducing Social Context Cues: Electronic Mail in Organizational Communication," *Management Science* 32 (1986): 1492–512.

54. John R. Wilke, "Computer Links Erode Hierarchical Nature of Workplace Culture," *The Wall Street Journal*, 9 December 1993, A1, A10; Huber, "A Theory of the Effects of Advanced Information Technologies"; Stephen D. Soloman, "Use Technology to Manage People," *Small Business Report* (September 1990): 46–51.

55. Huber, "A Theory of the Effects of Advanced Information Technologies."

56. *Ibid.*

57. John R. Wilke, "Computer Links Erode Hierarchical Nature of Workplace Culture."

58. Gleckman, et al., "The Technology Payoff"; Shoshanna Zuboff, *In the Age of the Smart Machine* (New York: Basic Books, 1984).

59. Lynda M. Applegate, James I. Cash, Jr., and D. Quinn Mills, "Information Technology and Tomorrow's Manager," *Harvard Business Review* (November–December 1988): 128–36.

60. Wilke, "Computer Links."

61. Applegate, Cash, and Mills, "Information Technology and Tomorrow's Manager."

5

chapter five

Organization Size and Life Cycle

While reading this chapter, think about your answers to the following questions:

- What are the advantages and disadvantages of large versus small organizations?

- What are the strengths and weaknesses of bureaucracy, and when can bureaucratic characteristics be used to make organizations more effective?

- How do size and organizational life cycle influence structural characteristics?

During the twentieth century, large organizations have become widespread, and over the past thirty years, bureaucracy has been a major topic of study in organization theory.[1] Today, most large organizations have bureaucratic characteristics. They provide us with abundant goods and services, and they surprise us with astonishing feats—astronauts to the moon, thousands of airline flights daily without an accident—that are testimony to their effectiveness. On the other hand, bureaucracy is also accused of many sins, including inefficiency, rigidity, and demeaning, routinized work that alienates both employees and the customers an organization tries to serve.[2]

As the twenty-first century approaches, companies around the world are combining the advantages of bigness with "the human scale, sharp focus, and fervent entrepreneurship of smallness."[3] They are looking for ways to be flexible and responsive in a rapidly changing marketplace. For example, at Matsushita Electric, the world's largest consumer electronics company, President Yoichi Morishita has been slashing headquarters staff and decentralizing management to get the giant company acting with the speed and simplicity of a small, entrepreneurial firm.[4] In the 1970s and 1980s, growth and large size were considered natural and desirable; but in the 1990s, small—or at least the ability to behave as a small company—is beautiful.[5]

PURPOSE OF THIS CHAPTER

In this chapter, we will explore the question of large versus small organization and how size is related to structural characteristics. Organization size is a contextual variable that influences organizational design and functioning just as do the contextual variables—technology, environment, goals—discussed in previous chapters. In the first section, we will look at the advantages of large versus small size. Then, we will examine the historical need for bureaucracy as a means to control large organizations and how managers today attack bureaucracy in some large organizations. Next, we will explore what is called an organization's life cycle and the structural characteristics at each stage. By the end of this chapter, you should understand the nature of bureaucracy, its strengths and weaknesses, and when to use bureaucratic characteristics to make an organization effective.

ORGANIZATION SIZE: IS BIGGER BETTER?

The question of big versus small begins with the notion of growth and the reasons so many organizations feel the need to grow large.

Pressures for Growth

Why do organizations grow? Why should they grow? Following are **reasons organizations grow:**

Organizational Goals. In the early 1990s, America's management guru, Peter Drucker, declared that "the *Fortune* 500 is over;" yet the dream of practically every businessperson is still to have his or her company become a member of the

Fortune 500 list—to grow fast and to grow large.[6] Sometimes this goal is more urgent than to make the best products or show the greatest profits. Some observers believe the United States is entering a new era of "bigness," as companies strive to acquire the size and resources to compete on a global scale, to invest in new technology, and to control distribution channels and guarantee access to markets. In the first nine months of 1995 alone, more than $270 billion worth of mergers and acquisitions were announced.[7] For example, Kimberly Clark Corporation acquired Scott Paper Company because Scott had strength in European markets that Kimberly lacked. Pharmaceutical companies such as Upjohn and Sweden's Pharmacia are merging to gain stronger market presence and the clout to negotiate deals with large purchasers.

Executive Advancement. Growth is often necessary to attract and keep quality managers. Growing organizations, both public and private, are exciting places to work. There are many challenges and opportunities for advancement when the number of employees is expanding.[8]

Economic Health. Many executives have found that firms must grow to stay economically healthy. To stop growing is to suffocate. To be stable or to relax means customers may not have their demands fully met or that competitors will meet customer needs and increase market share at the expense of your company. Hewlett-Packard, which continues to grow and succeed, has developed a philosophy of killing off its own products with new technology before its rivals have the chance to do so. Intel, an $11.5 billion company with a near-monopoly on the lucrative microprocessor market, is able to lavish more than $1 billion a year on research and development, compared to around $275 million spent by Advanced Micro Devices, Intel's nearest competitor.[9] Scale is still crucial to economic health in some industries. For example, greater size gives marketing-intensive companies, such as beverage distributors Coca-Cola and Anheuser-Busch, power in the marketplace and thus increased revenues.[10]

Large Versus Small

Organizations feel compelled to grow, but how much and how large? What size organization is better poised to compete in a global environment? The arguments are summarized in Exhibit 5.1.

Large. Huge resources and economies of scale are needed for many organizations to compete globally. Only large organizations can build a massive pipeline in Alaska. Only a large corporation like Boeing can afford to build a 747, and only a large American Airlines can buy it. Only a large Merck can invest hundreds of millions in new drugs that must be sold worldwide to show a profit. Only a large McDonald's can open a new restaurant somewhere in the world every seventeen hours.

Large companies also are standardized, often mechanistically run, and complex. The complexity offers hundreds of functional specialties within the organization to perform complex tasks and to produce complex products. Moreover, large organizations, once established, can be a presence that stabilizes a market for years. Managers can join the company and expect a career reminiscent of the "organization men" of the 1950s and 1960s. The organization can provide longevity, raises, and promotions.

Exhibit 5.1

Differences between Large and Small Organizations

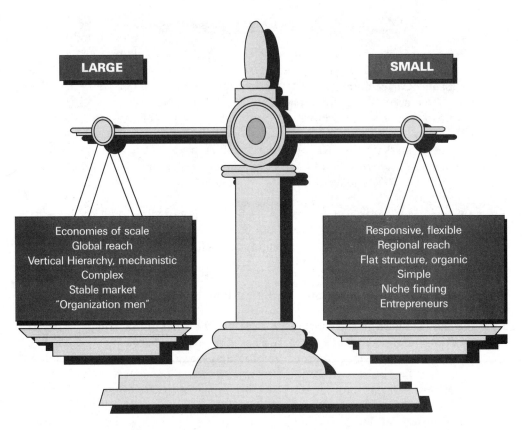

Source: Based on John A. Byrne, "Is Your Company Too Big?" *Business Week*, 27 March 1989, 84–94.

Small. The competing argument says small is beautiful because the crucial requirements for success in a global economy are responsiveness and flexibility in fast-changing markets. While the U.S. economy contains many large organizations, research shows that as global trade has accelerated, smaller organizations have become the norm. Huge investments are giving way to flexible manufacturing and niche marketing as the ways to succeed. The rapidly growing service sector, as discussed in the previous chapter, has also contributed to a decrease in average organization size, as most service companies remain small to be more responsive to customers.[11]

Despite the fact that recent mergers are creating giant companies in some industries, the average size of organizations is decreasing, not only in the United States but in Britain and Germany as well. Exhibit 5.2 reflects the decrease in the average number of employees per firm for the three countries. Small organizations have a flat structure and an organic, free-flowing management style that encourages entrepreneurship and innovation. Today's leading biotechnological drugs, for example, were all discovered by small firms, such as Chiron, which developed the hepatitis B vaccines, rather than by huge pharmaceutical companies, such as Merck.[12] Moreover, the personal involvement of employees in small firms encourages motivation and commitment because employees personally identify with the company's mission.

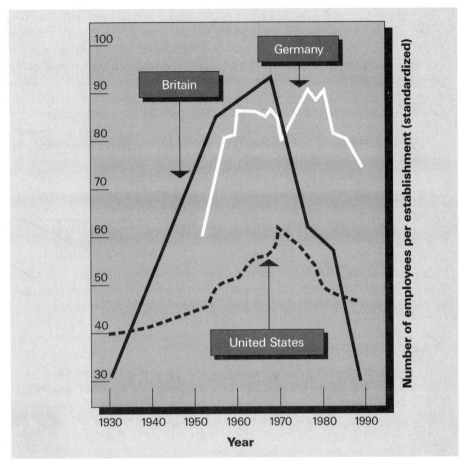

Exhibit 5.2

Average Size of Industrial Firms in Three Countries

Source: Tom Peters, "Rethinking Scale," *California Management Review* (Fall 1992): 7–29.
Used with permission.

Big-Company/Small-Company Hybrid. The paradox is that the advantages of small companies enable them to succeed and, hence, grow large. *Fortune* magazine reported that the fastest growing companies in America are small firms characterized by an emphasis on putting the customer first and being fast and flexible in responding to the environment.[13] But small companies can become victims of their own success as they grow large, shifting to a mechanistic structure emphasizing vertical hierarchies and spawning "organization men" rather than entrepreneurs.

The solution is what Jack Welch, chairman of General Electric, calls the "big-company/small-company hybrid" that combines a large corporation's resources and reach with a small company's simplicity and flexibility. This approach is being taken seriously by many large companies, including Johnson & Johnson, Hewlett-Packard, AT&T, and General Motors. These companies have all undergone massive reorganizations into groups of small companies to capture the mind-set and advantages of smallness. The $14 billion giant Johnson & Johnson is actually a group of 168 separate companies. When a new product is created in one of J&J's 56 labs, a new company is created along with it.[14] Percy Barnevik, CEO of power equipment giant Asea Brown Boveri Ltd. (ABB), blasted a 200,000-employee global enterprise into 5,000 units, averaging just 40 people each.[15]

A full-service, global firm needs a strong resource base and sufficient complexity and hierarchy to serve clients around the world. Large or growing companies can retain the flexibility and customer-focus of smallness by decentralizing authority and cutting layers of the hierarchy. At Nucor Corporation, a rapidly growing steelmaker with annual sales topping $2 billion, headquarters is staffed by only 23 people. Nucor's plant managers handle everything from marketing to personnel to production. Hewlett-Packard has decentralized almost every aspect of its business; for example, instead of relying on a central research and development staff, HP hands over most of its $2 billion research budget to its four operating groups to spend as they wish.[16]

ORGANIZATION SIZE AND BUREAUCRACY

The systematic study of bureaucracy was launched by Max Weber, a sociologist who studied government organizations in Europe and developed a framework of administrative characteristics that would make large organizations rational and efficient.[17] Weber wanted to understand how organizations could be designed to play a positive role in the larger society.

What is Bureaucracy?

Although Weber perceived **bureaucracy** as a threat to basic personal liberties, he also recognized it as the most efficient possible system of organizing. He predicted the triumph of bureaucracy because of its ability to ensure more efficient functioning of organizations in both business and government settings. Weber identified a set of organizational characteristics, listed in Exhibit 5.3, that could be found in successful bureaucratic organizations.

Rules and standard procedures enable organizational activities to be performed in a predictable, routine manner. Specialized duties meant that each employee had a clear task to perform. Hierarchy of authority provided a sensible mechanism for supervision and control. Technical competence was the basis by which people were hired rather than friendship, family ties, and favoritism that dramatically reduced work performance. The separation of the position from the position holder meant that individuals did not own or have an inherent right to the job, thus promoting efficiency. Written records provided an organizational memory and continuity over time.

Although bureaucratic characteristics carried to an extreme are widely criticized today, the rational control introduced by Weber was a significant idea and a new form of organization. Bureaucracy provided many advantages over organization forms based upon favoritism, social status, family connections, or graft,

Exhibit 5.3

Weber's Dimensions of Bureaucracy and Bases of Organizational Authority

Bureaucracy	Legitimate Bases of Authority
1. Rules and procedures	1. Rational-legal
2. Specialization and division of labor	2. Traditional
3. Hierarchy of authority	3. Charismatic
4. Technically qualified personnel	
5. Separate position and incumbent	
6. Written communications and records	

which are often unfair. For example, in Mexico, a retired American lawyer had to pay a five hundred-dollar bribe to purchase a telephone, then discovered that a government official had sold his telephone number to another family. In China, the tradition of giving government posts to relatives is widespread even under communism. China's emerging class of educated people doesn't like seeing the best jobs going to children and relatives of officials.[18] By comparison, the logical and rational form of organization described by Weber allows work to be conducted efficiently and according to established rules.

Bases of Authority

The ability of an organization to function efficiently depends upon its authority structure. Proper authority provides managers with the control needed to make the bureaucratic form of organization work. Weber argued that legitimate, rational authority was preferred over other types of control (for example, payoffs or favoritism) as the basis for internal decisions and activities. Within the larger society, however, Weber identified three types of authority that could explain the creation and control of a large organization.[19]

1. **Rational-legal authority** is based on employees' beliefs in the legality of rules and the right of those elevated to authority to issue commands. Rational-legal authority is the basis for both creation and control of most government organizations and is the most common base of control in organizations worldwide.
2. **Traditional authority** is the belief in traditions and in the legitimacy of the status of people exercising authority through those traditions. Traditional authority is the basis for control for monarchies and churches and for some organizations in Latin America and the Persian Gulf.
3. **Charismatic authority** is based upon devotion to the exemplary character or to the heroism of an individual person and the order defined by him or her. Revolutionary military organizations are often based on the leader's charisma, as are North American organizations led by charismatic individuals such as Lee Iacocca or Jack Welch.

More than one type of authority—such as long tradition and the leader's special charisma—may exist in today's organizations, but *rational-legal authority* is the most widely used form to govern internal work activities and decision making, especially in large organizations.

SIZE AND STRUCTURAL CHARACTERISTICS

In the field of organization theory, organization size has been described as an important variable that influences structural design. Should an organization become more bureaucratic as it grows larger? In what size organizations are bureaucratic characteristics most appropriate? More than one hundred studies have attempted to answer these questions.[20] Most of these studies indicate that large organizations are different from small organizations along several dimensions of bureaucratic structure, including formalization, centralization, complexity, and personnel ratios.

Formalization

Formalization, as described in Chapter 1, refers to rules, procedures, and written documentation, such as policy manuals and job descriptions, that prescribe the rights and duties of employees.[21] The evidence supports the conclusion that large organizations are more formalized. The reason is that large organizations rely on rules, procedures, and paperwork to achieve standardization and control across their large numbers of employees and departments, whereas top managers can use personal observation to control a small organization.[22] In large firms like IBM, Banc One, and AT&T, formal procedures allow top administrators to extend their reach, and rules are established to take the place of personal surveillance for such matters as sexual harassment, smoking bans, and flexible work hours.

Formalization may also promote more formal and impersonal modes of behavior and interaction in large bureaucratic organizations, as opposed to the spontaneous, casual behavior and social interaction often observed in small, loosely-knit organizations.[23]

Decentralization

Centralization refers to the level of hierarchy with authority to make decisions. In centralized organizations, decisions tend to be made at the top. In decentralized organizations, similar decisions would be made at a lower level.

Decentralization represents a paradox because, in the perfect bureaucracy, all decisions would be made by the top administrator, who would have perfect control. However, as an organization grows larger and has more people and departments, decisions cannot be passed to the top, or senior managers would be overloaded. Thus, the research on organization size indicates that larger organizations (for example, Campbell Soup Company and American Airlines) permit greater decentralization.[24] CEO Mike Quinlan of McDonald's pushes decisions as far down the hierarchy as he can; otherwise, McDonald's decision making would be too slow. Moreover, McDonald's has many rules that define boundaries within which decisions can be made, thereby facilitating decentralization.

Complexity

As discussed in Chapter 1, **complexity** refers to both the number of levels in the hierarchy (vertical complexity) and the number of departments or jobs (horizontal complexity). Large organizations show a definite pattern of greater complexity.[25] The explanation for the relationship between size and complexity is straightforward. First, the need for additional specialties occurs more often in large organizations. For example, a study of new departments reported that new administrative departments were often created in response to problems of large size.[26] A planning department was established in a large organization because a greater need for planning arose after a certain size was reached. Second, as departments within the organization grow in size, pressure to subdivide arises. Departments eventually get so large that managers cannot control them effectively. At this point, subgroups will lobby to be subdivided into separate departments.[27]

Finally, vertical complexity traditionally has been needed to maintain control over a large number of people. As the number of employees increases, additional levels of hierarchy keep spans of control from becoming too large.

Personnel Ratios

The next characteristic of bureaucracy is **personnel ratios** for administrative, clerical, and professional support staff. The most frequently studied ratio is the administrative ratio. In 1957, C. Northcote Parkinson published *Parkinson's Law,* which argued that work expands to till the time available for its completion. Parkinson suggested that administrators were motivated to add more administrators for a variety of reasons, including the enhancement of their own status through empire building. Parkinson used his argument, called **Parkinson's law,** to make fun of the British Admiralty. During a fourteen-year period from 1914 to 1928, the officer corps increased by 78 percent, although the total navy personnel decreased by 32 percent and the number of warships in use decreased by approximately 68 percent.[28]

In the years since Parkinson's book, the administrative ratio has been studied in school systems, churches, hospitals, employment agencies, and other business and voluntary organizations.[29] Two patterns have emerged.

The first pattern is that the ratio of top administration to total employment is actually smaller in large organizations.[30] This is the opposite of Parkinson's argument and indicates that organizations experience administrative economies as they grow larger. Larger organizations have large departments, more regulations, and a greater division of labor. These mechanisms require less supervision from the top. Increasing bureaucratization is a substitute for personal supervision from the administrators.

The second pattern concerns other staff support ratios. Recent studies have subdivided support personnel into subclassifications, such as clerical and professional staff.[31] These support groups tend to increase in proportion to organization size. The clerical ratio increases because of the greater communication (memos, letters) and paperwork requirements (policy manuals, job descriptions) in large organizations. The professional staff ratio increases because of the greater need for specialized skills in complex organizations. In a small organization, an individual may be a jack-of-all-trades. In a large organization, people are assigned full time to support activities to help make production employees more efficient.

Exhibit 5.4 illustrates administrative and support ratios for small and large organizations. As organizations increase in size, the administrative ratio declines and the ratios for other support groups increase.[32] The net effect for direct workers is that they decline as a percentage of total employees. Recent studies show that corporate America in general needs to reduce its overhead costs to remain competitive. Large Japanese companies, such as Toyota Motor Corporation and Matsushita Electric are also facing the need to reduce overhead costs. Japanese factories are highly productive, but companies are finding that profits are being dragged down by bloated administrative and clerical staffs. Shintaro Hori, a vice-president of Bain & Company Japan, estimates that Japanese companies in general have 15 to 20 percent more support workers than they need.[33]

An interesting pattern emerges from recent research on organizations during periods of growth and decline. In rapidly growing organizations, administrators grow faster than line employees; in declining organizations, they decline more slowly. This implies that administrative and staff personnel often are the first hired and last fired.[34] For example, when the University of Michigan was undergoing rapid growth, faculty increased by 7 percent, but professional nonfaculty

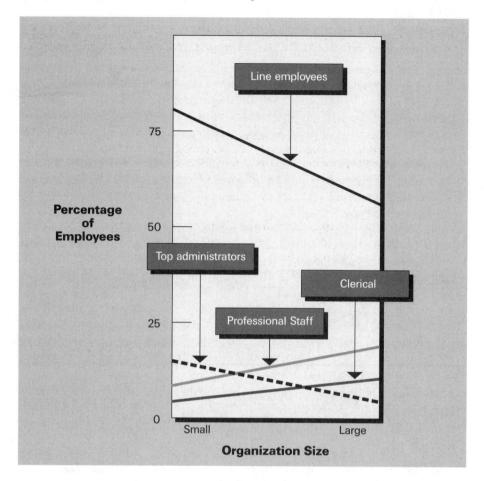

employees increased by 26 percent, and executive, administrative, and managerial employees increased by 40 percent.[35] If the University of Michigan should suddenly decline rapidly, the administration may decline more slowly than professional and faculty employees.

In summary, top administrators typically do not comprise a disproportionate number of employees in large organizations; in fact, they are a smaller percentage of total employment. However, the idea that proportionately greater overhead is required in large organizations is supported. The number of people in clerical and professional departments increases at a faster rate than does the number of people who work in the technical core of a growing organization.

The differences between small and large organizations are summarized in Exhibit 5.5. Large organizations have many characteristics that distinguish them from small organizations: more rules and regulations; more paperwork, written communication, and documentation; greater specialization; more decentralization; a lower percentage of people devoted to top administration; and a larger percentage of people allocated to clerical, maintenance, and professional support staff.

However, size by itself does not cause these organizational characteristics. Recall from previous chapters that goals, environment, and technology also influence structure. For example, an organization operating in a complex environment

Greater organization size is associated with:
1. Increased number of management levels (vertical complexity)
2. Greater number of jobs and departments (horizontal complexity)
3. Increased specialization of skills and functions
4. Greater formalization
5. Greater decentralization
6. Smaller percentage of top administrators
7. Greater percentage of technical and professional support staff
8. Greater percentage of clerical and maintenance support staff
9. Greater amount of written communications and documentation

Exhibit 5.5
Relationship between Size and Other Organization Characteristics

will need additional departments, and a changing environment creates the need for less formalization. Thus, while large organizations will appear different from small organizations, these relationships are not rigid. The impact of other contextual variables can modify bureaucratic structure.

BUREAUCRACY IN A CHANGING WORLD

Weber's prediction of the triumph of bureaucracy proved accurate. Bureaucratic characteristics have many advantages and have worked extremely well for many of the needs of the industrial age.[36] By establishing a hierarchy of authority and specific rules and procedures, bureaucracy provided an effective way to bring order to large groups of people and prevent abuses of power. Impersonal relationships based on roles rather than people reduced the favoritism and nepotism characteristic of many pre-industrial organizations. Bureaucracy also provided for systematic and rational ways to organize and manage tasks too complex to be understood and handled by a few individuals, thus greatly improving the efficiency and effectiveness of large organizations.

The world is rapidly changing, however, and the machine-like bureaucratic system of the industrial age no longer works so well as organizations face new challenges. With global competition and uncertain environments, many organizations are fighting against increasing complexity and professional staff ratios. The problems caused by large bureaucracies have perhaps nowhere been more evident than in the U.S. government. From the bureaucratic obstacles to providing emergency relief following Hurricane Andrew to the bungling by the U.S. Marshal's Service that put a convicted drug kingpin back on the streets, such actions by federal government agencies show how excessive bureaucracy can impede the effectiveness and productivity of organizations.[37]

Companies like Burlington Northern, Dana, and Hanson Industries have thirty-five to forty thousand employees and fewer than one hundred staff people working at headquarters. Aluminum Company of America (Alcoa) is cutting out two levels of top management, along with about two dozen headquarters staff jobs, giving business-unit managers unprecedented decision-making authority. The point is to not overload headquarters with accountants, lawyers, and financial analysts who will inhibit the autonomy and flexibility of divisions.[38] When Jack Welch laid off more than 100,000 employees during his tenure at General Electric, many of those affected were middle managers, senior managers, and staff professionals. Of course, many companies must be large to have sufficient resources and complexity to produce products for a global environment; but companies such as Johnson & Johnson, Wal-Mart, 3M, Coca-Cola, Emerson Electric, and Heinz are striving toward greater decentralization and leanness. They are giving front-line workers more authority and responsibility to define and direct their own jobs, often by creating self-directed teams that find ways to coordinate work, improve productivity, and better serve customers.

Another attack on bureaucracy is from the increasing professionalism of employees. Professionalism was defined in Chapter 1 as the length of formal training and experience of employees. More employees need college degrees, MBAs, and other professional degrees to work as attorneys, researchers, or doctors at General Motors, Kmart, and Bristol-Myers Squibb Company. Studies of professionals show that formalization is not needed because professional training regularizes a high standard of behavior for employees that acts as a substitute for bureaucracy.[39] Companies also enhance this trend when they provide ongoing training for *all* employees, from the front office to the shop floor, in a push for continuous individual and organizational learning. Increased training substitutes for bureaucratic rules and procedures that can constrain the creativity of employees to solve problems and increase organizational capability.

In addition, a form of organization called the *professional partnership* has emerged that is made up completely of professionals.[40] These organizations include medical practices, law firms, and consulting firms, such as Touche Ross and Price Waterhouse. The general findings concerning professional partnerships is that branches have substantial autonomy and decentralized authority to make necessary decisions. They work with a consensus orientation rather than top-down direction typical of traditional business and government organizations. Thus, the trend of increasing professionalism combined with rapidly changing environments is leading to less bureaucracy in corporate North America.

ORGANIZATIONAL LIFE CYCLE

A useful way to think about organizational growth and change is provided by the concept of a **life cycle,**[41] which suggests that organizations are born, grow older, and eventually die. Organization structure, leadership style, and administrative systems follow a fairly predictable pattern through stages in the life cycle. Stages are sequential in nature and follow a natural progression.

Stages of Life Cycle Development

Recent work on organizational life cycle suggests that four major stages characterize organizational development.[42] These stages are illustrated in Exhibit 5.6 along with the problems associated with transition to each stage. Growth is not easy. Each time an organization enters a new stage in the life cycle, it enters a whole new ball game with a new set of rules for how the organization functions internally and how it relates to the external environment.[43]

1. **Entrepreneurial Stage.** When an organization is born, the emphasis is on creating a product and surviving in the marketplace. The founders are entrepreneurs, and they devote their full energies to the technical activities of production and marketing. The organization is informal and nonbureaucratic.

Exhibit 5.6 *Organizational Life Cycle*

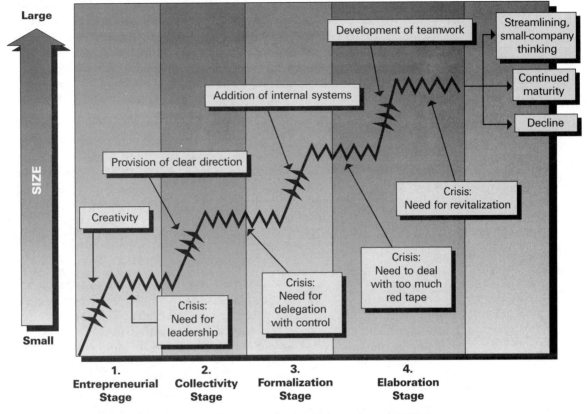

Large

SIZE

Small

Creativity

Provision of clear direction

Addition of internal systems

Development of teamwork

Streamlining, small-company thinking

Continued maturity

Decline

Crisis: Need for leadership

Crisis: Need for delegation with control

Crisis: Need to deal with too much red tape

Crisis: Need for revitalization

1. Entrepreneurial Stage

2. Collectivity Stage

3. Formalization Stage

4. Elaboration Stage

ORGANIZATION STAGES OF DEVELOPMENT

Source: Adapted from Robert E. Quinn and Kim Cameron, "Organizational Life Cycles and Shifting Criteria of Effectiveness: Some Preliminary Evidence," *Management Science* 29 (1983): 33–51; and Larry E. Greiner, "Evolution and Revolution as Organizations Grow," *Harvard Business Review* 50 (July–August 1972): 37–46.

The hours of work are long. Control is based on the owners' personal supervision. Growth is from a creative new product or service. Apple Computer was in the **entrepreneurial stage** when it was created by Steven Jobs and Stephen Wozniak in Wozniak's parents' garage. Software companies like Microsoft and Lotus Development were in the entrepreneurial stage when their original software programs were written and marketed.

Crisis: Need for Leadership. As the organization starts to grow, the larger number of employees causes problems. The creative and technically oriented owners are confronted with management issues, but they may prefer to focus their energies on making and selling the product or inventing new products and services. At this time of crisis, entrepreneurs must either adjust the structure of the organization to accommodate continued growth or else bring in strong managers who can do so. When Apple began a period of rapid growth, A. C. Markkula was brought in as a leader because neither Jobs nor Wozniak was qualified or cared to manage the expanding company.

2. **Collectivity Stage.** If the leadership crisis is resolved, strong leadership is obtained and the organization begins to develop clear goals and direction.

Departments are established along with a hierarchy of authority, job assignments, and a beginning division of labor. Employees identify with the mission of the organization and spend long hours helping the organization succeed. Members feel part of a collective, and communication and control are mostly informal, although a few formal systems begin to appear. Apple Computer was in the **collectivity stage** during the rapid growth years from 1978 to 1981. Employees threw themselves into the business as the major product line was established and more than two thousand dealers signed on.

Crisis: Need for Delegation. If the new management has been successful, lower-level employees gradually find themselves restricted by the strong top-down leadership. Lower-level managers begin to acquire confidence in their own functional areas and want more discretion. An autonomy crisis occurs when top managers, who were successful because of their strong leadership and vision, do not want to give up responsibility. Top managers want to make sure that all parts of the organization are coordinated and pulling together. The organization needs to find mechanisms to control and coordinate departments without direct supervision from the top.

3. **Formalization Stage.** The **formalization stage** involves the installation and use of rules, procedures, and control systems. Communication is less frequent and more formal. Engineers, human resource specialists, and other staff may be added. Top management becomes concerned with issues such as strategy and planning, and leaves the operations of the firm to middle management. Product groups or other decentralized units may be formed to improve coordination. Incentive systems based upon profits may be implemented to ensure that managers work toward what is best for the overall company. When effective, the new coordination and control systems enable the organization to continue growing by establishing linkage mechanisms between top management and field units. Apple Computer was in the formalization stage in the mid 1980s.

Crisis: Too Much Red Tape. At this point in the organization's development, the proliferation of systems and programs may begin to strangle middle-level executives. The organization seems bureaucratized. Middle management may resent the intrusion of staff people. Innovation may be restricted. The organization seems too large and complex to be managed through formal programs. It was at this stage of Apple's growth that Jobs resigned from the company and CEO John Sculley took full control to face his own management challenges.

4. **Elaboration Stage.** The solution to the red tape crisis is a new sense of collaboration and teamwork. Throughout the organization, managers develop skills for confronting problems and working together. Bureaucracy may have reached its limit. Social control and self-discipline reduce the need for additional formal controls. Managers learn to work within the bureaucracy without adding to it. Formal systems may be simplified and replaced by manager teams and task forces. To achieve collaboration, teams are often formed across functions or divisions of the company. The organization may also be split into multiple divisions to maintain a small-company philosophy. Apple Computer is currently in the **elaboration stage** of the life cycle, as are such large companies as Caterpillar and Motorola.

Crisis: Need for Revitalization. After the organization reaches maturity, it may enter periods of temporary decline.[44] A need for renewal may occur every ten to twenty years. The organization shifts out of alignment with the environment or perhaps becomes slow moving and overbureaucratized and must go through a stage of streamlining and innovation. Top managers are often replaced during this period. At Apple, the top spot has changed hands twice in the company's struggle to revitalize. Both John Sculley and his successor, Michael Spindler, were forced to resign, and Gilbert Amelio recently took the reins to try to revive Apple's sales and profits.

Both Sculley and Spindler slashed thousands of jobs at Apple in an effort to control costs and improve profit margins. Amelio is facing some of the most daunting challenges of any Apple CEO to date.[45] The company faces the simultaneous needs for innovative new products and major cost-cutting to remain competitive. Organizations need bold leadership to face the crisis at this stage of the life cycle and move forward into a new era. If mature organizations do not go through periodic revitalizations, they will decline, as shown in the last stage of Exhibit 5.6.

Eighty-four percent of businesses that make it past the first year still fail within five years because they can't make the transition from the entrepreneurial stage.[46] And the transitions become even more difficult as organizations progress through future stages of the life cycle. Organizations that do not successfully resolve the problems associated with these transitions are restricted in their growth and may even fail.

Organizational Characteristics During the Life Cycle

As organizations evolve through the four stages of the life cycle, changes take place in structure, control systems, innovation, and goals. The organizational characteristics associated with each stage are summarized in Exhibit 5.7.

Entrepreneurial. Initially, the organization is small, nonbureaucratic, and a one-person show. The top manager provides the structure and control system. Organizational energy is devoted to survival and the production of a single product or service.

Collectivity. This is the organization's youth. Growth is rapid, and employees are excited and committed to the organization's mission. The structure is still mostly informal, although some procedures are emerging. Strong charismatic leaders like Bill Gates of Microsoft provide direction and goals for the organization. Continued growth is a major goal.

Formalization. At this point, the organization is entering midlife. Bureaucratic characteristics emerge. The organization adds staff support groups, formalizes procedures, and establishes a clear hierarchy and division of labor. Innovation may be achieved by establishing a separate research and development department. Major goals are internal stability and market expansion. Top management has to delegate, but it also implements formal control systems.

At Dell Computer, for example, entrepreneurial whiz-kid Michael Dell has hired experienced managers, including some industry veterans from Apple, to help him develop and implement formal planning, management, and budgeting systems. Dell, who at the age of 31 is 14 years younger than the youngest of his

Exhibit 5.7 *Organizational Characteristics during Four Stages of Life Cycle*

Characteristic	1. Entrepreneurial Nonbureaucratic	2. Collectivity Prebureaucratic	3. Formalization Bureaucratic	4. Elaboration Very Bureaucratic
Structure	Informal, one-person show	Mostly informal, some procedures	Formal procedures, division of labor, new specialities added	Teamwork within bureaucracy, small-company thinking
Products or services	Single product or service	Major product or service, with variations	Line of products or services	Multiple product or service lines
Reward and control systems	Personal, paternalistic	Personal, contribution to success	Impersonal, formalized systems	Extensive, tailored to product and department
Innovation	By owner-manager	By employees and managers	By separate innovation group	By institutionalized R&D
Goal	Survival	Growth	Internal stability, market expansion	Reputation, complete organization
Top management style	Individualistic, entrepreneurial	Charismatic, direction-giving	Delegation with control	Team approach, attack bureaucracy

Source: Adapted from Larry E. Greiner, "Evolution and Revolution as Organizations Grow," *Harvard Business Review* 50 (July–August 1972): 37–46; G. L. Lippitt and W. H. Schmidt, "Crises in a Developing Organization," *Harvard Business Review* 45 (November–December 1967): 102–12; B. R. Scott, "The Industrial State: Old Myths and New Realities," *Harvard Business Review* 51 (March–April 1973): 133–48; Robert E. Quinn and Kim Cameron, "Organizational Life Cycles and Shifting Criteria of Effectiveness," *Management Science* 29 (1983): 33–51.

senior managers, says, "I'm very content to hire and delegate."[47] At the formalization stage, organizations may also develop complementary products to offer a complete product line.

Elaboration. The mature organization is large and bureaucratic, with extensive control systems, rules, and procedures. Organization managers attempt to develop a team orientation within the bureaucracy to prevent further bureaucratization. Top managers are concerned with establishing a complete organization. Organizational stature and reputation are important. Innovation is institutionalized through an R&D department. Management may attack the bureaucracy and streamline it.

Summary. Growing organizations move through stages of a life cycle, and each stage is associated with specific characteristics of structure, control systems, goals, and innovation. The life cycle phenomenon is a powerful concept used for understanding problems facing organizations and how managers can respond in a positive way to move an organization to the next stage.

SUMMARY OF KEY ISSUES

The material covered in this chapter contains several important ideas about organizations. One is that bureaucratic characteristics, such as rules, division of labor, written records, hierarchy of authority, and impersonal procedures, become important as organizations grow large and complex. Bureaucracy is a logical form of organizing that lets firms use resources efficiently. However, in many large corporate and government organizations, bureaucracy has come under attack with attempts to decentralize authority, flatten organization structure, reduce rules and written records, and create a small-company mind-set. These companies are willing to trade economies of scale for responsive, adaptive organizations. Many companies are subdividing into small divisions to gain small-company advantages.

In large organizations, Parkinson's notion that top administrators build empires is not found. Greater support is required, however, from clerical and professional staff specialists in large organizations. This is a logical outcome of employee specialization and the division of labor. By dividing an organization's tasks and having specialists perform each part, the organization can become more efficient. Many organizations today need to reduce their overhead costs by cutting support personnel.

Organizations evolve through distinct life cycle stages as they grow and mature. Organization structure, internal systems, and management issues are different for each stage of development. Growth creates crises and revolutions along the way toward large size. A major task of managers is to guide the organization through the entrepreneurial, collectivity, formalization, and elaboration stages of development.

In the final analysis, large organization size and accompanying bureaucracy have many advantages, but they also have shortcomings. Large size and bureaucratic characteristics are important but can impede an organization that must act as if it is small, is a professional partnership, or needs to survive in a rapidly changing environment.

Discussion Questions

1. Describe the three bases of authority identified by Weber. Is it possible for each of these types of authority to function at the same time within an organization?
2. Discuss the key differences between large and small organizations. Which kinds of organizations would be better off acting as large organizations, and which are best trying to act as big-company/small-company hybrids?
3. How would you define organization size? What problems can you identify with using number of employees as a measure of size?
4. The manager of a medium-sized manufacturing plant once said, "We can't compete on price with the small organizations because they have lower overhead costs." Based upon the discussion in this chapter, would you agree or disagree with that manager? Why?
5. Why do large organizations tend to be more formalized?
6. If you were managing a department of college professors, how might you structure the department differently than if you were managing a department of bookkeepers? Why?
7. Apply the concept of life cycle to an organization with which you are familiar, such as a university or a local business. What stage is the organization in now? How did the organization handle or pass through its life cycle crises?
8. Discuss advantages and disadvantages of rules and regulations.
9. Should a "no growth" philosophy of management be taught in business schools? Is a no-growth philosophy more realistic for today's economic conditions?

Notes

1. James Q. Wilson, *Bureaucracy* (Basic Books: 1989).

2. Charles Perrow, *Complex Organizations: A Critical Essay* (Glenview, Ill.: Scott, Foresman, 1979), 4.

3. Richard A. Melcher, "How Goliaths Can Act Like Davids," *Business Week/Enterprise*, 1993, 192–201.

4. Robert Neff, "Tradition Be Damned," *Business Week*, 31 October 1994, 108–10.

5. Kim S. Cameron, "Organizational Downsizing," in George P. Huber and William H. Glick, eds., *Organizational Change and Redesign* (New York: Oxford University Press, 1992).

6. Tom Peters, "Rethinking Scale," *California Management Review* (Fall 1992): 7–29.

7. Michael J. Mandel, Christopher Farrell, and Catherine Yang, "Land of the Giants," *Business Week*, 11 September 1995, 34–35; Michael J. Mandel, "A Dangerous Concentration?" *Business Week*, 29 April 1996, 96–97.

8. William H. Starbuck, "Organizational Growth and Development," in James March, ed., *Handbook of Organizations* (New York: Rand McNally, 1965), 451–522; John Child, *Organizations* (New York: Harper & Row, 1977), ch. 7.

9. Wendy Zellner, Robert D. Hof, Richard Brandt, Stephen Baker, and David Greising, "Go-Go Goliaths," *Business Week*, 13 February 1995, 64–70.

10. James B. Treece, "Sometimes, You've Still Gotta Have Size," *Business Week/Enterprise*, 1993, 200–01.

11. Glenn R. Carroll, "Organizations . . . The Smaller They Get," *California Management Review*, Vol. 37, No. 1, Fall 1994, 28–41.

12. Alan Deutschman, "America's Fastest Risers," *Fortune*, 7 October 1991, 46–57.

13. *Ibid.*

14. Melcher, "How Goliaths Can Act Like Davids."

15. Tom Peters, *The Pursuit of WOW: Every Person's Guide to Topsy-Turvy Times* (New York: Vintage, 1994), 31.

16. Wendy Zellner, Robert D. Hof, Richard Brandt, Stephen Baker, and David Greising, "Go-Go Goliaths," *Business Week*, 13 February 1995, 64–70.

17. Max Weber, *The Theory of Social and Economic Organizations*, translated by A. M. Henderson and T. Parsons (New York: Free Press, 1947).

18. John Crewdson, "Corruption Viewed as a Way of Life," *Bryan-College Station Eagle*, 28 November 1982, 13A; Barry Kramer, "Chinese Officials Still Give Preference to Kin, Despite Peking Policies," *The Wall Street Journal*, 29 October 1985, 1, 21.

19. Weber, *Theory of Social and Economic Organizations*, 328–40.

20. Allen C. Bluedorn, "Pilgrims' Progress: Trends and Convergence in Research on Organizational Size and Environment," *Journal of Management Studies* 19 (Summer 1993): 163–91; John R. Kimberly, "Organizational Size and the Structuralist Perspective: A Review, Critique, and Proposal," *Administrative Science Quarterly* (1976): 571–97; Richard L. Daft and Selwyn W. Becker, "Managerial, Institutional, and Technical Influences on Administration: A Longitudinal Analysis," *Social Forces* 59 (1980): 392–413.

21. James P. Walsh and Robert D. Dewar, "Formalization and the Organizational Life Cycle," *Journal of Management Studies* 24 (May 1987): 215–31.

22. Nancy M. Carter and Thomas L. Keon, "Specialization as a Multidimensional Construct," *Journal of Management Studies* 26 (1989): 11–28; Cheng-Kuang Hsu, Robert M. March, and Hiroshi Mannari, "An Examination of the Determinants of Organizational Structure," *American Journal of Sociology* 88 (1983): 975–96; Guy Geeraerts, "The Effect of Ownership on the Organization Structure in Small Firms," *Administrative Science Quarterly* 29 (1984): 232–37; Bernard Reimann, "On the Dimensions of Bureaucratic Structure: An Empirical Reappraisal," *Administrative Science Quarterly* 18 (1973): 462–76; Richard H. Hall, "The Concept of Bureaucracy: An Empirical Assessment," *American Journal of Sociology* 69 (1963): 32–40; William A. Rushing, "Organizational Rules and Surveillance: A Proposition in Comparative Organizational Analysis," *Administrative Science Quarterly* 10 (1966): 423–43.

23. David A. Morand, "The Role of Behavioral Formality and Informality in the Enactment of Bureaucratic Versus Organic Organizations," *Academy of Management Review*, Vol. 20, No. 4, 1995, 831–72.

24. Jerald Hage and Michael Aiken, "Relationship of Centralization to Other Structural Properties," *Administrative Science Quarterly* 12 (1967): 72–91.

25. Guy Geeraerts, "The Effect of Ownership on the Organization Structure in Small Firms"; Hsu, Marsh, and Mannari, "An Examination of the Determinants of Organizational Structure"; Robert Dewar and Jerald Hage, "Size, Technology, Complexity, and Structural Differentiation: Toward a Theoretical Synthesis," *Administrative Science Quarterly* 23 (1978): 111–36.

26. Richard L. Daft and Patricia J. Bradshaw, "The Process of Horizontal Differentiation: Two Models," *Administrative Science Quarterly* 25 (1980): 441–56.

27. Peter M. Blau, *The Organization of Academic Work* (New York: Wiley Interscience, 1973).

28. Peter Brimelow, "How Do You Cure Injelitance?" *Forbes*, 7 August 1989, 42–44.

29. Jeffrey D. Ford and John W. Slocum, Jr., "Size, Technology, Environment and the Structure of Organizations," *Academy of Management Review* 2 (1977): 561–75; John D. Kasarda, "The Structural Implications of Social System Size: A Three-Level Analysis," *American Sociological Review* 39 (1974): 19–28.

30. Graham Astley, "Organizational Size and Bureaucratic Structure," *Organization Studies* 6 (1985): 201–28; Spyros K. Lioukas and Demitris A. Xerokostas, "Size and Administrative Intensity in Organizational Divisions," *Management Science* 28 (1982): 854–68; Peter M. Blau, "Interdependence and Hierarchy in Organizations," *Social Science Research* 1 (1972): 1–24; Peter M. Blau and R. A. Schoenherr, *The Structure of Organizations* (New York: Basic Books, 1971); A. Hawley, W. Boland, and M. Boland, "Population Size and Administration in Institutions of Higher Education," *American Sociological Review* 30 (1965): 252–55; Richard L. Daft, "System Influence on Organization Decision-Making: The Case of Resource Allocation," *Academy of Management Journal* 21 (1978): 6–22; B. P. Indik, "The Relationship between Organization Size and the Supervisory Ratio," *Administrative Science Quarterly* 9 (1964): 301–12.

31. T. F. James, "The Administrative Component in Complex Organizations," *Sociological Quarterly* 13 (1972): 533–39; Daft, "System Influence on Organization Decision-Making"; E. A. Holdaway and E. A. Blowers, "Administrative Ratios and Organization Size: A Longitudinal Examination," *American Sociological Review* 36 (1971): 278–86; John Child, "Parkinson's Progress: Accounting for the Number of Specialists in Organizations," *Administrative Science Quarterly* 18 (1973): 328–48.

32. Richard L. Daft and Selwyn Becker, "School District Size and the Development of Personnel Resources," *Alberta Journal of Educational Research* 24 (1978): 173–87.

33. Andrew Pollack, "Think Japan Inc. Is Lean and Mean? Step Into This Office," *The New York Times*, 20 March 1994, Section 3, p. 11.

34. Robert M. Marsh and Hiroshi Mannari, "The Size Imperative? Longitudinal Tests," *Organization Studies* 10 (1989): 83–95.

35. Karen Grassmuck, "U-M's Work Force: A Growth Industry," *Ann Arbor (Mich.) News* 17 April 1989, A1, A4.

36. Based on Gifford and Elizabeth Pinchot, *The End of Bureaucracy and the Rise of the Intelligent Organization* (San Francisco: Berrett-Koehler Publishers, 1993), 21–39.

37. Bob Davis, "Federal Relief Agency Is Slowed by Infighting, Patronage, Regulations," *The Wall Street Journal*, 31 August 1992, A1, A12; Paul M. Barrett, "Bureaucratic Bungling Helps Fugitives Evade Capture by Feds," *The Wall Street Journal*, 7 August 1991, A1, A6.

38. Michael Schroeder, "The Recasting of Alcoa," *Business Week*, 9 September 1991, 62–64; Thomas Moore, "Goodbye Corporate Staff," *Fortune*, 21 December 1987, 65–76.

39. Philip M. Padsakoff, Larry J. Williams, and William D. Todor, "Effects of Organizational Formalization on Alienation Among Professionals and Nonprofessionals," *Academy of Management Journal* 29 (1986): 820–31.

40. Royston Greenwood, C. R. Hinings, and John Brown, "'P2-Form' Strategic Management: Corporate Practices in Professional Partnerships," *Academy of Management Journal* 33 (1990): 725–55; Royston Greenwood and C. R. Hinings, "Understanding Strategic Change: The Contribution of Archtypes," *Academy of Management Journal* 36 (1993): 1052–81.

41. John R. Kimberly, Robert H. Miles, and Associates, *The Organizational Life Cycle* (San Francisco: Jossey-Bass, 1980); Ichak Adices, "Organizational Passages—Diagnosing and Treating Lifecycle Problems of Organizations," *Organizational Dynamics* (Summer 1979): 3–25; Danny Miller and Peter H. Friesen, "A Longitudinal Study of the Corporate Life Cycle," *Management Science* 30 (October 1984): 1161–83; Neil C. Churchill and Virginia L. Lewis, "The Five Stages of Small Business Growth," *Harvard Business Review* 61 (May–June 1983): 30–50.

42. Larry E. Greiner, "Evolution and Revolution as Organizations Grow," *Harvard Business Review* 50 (July–August 1972): 37–46; Robert E. Quinn and Kim Cameron, "Organizational Life Cycles and Shifting Criteria of Effectiveness: Some Preliminary Evidence," *Management Science* 29 (1983): 33–51.

43. George Land and Beth Jarman, "Moving beyond Breakpoint," in Michael Ray and Alan Rinzler, eds., *The New Paradigm* (New York: Jeremy P. Tarcher/ Perigee Books, 1993), 250–66; Michael L. Tushman, William H. Newman, and Elaine Romanelli, "Convergence and Upheaval: Managing the Unsteady Pace of Organizational Evolution," *California Management Review* 29 (1987): 1–16.

44. David A. Whetten, "Sources, Responses, and Effects of Organizational Decline," in John R. Kimberly, Robert H. Miles, and Associates, *The Organizational Life Cycle* (San Francisco: Jossey-Bass, 1980), 342–74.

45. Kathy Rebello, Robert D. Hof, and Peter Burrows, "Inside Apple's Boardroom Coup," *Business Week*, 19 February 1996, 28–30.

46. George Land and Beth Jarman, "Moving Beyond Breakpoint."

47. Scott McCartney, "Michael Dell—and His Company—Grow Up," *The Wall Street Journal*, 31 January 1995, B1.

6

chapter six

Fundamentals of Organization Structure

While reading this chapter, think about your answers to the following questions:

- How can vertical and horizontal linkages be designed to provide needed coordination and information sharing in organizations?

- How is structure related to an organization's competitive strategy?

- What are the fundamental approaches to organization structure and under what conditions is each approach most effective?

- What are the symptoms of structural deficiency?

Every organization wrestles with the problem of how to organize. Structural changes are needed as the environment, technology, size, or competitive strategy changes. Xerox Corporation restructured itself from one large, hierarchical company into nine independent product divisions. The new structure allows collaboration within each division that helps provide fast transition of new technology into new products for the marketplace. The telecommunications industry was stunned by AT&T breaking into three decentralized businesses to go after growth opportunities in every part of the global information industry.[1] The challenge for managers is to understand how to design organization structure to achieve their company's goals.

PURPOSE OF THIS CHAPTER

The general concept of organization structure has been discussed in previous chapters. Structure includes such things as the number of departments in an organization, the span of control, and the extent to which the organization is formalized or centralized. The purpose of this chapter is to bring together these ideas to show how to design structure as it appears on the organization chart.

The material on structure is presented in the following sequence. First, structure is defined. Second, an information-processing perspective on structure explains how vertical and horizontal linkages are designed to provide needed information capacity. Third, basic organization design options are presented. Fourth, strategies for grouping organizational activities into functional, divisional, hybrid, or matrix structures are discussed. By the end of this chapter, you will understand how organization structure can help companies achieve their goals.

STRUCTURE AND STRATEGY

Organization **structure** is reflected in the organization chart. The organization chart is the visible representation for a whole set of underlying activities and processes in an organization. The three key components in the definition of organization structure are:

1. Organization structure designates formal reporting relationships, including the number of levels in the hierarchy and the span of control of managers and supervisors.
2. Organization structure identifies the grouping together of individuals into departments and of departments into the total organization.
3. Organization structure includes the design of systems to ensure effective communication, coordination, and integration of effort across departments.[2]

These three elements of structure pertain to both vertical and horizontal aspects of organizing. For example, the first two elements are the structural framework, which is the vertical hierarchy drawn on the organization chart.[3] The third element pertains to the pattern of interactions among organizational employees. An ideal structure encourages employees to provide horizontal information and coordination where and when it is needed.

Exhibit 6.1 illustrates that structural design is influenced by the environment, goals, technology, and size. Each of these key contextual variables was discussed at length in a previous chapter. Recall that an environment can be stable or unstable; managements goals and strategies may stress internal efficiency or adaptation to external markets; production technologies can be routine or non-routine; and an organization's size may be large or small. Each variable influences the correct structural design. Moreover, environment, technology, goals, and size may also influence one another. Human processes (such as leadership and culture) within the organization also influence structure as indicated in the center of Exhibit 6.1. These processes will be discussed in later chapters.

Of these contextual variables, the connection between competitive strategy and structure is of particular interest and has been widely studied. Structure typically reflects organizational strategy, and a change in product or market strategy frequently leads to a change in structure.[4] Once a company formulates a strategy by which it plans to achieve an advantage in the marketplace, leaders design or redesign the structure to coordinate organizational activities to best achieve that advantage. For example, an organization that adopts a strategy to produce a single or only a few products or services for a limited market generally operates well with a centralized, functional structure. Organizational goals stress internal efficiency and technical quality. Apple Computer in the early 1980s provides an example: the company essentially produced a single product, the Macintosh, that was sold to a single type of customer, computer dealers.[5]

Often, a company's strategy will evolve to the greater complexity of producing multiple products or services and expanding to new markets. When organizations diversify, structure may evolve into a decentralized, divisional form to promote flexibility and speed decision making. Goals stress adaptation to the external environment. In the late 1980s, under John Sculley's leadership, Apple

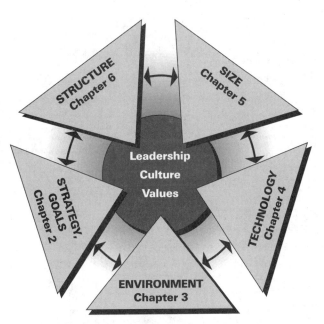

Exhibit 6.1
Organization Contextual Variables that Influence Structure

Source: Adapted from Jay R. Galbraith, *Competing with Flexible Lateral Organizations,* 2nd ed. (Reading, Mass.: Addison-Wesley Publishing, 1994), ch.1; and Jay R. Galbraith, *Organization Design* (Reading, Mass.: Addison-Wesley, 1977), ch. 1.

Computer shifted to a structure based on geographic divisions to facilitate manufacture and sales of a variety of computers to a larger customer base worldwide. Exhibit 6.2 illustrates the difference between the functional and the divisional structure as reflected in the organization chart.

Sometimes, an organization faces a simultaneous need for internal efficiency, a strength of the functional structure, and for external adaptation, a strength of the divisional structure. Strategy in this case may require that the organization evolve to the matrix structure, the most well-known dual-reporting structure used by organizations, also illustrated in Exhibit 6.2. The matrix and other basic organization designs will be discussed in detail later in this chapter.

INFORMATION-PROCESSING PERSPECTIVE ON STRUCTURE

The concepts in previous chapters—technology, goals, environment, size—impose different information-processing requirements on organizations. A non-routine technology or an uncertain environment, for example, requires employees to process more information to understand and respond to unexpected events. Reciprocal interdependence between departments requires substantially more communication and coordination than is needed for pooled interdependence. Thus, the organization must be designed to encourage information flow in both vertical and horizontal directions necessary to achieve the

Exhibit 6.2 *Three Fundamental Approaches to Structural Design*

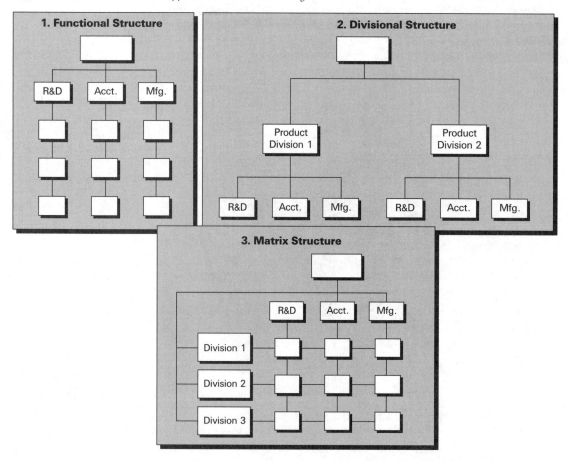

organization's overall task.[6] Exhibit 6.3 illustrates how structure should fit the information requirements of the organization: if it does not, people will either have too little information or will spend time processing information not vital to their tasks, thus reducing effectiveness.[7]

Vertical Information Linkages

Organization design should facilitate the communication among employees and departments that is necessary to accomplish the organization's overall task. *Linkage* is defined as the extent of communication and coordination among organizational elements. **Vertical linkages** are used to coordinate activities between the top and bottom of an organization. Employees at lower levels should carry out activities consistent with top-level goals, and top executives must be informed of activities and accomplishments at the lower levels. Organizations may use any of a variety of structural devices to achieve vertical linkage, including hierarchical referral, rules and procedures, plans and schedules, positions or levels added to the hierarchy, and formal management information systems.[8]

Hierarchical Referral. The first vertical device is the hierarchy, or chain of command, which is illustrated by the vertical lines in Exhibit 6.2. If a problem arises that employees don't know how to solve, it can be referred up to the next level in the hierarchy. When the problem is solved, the answer is passed back down to lower levels. The lines of the organization chart act as communication channels.

Rules and Plans. The next linkage device is the use of rules and plans. To the extent that problems and decisions are repetitious, a rule or procedure can be established so employees know how to respond without communicating directly with their manager. Rules provide a standard information source enabling employees to be coordinated without actually communicating about every job. A plan also provides standing information for employees. The most widely used plan is the budget. With carefully designed budget plans, employees at lower levels can be left on their own to perform activities within their resource allotment.

Exhibit 6.3 *Information-Processing Approach to Structural Design*

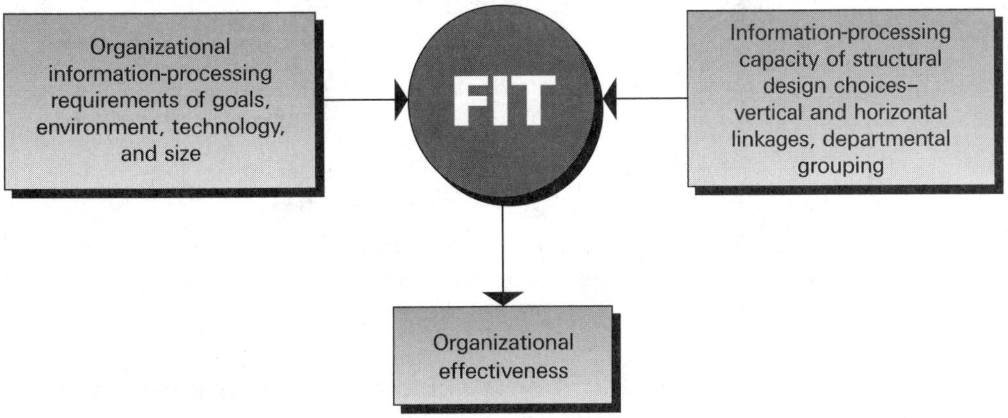

Source: Based on Richard L. Daft and Robert H. Lengel, "Organizational Information Requirements, Media Richness and Structural Design," *Management Science* 32 (1986): 554–71; and David Nadler and Michael Tushman, *Strategic Organization Design* (Glenview, Ill.: Scott Foresman, 1988).

Adding Positions to Hierarchy. When many problems occur, planning and hierarchical referral may overload managers. In growing or changing organizations, additional vertical linkages may be required. One technique is to add positions to the vertical hierarchy. In some cases, an assistant will be assigned to help an overloaded manager. In other cases, positions in the direct line of authority may be added. Such positions reduce the span of control and allow closer communication and control.

Vertical Information Systems. Vertical information systems are another strategy for increasing vertical information capacity **Vertical information systems** include the periodic reports, written information, and computer-based communications distributed to managers. Information systems make communication up and down the hierarchy more efficient. For example, Chairman Bill Gates of Microsoft communicates regularly with employees through his company's electronic mail system. He responds to a dozen individual messages each day. At Xerox, some 40,000 customers are polled each month, and this data is aggregated, summarized, and transferred up the hierarchy to managers.

Structural mechanisms that can be used to achieve vertical linkage and coordination are summarized in Exhibit 6.4. These structural mechanisms represent alternatives managers can use in designing an organization. Depending upon the amount of coordination needed in the organization, several of the linkage mechanisms in Exhibit 6.4 may be used.

Horizontal Information Linkages

Horizontal communication overcomes barriers between departments and provides opportunities for coordination among employees to achieve unity of effort and organizational objectives. **Horizontal linkage** refers to the amount of communication and coordination horizontally across organizational departments. Its importance was discovered by Lee Iacocca when he took over Chrysler Corporation.

Exhibit 6.4

Ladder of Mechanisms for Vertical Linkage and Control

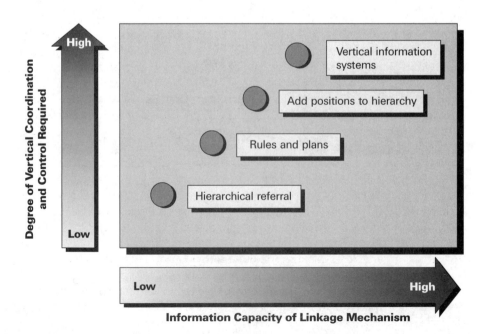

What I found at Chrysler were thirty-five vice presidents, each with his own turf. . . . I couldn't believe, for example, that the guy running engineering departments wasn't in constant touch with his counterpart in manufacturing. But that's how it was. Everybody worked independently. I took one look at that system and I almost threw up. That's when I knew I was in really deep trouble.

. . . Nobody at Chrysler seemed to understand that interaction among the different functions in a company is absolutely critical. People in engineering and manufacturing almost have to be sleeping together. These guys weren't even flirting.[9]

Today, horizontal communication has evolved to a high level at Chrysler and has had a significant positive impact. Chrysler puts everyone who's working on a specific vehicle project—designers, engineers, and manufacturers, along with representatives from marketing, finance, purchasing, and even outside suppliers, together on a single floor. The team concept has significantly improved horizontal coordination to help Chrysler become the world's most successful automaker.[10]

The need for horizontal coordination increases as the amount of uncertainty increases, such as when the environment is changing, the technology is nonroutine and interdependent, and goals stress innovation and flexibility. Horizontal linkage mechanisms often are not drawn on the organization chart, but nevertheless are part of organization structure. The following devices are structural alternatives that can improve horizontal coordination and information flow.[11] Each device enables people to exchange information.

Information Systems. A significant method of providing horizontal linkage in today's organizations is the use of cross-functional information systems. Computerized information systems can enable managers or front-line workers throughout the organization to routinely exchange information about problems, opportunities, activities, or decisions. Bow Valley Energy, a $264 million exploration and production company, redesigned its computer information system to improve cross-functional information flow among its geologists, geophysicists, production engineers, and contract managers worldwide.[12]

Direct Contact. A somewhat higher level of horizontal linkage is direct contact between managers or employees affected by a problem. To revive customer loyalty by improving service and quality, CEO Louis Morris began encouraging communication across department lines at Simplicity Pattern Company, so that creative design managers were talking with managers in sales and financing.[13] One way to promote direct contact is to create special **liaison role**. A liaison person is located in one department but has the responsibility for communicating and achieving coordination with another department. Liaison roles often exist between engineering and manufacturing departments because engineering has to develop and test products to fit the limitations of manufacturing facilities.

Task Forces. Direct contact and liaison roles usually link only two departments. When linkage involves several departments, a more complex device such as a task force is required. A **task force** is a temporary committee composed of representatives from each department affected by a problem.[14] Each member represents the interest of a department and can carry information from the meeting back to that department.

Task forces are an effective horizontal linkage device for temporary issues. They solve problems by direct horizontal coordination and reduce the information load on the vertical hierarchy. Typically, they are disbanded after their tasks are accomplished.

Xerox used a task force of twenty hand-picked members to develop its application for the Malcolm Baldrige National Quality Award. Book publishers coordinate the editing, production, advertising, and distribution of a special book with a temporary task force.

Full-Time Integrator. A stronger horizontal linkage device is to create a full-time position or department solely for the purpose of coordination. A full-time **integrator** frequently has a title, such as product manager, project manager, program manager, or brand manager. Unlike the liaison person described earlier, the integrator does not report to one of the functional departments being coordinated. He or she is located outside the departments and has the responsibility for coordinating several departments.

The brand manager for Planters Peanuts, for example, coordinates the sales, distribution, and advertising for that product. Gillette Company created product line managers for multinational coordination. A product line manager coordinates marketing and sales strategies for Trac II across fifteen countries, achieving savings by using similar advertising and marketing techniques in each country.

As part of its recent restructuring, General Motors is setting up brand managers who will be responsible for marketing and sales strategies for each of GM's new models.[15]

The integrator can also be responsible for an innovation or change project, such as developing the design, financing, and marketing of a new product. An organization chart that illustrates the location of project managers for new product development is shown in Exhibit 6.5.

The project managers are drawn to the side to indicate their separation from other departments. The arrows indicate project members assigned to the new product development. New Product A, for example, has a financial accountant assigned to keep track of costs and budgets. The engineering member provides design advice, and purchasing and manufacturing members represent their areas. The project manager is responsible for the entire project. He or she sees that the new product is completed on time, is introduced to the market, and achieves other project goals. The horizontal lines in Exhibit 6.5 indicate that project managers do not have formal authority over team members with respect to giving pay raises, hiring, or firing. Formal authority rests with the managers of the functional departments, who have formal authority over subordinates.

Integrating roles require excellent people skills. Integrators in most companies have a lot of responsibility but little authority The integrator has to use expertise and persuasion to achieve coordination. He or she spans the boundary between departments and must be able to get people together, maintain their trust, confront problems, and resolve conflicts and disputes in the interest of the organization.[16] The integrator must be forceful in order to achieve coordination, but must stop short of alienating people in the line departments.

Teams. Project teams tend to be the strongest horizontal linkage mechanism. **Teams** are permanent task forces and are often used in conjunction with a full-time integrator. When activities between departments require strong coordination over a long period of time, a cross-functional team is often the solution.

Exhibit 6.5 *Project Manager Location in the Structure*

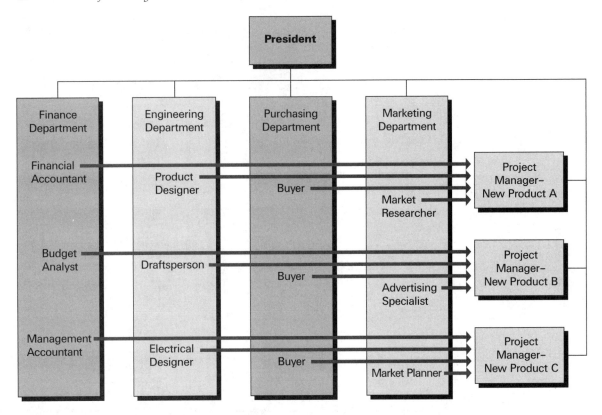

Special project teams may be used when organizations have a large-scale project, a major innovation, or a new product line, such as Chrysler's Neon.

Boeing used around 250 teams to design and manufacture the new 777 aircraft. Some teams were created around sections of the plane, such as the wing, cockpit, or engines, while others were developed to serve specific customers, such as United Airlines or British Airways. Boeing's teams had to be tightly integrated and coordinated to accomplish this massive project. Even the U.S. Department of the Navy has discovered the power of cross-functional teams to improve horizontal coordination and increase productivity.[17]

The Rodney Hunt Company develops, manufactures, and markets heavy industrial equipment and uses teams to coordinate each product line across the manufacturing, engineering, and marketing departments. These teams are illustrated by the dashed lines and shaded areas in Exhibit 6.6. Members from each team meet the first thing each day as needed to resolve problems concerning customer needs, backlogs, engineering changes, scheduling conflicts, and any other problem with the product.

The mechanisms for achieving horizontal linkages in organizations are summarized in Exhibit 6 7. These devices represent alternatives that managers can select to achieve horizontal coordination in any organization. The higher-level devices provide more horizontal information capacity. If communication is insufficient, departments will find themselves out of synchronization, and they will not contribute to the overall goals of the organization.

Exhibit 6.6 *Teams Used for Horizontal Coordination at Rodney Hunt Company*

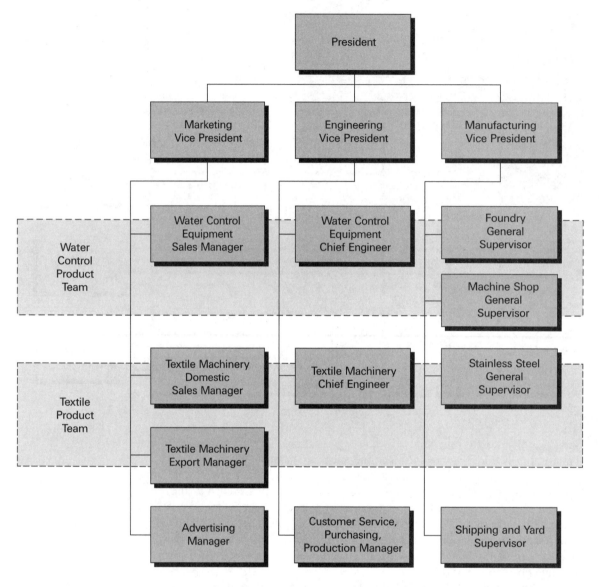

ORGANIZATION DESIGN ALTERNATIVES

The overall design of organization structure indicates three things—needed work activities, reporting relationships, and departmental groupings.

Work Activities

Departments are created to perform tasks considered strategically important to the company. For example, when moving huge quantities of supplies in the Persian Gulf, the U.S. Army's logistics commander created a squad of fifteen soldiers called Ghostbusters who were charged with getting out among the troops, identifying logistics problems, and seeing that the problems got fixed. The fiberglass group at

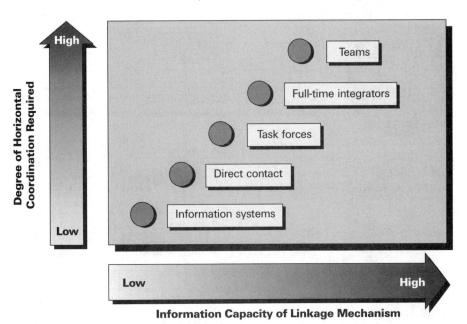

Exhibit 6.7
Ladder of Mechanisms for Horizontal Linkage and Coordination

Manville set a priority on growth and, hence, created a department that was simply called Growth Department. Defining a specific department is a way to accomplish tasks deemed valuable by the organization to accomplish its goals.

Reporting Relationships

Reporting relationships, often called the chain of command, are represented by vertical lines on an organization chart. The chain of command should be an unbroken line of authority that links all persons in an organization and shows who reports to whom. In a large organization like Standard Oil Company, one hundred or more charts are required to identify reporting relationships among thousands of employees. The definition of departments and the drawing of reporting relationships defines how employees are to be grouped into departments.

Departmental Grouping Options

Options for departmental grouping, including functional grouping, divisional grouping, geographic grouping, and multifocused grouping, are illustrated in Exhibit 6 8. **Departmental grouping** has impact on employees because they share a common supervisor and common resources, are jointly responsible for performance, and tend to identify and collaborate with one another.[18] For example, at Albany Ladder Company, the credit manager was shifted from the finance department to the marketing department. By being grouped with marketing, the credit manager started working with sales people to increase sales, thus becoming more liberal with credit than when he was located in the finance department.

 Functional grouping places employees together who perform similar functions or work processes or who bring similar knowledge and skills to bear. For example, all marketing people would work together under the same supervisor, as would manufacturing and engineering people. All people associated with the

Exhibit 6.8

Structural Design Options for Grouping Employees into Departments

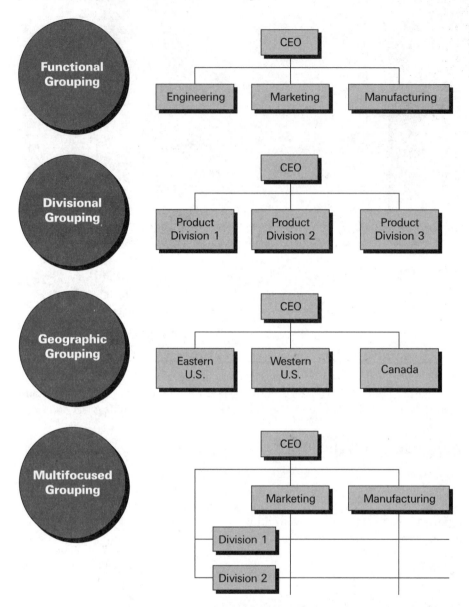

Source: Adapted from David Nadler and Michael Tushman, *Strategic Organization Design* (Glenview, Ill.: Scott Foresman, 1988), 68.

assembly process for generators would be grouped together in one department. All chemists may be grouped in a department different from biologists because they represent different disciplines.

Divisional grouping means people are organized according to what the organization produces. All people required to produce toothpaste—including the marketing, manufacturing, and sales people are grouped together under one executive. In huge corporations such as PepsiCo, the product lines may represent independent businesses, such as Taco Bell, Frito Lay, and Pepsi Cola.

Geographic grouping means resources are organized to serve customers or clients in a particular geographical area. For example, all the activities required to serve the Eastern United States or Canada or Latin America might be grouped together. This grouping focuses employees on meeting the specific needs of customers in a particular country or region.

Multifocused grouping means an organization embraces two structural grouping alternatives simultaneously. These structural forms are often called matrix or hybrid and will be discussed in more detail later in this chapter. An organization may need to group by function and product division simultaneously or perhaps by product division and geography.

The organizational forms described in Exhibit 6.8 provide the overall options within which the organization chart is drawn and the detailed structure is designed. Each structural design alternative has significant strengths and weaknesses, to which we now turn.

FUNCTIONAL, DIVISIONAL, AND GEOGRAPHICAL DESIGNS

Functional grouping and divisional grouping are the two most common approaches to structural design.

Functional Structure

In a **functional structure,** activities are grouped together by common function from the bottom to the top of the organization. All engineers are located in the engineering department, and the vice president of engineering is responsible for all engineering activities. The same is true in marketing, research and development, and manufacturing. An example of the functional organization structure is shown in part 1 of Exhibit 6.2 earlier in this chapter.

Exhibit 6.9 summarizes the organizational characteristics typically associated with the functional structure. This structure is most effective when the environment is stable and the technology is relatively routine with low interdependence across functional departments. Organizational goals pertain to internal efficiency and technical specialization. Size is small to medium. Each of these characteristics is associated with a low need for horizontal coordination. The stable environment, routine technology, internal efficiency, and small size mean the organization can be controlled and coordinated primarily through the vertical hierarchy. Within the organization, employees are committed to achieving the operative goals of their respective functional departments. Planning and budgeting is by function and reflects the cost of resources used in each department. Formal authority and influence within the organization rests with upper managers in the functional departments.

One strength of the functional structure is that it promotes economy of scale within functions. Economy of scale means all employees are located in the same place and can share facilities. Producing all products in a single plant, for example, enables the plant to acquire the latest machinery. Constructing only one facility instead of separate facilities for each product line reduces duplication and waste. The functional structure also promotes in-depth skill development of employees. Employees are exposed to a range of functional activities within their own department. The functional form of structure is best for small to medium-sized organizations when only one or a few products are produced.[19]

Exhibit 6.9
*Summary of
Functional
Organization
Characteristics*

Context
Structure: Functional Environment: Low uncertainty, stable Technology: Routine, low interdependence Strategy, Goals: Internal efficiency, technical quality
Internal Systems
Operative goals: Functional goal emphasis Planning and budgeting: Cost basis—budget, statistical reports Formal authority: Functional managers
Strengths
1. Allows economies of scale within functional departments 2. Enables in-depth skill development 3. Enables organization to accomplish functional goals 4. Is best in small to medium-sized organizations 5. Is best with only one or a few products
Weaknesses
1. Slow response time to environmental changes 2. May cause decisions to pile on top, hierarchy overload 3. Leads to poor horizontal coordination among departments 4. Results in less innovation 5. Involves restricted view of organizational goals

Source: Adapted from Robert Duncan, "What Is the Right Organization Structure? Decision Tree Analysis Provides the Answer," *Organizational Dynamics* (Winter 1979): 429.

The main weakness of the functional structure is a slow response to environmental changes that require coordination across departments. If the environment is changing or the technology is nonroutine and interdependent, the vertical hierarchy becomes overloaded. Decisions pile up, and top managers do not respond fast enough. Other disadvantages of the functional structure are that innovation is slow because of poor coordination, and each employee has a restricted view of overall goals.

Functional Structure with Horizontal Linkages

Today, there is a shift toward flatter, more horizontal structures because of the uncertain environment. Very few of today's successful companies can maintain a strictly functional structure. Organizations compensate for the vertical functional hierarchy by installing horizontal linkages, as described earlier in this chapter.

Managers improve horizontal coordination by using information systems, direct contact between departments, full-time integrators or project managers (illustrated in Exhibit 6.5), task forces, or teams (illustrated in Exhibit 6.6). Not-for-profit organizations are also recognizing the importance of horizontal linkages. An interesting example occurred at Karolinska Hospital in Stockholm, Sweden, where horizontal linkage mechanisms have dramatically improved productivity as well as patient care. Hospital managers reorganized work flow at Karolinska around patient care—instead of bouncing a patient from department to department, Karolinska now envisions the illness to recovery period as a process with pit stops in admission, X-ray, surgery, etc.

The most interesting aspect of the reorganization was the creation of the new position of "nurse coordinator." Nurse coordinators serve as full-time integrators, looking for situations where the baton is dropped in the handoff between or within departments. Horizontal linkages have dramatically improved performance at Karolinska. Even though 3 out of 15 operating theaters have been closed due to funding cuts, the high coordination has enabled the hospital to perform 3,000 more operations annually, a 25 percent increase, and waiting times for surgery have been reduced from eight months to only three weeks.[20]

Karolinska Hospital is using horizontal linkages to overcome some of the disadvantages of the functional structure. Full-time integrators span the boundaries between departments and coordinate activities to serve the needs of patients as well as the interests of the organization. We will talk more about this trend toward horizontal organizing in the next chapter.

Divisional Structure

The term **divisional structure** is used here as the generic term for what is sometimes called *product structure* or *strategic business units*. With this structure, divisions can be organized according to individual products, services, product groups, major projects or programs, divisions, businesses, or profit centers. The distinctive feature of a divisional structure is that grouping is based on organizational outputs.

The difference between a divisional structure and a functional structure is illustrated in Exhibit 6.10. The functional structure can be redesigned into separate product groups, and each group contains the functional departments of R&D, manufacturing, accounting, and marketing. Coordination across functional departments within each product group is maximized. The divisional structure promotes flexibility and change because each unit is smaller and can adapt to the needs of its environment. Moreover, the divisional structure decentralizes decision making, because the lines of authority converge at a lower level in the hierarchy. The functional structure, by contrast, forces decisions all the way to the top before a problem affecting several functions can be resolved.

The divisional structure fits the context summarized in Exhibit 6.11.[21] This form of structure is excellent for achieving coordination across functional departments. When the environment is uncertain, the technology is nonroutine and interdependent across departments, and goals are external effectiveness and adaptation, then a divisional structure is appropriate.

Large size is also associated with divisional structure. Giant, complex organizations such as General Electric, PepsiCo, and Johnson & Johnson are subdivided into a series of smaller, self-contained organizations for better control and coordination. In these large companies, the units are sometimes called divisions, businesses, or strategic business units.

An example of a divisional structure is Time Warner, Inc. Principal operating divisions include Warner Music, the world's largest record company, including the labels Warner Brothers, Elektra, and Atlantic; HBO, the leading pay cable television channel; Warner Brothers, maker of movies such as *Batman Forever* and television series such as "Friends"; and Time, Inc., which includes magazine publishers for *Time, Fortune*, and *People* as well as book publishers such as Little, Brown & Company.[22]

Exhibit 6.10 *Reorganization from Functional Structure to Divisional Structure at Info-Tech*

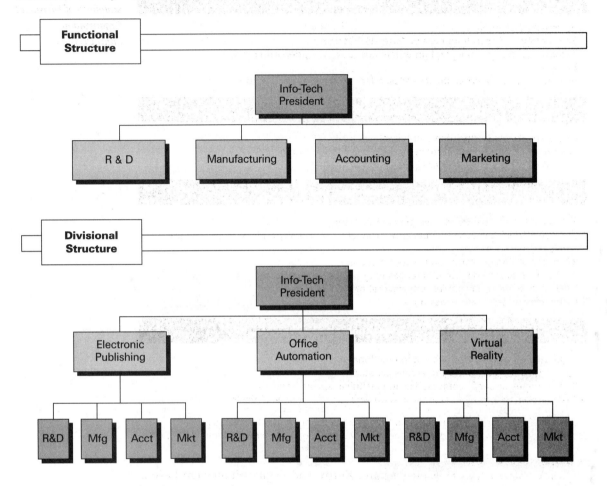

The divisional structure has several strengths. It is suited to fast change in an unstable environment and provides high product visibility. Since each product is a separate division, clients are able to contact the correct division and achieve satisfaction. Coordination across functions is excellent. Each product can adapt to requirements of individual customers or regions. The divisional structure typically works best in organizations that have multiple products or services and enough personnel to staff separate functional units. At corporations like Johnson & Johnson and PepsiCo, decision making is pushed down to the lowest levels. Each division is small enough to be quick on its feet, responding rapidly to changes in the market.

One disadvantage of using divisional structuring is that the organization loses economies of scale. Instead of fifty research engineers sharing a common facility in a functional structure, ten engineers may be assigned to each of five product divisions. The critical mass required for in-depth research is lost, and physical facilities have to be duplicated for each product line. Another problem is that product lines become separate from each other, and coordination across product lines can be difficult. As one Johnson & Johnson executive said, "We have to keep reminding ourselves that we work for the same corporation."[23]

Exhibit 6.11
Summary of Divisional Organization Characteristics

Context
Structure: Divisional Environment: Moderate to high uncertainty, changing Technology: Non-routine, high interdependence among departments Size: Large Strategy, Goals: External effectiveness, adaptation, client satisfaction

Internal Systems
Operative goals: Product line emphasis Planning and budgeting: Profit center basis—cost and income Formal authority: Product managers

Strengths
1. Suited to fast change in unstable environment 2. Leads to client satisfaction because product responsibility and contact points are clear 3. Involves high coordination across functions 4. Allows units to adapt to differences in products, regions, clients 5. Best in large organizations with several products 6. Decentralizes decision making

Weaknesses
1. Eliminates economies of scale in functional departments 2. Leads to poor coordination across product lines 3. Eliminates in-depth competence and technical specialization 4. Makes integration and standardization across product lines difficult

Source: Adapted from Robert Duncan, "What Is the Right Organization Structure? Decision Tree Analysis Provides the Answer," *Organizational Dynamics* (Winter 1979): 431.

Companies such as Hewlett-Packard, Xerox, and Digital Equipment have a large number of divisions and have had real problems with horizontal coordination. The software division may produce programs that are incompatible with business computers sold by another division. Customers are frustrated when a sales representative from one division is unaware of developments in other divisions. Task forces and other linkage devices are needed to coordinate across divisions. A lack of technical specialization is also a problem in a divisional structure. Employees identify with the product line rather than with a functional specialty. R&D personnel, for example, tend to do applied research to benefit the product line rather than basic research to benefit the entire organization.

Geographical Structure

Another basis for structural grouping is the organization's users or customers. The most common structure in this category is geography. Each region of the country may have distinct tastes and needs. Each geographic unit includes all functions required to produce and market products in that region. For multinational corporations, self-contained units are created for different countries and parts of the world.

As discussed earlier in the chapter, Apple Computer reorganized from a functional to a geographical structure to facilitate manufacture and delivery of

Apple computers to customers around the world. Exhibit 6.12 contains a partial organization structure illustrating the geographical thrust. Apple used this structure to focus managers and employees on specific geographical customers and sales targets. In Canada, department stores frequently use a geographical structure with a separate entity for Quebec because customers there are physically smaller, use a different language, and have different tastes than those in Ontario or the Maritime Provinces. The regional structure allows Apple or a Canadian department store chain to focus on the needs of customers in a geographical area.

The strengths and weaknesses of a geographic divisional structure are similar to the divisional organization characteristics listed in Exhibit 6.11. The organization can adapt to specific needs of its own region, and employees identify with regional goals rather than with national goals. Horizontal coordination within a region is emphasized rather than linkages across regions or to the national office.

Exhibit 6.12 *Geographical Structure for Apple Computer*

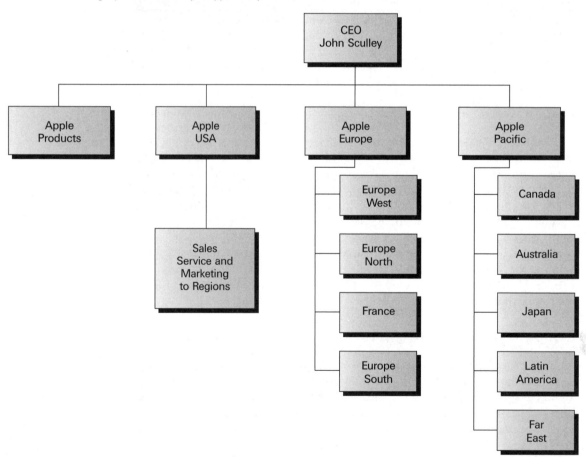

Source: Based on John Markoff, "John Sculley's Biggest Test," *New York Times,* 26 February 1989, Sec. 3, pp. 1, 26.

HYBRID STRUCTURE

As a practical matter, many structures in the real world do not exist in the pure form of functional, divisional, or geographic. An organization's structure may be multifocused in that both product and function, or product and geography, are emphasized at the same time. One type of structure that combines characteristics of both is called the **hybrid structure**.

Characteristics

When a corporation grows large and has several products or markets, it typically is organized into self-contained units of some type. Functions that are important to each product or market are decentralized to the self-contained units. However, some functions are also centralized and located at headquarters. Headquarters' functions are relatively stable and require economies of scale and in-depth specialization. By combining characteristics of the functional and divisional structures, corporations can take advantage of the strengths of each and avoid some of the weaknesses. Xerox Corporation recently reorganized into a hybrid structure, with nine nearly independent product divisions and three geographical sales divisions. CEO Paul Allaire thinks the hybrid structure can provide the coordination and flexibility needed to help Xerox get products to market faster and thrive in a competitive environment.[24]

Sun Petroleum Products also restructured from a functional to a hybrid structure to be more responsive to changing markets. Sun combined three product divisions with several functional departments to create the new hybrid structure illustrated in Exhibit 6. 13. Each product line vice president is now in charge of both marketing and manufacturing for that product, so coordination is easy to achieve. Each product line vice president also has planning, supply, and manufacturing departments reporting to him or her. The vice president in charge of refinery facilities is in charge of a functional department because there are major economies of scale by having all refineries work together. The output of these refineries becomes the input to the fuels, lubricants, and chemicals divisions. Other departments centralized as functional departments to achieve economies of scale are human resources, technology, financial services, and resources and strategy. Each of these departments provides services for the entire organization. The new structure is just right for SPPC because of the company's large size, moderate environmental change, interdependence, and goal of adapting to the environment.[25]

Strengths and Weaknesses

The hybrid structure typically appears in a context similar to that of the divisional structure. Hybrid structures tend to be used in an uncertain environment because product divisions are designed for innovation and external effectiveness. Technologies may be both routine and nonroutine, and interdependencies exist across the functions in product groupings. Size is typically large to provide sufficient resources for duplication of resources across product divisions. The organization has goals of client satisfaction and innovation, as well as goals of efficiency with respect to functional departments.

As summarized in Exhibit 6.14, a major strength of the hybrid structure is that it enables the organization to pursue adaptability and effectiveness within the

Exhibit 6.13 *Sun Petroleum Products Company's Hybrid Organization*

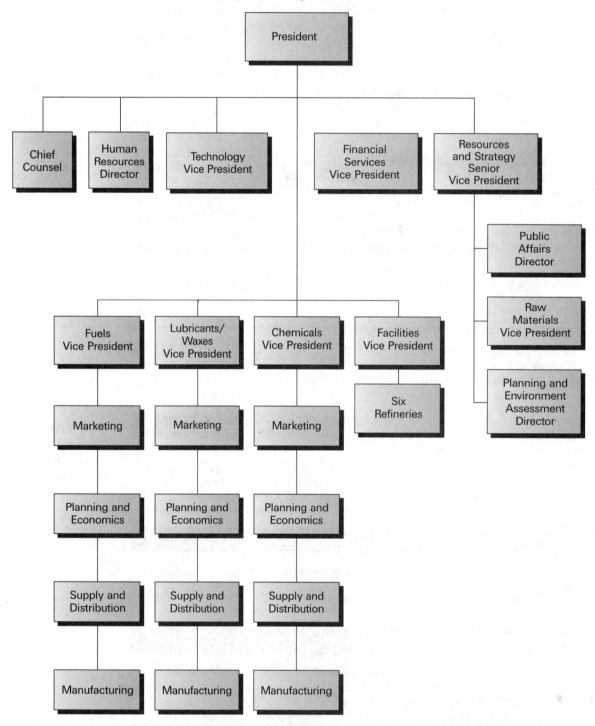

product divisions simultaneously with efficiency in the functional departments. Thus, the organization can attain the best of both worlds. This structure also provides alignment between product division and corporate goals. The product groupings provide effective coordination within divisions, and the central functional departments provide coordination across divisions.

One weakness of the hybrid structure is administrative overhead. Some organizations experience a buildup of corporate staffs to oversee divisions. Some corporate functions duplicate activities undertaken within product divisions. If uncontrolled, administrative overhead can increase as the headquarters staff grows large. Decisions then become more centralized, and the product divisions lose the ability to respond quickly to market changes. As described in Chapter 5 on size, companies such as Nucor, Hanson Industries, and Burlington Northern have resisted administrative overhead by keeping headquarters staffs at fewer than 100 people despite having as many as 3,300 employees in product divisions. Managers in these companies minimize headquarters staffs to reduce bureaucracy and encourage division flexibility.[26]

An associated weakness is the conflict between corporate and divisional personnel. Headquarters functions typically do not have line authority over divisional activities. Division managers may resent headquarters' intrusions, and headquarters managers may resent the desire of divisions to go their own way. Headquarters executives often do not understand the unique needs of the individual divisions that are trying to satisfy different markets.

The hybrid structure is often preferred to either the pure functional or pure divisional structure. It overcomes many of the weaknesses of these other structures and provides some advantages of both.

Exhibit 6.14
Summary of Hybrid Organization Characteristics

Context

Structure: Hybrid
Environment: Moderate to high uncertainty, changing customer demands
Technology: Routine or non-routine, with some interdependencies between functions
Size: Large
Strategy, Goals: External effectiveness and adaptation plus efficiency within some functions

Internal Systems

Operative goals: Product line emphasis, some functional emphasis
Planning and budgeting: Profit center basis for divisions; cost basis for central functions
Formal authority: Product managers; coordination responsibility resting with functional managers

Strengths

1. Allows organization to achieve adaptability and coordination in product divisions and efficiency in centralized functional departments
2. Results in better alignment between corporate and division-level goals
3. Achieves coordination both within and between product lines

Weaknesses

1. Has potential for excessive administrative overhead
2. Leads to conflict between division and corporate departments

MATRIX STRUCTURE

Another way to achieve focus on multiple outcomes is with the **matrix structure**. The matrix can be used when one sector of the environment requires technological expertise, for example, and another sector requires rapid change within each product line. The matrix structure often is the answer when organizations find that neither the functional, divisional, geographical, nor hybrid structures combined with horizontal linkage mechanisms will work.

The matrix is a strong form of horizontal linkage. The unique characteristic of the matrix organization is that both product division and functional structures (horizontal and vertical) are implemented simultaneously, as shown in Exhibit 6.15. Rather than divide the organization into separate parts as in the hybrid structure, the product managers and functional managers have equal authority within the organization, and employees report to both of them. The matrix structure is similar to the use of full-time integrators or product managers described earlier in this chapter (Exhibit 6.5), except that in the matrix structure the product managers (horizontal) are given formal authority equal to that of the functional managers (vertical).

Conditions for the Matrix

A dual hierarchy may seem an unusual way to design an organization, but the matrix is the correct structure when the following conditions are met.[27]

- *Condition 1*. Pressure exists to share scarce resources across product lines. The organization is typically medium-sized and has a moderate number of product lines. It feels pressure for the shared and flexible use of people and equipment across those products. For example, the organization is not large enough to assign engineers full-time to each product line, so engineers are assigned part-time to several products or projects.
- *Condition 2*. Environmental pressure exists for two or more critical outputs, such as for technical quality (functional structure) and frequent new products (divisional structure). This dual pressure means a balance of power is needed between the functional and product sides of the organization, and a dual-authority structure is needed to maintain that balance.
- *Condition 3*. The environmental domain of the organization is both complex and uncertain. Frequent external changes and high interdependence between departments require a large amount of coordination and information processing in both vertical and horizontal directions.

Under these three conditions, the vertical and horizontal lines of authority must be given equal recognition. A dual-authority structure is thereby created so the balance of power between them is equal.

Referring again to Exhibit 6.15, assume the matrix structure is for a clothing manufacturer. Product A is footwear, product B is outerwear, product C is sleepwear, and so on. Each product line serves a different market and customers. As a medium-size organization, the company must effectively use people from manufacturing, design, and marketing to work on each product line. There are not enough designers to warrant a separate design department for each product line, so the designers are shared across product lines. Moreover, by keeping the manufacturing, design, and marketing functions intact, employees can develop the in-depth expertise to serve all product lines efficiently.

Exhibit 6.15 *Dual-Authority Structure in a Matrix Organization*

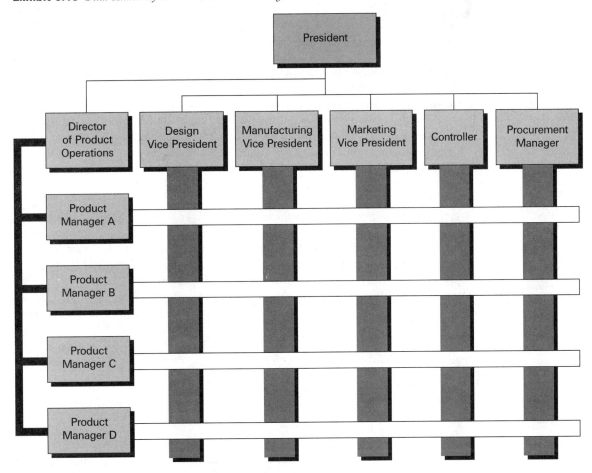

Key Matrix Roles

The unique aspect of matrix structure as reflected in Exhibit 6.15 is that employees have two bosses. Working within a matrix structure most managers because it requires a new set of required for a single-authority structure key roles have specific responsibili bosses, and two-boss employees. Th Business matrix in Exhibit 6.16. In th the academic departments of manage which represent the vertical hierarchy. to the program directors for the underg

Top Leader. The dean is the **top leader**, tures. The primary responsibility for this between the functional managers (depar (program directors). The top leader must and encourage direct contact and group p heads and program directors, which will e coordination.

Matrix Boss. The problem for **matrix bosses**—department heads and program directors in Exhibit 6.16—is that they do not have complete control over their subordinates. Matrix bosses must work with each other to delineate activities over which they are responsible. The department head's responsibilities pertain to functional expertise, rules, and teaching standards. The program director is responsible for coordinating the whole program. This person has authority over subordinates for such activities as class scheduling, exams, and preventing overlapping of course content. Matrix bosses must be willing to confront one another on disagreements and conflicts. They must also collaborate on such things as performance reviews, promotions, and salary increases, since professors report to both of them. These activities require a great deal of time, communication, patience, and skill at working with people, which are all part of matrix management.

Two-Boss Employees. The **two-boss employee** often experiences anxiety and stress. Conflicting demands are imposed by the matrix bosses. The finance professor in Exhibit 6.16, for example, must cope with conflicting demands imposed by the finance department head and the MBA program director. The department head's demand to do research is in direct conflict with the MBA program director's demand that time be spent reading and developing teaching materials for use in the MBA program. The two-boss employee must confront both the department head and the MBA program director on these demands and reach a joint decision about how to spend his or her time. Two-boss employees must maintain an effective relationship with both managers, and they should display a dual loyalty toward both their departments and their programs.

Strengths and Weaknesses

The matrix structure is best when environmental uncertainty is high and when goals reflect a dual requirement, such as for both product and functional goals. The dual authority structure facilitates communication and coordination to cope with rapid environmental change and enables an equal balance between product and functional bosses. The matrix is also good for nonroutine technologies that have interdependencies both within and across functions. The matrix is an organic structure that facilitates discussion and adaptation to unexpected problems. It tends to work best in organizations of moderate size with a few product lines. The matrix is not needed for only a single-product line, and too many product lines make it difficult to coordinate both directions at once.

The matrix structure has been used in organizations for more than thirty years. Although horizontal linkages are increasingly popular, empirical evidence of specific advantages is still relatively sparse. Exhibit 6.17 summarizes the strengths and weaknesses of the matrix structure based on what we know of organizations that use it.[28]

Internal systems reflect the dual organization structure. Two-boss employees are aware of and adopt subgoals for both their functions and their products. Dual planning and budgeting systems should be designed, one for the functional hierarchy and one for the product line hierarchy. Power and influence are shared equally by functional and product heads.

The strength of the matrix is that it enables an organization to meet dual demands from the environment. Resources (people, equipment) can be flexibly allocated across different products, and the organization can adapt to

Exhibit 6.16 *Key Positions in a College of Business Matrix Structure*

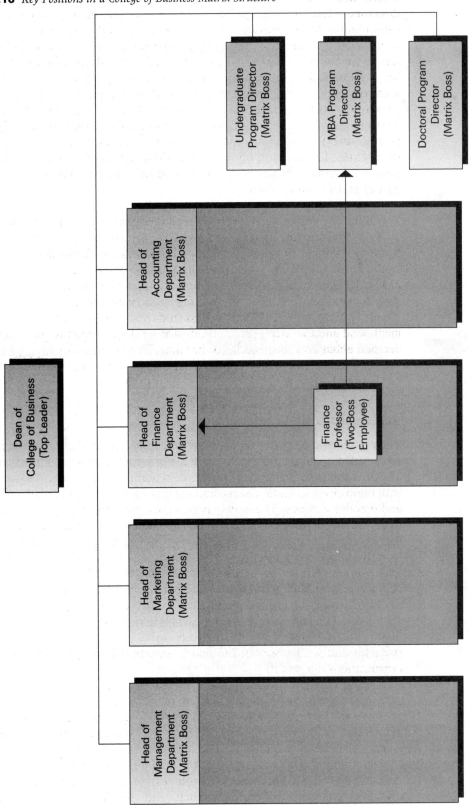

changing external requirements.[29] This structure also provides an opportunity for employees to acquire either functional or general management skills, depending on their interests.

One disadvantage of the matrix is that some employees experience dual authority, which is frustrating and confusing. They need excellent interpersonal and conflict-resolution skills, which may require special training in human relations. The matrix also forces managers to spend a great deal of time in meetings.[30] If managers do not adapt to the information and power sharing required by the matrix, the system will not work. Managers must collaborate with one another rather than rely on vertical authority in decision making.

All kinds of organizations have experimented with the matrix, including consulting firms, hospitals, banks, insurance companies, government, and many types of industrial firms.[31]

This structure has been used successfully by companies such as IBM, Unilever, and Ford Motor Company, which have fine-tuned the matrix to suit their particular goals and cultures. The matrix can be highly effective in a complex, rapidly changing environment where the organization needs to be flexible and adaptable.[32] However, the matrix is not a cure-all for structural problems. Many organizations have found the matrix described here, sometimes called a balanced matrix, difficult to install and maintain because one side of the authority structure

Exhibit 6.17

Summary of Matrix Organization Characteristics

Context
Structure: Matrix Environment: High uncertainty Technology: Nonroutine, many interdependencies Size: Moderate, a few product lines Strategy, Goals: Dual—product innovation and technical specialization

Internal Systems
Operative goals: Equal product and functional emphasis Planning and budgeting: Dual systems—by function and by product line Formal authority: Joint between functional and product heads

Strengths
1. Achieves coordination necessary to meet dual demands from environment 2. Flexible sharing of human resources across products 3. Suited to complex decisions and frequent changes in unstable environment 4. Provides opportunity for functional and product skill development 5. Best in medium-sized organizations with multiple products

Weaknesses
1. Causes participants to experience dual authority, which can be frustrating and confusing 2. Means participants need good interpersonal skills and extensive training 3. Is time-consuming; involves frequent meetings and conflict resolution sessions 4. Will not work unless participants understand it and adopt collegial rather that vertical-type relationships 5. Requires dual pressure from environment to maintain power balance

Source: Adapted from Robert Duncan, "What Is the Right Organization Structure? Decision Tree Analysis Provides the Answer," *Organizational Dynamics* (Winter 1979): 429.

often dominates. Recognizing this tendency, two variations of matrix structure have evolved—the **functional matrix** and the **project matrix**. In a functional matrix, the functional bosses have primary authority, and project or product managers simply coordinate product activities. In a project matrix, by contrast, the project or product manager has primary responsibility, and functional managers simply assign technical personnel to projects and provide advisory expertise as needed. For many organizations, one of these approaches works better than the balanced matrix and dual lines of authority.[33]

SYMPTOMS OF STRUCTURAL DEFICIENCY

Each form of structure—functional, divisional, hybrid, matrix—represents a tool that can help managers make an organization more effective depending on the demands of its situation. Senior managers periodically evaluate organization structure to determine whether it is appropriate to changing organization needs. Many organizations try one organization structure, then reorganize to another structure in an effort to find the right fit between internal reporting relationships and the needs of the external environment. Compaq Computer Corporation, for example, switched from a functional structure to a divisional structure for about a year to develop new products and then switched back to a functional structure to reduce competition among its product lines.[34]

As a general rule, when organization structure is out of alignment with organization needs, one or more of the following **symptoms of structural deficiency** appear.[35]

- *Decision making is delayed or lacking in quality*. Decision makers may be overloaded because the hierarchy funnels too many problems and decisions to them. Delegation to lower levels may be insufficient. Another cause of poor-quality decisions is that information may not reach the correct people. Information linkages in either the vertical or horizontal direction may be inadequate to ensure decision quality.
- *The organization does not respond innovatively to a changing environment*. One reason for lack of innovation is that departments are not coordinated horizontally. The identification of customer needs by the marketing department and the identification of technological developments in the research department must be coordinated. Organization structure also has to specify departmental responsibilities that include environmental scanning and innovation.
- *Too much conflict is evident*. Organization structure should allow conflicting departmental goals to combine into a single set of goals for the entire organization. When departments act at cross purposes or are under pressure to achieve departmental goals at the expense of organizational goals, the structure is often at fault. Horizontal linkage mechanisms are not adequate.

SUMMARY OF KEY ISSUES

Organization structure must accomplish two things for the organization. It must provide a framework of responsibilities, reporting relationships, and groupings, and it must provide mechanisms for linking and coordinating organizational elements into a coherent whole. The structure is reflected on the organization chart.

Linking the organization into a coherent whole requires the use of information systems and linkage devices in addition to the organization chart.

It is important to understand the information-processing perspective on structure. Organization structure can be designed to provide vertical and horizontal information linkages based upon the information processing required because of an uncertain environment, technology, size, or strategy and goals. Early organization theorists stressed vertical design and relied on vertical linkages, such as the hierarchy, planning, and new positions, to provide coordination. Vertical linkages are not sufficient for most organizations in today's complex and rapidly changing world.

The trend is toward flatter, more horizontal structures. Many organizations are breaking down the vertical hierarchy in favor of cross-functional teams. Other ways organizations provide horizontal linkages are through temporary task forces; regular, direct contact between managers across department lines; and through full-time integrators, such as product managers.

Alternatives for grouping employees and departments into overall structural design include functional grouping, divisional grouping, geographic grouping, and multifocused (hybrid, matrix) grouping. The best organization design achieves the correct balance between vertical and horizontal coordination. The choice among functional, divisional and hybrid structures determines vertical priority and, hence, where coordination and integration will be greatest. Horizontal linkage mechanisms complement the vertical dimension to achieve the integration of departments and levels into an organizational whole. The matrix organization implements an equal balance between the vertical and horizontal dimensions of structure.

Finally, an organization chart is only so many lines and boxes on a piece of paper. A new organization structure will not necessarily solve an organization's problems. The organization chart simply reflects what people should do and what their responsibilities are. The purpose of the organization chart is to encourage and direct employees into activities and communications that enable the organization to achieve its goals. The organization chart provides the structure, but employees provide the behavior. The chart is a guideline to encourage people to work together, but management must implement the structure and carry it out.

Discussion Questions

1. What is the definition of *organization structure*? Does organization structure appear on the organization chart? Explain.
2. How do rules and plans help an organization achieve vertical integration?
3. When is a functional structure preferable to a divisional structure?
4. Large corporations tend to use hybrid structures. Why?
5. How does organizational context influence the choice of structure? Are some contextual variables more important than others? Discuss.
6. What is the difference between a task force and a team? Between liaison role and integrating role? Which of these provides the greatest amount of horizontal coordination?
7. What conditions usually have to be present before an organization should adopt a matrix structure?

8. The manager of a consumer products firm said, "We use the brand manager position to train future executives." Do you think the brand manager position is a good training ground? Discuss.

9. In a matrix organization, how do the role requirements of the top leader differ from the role requirements of the matrix bosses?

10. In your opinion, what is the value of an information-processing perspective on structure?

Notes

1. Lisa Driscoll, "The New, New Thinking at Xerox," *Business Week*, 22 June 1992; Evan Ramstad, "AT&T Remakes Itself," *The Tennessean,* 21 September 1995, 2E, 4E.

2. John Child, *Organization* (New York: Harper & Row, 1984).

3. Stuart Ranson, Bob Hinings, and Royston Greenwood, "The Structuring of Organizational Structures," *Administrative Science Quarterly* 25 (1980): 1–17; Hugh Willmott, "The Structuring of Organizational Structure: A Note," *Administrative Science Quarterly* 26 (1981): 470–74.

4. This discussion is based on Jay R. Galbraith, *Competing with Flexible Lateral Organizations*, 2nd edition (Reading, Mass.: Addison-Wesley Publishing, 1994), ch. 2; Terry L. Amburgey and Tina Dacin, "As The Left Foot Follows the Right? The Dynamics of Strategic and Structural Change," *Academy of Management Journal*, 1994, Vol. 37, No. 6, 1427–1452; and Raymond E. Miles and W. E. Douglas Creed, "Organizational Forms and Managerial Philosophies: A Descriptive and Analytical Review," *Research in Organizational Behavior*, Vol. 17, 1995, 333–72.

5. Jay R. Galbraith, *Competing with Flexible Lateral Organizations*.

6. David Nadler and Michael Tushman, *Strategic Organization Design* (Glenview, Ill.: Scott Foresman, 1988).

7. Ibid.

8. Based on Jay R. Galbraith, *Designing Complex Organizations* (Reading, Mass.: Addison-Wesley, 1973) and *Organization Design* (Reading, Mass.: Addison-Wesley, 1977), 81–127.

9. Lee Iacocca with William Novak, *Iacocca: An Autobiography* (New York: Phantom Books, 1984), 152–53.

10. Alex Taylor III, "Will Success Spoil Chrysler?" *Fortune*, 10 January 1994, 88–92.

11. Based on Galbraith, *Designing Complex Organizations*.

12. Bob Lindgren, "Going Horizontal," *Enterprise*, April 1994, 20–25.

13. Barbara Ettorre, "Simplicity Cuts a New Pattern," *Management Review* (December 1993): 25–29.

14. Walter Kiechel III, "The Art of the Corporate Task Force," *Fortune*, 28 January 1991, 104–05; William J. Altier, "Task Forces: An Effective Management Tool," *Management Review* (February 1987): 52–57.

15. Keith Naughton and Kathleen Kerwin, "At GM, Two Heads May Be Worse Than One," *Business Week*, 14 August 1995, 46.

16. Paul R. Lawrence and Jay W. Lorsch, "New Managerial Job: The Integrator," *Harvard Business Review* (November–December 1967): 142–51.

17. Jay R. Galbraith, *Competing with Flexible Lateral Organizations*, 2nd ed. (Reading Mass.: Addison-Wesley Publishing Company, 1994), 17–18; Laurie P. O'Leary, "Curing the Monday Blues: A U.S. Navy Guide for Structuring Cross-Functional Teams," *National Productivity Review*, Spring 1996, 43–51.

18. Henry Mintzberg, *The Structuring of Organizations* (Englewood Cliffs, N.J.: Prentice Hall, 1979).

19. Based on Robert Duncan, "What Is the Right Organization Structure?" *Organizational Dynamics* (Winter 1979): 59–80; W. Alan Randolph and Gregory G. Dess, "The Congruence Perspective of

Organization Design: A Conceptual Model and Multivariate Research Approach," *Academy of Management Review* 9 (1984); 114–27.

20. Rahul Jacob, "The Struggle to Create an Organization for the 21st Century," *Fortune*, 3 April 1995, 90–99.

21. Based on Duncan, "What Is the Right Organization Structure?"

22. Mark Landler, "Shake-Up at Warner Music Group Results in Ouster of Its Chairman," *The New York Times*, 4 May 1995, C1, C7.

23. Joseph Weber, "A Big Company That Works," *Business Week*, 4 May 1992, 124–32.

24. Lisa Driscoll, "The New, New Thinking at Xerox," *Business Week* 22 June 1992, 120–21.

25. Adapted from Linda S. Ackerman, "Transition Management: An In-depth Look at Managing Complex Change," *Organizational Dynamics* (Summer 1982): 46–66.

26. Terrence P. Pare, "How to Cut the Cost of Headquarters," *Fortune*, 11 September 1989, 189–96; Thomas Moore, "Goodbye, Corporate Staff," *Fortune*, 21 December 1987, 65–76.

27. Stanley M. Davis and Paul R. Lawrence, *Matrix* (Reading, Mass.: Addison-Wesley, 1977), 11–24.

28. Robert C. Ford and W. Alan Randolph, "Cross-Functional Structures: A Review and Integration of Matrix Organizations and Project Management," *Journal of Management* 18 (June 1992): 267–94; Duncan, "What Is the Right Organization Structure?"

29. Lawton R. Burns, "Matrix Management in Hospitals: Testing Theories of Matrix Structure and Development," *Administrative Science Quarterly* 34 (1989): 349–68.

30. Christopher A. Bartlett and Sumantra Ghoshal, "Matrix Management: Not a Structure, a Frame of Mind," *Harvard Business Review* (July–August 1990): 138–45.

31. Davis and Lawrence, *Matrix*, 155–80.

32. Robert C. Ford and W. Alan Randolph, "Cross-Functional Structures: A Review and Integration of Matrix Organization and Project Management," *Journal of Management*, Vol. 18, No. 2, 1992, 267–94; and Paula Dwyer with Pete Engardio, Zachary Schiller and Stanley Reed, "Tearing Up Today's Organization Chart," *Business Week*/21st Century Capitalism, 18 November 1994, 80–90.

33. Erik W. Larson and David H. Gobeli, "Matrix Management: Contradictions and Insight," *California Management Review* 29 (Summer 1987): 126–38.

34. Jo Ellen Davis, "Who's Afraid of IBM?" *Business Week*, 29 June 1987, 68–74.

35. Based on Child, *Organization*, ch. 1.

7

chapter seven

Contemporary Designs for Global Competition

While reading this chapter, think about your answers to the following questions:

- Why are new horizontal and network structures being used by organizations today?

- What is reengineering? What impact does it have on organization structure, culture, and information systems?

- What are the various stages of international development and what structures can be used to fit each stage?

- What is the difference between a globalization strategy and a multidomestic strategy?

- What is the transnational model and why is it becoming increasingly important?

Globalization is a fact of life in today's business world and companies large and small are looking for new ways to fight on the increasingly competitive global battleground. Dozens of America's top manufacturers, including Gillette, Xerox, Hewlett-Packard, Dow Chemical, 3M, and DuPont, sell more of their products outside of the United States than they do at home. In terms of profits, Coca-Cola made more money in both the Pacific and Western Europe than it did in the United States, and nearly 70 percent of General Motors' profit in recent years has been from non-U.S. operations.

Even more ominous for North American companies is the arrival on North American shores of foreign competitors in enormous numbers and strength. Companies such as Nestlé (Switzerland), Michelin (France), Sony and Honda (Japan), Bayer (Germany), Northern Telecom (Canada), and Unilever (United Kingdom) all receive more than 40 percent of annual sales from foreign countries.[1] They are in North America competing vigorously for markets.

Today, no company is isolated from global influence, and global competition continues to escalate with rapid advances in technology and communications. Consider Hong Kong's Johnson Electric Holdings Ltd., a $195 million producer of micromotors that power hair dryers, blenders, and automobile features such as power windows and door locks. With factories in south China and a research and development lab in Hong Kong, Johnson is thousands of miles away from a leading auto maker. Yet the company has cornered the market for electric gizmos for Detroit's Big Three by using new information technology. Johnson design teams "meet" face-to-face for two hours each morning with their customers in the U.S. and Europe via videoconferencing. The company's processes and procedures are so streamlined that Johnson can take a concept and deliver a prototype to the U.S. in six weeks.[2] North American companies simply have no choice about global competition. No company is safe and no employee immune to its impact.

PURPOSE OF THIS CHAPTER

This chapter will introduce new approaches to organization design that enable organizations to compete effectively in a global environment. First, we will discuss the grim reality of worldwide competition. Then we will examine new designs for domestic advantage, including a shift from vertical to horizontal management, the radical redesign of business processes known as *reengineering*, and the use of network structures. Finally, we will discuss how companies can best organize for worldwide advantage, ranging from adding an export department to establishing a worldwide matrix structure or transnational model. By the end of the chapter, you will understand how to apply organization design innovations to a variety of domestic and international situations.

GLOBAL FORCES AT WORK

It is hard to deny the impact of globalization on each of us. We buy goods and services from around the world. Many U.S. workers are already working for foreign bosses. Even if you live and work in a small city, an international thrust for your company may be just around the corner, with rewards going to employees who can speak a foreign language or who have international abilities.

Globalization is so pervasive that it is hard to sort out, but the boxes in Exhibit 7.1 identify some of the key elements.[3] International forces at work today include the dominant economies of Japan and Germany, which sponsor powerhouse international companies and have huge positive trade balances with the United States. This means the end of U.S. company dominance and the onset of intense competition among high-wage nations. Newly industrialized countries such as Korea, Taiwan, and Spain are fast-growing and rapidly becoming industrialized. Their companies produce low-cost, high quality commodities and are moving into high-value items, such as automobiles and high-technology electronic goods. The shift toward market economies in eastern Europe and the former Soviet republics is rapidly producing more sources of goods, potential new markets, and, to some extent, an unpredictable future about how these countries will affect globalization.

More uncertainty will be caused by international blocs, including: the European Union agreement to drop internal trade barriers, spawning even larger more competitive international companies and erecting barriers to outsiders; the "yen bloc" that includes Asian powerhouse nations; and the North American Free Trade Agreement. These power blocs will shape the world economy into the twenty-first century and will certainly mean the end of U.S. domination of international trade policy.

What are the outcomes for individuals and businesses within the United States and Canada—or any other country for that matter? One outcome is economic volatility: No one knows whether oil will cost fifteen or twenty dollars a barrel next year. Likewise, currency values fluctuate based on inflation, trade balances, and capital investments over which no single country has control. Products we buy today, such as an IBM PC or a Black & Decker appliance, may include components from a dozen nations. No company or country can provide global economic leadership; every company and country is subordinate to larger economic forces.

No wonder we've seen the dramatic restructuring of traditional industries in the United Slates through leveraged buyouts, mergers, and breakups. These companies were striving for greater efficiency within an increasingly turbulent and competitive international environment. Indeed, the spinoffs and breakups of previous mergers may turn out to be a bigger story than the mergers, because the smaller players are efficient and well managed. Also, expect new and rapidly emerging industries, such as information technology, that already contributes 20 percent directly to gross national product. Biotechnology is just underway and may foster its own industrial revolution. People who grew up feeling comfortable and secure working for a manufacturing firm appreciate just how elusive stability and security are in the new world order.

The impact at a personal level is illustrated in the righthand column of Exhibit 7.1. Companies operating nationally, such as Wal-Mart or Quad/Graphics, are adopting new organizational forms that include less hierarchy and more self-managed teams and dynamic network structures that provide autonomy to clusters of people and activities. These organizational forms utilize human resources better than ever before and enable companies to fend off international competition.

Another outcome is perpetual change—enduring turbulence that organizations must learn to accept as the norm. Employees and organizations need to begin thinking of themselves as global players; they must try to use global

Exhibit 7.1 *Global Forces Influencing Domestic Organizations*

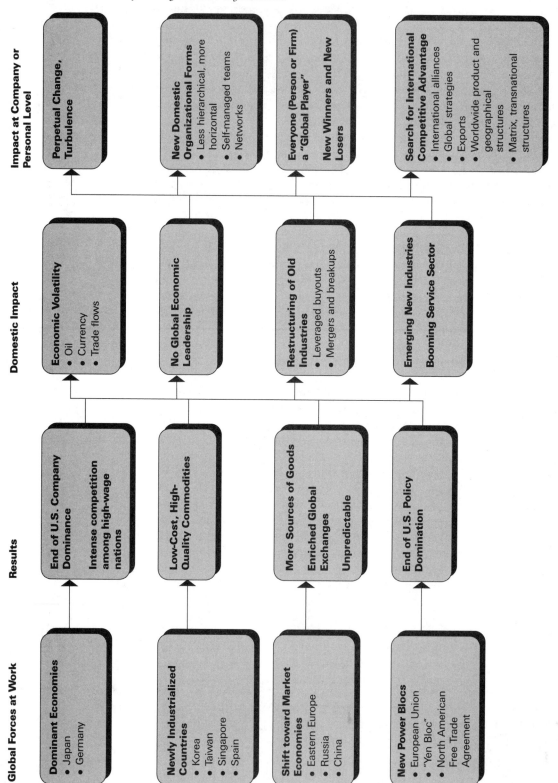

Source: Adapted from Tom Peters, "Prometheus Barely Unbound," *Academy of Management Executive* 4 (1990): 71.

alliances to advantage, sell to global markets, and be ready to meet global competition. This is especially true for Americans, who grew up believing in the superiority and invincibility of the U.S. economy.

All of this turbulence creates new winners and new losers. New winners are companies thriving under the new rules of the game—Nucor in steel, Compaq in computers, MCI in telecommunications—companies not even in existence 25 years ago. Moreover, companies are learning to search for international competitive advantage through international alliances and joint ventures. Even small companies are learning to produce quality products that can compete overseas and, hence, are adding export departments. Larger companies have learned to organize themselves into worldwide product or geographical structures. A few global firms have attained a quality of being transnational—almost without a home country—and are held together through complex international matrix or transnational structures that allow them to be global and local in 50 or more countries at the same time.

These international forces and the impact on individuals and companies mean that things must be done faster, organizations must be flexible, and innovation and improvement are paramount. Companies must be designed for maximum domestic or worldwide advantage.

In the next section we will discuss some new organization designs for domestic advantage and then we will look at worldwide organization designs.

NEW DESIGNS FOR DOMESTIC ADVANTAGE

The functional organization structure described in Chapter 6 was the first to be used by large firms and eventually became associated with bureaucracy. The divisional structure was the next innovation in structure and provided a way to subdivide huge firms like General Motors and Sears Roebuck into more manageable profit centers. Then came the notion of cross-functional teams that worked horizontally to coordinate across departments. Horizontal teams evolved into the matrix structure that has two hierarchies simultaneously.

The most recent organization design innovations are a significant shift toward horizontal rather than vertical management, the redesign of business processes referred to as reengineering, and the use of dynamic network structures. These approaches harness human resources in new ways to give companies a competitive advantage.

The Horizontal Corporation

Many of today's corporations are shifting away from the top-heavy functionally organized structures of the past to a form that virtually eliminates both the vertical hierarchy and old departmental boundaries. The newly emerging **horizontal corporation** is illustrated in Exhibit 7.2 and has the following characteristics:

1. Structure is created around work flows or processes rather than departmental functions. Boundaries between traditional departments are obliterated. At Chrysler, for example, the structure is designed around the core processes of new car development.
2. The vertical hierarchy is flattened, with perhaps only a few senior executives in traditional support functions such as finance and human resources.

3. Management tasks are delegated to the lowest level. Most employees work in multidisciplinary, self-directed teams organized around a process, such as new product development. Kodak, for example, did away with its senior vice presidents in charge of such functions as administration, manufacturing, and R&D and replaced them with self-directed teams. The company has over 1,000 such teams working on various processes and programs.

4. Customers drive the horizontal corporation. For the horizontal design to work, processes must be based on meeting customer needs. Employees are brought into direct, regular contact with customers as well as suppliers. Sometimes, representatives of these outside organizations serve as full-fledged team members.[4]

Self-Directed Teams. Self-directed teams are the building blocks of the new horizontal organization. A **self-directed team** is an outgrowth of earlier team approaches.[5] For example, many companies have used cross-functional teams to achieve coordination across departments and task forces to accomplish temporary projects. Other companies have experimented with problem-solving teams of voluntary hourly employees who meet to discuss ways to improve quality, efficiency, and work environment.

Self-directed teams, also called self-managed teams, typically consist of five to thirty workers with different skills who rotate jobs and produce an entire product or service and who take over managerial duties, such as work and vacation scheduling, ordering materials, and hiring new members. To date, several hundred companies in Canada and the United States have experimented with a self-directed team design.[6] These companies include AT&T, Xerox, General Mills, Federal Express, Ryder Systems, and Motorola.

The self-directed team design consists of permanent teams that include the following three elements:

1. The team is given access to resources, such as materials, information, equipment, machinery, and supplies, needed to perform a complete task.
2. The team includes a range of employee skills, such as engineering, manufacturing, finance and marketing. The team eliminates barriers between departments, functions, disciplines, or specialties. The team members are cross-trained to perform one another's jobs, and the combined skills are sufficient to perform a major organizational task.
3. The team is empowered with decision-making authority, which means members have the freedom to plan, solve problems, set priorities, spend money, monitor results, and coordinate activities with other departments or teams. The team must have autonomy to do what is necessary to accomplish the task.[7]

In Canada, Campbell Soup Company Ltd. designed self-directed teams to make its operations competitive with U.S. operations, achieving an "impossible" assignment of finding $700,000 of savings in three months.[8]

General Mills has increased the productivity of its plants by 40 percent using self-directed teams. At its cereal plant in Lodi, California, workers are in charge of all activities, including designing the work process, purchasing equipment, and scheduling, operating, and maintaining machinery. The company has discovered that teams generally set higher goals for themselves than management would have set for them.[9]

Exhibit 7.2
*The Horizontal
Corporation*

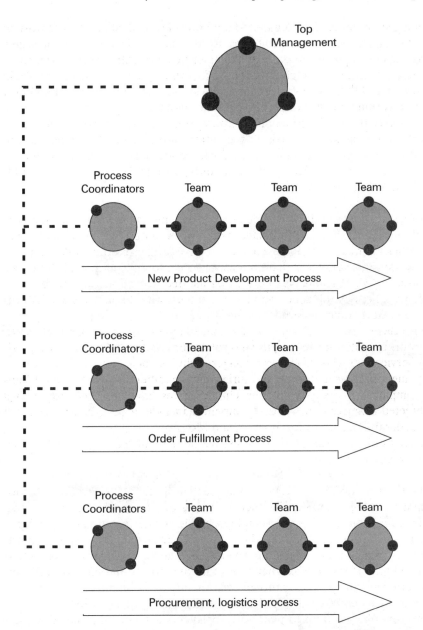

Source: Based on John A. Byrne, "The Horizontal Corporation." *Business Week*, 20 December 1993, 76–81; and Thomas A. Stewart, "The Search for the Organization of Tomorrow," *Fortune*, 18 May 1992, 92–98.

From Vertical to Horizontal. Experimentation with teams and horizontal structures often begins at the lower levels of organizations, but today, more companies are shifting their entire structures to horizontal modes. Some start-up companies, such as Astra-Merck Group, a stand-alone company created to market anti-ulcer and blood-pressure medicine from Sweden's Astra, are structuring themselves as horizontal organizations from the beginning. Astra-Merck is organized around processes, such as drug development and product distribution, rather than divided into functional departments.

Eastman Chemical Company, a $3.5 billion stand-alone unit of Eastman-Kodak, replaced several of its senior vice presidents with self-directed teams. The company calls its new organization chart "the pizza chart," because it looks like a round pizza with several slices of pepperoni on top. Each slice of pepperoni (small circles) on the pizza represents a self-directed team that is responsible for a work flow, such as cellulose technology. The president of the company is in the center of the pizza. Surrounding him are the self-directed teams, with the white space in between reflecting where the interaction among teams should take place. As Ernest W. Deavenport Jr., the "head pepperoni," says, "We did it in circular form to show that everyone is equal in the organization. No one dominates the other."[10]

Advantages and Disadvantages. The horizontal structure with self-directed teams has yielded excellent results in many organizations. But, as with all structures, it has disadvantages as well as advantages. The most significant advantage is that it delivers dramatic improvements in speed and efficiency. Rapid response time and quicker decisions mean greater customer satisfaction. Second, there are reduced, practically nonexistent, barriers among departments, which means achieving cooperation with the total task in mind. Third, there is better morale because employees are enthused about their involvement and participation. Finally, administrative overhead is reduced because teams take on the administrative tasks.

However, shifting to a horizontal structure can be a lengthy and difficult process, requiring major changes in job design, management philosophy, and information and reward systems.[11] Simply defining the processes around which teams are to be organized can be mind-boggling. The 16,000-employee Network Systems Division of AT&T eventually counted up 130 processes, then began working to pare them down to 13 core ones.[12]

In addition, managers need to be trained to understand the concept of participative management and develop new skills to become coaches and facilitators rather than "supervisors." Employees need training to work effectively in a team environment. Information systems may need to be redesigned to give team members the information they need, not only from within the organization but from customers and suppliers as well. Employees have to spend more time in lengthy meetings to coordinate and reach consensual decisions. Finally, reward systems should support team performance and commitment.

In the shift to horizontal structures and self-directed teams, there is also a danger that the company will organize around processes without analyzing and linking processes to its key goals, in which case the new structure may bring about more negative than positive results. In the next section, we discuss reengineering, which can prevent this from happening.

Reengineering

The shift to a horizontal structure often goes hand-in-hand with reengineering, a popular management concept sweeping through corporate America. **Reengineering** is a cross-functional initiative involving the radical redesign of business processes to bring about simultaneous changes in organization structure, culture, and information technology and produce dramatic performance improvements in areas such as customer service, quality, cost, and speed.[13] Hoechst Celanese Corp., Union Carbide, DuPont Co., Pepsi-Cola North

America, Pacific Bell, and BellSouth Telecommunications are among the dozens of companies involved in major reengineering efforts. After reengineering, Union Carbide cut $400 million out of fixed costs in just three years. Hoechst Celanese identified $70 million in cost savings and productivity improvements over a two year period, without making massive job cuts.[14] Many more organizations have reengineered one or a few specific processes; a 1994 Price Waterhouse poll, for example, revealed that an astounding 78 percent of Fortune 500 companies and 68 percent of British firms were reengineering one process or another.[15] Organizations are finding that the old ways of doing things no longer work in the emerging post-modern world. Reengineering is one method companies are using to reinvent themselves to meet new challenges.

Reengineering basically means taking a clean slate approach, pushing aside all the notions of how work is done now and looking at how work can best be designed for optimal performance. The idea is to squeeze out the dead space and time lags in work flows. Successful reengineering efforts are customer-driven. For example, looking at work processes "from the outside in" means BellSouth's cost-cutting zeroes in on eliminating work content that is internally focused and does not add value for the customer—staff dealing with staff, hand-offs from one group to another, etc.[16] When reengineering forces companies to examine work and workflow in terms of customer value, the organization is more likely to organize processes around key goals and core competencies. Reengineering also brings about fundamental changes in organization structure, culture, and information systems.

Organization Structure. Because reengineering examines work processes that cross functional boundaries, it is almost always associated with a shift to a more horizontal structure. Pepsi-Cola North America scrapped its functional, hierarchical organization for one designed around serving customers. Seven layers of management were cut to four. Similarly, after reengineering at Premier Bank of Louisiana, the organization structure is becoming increasingly flatter, with fewer management layers, the elimination of checking/reworking positions, and a reduction in centralized control both at headquarters and the regional levels. Exhibit 7.3 illustrates the evolution from the vertical to the horizontal organization as the design of work shifts from a focus on function to a focus on process. Most reengineering projects have landed companies somewhere in the middle of the evolutionary scale; few companies have shifted to an organization structure based entirely on horizontal processes.[17]

Culture. As structure becomes flatter and more authority is pushed down to lower levels, corporate culture changes. Lower-level employees are empowered to make decisions and held accountable for performance improvements. Trust and tolerance of mistakes become key cultural values. Since reengineering at BellSouth, some employees have actually earned cash awards for their failures. According to Richard Harder, vice president for organization planning and development, "You need some worthy failures in your efforts to change behavior." At Premier Bank, where teams have been empowered to make decisions to best serve customers, questioning and experimentation have become part of the culture.[18]

Information Systems. In traditionally organized companies, information systems have generally linked people within functional departments, but as work flow shifts to processes rather than functions, information systems need to cross

Exhibit 7.3 *Reengineering from Vertical to Horizontal Structure*

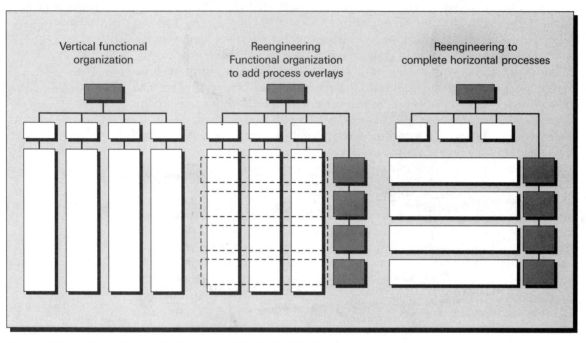

Source: Adapted from George Stalk, Jr. and Jill E. Black, "The Myth of the Horizontal Organization," *Canadian Business Review*, Winter 1994, 26–31.

boundaries as well.[19] The Gillette Company of Boston reengineered to cut its order cycle time from 10-15 days down to 1 or 2 days. Information systems are being redesigned so that the customer-service representative who takes the order can quickly access customer intelligence, up-to-date inventory information, pricing data, and worldwide delivery schedules from her or his PC or workstation.

Reengineering can lead to stunning results, but, as with all business ideas, it has its drawbacks. Reengineering is expensive, time-consuming, and usually painful. Leaders should be aware that it is a long-term process requiring major shifts in thinking and significant changes in organizational infrastructure.

Dynamic Network Design

Another major trend of the 1990s is the choice companies are making to limit themselves to only a few activities that they do extremely well and let outside specialists handle the rest. These network organizations, sometimes also called *modular corporations*, are flourishing particularly in fast-moving industries, such as apparel and electronics, but even companies in such industries as steel and chemicals are shifting toward this type of structure.[20]

The **dynamic network** structure incorporates a free market style to replace the traditional vertical hierarchy. A company keeps key activities in-house and then outsources other functions, such as sales, accounting, and manufacturing, to separate companies or individuals who are coordinated or brokered by a small headquarters. In most cases, these separate organizations are connected electronically to a central office.[21] An illustration of how this organization might look is in Exhibit 7.4.

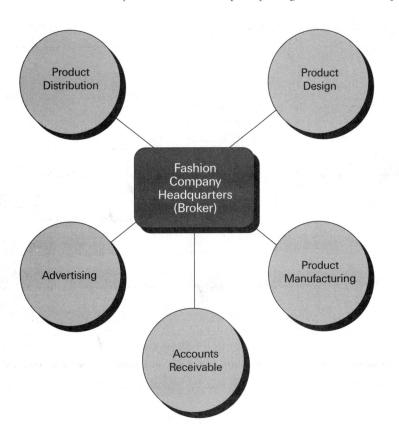

Exhibit 7.4
Dynamic Network Structure

For example, Lewis Galoob Toys, Inc., sold $58 million worth of toys with only 115 employees. Galoob contracts out manufacturing and packaging to contractors in Hong Kong, toy design to independent inventors, and sales to independent distribution representatives. Galoob never touches a product and does not even collect the money. The company is held together with phones, telexes, and other electronic technology.[22]

The free market aspect means subcontractors flow in and out of the system as needed. Much like building blocks, parts of the network can be added or taken away to meet changing needs.[23] One company, TopsyTail, Inc., used the network approach to grow into an $80 million company with only two full-time employees. TopsyTail started by farming out the tooling and injection molding of its plastic hair product, saving at least $5 million in start-up costs. Today, TopsyTail's production partners include a tool maker, two injection molders, a package designer, a logo designer, freelance photographers, and a printer. The company also outsources packaging and shipping to three fulfillment houses, television commercials to a video production company, customer mailings to a mailing list firm, and publicity to a public relations firm. Four distributing companies sell TopsyTail products in the U. S., Canada, Mexico, the Pacific Rim, Europe, and South Africa.[24]

Advantages and Disadvantages. The advantages of the dynamic network structure are several. The structure is unbelievably lean, with almost no administrative overhead because work activities are contracted and coordination is electronic.

As illustrated by the previous example, the approach can help new entrepreneurs get products to market quickly without having to incur huge start-up costs. In mature industries that are beginning to stagnate, the network structure can reinvigorate companies by enabling them to develop new products without huge investments. Another significant advantage of the network approach is its flexible, rapid response—the ability to arrange and rearrange resources to meet changing needs and best serve customers. Managerial and technical talent can be focused on key activities that provide competitive advantage, while other functions are outsourced.[25]

The disadvantages are related to the unusual nature of this organization design. For one thing, there is little hands-on control. Operations are not under one roof and managers must adjust to relying on independent subcontractors to do the work. Companies can experience problems with quality control when many different subcontractors are involved. In addition, some companies have found that subcontractors tend to dramatically raise prices once the company becomes hooked on their products or services.[26] Moreover, it can be difficult with a network structure to define the organization, since it may change from week to week as the set of subcontractors changes. Likewise the organization can occasionally lose a part if a subcontractor defects or goes out of business and can't be replaced. A final disadvantage is weakened employee loyalty. A cohesive corporate culture for the larger organization is difficult to establish. Turnover tends to be high because employees are committed only to their own task or subcontractor and they may be dismissed at any time in favor of a new contractor.

ORGANIZATIONAL DESIGNS FOR GLOBAL ADVANTAGE

Companies in the 1990s must think globally to remain competitive. At least 70 to 85 percent of the U.S. economy is feeling the impact of foreign competition.[27] The global environment is a huge potential market. International expansion can lead to greater profits, efficiency, and responsiveness. Of course, no company can become a global giant overnight. The change from domestic to international usually occurs through stages of development similar to the life cycle described in Chapter 5.

Stages of International Development

Exhibit 7.5 summarizes the four stages many companies go through as they evolve toward full-fledged global operations.[28] In stage one, the **domestic stage**, the company is domestically oriented, but managers are aware of the global environment and may want to consider initial foreign involvement to expand production volume. Market potential is limited and is primarily in the home country. The structure of the company is domestic, typically functional or divisional, and initial foreign sales are handled through an export department. The details of freight forwarding, customs problems, and foreign exchange are handled by outsiders.

In stage two, the **international stage**, the company takes exports seriously and begins to think multidomestically. **Multidomestic** means competitive issues in each country are independent of other countries; the company deals with each country individually. The concern is with international competitive positioning compared with other firms in the industry. At this point, an international division has replaced the export department, and specialists are hired to handle sales, service, and warehousing abroad. Multiple countries are identified as potential markets.

Exhibit 7.5 *Four Stages of International Evolution*

	I. Domestic	II. International	III. Multinational	IV. Global
Strategic Orientation	Domestically oriented	Export-oriented, multidomestic	Multinational	Global
Stage of Development	Initial foreign involvement	Competitive positioning	Explosion	Global
Structure	Domestic structure, plus export department	Domestic structure, plus international division	Worldwide, geographic product	Matrix, transnational
Market Potential	Moderate, mostly domestic	Large, multidomestic	Very large, multinational	Whole world

Source: Based on Nancy J. Adler, *International Dimensions of Organizational Behavior* (Boston: PWS-Kent, 1991), 7–8; and Theodore T. Herbert, "Strategy and Multinational Organization Structure: An Interorganizational Relationships Perspective," *Academy of Management Review* 9 (1984): 259–71.

In stage three, the **multinational stage**, the company is becoming a truly multinational company, which means it has marketing and production facilities in many countries and has more than one-third of its sales outside the home country. Explosion occurs as international operations take off, and the company has business units scattered around the world along with suppliers, manufacturers, and distributors.

The fourth and ultimate stage is the **global stage**, which means the company transcends any single country. The business is not merely a collection of domestic industries; rather, subsidiaries are interlinked to the point where competitive position in one country significantly influences activities in other countries.[29] Truly **global companies** no longer think of themselves as having a single home country, and, indeed, have been called "stateless" corporations.[30] This represents a new and dramatic evolution from the multinational company of the 1960s and 1970s.

Global companies operate in truly global fashion, and the entire world is their marketplace. Organization structure at this stage can be extremely complex and often evolves into an international matrix or transnational model, which will be discussed later in this chapter.

Global companies such as Procter & Gamble, Unilever, and Matsushita Electric may operate in 40 to 75 counties. The structural problem of holding together this huge complex of subsidiaries scattered thousands of miles apart is immense. Before turning to a discussion of specific structures, let's briefly consider two additional approaches to international activity, international alliances and global teams.

International Strategic Alliances

Strategic alliances are perhaps the hottest way to get involved in international operations. Typical alliances include licensing, joint ventures, and consortia.[31] Licensing agreements are frequently entered into by manufacturing firms to capitalize on the diffusion of new technology quickly and inexpensively while getting the advantage of lucrative worldwide sales. For example, Merck, Eli Lilly, and Bayer cross-license their newest drugs to one another to support industry-wide innovation and advertising and offset the high fixed costs of research and distribution.[32] **Joint ventures** are separate entities created with two or more active firms as sponsors. This is another approach to sharing development and production costs and penetrating new markets. It is estimated that the rate of joint venture formation between U.S. and international companies has been growing by 27 percent annually since 1985. Joint ventures may be with either customers or competitors. Merck has put together major ventures with such competitors as Johnson & Johnson and AB Astra of Sweden.[33] A manufacturer may seek a joint venture to distribute its new technology and products through another country's distribution channels and markets.

The agreement between Toyota and General Motors to construct a Chevrolet Nova plant in California was Toyota's way of distributing its technology to the United States. Texas Instruments sought long-term alliances with its biggest customers in Japan, including Sony, to gain subsidiaries in Japan. Over time, TI bought out Sony's share and ended up with four major plants in Japan producing semiconductors for the rest of TI's worldwide operations.[34]

Given the expense of new technology, **consortia** of organizations are likely to be the wave of the future. Rather than one-on-one competition among individual firms, groups of independent companies—suppliers, customers, and even competitors—will join together to share skills, resources, costs, and access to one another's markets.

Managers must learn to cooperate as well as compete.[35] For example, Airbus Industrie is a European consortium of businesses backed by the governments of Germany, France, the United Kingdom, and Spain to produce commercial aircraft. Airbus is slowly gaining market share and is successfully selling aircraft worldwide.

A type of consortia, called the *virtual organization*, is increasingly being used in the United States and offers a promising avenue for worldwide competition in the future. The virtual organization is a continually evolving group of companies that unite to exploit specific opportunities or attain specific strategic advantages and then disband when objectives are met. A company may be involved in multiple alliances at any one time. Some U.S. executives believe shifting to a consortia or virtual approach is the best way for U.S. companies to remain competitive in the global marketplace.[36]

Global Work Teams

The reality of today's business world as a global work environment has led some companies to establish global work teams to expand their products and operations into international markets.[37] **Global teams,** also called *transnational teams*, are work groups made up of multinational members whose activities span multiple countries. For example, Heineken formed the European Production Task Force, a 13-member team representing five countries, to wrestle with the question of how the company's production facilities throughout Europe could best be configured to cope with the challenges of the 21st century.[38] Global teams have been used in various ways. Some, such as Heineken's, help organizations achieve global efficiencies by developing regional or worldwide cost advantages and standardizing designs and operations. Other global teams help their companies be more locally responsive by meeting the needs of different regional markets, consumer preferences, and political and legal systems. A third primary use of global teams is to contribute to continuous organizational learning and adaptation on a global level.[39] The most advanced use of global teams involves simultaneous contributions in all of these strategic areas.

Global work teams bring unique problems to the concept of teamwork. Team leaders and members must learn to accommodate one another's cultural values and backgrounds and work together smoothly, usually in conditions of rapid change. One model for global team effectiveness, called the GRIP model, suggests that teams focus on developing common understanding in four critical areas: goals, relationships, information, and work processes, thus enabling the team to "get a grip" on its collaborative work at a very high level.[40] The need for and use of global work teams is likely to grow. Teams that effectively blend their varied backgrounds and interests into a teamwork culture focused on serving the organization's international goals can significantly enhance a company's global competitiveness.

INTERNATIONAL STRATEGY AND ORGANIZATION DESIGN FIT

As we discussed in Chapter 6, an organization's structure must fit its situation by providing sufficient information processing for coordination and control while focusing employees on specific functions, products, or geographic regions. Organization design for international structure follows a similar logic, with special interest on global versus local strategic opportunities.

Model for Global Versus Local Opportunities

A major strategic issue for firms venturing into the international domain is whether (and when) to use a globalization rather than a multidomestic strategy. The **globalization strategy** means that product design and advertising strategy are standardized throughout the world.[41] For example, the Japanese took business away from Canadian and American companies by developing similar high-quality, low-cost products for all countries. The Canadian and American companies incurred higher costs by tailoring products to specific countries. Black & Decker became much more competitive internationally when it standardized its line of power hand tools. Other products, such as Coca-Cola and Levi blue jeans, are naturals for globalization, because only advertising and marketing need to be tailored for different regions.

A **multidomestic strategy** means that competition in each country is handled independently of competition in other countries. Thus, a multidomestic strategy would encourage product design, assembly, and marketing tailored to the specific needs of each country. Some companies have found that their products do not thrive in a single global market. The French do not drink orange juice for breakfast, and laundry detergent is used to wash dishes, not clothes, in parts of Mexico. Parker Pen experienced a disaster when it reduced from five hundred to one hundred pen styles because the different styles were valued in different countries.

The model in Exhibit 7.6 illustrates how organization design and international strategy fit.[42] Companies can be characterized by whether their product and service lines have potential for globalization, which means advantages through worldwide standardization. Companies that sell diverse products or services across many countries have a globalization strategy. On the other hand, some companies have products and services appropriate for a multidomestic strategy, which means local-country advantages through differentiation and customization.

As indicated in Exhibit 7.6, when a company is low with respect to developing either a globalization or multidomestic strategy, simply using an international division with the domestic structure is an appropriate way to handle international business. For some businesses, however, the basis for advantage may be a globalization strategy—selling the same products worldwide—in which case a global product division structure is appropriate. This structure will provide product managers with authority to handle their product lines worldwide. When a company's strategy is multidomestic through locally based customization, then a worldwide geographical structure is appropriate, with each country or region having subsidiaries modifying products and services to fit that locale.

In many instances, companies will have both global and local opportunities simultaneously, in which case the matrix structure or transnational model can be used. Part of the product line may need to be standardized globally, and other parts tailored to the needs of local countries, in which case the matrix structure may work. When the company achieves truly global size and scope beyond what can be handled by the matrix, the transnational model may be used. Next, we will discuss each of the structures in Exhibit 7.6 in more detail.

Exhibit 7.6

Model to Fit Organization Structure to International Advantages

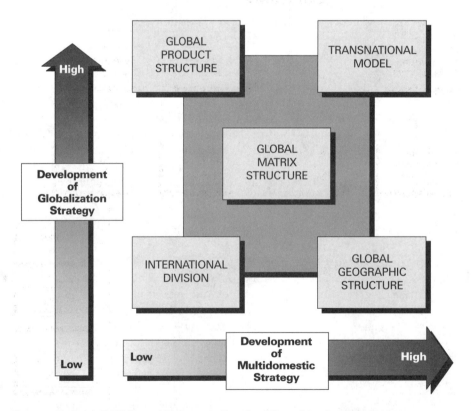

Source: Roderick E. White and Thomas A. Poynter, "Organizing for Worldwide Advantage," *Business Quarterly* (Summer 1989): 84–89. Adapted by permission of *Business Quarterly*, published by the Western Business School, the University of Western Ontario, London, Ontario, Canada.

International Division

As companies begin to explore international opportunities, they typically start with an export department that grows into an **international division**. The international division has a status equal to the other major departments or divisions within the company and is illustrated in Exhibit 7.7. The international division has its own hierarchy to handle business (licensing, joint ventures) in various countries, selling the products and services created by the domestic divisions, opening subsidiary plants, and in general moving the organization into more sophisticated international operations.

Although functional structures are often used domestically, they are less frequently used to manage a worldwide business.[43] Lines of functional hierarchy running around the world would extend too long, so some form of product or geographical structure is used to subdivide the organization into smaller units. Firms typically start with an international department and, depending on their strategy, later use product or geographic divisional structures, to which we will now turn.

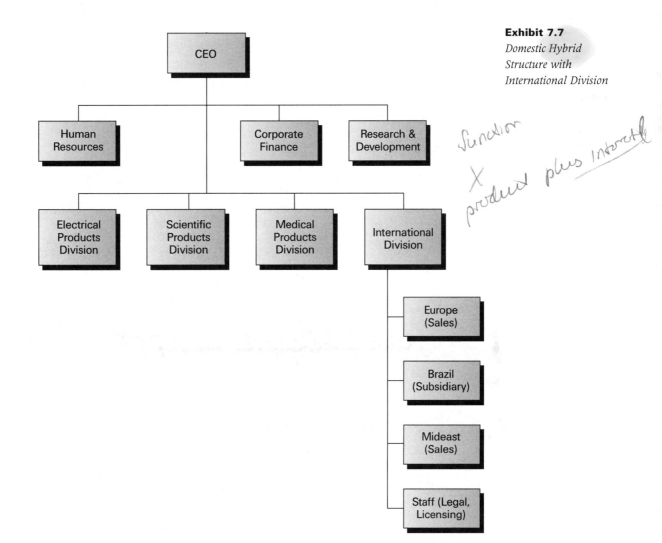

Exhibit 7.7
Domestic Hybrid Structure with International Division

STRUCTURAL DESIGNS FOR GLOBAL OPERATIONS

The international arena produces complex structures because of defined national boundaries and great distances. The structures most typically used by international firms are the global product structure and global geographic structure.

Global Product Division Structure

In a **global product structure,** the product divisions take responsibility for global operations in their specific product area. Each product division can organize for international operations as it sees fit. Each division manager is responsible for planning, organizing, and controlling all functions for the production and distribution of its products for any market around the world. The product-based structure works best when a division handles products that are technologically similar and can be standardized for marketing worldwide. As we saw in Exhibit 7.6, the global product structure works best when the company has opportunities for worldwide production and sale of standard products for all markets, thus providing economies of scale and standardization of production, marketing, and advertising.

Eaton Corporation has used a form of worldwide product structure, as illustrated in Exhibit 7.8. In this structure, the automotive components group, industrial group, and so on are responsible for manufacture and sale of products worldwide. The vice president of international is responsible for coordinators in each region, including a coordinator for Japan, Australia, South America, and northern Europe. The coordinators find ways to share facilities and improve production and delivery across all product lines sold in their region. These coordinators provide the same function as integrators described in Chapter 6.

The product structure is great for standardizing production and sales around the globe, but it also has problems. Often the product divisions do not work well together, competing instead of cooperating in some countries; and some countries may be ignored by product managers. The solution adopted by Eaton Corporation of using country coordinators who have a clearly defined role is a superb way to overcome these problems.

Global Geographic Division Structure

A worldwide regional organization divides the world into regions, each of which reports to the CEO. Each region has full control of functional activities in its geographical area. Companies that use this **global geographic structure** tend to have mature product lines and stable technologies. They find low-cost manufacturing within countries as well as different needs across countries for marketing and sales. Strategically, this structure can exploit many opportunities for regional or locally based competitive advantages.[44]

The problems encountered by senior management using a global geographic structure result from the autonomy of each regional division. For example, it is difficult to do planning on a global scale—such as new product R&D—because each division acts to meet only the needs of its region. New domestic technologies and products can be difficult to transfer to international markets because each division feels it will develop what it needs. Likewise, it is difficult to rapidly introduce products developed offshore into domestic markets; and there is often duplication of line and staff managers across regions. Companies such as Dow

Exhibit 7.8 *Partial Global Product Structure Used by Eaton Corporation*

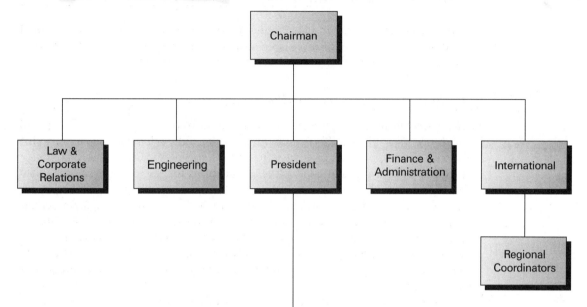

Source: Based on *New Directions in Multinational Corporate Organization* (New York: Business International Corp., 1981).

Chemical find ways to take advantage of the geographic structure while overcoming these problems.

For several years, Dow used a geographic structure of the form illustrated in Exhibit 7.9. Dow handled the problems of coordination across regions by creating a corporate-level product department to provide long-term planning and worldwide product coordination and communication. Six corporate product directors act as staff coordinators and also have authority to approve large capital investments and to move manufacturing of a product from one geographic location to another to best serve corporate needs. With this structure, Dow maintains its focus on each region and achieves coordination for overall planning, savings in administrative staff, and manufacturing and sales efficiency.[45]

Global Matrix Structure

We've discussed how Eaton used a global product division structure and found ways to coordinate across worldwide divisions. Dow Chemical used a global geographic division structure and found ways to coordinate across geographical regions. Each of these companies emphasized a single dimension. Recall from Chapter 6 that a matrix structure provides a way to achieve vertical and horizontal coordination

Exhibit 7.9 *Global Geographic Division Structure*

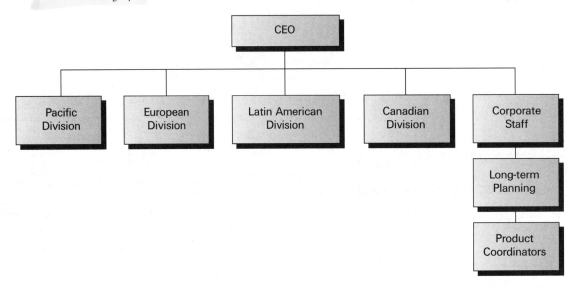

simultaneously along two dimensions. Matrix structures used by multinational corporations are similar to those described in Chapter 6, except that geographical distances for communication are greater and coordination is more complex.

The matrix works best when pressure for decision making balances the interests of both product standardization and geographical localization and when coordination to share resources is important. An excellent example of a **global matrix structure** that works extremely well is Asea Brown Boveri (ABB), an electrical equipment corporation headquartered in Zurich.

ABB owns 1,300 subsidiary companies, divided into 5,000 profit centers located in 140 countries. ABB uses a complex global matrix structure similar to Exhibit 7.10 to achieve worldwide economies of scale combined with local flexibility and responsiveness.

At the top are the chief executive officer and an international committee of top managers who hold frequent meetings around the world. Along one side of the matrix are sixty-five or so business areas located worldwide, into which ABB's products and services are grouped. Each business area leader is responsible for handling business on a global scale, allocating export markets, establishing cost and quality standards, and creating mixed-nationality teams to solve problems.

Along the other side of the matrix is a country structure: ABB has more than one hundred country managers, most of them citizens of the country in which they work. They run national companies and are responsible for local balance sheets, income statements, and career ladders. The matrix structure converges at the level of the 1,300 local companies. The presidents of local companies report to two bosses—the business arealeader, who is usually located outside the country, and the country president who runs the company of which the local organization is a subsidiary.[46]

In the language of Chapter 6, the CEO is the "top leader," the business area and country managers are "matrix bosses," and the presidents of local company affiliates are "two-boss employees." ABB is a large, successful company that manages to achieve the benefits of both product and geographic organizations through this matrix structure.

Exhibit 7.10 *Global Matrix Structure*

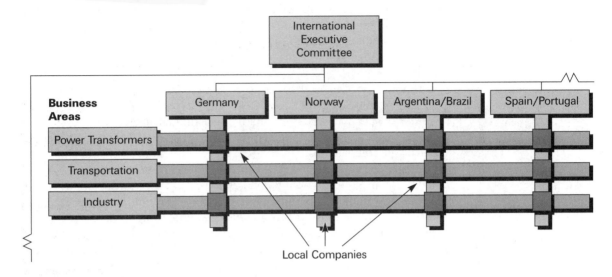

Local Companies

Transnational Model

The **transnational model** of organization structure may occur for huge multinational firms with subsidiaries in many countries that try to exploit both global and local advantages, and perhaps technological superiority, rapid innovation, and functional control. The matrix is effective for handling two issues (product and geographic), but more than two competitive issues requires a more complex form of structure. The transnational model represents the most current thinking about the kind of structure needed by complex global organizations such as N.V. Philips, illustrated in Exhibit 7.11. Headquartered in the Netherlands, Philips has operating units in 60 countries and is typical of global companies, such as Heinz, Unilever, or Procter & Gamble.[47]

The units in Exhibit 7.11 are far-flung. Achieving coordination, a sense of participation and involvement by subsidiaries, and a sharing of information, new technologies, and customers requires a complex and multidimensional form of structure. For example, a global corporation like Philips is so large that size itself is a problem when coordinating global operations. In addition, some subsidiaries may become so large that they no longer fit a narrow strategic role assigned to them by headquarters. While being part of a large organization, they also need autonomy for themselves and need to have impact on other parts of the organization.

The transnational model is much more than just an organization chart. It is a state of mind, a set of values, a shared desire to make a worldwide system work, and an idealized organization structure for effectively managing such a system. The transnational model cannot be given a precise definition, but the following characteristics distinguish it from and move it beyond a matrix structure.[48]

1. *The transnational model differentiates into many centers of different kinds.* The matrix structure had a single headquarters, a single center of control for each country, and a single center for each product line. The transnational operates on a principle of "flexible centralization." A transnational may

centralize some functions in one country, some in another, yet decentralize still other functions among its many geographically dispersed operations. An R&D center may be centralized in Holland and a purchasing center located in Sweden, while financial accounting responsibilities are decentralized to operations in many countries. A unit in Hong Kong may be responsible for coordinating activities across Asia, while activities for all other countries are coordinated by a large division headquarters in London.

2. *Subsidiary managers initiate strategy and innovations that become strategy for the corporation as a whole.* In traditional structures, managers have a strategic role only for their division. In a transnational, various centers and subsidiaries can shape the company from the bottom up because there is no notion of a single headquarters, no clear top-down corporate level responsibility.

   Managers at all levels in any country have authority to develop creative responses and initiate programs in response to emerging local trends, then disperse their innovations worldwide. Transnational companies recognize that different parts of the organization possess different capabilities. In addition, environmental demands and opportunities vary from country to country, and exposing the whole organization to this broader range of environmental stimuli can trigger greater learning and innovation. By ensuring that the entire organization has access to the combined knowledge, abilities, and intellectual capacities of all divisions and all employees, transnationals engage in continuous worldwide learning.

3. *Unification and coordination are achieved through corporate culture, shared vision and values, and management style rather than through the vertical hierarchy.* The transnational is essentially a horizontal structure. It is diverse, extended, and exists in a fluctuating environment so that standard rules, procedures, and close supervision are not appropriate.

   The very nature of the transnational organization dramatically expands the difficulty of unifying and coordinating operations. To achieve unity and coordination, organization leaders build a context of shared vision, values, and perspectives among managers, who in turn cascade these elements down through all parts of the organization. For example, people are often promoted by rotation through different jobs, divisions, and countries. Moreover, long experience with the company is highly valued because these people have been strongly socialized into the corporate culture. Experience plus rotation through different divisions and regions means that people share corporate culture and values sufficient for unity of purpose.

4. *Alliances are established with other company parts and with other companies.* Although resources and functions are widely dispersed, the transnational may integrate them through strong interdependencies. A world-scale production plant in Singapore may depend on world-scale component plants in Australia, Mexico, and Germany; major sales subsidiaries in turn depend on Singapore for finished products. In addition, each part of the organization can serve as an independent catalyst, bringing together unique elements with synergistic potential, perhaps other firms or subsidiaries from different countries, to improve its performance. These alliances may include joint ventures, cooperation with governments, and licensing arrangements.

The transnational model is truly a complex and "messy" way to conceptualize organization structure, but it is becoming increasingly relevant for large, global firms that treat the whole world as their playing field and do not have a single

Exhibit 7.11 *International Organizational Units and Interlinkages within N.V. Philips*

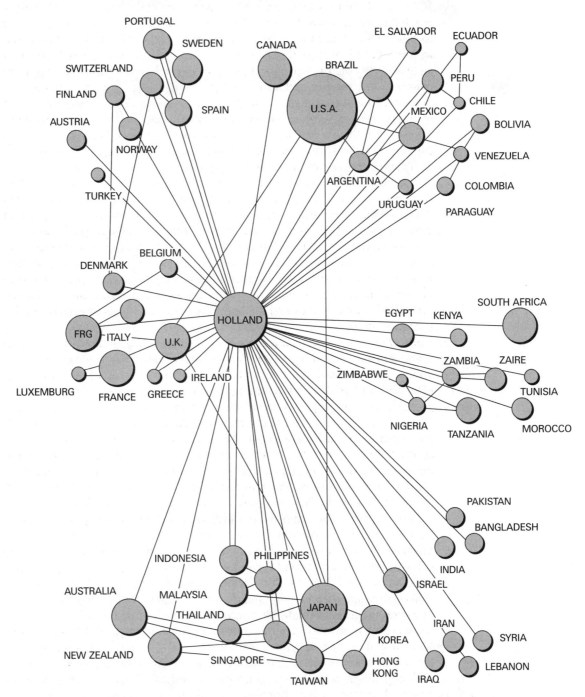

Source: Sumantra Ghoshal and Christopher A. Bartlett, "The Multinational Corporation as an Interorganizational Network," *Academy of Management Review* 15 (1990): 605. Used by permission.

country base. The autonomy of organizational parts gives strength to smaller units and allows the firm to take advantage of rapid change and competitive opportunities. To achieve this end a broad range of people throughout the global firm must develop capacity for strategic thinking and strategic action. Managers must follow their own instincts, using worldwide resources to achieve their local objectives. Strategy is the result of action in the sense that company parts seek to improve on their own rather than waiting for a strategy from the top. Indeed, each part of the company must be aware of the whole organization so its local actions will complement and enhance other company parts.

SUMMARY OF KEY ISSUES

The concepts about organization design in this chapter build upon the approaches to organizational structure and design described in Chapter 6. Significant global forces are causing American companies to find innovative designs and to extend operations overseas. The international forces include the dominant economies of Japan and Germany, newly industrialized countries, a shift toward market economies in Eastern Europe, and new power blocs. One response to these pressures is for domestic organizations to become more competitive. One significant innovation is the shift away from top-heavy, functionally organized structures toward horizontal structures. With a horizontal structure the focus is on processes rather than function, the hierarchy is flattened, and self-directed teams are empowered to make the decisions necessary to satisfy the customer.

The shift to a horizontal structure often begins with reengineering, one of the hottest concepts in management today. Reengineering means looking at how work processes can be designed for optimal performance in today's rapidly changing environment. Reengineering brings about changes in organization structure, culture, and information systems, and can produce dramatic results.

Another innovation is the dynamic network structure, which uses a free market approach rather than a vertical hierarchy. Separate companies or individuals are coordinated through contracts with a small headquarters organization. New contractors can be added as needed to respond immediately to changes in the environment.

Many companies are developing overseas operations to take advantage of the world markets. One way companies get involved internationally is through international strategic alliances, such as joint ventures or a consortia of independent organizations that share resources and access to one another's markets. Global work teams, made up of multinational members whose activities span multiple countries, are increasingly being used to help companies expand their operations into international markets.

Organizations typically evolve through four stages, beginning with a domestic orientation, shifting to an international orientation, then a multinational orientation, finally to a global orientation that sees the whole world as a potential market. Organizations initially use an export department, then an international division, and finally develop into a worldwide geographic or product division structure. Huge global companies may use a matrix or a transnational form of structure.

A global product structure is typically best when a company has many opportunities for globalization, which means products can be standardized and sold worldwide. A global geographic structure is typically used when a company's products and services have local country advantages, which means they do best when tailored to local needs and cultures. When an international company must succeed on two dimensions—global and local—simultaneously, the matrix structure is appropriate. When global companies must compete on multiple dimensions simultaneously, they may evolve toward a transnational model, which is a form of horizontal organization. The transnational differentiates into multiple centers; subsidiary managers initiate strategy and innovations for the company as a whole; and unity and coordination is achieved through corporate culture and shared values.

Discussion Questions

1. What do you see as the primary differences between horizontal corporations and traditional, functionally organized corporations?
2. What are the consequences to organizations of no single company or country being able to dominate global commerce?
3. How do self-directed teams differ from the cross-functional teams described in Chapter 6?
4. Would you like to work on a self-directed team where decisions are made by the team rather than by individuals and individual rewards are subordinated to team rewards? Discuss.
5. Because reengineering focuses on work processes that cut across functional boundaries, it leads to changes in organization structure. Why does this also cause significant changes in organizational culture and information systems?
6. How does the dynamic network structure enable an organization to respond rapidly in a changing, competitive environment?
7. Under what conditions should an organization consider a global product structure as opposed to a global geographic structure?
8. How does an international matrix structure differ from the domestic matrix structure described in Chapter 6?
9. Why do you think firms should join strategic alliances? Would they be better served to go it alone in international operations? Explain.
10. Describe the transnational model. Does this model seem workable in a huge global firm? Discuss.

Notes

1. William J. Holstein, "The Stateless Corporation," *Business Week*, 14 May 1990, 98–105.

2. Pete Engardio, with Robert D. Hof, Elisabeth Malkin, Neil Gross, and Karen Lowry Miller, "High-Tech Jobs All Over the Map," *Business Week*/21st Century Capitalism, 18 November 1994, 112–17.

3. Based on Tom Peters, "Prometheus Barely Unbound," *Academy of Management Executive* 4 (November 1990): 70–84.

4. John A. Byrne, "The Horizontal Corporation"; *Business Week*, 20 December 1993, 76-81. Thomas A. Stewart, "The Search for the Organization of Tomorrow," *Fortune*, 18 May 1992, 92–98.

5. Jack D. Orsburn, Linda Moran, Ed Musselwhite, and John H. Zenger, *Self-Directed Work Teams: The New American Challenge* (Homewood, Ill.: Business One Irwin, 1990).

6. Charles C. Mainz, David E. Keating, and Anne

Donnellon, "Preparing for an Organizational Change to Employee Self-Managed Teams: The Managerial Transition," *Organizational Dynamics* (Autumn 1990): 15–26.

7. Thomas Owens, "The Self-Managing Work Team," *Small Business Reports* (February 1991): 53–65; D. Brian Harrison and Henry P. Conn, "Mobilizing Abilities Through Teamwork," *Canadian Business Review*, Autumn 1994, 20–23.

8. Wendy Trueman, "Alternate Visions," *Canadian Business*, March 1991, 29–33.

9. Gregory G. Dess, Abdul M. A. Rasheed, Kevin J. McLaughlin, and Richard L. Priem, "The New Corporate Architecture," *Academy of Management Executive* 1995, Vol. 9, No. 3, 7–20.

10. Byrne, "The Horizontal Corporation."

11. Susan G. Cohen, "New Approaches to Teams and Teamwork," in Jay R. Galbraith, Edward E. Lawler III, & Associates, *Organizing for the Future: The New Logic for Managing Complex Organizations*, (San Francisco, Calif.: Jossey-Bass, 1993), 194–226.

12. Byrne, "The Horizontal Corporation."

13. Donna B. Stoddard, Sirkka L. Jarvenpaa, and Michael Littlejohn, "The Reality of Business Reengineering: Pacific Bell's Centrex Provisioning Process," *California Management Review*, Vol. 38, No. 3, Spring 1996, 57–76.

14. Thomas A. Stewart, "Reengineering: The Hot New Managing Tool," *Fortune*, 23 August 1993, 41–48; Brian S. Moskal, "Reengineering Without Downsizing," *IW*, 19 February 1996, 23–28.

15. S. L. Mintz, "The Reengineers: A Guide for the Perplexed," *CFO*, October 1994, 42–54.

16. A. J. Vogl, "Plugging in Change," *Across the Board*, October 1995, 24–31.

17. George Stalk, Jr. and Jill E. Black, "The Myth of the Horizontal Organization," *Canadian Business Review*, Winter 1994, 26–31.

18. A. J. Vogl, "Plugging in Change"; T. Wood Parker, "Real-World Reengineering: Supporting Organizational Change at Premier Bank," *National Productivity Review,* Spring 1996, 67-80.

19. Bob Lindgren, "Going Horizontal," *Enterprise*, April 1994, 20–25.

20. Charles C. Snow, Raymond E. Miles, and Henry J. Coleman, Jr., "Managing 21st Century Network Organizations," *Organizational Dynamics* 20 (Winter 1992); 5–19; Shawn Tully, "The Modular Corporation," *Fortune*, 8 February 1993, 106–14.

21. Raymond E. Miles and Charles C. Snow, "Fit Failure and the Hall of Fame," *California Management Review* 26 (Spring 1984): 10–28.

22. Richard L. Daft, *Management* 2d ed. (Chicago: Dryden Press, 1991).

23. Gregory G. Dess, Abdul M. A. Rasheed, Kevin J. McLaughlin, and Richard L. Priem, "The New Corporate Architecture," *Academy of Management Executive*, 1995, Vol. 9, No. 3, 7–20.

24. Echo Montgomery Garrett, "Innovation + Outsourcing = Big Success," *Management Review*, September 1994, 17–20.

25. Raymond E. Miles and Charles C. Snow, "The New Network Firm: A Spherical Structure Built on a Human Investment Philosophy," *Organizational Dynamics*, Spring 1995, 5–18, and Gregory G. Dess, Abdul M. A. Rasheed, Kevin J. McLaughlin, and Richard L. Priem, "The New Corporate Architecture."

26. Donna Brown, "Outsourcing: How Corporations Take Their Business Elsewhere," *Management Review* (February 1992): 16–19.

27. Snow, Miles, and Coleman, "Managing 21st Century Network Organizations."

28. Based heavily on Nancy J. Adler, *International Dimensions of Organizational Behavior*, 2d ed. (Boston: PWS-Kent, 1991); Theodore T. Herbert "Strategy and Multinational Organizational Structure: An Interorganizational Relationships Perspective," *Academy of Management Review* 9 (1984): 259–71; Laura K. Rickey, "International Expansion—U.S. Corporations: Strategy, Stages of Development and Structure," (Unpublished manuscript, Vanderbilt University, 1991).

29. Michael E. Porter, "Changing Patterns of International Competition," *California Management Review* 28 (Winter 1986): 9–40.

30. Holstein, "The Stateless Corporation."

31. David Lei and John W. Slocum, Jr., "Global Strategic Alliances: Payoffs and Pitfalls," *Organizational Dynamics* (Winter 1991): 17–29.

32. Ibid.

33. Stratford Sherman, "Are Strategic Alliances Working?" *Fortune*, 21 September 1992, 77–78; David Lei, "Strategies for Global Competition," *Long-Range Planning* 22 (1989): 102–09.

34. Lei, "Strategies For Global Competition."

35. Kathryn Rudie Harrigan, "Managing Joint Ventures: Part I," *Management Review* (February 1987): 24–41.

36. Kevin Kelly and Otis Port, with James Treece, Gail DeGeorge, and Zachary Schiller, "Learning from Japan," *Business Week*, 27 January 1992, 52–60; Dess, Rasheed, McLaughlin, and Priem, "The New Corporate Architecture."

37. Mary O'Hara-Devereaux and Robert Johansen, *Globalwork: Bridging Distance, Culture & Time* (San Francisco: Jossey-Bass, 1994).

38. Charles C. Snow, Scott A. Snell, Sue Canney Davison, and Donald C. Hambrick, "Use Transnational Teams to Globalize Your Company," *Organizational Dynamics*, Spring 1996, Vol. 24, No. 4, 50–67.

39. Ibid.

40. Mary O'Hara-Devereaux and Robert Johansen, *Globalwork: Bridging Distance, Culture & Time*, 227–28.

41. Kenichi Ohmae, "Managing in a Borderless World," *Harvard Business Review* (May–June 1989): 152–61.

42. Sumantra Ghoshal and Nitin Nohria, "Horses for Courses: Organizational Forms for Multinational Corporations," *Sloan Management Review* (Winter 1993): 23–25; Roderick E. White and Thomas A. Poynter, "Organizing for Worldwide Advantage," *Business Quarterly* (Summer 1989): 84–89.

43. John D. Daniels, Robert A. Pitts, and Marietta J. Tretter, "Strategy and Structure of U.S. Multinationals: An Exploratory Study," *Academy of Management Journal* 27 (1984): 292–307.

44. *New Directions in Multinational Corporate Organization* (New York: Business International Corporation, 1981).

45. Ibid.

46. William Taylor, "The Logic of Global Business: An Interview with ABB's Percy Barnevik," *Harvard Business Review* (March–April 1991): 91–105; Carla Rapoport, "A Tough Swede Invades the U.S.," *Fortune*, 29 January 1992, 76–79; Raymond E. Miles and Charles C. Snow, "The New Network Firm: A Spherical Structure Built on a Human Investment Philosophy," *Organizational Dynamics*, Spring 1995, 5–18; Manfred F.R. Kets de Vries, "Making a Giant Dance," *Across the Board*, October 1994, 27–32.

47. Sumantra Ghoshal and Christopher A. Bartlett, "The Multinational Corporation as an Interorganizational Network," *Academy of Management Review* 15 (1990): 603–25.

48. Gunnar Hedlund and Dag Rolander, "Action in Heterarchies: New Approaches to Managing the MNC," in Christopher A. Bartlett, Yves Doz, and Gunnar Hedlund, eds., *Managing the Global Firm* (New York: Routledge, 1990), 15–46; Gunnar Hedlund, "The Hypermodern MNC—A Heterarchy?" *Human Resource Management* 25 (Spring 1986): 9–35; Christopher A. Bartlett and Sumantra Ghoshal, *Managing Across Borders: The Transnational Solution* (Boston, Mass.: Harvard Business School Press), 1989.

part four

Organization Design Processes

4

chapter eight

Innovation and Change

While reading this chapter, think about your answers to the following questions:

- What five elements typically are needed for successful change to occur?

- What is the difference between radical change and incremental change?

- What are four types of change organizations can use to achieve strategic advantage?

- Why are different structures and management processes typically associated with each type of change?

- Why are total quality management and reengineering discussed in connection with people and culture change?

W hen asked about 3M's strategy, CEO L. D. DiSimone says, "We're going to do two principal things: be very innovative, and satisfy our customers in all aspects." The 3M Company, whose name is synonymous with innovation, has achieved its goal of getting 30 percent of sales from products less than four years old so consistently that it is considering raising the bar.[1] At 3M, innovation is a primary goal preached by top management and supported throughout the organization. Employees are encouraged to experiment and take risks. Strong cross-functional coordination and communication helps identify customer needs, turn new ideas into new products, and get them to the marketplace fast.

   Innovation is not limited to 3M. Today, every organization must change to survive. New discoveries and inventions quickly replace standard ways of doing things. The pace of change is revealed in the fact that the parents of today's college-age students grew up without cable television, VCRs, crease-resistant clothing, personal computers, compact disc players, video games, and talking checkout machines in supermarkets.

PURPOSE OF THIS CHAPTER

This chapter will explore how organizations change and how managers direct the innovation and change process. The next section describes the difference between incremental and radical change, the four types of change—technology, product, structure, people—occurring in organizations, and how to manage change successfully. The organization structure and management approach for facilitating each type of change is then discussed.

INNOVATE OR PERISH: THE STRATEGIC ROLE OF CHANGE

If there is one theme or lesson that emerges from previous chapters, it is that organizations must run fast to keep up with changes taking place all around them. Organizations must modify themselves not just from time to time, but all of the time. Large organizations must find ways to act like small, flexible organizations. Manufacturing firms need to reach out for new computer-integrated manufacturing technology and service firms for new information technology. Today's organizations must poise themselves to innovate and change, not only to prosper but merely to survive in a world of increased competition.[2] As illustrated in Exhibit 8.1, there are a number of environmental forces driving this need for major organizational change. Powerful forces associated with advancing technology, international economic integration, the maturing of domestic markets, and the shift to capitalism in formerly communist regions have brought about a globalized economy that impacts every business, from the largest to the smallest, creating more threats as well as more opportunities. To recognize and manage the threats and take advantage of the opportunities, today's companies are undergoing dramatic changes in all areas of their operations. As we saw in Chapter 7, many organizations are responding to global forces by reengineering business processes and shifting to a horizontal organization structure with self-directed teams. Some are adopting structural innovations, such as the network, to focus on their core competencies while outside specialists handle other activities. Others become involved in joint ventures, consortia, or virtual organizations to extend operations and markets internationally. In addition to these structural changes, today's organizations face the need for dramatic strategic and cultural change and for rapid innovations in technology and products.

In the past, stability was the norm and change occurred incrementally and infrequently. Today, organizational change is often dramatic and constant. For example, a key element in the success of PepsiCo in recent years has been its passion for change. Wayne Calloway, former CEO, insisted that the worst rule of management is "if it ain't broke, don't fix it." Calloway preached that in today's economy, "if it ain't broke, you might as well break it yourself, because it soon will be.[3]

Exhibit 8.1 *Forces Driving the Need for Major Organizational Change*

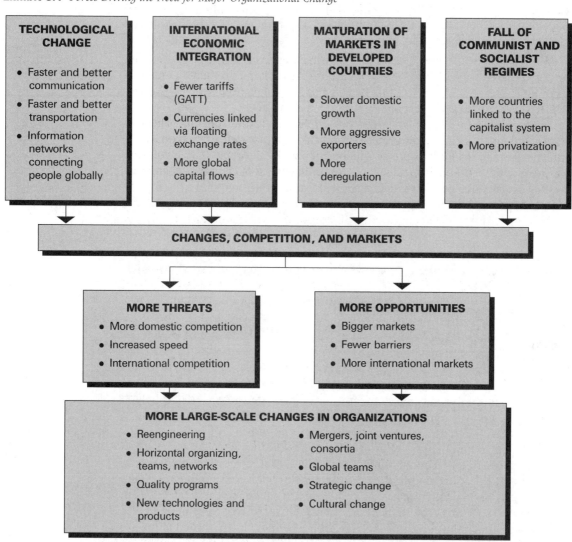

Source: From *The New Rules: How to Succeed in Today's Post-Corporate World* by John P. Kotter. Copyright © 1995 by John P. Kotter. Adapted with permission of The Free Press, a Division of Simon & Schuster.

Incremental Versus Radical Change

The changes used to adapt to the environment can be evaluated according to scope—that is, the extent to which changes are incremental or radical for the organization.[4] As summarized in Exhibit 8.2 **incremental change** represents a series of continual progressions that maintain the organization's general equilibrium and often affect only one organizational part. **Radical change,** by contrast, breaks the frame of reference for the organization, often creating a new equilibrium because the entire organization is transformed. For example, an incremental change is the implementation of sales teams in the marketing department, while a radical change is reengineering the organization to develop new products in only one year instead of four and maintaining one year as the new equilibrium.

For the most part, incremental change occurs through the established structure and management processes, and it may include new technologies—such as computer-integrated manufacturing technologies—and product improvements. Radical change involves the creation of a new structure and management processes. The technology is likely to be breakthrough, and new products thereby created will establish new markets.

As we have just discussed, there is a growing emphasis on the need for radical change because of today's turbulent, unpredictable environment.[5] Indeed, some experts argue that firms must be constantly changing their structures and management processes in response to changing demands.

One example of radical change was the revolution at Motorola that achieved an astounding six sigma quality (only 3.4 mistakes per million parts produced). This level of quality, previously considered impossible, became the new norm. Motorola is now aiming for the same level of quality in its administrative functions, such as financial recordkeeping and reporting.[6]

Corporate transformations and turnarounds are also considered radical change. A good example of a radical corporate transformation is Globe Metallurgical, Inc., which was a typical Rust Belt company in the early 1980s: old-fashioned, bureaucratic, slow-moving, and unresponsive to customers. Costs were high and quality was low. When Arden Sims took over as chief executive in 1984, the company was in a death spiral, sure to be run out of business by foreign competition. Over a period of eight years, Sims transformed Globe into today's top source for specialty metals for the chemical and foundry industries worldwide. The transformation involved fundamental changes in management systems, work structures, products, technology, and worker attitudes. Globe became the first small company to win a Malcolm Baldrige National Quality Award.[7]

Strategic Types of Change

Managers can focus on four types of change within organizations to achieve strategic advantage. These four types of change are summarized in Exhibit 8.3 as products and services, strategy and structure, people and culture, and technology. We touched on overall leadership and organizational strategy in Chapter 2, and we will touch these topics again along with corporate culture in Chapter 10. These factors provide an overall context within which the four types of change serve as a competitive wedge to achieve an advantage in the international environment. Each company has a unique configuration of products and services,

Exhibit 8.2

Incremental Versus Radical Change

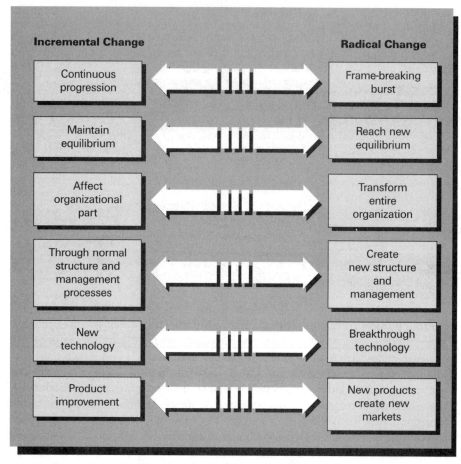

Incremental Change	Radical Change
Continuous progression	Frame-breaking burst
Maintain equilibrium	Reach new equilibrium
Affect organizational part	Transform entire organization
Through normal structure and management processes	Create new structure and management
New technology	Breakthrough technology
Product improvement	New products create new markets

Source: Based on Alan D. Meyer, James B. Goes, and Geoffrey R. Brooks, "Organizations in Disequilibrium: Environmental Jolts and Industry Revolutions," in George Huber and William H. Glick, eds., *Organizational Change and Redesign* (New York: Oxford University Press, 1992), 66–111; and Harry S. Dent, Jr., "Growth through New Product Development," *Small Business Reports* (November 1990): 30–40.

strategy and structure, people and culture, and technologies that can be focused for maximum impact upon the company's chosen markets.[8]

Technology changes are changes in an organization's production process, including its knowledge and skill base, that enable distinctive competence. These changes are designed to make production more efficient or to produce greater volume. Changes in technology involve the techniques for making products or services. They include work methods, equipment, and work flow. For example, in a university, technology changes are changes in techniques for teaching courses. As another example, Globe Metallurgical changed its production process using breakthrough furnace technology.

Product and service changes pertain to the product or service outputs of an organization. New products include small adaptations of existing products or entirely new product lines. New products are normally designed to increase the market share or to develop new markets, customers, or clients. Globe Metallurgical shifted its product line to high-margin specialty metals, which helped take the company global and into highly profitable niche markets. The Saturn automobile developed by General Motors is a product change.

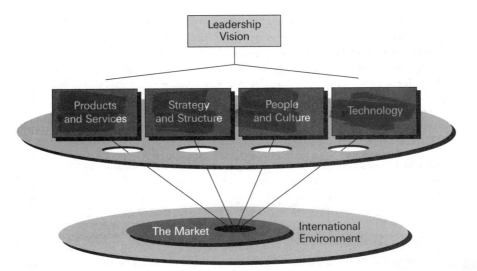

Exhibit 8.3
The Four Types of Change Provide a Strategic Competitive Wedge

Source: Joseph E. McCann, "Design Principles for an Innovating Company," *Academy of Management Executive* 5 (May 1991): 76–93. Used with permission.

Strategy and structure changes pertain to the administrative domain in an organization. The administrative domain involves the supervision and management of the organization. These changes include changes in organization structure, strategic management, policies, reward systems, labor relations, coordination devices, management information and control systems, and accounting and budgeting systems. Structure and system changes are usually top-down, that is, mandated by top management, whereas product and technology changes may often come from the bottom up. The structure at Globe Metallurgical was changed after managers discovered the power of flexible work teams when they were forced to run the furnaces during a year-long strike. When workers came back on the job, management instituted a new team structure. A system change instituted by management in a university might be a new merit pay plan. Corporate downsizing is another example of top-down structure change.

People and culture changes refer to changes in the values, attitudes, expectations, beliefs, abilities, and behavior of employees. An organization may wish to hire only the best people or to upgrade the leadership ability of key managers. Changes in communication networks and improved problem-solving and planning skills of employees are people changes. In transformations and turnarounds, the entire culture of the organization is changed. In the old days at Globe Metallurgical, employees were suspicious of management, who dictated new policies without consulting workers. One of the results of Globe's transformation is a new culture that values employee empowerment and involvement, a new respect for management, and a new commitment to quality.

Change Interdependence. The four types of changes in Exhibit 8.3 are interdependent—a change in one often means a change in another. A new product may require changes in the production technology, or a change in structure may require new employee skills. For example, when Shenandoah Life Insurance Company acquired new computer technology to process claims, the technology was not fully utilized until clerks were restructured into teams of five to seven members that were compatible with the technology. The structural change was an outgrowth of the technology change. In a manufacturing company, engineers introduced robots and advanced manufacturing technologies, only to find that the technology placed greater demands on employees. Upgrading employee skills required a change in wage systems. Organizations are interdependent systems, and changing one part often has implications for other organization elements.

Elements for Successful Change

Regardless of the type or scope of change, there are identifiable stages of innovation, which generally occur as a sequence of events, though innovation stages may overlap.[9]

In the research literature on innovation, **organizational change** is considered the adoption of a new idea or behavior by an organization.[10] **Organizational innovation**, in contrast, is the adoption of an idea or behavior that is new to the organization's industry, market, or general environment.[11] The first organization to introduce a new product is considered the innovator, and organizations that copy are considered to adopt changes. For purposes of managing change, however, the terms *innovation* and *change* will be used interchangeably because the **change process** within organizations tends to be identical whether a change is early or late with respect to other organizations in the environment.

Innovations typically are assimilated into an organization through a series of steps or elements. Organization members first become aware of a possible innovation, evaluate its appropriateness, and then evaluate and choose the idea.[12] The required elements of successful change are summarized in Exhibit 8.4. For a change to be successfully implemented, managers must make sure each element occurs in the organization. If one of the elements is missing, the change process will fail.

1. Ideas. Although creativity is a dramatic element of organizational change, creativity within organizations has not been widely and systematically studied. No company can remain competitive without new ideas; change is the outward expression of those ideas.13 An idea is a new way of doing things. It may be a new product or service, a new management concept, or a new procedure for working together in the organization. Ideas can come from within or from outside the organization.

2. *Need.* Ideas are generally not seriously considered unless there is a perceived need for change. A perceived need for change occurs when managers see a gap between actual performance and desired performance in the organization. For example, IBM executives perceived a strong need for structural change after the company posted operating losses for two consecutive years. Sometimes, ideas are generated to meet a perceived need; other times, a new idea occurs first and will stimulate consideration of problems it will solve or opportunities it provides.

3. *Adoption.* Adoption occurs when decision makers choose to go ahead with a proposed idea. Key managers and employees need to be in agreement to support the change. For a major organizational change, the decision might require the signing of a legal document by the board of directors. For a small change, adoption might occur with informal approval by a middle manager. When Ray Kroc was CEO of McDonald's, he made the adoption decision about innovations such as the Big Mac and Egg McMuffin.

Exhibit 8.4 *Sequence of Elements for Successful Change*

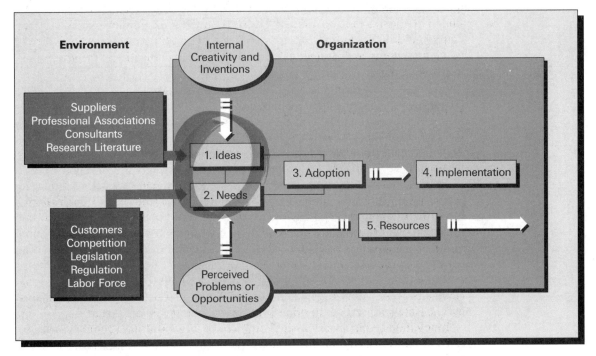

4. *Implementation.* Implementation occurs when organization members actually use a new idea, technique, or behavior. Materials and equipment may have to be acquired, and workers may have to be trained to use the new idea. Implementation is a very important step because without it, previous steps are to no avail. Implementation of change is often the most difficult part of the change process. Until people use the new idea, no change has actually taken place.

5. *Resources.* Human energy and activity are required to bring about change. Change does not happen on its own; it requires time and resources, for both creating and implementing a new idea. Employees have to provide energy to see both the need and the idea to meet that need. Someone must develop a proposal and provide the time and effort to implement it.

At 3M there is an unwritten but widely understood rule that its 8,300 researchers can spend up to 15 percent of their time working on any idea of their choosing, without management approval. Most innovations go beyond ordinary budget allocations and require special funding. At 3M, exceptionally promising ideas become "pacing programs" and receive high levels of funding for further development.

At S. C. Johnson & Son, a $250,000 seed fund has been set up for anyone with a promising new product idea. Other companies use committees and task forces, as described in Chapter 6, to focus resources on a change.

One point about Exhibit 8.4 is especially important. Needs and ideas are listed simultaneously at the beginning of the change sequence. Either may occur first. Many organizations adopted the computer, for example, because it seemed a promising way to improve efficiency. The search for a polio vaccine, on the other hand, was stimulated by a severe need. Whether the need or the idea occurs first, for the change to be accomplished, each of the steps in Exhibit 8.4 must be completed.

TECHNOLOGY CHANGE

In today's rapidly changing world, any company that isn't constantly developing, acquiring, or adapting new technology will likely be out of business in a few years. However, organizations face a contradiction when it comes to technology change, for the conditions that promote new ideas are not generally the best for implementing those ideas for routine production. An innovative organization is characterized by flexibility, empowered employees, and the absence of rigid work rules.[14] As discussed earlier in this book, an organic, free-flowing organization is typically associated with change and is considered the best organization form for adapting to a chaotic environment.

The flexibility of an organic organization is attributed to people's freedom to create and introduce new ideas. Organic organizations encourage a bottom-up innovation process. Ideas bubble up from middle- and lower-level employees because they have the freedom to propose ideas and to experiment. A mechanistic structure, on the other hand, stifles innovation with its emphasis on rules and regulations, but it is often the best structure for efficiently producing routine products. The challenge for organizations is to create both organic and mechanistic conditions within organizations to achieve both innovation and efficiency. To achieve both aspects of technological change, many organizations use the ambidextrous approach.

The Ambidextrous Approach

Recent thinking has refined the idea of organic versus mechanistic structures with respect to innovation creation versus innovation utilization. For example, sometimes an organic structure generates innovative ideas but is not the best structure for using those ideas.[15] In other words, the initiation and the utilization of change are two distinct processes. Organic characteristics such as decentralization and employee freedom are excellent for initiating ideas; but these same conditions often make it hard to use a change because employees are less likely to comply. Employees can ignore the innovation because of decentralization and a generally loose structure.

How does an organization solve this dilemma? One approach is for the organization to be **ambidextrous**—to incorporate structures and management processes that are appropriate to both the creation and use of innovation.[16] The organization can behave in an organic way when the situation calls for the initiation of new ideas and in a mechanistic way to implement and use the ideas.

An example of the ambidextrous approach is the Freudenberg-NOK auto parts factory in Ligonier, Indiana. Shifting teams of twelve, including plant workers, managers, and outsiders, each spend three days creating ideas to cut costs and boost productivity in various sections of the plant. At the end of the three days, team members go back to their regular jobs, and a new team comes in to look for even more improvements. Over a year's time, there are approximately forty of these GROWTTH (Get Rid of Waste Through Team Harmony) teams roaming through the sprawling factory. Management has promised that no one will be laid off as a result of suggestions from GROWTTH teams, which further encourages employees to both create and use innovations.[17]

Techniques for Encouraging Technology Change

Freudenberg-NOK has created both organic and mechanistic conditions in the factory. Some of the techniques used by many companies to maintain an ambidextrous approach are switching structures, separate creative departments, venture teams, and corporate entrepreneurship.

Switching Structures. **Switching structures** means an organization creates an organic structure when such a structure is needed for the initiation of new ideas.[18] Some of the ways organizations have switched structures to achieve the ambidextrous approach are as follows.

- Philips Corporation, a building materials producer in Ohio, each year creates groups of five employees from various departments—up to 150 teams—to work together for five days to improve Philips products. After the five days of organic brainstorming and problem solving, the company switches back to running things on a more mechanistic basis as the improvements are implemented into the system.[19]
- Lockheed's famous Skunk Works, a secret research and development subsidiary, was purposely isolated from the corporation's sprawling bureaucracy. Staffed with creative mavericks not afraid to break conventions, Skunk Works has been responsible for some of Lockheed's greatest innovations. Chief Executive Daniel M. Tellup counts on the innovators at Skunk Works to help Lockheed maintain its technological edge as the defense industry shrinks and becomes more competitive.[20]
- The NUMMI plant, a Toyota subsidiary located in Fremont, California, creates a separate, organically organized cross-functional subunit, called the Pilot Team, to design production processes for new car and truck models. When the model they are preparing moves into production, workers return to their regular jobs on the shop floor.[21]

Each of these organizations found creative ways to be ambidextrous, establishing organic conditions for developing new ideas in the midst of more mechanistic conditions for implementing and using those ideas.

Creative Departments. In many large organizations the initiation of innovation is assigned to separate **creative departments.**[22] Staff departments, such as research and development, engineering, design, and systems analysis, create changes for adoption in other departments. Departments that initiate change are organically structured to facilitate the generation of new ideas and techniques. Departments that use those innovations tend to have a mechanistic structure more suitable for efficient production. Exhibit 8.5 indicates how one department is responsible for creation and another department implements the innovation.

Raytheon's New Products Center, in operation for twenty-five years, illustrates how creativity and entrepreneurial spirit can coexist with discipline and controls. The center has been responsible for many technical innovations, including industry-leading combination ovens, which added microwave capabilities to

Exhibit 8.5

*Division of Labor
between
Departments to
Achieve Changes
in Technology*

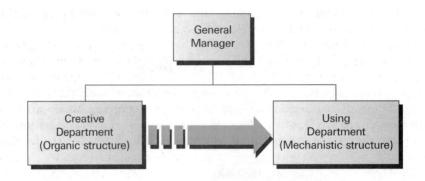

conventional stoves. The New Products Center provides autonomy and freedom for staff to explore new ideas, yet staff must also establish a working relationship with other departments so that innovations meet a genuine need for Raytheon departments.[23]

Venture Teams. **Venture teams** are a recent technique used to give free reign to creativity within organizations. Venture teams are often given a separate location and facilities so they are not constrained by organizational procedures. Dow Chemical created an innovation department that has virtually total license to establish new venture projects for any department in the company. Convergent Technologies uses the name "strike force" for a separate team that will develop a new computer. The team is cut loose to set up its own company and pursue members' ideas. The venture groups are kept small so they have autonomy and no bureaucracy emerges.

A new venture team is a small company within a large company. To giant companies like Eastman Kodak and AT&T, new venture teams are essential to free creative people from the bureaucracy. Eastman Kodak has launched fourteen new ventures since 1984. Each is like a company-within-a-company that explores such ideas as computerized photo imaging, lithium batteries, or technology to project computer images on a large screen. AT&T has created eleven venture companies, one of which developed Pixel Machines, which offer striking capability to produce sharp pictures on a computer terminal. These venture companies are carefully nurtured and are given freedom from the AT&T bureaucracy.[24]

Corporate Entrepreneurship. Corporate entrepreneurship attempts to develop an internal entrepreneurial spirit, philosophy, and structure that will produce a higher than average number of innovations.[25] Corporate entrepreneurship may involve the use of creative departments and new venture teams as described above, but it also attempts to release the creative energy of all employees in the organization. The most important outcome is to facilitate **idea champions**, which go by a variety of names, including advocate, intrapreneur, or change agent. Idea champions provide the time and energy to make things happen. They fight to overcome natural resistance to change and to convince others of the merit of a new idea.[26] For example, when Texas Instruments reviewed fifty successful and unsuccessful technical projects, one fascinating finding emerged. Every failure was characterized by the absence of a volunteer champion. There was no one who passionately believed in the idea, who pushed the idea through all the necessary obstacles to make it work. Texas Instruments took this finding so seriously that now its number one criterion for approving new technical projects is the presence of a zealous champion.[27]

Companies encourage idea champions by providing freedom and slack time to creative people. IBM and General Electric allow employees to develop new technologies without company approval. Known as "bootlegging," the unauthorized research often pays big dividends. As one IBM executive said, 'We wink at it. It pays off. It's just amazing what a handful of dedicated people can do when they are really turned on."[28]

Idea champions usually come in two types. The **technical or product champion** is the person who generates or adopts and develops an idea for a technological innovation and is devoted to it, even to the extent of risking position or prestige. The **management champion** acts as a supporter and sponsor to shield and promote an idea within the organization.[29] The management champion sees the potential application and has the prestige and authority to get it a fair hearing and to allocate resources to it. Technical and management champions often work together because a technical idea will have a greater chance of success if a manager can be found to sponsor it. At Black & Decker, Peter Chaconas is a technical champion. He invented the Piranha circular saw blade, which is a best-selling tool accessory. Next, he invented the Bullet, which is a bit for home power drills and is the first major innovation in this product in almost 100 years. Chaconas works full-time designing products and promoting their acceptance. Randy Blevins, his boss, acts as management champion for Chaconas's ideas.[30]

NEW PRODUCTS AND SERVICES

Many of the concepts described for technology change are also relevant to the creation of new products and services. However, in many ways, new products and services are a special case of innovation because they are used by customers outside the organization. Since new products are designed for sale in the environment, uncertainty about the suitability and success of an innovation is very high.

New Product Success Rate

Research has explored the enormous uncertainty associated with the development and sale of new products.[31] To understand what this uncertainty can mean to organizations, just consider such flops as RCA's VideoDisc player, which lost an estimated $500 million, or Time Incorporated's *TV-Cable Week*, which lost $47 million. Producing new products that fail is a part of business in all industries. One survey examined 200 projects in 19 chemical, drug, electronics, and petroleum laboratories to learn about success rates. To be successful, the new product had to pass three stages of development: technical completion, commercialization, and market success. The findings about success rates are given in Exhibit 8.6.

On the average, only 57 percent of all projects undertaken in the R&D laboratories achieved technical objectives, which means all technical problems were solved and the projects moved on to production. Of all projects that were started, however, less than one-third (31 percent) were fully marketed and commercialized. Several projects failed at this stage because production estimates or test market results were unfavorable.

	Probability
Technical completion (technical objectives achieved)	.57
Commercialization (full-scale marketing)	.31
Market success (earns economic returns)	.12

Source: Based on Edwin Mansfield, J. Rapaport, J. Schnee, S. Wagner, and M. Hamburger, *Research and Innovation in Modern Corporations* (New York: Norton, 1971), 57.

Finally, only 12 percent of all projects originally undertaken achieved economic success. Most of the commercialized products did not earn sufficient returns to cover the cost of development and production. This means that only about one project in eight returns a profit to the company. New product development is thus very risky.

Reasons for New Product Success

The next question to be answered by research was, "Why are some products more successful than others?" Further studies indicated that innovation success was related to collaboration between technical and marketing departments. Successful new products and services seemed to be technologically sound and also carefully tailored to customer needs.[32] A study called Project SAPPHO examined 17 pairs of new product innovations, with one success and one failure in each pair, and concluded the following:

1. Successful innovating companies had a much better understanding of customer needs and paid much more attention to marketing.
2. Successful innovating companies made more effective use of outside technology and outside advice, even though they did more work in-house.
3. Top management support in the successful innovating companies was from people who were more senior and had greater authority.

Thus, there is a distinct pattern of tailoring innovations to customer needs, making effective use of technology, and having influential top managers support the project. These ideas taken together indicate that the effective design for new product innovation is associated with horizontal linkage across departments.

Horizontal Linkage Model

The organization design for achieving new product innovation involves three components—departmental specialization, boundary spanning, and horizontal linkages. These components are similar to the differentiation and integration ideas in Chapter 3 and the information linkage mechanisms in Chapter 6. Exhibit 8.7 illustrates these components in the **horizontal linkage model**.

Specialization. The key departments in new product development are R&D, marketing, and production. The specialization component means that the personnel in all three of these departments are highly competent at their own tasks. The three departments are differentiated from each other and have skills, goals, and attitudes appropriate for their specialized functions.

Boundary Spanning. This component means each department involved with new products has excellent linkage with relevant sectors in the external environment. Personnel in R&D are linked to professional associations and to colleagues in other R&D departments. They are aware of recent scientific developments. Marketing personnel are closely linked to customer needs. They listen to what customers have to say, and they analyze competitor products and suggestions by distributors. For example, Kimberly-Clark had astonishing success with its Huggies Pull-Ups training pants because of market research, which meant working with hundreds of customers individually and in groups to learn their needs.[33]

Horizontal Linkages. This component means that technical, marketing, and production people share ideas and information. Research people inform marketing of new technical developments to learn whether the developments are applicable to customers. Marketing people provide customer complaints and information to R&D to use in the design of new products. People from both R&D and marketing coordinate with production because new products have to fit within production capabilities so costs are not exorbitant. The decision to launch a new product is ultimately a joint decision among all three departments.

At General Electric, members of the R&D department have a great deal of freedom to imagine and invent, and then they have to shop their ideas around other departments and divisions, sometimes finding applications for new technologies that are far from their original intentions. As a result, one study shows that of 250 technology products GE undertook to develop over a four-year period, 150 of them produced major applications, far above the U.S. average of about one success out of ten. Boeing's engineers and manufacturers worked side-by-side on the new 777 project, sometimes bringing in representatives from outside suppliers, airline customers, maintenance, and finance.[34] Famous innovation failures—such as Weyerhaeuser's UltraSoft diapers, General Mills' Benefit cereal, Anheuser-Busch's LA Beer, and RJR Nabisco's Premier smoke-

Exhibit 8.7 *Horizontal Linkage Model for New Product Innovations*

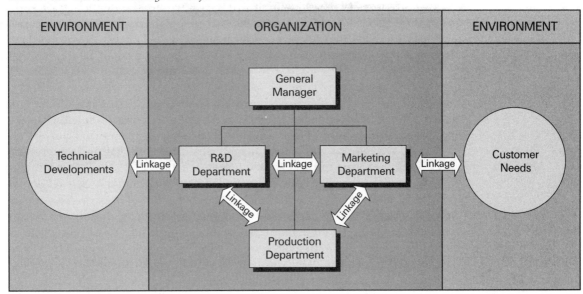

less cigarettes—usually violate the horizontal linkage model. Employees fail to connect with customer needs, or internal departments fail to adequately share needs and coordinate with one another.

Companies are increasingly using cross-functional teams for product development to ensure a high level of communication and coordination from the beginning. The functional diversity increases both the amount and the variety of information for new product development, enabling the design of products that meet customer needs and circumventing manufacturing and marketing problems.[35]

Achieving Competitive Advantage with Product Innovation

For many companies, creating new products is a critical way to adapt and survive in a rapidly changing environment.[36] Getting new products to market fast and developing products that can compete in a competitive international market, are key issues for companies like Xerox, Hewlett-Packard, and Chrysler. One authority on time-based competition has said that the old paradigm for success—"provide the most value for the least cost"—has been updated to "provide the most value for the least cost in the least elapsed time."[37]

To gain business, companies are learning to develop new products and services incredibly fast. Whether the approach is called the horizontal linkage model, concurrent engineering, companies without walls, the parallel approach, or simultaneous coupling of departments, the point is the same—get people working together simultaneously on a project rather than in sequence. Many companies are learning to sprint to market with new products.

By breaking down the walls between functions, Chrysler delivered its new Neon in a speedy forty-two months, and has now cut the time it takes to go from concept to production to less than three years.[38] Hewlett-Packard has made speed a top priority, getting products out the door twice as fast and urging employees to rethink every process in terms of speed. A printer that once took fifty-four months to develop is now on the market in twenty-two. Speed is becoming a major competitive issue and requires the use of cross-functional teams and other horizontal linkages.[39]

Another critical issue is designing products that can compete on a global scale and successfully marketing those products internationally. Chrysler is already making and selling 50,000 Jeep Cherokees a year in China and is opening a small factory in Vietnam. Ford is enhancing its global competitiveness by using global teleconferencing to link car design teams into a single unified group. Black & Decker has also been redesigning its product development process to become a stronger international player. To make global product development faster and more effective, new products are developed by cross-functional Project Delivery Teams, which are answerable to a Global Business Unit Team.[40]

Failing to pay attention to global horizontal linkages can hurt companies trying to compete internationally. The Dutch giant Philips Electronics NV was certain its compact-disk interactive player called "The Imagination Machine" would be a hit in the crucial U.S. market, and ultimately, the rest of the world. Five years later, the product, which was promoted as an interactive teaching aid and was so complex it required a 30-minute sales demonstration, had all but disappeared from the shelves. Marketing employees, salespeople, and major customers had crucial information that would have helped Philips understand the U.S. market, but by the time executives gathered the information and tried to change course, it was too late. "We should have done things differently," said one Philips executive. "The world isn't as easy as it seems."[41] When companies enter the arena of intense international competition, horizontal coordination across countries is essential to new product development.

STRATEGY AND STRUCTURE CHANGE

The preceding discussion focused on new production processes and products which are based in the technology of an organization. The expertise for such innovation lies within the technical core and professional staff groups such as research and engineering. This section turns to an examination of structural and strategy changes.

All organizations need to make changes in their strategies and structures from time to time. In the past, when the environment was relatively stable, most organizations focused on small, incremental changes to solve immediate problems or take advantage of new opportunities. However, over the past decade, companies throughout the world have faced the need to make radical changes in strategy, structure, and management processes to adapt to new competitive demands.[42] Many organizations are reducing the work force, cutting out layers of management, and decentralizing decision-making. There is a strong shift toward more horizontal structures, with teams of front-line workers empowered to make decisions and solve problems on their own. Some companies are breaking totally away from traditional organization forms and moving toward network strategies and structures. Global competition and rapid technological change will likely lead to even greater strategy-structure realignments over the next decade.

These types of changes are the responsibility of the organization's top managers, and the overall process of change is typically different from the process for innovation in technology or new products.

The Dual-Core Approach

The dual-core approach compares administrative and technical changes. Administrative changes pertain to the design and structure of the organization itself, including restructuring, downsizing, teams, control systems, information systems, and departmental grouping. Research into administrative change suggests two things. First, administrative changes occur less frequently than do technical changes. Second, administrative changes occur in response to different environmental sectors and follow a different internal process than do technology-based changes.[43] The **dual-core approach** to organizational change identifies the unique processes associated with administrative change.[44]

Organizations—schools, hospitals, city governments, welfare agencies, government bureaucracies, and many business firms—can be conceptualized as having two cores: a technical core and an administrative core. Each core has its own employees, tasks, and environmental domain. Innovation can originate in either core.

The administrative core is above the technical core in the hierarchy. The responsibility of the administrative core includes the structure, control, and coordination of the organization itself and concerns the environmental sectors of government, financial resources, economic conditions, human resources, and competitors. The technical core is concerned with the transformation of raw materials into organizational products and services and involves the environmental sectors of customers and technology.[45]

The findings from research comparing administrative and technical change suggest that a mechanistic organization structure is appropriate for frequent administrative changes, including changes in goals, strategy, structure, control systems, and personnel.[46] For example, administrative changes in policy, regulations, or control systems are more critical than technical changes in many government organizations that are bureaucratically structured. Organizations that successfully adopt many administrative changes often have a larger administrative ratio, are larger in size, and are centralized and formalized compared with organizations that adopt many technical changes.[47] The reason is the top-down implementation of changes in response to changes in the government, financial, or legal sectors of the environment. In contrast, if an organization has an organic structure, lower-level employees have more freedom and autonomy and, hence, may resist top-down initiatives. An organic structure is more often used when changes in organizational technology or products are important to the organization.

The innovation approaches associated with administrative versus technical change are summarized in Exhibit 8.8. Technical change, such as changes in production techniques and innovation technology for new products, is facilitated by an organic structure, which allows ideas to bubble upward from lower- and middle-level employees. Organizations that must adopt frequent administrative changes tend to use a top-down process and a mechanistic structure. For example, policy changes, such as the adoption of tough no-smoking policies by companies like Park Nicollet Medical Center in Minnesota, are facilitated by a top-down approach. Downsizing and restructuring are nearly always managed top-down, such as when Ronald E. Compton, CEO of Aetna Life and Casualty Company, announced plans to slash over 4,000 jobs and drop two of the company's product lines.[48]

The point of the dual-core approach is that many organizations—especially not-for-profit and government organizations—must adopt frequent administrative

Exhibit 8.8
Dual-Core Approach to Organization Change

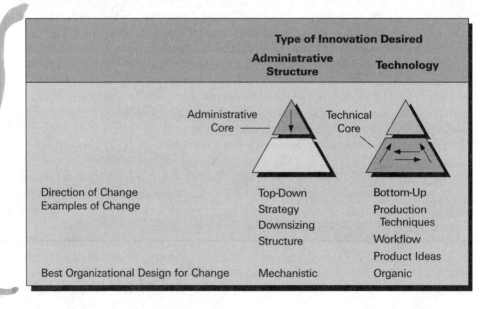

	Type of Innovation Desired	
	Administrative Structure	Technology
	Administrative Core	Technical Core
Direction of Change	Top-Down	Bottom-Up
Examples of Change	Strategy	Production Techniques
	Downsizing	Workflow
	Structure	Product Ideas
Best Organizational Design for Change	Mechanistic	Organic

changes, so a mechanistic structure may be appropriate. For example, research into civil service reform found that the implementation of administrative innovation was extremely difficult in organizations that had an organic technical core. The professional employees in a decentralized agency could resist civil service changes. By contrast, organizations that were considered more bureaucratic in the sense of high formalization and centralization adopted administrative changes readily.[49]

What about business organizations that normally are technologically innovative in bottom-up fashion but suddenly face a crisis and need to reorganize? Or consider a technically innovative, high-tech firm that must reorganize frequently or must suddenly cut back to accommodate changes in production technology or the environment. Technically innovative firms may suddenly have to restructure, reduce the number of employees, alter pay systems, disband teams, or form a new division.[50] The answer is to use a top-down change process. The authority for strategy and structure change lies with top management, who should initiate and implement the new strategy and structure to meet environmental circumstances. Employee input may be sought, but top managers have the responsibility to direct the change. Downsizing, restructuring, and reorganizing are common terms for what happens in times of rapid change and global competition. Often, strong top-down changes follow the installation of new top management.

When Carol Bartz took over as CEO of Autodesk, Inc., the world's sixth largest PC software company, profits were falling and stock prices declining sharply. Bartz came in with a mandate for change and introduced a first for the company: a management hierarchy. To ease the stress on freethinking employees accustomed to "doing their own thing," she instituted a series of brown-bag chats to hear their side and build faith in the new structure. Although the change was not easy, Autodesk's revenues have doubled since Bartz joined the company.[51] She recognized that it is important for top management to communicate with employees, while being responsible for firmly directing restructuring changes. Restructuring and especially downsizing can be painful and difficult, so top managers should move quickly and authoritatively to make both as humane as possible.[52]

PEOPLE AND CULTURE CHANGE

Organizations are made up of people and their relationships with one another. Changes in strategy, structure, technologies, and products do not happen on their own, and changes in any of these areas involve people changes as well. The target of people change is the values, skills, and attitudes of individual employees. Employees must learn how to use new technologies, or market new products, or work effectively in a team-based structure.

In a world where any organization can purchase new technology, the motivation, skill, and commitment of employees can provide the competitive edge. Human resource systems can be designed to attract, develop, and maintain an efficient force of employees.

Sometimes achieving a new way of thinking requires a focused change on the underlying corporate culture values and norms. In the last decade, numerous large corporations, including DuPont, Rockwell, and Amoco, have undertaken some type of culture change initiative. Changing corporate culture fundamentally shifts how work is done in an organization and generally leads to renewed commitment and empowerment of employees and a stronger bond between the company and its customers.[53]

Some recent trends that generally lead to significant changes in corporate culture are reengineering, the shift to horizontal forms of organizing, and the implementation of total quality management programs, all of which require employees to think in new ways about how work is done.

Organizational development programs also focus on changing old culture values to new ways of thinking, including greater employee participation and empowerment and developing a shared companywide vision.

Reengineering/Horizontal Organization

As described in the previous chapter, reengineering is a cross-functional initiative involving the radical redesign of business processes to produce dramatic performance improvements. Because the focus is on process rather than function, reengineering generally leads to a shift in organization structure from vertical to horizontal, requiring major changes in corporate culture and management philosophy.

In the horizontal organization, managers and front-line workers need to understand and embrace the concepts of teamwork, empowerment, and cooperation. Everyone throughout the organization needs to share a common vision and goals so they have a framework within which to make decisions and solve problems. Managers shift their thinking to view workers as colleagues rather than "cogs in a wheel," while workers learn to accept not only greater freedom and power, but also the higher level of responsibility—and stress—that comes with it. Mutual trust, risk-taking, and tolerance for mistakes become key cultural values in the horizontal organization. Most top managers have little experience dealing with the complexities of human behavior; yet, they should remember that significant people and culture changes are crucial to the success of reengineering and the shift to horizontal forms of organization.

Total Quality Management

The approach known as **total quality management** infuses quality values throughout every activity within a company. The concept is simple: no longer are quality control departments and other formal control systems in charge of checking parts and improving quality. Companies are training their workers and then trusting them to infuse quality into everything they do. The results of TQM programs can be staggering. After noticing that Ford Motor Company cut $40 billion out of its operating budget by adopting quality principles and changing corporate culture, the Henry Ford Health System instituted a quality program. Gail Warden, CEO, says of quality programs at Henry Ford and other U.S. health care institutions, "We have to change the way we practice medicine" to get health care costs down and remain competitive in the rapidly changing health care industry.[54]

By requiring organizationwide participation in quality control, TQM requires a major shift in mind-set for both managers and workers. In TQM, workers must be trained, involved, and empowered in a way that many managers at first find frightening. One way in which workers are involved is through **quality circles**, groups of six to twelve volunteer workers who meet to analyze and solve problems.

Another technique of total quality management is known as **benchmarking,** a process whereby companies find out how others do something better than they do and then try to imitate or improve on it. Through research and field trips by small teams of workers, companies compare their products, services, and business practices with those of their competitors and other companies. Xerox, AT&T, DuPont, Eastman Kodak, and Motorola are constantly benchmarking. Ford Motor Company shamelessly benchmarked more than 200 features of the Ford Taurus against seven competitors, including the Honda Accord, Chevy Lumina, and Nissan Maxima, helping to make the Taurus one of the top-selling cars.[55]

While the focus of total quality programs is generally on improving quality and productivity, it always involves a significant people and culture change. Managers should be prepared for this aspect before undertaking quality programs.

Organizational Development

One method of bringing about culture change is known as organizational development, which focuses on the development and fulfillment of people to bring about improved performance. In the 1970s, **organizational development** evolved as a separate field in the behavioral sciences focused on examining how work is done and how people who do the work feel about their efficiency and effectiveness. Rather than using a step-by-step procedure to solve a specific problem, organizational development is a process of fundamental change in an organization's culture.[56]

Organizational development uses knowledge and techniques from the behavioral sciences to improve performance through trust, open confrontation of problems, employee empowerment and participation, the design of meaningful work, cooperation between groups, and the full use of human potential. Its practitioners believe the best performance occurs by breaking down hierarchical and authoritarian approaches to management. However, consistent with the arguments in the environment and technology chapters, research has shown that the OD approach may not enhance performance or satisfaction in stable business environments and for routine tasks.[57]

Changing organizational culture is not easy, but organizational development techniques can smooth the process. For example, OD can help managers and employees think in new ways about human relationships, making the transition to more participative management less stressful. The U.S. Agriculture Department's Animal and Plant Health Inspection Service (APHIS) began its OD unit after an experimental team approach among plant protection and quarantine workers at Miami International Airport failed. Workers were frustrated and demoralized because neither they nor their supervisors had the necessary skills to work in a team environment. Organizational development specialists were hired to help develop the change in mindset needed for a team approach. The APHIS organization development unit has continued to grow and has helped the agency win a string of Hammer Awards from Vice President Al Gore for its aggressive approach to reinventing government.[58]

Organizational Development Culture Change Interventions

Organizational development interventions involve training of specific groups or of everyone in the organization. For OD intervention to be successful, senior management in the organization must see the need for OD and provide enthusiastic support for the change. Techniques used by many organizations for improving people skills through OD include the following.

Survey Feedback. Organizational personnel are surveyed about their job satisfaction, attitudes, performance, leader behavior, climate, and quality of work relationships. A consultant feeds back the data to stimulate a discussion of organizational problems. Plans are then made for organizational change.[59]

Off-Site Meetings. The process of change may begin with an off-site meeting to formulate a vision for the desired outcome of the process, create a microcosm of the new culture, and devise ways to instill new cultural values throughout the organization. Off-site meetings limit interference and distractions, enabling participants to focus on a new way of doing things. At MasterBrand Industries, for example, the culture change process began with an off-site meeting of 75 key managers who would be the catalysts for remaking MasterBrand into a cross-functional team-based organization. The managers formed into "advocate teams" that examined all the company's activities from a cross-functional perspective and began to develop a cooperative team spirit. The goal of the three-day conference was to break down vertical walls that had isolated departments and sow the seeds of a self-sustaining team culture from top management down to the shop floor.[60]

Team Building. **Team building** activities promote the idea that people who work together can work as a team. A work team can be brought together to discuss conflicts, goals, the decision-making process, communication, creativity, and leadership. The team can then plan to overcome problems and improve results.[61] Team building activities are also used in many companies to train task forces, committees, and new product development groups.

Intergroup Activities. Representatives from different groups are brought together in a mutual location to surface conflict, diagnose its causes, and plan improvement in communication and coordination. This type of intervention has been applied to union-management conflict, headquarters-field office conflict, interdepartmental conflict, and mergers.[62]

In today's world, the work force is becoming more and more diverse, and organizations are constantly changing in response to environmental uncertainty and increasing international competition. Organizational development interventions can respond to these new realities as organizations head toward the 21st century.[63]

SUMMARY OF KEY ISSUES

Organizations face a dilemma. Managers prefer to organize day-to-day activities in predictable, routine manner. However, change—not stability—is the natural order of things in today's global environment. Thus, organizations need to build in change as well as stability, to facilitate innovation as well as efficiency.

Most change in organizations is incremental, but there is a growing emphasis on the need for radical change. Four types of change—products and services, strategy and structure, people and culture, and technology—may give an organization a competitive edge, and managers can make certain each of the necessary ingredients for change is present.

For technical innovation, which is of concern to most organizations, an organic structure that encourages employee autonomy works best because it encourages a bottom-up flow of ideas. Other approaches are to establish a separate department charged with creating new technical ideas, establish venture teams, and encourage idea champions. New products and services generally require cooperation among several departments, so horizontal linkage is an essential part of the innovation process.

For changes in strategy and structure, a top-down approach is typically best. These innovations are in the domain of top administrators who take responsibility for restructuring, for downsizing, and for changes in policies, goals, and control systems.

People changes are also generally the responsibility of top management. Sometimes, the entire corporate culture must change. Some recent trends that lead to significant changes in corporate culture are reengineering, the shift to horizontal forms of organizing, and the implementation of total quality management programs, all of which require employees to think in new ways. Organizational development is another process for bringing about culture change by focusing on the development and fulfillment of people to bring about improved performance. All of these approaches typically favor organic conditions that lead to employee participation in decisions, interesting work, and the freedom to initiate ideas to improve their jobs.

Discussion Questions

1. How is the management of radical change likely to differ from the management of incremental change?
2. How are organic characteristics related to changes in technology? To administrative changes?
3. Describe the dual-core approach. How does administrative change normally differ from technology change? Discuss.
4. How might organizations manage the dilemma of needing both stability and change? Discuss.
5. "Bureaucracies are not innovative." Discuss.
6. A noted organization theorist said, "Pressure for change originates in the environment; pressure for stability originates within the organization." Do you agree? Discuss.
7. Of the five elements required for successful change, which element do you think managers are most likely to overlook? Discuss.
8. Why do total quality management programs lead to significant culture changes when these programs are aimed at improving quality and productivity? Discuss.
9. The manager of R&D for a drug company said only 5 percent of the company's new products ever achieve market success. He also said the industry average is 10 percent and wondered how his organization might increase its success rate. If you were acting as a consultant, what advice would you give him concerning organization structure?

Notes

1. L. D. DiSimone, comments about 3M in "How Can Big Companies Keep the Entrepreneurial Spirit Alive?" *Harvard Business Review*, November–December 1995, 184–85, and Thomas A. Stewart, "3M Fights Back," *Fortune*, 5 February 1996, 94–99.

2. Based on John P. Kotter, *Leading Change* (Boston, Mass.: Harvard Business School Press, 1996), 18–20.

3. Laura Zinn, "Pepsi's Future Becomes Clearer," *Business Week*, 1 February 1993, 74–75; Patricia Sellers, "Pepsi Keeps on Going after No. 1," *Fortune*, 11 March 1991, 61–70.

4. David A. Nadler and Michael L. Tushman, "Organizational Frame Bending: Principles for Managing Reorientations," *Academy of Management Executive* 3 (1989): 199–204.

5. William H. Davidow and Michael S. Malone, *The Virtual Corporation* (New York: Harper-Collins, 1992); Gregory G. Dess, Abdul M. A. Rasheed, Kevin J. McLaughlin, and Richard L. Priem, "The New Corporate Architecture," *Academy of Management Executive*, 1995, Vol. 9, No. 3, 7–20.

6. Barbara Ettorre, "How Motorola Closes Its Books In Two Days," *Management Review,* March 1995, 40–44.

7. Bruce Rayner, "Trial-by-Fire Transformation: An Interview With Globe Metallurgical's Arden C. Sims," *Harvard Business Review,* (May–June 1992): 117–29.

8. Joseph E. McCann, "Design Principles for an Innovating Company," *Academy of Management Executive* 5 (May 1991): 76–93.

9. Richard A. Wolfe, "Organizational Innovation: Review, Critique and Suggested Research Directions," *Journal of Management Studies* 31:3 (May 1994), 405–31.

10. John L. Pierce and Andre L. Delbecq, "Organization Structure, Individual Attitudes and Innovation," *Academy of Management Review* 2 (1977): 27–37; Michael Aiken and Jerald Hage, "The Organic Organization and Innovations," *Sociology* 5 (1971): 63–82.

11. Richard L. Daft, "Bureaucratic versus Nonbureaucratic Structure in the Process of Innovation and Change," in Samuel Bacharach, ed., *Perspectives in Organizational Sociology: Theory and Research* (Greenwich, Conn.: JAI Press, 1982), 129–66.

12. Alan D. Meyer and James B. Goes, "Organizational Assimilation of Innovations: A Multilevel Contextual Analysis," *Academy of Management Journal* 31 (1988): 897–923.

13. Richard W. Woodman, John E. Sawyer, and Ricky W. Griffin, "Toward a Theory of Organizational Creativity," *Academy of Management Review* 18 (1993): 293–321; Alan Farnham, "How to Nurture Creative Sparks," *Fortune*, 10 January 1994, 94–100.

14. D. Bruce Merrifield, "Intrapreneurial Corporate Renewal," *Journal of Business Venturing* 8 (September 1993): 383–89; Linsu Kim, "Organizational Innovation and Structured" *Journal of Business Research* 8 (1980): 225–45; Tom Burns and G. M. Stalker, *The Management of Innovation* (London: Tavistock Publications, 1961).

15. James Q. Wilson, "Innovation in Organization: Notes toward a Theory," in James D. Thompson, ed., *Approaches to Organizational Design* (Pittsburgh: University of Pittsburgh Press, 1966), 193–218.

16. J. C. Spender and Eric H. Kessler, "Managing the Uncertainties of Innovation: Extending Thompson (1967)," *Human Relations* Vol. 48, No. 1, 1995, 35–56; Robert B. Duncan, "The Ambidextrous Organization: Designing Dual Structures for Innovation," in Ralph H. Killman, Louis R. Pondy, and Dennis Slevin, eds., *The Management of Organization*, Vol. 1 (New York: North-Holland, 1976), 167–88.

17. James B. Treece, "Improving the Soul of an Old Machine," *Business Week*, 25 October 1993, 134–36.

18. Edward F. McDonough III and Richard Leifer, "Using Simultaneous Structures to Cope with Uncertainty," *Academy of Management Journal* 26 (1983): 727–35.

19. John McCormick and Bill Powell, "Management for the 1990s," *Newsweek*, 25 April 1988, 47–48.

20. Eric Schine, "Out at the Skunk Works, the Sweet Smell of Success," *Business Week*, 26 April 1993, 101.

21. Paul S. Adler, Barbara Goldoftas, and David I. Levine, "Flexibility Versus Efficiency? A Case Study of Model Changeovers in the Toyota Production System," Working Paper, School of Business Administration, University of Southern California, Los Angeles, 1996.

22. Judith R. Blau and William McKinley, "Ideas, Complexity, and Innovation," *Administrative Science Quarterly* 24 (1979): 200–19.

23. Rosabeth Moss Kanter, Jeffrey North, Lisa Richardson, Cynthia Ingols, and Joseph Zolner, "Engines of Progress: Designing and Running Entrepreneurial Vehicles in Established Companies: Raytheon's New Product Center, 1969–1989," *Journal of Business Venturing* 6 (March 1991): 145–63.

24. Rosabeth Moss Kanter, Lisa Richardson, Jeffrey North, and Erika Morgan, "Engines of Progress: Designing and Running Entrepreneurial Vehicles in Established Companies: The New Venture Process at Eastman Kodak, 1983–1989," *Journal of Business Venturing* 6 (January 1991): 63–82; Gene Bylinsky, "The New Look at America's Top Lab," *Fortune*, 1 February 1988, 60–64.

25. Daniel F. Jennings and James R. Lumpkin, "Functioning Modeling Corporate Entrepreneurship: An Empirical Integrative Analysis," *Journal of Management* 15 (1989): 485–502.

26. Jane M. Howell and Christopher A. Higgins, Champions of Technology Innovation," *Administrative Science Quarterly* 35 (1990): 317–41; Jane M. Howell and Christopher A. Higgins, "Champions of Change: Identifying, Understanding, and Supporting Champions of Technology Innovations," *Organizational Dynamics* (Summer 1990): 40–55.

27. Thomas J. Peters and Robert H. Waterman, Jr., *In Search of Excellence* (New York: Harper & Row, 1982).

28. Ibid., 205.

29. Peter J. Frost and Carolyn P. Egri, "The Political Process of Innovation," in L. L. Cummings and Barry M. Staw, eds., *Research in Organizational Behavior*, Vol. 13 (New York: JAI Press, 1991), 229–95; Jay R. Galbraith, "Designing the Innovating Organization," *Organizational Dynamics* (Winter 1982): 5–25; Marsha Sinatar, "Entrepreneurs, Chaos, and Creativity—Can Creative People Really Survive Large Company Structure?" *Sloan Management Review* (Winter 1985): 57–62.

30. "Black & Decker Inventory Makes Money for Firm By Just Not 'Doing the Neat Stuff,'" *Houston Chronicle*, 25 December 1987, Sec. 3. p. 2.

31. Christopher Power with Kathleen Kerwin, Ronald Grover, Keith Alexander, and Robert D. Hof, "Flops," *Business Week*, 16 August 1993, 76–82; Modesto A. Maidique and Billie Jo Zirger, "A Study of Success and Failure in Product Innovation: The Case of the U.S. Electronics Industry," *IEEE Transactions in Engineering Management* 31 (November 1984): 192–203; Edwin Mansfield, J. Rapaport, J. Schnee, S. Wagner, and M. Hamburger, *Research and Innovation in Modern Corporations* (New York. Norton, 1971); Antonio J. Bailetti and Paul F. Litva, "Integrating Customer Requirements into Product Designs," *Journal of Product Innovation Management* 12 (1995): 3–15.

32. Shona L. Brown and Kathleen M. Eisenhardt, "Product Development: Past Research, Present Findings, and Future Directions," *Academy of Management Review* 1995, Vol. 20, No. 2, 343–78; F. Axel Johne and Patricia A. Snelson, "Success Factors in Product Innovation: A Selective Review of the Literature," *Journal of Product Innovation Management* 5 (1988): 114–28; Science Policy Research Unit, University of Sussex, *Success and Failure in Industrial Innovation* (London: Centre for the Study of Industrial Innovation, 1972).

33. Ronald B. Lieber, "Storytelling: A New Way to Get Close to Your Customer," *Fortune*, 3 February 1997, 102–08.

34. Amal Kumar Naj, "GE's Latest Invention: A Way to Move Ideas from Lab to Market," *The Wall Street Journal*, 14 June 1990, Al, A9; Dora Jones Yang, "Boeing Knocks Down the Walls Between the Dreamers and the Doers," *Business Week*, 28 October 1991, 120–21.

35. Shona L. Brown and Kathleen M. Eisenhardt, "Product Development: Past Research Present Findings, and Future Directions," *Academy of Management Review*, 1995, Vol. 20, No. 2, 343–78, and Dan Dimancescu and Kemp Dwenger, "Smoothing the Product Development Path," *Management Review* (January 1996): 36–41.

36. Kathleen M. Eisenhardt and Behnam N. Tabrizi, "Accelerating Adaptive Processes: Product Innovation in the Global Computer Industry," *Administrative Science Quarterly*, 40 (1995): 84–110.

37. George Stalk, Jr., "Time and Innovation," *Canadian Business Review*, Autumn 1993, 15–18.

38. Marshall Loeb, "Empowerment That Pays Off," *Fortune*, 20 March 1995, 145–46.

39. Robert D. Hof, "From Dinosaur to Gazelle: HP's Evolution Was Painful but Necessary." *Business*

Week/Reinventing America, 1992, 65; Karne Bronikowski, "Speeding New Products to Market," *Journal of Business Strategy* (September–October 1990): 34–37.

40. Dan Dimancescu and Kemp Dwenger, "Smoothing the Product Development Path," *Management Review*, January 1996, 36–41.

41. Jeffrey A. Trachtenberg, "How Philips Flubbed Its U. S. Introduction of Electronic Product," *The Wall Street Journal*, 28 June 1996, A1.

42. Raymond E. Miles, Henry J. Coleman, Jr., and W. E. Douglas Creed, "Keys to Success in Corporate Redesign," *California Management Review*, Vol. 37, No. 3, Spring 1995, 128–45.

43. Fariborz Damanpour and William M. Evan, "Organizational Innovation and Performance: The Problem of 'Organizational Lag,'" *Administrative Science Quarterly* 29 (1984): 392–409; David J. Teece, "The Diffusion of an Administrative Innovation," *Management Science* 26 (1980): 464–70; John R. Kimberly and Michael J. Evaniski, "Organizational Innovation: The Influence of Individual, Organizational and Contextual Factors on Hospital Adoption of Technological and Administrative Innovation," *Academy of Management Journal* 24 (1981): 689–713; Michael K. Moch and Edward V. Morse, "Size, Centralization, and Organizational Adoption of Innovations," *American Sociological Review* 42 (1977): 716–25, Mary L. Fennell, "Synergy, Influence, and Information in the Adoption of Administrative Innovation," *Academy of Management Journal* 27 (1984): 113–29.

44. Richard L. Daft, "A Dual-Core Model of Organizational Innovation," *Academy of Management Journal* 21 (1978): 193–210.

45. Daft, "Bureaucratic versus Nonbureaucratic Structure"; Robert W. Zmud, "Diffusion of Modern Software Practices: Influence of Centralization and Formalization," *Management Science* 28 (1982): 1421–31.

46. Daft, "A Dual-Core Model of Organizational Innovation"; Zmud, "Diffusion of Modern Software Practices."

47. Fariborz Damanpour, "The Adoption of Technological, Administrative, and Ancillary Innovations: Impact of Organizational Factors," *Journal of Management* 13 (1987): 675–88.

48. Mark Landler with Ronald Grover, "Aetna's Heavy Ax," *Business Week*, 14 February 1994, 32.

49. Gregory H. Gaertner, Karen N. Gaertner, and David M. Akinnusi, "Environment, Strategy, and the Implementation of Administrative Change: The Case of Civil Service Reform," *Academy of Management Journal* 27 (1984): 525–43.

50. Claudia Bird Schoonhoven and Mariann Jelinek, "Dynamic Tension in Innovative, High Technology Firms: Managing Rapid Technology Change Through Organization Structure," in Mary Ann Von Glinow and Susan Albers Mohrman, eds., *Managing Complexity in High Technology Organizations* (New York: Oxford University Press, 1990), 90–118.

51. Lawrence M. Fisher, "Imposing a Hierarchy on a Gaggle of Techies," *New York Times*, 29 November 1992, F4; and Katherine and Richard Green "Executive Privilege: The 20 Best-Paid Women in Corporate America," *Working Woman*, January 1997, 27–30, 58–68.

52. David Ulm and James K. Hickel, "What Happens After Restructuring?" *Journal of Business Strategy* (July–August 1990): 37–41; John L. Sprague, "Restructuring and Corporate Renewal: A Manager's Guide," *Management Review* (March 1989): 34–36.

53. Benson L. Porter and Warrington S. Parker, Jr., "Culture Change," *Human Resource Management* 31 (Spring–Summer 1992): 45–67.

54. Ron Winslow, "Healthcare Providers Try Industrial Tactics to Reduce Their Costs," *The Wall Street Journal*, 3 November 1993, A1, A16.

55. Jeremy Main, "How to Steal the Best Ideas Around," *Fortune*, 19 October 1992, 102–06.

56. W. Warner Burke, *Organization Development: A Process of Learning and Changing*, 2nd ed. (Reading, Mass.: Addison-Wesley Publishing, 1994).

57. Michael Beer and Elisa Walton, "Developing the Competitive Organization: Interventions and Strategies," *American Psychologist* 45 (February 1990): 154–61.

58. James Thompson, "Rogue Workers, Change Agents," *Government Executive*, April 1996, 46–49.

59. David A. Nadler, *Feedback and Organizational Development: Using Databased Methods* (Reading, Mass.: Addison-Wesley, 1977), 5–8.

60. Patrick Flanagan, "The ABCs of Changing Corporate Culture," *Management Review*, July 1995, 57–61.

61. Wendell L. French and Cecil H. Bell, Jr., *Organization Development* (Englewood Cliffs, N.J.: Prentice-Hall, 1978), 117–29.

62. Paul F. Buller, "For Successful Strategic Change: Blend OD Practices with Strategic Management," *Organizational Dynamics* (Winter 1988): 42–55.

63. Jyotsna Sanzgiri and Jonathan Z. Gottlieb, "Philosophic and Pragmatic Influences on the Practice of Organization Development, 1950–2000," *Organizational Dynamics* (Autumn 1992): 57–69.

9

chapter nine

Information Technology and Organizational Control

While reading this chapter, think about your answers to the following questions:

- How can managers design information support systems to meet the information processing requirements of diverse divisions or departments?

- How might information technology be used to achieve strategic advantage through low-cost leadership or differentiation?

- What are the differences among market, bureaucratic, and clan control and the conditions under which each should be emphasized in an organization?

Information and control are essential components of organizations. Today, companies in all industries are taking advantage of new information technology to improve organizational control and decision making and to maintain a competitive edge in the face of increasing global competition and rising customer demands for speed, quality, and value. Information technology can empower employees by giving them the complete information they need to do their jobs well and opportunities to propose new ways of doing things. It can also increase the brainpower of the organization and enable the company to move to a higher level of quality and customer service.

PURPOSE OF THIS CHAPTER

Managers spend 80 percent of their time actively exchanging information.[1] They need this information to hold the organization together. For example, the vertical and horizontal information linkages described in Chapter 6 are designed to provide managers with relevant data for decision making and evaluation. Moreover, control systems depend on information. The first part of this chapter examines information processing requirements in organizations and then evaluates how technology helps meet the requirements and provides a strategic advantage. Then we will examine mechanisms of organizational control and how information technology assists in management control.

INFORMATION REQUIREMENTS

Information is the lifeblood of organizations because information feeds decision making about such things as structure, technology, and innovation and because information is the lifeline to suppliers and customers. Organizations should be designed to provide both the correct amount and richness of information to managers. Before moving into information technology and design, however, one must understand what information is.

Information is that which alters or reinforces understanding, while **data** are the input of a communication channel.[2] Data are tangible and include the number of words, telephone calls, or pages of computer printout sent or received. Data do not become information unless people use it to improve their understanding. Managers want information, not data. Organizational information systems should provide information rather than data to managers.

Information Amount and Richness

The factors that shape organizational information processing are summarized in Exhibit 9.1. Changes in the environment, large size, and nonroutine or interdependent technologies may create both higher uncertainty and higher ambiguity for managers in organizations.[3] **Uncertainty** is the absence of information; when uncertainty is high, a great amount of information has to be acquired and processed.[4] **Information amount** is the volume of data about organizational activities that is gathered and interpreted by organization participants. Under

Exhibit 9.1

*Uncertainty and
Ambiguity Influence
Information
Processing Amount
and Channels*

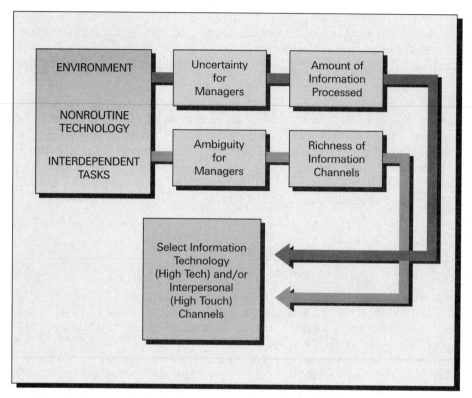

conditions of high uncertainty, data can be gathered that will answer questions and reduce uncertainty. Often this data can be provided by technology-based information systems, called **high tech** for short.

Information ambiguity means issues cannot be objectively analyzed and understood, and additional data cannot be gathered that will resolve an issue. Encountering an ambiguous situation means managers process richer information and discuss the situation with each other to create a solution, since external data does not provide an answer. Face-to-face discussion is **high touch** and enables managers to understand ill-defined issues and reach agreement to the best of their ability about how to respond.

The formal definition of **information richness** is the information carrying capacity of data.[5] Some data are highly informative and provide deeper, richer understanding to managers, especially for ambiguous issues. The communication channels used in organizations can be roughly organized into a continuum of four categories ranging from highest to lowest in richness. Channels low in richness are considered lean because they are effective for conveying a large amount of data and facts.

1. Face-to-face is the richest medium. It provides many cues, such as body language and facial expression. Immediate feedback allows understanding to be checked and corrected. This channel is best for mitigating ambiguity, enabling managers to create a shared understanding.
2. Telephone and other personal electronic media such as voice mail are next in richness, representing a relatively rich channel because feedback is fast and messages are personally focused, although visual cues are missing.
3. Written, addressed documents—such as letters, memos, notes, and faxes—are lower still in richness. Feedback is slow compared with richer media, and visual cues are minimal.

4. Written, impersonally addressed documents—including bulletins, standard computer reports, computer databases, and printouts—are the leanest channels. These documents are not amendable to feedback and are often quantitative in nature. This channel is best for conveying a large amount of precise data to numerous people.

At Connor Formed Metal Products, a job-shop manufacturer of springs and other components, computer technology is used to automatically figure price, production, and delivery answers when a customer calls with a new order. A lean channel such as impersonal computer technology is effective for this application because uncertainty is high and a substantial amount of data must be processed to calculate answers. However, when a managerial problem is ambiguous, computer technology is not as effective as face-to-face communication. For example, a company wanted to develop a new concept for a restaurant and there was no database that would tell it which concept would succeed. The response was to pick a date or a place as a restaurant theme and to form a team of experts to *create* a solution. The team included chefs, architects, designers, and artists. The group stayed focused on this issue and brainstormed for several days until they created all of the details for the restaurant. The result, Ed Debevic's, has been a smashing success in Beverly Hills and Chicago.[6]

In today's global business world, face-to-face communication may not always be possible. New forms of communication such as videoconferencing and groupware, which enable colleagues around the world to share information and ideas, are increasingly and effectively being used for ambiguous problems.

INFORMATION TECHNOLOGY AND THE ORGANIZATION

Recall from Chapter 4 that advanced information technology—including executive information systems, groupware, and work flow automation—has impact on organization structure.

We will first examine this impact on structure and then discuss how information systems have gradually evolved toward a variety of applications at all levels in organizations.

New Organization Structures and Information Technology

An important aspect of organizational structure is the way in which the parts of an organization communicate and coordinate with one another and with other organizations.[7] As we discussed in previous chapters, vertical linkages coordinate activities between the top and bottom of the organization, while horizontal linkages are used to coordinate activities across departments. Advances in information technology can reduce the need for middle managers and administrative support staff, resulting in leaner organizations with fewer hierarchical levels. In some organizations, such as Microsoft and Andersen Consulting, front-line employees communicate directly with top managers through e-mail. Information technology can also provide stronger linkages across departments and plays a significant role in the shift to horizontal forms of organizing. Coordination no longer depends on physical proximity; teams of workers from various functions can communicate and collaborate electronically.

New technology enables the electronic communication of richer, more complex information and removes the barriers of time and distance that have traditionally defined organization structure. A special kind of team, the virtual team, uses computer technology to tie together geographically distant members working toward a common goal. Virtual teams can be formed within an organization whose plants and offices are scattered across the country or around the world. Whirlpool Corp.'s North American Appliance Group in Evansville, Indiana, used a virtual team made up of members from the U.S., Brazil, and Italy to develop its chlorofluorocarbon-free refrigerator. A company may also use virtual teams in partnership with suppliers or even competitors to pull together the best minds to complete a project or speed a new product to market.[8]

An organization structure that takes the virtual approach a step further is the network, described in Chapter 7. Key activities are performed by a headquarters organization, with other functions outsourced to separate companies or individuals connected electronically to the central office. The speed and ease of electronic communication makes networking a viable option for companies looking for ways to keep costs low but expand activities or market visibility.

Almost every organization today uses some level of information technology to support its activities and enhance vertical and horizontal coordination. The following section examines the specific evolution of information technology applications within organizations.

Information Technology Evolution

The evolution of information technology is illustrated in Exhibit 9.2. First-line management is typically characterized with well-defined, programmed problems about operational issues and past events. Top management, by contrast, is concerned with uncertain, ambiguous issues, such as strategy, planning, and other nonprogrammed events, about which decisions must be made. As the complexity of computer-based information technology has increased, applications have grown to include nonprogrammed issues at top management levels.[9]

The initial applications were based on the notion of machine room efficiency—that is, current tasks could be performed more efficiently with the use of computer technology. The goal was to reduce labor costs by having computers take over some tasks. These systems became known as **transaction processing systems (TPS)**, which automate the organization's routine, day-to-day business transactions. Routine transactions include sending bills to customers, depositing checks in the bank, or placing orders. For example, American Airlines introduced Sabre in the 1960s to keep track of customer reservations, by far its biggest set of daily transactions.

In the next stage, technology became a business resource. Through the application of management information systems and decision support systems, managers had tools to improve performance of departments and the organization as a whole. As databases accumulated from transaction processing systems, managers began envisioning ways the computer could help them make important decisions by using data in summary form.

A **management information system** (MIS) is a system that generally contains comprehensive data about all transactions within an organization. MISs can provide data to help managers make decisions and perform their management functions. However, while these vast, comprehensive databases are vital to businesses, they do not present information in the fast and flexible ways most

Exhibit 9.2

Evolution of Organizational Applications of Information Technology

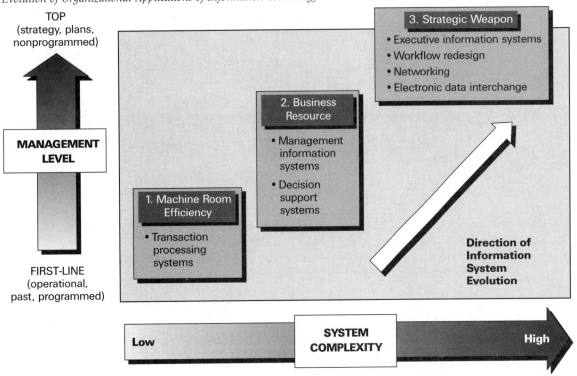

managers regularly need. An **executive information system** (EIS) is a higher-level application because it focuses on information as opposed to data: this interactive system helps top managers monitor and control organizational operations by processing and presenting data in usable form. A **decision support system** (DSS) provides specific benefits to managers at all levels of the organization because it enables them to retrieve, manipulate, and display information from integrated databases for making specific decisions.[10] For example Frito-Lay, Inc. uses information technology so well that the DSS has become a strategic weapon, enabling the company to gain market share. Frito-Lay has developed a huge database that draws upon information fed into it by 10,000 sales people reporting each day with hand-held computers on about 100 product lines selling in 400,000 stores. This database builds a powerful decision support system for managers. In one case, sales were observed to be slumping in San Antonio and Houston, and an analysis of data for the south Texas area showed that something was clearly wrong. Executives learned that a competitor had introduced a white-corn tortilla chip that was winning shelf space and market share. Having identified the problem, Frito-Lay introduced within three months a white-corn version of Tostitos and soon won back its market share.[11]

Using information technology such as executive information systems as a strategic weapon is the highest level of application (Exhibit 9.2). Workflow redesign, networks, and electronic data interchange systems are other ways organizations use information technology in their strategy. **Networking**, which links computers within or between organizations and enables coworkers within a business or even in separate companies to share information and cooperate on projects, is rapidly becoming a primary strategic weapon for many companies.

Networks take many forms. Companies can establish their own local area network (LAN) or wide area network (WAN) or communicate directly via the Internet, an amorphous, rapidly growing web of corporate, educational, and research computer networks around the world. For Sterling Software, Inc., a Dallas software maker, the Internet enables 3,600 employees across 75 worldwide offices to keep in touch with each other, with headquarters, and with customers.[12] The fastest growing form of corporate networking is called the **intranet,** a private internal network that uses the infrastructure and standards of the Internet and the World Wide Web but is cordoned off from the public with the use of software programs known as "firewalls."[13]

Before turning to a further discussion of the strategic use of information technology, let's explore a model for tailoring information support systems to organizational needs.

A MODEL FOR DESIGNING INFORMATION SUPPORT SYSTEMS

Organizations can be designed to provide the right kind of information to managers. So can information support systems. Frito-Lay enjoys success with its decision support system because it applied technology to measurable, analyzable problems. Some problems, especially at the top management level, are handled by face-to-face discussions. The application of MIS, EIS, and DSS to the right task is essential for its successful application.

A framework for applying information concepts to organizational departments is given in Exhibit 9.3. This framework is based upon Perrow's concept of department technology, which was discussed in Chapter 4. Technology represents the pattern of issues and tasks performed in different parts of the organization. Exhibit 9.3 identifies the two relationships that determine information requirements based upon the type of task performed by a department.

1. When task variety is high, problems are frequent, wide ranging, and unpredictable. Uncertainty is greater, so the amount of information needed also will be greater. Employees spend more time processing information, and they need access to high tech sources and large databases. When variety is low, the amount of information processed is less.[14]
2. When tasks are unanalyzable and hence lead to ambiguous problems, employees need rich, high touch information.[15] Face-to-face discussions and telephone conversations transmit multiple information cues in a short time. When tasks are simple, managers will use lean media. Then the underlying problem is clear, so only simple, written or computer-based information is needed.

The implication of these relationships is reflected in the framework in Exhibit 9.3. Organization structure and information support systems should be designed to provide department managers and employees with the appropriate amount and richness of information. *Routine* activities have only a few problems which are well understood. For such activities, the amount of information can be small and directed toward clear applications. Written procedures and economic order

Exhibit 9.3 *Task Characteristics and Information-Processing Requirements*

Craft Technology
Small amount of rich information, personal observation, occasional face-to-face and group meetings. Little MIS, DSS support. High touch. For example, **fine furniture making.**

Nonroutine Technology
Large amount of rich information—frequent face-to-face and group meetings, unscheduled discussions, substantial MIS, DSS support. High tech and high touch. For example, **strategy formulation.**

Routine Technology
Small amounts of clear, often quantitative information—written reports, procedures, schedules, some MIS and database support. For example, **credit checking.**

Engineering Technology
Large amounts of primarily quantitative information—large computer databases, written and technical materials, reliance on MIS, DSS support, high tech. For example, **architectural engineering.**

(Vertical axis) **ANALYZABILITY:** Greater ambiguity increases need for richer information — Analyzable to Unanalyzable

(Horizontal axis) Low — High
TASK VARIETY:
Greater uncertainty increases need for more information

quantity (EOQ) reorder systems for inventory control are examples of information support used for a routine task.

Engineering tasks have high variety, which increases the demand for information. With these tasks, managers and employees typically need access to large databases and high tech decision support systems. A large information base is appropriate. The huge number of engineering blueprints that support an engineering project is an example of a large database that can be stored on a computer. So is the large database made available to airline reservation agents.

Craft departments require a different form of information. Here, task variety is not high, but problems are ambiguous and hard to analyze. Problems are handled on the basis of high touch experience and judgment. There are many intangibles, so managers need rich information. An example of a craft organization is a psychiatric care unit. The process of therapeutic change is not well understood.

MIS information about costs and benefits cannot be directly related to the healing process. When psychiatrists are unclear about an issue, they discuss it face-to-face among themselves until they reach a solution.

Nonroutine departments are characterized by many problems that are ambiguous. Large amounts of rich information have to be accessible or gathered. Managers spend time in both scheduled and unscheduled meetings. For technical problems in these departments, management information and decision support systems are valuable. Managers may need to interact directly with databases to ask "what if" questions. Strategic planning units and basic research departments are examples of nonroutine tasks that use both high tech and high touch information.

The underlying tasks determine the pattern of issues and information needs confronting managers. The information support systems and organization structure should provide information to managers based upon the pattern of decisions to be made. More information should be available when tasks have many problems, and richer information should be provided when tasks are poorly defined and unanalyzable. When information systems are poorly designed, problem solving and decision processes will be ineffective, and managers may not understand why.

As discussed earlier, information technology in recent years has been adapted to a strategic role at the top of organizations as illustrated in Exhibit 9.2. Studies have shown that the appropriate use of information technology, such as executive information systems and decision support systems, can improve the efficiency and effectiveness of the strategic decision making process. Information technology enhances the ability of top managers to identify problems as well as the speed at which they generate solutions.[16]

The Strategic Advantage of Information Technology

Managers are increasingly considering the role of information management in their constant search for the right combination of strategy, motivation, technology, and business design to maintain a competitive edge in today's rapidly changing world.[17]

Recall from Chapter 2 that two of the competitive strategies firms can adopt are *low-cost leadership* and *differentiation*. The low-cost leader incurs low production costs and can price its product or service offerings low enough so it makes a profit while rival firms are sustaining losses. Differentiation means a firm offers a unique product or service based on product features, superb service, or rapid delivery. An important question for top managers is whether information technology can be used to achieve cost leadership or differentiation. Information technology might be used to create barriers to entry for new firms, high product switching costs for competitors, or efficient relationships with suppliers that can alter competitive balance with respect to cost leadership or differentiation.[18]

The American Airlines Sabre system, originally installed to keep track of reservations, evolved into a strategic weapon. More than 85,000 Sabre terminals have been installed at travel agencies in 47 countries, keeping track of fares and schedules for 665 airlines, 20,000 hotels, and 52 rental car companies. This information service differentiates American and is an enormous profit maker. It has also increased American's efficiency by enabling it to load as many as 1.5 million new fares daily to meet competition and to make precise calculations for flight plans, aircraft weight, fuel requirements, and takeoff power settings for 2,300 American flights each day.[19] Other organizations find other ways of using information technology for strategic advantage.

Wal-Mart's pioneering use of computer networks to conduct business electronically squeezed time and costs out of unwieldy supply chains and made the company the largest retailer in the world. Wal-Mart uses technology to convert information into action almost immediately, keeping it a step ahead of the competition.[20]

Exhibit 9.4 lists a few ways information technology can be used to give companies a strategic edge over competitors.

Low-Cost Leadership

Perhaps the most obvious way information technology can lower cost is through *operational efficiency*; but this means more than simply doing the same work faster. One element of operational efficiency has been the development of *executive information systems*, as discussed earlier in this chapter. Executive information systems use computer technology to facilitate the highest levels of strategic decision making, helping senior managers diagnose problems and develop solutions. Executive information systems can shape masses of numbers into simple, colorful charts and can be operated without in-depth computer skills. For example, the CEO of Duracell used EIS to compare the performance of hourly and salaried work forces in the United States and overseas. Within seconds, he had a crisp color table showing that U.S. workers produced more sales. Asking for more data, he discovered that salespeople overseas spent too much time calling on small stores. The EIS provided sufficient information to diagnose and solve this problem.[21]

Another way to improve efficiency is **workflow redesign**, which means reengineering (described in Chapter 7) work processes to fit new information technology rather than simply layering new computerized workflow systems on top of old work processes.

For example, at Texas Commerce Bank, workflow redesign is part of a $42 million reengineering effort. Consumers seeking a loan used to wait at least two weeks before their applications were approved. Thanks to workflow redesign, nine out of ten customers now have their applications processed in just three hours, and rush applications are handled in as little as 30 minutes. A sophisticated computer system and workflow software routes applications for processing to whichever loan officer is available.[22]

Advances in information technology are also leading to greater *interdepartmental coordination* as well as growing linkages between organizations. Thanks to networks and intranets, boundaries between departments within organizations as well as between organizations seem to dissolve, making a division or company across the world seem as close as one down the hall. Networks allow computers

Low-Cost Leadership	Differentiation
Operational efficiency	Lock in customers
Interdepartmental coordination	Customer service
Rapid resupply	Product development, market niches

Exhibit 9.4
Strategic Advantages from Information Technology

to talk to one another about all aspects of business, such as customer orders, parts required, invoices, manufacturing dates, and market share slippage.[23]

One specific type of interorganizational linkage, **electronic data interchange** (EDI), ties businesses with suppliers. EDI, which links a computer at one company to a computer at another for the transmission of business data such as sales statistics, without human interference, can enable businesses to achieve low-cost leadership through *rapid resupply*.

One study found that the use of EDI to coordinate material movements byChrysler assembly plants and its suppliers resulted in annual savings of about $220 million.[24] Campbell Soup Company invested $30 million to redesign its order processing system around EDI, a move the company predicts will save $18 million a year and speed deliveries. The EDI systems can detect when a customer like Flemings Co. runs low on Campbell's tomato soup, for instance, and ensure that the warehouse is restocked automatically.[25] Some large retailers with a low-cost strategy, such as Wal-Mart and JCPenney, are requiring that suppliers become EDI-capable.

Differentiation

A way to differentiate a company is to *lock in customers* with information technology. The innovator of this strategy was American Hospital Supply Corporation. Senior executives decided to give computer terminals free to hospitals around the country, linking hospital purchasers directly with AHS, enabling customers to directly place orders for any of more than 100,000 products. AHS immediately gained sales and market share at competitors' expense.[26] Fruit of the Loom is connecting its wholesalers to the Internet at virtually no cost to them to compete with Hanes and other brands in the market for blank T-shirts sold through novelty stores and at special events.

This approach can be upgraded to electronic data interchange so supplies are reordered automatically. EDI is gradually replacing traditional paper document flows. It is estimated that by the end of the decade, at least 75 percent of all interorganization transactions will be handled via EDI, over either private networks or the Internet.[27]

Exhibit 9.5 shows how EDI can be used to connect several organizations to facilitate trade on both domestic and international levels. Companies that are not plugged into this technology will be at a competitive disadvantage.

Improving customer service can differentiate a company from competitors. For example, automating the sales force can dramatically reduce the time it takes to close an order as well as increase the rate of successful closes. Deere Power Systems, a division of John Deere that makes diesel engines and other heavy equipment, found that its salespeople might spend a full day logging into various computer systems and calling different departments for information before going on a call. In the meantime, competitors would step in and beat Deere to the deal. With new information technology, departments that once kept information to themselves are sharing it on a network, and a salesperson is generally able to get all the information needed for a call in half a day or less.[28]

A third dimension of differentiation is *new product development* for *specialized market niches*. Coleco, for example, used computers to design millions of its wildly successful Cabbage Patch dolls, each of which was unique. Moreover, many companies, like J.P. Morgan, General Electric, and Xerox, are

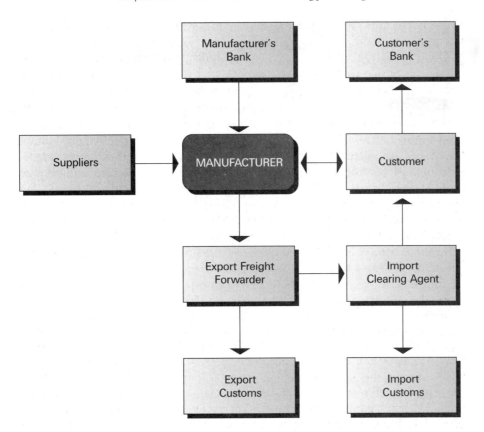

Exhibit 9.5
*Electronic Data
Interchange for
International
Transactions*

using the resources of the Internet to spot unutilized niches, detect needs for
new products or services, learn about their competitors, and stay up-to-date on
the latest technological advances.[29]

Companies constantly look for new ways to use information technology to
gain a step on competitors. Trucking company Schneider National's investment
in information technology helped the company cut costs, improve on-time reliability, and increase revenues. Schneider also uses information technology for
organizational control. Top managers meet each morning to analyze information
and direct activities and resources to meet the company's strategic goals.[30] A
large part of organizational information processing pertains to control, which is
a major responsibility of management and to which we now turn.

STRATEGIC CONTROL

Strategic control is the overall evaluation of the strategic plan, organizational
activities, and results that provides information for future action.[31] Exhibit 9.6
illustrates a simplified model of strategic control. The cycle of control includes
the strategic plan, measuring production activities to determine whether they are
on target, and assuring control by correcting or changing activities as needed.
Note in Exhibit 9.6 that strategic control also includes the measurement of
inputs to the production activity, as well as outputs, and continuous information
about the external environment to determine whether the strategic plan is
responding to emerging developments.

Strategic control differs from **operational control**, which is a short-term cycle that includes the four stages of target-setting, measurement of performance, comparison of performance against standards, and feedback.[32] Operational control tends to focus on a specific department or activity and to be short-term.

Strategic control typically uses both feedback and "feedforward" information. Feedback control measures outputs, and control information is fed back and compared to targets to make required changes. Feedforward control measures inputs on the front end of the process, both with respect to production activities and environmental changes that may affect strategic plans. Feedforward control enables the organization to be proactive and change plans earlier than would be possible with output data alone and before the organization gets out of alignment with external needs. Strategic control is an ongoing process that requires monitoring not only conditions within the organization but also in the external environment.

Strategic control directs the activities of the firm toward strategic objectives. For example, Frito-Lay uses the information system described earlier for strategic control. Frito-Lay establishes targets in each region of the country for snack food sales. The hand-held computers used by 10,000 salespeople provide daily information on actual sales levels. This data is compared, and feedback is used to change strategies, products, or marketing approaches to improve sales as needed. The control system reflects the strategic direction of the firm.[33]

Exhibit 9.6 *A Simplified Model of Strategic Control*

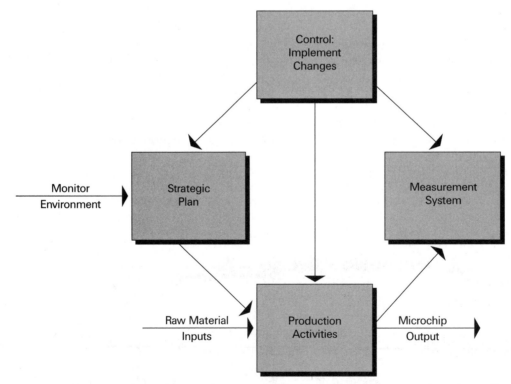

Source: Adapted from David Asch, "Strategic Control: A Problem Looking for a Solution," *Long Range Planning* 25 (1992): 105–10.

Theory X (handwritten)

MAJOR CONTROL APPROACHES

Managers at the top and middle levels of an organization can choose among three overall approaches for control. These approaches come from a framework for organizational control proposed by William Ouchi of the University of California at Los Angeles. Ouchi suggested three control strategies that organizations could adopt—market, bureaucratic, and clan.[34] Each form of control uses different types of information. However, all three types may appear simultaneously in an organization. The requirements for each control strategy are given in Exhibit 9.7.

Market Control

Market control occurs when price competition is used to evaluate the output and productivity of an organization. The idea of market control originated in economics.[35] A dollar price is an efficient form of control because managers can compare prices and profits to evaluate the efficiency of their corporation. Top managers nearly always use the price mechanism to evaluate performance in corporations. Corporate sales and costs are summarized in a profit-and-loss statement that can be compared against performance in previous years or with that of other corporations.

The use of market control requires that outputs be sufficiently explicit for a price to be assigned and that competition exist. Without competition, the price will not be an accurate reflection of internal efficiency. A few traditionally not-for-profit organizations are turning to market control.

For example, the city of Indianapolis requires its departments to bid against private companies. When the city's transportation department was underbid by a private company on a contract to fill potholes, the city's union workers made a counterproposal that involved eliminating most of the department's middle managers and reengineering union jobs to save money. Eighteen supervisors were laid off, costs were cut by 25 percent, and the department won the bid.[36]

Market control is used primarily at the level of the entire organization, but it also can be used in product divisions. Profit centers are self-contained product divisions, such as those described in Chapter 6. Each division contains resource inputs needed to produce a product. Each division can be evaluated on the basis of profit or loss compared with other divisions.

Asea Brown Boveri (ABB), a multinational electrical contractor and manufacturer of electrical equipment, includes three different types of profit centers, all operating according to their own bottom lines and interacting through buying and selling with one another and with outside customers. Some firms even require that individual departments interact with one another at market prices, buying and selling products or services among themselves.[37] Companies are finding that they can apply the market control concept to internal departments such as accounting, data processing, legal departments, and information services.

Type	Requirements
Market	Prices, competition, exchange relationship
Bureaucracy	Rules, standards, hierarchy, legitimate authority
Clan	Tradition, shared values and beliefs, trust

Exhibit 9.7

Three Organizational Control Strategies

The trend toward creating internal markets is closely related to current trends toward outsourcing and network structures, described in Chapter 7. With outsourcing, companies farm out certain tasks to other firms that can provide high-quality services at low costs. Many banks outsource the processing of credit cards to companies that can do it more cheaply. Ford Motor Company has cut costs by developing good outsourcing relationships with independent suppliers of auto parts. One survey found that about 86 percent of major corporations, including American Airlines, DuPont, Exxon, Honda, IBM, and Johnson & Johnson, now outsource some of their services.[38]

Bureaucratic Control

Bureaucratic Control is the use of rules, policies, hierarchy of authority, written documentation, standardization, and other bureaucratic mechanisms to standardize behavior and assess performance. Bureaucratic control uses the bureaucratic characteristics defined by Weber and discussed in Chapter 5 on bureaucracy. The primary purpose of bureaucratic rules and procedures is to standardize and control employee behavior.

Within a large organization, thousands of work behaviors and information exchanges take place both vertically and horizontally. Rules and policies evolve through a process of trial and error to regulate these behaviors. Bureaucratic control mechanisms are used when behavior and methods of processing information are too complex or ill-defined to be controlled with a price mechanism.

Some degree of bureaucratic control is used in virtually every organization. Rules, regulations, and directives contain information about a range of behaviors. Bureaucratic mechanisms are especially valuable in not-for-profit organizations for which prices and competitive markets often do not exist.

Management Control Systems. Management control systems are broadly defined as the formalized routines, reports, and procedures that use information to maintain or alter patterns in organizational activity.[39] The management information and strategic control systems discussed earlier in this chapter are critical tools to help managers control organizational operations. Control systems include the formalized information-based activities for planning, budgeting, performance evaluation, resource allocation, and employee rewards. These systems operate as feedback systems, with the targets set in advance, outcomes compared with targets, and variance reported to managers for remedial actions.[40] Advances in technology have dramatically improved the efficiency and effectiveness of these systems.

In the past, most organizations relied largely on financial accounting measures as the basis for measuring organization performance, but today's companies realize that a balanced view of both financial and operational measures is needed for successful organization control in a competitive and rapidly changing environment.[41] The four control system elements listed in Exhibit 9.8 are often considered the core of management control systems. These four elements include the budget, periodic nonfinancial statistical reports, reward systems, and standard operating procedures.[42] The management control system elements enable middle and upper management to both monitor and influence major departments.

The operating budget is used to set financial targets for the year and then report costs on a monthly or quarterly basis. Periodic statistical reports are used to evaluate and monitor nonfinancial performance. These reports typically are computer-based and may be available daily, weekly, or monthly.

Subsystem	Content and Frequency
Budget	Financial, resource expenditures, monthly
Statistical reports	Nonfinancial outputs, weekly or monthly, often computer-based
Reward systems	Annual evaluation of managers based on department goals and performance
Operating procedures	Rules and regulations, policies that prescribe correct behavior, continuous

Exhibit 9.8
Management Control Systems Used as Part of Bureaucratic Control

Source: Based on Richard L. Daft and Norman B. Macintosh, "The Nature and Use of Formal Control Systems for Management Control and Strategy Implementation," *Journal of Management* 10 (1984): 43–66.

Reward systems offer incentives for managers and employees to improve performance and meet departmental goals. Managers and superiors may sit down and evaluate how well previous goals were met, set new goals for the year, and establish rewards for meeting the new targets. Operating procedures are traditional rules and regulations. Managers use all of these systems to correct variances and bring activities back into line.

One finding from research into management control systems is that each of the four control systems focuses on a different aspect of the production process. These four systems thus form an overall management control system that provides middle managers with control information about resource inputs, process efficiency, and output.[43] Moreover, the use of and reliance on control systems depend on the strategic targets set by top management. The relationship of strategy, management control systems, and departmental activities is illustrated in Exhibit 9.9.

The budget is used primarily to allocate resource inputs. Managers use the budget for planning the future and reducing uncertainty about the availability of human and material resources needed to perform department tasks. Whereas the budget deals with resource inputs, computer-based statistical reports are used to control outputs. These reports contain data about output volume and quality and other indicators that provide feedback to middle management about departmental results. The reward system and operating procedures are directed at the production process.

Operating procedures give explicit guidelines about appropriate behaviors. Reward systems provide incentives to meet goals and can help guide and correct employee activities. Managers also use direct supervision to keep departmental work activities within desired limits.

Technology Overcontrol. Taken together, the management control subsystems described in Exhibit 9.9 provide important information within the overall bureaucratic control framework used to monitor and influence departmental performance. However, the information technology described earlier in this chapter can be used to increase the speed and intensity of control over employees. As businesses continue to try to squeeze out more productivity in today's competitive environment, they sometimes turn to electronic technology to track workers' every move.

At Schneider National, described earlier, each truck's speed is constantly monitored by computer; if drivers stay within the speed limit, the company offers financial rewards. In addition to lowering accident rates, Schneider has cut fuel costs by preventing truckers from speeding. Some organizations have

Exhibit 9.9

*Four Management
Control Subsystems
and Focus of Control*

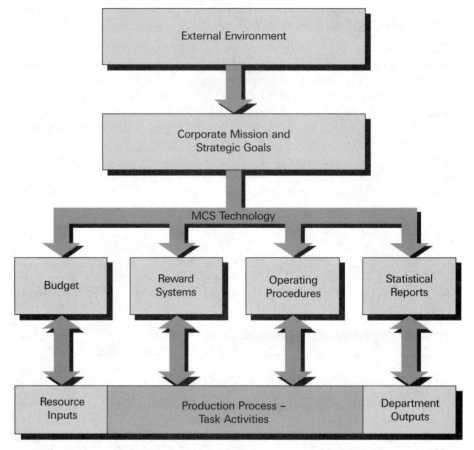

Source: Adapted from Richard L. Daft and Norman B. Macintosh, "The Nature and Use of Formal Control Systems for Management Control and Strategy Implementation," *Journal of Management* 10 (1984): 43–66.

taken the use of computer control to the point of overkill, believing that carefully monitored workers will perform more efficiently. Organizations count the number of elapsed seconds per phone call, the number of keystrokes per minute, and every other measurable behavior related to the job, creating stress for employees.

Unions and employee associations are fighting back, and several organizations have reduced control and discovered that performance actually improved.[44] Canada Bell started monitoring employees in groups rather than individually, responding only if the group average fell below target levels. This has not been needed, however, because overall performance increased. Northwestern Bell and Federal Express decreased monitoring and found that productivity remained high and employee satisfaction increased. In one study, "monitored" service workers reported that production quantity was high but work quality was poor. "Unmonitored" employees reported that work quality, service accuracy, and teamwork were more important than work quantity. On average, the unmonitored workers provided better customer service, taking more time to do the job right rather than trying to save seconds at the expense of customers or fellow employees.[45]

Synthetic solutions / virtual solutions

— " cultured — see next chap, p 239/

Clan Control

Clan control is the use of social characteristics, such as corporate culture, shared values, commitment, traditions, and beliefs, to control behavior. Organizations that use clan control require shared values and trust among employees.[46] Clan control is important when ambiguity and uncertainty are high. High uncertainty means the organization cannot put a price on its services, and things change so fast that rules and regulations are not able to specify every correct behavior. Under clan control, people may be hired because they are committed to the organization's purpose, such as in a religious organization. New employees may be subjected to a long period of socialization to gain acceptance by colleagues. Clan control is most often used in small, informal organizations with a strong culture, because of personal involvement in and commitment to the organization's purpose. In addition, the increasing use of computer networks, which can lead to a democratic spread of information throughout the organization, may force many companies to depend less on bureaucratic control and more on shared values that guide individual actions for the corporate good.[47]

Traditional control mechanisms based on strict rules and close supervision are ineffective for controlling behavior in conditions of high uncertainty and rapid change.[48] Companies that shift to the new management paradigm of decentralization, horizontal teams, network structures, and employee participation generally use clan control or *self control*.

Whereas clan control is a function of being socialized into a group, self control stems from individual values, goals, and standards. The organization attempts to induce a change such that individual employees' own internal values and work preferences are brought in line with the organization's values and goals.[49] With self control, employees generally set their own goals and monitor their own performance, yet companies relying on self control need strong leaders who can clarify boundaries within which employees can exercise their own knowledge and discretion.

Clan or self control may also be used in certain departments, such as research and development, where uncertainty is high and performance is difficult to measure. Managers of departments that rely on these informal control mechanisms must not assume that the absence of written, bureaucratic control means no control is present. Clan control is invisible yet very powerful. One recent study found that the actions of employees were controlled even more powerfully and completely with clan control than with a bureaucratic hierarchy.[50] When clan control works, bureaucratic control is not needed.

CONTINGENCY CONTROL MODEL

A question for organization designers is when to emphasize each control strategy. A **contingency control model** that describes contingencies associated with market, bureaucratic, and clan control is shown in Exhibit 9.10. Each type of control often appears in the same organization, but one form of control will usually dominate.[51]

Bureaucratic control mechanisms are by far the most widely used control strategy. Some form of bureaucratic control combined with internal management control systems is found in almost every organization. Bureaucratic control is used more exclusively when organizations are large and when the environment and technology are certain, stable, and routine. It is also associated with the

Exhibit 9.10 *Contingency Model for Organizational Control Strategies*

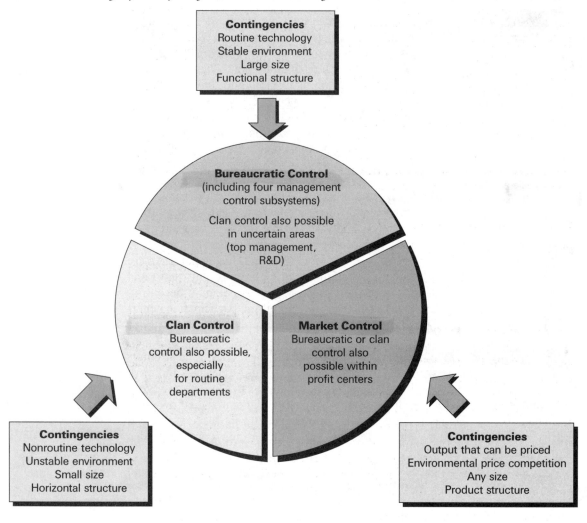

functional structure described in Chapter 6. Bureaucratic control emphasizes a vertical information and control process.

Clan control is almost the opposite of bureaucratic control. When organizations are small and when the environment and technology are uncertain, unstable, and nonroutine, then trust, tradition, and shared culture and values are important sources of control. Clan control is best when horizontal information sharing and coordination are needed, as they are with a matrix, team-based, or horizontal organization structure. Rules and budgets will be used, of course, but trust, values, and commitment will be the primary reason for employee compliance.

Research on self control is just emerging, but this type of control seems most appropriate in organizations that are shifting to what has been called the learning organization, an organization in which everyone is engaged in identifying and solving problems, enabling the organization to continuously experiment, improve, and increase its capability. The learning organization involves changing employee behaviors and attitudes and will be discussed in detail in Chapter 15.

Market control has limited applications, but its use is growing. It is used when costs and outputs can be priced and a market is available for price competition. The technology must produce outputs that can be defined and priced, and competition must exist in the environment. Market control can be used in organizations of any size so long as costs can be identified and outputs are competitively priced. It is frequently used in self-contained product divisions of a business corporation, as described in Chapter 6. Each such division is a profit center. When applicable, market control is efficient because performance information is summarized in a profit-and-loss statement.

The balance among control strategies may differ from organization to organization. The use of each strategy reflects the structure, technology, and environment, as well as the ability to price output. When managers emphasize the correct type of control, the outcome can be very positive.

Balancing Empowerment and Control

Many managers are giving up some of their control and empowering workers at low organization levels to make decisions and act independently. Tight management control can constrain creativity and limit flexibility and innovation, organizational characteristics that are becoming increasingly important in an era of rapid change. Yet managers must still maintain adequate control to ensure that departments and organizations meet their goals.

Most managers are accustomed to relying on control systems that measure the progress of individuals and departments toward strategically important goals. While such systems are still an important part of control in empowered companies, they should be balanced with other mechanisms, including shared belief systems, boundary systems that set the limits for employee behavior (including ethical statements and codes of conduct) and interactive information systems that enable managers to stay abreast of what is happening in the organization and involve themselves regularly and personally in the activities and decisions of employees. A balanced approach to control can help managers unleash the creativity of employees while ensuring that activities are directed toward meeting strategic goals.

SUMMARY OF KEY ISSUES

An organization's situation creates uncertainty and ambiguity for managers, which translates into requirements for information amount and richness. Determining how manager and department information needs differ along these two dimensions and how to design information support systems are key problems for organizations to solve. Generally, as ambiguity of managerial tasks increases, more rich, personal information is required. Well-defined tasks that are complex and of high variety require a large amount of precise, quantitative data.

Information technology impacts organization structure by removing barriers of time and distance. Advanced technology has played a significant role in the shift to horizontal forms of organizing, with fewer hierarchical levels and more self-directed teams, and in the trend toward network structures. Within organizations, information systems have evolved to a variety of applications to meet information needs.

Initial transaction processing systems were applied to well-defined tasks at lower levels, and they increased efficiency. Then management information systems and decision support systems were developed as business resources at the middle- and upper-management levels. Finally, executive information systems are being used at top levels of management as a strategic weapon. Advances in networking technology are leading to greater cooperation between departments as well as between organizations. Interorganization linkages, such as electronic data interchange and communication via the Internet, also provide strategic advantages.

Information technology plays an important role in helping organizations achieve a competitive advantage through low-cost leadership or differentiation. Information technology can increase operational efficiency, coordination, and the speed of resupply, and can lock in customers, improve customer service, and enhance product development.

A large part of information processing pertains to control. The concepts of market, bureaucratic, and clan control help explain how control is exercised in organizations. Market control is used where product or service outputs can be priced and competition exists. Clan control, and more recently, self control, are associated with uncertain and rapidly changing organizational processes and rely on commitment, tradition, and shared values for control. Bureaucratic control relies on the bureaucratic characteristics of organizations described in Chapter 5, as well as on the four internal management control systems of budgets, statistical reports, operating procedures, and reward systems. In organizations where employees are empowered to make decisions and act independently, managers are taking a balanced approach to control, helping to unleash employee creativity while also ensuring that activities are directed toward meeting organizational goals.

Discussion Questions

1. How do uncertainty and ambiguity affect information processing requirements and the design of information support systems?
2. To what extent can information technology meet the needs of top managers for rich information? Do you think technology will ever enable top managers to do their job without face-to-face communication? Discuss.
3. How might the Internet provide a competitive advantage to a company?
4. The manager of a computer processing department told his employees: "Top managers need the same control data everyone else needs, except that we'll aggregate it for the company as a whole." Agree or disagree with the manager's philosophy, and explain why.
5. An organization consultant argued that managers need information that is independent of computers. Explain why you agree or disagree with her point of view.
6. In writing about types of control, William Ouchi said, "The Market is like the trout and the Clan is like the salmon, each a beautiful highly specialized species which requires uncommon conditions for its survival. In comparison, the bureaucratic method of control is the catfish—clumsy, ugly, but able to live in the widest range of environments and ultimately, the dominant species." Discuss what Ouchi meant with that analogy.
7. Government organizations often seem more bureaucratic than for-profit organizations. Could this partly be the result of the type of control used in government organizations? Explain.
8. Discuss the following statements: "Things under tight control are better than things under loose control." "The more data managers have, the better decisions they make."

Notes

1. Henry Mintzberg, *The Nature of Managerial Work* (New York: Harper & Row, 1972), 39.

2. Richard L. Daft and Norman B. Macintosh, "A Tentative Exploration into the Amount and Equivocality of Information Processing in Organizational Work Units," *Administrative Science Quarterly* 26 (1981): 207–24.

3. Michael L. Tushman and David A. Nadler, "Information Processing as an Integrating Concept in Organizational Design," *Academy of Management Review* 3 (1978): 613–24; Samuel B. Bacharach and Michael Aiken, "Communication in Administrative Bureaucracies," *Academy of Management Journal* 20 (1977): 365–77.

4. Jay R. Galbraith, *Organization Design* (Reading, Mass.: Addison-Wesley, 1977), 35–36; William E. Souders and Ruby K. Moenaert, "Integrating Marketing and R&D Project Personnel within Innovation Projects: An Information Uncertainty Model," *Journal of Management Studies* 29 (July 1992): 485–512.

5. Richard L. Daft, Robert H. Lengel, and Linda Klebe Trevino, "Message Equivocality, Media Selection, and Manager Performance: Implications for Information Systems," *MIS Quarterly* 11 (1987): 355–66; Richard L. Daft and Robert H. Lengel, "Information Richness: A New Approach to Managerial Behavior and Organization Design," in Barry Staw and Larry L. Cummings, eds., *Research in Organizational Behavior*, Vol. 6 (Greenwich, Conn.: JAI Press, 1984), 191–233; Robert H. Lengel, "Managerial Information Processing and Communication-Media Source Selection Behavior," (Unpublished Ph.D. Dissertation, Texas A&M University, 1982).

6. Erik Larson, "The Man with the Golden Touch," *Inc.*, October 1988, 67–77.

7. Based on Janet Fulk and Gerardine DeSanctis, "Electronic Communication and Changing Organizational Forms," *Organization Science*, Vol. 6, No. 4, July–August 1995, 337–49.

8. Beverly Geber, "Virtual Teams," *Training*, April 1995, 36–40.

9. David W. L. Wightman, "Competitive Advantage through Information Technology," *Journal of General Management* 12 (Summer 1987): 36–45; M. J. Bissett, "Competitive Advantage—Through Controlling the Middle Ground," (Paper presented at Southcourt Conference: Improving Business-Based IT Strategy, October 1986).

10. Robin Matthews and Anthony Shoebridge, "EIS: A Guide for Executives," *Long Range Planning* 25, No. 6 (1992): 94–101; Jeffrey P. Stamen, "Decision Support Systems Help Planners Hit Their Targets," *Journal of Business Strategy*, March/April 1990, 30–33.

11. Jeffrey Rothfeder, Jim Bartimo and Lois Therrien, "How Software Is Making Food Sales a Piece of Cake," *Business Week,* 2 July 1990, 54–55.

12. Rick Tetzeli, "The Internet and Your Business," *Fortune,* 7 March 1994, 86–96.

13. Amy Cortese, "Here Comes the Intranet," *Business Week,* 26 February 1996, 76-84; and Alison L. Sprout, "The Internet Inside Your Company," *Fortune,* 27 November 1995, 161–68.

14. Richard L. Daft and Robert Lengel, "Organizational Information Requirements, Media Richness and Structural Design," *Management Science* 32 (1986): 554–71; Daft and Macintosh, "A Tentative Exploration," W. Alan Randolph, "Matching Technology and the Design of Organization Units," *California Management Review* 22–23 (1980–1981): 39–48; Michael L. Tushman "Technical Communications in R&D Laboratories: The Impact of Project Work Characteristics," *Academy of Management Journal* 21 (1978): 624–45.

15. Robert H. Lengel and Richard L. Daft, "The Selection of Communication Media as an Executive Skill," *Academy of Management Executive* 2 (August 1988): 225–32.

16. Steve Molloy and Charles R. Schwenk, "The Effects of Information Technology on Strategic Decision-Making," *Journal of Management Studies* 32:3, May 1995, 283–311, and Dorothy E. Leidner and Joyce J. Elam, "The Impact of Executive Information Systems on Organizational Design, Intelligence, and Decision Making," *Organization Science*, Vol. 6, No. 6, (November–December 1995), 645–64.

17. Renae Broderick and John W. Boudreau, "Human Resource Management, Information Technology

and the Competitive Edge," *Academy of Management Executive* 6, No. 2 (1992): 7–17.

18. Mark C. S. Lee and Dennis A. Adams, "A Manager's Guide to the Strategic Potential of Information Systems," *Information and Management* (1990): 169–82; Wightman, "Competitive Advantage Through Information Technology."

19. Kenneth Labich, "American Takes on the World," *Fortune,* 24 September 1990, 40–48.

20. John W. Verity, "Invoice? What's An Invoice?" *Business Week,* 10 June 1995, 110–12, and Bill Saporito, "What Sam Walton Taught America," *Fortune,* 4 May 1992, 104–05.

21. Fess Crockett, "Revitalizing Executive Information Systems," *Sloan Management Review* (Summer 1992): 39–47; Jeremy Main, "At Last, Software CEOs Can Use," *Fortune,* 13 March 1989, 77–81.

22. Doug Bartholomew, "A Better Way to Work," *Information Week,* 11 September 1995, 32–40.

23. Myron Magnet, "Who's Winning the Information Revolution," *Fortune,* 30 November 1992, 110–17; Jeremy Main, "Computers of the World, Unite!" *Fortune,* 24 September 1990, 114–22.

24. Tridas Mukhopadhyay, Sunder Kekre, and Suresh Kalathur, "Business Value of Information Technology: A Study of Electronic Data Interchange," *MIS Quarterly,* June 1995, 137–56.

25. Verity, "Invoice? What's An Invoice?"

26. Robert I. Benjamin, John F. Rockart, Michael S. Scott Morton, and John Wyman, "Information Technology: A Strategic Opportunity," *Sloan Management Review* 25 (Spring 1984): 3–10.

27. N. Venketraman, "IT-Enabled Business Transformation: From Automation to Business Scope Redefinition," *Sloan Management Review* (Winter 1994): 73–87.

28. John W. Verity, "Taking a Laptop on a Call," *Business Week,* 25 October 1993, 124–25.

29. Rick Tetzeli, "The Internet and Your Business," *Fortune,* 7 March 1994, 86–96.

30. Warren Cohen, "Taking It to the Highway," *U.S. News and World Report,* 18 September 1995, 84–87.

31. John F. Preble, "Towards a Comprehensive System of Strategic Control," *Journal of Management*

Studies 29 (July 1992): 391–409; David Asch, "Strategic Control: A Problem Looking for a Solution," *Long Range Planning* 25, No. 2 (1992): 105–10.

32. T. K. Das, "Organizational Control: An Evolutionary Perspective," *Journal of Management Studies* 26 (1989): 459–75; Kenneth A. Merchant, *Control in Business Organizations* (Marshfield, Mass.: Pitman, 1985); William G. Ouchi, "The Relationship between Organizational Structure and Organizational Control," *Administrative Science Quarterly* 22 (1977): 95–113.

33. Michael Goold, "Strategic Control in the Decentralized Firm," *Sloan Management Review* (Winter 1991): 69–81; Robert Simons, "Strategic Orientation and Top Management Attention to Control Systems," *Strategic Management Journal* 12 (1991): 49–62.

34. William G. Ouchi, "Markets, Bureaucracies, and Clans," *Administrative Science Quarterly* 25 (1980): 129–41; idem, "A Conceptual Framework for the Design of Organizational Control Mechanisms," *Management Science* 25 (1979): 833–48.

35. Oliver A. Williamson, *Markets and Hierarchies: Analyses and Antitrust Implications* (New York: Free Press, 1975).

36. Anita Micossi, "Creating Internal Markets," *Enterprise,* April 1994, 43–44.

37. Raymond E. Miles, Henry J. Coleman, Jr., and W. E. Douglas Creed, "Keys to Success in Corporate Redesign," *California Management Review,* Vol. 37, No. 3, Spring 1995, 128–45.

38. John A. Byrne, "Has Outsourcing Gone Too Far?" *Business Week,* 1 April 1996, 26–28.

39. Simons, "Strategic Organizations and Top Management Attention to Control Systems."

40. Stephen G. Green and M. Ann Welsh, "Cybernetics and Dependents: Reframing the Control Concept," *Academy of Management Review* 13 (1988): 287–301.

41. Robert S. Kaplan and David P. Norton, "The Balanced Scorecard—Measures That Drive Performance," *Harvard Business Review* (January–February 1992): 71–79; Robert G. Eccles, "The Performance Measurement Manifesto," *Harvard Business Review,* (January– February 1991): 131–37.

42. Richard L. Daft and Norman B. Macintosh, "The Nature and Use of Formal Control Systems for Management Control and Strategy Implementation," *Journal of Management* 10 (1984): 43–66.

43. Ibid.; Scott S. Cowen and J. Kendall Middaugh II, "Matching an Organization's Planning and Control System to Its Environment," *Journal of General Management* 16 (1990): 69–84.

44. Marlene C. Piturro, "Employee Performance Monitoring . . . or Meddling?" *Management Review* (May 1989): 31–33.

45. Rebecca A. Grant, Christopher A. Higgins, and Richard H. Irving, "Computerized Performance Monitors: Are They Costing You Customers?" *Sloan Management Review* (Spring 1988): 39–45.

46. Ouchi, "Markets, Bureaucracies, and Clans."

47. Stratford Sherman, "The New Computer Revolution," *Fortune,* 14 June 1993, 56–80.

48. Richard Leifer and Peter K. Mills, "An Information Processing Approach for Deciding Upon Control Strategies and Reducing Control Loss in Emerging Organizations," *Journal of Management*, Vol. 22, No. 1, 1996, 113–37.

49. Leifer and Mills, "An Information Processing Approach for Deciding Upon Control Strategies," and Laurie J. Kirsch, "The Management of Complex Tasks in Organizations: Controlling the Systems Development Process," *Organization Science*, Vol. 7, No. 1, January–February 1996, 1–21.

50. James R. Barker, "Tightening the Iron Cage: Concertive Control in Self-Managing Teams," *Administrative Science Quarterly* 38 (1993): 408–37.

51. Carol R. Snodgrass and Edward J. Szewczak, "The Substitutability of Strategic Control Choices: An Empirical Study," *Journal of Management Studies* 27 (1990): 535–53.

10

chapter ten

Organizational Culture
and Ethical Val~~ues~~

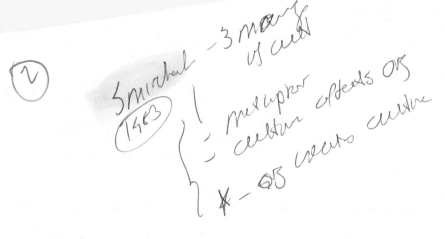

W ... answers to the following questions:

- ... important to performance?

- S ... erson interpret an organization's
  c ...

- H ... ve or positive outcomes?

- H ... nd the external environment?

- W ... ated to behavior governed by
  la ...

- Wh ... res and systems can leaders use
  to s ... and performance outcomes?

Herb Kelleher, CEO and president of Southwest Airlines, believes the key to good business is to do what your customer wants and be happy in your work. It's a philosophy that has made Southwest the most consistently profitable airline in the industry and earned the company a string of awards from the U.S. Department of Transportation. While other airlines may imitate some of Southwest's low-cost operating practices, the characteristic that truly makes Southwest successful can never be cloned. That characteristic, known as the "Southwest Spirit," is the company's unique corporate culture.

Every employee is treated as an individual and an important part of the Southwest family. Southwest also believes a fun atmosphere builds a strong sense of community, counterbalances the stress of hard work, and enhances customer service. Employees are given the flexibility to let their own individual personalities come out in serving customers. Passengers on a recent flight, for example, had a bunny-eared flight attendant pop out of an overhead bin to greet them. Southwest Airlines has definite values that make it unique. Southwest has created a culture that engages employees' hearts and minds as well as their bodies. A Culture Committee, made up of employees representing a cross-section of departments, meets four times a year to make sure the Southwest Spirit stays alive.[1]

Organizational success or failure is often attributed to culture. Firms such as 3M and Johnson & Johnson have been praised for their innovative cultures. Corporate culture also has been implicated in problems faced by IBM, Sears, Bank of America, and General Motors, where changing their cultures is considered essential for ultimate success.[2]

PURPOSE OF THIS CHAPTER

This chapter explores ideas about corporate culture and associated ethical values and how these are influenced by organizations. The first section will describe the nature of corporate culture, its origins and purpose, and how to identify and interpret culture through ceremonies, stories, and symbols. Then we turn to ethical values in organizations and how leaders shape cultural and ethical values in a direction suitable for strategy and performance outcomes.

ORGANIZATIONAL CULTURE

The popularity of the organizational culture topic raises a number of questions. Can we identify cultures? Can culture be aligned with strategy? How can cultures be managed or changed? The best place to start is by defining culture and explaining how it can be identified in organizations.

What Is Culture?

Culture is the set of values, guiding beliefs, understandings, and ways of thinking that is shared by members of an organization and is taught to new members as correct.[3] It represents the unwritten, feeling part of the organization. Everyone participates in culture, but culture generally goes unnoticed. It is only when organizations try to implement new strategies or programs that go against basic culture norms and values that they come face to face with the power of culture.

Organizational culture exists at two levels, as illustrated in Exhibit 10.1. On the surface are visible artifacts and observable behaviors—the ways people dress and act, the symbols, stories, and ceremonies that are shared among organization members. But the visible elements of culture reflect deeper values in the minds of organization members. These underlying values, assumptions, beliefs, and thought processes are the true culture.[4] The attributes of culture display themselves in many ways but typically evolve into a patterned set of activities carried out through social interactions.[5] Those patterns can be used to interpret culture.

Emergence and Purpose of Culture

Culture provides members with a sense of organizational identity and generates a commitment to beliefs and values that are larger than themselves. Though ideas that become part of culture can come from anywhere within the organization, an organization's culture generally begins with a founder or early leader who articulates and implements particular ideas and values as a vision, philosophy, or business strategy. When these ideas and values lead to success, they

Exhibit 10.1
Levels of Corporate Culture

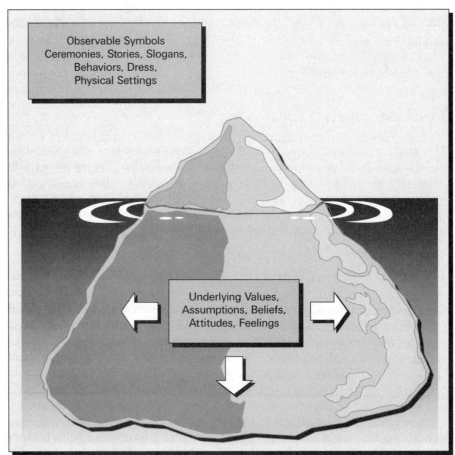

Observable Symbols Ceremonies, Stories, Slogans, Behaviors, Dress, Physical Settings

Underlying Values, Assumptions, Beliefs, Attitudes, Feelings

become institutionalized, and an organizational culture emerges that reflects the vision and strategy of the founder or leader, as it did at Southwest Airlines.[6]

Cultures serve two critical functions in organizations: (1) to integrate members so that they know how to relate to one another, and (2) to help the organization adapt to the external environment. **Internal integration** means that members develop a collective identity and know how to work together effectively. It is culture that guides day-to-day working relationships and determines how people communicate within the organization, what behavior is acceptable or not acceptable, and how power and status is allocated. **External adaptation** refers to how the organization meets goals and deals with outsiders. Culture helps guide the daily activities of workers to meet certain goals. It can help the organization respond rapidly to customer needs or the moves of a competitor. We will discuss culture and adaptation in more detail later in the chapter.

Interpreting Culture

To identify and interpret the content of culture requires that people make inferences based on observable artifacts. Artifacts can be studied but are hard to decipher accurately. An award ceremony in one company may have a different meaning than in another company. To decipher what is really going on in an organization requires detective work and probably some experience as an insider. Some of the typical and important observable aspects of culture are rites and ceremonies, stories, symbols, and language.

Rites and Ceremonies. Important artifacts for culture are **rites and ceremonies**, the elaborate, planned activities that make up a special event and are often conducted for the benefit of an audience. Managers can hold rites and ceremonies to provide dramatic examples of what a company values. These are special occasions that reinforce specific values, create a bond among people for sharing an important understanding, and can anoint and celebrate heroes and heroines who symbolize important beliefs and activities.[7]

Four types of rites that appear in organizations are summarized in Exhibit 10.2. *Rites of passage* facilitate the transition of employees into new social roles. *Rites of enhancement* create stronger social identities and increase the status of employees. *Rites of renewal* reflect training and development activities that improve organization functioning. *Rites of integration* create common bonds and good feelings among employees and increase commitment to the organization. The following examples illustrate how these rites and ceremonies are used by top managers to reinforce important cultural values.

- In a major bank, election as an officer was seen as the key event in a successful career. A series of activities accompanied every promotion to bank officer, including a special method of notification, taking the new officer to the officers' dining room for the first time, and the new officer buying drinks on Friday after his or her notification.[8] This is a rite of passage.
- Mary Kay Cosmetics Company holds elaborate awards ceremonies, presenting gold and diamond pins, furs, and pink Cadillacs to high-achieving sales consultants. Their most successful consultants are introduced by film clips like the kind used to introduce award nominees in the entertainment industry.[9] This is a rite of enhancement.
- An important annual event at McDonald's is the nationwide contest to determine the best hamburger cooking team in the country. The contest encourages

Exhibit 10.2

A Typology of Organizational Rites and Their Social Consequences

Type of Rite	Example	Social Consequences
Passage	Induction and basic training, U.S. Army	Facilitate transition of persons into social roles and statuses that are new for them
Enhancement	Annual awards night	Enhance social identities and increase status of employees
Renewal	Organizational development activities	Refurbish social structures and improve organization functioning
Integration	Office Christmas party	Encourage and revive common feelings that bind members together and commit them to the organization

Source: Adapted from Harrison M. Trice and Janice M. Beyer, "Studying Organizational Cultures through Rites and Ceremonials," *Academy of Management Review* 9 (1984): 653–59. Used with permission.

all stores to reexamine the details of how they cook hamburgers. The ceremony is highly visible and communicates to all employees the McDonald's value of hamburger quality.[10] This is a rite of renewal.

• Whenever a Wal-Mart executive visits one of the stores, he or she leads employees in the Wal-Mart cheer: "Give me a W! Give me an A! Give me an L! Give me a squiggly! (where all do a version of the twist.) Give me an M! Give me an A! Give me an R! Give me a T! What's that spell? Wal-Mart! What's that spell? Wal-Mart! Who's No. 1? THE CUSTOMER!" The cheer strengthens bonds among employees and reinforces their commitment to common goals.[11] This is a rite of integration.

Stories. **Stories** are narratives based on true events that are frequently shared among organizational employees and told to new employees to inform them about an organization. Many stories are about company heroes who serve as models or ideals for serving cultural norms and values. Some stories are considered **legends** because the events are historic and may have been embellished with fictional details. Other stories are **myths**, which are consistent with the values and beliefs of the organization but are not supported by facts.[12] Stories keep alive the primary values of the organization and provide a shared understanding among all employees. Examples of how stories shape culture are as follows:

• Two stories that symbolize the "HP way" at Hewlett-Packard involve the hero founders, David Packard and Bill Hewlett. After work hours one evening, Packard was wandering around the Palo Alto lab. He discovered a prototype constructed of inferior materials. Packard destroyed the model and left a note saying, "That's not the HP way. Dave." Similarly, Bill Hewlett is said to have gone to a plant on Saturday and found the lab stockroom door locked. He cut the padlock and left a note saying, "Don't ever lock this door again. Thanks, Bill." Hewlett wanted the engineers to have free access to components, and even to take them home, to stimulate the creativity that is part of the HP way.[13]

• For years, workers at U.S. Paper Mills Corporation have been hearing this story about the company's founder and principal stockholder: One morning, when Walter Cloud saw a worker trying to unclog the drain of a blending vat using an extension pole, he quickly jumped over the edge of the vat and reached through the 3-feet deep muck to unclog the drain with his hand. Brushing himself off, Cloud then asked the worker, "Now, what are you going to do the next time you need to unclog a drain?" By telling and retelling this story, workers at the mill communicate the importance of jumping in to do whatever needs to be done.14

Symbols. Another tool for interpreting culture is the symbol. A **symbol** is something that represents another thing. In one sense, ceremonies, stories, slogans, and rites are all symbols. They symbolize deeper values of an organization. Another symbol is a physical artifact of the organization. Physical symbols are powerful because they focus attention on a specific item. Examples of physical symbols are as follows:

- Nordstrom department store symbolizes the importance of supporting lower-level employees with the organization chart in Exhibit 10.3. Nordstrom is known for its extraordinary customer service, and the organization chart symbolizes that managers are to support the employees who *give* the service rather than be managers who control them.[15]
- President Bill Arnold of Nashville's Centennial Medical Center symbolized his commitment to an open door policy by ripping his office door from its hinges and suspending it from the ceiling where all employees could see it.[16]

Language. The final technique for influencing culture is **language**. Many companies use a specific saying, slogan, metaphor, or other form of language to convey special meaning to employees. Slogans can be readily picked up and repeated by employees as well as customers of the company. At Speedy Muffler in Canada, the saying "At Speedy you're somebody" applies to employees and customers alike. Other significant uses of language to shape culture are as follows:

- T. J. Watson, Jr., son of the founder of International Business Machines, used the metaphor "wild ducks" to describe the type of employees needed by IBM. His point was, "You can make wild ducks tame, but you can never make tame ducks wild again."[17] Wild ducks symbolized the freedom and opportunity that must be available to keep from taming creative employees at IBM.
- At Sequins International, where 80 percent of the employees are Hispanic, words from W. Edwards Deming, "You don't have to please the boss; you have to please the customer," are embroidered in Spanish on the pockets of workers' jackets. Employees work in teams and are empowered to make quality and customer satisfaction improvements.[18]

Recall that culture exists at two levels—the underlying values and assumptions and the visible artifacts and observable behaviors. The slogans, symbols, and ceremonies described above are artifacts that reflect underlying company values. These visible artifacts and behaviors can be used by managers to shape company values and to strengthen organizational culture. Now we will discuss how a strong corporate culture can have either positive or negative outcomes.

Culture Strength and Adaptation

When an organizational culture is strong, it can have a powerful impact, though not necessarily always a positive one. **Culture strength** refers to the degree of

Exhibit 10.3

*Organization Chart
for Nordstrom, Inc.*

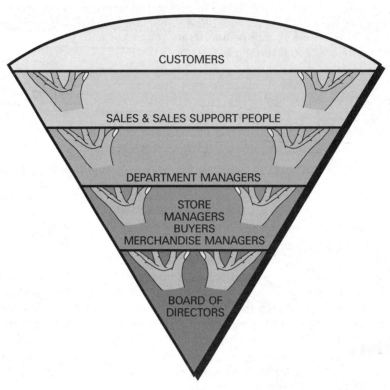

Source: Used with permission of Nordstrom, Inc.

agreement among members of an organization about the importance of specific values. If widespread consensus exists about the importance of those values, the culture is cohesive and strong; if little agreement exists, the culture is weak.[19]

A strong culture is typically associated with the frequent use of ceremonies, symbols, stories, heroes, and slogans. These elements increase employee commitment to the values and strategy of a company.

However, research into some two hundred corporate cultures found that a strong culture does not ensure success unless the culture is one that encourages a healthy adaptation to the external environment.[20] A strong culture that does not encourage adaptation can be more damaging to an organization's success than having a weak culture. Consider the case of IBM in Chapter 1, where a strong corporate culture actually precluded adaptation.

As illustrated in Exhibit 10.4, adaptive corporate cultures have different values and behavior patterns than unadaptive cultures. In adaptive cultures, managers are concerned about customers and employees, and they strongly value processes that contribute to useful change. Behavior is flexible; managers initiate change when needed, even if it involves risk. In an unadaptive corporate culture, on the other hand, managers are more concerned about themselves or some pet project. Their values discourage risk-taking and change. Thus, while strong, healthy cultures help organizations adapt to the external environment, strong, unhealthy cultures can encourage an organization to march resolutely in the wrong direction.

Exhibit 10.4 *Adaptive versus Nonadaptive Corporate Cultures*

	Adaptive Corporate Cultures	**Unadaptive Corporate Cultures**
Core Values	Managers care deeply about customers, stockholders, and employees. They also strongly value people and processes that can create useful change (for example, leadership initiatives up and down the management hierarchy).	Managers care mainly about themselves, their immediate work group, or some product (or technology) associated with that work group. They value the orderly and risk-reducing management process much more highly than leadership initiatives.
Common Behavior	Managers pay close attention to all their constituencies, especially customers, and initiate change when needed to serve their legitimate interests, even if it entails taking some risks.	Managers tend to be somewhat isolated, political, and bureaucratic. As a result, they do not change their strategies quickly to adjust to or take advantage of changes in their business environments.

Source: Adapted and reprinted with the permission of The Free Press, an imprint of Simon & Schuster, from *Corporate Culture and Performance* by John P. Kotter and James L. Heskett. Copyright © 1992 by Kotter Associates, Inc. and James L. Heskett.

The Hewlett-Packard stories discussed earlier reinforced an adaptive internal culture consistent with the "HP Way." Insistence on product quality, recognition of employee achievement, and respect for individual employees are the values responsible for HP's success.

STRATEGY AND CULTURE

Strategy and the external environment are big influences on corporate culture. Corporate culture should embody what the organization needs to be effective within its environment. For example, if the external environment requires flexibility and responsiveness, the culture should encourage adaptability. The correct relationship between cultural values and beliefs, organizational strategy, and the business environment can enhance organizational performance.

Studies of culture and effectiveness have proposed that the fit among strategy, environment, and culture is associated with four categories of culture, which are illustrated in Exhibit 10.5.[21] These categories are based on two factors: (1) the extent to which the competitive environment requires flexibility or stability and (2) the extent to which the strategic focus and strength is internal or external. The four categories associated with these differences are adaptability/entrepreneurial, mission, clan, and bureaucratic.

The Adaptability/Entrepreneurial Culture

The **adaptability/entrepreneurial culture** is characterized by strategic focus on the external environment through flexibility and change to meet customer needs. The culture encourages norms and beliefs that support the capacity of the organization to detect, interpret, and translate signals from the environment into new behavior responses.

This type of company doesn't just react quickly to environmental changes, however; it actively creates change. Innovation, creativity, and risk-taking are valued and rewarded.

Exhibit 10.5

*Relationship of
Environment and
Strategy to Corporate
Culture*

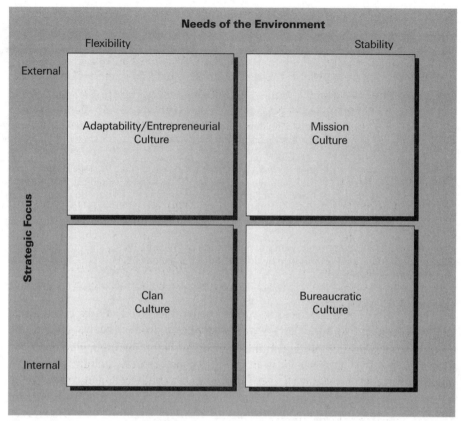

Source: Based on Daniel R. Denison and Aneil K. Mishra, "Toward a Theory of Organizational Culture and Effectiveness," *Organization Science*, Vol. 6, No. 2, March–April 1995, 204–23; R. Hooijberg and F. Petrock, "On Cultural Change: Using the Competing Values Framework to Help Leaders Execute a Transformational Strategy," *Human Resource Management* 32 (1993), 29–50; and R. E. Quinn, *Beyond Rational Management: Mastering the Paradoxes and Competing Demands of High Performance* (San Francisco: Jossey-Bass, 1988).

An example of the adaptability/entrepreneurial culture is 3M, a company whose values promote individual initiative and entrepreneurship. All new employees attend a class on risk-taking, where they are told to pursue their ideas even if it means defying their supervisors. Marketing, electronics, and cosmetic companies may also use this type of culture because they must move quickly to satisfy customers.

The Mission Culture

An organization concerned with serving specific customers in the external environment, but without the need for rapid change, is suited to the mission culture. The **mission culture** is characterized by emphasis on a clear vision of the organization's purpose and on the achievement of goals, such as sales growth, profitability, or market share, to help achieve the purpose. Individual employees may be responsible for a specified level of performance and the organization promises specified rewards in return. Managers shape behavior by envisioning and communicating a desired future state for the organization. Because the environment is stable, they can translate the vision into measurable goals and evaluate employee performance for meeting them. In some cases, mission cultures reflect a high level of competitiveness and a profit-making orientation.

One example is PepsiCo, where former CEO Wayne Calloway set a vision to be the best consumer products company in the world. Managers who met the high performance standards were generously rewarded—first-class air travel, fully loaded company cars, stock options, bonuses, and rapid promotion. Annual performance reviews focused specifically on meeting performance goals, such as sales targets or marketing goals.[22]

The Clan Culture

The **clan culture** has a primary focus on the involvement and participation of the organization's members and on rapidly changing expectations from the external environment. This culture is similar to the clan form of control described in Chapter 9. More than any other, this culture focuses on the needs of employees as the route to high performance. Involvement and participation create a sense of responsibility and ownership and, hence, greater commitment to the organization.

Southwest Airlines, described at the beginning of this chapter, is an example of a clan culture. The most important value is taking care of employees. In so doing, the organization is able to adapt to competition and changing markets. Companies in the fashion and retail industries also use this culture because it releases the creativity of employees to respond to rapidly changing tastes.

The Bureaucratic Culture

The **bureaucratic culture** has an internal focus and a consistency orientation for a stable environment. This organization has a culture that supports a methodical approach to doing business. Symbols, heroes, and ceremonies support cooperation, tradition, and following established policies and practices as a way to achieve goals. Personal involvement is somewhat lower here, but that is outweighed by a high level of consistency, conformity, and collaboration among members. This organization succeeds by being highly integrated and efficient.

One example of a bureaucratic culture is Safeco Insurance Company, considered by some to be stuffy and regimented. Employees take their coffee breaks at an assigned time, and the dress codes specify white shirts and suits for men and no beards. However, employees like this culture. Reliability counts. Extra work is not required. The culture is appropriate for the insurance company, which succeeds because it can be trusted to deliver on insurance policies as agreed.[23]

ETHICAL VALUES IN ORGANIZATIONS

Of the values that make up an organization's culture, ethical values are now considered among the most important. Ethical standards are becoming part of the formal policies and informal cultures of many organizations, and courses in ethics are taught in many business schools. **Ethics** is the code of moral principles and values that governs the behaviors of a person or group with respect to what is right or wrong. Ethical values set standards as to what is good or bad in conduct and decision making.[24]

Ethics is distinct from behaviors governed by law. The **rule of law** arises from a set of codified principles and regulations that describe how people are required to act, are generally accepted in society, and are enforceable in the courts.[25]

The relationship between ethical standards and legal requirements is illustrated in Exhibit 10.6. Ethical standards for the most part apply to behavior not covered by the law, and the rule of law covers behaviors not necessarily covered by ethical standards. Current laws often reflect combined moral judgments, but not all moral judgments are codified into law. The morality of aiding a drowning person, for example, is not specified by law, and driving on the right hand side of the road has no moral basis; but in areas such as robbery or murder, rules and moral standards overlap.

Many people believe that if you are not breaking the law, then you are behaving in an ethical manner, but ethics often goes far beyond the law.[26] Many behaviors have not been codified, and managers must be sensitive to emerging norms and values about those issues. **Managerial ethics** are principles that guide the decisions and behaviors of managers with regard to whether they are right or wrong in a moral sense. The notion of **social responsibility** is an extension of this idea and refers to management's obligation to make choices and take action so that the organization contributes to the welfare and interest of society as well as to itself.[27]

Examples of the need for managerial ethics are as follows:[28]

- The supervisor of a travel agency was aware that she and her agents could receive large bonuses for booking one hundred or more clients each month with an auto rental firm, although clients typically wanted the rental agency selected on the basis of lowest cost.
- The executive in charge of a parts distribution facility told employees to tell phone customers that inventory was in stock even if it was not. Replenishing the item took only one to two days, no one was hurt by the delay, and the business was kept from competitors.
- The project manager for a consulting project wondered whether some facts should be left out of a report because the marketing executives paying for the report would look bad if the facts were reported.

Exhibit 10.6

Relationship between the Rule of Law and Ethical Standards

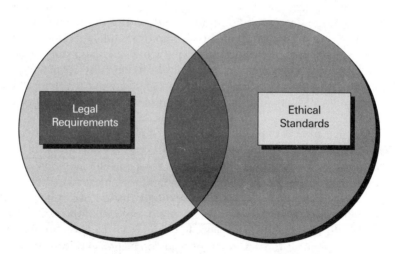

Source: LaRue Tone Hosmer, *The Ethics of Management,* 2d ed. (Homewood, Ill.: Irwin, 1991).

- A North American manufacturer operating abroad was asked to make cash payments (a bribe) to government officials and was told it was consistent with local customs, despite being illegal in North America.

These issues are exceedingly difficult to resolve and often represent dilemmas. An ethical dilemma arises when each alternative choice or behavior seems undesirable because of a potentially negative ethical consequence. Right or wrong cannot be clearly identified. These choices can be aided by establishing ethical values within the organization as part of corporate culture. Corporate culture can embrace the ethical values needed for business success.

HOW LEADERS SHAPE CULTURE AND ETHICS

A report issued by the Business Roundtable—an association of chief executives from 250 large corporations—discussed ethics, policy, and practice in one hundred member companies, including GTE, Xerox, Johnson & Johnson, Boeing, and Hewlett-Packard.[29] In the experience of the surveyed companies, the single most important factor in ethical decision making was the role of top management in providing commitment, leadership, and example for ethical values. The CEO and other top managers must be committed to specific values and must give constant leadership in tending and renewing those values. Values can be communicated in a number of ways—speeches, company publications, policy statements, and, especially, personal actions. Top leaders are responsible for creating and sustaining a culture that emphasizes the importance of ethical behavior for all employees every day. When the CEO engages in unethical practices or fails to take firm and decisive action in response to the unethical practices of others, this attitude filters down through the organization. Formal ethics codes and training programs are worthless if leaders do not set and live up to high standards of ethical conduct.[30]

The following sections examine how managers signal and implement values through leadership as well as through the formal systems of the organization.

Value-Based Leadership

The underlying value system of an organization cannot be managed in the traditional way. Issuing an authoritative directive, for example, has little or no impact on an organization's value system.

Organizational values are developed and strengthened primarily through **value-based leadership**, a relationship between a leader and followers that is based on shared, strongly internalized values that are advocated and acted upon by the leader.[31] Leaders influence cultural and ethical values by clearly articulating a vision for organizational values that employees can believe in, communicating the vision throughout the organization, and institutionalizing the vision through everyday behavior, rituals, ceremonies, and symbols, as well as through organizational systems and policies.

Leaders must remember that every statement and action has impact on culture and values, perhaps without their realizing it. Employees learn about values, beliefs and goals from watching managers, just as students learn which topics are important for an exam, what professors like, and how to get a good grade from watching professors. To be effective value-based leaders, executives often use symbols, ceremonies, speeches, and slogans that match the values.

Most important, actions speak louder than words, so value-based leaders "walk their talk."[32] At Eastman Kodak, for example, CEO George Fisher has emphasized the organization's commitment to social responsibility by linking a portion of his own pay to social factors.[33]

Value-based leaders engender a high level of trust and respect from employees, based not only on their stated values but also on the courage, determination, and self-sacrifice they demonstrate in upholding the values. Leaders can use this respect and trust to motivate employees toward high performance and a sense of purpose in achieving the organizational vision. When leaders are willing to make personal sacrifices for the sake of values, employees also become more willing to do so. This element of self-sacrifice puts a somewhat spiritual connotation on the process of leadership. Indeed, one writer in organization theory, Karl Weick, has said, "Managerial work can be viewed as managing myth, symbols, and labels . . . ; because managers traffic so often in images, the appropriate role for the manager may be evangelist rather than accountant."[34]

An excellent example of a value-based leader is Max De Pree, retired CEO of Herman Miller, whose books, *Leadership is an Art* and *Leadership Jazz*, offer insights into his success as a leader. De Pree defines his "covenant" model of leadership as an emotional bond creating mutual trust built on shared goals and values. De Pree believes effective leadership can occur only when there is a "sacred" relationship between leaders and followers.

De Pree was a hero to his workers. He symbolized hard work, integrity, and a constant awareness of how his decisions affected those who followed his leadership. He believed that leadership should "[liberate] people to do what is required of them in the most effective and humane way possible." De Pree worked to create and sustain an environment in which each employee wanted to do his or her best, helping the company gain recognition by *Fortune* magazine as one of the ten best managed, most innovative companies in America.[35]

Formal Structure and Systems

Another set of tools leaders can use to shape cultural and ethical values is the formal structure and systems of the organization. These systems have been especially effective in recent years for influencing managerial ethics.

Structure. Managers can assign responsibility for ethical values to a specified position. This not only allocates organization time and energy to the problem but symbolizes to everyone the importance of ethics. One example is an **ethics committee,** which is a group of executives appointed to oversee company ethics. The committee provides rulings on questionable ethical issues and assumes responsibility for disciplining wrongdoers.

Many companies are setting up ethics offices that go beyond a "police" mentality to act more as counseling centers. Northrup Grumman, A Los Angeles defense contractor, set up an ethics office in the mid-1980s primarily to ferret out wrongdoers. Today, however, the department spends most of its time dealing with day-to-day ethical dilemmas, questions, and appeals for advice. The department is also responsible for training employees based on a statement of values intended to guide behavior.[36]

Another example is an **ethics ombudsperson**, who is a single manager, perhaps with a staff, who serves as the corporate conscience. As work forces become more diverse and organizations continue to emphasize greater employee involvement, it is likely that more and more companies will assign ombudspersons to listen to grievances, investigate ethical complaints, and point out employee concerns and possible ethical abuses to top management. For the system to work, it is necessary for the person in this position to have direct access to the chairman or CEO, as does the corporate ombudsman for Pitney Bowes.[37]

Disclosure Mechanisms. The ethics office, committee, or ombudsperson provide mechanisms for employees to voice concerns about ethical practices. One important function is to establish supportive policies and procedures about whistle-blowing. **Whistle-blowing** is employee disclosure of illegal, immoral, or illegitimate practices on the part of the organization.[38] One value of corporate policy is to protect whistle-blowers so they will not be transferred to lower-level positions or fired because of their ethical concerns. A policy can also encourage whistle-blowers to stay within the organization—for instance, to quietly blow the whistle to responsible managers.[39] Whistle-blowers have the option to stop organizational activities by going to newspaper or television reporters, but as a last resort.

Although whistle-blowing has become widespread in recent years, it is still risky for employees, who can lose their jobs or be ostracized by coworkers. Sometimes managers believe a whistle-blower is out of line and think they are acting correctly to fire or sabotage that employee. As ethical problems in the corporate world increase, many companies are looking for ways to protect whistle-blowers. In addition, calls are increasing for legal protection for those who report illegal or unethical business activities.[40]

When there are no protective measures, whistle-blowers suffer, and the company may continue its unethical or illegal practices. After exposing fraud in the real estate funds he managed for Prudential Insurance Company of America, Mark Jorgensen suffered ostracism by his supervisor and colleagues, was accused by company lawyers of breaking the law, and was eventually dismissed. Although the company later offered Jorgensen an apology and his job back (which he declined), this could not make up for the months of despair he and his family suffered.[41]

Although many whistle-blowers are prepared to suffer financial loss to maintain ethical standards, many companies have created a climate in which employees feel free to point out problems. A growing number of corporations, including Texas Instruments, Nynex, Raytheon, Pacific Bell, and Northern Telecom, are setting up ethics hot lines that give employees a confidential way to report misconduct.

Code of Ethics. A recent study by the Center for Business Ethics found that 90 percent of *Fortune* 500 companies and almost half of all other companies have developed a corporate *code of ethics*.[42] The code clarifies company expectations of employee conduct and makes clear that the company expects its personnel to recognize the ethical dimensions of corporate behavior.

Some companies use broader mission statements within which ethics is a part. These statements define ethical values as well as corporate culture and contain language about company responsibility, quality of product, and treatment of employees. GTE, Norton, and Chemical Bank all have established statements of cultural and ethical values.[43] Northern Telecom's *Code of Business Conduct*, which is provided to all employees in booklet form and is also available on the Internet, is a set of standards and guidelines that illustrate how the company's core values and mission translate into ethical business practices.

A code of ethics states the values or behaviors that are expected as well as those that will not be tolerated or backed up by management's action. A code of ethics or larger mission statement is an important tool in the management of organizational values.

Training Programs. To ensure that ethical issues are considered in daily decision making, companies can supplement a written code of ethics with employee training programs.[44] A recent survey showed that 45 percent of responding companies were including ethics training in employee seminars. McDonnell Douglas has a corporate-wide ethics training program that all management and nonmanagement employees attend.[45] These training programs include case examples to give employees a chance to wrestle with ethical dilemmas. Training also provides rules or guidelines for decision making, and it discusses codes of ethics and mission statements.

Texas Instruments provides an eight-hour ethics training course for each employee and also incorporates an ethics component into every course it offers. For example, a new course on how to use Windows 95 included information on the ethics of copying and distributing software.

In an important step, ethics programs also include frameworks for ethical decision making that can help managers act autonomously and still think their way through a difficult decision. This training has been an important catalyst for establishing ethical behavior and integrity as critical components of strategic competitiveness.[46]

SUMMARY OF KEY ISSUES

This chapter covered a range of material on corporate culture, the importance of cultural and ethical values, and techniques managers can use to influence these values.

Culture is the set of key values, beliefs, and understandings shared by members of an organization. Organizational cultures serve two critically important functions—to integrate members so that they know how to relate to one another and to help the organization adapt to the external environment. Culture can be observed and interpreted through rites and ceremonies, stories and heroes, symbols, and language. Strong corporate cultures can be either adaptive or unadaptive. Adaptive cultures have different values and different behavior patterns than unadaptive cultures. Strong but unhealthy cultures can be detrimental to a company's chances for success. Four types of cultures that may exist in organizations are adaptability/entrepreneurial culture, mission culture, clan culture, and bureaucratic culture. Leaders can shape organizational culture and ethics. One important idea is value-based leadership, which means leaders define a vision of proper values, communicate it throughout the organization, and institutionalize it through everyday behavior, rituals, ceremonies, and symbols.

We also discussed formal systems that are important for shaping ethical values. Formal systems include an ethics committee, an ethics ombudsperson, disclosure mechanisms for whistle-blowing, ethics training programs, and a code of ethics or mission statement that specifies ethical values.

Discussion Questions

1. Describe observable symbols, ceremonies, dress, or other aspects of culture and the underlying values they represent for an organization where you have worked.
2. Discuss how a strong corporate culture could be negative as well as positive for an organization.
3. Do you think a bureaucratic culture would be less employee-oriented than clan culture? Discuss.
4. Discuss the differences between rites of enhancement, renewal, and integration.
5. Why is value-based leadership so important to the influence of culture? Does a symbolic act communicate more about company values than an explicit statement? Discuss.
6. What importance would you attribute to leadership statements and actions for influencing ethical values and decision making in an organization?
7. Codes of ethics have been criticized for transferring responsibility for ethical behavior from the organization to the individual employee. Do you agree? Do you think a code of ethics is valuable for an organization?

Notes

1. Brenda Paik Sunoo, "How Fun Flies At Southwest Airlines," *Personnel Journal*, June 1995, 62–73; Kristin Dunlap Godsey, "Slow Climb to New Heights: Combine Strict Discipline with Goofy Antics and Make Billions," *Success*, October 1996, 20–26; "Southwest Airlines' Herb Kelleher: Unorthodoxy at Work," an interview with William G. Lee, *Management Review*, January 1995, 9–12.

2. Charles O'Reilly, "Corporations, Culture, and Commitment: Motivation and Social Control in Organizations," *California Management Review* 31 (Summer 1989): 9–25.

3. W. Jack Duncan, "Organizational Culture: 'Getting a Fix' on an Elusive Concept," *Academy of Management Executive* 3 (1989): 229–36; Linda Smircich, "Concepts of Culture and Organizational Analysis," *Administrative Science Quarterly* 28 (1983): 339–58; Andrew D. Brown and Ken Starkey, "The Effect of Organizational Culture on Communication and Information," *Journal of Management Studies* 31:6 (November 1994): 807–28.

4. Edgar H. Schein, "Organizational Culture," *American Psychologist* 45 (February 1990): 109–19.

5. Harrison M. Trice and Janice M. Beyer, "Studying Organizational Cultures through Rites and Ceremonials," *Academy of Management Review* 9 (1984): 653–69; Janice M. Beyer and Harrison M. Trice, "How an Organization's Rites Reveal Its Culture," *Organizational Dynamics* 15 (Spring 1987): 5–24; Steven P. Feldman, "Management in Context: An Essay on the Relevance of Culture to the Understanding of Organizational Change," *Journal of Management Studies* 23 (1986): 589–607; Mary Jo Hatch, "The Dynamics of Organizational Culture," *Academy of Management Review* 18 (1993): 657–93.

6. This discussion is based on Edgar H. Schein, *Organizational Culture and Leadership*, 2d ed. (Homewood, Ill.: Richard D. Irwin, 1992); John P. Kotter and James L. Heskett, *Corporate Culture and Performance* (New York: Free Press, 1992).

7. Charlotte B. Sutton, "Richness Hierarchy of the Cultural Network: The Communication of Corporate Values" (Unpublished manuscript, Texas A&M University, 1985); Terrence E. Deal and Allan A. Kennedy, "Culture: A New Look through Old Lenses," *Journal of Applied Behavioral Science* 19 (1983): 498–505.

8. Thomas C. Dandridge, "Symbols at Work" (Working paper, School of Business, State University of New York at Albany, 1978), 1.

9. Alan Farnham, "Mary Kay's Lessons in Leadership," *Fortune*, 30 September 1993, 68–77.

10. Thomas J. Peters and Robert H. Waterman, Jr., *In Search of Excellence* (New York: Harper & Row, 1982).

11. Don Hellriegle and John W. Slocum, Jr., *Management*, 7th ed. (Cincinnati, Ohio: South-Western College Publishing, 1996), 537.

12. Trice and Beyer, "Studying Organizational Cultures through Rites and Ceremonials."

13. Sutton, "Richness Hierarchy of the Cultural Network"; Deal and Kennedy, *Corporate Cultures*.

14. Gregory M. Bounds, Gregory H. Dobbins, and Oscar S. Fowler, *Management: A Total Quality Perspective* (Cincinnati, Ohio: South-Western College Publishing, 1995), 353–54.

15. "FYI," *Inc.*, April 1991, 14.

16. Nancy K. Austin, "Wacky Management Ideas that Work," *Working Woman*, November 1991, 42–44.

17. Richard Ott, "Are Wild Ducks Really Wild: Symbolism and Behavior in the Corporate Environment" (Paper presented at the Northeastern Anthropological Association, March 1979).

18. Barbara Ettorre, "Retooling People and Processes," *Management Review* (June 1995): 19–23.

19. Bernard Arogyaswamy and Charles M. Byles, "Organizational Culture: Internal and External Fits," *Journal of Management* 13 (1987): 647–59.

20. Kotter and Heskett, *Corporate Culture and Performance*.

21. Based on Daniel R. Denison, *Corporate Culture and Organizational Effectiveness* (New York: John Wiley & Sons, 1990), 11–15; Daniel R. Denison and Aneil K. Mishra, "Toward a Theory of Organizational Culture and Effectiveness," *Organization Science*, Vol. 6, No. 2 (March–April 1995): 204–23; R. Hooijberg and F. Petrock, "On Cultural Change: Using the Competing Values Framework to Help Leaders Execute a Transformational Strategy," *Human Resource Management* 32 (1993): 29–50; R. E. Quinn, *Beyond Rational Management: Mastering the Paradoxes and*

Competing Demands of High Performance (San Francisco: Jossey-Bass, 1988).

22. Brian Dumaine, "Those High Flying PepsiCo Managers," *Fortune,* 10 April 1989; L. Zinn, J. Berry, and G. Burns, "Will the Pepsi Brass Be Drinking Hemlock?" *Business Week*, 25 July 1994, 31; S. Lubove, "We Have a Big Pond to Play in," *Forbes,* 12 September 1993, 216–24; and J. Wolfe, "PepsiCo and the Fast Food Industry," in M. A. Hitt, R. D. Ireland, and R. E. Hoskisson, eds., *Strategic Management: Competitiveness and Globalization*, (St. Paul, Minn.: West Publishing, 1995), 879.

23. Carey Quan Jelernter, "Safeco: Success Depends Partly on Fitting the Mold," *Seattle Times*, 5 June 1986, D8.

24. Gordon F. Shea, *Practical Ethics* (New York: American Management Association, 1988); Linda K. Trevino, "Ethical Decision Making in Organizations: A Person-Situation Interactionist Model," *Academy of Management Review* 11 (1986): 601–17.

25. LaRue Tone Hosmer, *The Ethics of Management*, 2d ed., (Homewood, Ill.: Irwin, 1991).

26. Dawn-Marie Driscoll, "Don't Confuse Legal and Ethical Standards," *Business Ethics*, July/August 1996, 44.

27. Eugene W. Szwajkowski, "The Myths and Realities of Research on Organizational Misconduct," in James E. Post, ed., *Research and Corporate Social Performance and Policy*, Vol. 9 (Greenwich, Conn.: JAI Press, 1986), 103–22.

28. These incidents are from Hosmer, *The Ethics of Management.*

29. *Corporate Ethics: A Prime Business Asset.*

30. Andrew W. Singer, "The Ultimate Ethics Test," *Across the Board*, March 1992, 19–22; Ronald B. Morgan, "Self and Co-Worker Perceptions of Ethics and Their Relationships to Leadership and Salary," *Academy of Management Journal*, 36, No. 1 (February 1993): 200–14; and Joseph L. Badaracco, Jr., and Allen P. Webb, "Business Ethics: A View From the Trenches," *California Management Review* 37, No. 2 (Winter 1995): 8–28.

31. This discussion is based on Robert J. House, Andre Delbecq, and Toon W. Taris, "Value Based Leadership: An Integrated Theory and an Empirical Test," working paper.

32. Peters and Waterman, *In Search of Excellence.*

33. "Best Moves of 1995," *Business Ethics*, January/February 1996, 23.

34. Karl E. Weick, "Cognitive Processes in Organizations," in B. M. Staw, ed., *Research in Organizations*, Vol. 1 (Greenwich, Conn.: JAI Press, 1979), 42.

35. Patrick E. Murphy and Georges Enderle, "Managerial Ethical Leadership: Examples Do Matter," *Business Ethics Quarterly*, Vol. 5, Issue 1 (January 1995): 117–28.

36. Beverly Geber, "The Right and Wrong of Ethics Offices," *Training*, October 1995, 102–18.

37. Justin Martin, "New Tricks for an Old Trade," *Across the Board*, June 1992, 40–44.

38. Janet P. Near and Marcia P. Miceli, "Effective Whistle-Blowing," *Academy of Management Review*, Vol. 20, No. 3 (1995): 679–708.

39. Richard P. Nielsen, "Changing Unethical Organizational Behavior," *Academy of Management Executive* 3 (1989): 123–30

40. Jene G. James, "Whistle-Blowing: Its Moral Justification," in Peter Madsen and Jay M Shafritz, eds, *Essentials of Business Ethics* (New York: Meridian Books, 1990), 160–90; Janet P. Near, Terry Morehead Dworkin, and Marcia P. Miceli "Explaining the Whistle-Blowing Process: Suggestions from Power Theory and Justice Theory," *Organization Science* 4 (1993): 393–411.

41. Kurt Eichenwald, "He Told, He Suffered, Now He's a Hero," *The New York Times*, 29 May 1994, Section 3,1.

42. W. Carolyn Wiley, "The ABC's of Business Ethics: Definitions, Philosophies, and Implementation," *IM*, January/February 1995, 22–27.

43. Saul W. Gellerman, "Managing Ethics from the Top Down," *Sloan Management Review* (Winter 1989): 73–79; Donald Robin, Michael Giallourakis, Fred R. David, and Thomas E. Moritz, "A Different Look at Codes of Ethics," *Business Horizons* (January–February 1989): 66–71.

44. James Weber, "Institutionalizing Ethics into Business Organizations: A Model and Research Agenda," *Business Ethics Quarterly* 3 (1993): 419–36.

45. Susan J. Harrington, "What Corporate America is Teaching about Ethics," *Academy of Management Executive* 5 (1991): 21–30.

46. Harrington, "What Corporate America is Teaching about Ethics."

11

chapter eleven

Decision Making Processes

While reading this chapter, think about your answers to the following questions:

- What is the difference between programmed and nonprogrammed decisions, and how is today's environment affecting the frequency of these decisions in organizations?

- What is the difference between the rational approach to individual decision making and the bounded rationality perspective?

- What are three primary approaches to organizational decision making, and how do they relate to the problem identification or problem solution stages of a decision situation?

- Discuss the concepts of "decision learning" and "escalating commitment" and how they affect organizational decision making.

Every organization grows, prospers, or fails as a result of decisions by its managers, and decisions can be risky and uncertain, without any guarantee of success. Decision making must be done amid constantly changing factors, unclear information, and conflicting points of view. Intel Corporation, the leading supplier of microprocessors in the computer industry, was propelled to its current dominance by a decision CEO Andrew Grove made in the 1980s. Over the strong objections of other executives, Grove decided to take Intel out of the DRAM memory-chip business—a technology Intel had invented—and focus relentlessly on microprocessors. The decision proved to be a boon to the company, but the outcome was certainly not clear in 1985. A more recent decision by Grove—the initial refusal to replace faulty Pentium chips—put the company in the midst of a public relations disaster. Intel's reputation was not seriously damaged because Grove later agreed to a Pentium replacement policy and implemented new procedures to keep Intel in closer touch with customers.[1]

Many organizational decisions are complete failures. For example, Coca-Cola thought it had a sure-fire winner in its BreakMate, a miniature soda fountain designed for office use and targeted to small offices without enough workers to support a standard vending machine. But maintaining the machines proved to be a major headache. After pumping some $30 million into the biggest development project in its history, Coke never saw a profit and BreakMate fountains now sit gathering dust in storage sheds. Apple Computer is facing serious trouble because of a series of poor decisions, perhaps the most damaging being the failure to license its technology to other computer makers to permit Mac clones. If the decision had gone the other direction, many observers believe that Apple, not Microsoft, would now be ruling the computer business.[2]

However, managers also make many successful decisions every day. For example, Pepsi-Cola's quick and open response to reports of syringes found in cans of Pepsi enhanced the company's reputation. Lee Iacocca's decision to forgo an alliance with foreign auto makers and instead have Chrysler build the new Dodge Neon revived not only the company but perhaps the entire U.S. auto industry.[3]

PURPOSE OF THIS CHAPTER

At any time, an organization may be identifying problems and implementing alternatives for hundreds of decisions. Managers and organizations somehow muddle through these processes.[4] The purpose here is to analyze these processes to learn what decision making is actually like in organizational settings.

Decision-making processes can be thought of as the brain and nervous system of an organization. Decision making is the end use of the information and control systems described in Chapter 9. Decisions are made about organization strategy, structure, innovation, and acquisitions. This chapter explores how organizations can and should make decisions about these issues.

The first section of the chapter defines decision making. The next section examines how individual managers make decisions. Then several models of organizational decision making are explored. Each model is used in a different organizational situation. The final section in this chapter discusses special issues, such as decision mistakes.

DEFINITIONS

Organizational decision making is formally defined as the process of identifying and solving problems. The process contains two major stages. The **problem identification** stage is where information about environmental and organizational conditions is monitored to determine if performance is satisfactory and to diagnose the cause of shortcomings. The **problem solution** stage is where alternative courses of action are considered and one alternative is selected and implemented.

Organizational decisions vary in complexity and can be categorized as programmed or nonprogrammed.[5] **Programmed decisions** are repetitive and well defined, and procedures exist for resolving the problem. They are well structured because criteria of performance are normally clear, good information is available about current performance, alternatives are easily specified, and there is relative certainty that the chosen alternative will be successful. Examples of programmed decisions include decision rules, such as when to replace an office copy machine, when to reimburse managers for travel expenses, or whether an applicant has sufficient qualifications for an assembly-line job.

Nonprogrammed decisions are novel and poorly defined, and no procedure exists for solving the problem. They are used when an organization has not seen a problem before and may not know how to respond. Clear-cut decision criteria do not exist. Alternatives are fuzzy. There is uncertainty about whether a proposed solution will solve the problem. Typically, few alternatives can be developed for a nonprogrammed decision, so a single solution is custom-tailored to the problem.

The decision about how to deal with charges of faulty Pentium chips was a nonprogrammed decision. Intel had never faced this type of problem and did not have rules for dealing with it. Many nonprogrammed decisions involve strategic planning, because uncertainty is great and decisions are complex. For example, at Continental Airlines, new CEO Gordon M. Bethune decided to ground 41 planes, cut more than 4,200 jobs, and abolish cut-rate fares as part of his strategy to make the ailing airline profitable again. Bethune and other top managers had to analyze complex problems, evaluate alternatives, and make a choice about how to pull Continental out of its slump.[6]

Particularly complex nonprogrammed decisions have been referred to as "wicked" decisions, because simply defining the problem can turn into a major task. Wicked problems are associated with manager conflicts over objectives and alternatives, rapidly changing circumstances, and unclear linkages among decision elements. Managers dealing with a wicked decision may hit upon a solution that merely proves they failed to correctly define the problem to begin with.[7]

Today's managers and organizations are dealing with a higher percentage of nonprogrammed decisions because of the rapidly changing business environment. As outlined in Exhibit 11.1, today's environment has increased both the number and complexity of decisions that have to be made and created a need for new decision making processes. One example of how the environment affects organizations is the recent increase in the minimum wage. Managers at Popeye's Chicken & Biscuits have estimated that paying the higher wage will decrease operating profits by 25 percent or more and are considering decision alternatives such as cutting jobs or raising prices to meet the new conditions. Another example is globalization. The trend toward moving production to low-wage countries has managers all over corporate America struggling with ethical decisions concerning working conditions in the Third World and the loss of manufacturing jobs in small American communities.[8]

Today's Business Environment:

- Demands more large-scale change via new strategies, reengineering, restructuring, mergers, acquisitions, downsizing, new product or market development, etc.

↓

Decisions Made Inside the Organization:

- Are based on bigger, more complex, more emotionally charged issues
- Are made more quickly
- Are made in a less certain environment, with less clarity about means and outcomes
- Require more cooperation from more people involved in making and implementing decisions

↓

A New Decision Making Process:

- Is required because no one individual has the information needed to make all major decisions
- Is required because no one individual has the time and credibility needed to convince lots of people to implement the decision
- Relies less on hard data as a base for good decisions
- Is guided by a powerful coalition that can act as a team
- Permits decisions to evolve through trial and error and incremental steps as needed

---

Exhibit 11.1
*Decision Making in
Today's Environment*

Source: Adapted from John P. Kotter, *Leading Change* (Boston, Mass.: Harvard Business School Press, 1996), 56. Used with permission.

INDIVIDUAL DECISION MAKING

Individual decision making by managers can be described in two ways. First is the **rational approach**, which suggests how managers should try to make decisions. Second is the **bounded rationality perspective**, which describes how decisions actually have to be made under severe time and resource constraints. The rational approach is an ideal managers may work toward but never reach.

Rational Approach

The rational approach to individual decision making stresses the need for systematic analysis of a problem followed by choice and implementation in a logical step-by-step sequence. The rational approach was developed to guide individual decision making because many managers were observed to be unsystematic and arbitrary in their approach to organizational decisions. According to the rational approach, the decision process can be broken down into the following eight steps.[9]

1. *Monitor the decision environment.* In the first step, a manager monitors internal and external information that will indicate deviations from planned or acceptable behavior. He or she talks to colleagues and reviews financial statements, performance evaluations, industry indices, competitors' activities, and so forth. For example, during the pressure-packed five-week Christmas season, Linda Koslow, general manager of Marshall Fields' Oakbrook, Illinois, store, checks out competitors around the mall, eyeing whether they are marking down merchandise. She also scans printouts of her store's previous day's sales to learn what is or is not moving.[10]

2. *Define the decision problem.* The manager responds to deviations by identifying essential details of the problem: where, when, who was involved, who was affected, and how current activities are influenced. For Koslow, this means defining whether store profits are low because overall sales are less than expected or because certain lines of merchandise are not moving as expected.

3. *Specify decision objectives.* The manager determines what performance outcomes should be achieved by a decision.

4. *Diagnose the problem.* In this step, the manager digs below the surface to analyze the cause of the problem. Additional data may be gathered to facilitate this diagnosis. Understanding the cause enables appropriate treatment. For Koslow at Marshall Fields, the cause of slow sales may be competitors' marking down of merchandise or Marshall Fields' failure to display hot-selling items in a visible location.

5. *Develop alternative solutions.* Before a manager can move ahead with a decisive action plan, he or she must have a clear understanding of the various options available to achieve desired objectives. The manager may seek ideas and suggestions from other people. Koslow's alternatives for increasing profits could include buying fresh merchandise, running a sale, or reducing the number of employees.

6. *Evaluate alternatives.* This step may involve the use of statistical techniques or personal experience to assess the probability of success. The merits of each alternative are assessed as well as the probability that it will reach the desired objectives.

7. *Choose the best alternative.* This step is the core of the decision process. The manager uses his or her analysis of the problem, objectives, and alternatives to select a single alternative that has the best chance for success. At Marshall Fields, Koslow may choose to reduce the number of staff as a way to meet the profit goals rather than increase advertising or markdowns.

8. *Implement the chosen alternative.* Finally, the manager uses managerial, administrative and persuasive abilities and gives directions to ensure that the decision is carried out. The monitoring activity (step 1) begins again as soon as the solution is implemented. For Linda Koslow, the decision cycle is a continuous process, with new decisions made daily based on monitoring her environment for problems and opportunities.

The first four steps in this sequence are the problem identification stage of decision making, and the next four are the problem solution stage, as indicated in Exhibit 11.2. All eight steps normally appear in a manager's decision, although each step may not be a distinct element. Managers may know from experience exactly what to do in a situation, so one or more steps will be minimized.

The rational procedure works best for programmed decisions, when prob-

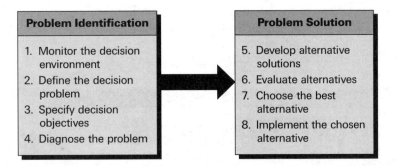

Exhibit 11.2
Steps in Rational Approach to Decision Making

lems, objectives, and alternatives are clearly defined and the decision maker has sufficient time for an orderly, thoughtful process. When decisions are nonprogrammed, ill defined, and piling on top of one another, the individual manager should still try to use the steps in the rational approach, but he or she often will have to take shortcuts by relying on intuition and experience. Deviations from the rational approach are explained by the bounded rationality perspective.

Bounded Rationality Perspective

The point of the rational approach is that managers should try to use systematic procedures to arrive at good decisions. When organizations are facing little competition and are dealing with well-understood issues, managers generally use rational procedures to make decisions.[11] Yet research into managerial decision making shows managers often are unable to follow an ideal procedure. In today's competitive environment, decisions often must be made very quickly. Time pressure, a large number of internal and external factors affecting a decision, and the ill-defined nature of many problems make systematic analysis virtually impossible. Managers have only so much time and mental capacity and, hence, cannot evaluate every goal, problem, and alternative. The attempt to be rational is bounded (limited) by the enormous complexity of many problems. There is a limit to how rational managers can be. For example, an executive in a hurry may have a choice of 50 ties on a rack but will take the first or second one that matches his suit. The executive doesn't carefully weigh all 50 alternatives because the short amount of time and the large number of plausible alternatives would be overwhelming. The manager simply selects the first tie that solves the problem and moves on to the next task.

Large organizational decisions are not only too complex to fully comprehend, but many other constraints impinge upon the decision maker, as illustrated in Exhibit 11.3. The circumstances are ambiguous, requiring social support, a shared perspective on what happens, and acceptance and agreement. For example, in a study of the decision making surrounding the Cuban missile crisis, the executive committee in the White House knew a problem existed but was unable to specify exact goals and objectives. The act of discussing the decision led to personal objections and finally to the discovery of desired objectives that helped clarify a course of action and possible consequences.[12] In addition, personal constraints—such as decision style, work pressure, desire for prestige, or simple feelings of insecurity—may restrict either the search for alternatives or the acceptability of an alternative. All of these factors limit a perfectly rational approach that should lead to an obviously ideal choice.[13] Even seemingly simple decisions, such as

Exhibit 11.3 *Constraints and Trade-offs during Nonprogrammed Decision Making*

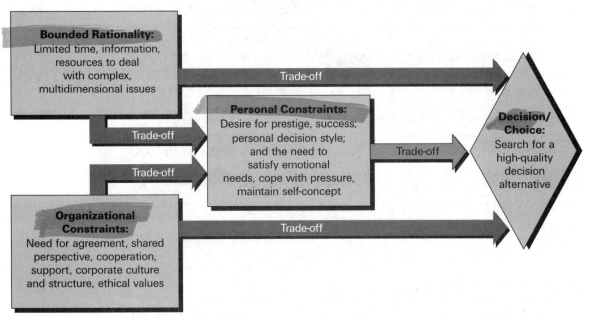

Source: Adapted from Irving L. Janis, *Crucial Decisions* (New York: Free Press, 1989); and A. L. George, *Presidential Decision Making in Foreign Policy: The Effective Use of Information and Advice* (Boulder, Colo,: Westview Press, 1980).

selecting a job upon graduation from college, can quickly become so complex that a bounded rationality approach is used. Graduating students have been known to search for a job until they have two or three acceptable job offers, at which point their search activity rapidly diminishes. Hundreds of firms may be available for interviews, and two or three job offers are far short of the maximum number that would be possible if students made the decision based on perfect rationality.

The bounded rationality perspective is often associated with intuitive decision processes. In **intuitive decision making**, experience and judgment rather than sequential logic or explicit reasoning are used to make decisions.[14] Intuition is not arbitrary or irrational because it is based on years of practice and hands-on experience, often stored in the subconscious. A manager using intuition based on long experience with organizational issues will more rapidly perceive and understand problems and develop a gut feeling or hunch about which alternative will solve a problem, thus speeding the decision making process.[15]

In a situation of great complexity or ambiguity, previous experience and judgment are needed to incorporate intangible elements, at both the problem identification and problem solution stage.[16] A study of manager problem finding showed that 30 of 33 problems were ambiguous and ill defined.[17] Bits and scraps of unrelated information from informal sources resulted in a pattern in the manager's mind. The manager could not "prove" a problem existed but knew intuitively that a certain area needed attention. A too simple view of a complex problem is often associated with decision failure,[18] and research shows managers are more likely to respond intuitively to a perceived threat to the organization than to an opportunity.[19]

For example, although IDS Financial Services was very profitable and grew rapidly in the early 1990s, a manager perceived a high turnover rate among the company's financial planners. She interpreted this as a weakness that could seriously threaten IDS's position in the increasingly competitive financial services industry. Other examples of problems that might be discovered through informal, intuitive processes are the possibility of impending legislation against the company, the need for a new product, customer dissatisfaction, and a need for reorganization by creating new departments.[20]

Intuitive processes are also used in the problem solution stage. A survey found that executives frequently made decisions without explicit reference to the impact on profits or to other measurable outcomes.[21] As we saw in Exhibit 11.3, many intangible factors—such as a person's concern about the support of other executives, fear of failure, and social attitudes—influence selection of the best alternative. These factors cannot be quantified in a systematic way, so intuition guides the choice of a solution. Managers may make decisions based on what they sense to be right rather than on what they can document with hard data.

A number of important decisions, some quite famous, have been based on hunch and intuition. For example, researchers who analyzed hard data warned film director George Lucas that his choice of *Star Wars* as the title of his film would turn away crowds at the box office, but Lucas stuck with his intuitive feeling that the title would work.[22]

Managers may walk a fine line between two extremes: making arbitrary decisions without careful study, and relying obsessively on numbers and rational analysis.[23] Remember that the bounded rationality perspective and the use of intuition applies mostly to nonprogrammed decisions. The novel, unclear, complex aspects of nonprogrammed decisions mean hard data and logical procedures are not available. A study of executive decision making found that managers simply could not use the rational approach for nonprogrammed decisions, such as when to buy a CT scanner for an osteopathic hospital or whether a city had a need for and could reasonably adopt a data processing system.[24] In those cases, managers had limited time and resources, and some factors simply couldn't be measured and analyzed. Trying to quantify such information could cause mistakes because it may oversimplify decision criteria.

ORGANIZATIONAL DECISION MAKING

Organizations are composed of managers who make decisions using both rational and intuitive processes; but organization-level decisions are not usually made by a single manager. Many organizational decisions involve several managers. Problem identification and problem solution involve many departments, multiple viewpoints and even other organizations, which are beyond the scope of an individual manager.

The processes by which decisions are made in organizations are influenced by a number of factors, particularly the organization's own internal structures as well as the degree of stability or instability of the external environment.[25] Research into organization-level decision making has identified three types of organizational decision-making processes: the management science approach, the Carnegie model, and the incremental decision process model.

Management Science Approach

The **management science approach** to organizational decision making is the analog to the rational approach by individual managers. Management science came into being during World War II.[26] At that time, mathematical and statistical techniques were applied to urgent, large-scale military problems that were beyond the ability of individual decision makers. Mathematicians, physicists, and operations researchers used systems analysis to develop artillery trajectories, antisubmarine strategies, and bombing strategies such as salvoing (discharging multiple shells simultaneously).

Management science yielded astonishing success for many military problems. This approach to decision making diffused into corporations and business schools, where techniques were studied and elaborated. Today, many corporations have assigned departments to use these techniques. The computer department develops quantitative data for analysis. Operations research departments use mathematical models to quantify relevant variables and develop a quantitative representation of alternative solutions and the probability of each one solving the problem. These departments also use such devices as linear programming, Bayesian statistics, PERT charts, and computer simulations.

Management science is an excellent device for organizational decision making when problems are analyzable and when the variables can be identified and measured. Mathematical models can contain a thousand or more variables, each one relevant in some way to the ultimate outcome. Management science techniques have been used to correctly solve problems as diverse as finding the right spot for a church camp, test marketing the first of a new family of products, drilling for oil, and radically altering the distribution of telecommunications services.[27] Other problems amenable to management science techniques are the scheduling of airline employees, telephone operators, and ambulance technicians.[28] By using mathematical formulations and techniques, Urgences Santé, the public agency responsible for coordinating ambulance service in the Montréal area, improved the quality of ambulance technicians' schedules as well as cut $250,000 a year from operating costs.[29]

Management science can accurately and quickly solve problems that have too many explicit variables for human processing. This system is at its best when applied to problems that are analyzable, measurable, and can be structured in a logical way.

Management science has also produced many failures.[30] In recent years, many banks have begun using computerized scoring systems to rate those applying for credit, but some argue that human judgment is needed to account for extenuating circumstances. In one case, a member of the Federal Reserve Board, the agency that sets interest rates and regulates banks, was denied a Toys 'R' Us credit card based on his computerized score.[31]

One problem with the management science approach, as discussed in Chapter 9, is that quantitative data are not rich. Informal cues that indicate the existence of problems have to be sensed on a more personal basis by managers.[32] The most sophisticated mathematical analyses are of no value if the important factors cannot be quantified and included in the model. Such things as competitor reactions, consumer "tastes," and product "warmth" are qualitative dimensions. In these situations, the role of management science is to supplement manager decision making. Quantitative results can be given to managers for discussion and interpretation along with their informal opinions, judgment, and intuition. The final decision can include qualitative factors as well as quantitative calculations.

Carnegie Model

The **Carnegie model** of organizational decision making is based upon the work of Richard Cyert, James March, and Herbert Simon, who were all associated with Carnegie-Mellon University.[33] Their research helped formulate the bounded rationality approach to individual decision making as well as provide new insights about organization decisions. Until their work, research in economics assumed that business firms made decisions as a single entity, as if all relevant information were funneled to the top decision maker for a choice. Research by the Carnegie group indicated that organization-level decisions involved many managers and that a final choice was based on a coalition among those managers. A **coalition** is an alliance among several managers who agree about organizational goals and problem priorities.[34] It could include managers from line departments, staff specialists, and even external groups, such as powerful customers, bankers, or union representatives.

Management coalitions are needed during decision making for two reasons. First, organizational goals are often ambiguous, and operative goals of departments are often inconsistent. When goals are ambiguous and inconsistent, managers disagree about problem priorities. They must bargain about problems and build a coalition around the question of which problems to solve. For example, months of discussion, bargaining, and planning took place before Chrysler decided not to abandon small-car production and began working on the new Neon.[35]

The second reason for coalitions is that individual managers intend to be rational but function with human cognitive limitations and other constraints, as described earlier. Managers do not have the time, resources, or mental capacity to identify all dimensions and to process all information relevant to a decision. These limitations lead to coalition-building behavior. Managers talk to each other and exchange points of view to gather information and reduce ambiguity. People who have relevant information or a stake in a decision outcome are consulted. Building a coalition will lead to a decision that is supported by interested parties.

The process of coalition formation has several implications for organizational decision behavior. First, decisions are made to satisfice rather than optimize problem solutions. **Satisficing** means organizations accept a "satisfactory" rather than a maximum level of performance, enabling them to achieve several goals simultaneously. In decision making, the coalition will accept a solution that is perceived as satisfactory to all coalition members. Second, managers are concerned with immediate problems and short-run solutions. They engage in what Cyert and March called problemistic search.[36] **Problemistic search** means managers look around in the immediate environment for a solution to quickly resolve a problem. Managers don't expect a perfect solution when the situation is ill defined and conflict-laden. This contrasts with the management science approach, which assumes that analysis can uncover every reasonable alternative. The Carnegie model says search behavior is just sufficient to produce a satisfactory solution and that managers typically adopt the first satisfactory solution that emerges. Third, discussion and bargaining are especially important in the problem identification stage of decision making. Unless coalition members perceive a problem, action will not be taken. The decision process described in the Carnegie model is summarized in Exhibit 11.4.

The Carnegie model points out that building agreement through a managerial coalition is a major part of organizational decision making. This is especially true at upper management levels. Discussion and bargaining are

Exhibit 11.4 *Choice Processes in the Carnegie Model*

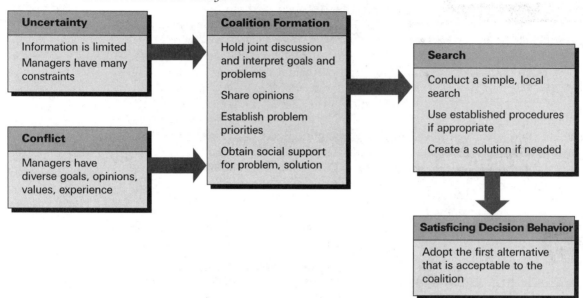

time-consuming, so search procedures are usually simple and the selected alternative satisfices rather than optimizes problem solution. When problems are programmed—are clear and have been seen before—the organization will rely on previous procedures and routines. Rules and procedures prevent the need for renewed coalition formation and political bargaining. Nonprogrammed decisions, however, require bargaining and conflict resolution.

One of the best and most visible coalition builders of recent years was former President George Bush, who would seek a broad-based coalition at the start of an important decision process. During the decision process regarding the Persian Gulf War, President Bush kept up a barrage of personal calls and visits to world leaders to gain agreement for his vision of forcing Saddam Hussein from Kuwait and for shaping a "new world order."[37]

Incremental Decision Process Model

Henry Mintzberg and his associates at McGill University in Montreal approached organizational decision making from a different perspective. They identified 25 decisions made in organizations and traced the events associated with these decisions from beginning to end.[38] Their research identified each step in the decision sequence. This approach to decision making, called the **incremental decision process model**, places less emphasis on the political and social factors described in the Carnegie model, but tells more about the structured sequence of activities undertaken from the discovery of a problem to its solution.[39]

Sample decisions in Mintzberg's research included choosing which jet aircraft to acquire for a regional airline, developing a new supper club, developing a new container terminal in a harbor, identifying a new market for a deodorant, installing a controversial new medical treatment in a hospital, and firing a star announcer.[40] The scope and importance of these decisions are revealed in the length of time taken to complete them. Most of these decisions took more than a year, and one-third of them took more than two years. Most of these decisions were nonprogrammed and required custom-designed solutions.

One discovery from this research is that major organization choices are usually a series of small choices that combine to produce the major decision. Thus, many organizational decisions are a series of nibbles rather than a big bite. Organizations move through several decision points and may hit barriers along the way. Mintzberg called these barriers *decision interrupts*. An interrupt may mean an organization has to cycle back through a previous decision and try something new. Decision loops or cycles are one way the organization learns which alternatives will work. The ultimate solution may be very different from what was initially anticipated.

The pattern of decision stages discovered by Mintzberg and his associates is shown in Exhibit 11.5. Each box indicates a possible step in the decision sequence. The steps take place in three major decision phases: identification, development, and selection.

Identification Phase. The identification phase begins with *recognition*. Recognition means one or more managers become aware of a problem and the need to make a decision. Recognition is usually stimulated by a problem or an opportunity. A problem exists when elements in the external environment change or when internal performance is perceived to be below standard. In the case of firing a radio announcer, comments about the announcer came from listeners, other announcers, and advertisers. Managers interpreted these cues until a pattern emerged that indicated a problem had to be dealt with.

The second step is *diagnosis*, which is where more information is gathered if needed to define the problem situation. Diagnosis may be systematic or informal, depending upon the severity of the problem. Severe problems do not have time for extensive diagnosis; the response must be immediate. Mild problems are usually diagnosed in a more systematic manner.

Development Phase. The development phase is when a solution is shaped to solve the problem defined in the identification phase. The development of a solution takes one of two directions. First, search procedures may be used to seek out alternatives within the organization's repertoire of solutions. For example, in firing the star announcer, managers asked what the radio station had done the last time an announcer had to be let go. To conduct the search, organization participants may look into their own memories, talk to other managers, or examine the formal procedures of the organization.

The second direction of development is to design a custom solution. This happens when the problem is novel so that previous experience has no value. Mintzberg found that in these cases, key decision makers have only a vague idea of the ideal solution. Gradually, through a trial-and-error process, a custom-designed alternative will emerge. Development of the solution is a groping, incremental procedure, building the solution brick by brick.

Selection Phase. The selection phase is when the solution is chosen. This phase is not always a matter of making a clear choice among alternatives. With custom-made solutions, selection is more an evaluation of the single alternative that seems feasible.

Evaluation and choice may be accomplished in three ways. The *judgment* form of selection is used when a final choice falls upon a single decision

Exhibit 11.5 *The Incremental Decision Process Model*

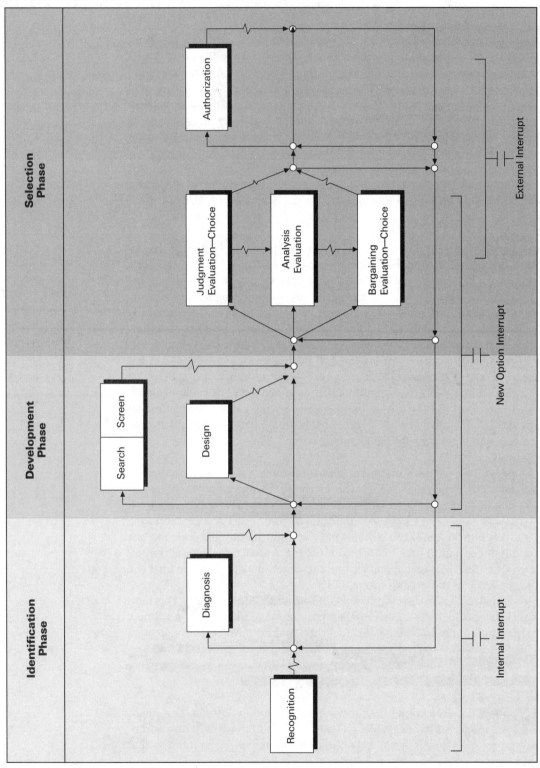

maker, and the choice involves judgment based upon experience. In *analysis*, alternatives are evaluated on a more systematic basis, such as with management science techniques. Mintzberg found that most decisions did not involve systematic analysis and evaluation of alternatives. *Bargaining* occurs when selection involves a group of decision makers. Each decision maker may have a different stake in the outcome, so conflict emerges. Discussion and bargaining occur until a coalition is formed, as in the Carnegie model described earlier.

When a decision is formally accepted by the organization, *authorization* takes place. The decision may be passed up the hierarchy to the responsible hierarchical level. Authorization is often routine because the expertise and knowledge rest with the lower decision makers who identified the problem and developed the solution. A few decisions are rejected because of implications not anticipated by lower-level managers.

Dynamic Factors. The lower part of the chart in Exhibit 11.5 shows lines running back toward the beginning of the decision process. These lines represent loops or cycles that take place in the decision process. Organizational decisions do not follow an orderly progression from recognition through authorization. Minor problems arise that force a loop back to an earlier stage. These are decision interrupts. If a custom-designed solution is perceived as unsatisfactory, the organization may have to go back to the very beginning and reconsider whether the problem is truly worth solving. Feedback loops can be caused by problems of timing, politics, disagreement among managers, inability to identify a feasible solution, turnover of managers, or the sudden appearance of a new alternative. For example, when a small Canadian airline made the decision to acquire jet aircraft, the board authorized the decision, but shortly after, a new chief executive was brought in and he canceled the contract, recycling the decision back to the identification phase. He accepted the diagnosis of the problem, but insisted upon a new search for alternatives. Then a foreign airline went out of business and two used aircraft became available at a bargain price. This presented an unexpected option, and the chief executive used his own judgment to authorize the purchase of the aircraft.[41]

Since most decisions take place over an extended period of time, circumstances change. Decision making is a dynamic process that may require a number of cycles before a problem is solved. An example of the incremental process and cycling that can take place is illustrated in Gillette's decision to create the Sensor razor, a process that took 13 years. The identification phase occurred when executives became aware of the need for a new razor and considered the idea of floating, thin blades that would make Gillette's cartridges easier to clean. During the development phase, engineers first tried to find established techniques. None fit the bill, so a trial and error custom design process followed. At the selection phase, some approaches were found too costly or too complicated to manufacture. In addition, a conflict broke out between two groups of managers over whether Gillette should create a permanent razor or orient the product toward inexpensive disposables. These decision interrupts caused Gillette to recycle back, reappraise goals, and redesign the razor. After redesign, the decision advanced back to the selection phase, where the Sensor passed the judgment of top executives and manufacturing and marketing budgets were quickly authorized.[42]

Integrating the Incremental Process and Carnegie Models

At the beginning of this chapter, decision making was defined as occurring in two stages: problem identification and problem solution. The Carnegie description of coalition building is especially relevant for the problem identification stage. When issues are ambiguous, or if managers disagree about problem severity, discussion, negotiation, and coalition building are needed. Once agreement is reached about the problem to be tackled, the organization can move toward a solution.

The incremental process model tends to emphasize the steps used to reach a solution. After managers agree upon a problem, the step-by-step process is a way of trying various solutions to see what will work. When problem solution is unclear, a trial-and-error solution may be designed.

The two models do not disagree with one another. They describe how organizations make decisions when either problem identification or solution is uncertain. The application of these two models to the stages in the decision process is illustrated in Exhibit 11.6. When both parts of the decision process are highly uncertain simultaneously, the organization is in an extremely difficult position. Decision processes in that situation may be a combination of Carnegie and incremental process models.

SPECIAL DECISION CIRCUMSTANCES

In a highly competitive world beset by global competition and rapid change, decision making seldom fits the traditional rational, analytical model. To cope in today's world, managers must learn to make decisions fast, especially in high-velocity environments, to learn from decision mistakes, and to avoid escalating commitment to an unsatisfactory course of action.

High-Velocity Environments

In some industries today, the rate of competitive and technological change is so extreme that market data is either unavailable or obsolete, strategic windows open and shut quickly, perhaps within a few months, and the cost of a decision error is company failure. Recent research has examined how successful companies make decisions in these **high-velocity environments**, especially to

Exhibit 11.6 *Organizational Decision Process When Either Problem Identification or Problem Solution is Uncertain*

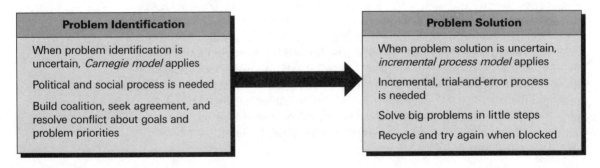

understand whether organizations abandon rational approaches or have time for incremental implementation.[43]

Comparing successful with unsuccessful decisions in high-velocity environments suggests the following guidelines.

- Successful decision makers track information in real time to develop a deep and intuitive grasp of the business. Two to three intense meetings per week with all key players are usual. Decision makers track operating statistics about cash, scrap, backlog, work in process, and shipments to constantly feel the pulse of what is happening. Unsuccessful firms were more concerned with future planning and forward-looking information, with only a loose grip on immediate happenings.
- During a major decision, successful companies began immediately to build multiple alternatives. Implementation of the choices may have run in parallel before the firm finally settled on a final choice. Slow-decision companies developed only a single alternative, moving to another only after the first one failed.
- Fast, successful decision makers sought advice from everyone and depended heavily on one or two savvy, trusted colleagues as counselors. Slow companies were unable to build trust and agreement among the best people.
- Fast companies involved everyone in the decision and tried for consensus; but if consensus did not emerge, the top manager made the choice and moved ahead. Waiting for everyone to be on board created more delays than warranted. Slow companies delayed decisions to achieve a uniform consensus.
- Fast, successful choices were well integrated with other decisions and the overall strategic direction of the company. Firms making less successful choices considered the decision in isolation from other decisions; the decision was made in the abstract.[44]

When speed matters, a slow decision is as ineffective as the wrong decision. As we discussed in Chapter 8, speed is a crucial competitive weapon in a growing number of industries, and companies can learn to make decisions fast. Managers must be plugged into the pulse of the company, must seek consensus and advice, and then be ready to take the risk and move ahead.

Decision Mistakes and Learning

Organizational decisions produce many errors, especially when made under high uncertainty. Managers simply cannot determine or predict which alternative will solve a problem. In these cases, the organization must make the decision—and take the risk—often in the spirit of trial and error. If an alternative fails, the organization can learn from it and try another alternative that better fits the situation. Each failure provides new information and learning. The point for managers is to move ahead with the decision process despite the potential for mistakes. "Chaotic action is preferable to orderly inaction."[45]

In many cases, managers have been encouraged to instill a climate of experimentation, even foolishness, to facilitate creative decision making. If one idea fails, another idea should be tried. Failure often lays the groundwork for success, as when technicians at 3M developed Post-it Notes based on a failed product—a not-very-sticky glue. Companies like Pepsi-Cola believe that if all their new products succeed, they're doing something wrong and not taking the necessary risks to develop new markets.[46]

Only by making mistakes can managers and organizations go through the process of **decision learning** and acquire sufficient experience and knowledge to perform more effectively in the future. Robert Townsend, who was president at Avis Corporation, gives the following advice:

Admit your mistakes openly, maybe even joyfully. Encourage your associates to do likewise by commiserating with them. Never castigate. Babies learn to walk by falling down. If you beat a baby every time he falls down, he'll never care much for walking.

My batting average on decisions at Avis was no better than a .333. Two out of every three decisions I made were wrong. But my mistakes were discussed openly and most of them corrected with a little help from my friends.[47]

Escalating Commitment

A much more dangerous mistake is to persist in a course of action when it is failing. Research suggests that organizations often continue to invest time and money in a solution despite strong evidence that it is not working. Two explanations are given for why managers **escalate commitment** to a failing decision. The first is that managers block or distort negative information when they are personally responsible for a negative decision. They simply don't know when to pull the plug. In some cases, they continue to throw good money after bad even when a strategy seems incorrect and goals are not being met.[48] An example of this distortion is the reaction at Borden when the company began losing customers following its refusal to lower prices on dairy products. When the cost of raw milk dropped, Borden hoped to boost the profit margins of its dairy products, convinced that customers would pay a premium for the brand name. Borden's sales plummeted as low-priced competitors mopped up, but top executives stuck with their premium pricing policy for almost a year. By then, the company's dairy division was operating at a severe loss. Other companies have done the same, such as when Emery Air Freight Corporation acquired Consolidated Freightways, Inc. In the year since acquiring Consolidated, Emery lost $100 million on it, but executives were reluctant to admit it was a bad choice, believing things were about to get better.[49] Negative information often doesn't sink in.

A second explanation for escalating commitment to a failing decision is that consistency and persistence are valued in contemporary society. Consistent managers are considered better leaders than those who switch around from one course of action to another. Even though organizations learn through trial-and-error, organizational norms value consistency. These norms may result in a course of action being maintained, resources being squandered, and learning being inhibited. Emphasis on consistent leadership was partly responsible for the Long Island Lighting Company's refusal to change course in the construction of the Shoreham Nuclear Power Plant, which was eventually abandoned—after an investment of more than $5 billion—without ever having begun operation. Shoreham's cost was estimated at $75 million when the project was announced in 1966, but by the time a construction permit was granted, LILCO had already spent $77 million. Opposition to nuclear power was growing. Critics continued to decry the huge sums of money being pumped into Shoreham. Customers complained that LILCO was cutting back on customer service and maintenance of current operations. But Shoreham officials seemed convinced that they would triumph in the end; their response to criticism was, "If people will just wait until the end, they are going to realize that this is a hell of an investment."

The end came in 1989, when a negotiated agreement with New York led LILCO to abandon the $5.5 billion plant in return for rate increases and a $2.5 billion tax write-off. By the time Governor Mario Cuomo signed an agreement with the company, LILCO had remained firmly committed to a losing course of action for more than 23 years.[50] Failure to admit a mistake and adopt a new course of action is far worse than an attitude that encourages mistakes and learning. Based upon what has been said about decision making in this chapter, one can expect companies to be ultimately successful in their decision making by adopting a learning approach toward solutions. They will make mistakes along the way, but they will resolve uncertainty through the trial-and-error process.

SUMMARY OF KEY ISSUES

The single most important idea in this chapter is that most organizational decisions are not made in a logical, rational manner. Most decisions do not begin with the careful analysis of a problem, followed by systematic analysis of alternatives, and finally implementation of a solution. On the contrary, decision processes are characterized by conflict, coalition building, trial and error, speed, and mistakes. Managers operate under many constraints that limit rationality; hence, intuition and hunches often are the criteria for choice.

Another important idea is that individuals make decisions, but organizational decisions are not made by a single individual. Organizational decision making is a social process. Only in rare circumstances do managers analyze problems and find solutions by themselves. Many problems are not clear, so widespread discussion and coalition building take place. Once goals and priorities are set, alternatives to achieve those goals can be tried. When a manager does make an individual decision, it is often a small part of a larger decision process. Organizations solve big problems through a series of small steps. A single manager may initiate one step but should be aware of the larger decision process in which it is embedded.

The greatest amount of conflict and coalition building occurs at the problem identification stage. Priorities must be established to indicate which goals are important and what problems should be solved first. If a manager attacks a problem other people do not agree with, the manager will lose support for the solution to be implemented. Thus, time and activity should be spent building a coalition in the problem identification stage of decision making. Then the organization can move toward solutions.

The incremental process model emphasizes the steps used to reach a solution. After managers agree upon a problem, the solution may unfold as a series of incremental trials that will gradually lead to an overall solution.

Finally, many organizations must make decisions with speed, which means staying in immediate touch with operations and the environment. Moreover, in an uncertain world, organizations will make mistakes, and mistakes made through trial and error should be encouraged. Encouraging trial-and-error increments facilitates organizational learning. On the other hand, an unwillingness to change from a failing course of action can have serious negative consequences for an organization. Norms for consistency and the desire to prove one's decision correct can lead to continued investment in a useless course of action.

Discussion Questions

1. A professional economist once told his class, "An individual decision maker should process all relevant information and select the economically rational alternative." Do you agree? Why or why not?
2. Why is intuition used in decision making?
3. The Carnegie model emphasizes the need for a political coalition in the decision process. When and why are coalitions necessary?
4. What are the three major phases in Mintzberg's incremental decision process model? Why might an organization recycle through one or more phases of the model?
5. An organization theorist once told her class, "Organizations never make big decisions. They make small decisions that eventually add up to a big decision." Explain the logic behind this statement.
6. Why would managers in high-velocity environments worry more about the present than the future? Discuss.
7. Are there decision-making situations in which managers should be expected to make the "correct" decision? Are there situations in which decision makers should be expected to make mistakes? Discuss.
8. Why are decision mistakes usually accepted in organizations but penalized in college courses and exams that are designed to train managers?

Notes

1. Robert D. Hof, "The Education of Andrew Grove," *Business Week*, 16 January 1995, 60–62.

2. John R. Emshwiller and Michael J. McCarthy, "Coke's Soda Fountain For Offices Fizzles, Dashing High Hopes," *The Wall Street Journal*, 14 June 1993, A1, A6; Walter S. Mossberg, "Apple of America's Eye Falls Victim to Pride," *The Wall Street Journal*, 24 January 1996, B1, and Kathy Rebello, Peter Burrows, and Ira Sager, "The Fall of an American Icon," *Business Week*, 5 February 1996, 34–42.

3. David Woodruff with Karen Lowry Miller, "Chrysler's Neon," *Business Week*, 3 May 1993, 116–26.

4. Charles Lindblom, "The Science of 'Muddling Through,'" *Public Administration Review* 29 (1954): 79–88.

5. Herbert A. Simon, *The New Science of Management Decision* (Englewood Cliffs, NJ.: Prentice-Hall, 1960) 1–8.

6. Wendy Zellner, "Back to Coffee, Tea, or Milk?" *Business Week*, 3 July 1995, 52–56.

7. Michael Pacanowsky, "Team Tools for Wicked Problems," *Organizational Dynamics*, Vol. 23, No. 3, Winter 1995, 36–51.

8. Bernard Wysocki, Jr., "A Popeyes Chain Frets Over How to Handle A Minimum-Pay Rise," *The Wall Street Journal*, 24 April 1996, A1; Doug Wallace, "What Would You Do? Southern Discomfort," *Business Ethics*, March/April 1996, 52–53; Renee Elder, "Apparel Plant Closings Rip Fabric of Community's Employment, *The Tennessean*, 3 November 1996, 1E.

9. Earnest R. Archer, "How to Make a Business Decision: An Analysis of Theory and Practice," *Management Review* 69 (February 1980): 54–61; Boris Blai, "Eight Steps to Successful Problem Solving," *Supervisory Management* (January 1986): 7–9.

10. Francine Schwadel, "Christmas Sales' Lack of Momentum Tests Store Managers' Mettle," *The Wall Street Journal*, 16 December 1987, 1.

11. James W. Dean, Jr., and Mark P. Sharfman, "Procedural Rationality in the Strategic Decision Making Process," *Journal of Management Studies* 30 (1993): 587–610.

12. Paul A. Anderson, "Decision Making by Objection and the Cuban Missile Crisis," *Administrative Science Quarterly* 28 (1983): 201–22.

13. Irving L. Janis, *Crucial Decisions: Leadership in Policymaking and Crisis Management* (New York: Free Press, 1989); Paul C. Nutt, "Flexible Decision Styles and the Choices of Top Executives," *Journal of Management Studies* 30 (1993): 695–721.

14. Herbert A. Simon, "Making Management Decisions: The Role of Intuition and Emotion," *Academy of Management Executive* 1 (February 1987) 57–64; Daniel J. Eisenberg, "How Senior Managers Think," *Harvard Business Review* 62, (November–December 1984): 80–90.

15. Stefan Wally and J. Robert Baum, "Personal and Structural Determinants of the Pace of Strategic Decision Making," *Academy of Management Journal*, Vol. 37, No. 4 (1994): 932–56; Orlando Behling and Norman L. Eckel, "Making Sense Out of Intuition," *Academy of Management Executive* 5, No. 1 (1991): 46–54.

16. Thomas F. Issack, "Intuition: An Ignored Dimension of Management," *Academy of Management Review* 3 (1978): 917–22.

17. Marjorie A. Lyles, "Defining Strategic Problems: Subjective Criteria of Executives," *Organizational Studies* 8 (1987): 263–80; Marjorie A. Lyles and Ian I. Mitroff, "Organizational Problem Formulation: An Empirical Study," *Administrative Science Quarterly* 25 (1980): 102–19.

18. Marjorie A. Lyles and Howard Thomas, "Strategic Problem Formulation: Biases and Assumptions Embedded in Alternative Decision-Making Models," *Journal of Management Studies* 25 (1988): 131–45.

19. Susan E. Jackson and Jane E. Dutton, "Discerning Threats and Opportunities," *Administrative Science Quarterly* 33 (1988): 370–87.

20. David A. Cowan, "Developing a Classification Structure of Organizational Problems: An Empirical Investigation," *Academy of Management Journal* 33 (1990): 366–90; David Greising, "Rethinking IDS from the Bottom up," *Business Week*, 8 February 1993, 110–12.

21. Ross Stagner, "Corporate Decision-Making: An Empirical Study," *Journal of Applied Psychology* 53 (1969): 1–13.

22. Annetta Miller and Dody Tsintar, "A Test for Market Research," *Newsweek*, 28 December 1987, 32–33; Oren Harari, "The Tarpit of Market Research," *Management Review* (March 1994): 42–44.

23. Ann Langley, "Between 'Paralysis By Analysis' and 'Extinction By Instinct,'" *Sloan Management Review* (Spring 1995): 63–76.

24. Paul C. Nutt, "Types of Organizational Decision Processes," *Administrative Science Quarterly* 29 (1984): 414–50.

25. Nandini Rajagopalan, Abdul M. A. Rasheed, and Deepak K. Datta, "Strategic Decision Processes: Critical Review and Future Decisions," *Journal of Management* 19 (1993): 349–84; Paul J. H. Schoemaker, "Strategic Decisions in Organizations: Rational and Behavioral Views," *Journal of Management Studies* 30 (1993): 107–29; Charles J. McMillan, "Qualitative Models of Organizational Decision Making," *Journal of Management Studies* 5 (1980): 22–39; Paul C. Nutt, "Models for Decision Making in Organizations and Some Contextual Variables Which Stimulate Optimal Use," *Academy of Management Review* 1 (1976): 84–98.

26. Hugh J. Miser, "Operations Analysis in the Army Air Forces in World War II: Some Reminiscences," *Interfaces* 23 (September–October 1993): 47–49; Harold J. Leavitt, William R. Dill, and Henry B. Eyring, *The Organizational World* (New York: Harcourt Brace Jovanovich, 1973), Ch. 6.

27. Stephen J. Huxley, "Finding the Right Spot for a Church Camp in Spain," *Interfaces* 12 (October 1982): 108–14; James E. Hodder and Henry E. Riggs, Pitfalls in Evaluating Risky Projects," *Harvard Business Review* (January–February 1985): 128–35.

28. Edward Baker and Michael Fisher, "Computational Results for Very Large Air Crew Scheduling Problems," *Omega* 9 (1981): 613–18; Jean Aubin, "Scheduling Ambulances," *Interfaces* 22 (March–April, 1992): 1–10.

29. Jean Aubin, "Scheduling Ambulances."

30. Harold J. Leavitt, "Beyond the Analytic Manager," *California Management Review* 11 (1975): 5–12; C. Jackson Grayson, Jr., "Management Science and Business Practice," *Harvard Business Review* 51 (July–August 1993): 41–48.

31. David Wessel, "A Man Who Governs Credit Is Denied a Toys 'R' Us Card," *The Wall Street Journal*, 14 December 1995, Bl .

32. Richard L. Daft and John C. Wiginton, "Language and Organization," *Academy of Management Review* (1979): 179–91.

33. Based on Richard M. Cyert and James G. March, *A Behavioral Theory of the Firm* (Englewood Cliffs, N.J.: Prentice-Hall, 1963); and James G. March and Herbert A. Simon, *Organizations* (New York: Wiley, 1958).

34. William B. Stevenson, Joan L. Pearce, and Lyman W. Porter, "The Concept of 'Coalition' in Organization Theory and Research," *Academy of Management Review* 10 (1985): 256–68.

35. David Woodruff with Karen Lowry Miller, "Chrysler's Neon," *Business Week*, 3 May 1993, 116–26.

36. Cyert and March, *Behavioral Theory of the Firm*, 120–22.

37. Ann Reilly Dowd, "How Bush Decided," *Fortune*, 11 February 1991, 45–46.

38. Based on Henry Mintzberg, Duru Raisinghani, and Andre Théorêt, "The Structure of 'Unstructured' Decision Processes," *Administrative Science Quarterly* 21 (1976): 246–75.

39. Lawrence T. Pinfield, "A Field Evaluation of Perspectives on Organizational Decision Making," *Administrative Science Quarterly* 31 (1986): 365–88.

40. Mintzberg, et al, "The Structure of 'Unstructured' Decision Processes."

41. Ibid., 270.

42. Keith. H. Hammonds, "How a $4 Razor Ends up Costing $300 Million," *Business Week*, 29 January 1990, 62–63.

43. L. J. Bourgeois III and Kathleen M. Eisenhardt, "Strategic Decision Processes in High Velocity Environments: Four Cases in the Microcomputer Industry," *Management Science* 34 (1988): 816–35.

44. Kathleen M. Eisenhardt, "Speed and Strategic Course: How Managers Accelerate Decision Making," *California Management Review* (Spring 1990): 39–54.

45. Karl Weick, *The Social Psychology of Organizing*, 2d ed. (Reading, Mass. Addison-Wesley, 1979), 243.

46. Power, et al., "Flops".

47. Robert Townsend, *Up the Organization* (New York: Knopf, 1974), 115.

48. Helga Drummond, "Too Little Too Late: A Case Study of Escalation in Decision Making," *Organization Studies*, Vol. 15, No. 4, 1994, 591–607; Joel Brockner, "The Escalation of Commitment to a Failing Course of Action: Toward Theoretical Progress," *Academy of Management Review* 17 (1992): 39–61; Barry M. Staw and Jerry Ross, "Knowing When to Pull the Plug," *Harvard Business Review* 65 (March–April 1987): 68–74; Barry M. Staw, "The Escalation of Commitment to a Course of Action," *Academy of Management Review* 6 (1981): 577–87.

49. Elizabeth Lesly, "Why Things Are So Sour at Borden," *Business Week*, 22 November 1993, 78–85; Joan O'C. Hamilton, "Emery Is One Heavy Load for Consolidated Freightways," *Business Week*, 26 March 1990, 62–64.

50. Jerry Ross and Barry M. Staw, "Organizational Escalation and Exit: Lessons from the Shoreham Nuclear Power Plant," *Academy of Management Journal* 36 (1993): 701–32.

chapter twelve

Power and Politics

While reading this chapter, think about your answers to the following questions:

- How is power distinguished from authority in organizations?

- What are the sources of power for top managers?

- How can lower level participants obtain power and exert influence up the organizational hierarchy?

- What four elements must be put into place to empower workers and how can managers successfully implement the empowerment process?

- What characteristics lead to power differences among departments?

- How can managers increase their power base, and what political tactics can help them achieve their desired outcomes?

The nature and use of power in organizations is rapidly changing. Top executives once were perceived to isolate themselves in fancy corner offices and dictate orders to others in the company. Today, executives like Andy Grove, CEO of Intel, work in cubicles just like everyone else at the company. Bill Gates of Microsoft, one of the richest men in the world, wears polo shirts to work and types out his own e-mail, responding to messages from anyone in the organization. Donald Tyson, former leader of Tyson Foods, showed up at work in the same brown uniform worn by his workers, with "Don" embroidered above the shirt pocket. These outward symbols reflect a trend that is sweeping North America and other parts of the world—turning power over to workers.[1]

Rather than top managers taking responsibility for making the company work, using power and authority to the fullest, many managers are giving power away as fast as they can, with astonishing results. Sometimes it's done by creating a high-involvement corporate culture, or perhaps through self-directed teams, or by using clan control, all of which have been discussed in previous chapters. The implications are enormous because if this trend continues, managers will have to learn power sharing rather than power grabbing, a new way to manage effectively in today's world.

PURPOSE OF THIS CHAPTER

Most organizations still operate under the old rules of power and politics. This chapter will explore power in organizations as a way to get things done. The following sections examine sources of power in organizations and the way power is used to attain organizational goals. Vertical and horizontal power are quite different, so these are discussed separately. We will also explore the new trend of worker empowerment to understand how it works. The latter part of the chapter looks at politics, which is the application of power and authority to achieve desired outcomes.

The study of power and politics is a natural extension of the previous chapter on decision making. Like decision making, politics involves the development of coalitions among executives. The dynamic processes associated with power and politics are thus similar in some respects to the processes associated with decision making.

INDIVIDUAL VERSUS ORGANIZATIONAL POWER

In popular literature, power is often described as a personal characteristic, and a frequent topic is how one person can influence or dominate another.[2] You probably recall from an earlier management or organizational behavior course that managers have five sources of personal power.[3] *Legitimate power* is the authority granted by the organization to the formal management position a manager holds. *Reward power* stems from the ability to bestow rewards, a promotion, raise, or a pat on the back, to other people. The authority to punish or recommend punishment is called *coercive power*. *Expert power* derives from a person's higher skill or knowledge about the tasks being performed. The last one, *referent power*, derives from a manager's personal characteristics that people admire and want to emulate or identify with out of respect and admiration. Each of these sources may be used by individuals within organizations.

Power in organizations, however, is often the result of structural characteristics.[4] Organizations are large, complex systems that contain hundreds, even thousands, of people. These systems have a formal hierarchy in which some tasks are more important regardless of who performs them. In addition, some positions have access to greater resources, or their contribution to the organization is more critical. Thus, the important power processes in organizations reflect larger organizational relationships, both horizontal and vertical, and organizational power usually is vested in the position, not in the person.

POWER VERSUS AUTHORITY

Power is an intangible force in organizations. It cannot be seen, but its effect can be felt. Power is often defined as the potential ability of one person (or department) to influence other persons (or departments) to carry out orders[5] or to do something they would not otherwise have done.[6] Other definitions stress that power is the ability to achieve the goals or outcomes that power holders desire.[7] The achievement of desired outcomes is the basis of the definition used here: **Power** is the ability of one person or department in an organization to influence other people to bring about desired outcomes. It is the potential to influence others within the organization, but with the goal of attaining desired outcomes for the power holders.

Power exists only in a relationship between two or more people, and it can be exercised in either vertical or horizontal directions. The source of power often derives from an exchange relationship in which one position or department provides scarce or valued resources to other departments. When one person is dependent on another person, a power relationship emerges in which the person with the resources has greater power.[8] When power exists in a relationship, the power holders can achieve compliance with their requests. For example, the following outcomes are indicators of power in an organization:

- A larger increase in budget than other departments
- Above-average salary increases for subordinates
- Production schedules favorable to the department
- Desired items on the agenda at policy meeting[9]

The inability to achieve a desired outcome came as a shock to Steve Jobs when he tried to oust John Sculley from Apple Computer. Sculley wrested control from Jobs after Jobs tried to fire him. The board of directors and senior managers supported Sculley, so Sculley, not Jobs, effectively had power.[10] Shortly after, Jobs, who had created Apple Computer, was forced from the company.

The concept of formal authority is related to power but is narrower in scope. **Authority** is also a force for achieving desired outcomes, but only as prescribed by the formal hierarchy and reporting relationships. Three properties identify authority:

1. *Authority is vested in organizational positions.* People have authority because of the positions they hold, not because of personal characteristics or resources.

2. *Authority is accepted by subordinates.* Subordinates comply because they believe position holders have a legitimate right to exercise authority.[11] Richard Ferris resigned as chairman of Allegis Corporation (now UAL, Inc.) because few people accepted his strategy of making Allegis a travel empire. Other senior managers, airline pilots, and board members preferred to see the company concentrate on its major business, United Airlines, and didn't accept Ferris's authority to implement his strategy.

3. *Authority flows down the vertical hierarchy.*[12] Authority exists along the formal chain of command, and positions at the top of the hierarchy are vested with more formal authority than are positions at the bottom.

Organizational power can be exercised upward, downward, and horizontally in organizations. Formal authority is exercised downward along the hierarchy and is the same as vertical power and legitimate power. The next section examines the use of vertical power as well as sources of power for lower participants. A later section examines the use of horizontal power in organizations, which is not defined by the vertical hierarchy and is determined by power relationships across departments.

VERTICAL POWER

All employees along the vertical hierarchy have access to some sources of power. Although any person may have access to almost any source of power, each level in the hierarchy tends to be concerned with different power issues and to rely on somewhat different power sources.

Power Sources for Top Management

The formal pyramid of authority provides power and authority to top management. Top management is responsible for a great number of people and many resources, and its authority is equal to those responsibilities. The chain of command converges at the top of the organization, so authority is great for top offices. The authority to govern granted to top management is reflected in both the formal organization structure and the decision authority defined by that structure.

> *The design of an organization, its structure, is first and foremost the system of control and authority by which the organization is governed. In the organizational structure, decision discretion is allocated to various positions and the distribution of formal authority is established. Furthermore, by establishing the pattern of prescribed communication and reporting requirements, the structure provides some participants with more and better information and more central locations in the communication network. . . . Thus, organizational structures create formal power and authority by designating certain persons to do certain tasks and make certain decisions, and create informal power through the effect on information and communication structures within the organization. Organizational structure is a picture of the governance of the organization and a determinant of who controls and decides organizational activities.*[13]

A large amount of power is allocated to senior management positions by the traditional organizational structure. The power of top management comes from four major sources: formal position, resources, control of decision premises and information, and network centrality.[14]

Formal Position. Certain rights, responsibilities, and prerogatives accrue to top positions. People throughout the organization accept the legitimate right of top managers to set goals, make decisions, and direct activities. Thus, the power from a formal position is sometimes called legitimate power.

Senior managers often use symbols and language to perpetuate their legitimate power. Reserving the top floor for senior executives and giving them wood-paneled offices are ways to communicate legitimate authority to others in the organization. When James Dutt was chairman of Beatrice, he had his picture hung in every facility worldwide. Such symbols reinforce the legitimacy of top management's authority. Most Americans accept the legitimate right of top managers to direct an organization. They believe that "those in authority have the right to expect compliance; those subject to authority have the duty to obey."[15]

Resources. Organizations allocate huge amounts of resources. Buildings are constructed, salaries are paid, and equipment and supplies are purchased. Each year, new resources are allocated in the form of budgets. These resources are allocated downward from top managers. In many companies, top managers own stock, which gives them property rights over resource allocation. A senior vice president with large shareholdings may sometimes be more powerful than the CEO.[16]

Top managers control the resources and, hence, can determine their distribution. Resources can be used as rewards and punishments, which are sources of power. Resource allocation also creates a dependency relationship. Lower-level participants depend upon top managers for the financial and physical resources needed to perform their tasks. Top management can exchange resources in the form of salaries, personnel, promotion, and physical facilities for compliance with the outcomes they desire.

Control of Decision Premises and Information. Control of **decision premises** means that top managers place constraints on decisions made at lower levels by specifying a decision frame of reference and guidelines. For example, when he was president of McDonnell Douglas, Sandy McDonnell prescribed a value of participative management, which was a frame of reference for the decisions of other managers. In one sense, top managers make big decisions, while lower-level participants make small decisions. Top management decides which goal an organization will try to achieve, such as increased market share. Lower-level participants then decide how the goal is to be reached. In one company, top management appointed a committee to select a new marketing vice president. The CEO provided the committee with detailed qualifications that the new vice president should have. He also selected people to serve on the committee. In this way, the CEO shaped the decision premises within which the marketing vice president would be chosen. Top manager actions and decisions such as these place limits on the decisions of lower-level managers and thereby influence the outcome of their decisions.[17]

The control of information can also be a source of power. Managers in today's organizations recognize that information is a primary business resource and that by controlling what information is collected, how it is interpreted, and how it is shared, they can influence how decisions are made.[18] Top managers often have access to more information than do other managers. This information can be released as needed to shape the decision outcomes of other people. For example, in one organization, Clark, Ltd., the senior manager controlled information given to the board of directors and thereby influenced the board's decision to purchase a large computer system.[19] The board of directors had formal authority to decide from which company the computer would be purchased. The management services group was asked to recommend which of six computer manufacturers should receive the order. Jim Kenny was in charge of the management services group, and Kenny disagreed with other managers about which computer to purchase. As shown in Exhibit 12.1, other managers had to go through Kenny to have their viewpoints heard by the board. Kenny shaped the board's thinking to select the computer he preferred by controlling information given to them.

Network Centrality. Top managers can locate themselves centrally in an organization. They can surround themselves with a network of loyal subordinates and use their networks to learn about events throughout the organization.[20] By placing managers whom they know in critical positions, top managers increase their power. They gain power by being well informed, having access to other people in the network, and having multiple people dependent upon them. They can use their central positions to build alliances and loyalty and, hence, be in a position to wield substantial power in the organization.

When Harvey Golub was named chief executive officer of American Express, the board of directors put him on a short leash, naming a board member as chairman and assigning a committee to keep tabs on the new CEO. But Golub moved quickly to put his imprint on the company and establish friendships and support among board members. He was named chairman within five months and then moved to surround himself with hand-picked top managers he trusted to be loyal and supportive.[21]

Exhibit 12.1

Information Flow for Computer Decision at Clark Ltd.

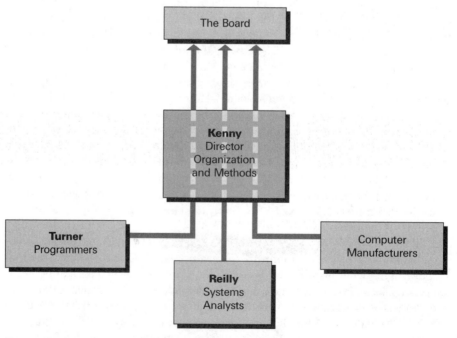

Source: Andrew M. Pettigrew, *The Politics of Organizational Decision-Making* (London: Tavistock, 1973), 235, with permission.

Power Sources for Middle Managers

The distribution of power down the hierarchy is influenced by organization design factors. Top managers will almost always have more power than middle managers, but the amount of power provided to any given position or organizational group can be built into the organization's structural design. The allocation of power to middle managers and staff is important because power enables employees to be productive. Managers need sufficient power and latitude to perform their jobs well. When positions are powerless, middle managers may seem ineffective and may become petty, dictatorial, and rules-minded.[22] Several factors that influence the amount of power along the hierarchy are shown in Exhibit 12.2. Power is the result of both task activities and network interactions. When a position is nonroutine, it encourages discretion, flexibility and creativity. When a job pertains to pressing organizational problems, power is more easily accumulated. Power is also increased when a position encourages contact with high-level people, brings visibility and recognition to employees, and facilitates peer networks both inside and outside the organization.

The variables in Exhibit 12.2 can be designed into specific roles or departments. For example, funds can be allocated to a department so members can attend professional meetings, thereby increasing their visibility and stature. Allowing people to approve their own decisions gives more discretion, reduces dependence on others, and increases power.

The logic of designing positions for more power assumes an organization does not have a limited amount of power to be allocated among high-level and low-level employees. The total amount of power in an organization can be increased by designing tasks and network interactions along the hierarchy so everyone has more influence. If the distribution of power is too heavily skewed toward the top so that middle managers are powerless, research suggests the organization will be less effective. A study by Rosabeth Moss Kanter showed that design factors prevented some middle managers and staff personnel from having enough power to accomplish their jobs.

Exhibit 12.2 *Ways in Which Vertical Design Contributes to Power at Middle-Manager Levels*

Design Factor	Generates Power When Factor Is	Generates Powerlessness When Factor Is
Task Activities		
Rules, precedents, and established routines in the job	Few	Many
Task variety and flexibility	High	Low
Rewards for unusual performance and innovation	Many	Few
Approvals needed for nonroutine decisions	Few	Many
Relation of tasks to current problem areas	Central	Peripheral
Network Interactions		
Physical location	Central	Distant
Publicity about job activities and contact with senior officials	High	Low
Participation in programs, conferences, meetings	High	Low
Participation in problem-solving task forces	High	Low

Source: Based on Rosabeth Moss Kanter, "Power Failure in Management Circuits," *Harvard Business Review* 57 (July–August 1979); 65–75.

> *Decision factors can leave an entire level of the hierarchy, such as first line supervisors, in a position of powerlessness. Their jobs may be overwhelmed with rules and precedents, and they may have little opportunity to develop an interaction network in the organization. Minority group members often have little power because management is overprotective, and thereby precludes opportunities for initiative and exposure needed for power accumulation. The same fate can befall staff specialists.*
>
> *As advisors behind the scenes, staff people must sell their programs and bargain for resources, but unless they get themselves entrenched in organizational power networks, they have little in the way of favors to exchange. They are not seen as useful to the primary tasks of the organization. . . . Lacking growth prospects themselves and working alone or in very small teams, they are not in a position to develop others or pass on power to them. They miss out on an important way in which power can be accumulated.*[23]

Without sufficient power, middle-level people cannot be productive. Power can be built into positions and departments through the design of task activities and interaction opportunities.

Power Sources for Lower-Level Participants

Positions at the bottom of an organization have less power than positions at higher levels. Often, however, people at the bottom levels obtain power disproportionate to their positions and are able to exert influence in an upward direction. Secretaries, maintenance people, word processors, computer programmers, and others find themselves being consulted in decisions or having great latitude and discretion in the performance of their jobs. The power of lower-level employees often surprises managers. The vice president of a university may be more reluctant to fire a secretary than to fire an academic department head. Why does this happen?

People at lower levels obtain power from several sources. Some of these sources are individual because they reflect the personality and skill of employees.[24] Other power sources are position based, as indicated in Exhibit 12.3. One study found that unexpectedly high levels of power came from expertise, physical location, information, and personal effort.[25] When lower-level participants become knowledgeable and expert about certain activities, they are in a position to influence decisions. Sometimes individuals take on difficult tasks and acquire specialized knowledge, and then become indispensable to managers above them. Power accumulation is also associated with the amount of effort and interest displayed. People who show initiative, work beyond what is expected, take on undesirable but important projects, and show an interest in learning about the company and the industry often find themselves with influence.[26]

Exhibit 12.3
Power Sources for Lower-Level Participants

Personal Sources	Position Sources
Expertise	Physical location
Effort	Information flow
Persuasion	Access
Manipulation	

Physical location also helps because some locations are in the center of things. Central location lets a person be visible to key people and become part of interaction networks. Likewise, certain positions are in the flow of organizational information. One example is the secretary to a senior executive. He or she can control information that other people want, and will be in a position to influence those people.

Additional personal sources of upward influence are persuasion and manipulation.[27] Persuasion is a direct appeal to upper management and is the most frequent type of successful upward influence.[28] Manipulation means arranging information to achieve the outcome desired by the employee. It differs from persuasion because, with manipulation, the true objective for using influence is concealed.

The final source of power is a position that provides access to other important people.[29] Access to powerful people and the development of relationships with them provide a strong base of influence. However, access, persuasion, and manipulation work as sources of power only if employees are willing to attempt influences that will provide desired outcomes.

THE TREND TOWARD EMPOWERMENT

A vertical hierarchy with greater power centralized at the top has been a distinctive feature of organizations almost since the appearance of the first large organization. Now we see a major shift away from this approach. Whether we are talking about organic structures, self-directed teams, or high-involvement cultures, the attempts to diffuse and share power are widespread. The notion of encouraging employees to participate fully in the organization is called empowerment. **Empowerment** is power sharing, or the delegation of power or authority to subordinates in the organization.[30] It means giving power to others in the organization so they can act more freely to accomplish their jobs.

In an environment characterized by intense global competition and new technology, many top managers believe giving up centralized control will promote speed, flexibility, and decisiveness. Indeed, fully 74 percent of CEOs reported in a recent survey that they are more participatory, more consensus-oriented, and now rely more on communication than on command. They are finding less value in being dictatorial, autocratic, or imperial.[31] The trend is clearly toward moving power out of the executive suite and into the hands of employees. This trend can be seen in a variety of manufacturing and service industries, including some of the best known companies in the world, such as Hewlett-Packard, Southwest Airlines, Boeing, General Electric, and Caterpillar.[32]

Reasons for Empowerment

Why are so many organizations empowering workers, and what advantages do these organizations achieve? One study suggests three primary reasons firms adopt empowerment: (1) as a strategic imperative to improve products or services; (2) because other firms in their industry are doing so (recall from Chapter 3 how firms tend to imitate similar organizations in the same environment); and (3) to create a unique organization with superior performance capabilities. Of the three reasons, the most compelling in terms of durability and success is the third—to create a unique organization that becomes the basis of sustainable competitive advantage.[33] The best-known example is

Southwest Airlines, discussed in Chapter 10. The strength of Southwest comes not from products or services but from a unique culture and management philosophy that emphasizes employee involvement and empowerment.[34]

Empowerment provides a basis of sustainable competitive advantage in several ways. For one thing, empowerment *increases* the total amount of power in the organization. Many managers mistakenly believe power is a zero-sum game, which means they must give up power in order for someone else to have more. Not true. Both research and managerial experience indicate that delegating power from the top creates a bigger power pie, so that everyone has more power.[35] Ralph Stayer, CEO of Johnsonville Foods, believes a manager's strongest power comes from committed workers: "Real power comes from giving it up to others who are in a better position to do things than you are."[36] The manager who gives away power gets commitment and creativity in return. Employees find ways to use their knowledge and abilities to make good things happen. Front-line workers often have a better understanding of how to improve a work process, satisfy a customer, or solve a production problem than do managers. In addition, employees are more likely to be committed to a decision or course of action when they are closely involved in the decision making process.[37] Managers' fear of power loss is the biggest barrier to empowerment of employees; but when they understand that they will actually gain power by delegating, the decision should be easy.

Empowerment also increases employee motivation. Research indicates that individuals have a need for *self-efficacy*, which is the capacity to produce results or outcomes and feel they are effective. Increasing employee power heightens motivation for task accomplishment because people improve their own effectiveness when they choose how to do a task and use their creativity.[38] Most people come into the organization with the desire to do a good job, and empowerment enables them to release the motivation already there. Their reward is a sense of personal mastery and competence.

Elements of Empowerment

Empowering employees means giving them four elements that enable them to act more freely to accomplish their jobs: information, knowledge, power, and rewards.[39]

Information. In companies where employees are fully empowered, such as Semco S/A, Brazil's largest manufacturer of marine and food processing equipment, no information is secret. At Semco, every employee has access to the books and any other information, including executive salaries. To show they're serious about sharing information, Semco management works with the labor union that represents its workers to train all employees—even messengers and cleaning people—to read balance sheets and cash flow statements.

Knowledge and Skills. Companies use training programs to give employees the knowledge and skills they need to personally contribute to company performance. For example, regular quality awareness workshops are held at Chrysler Canada's assembly plant in Bramalea, Ontario, so that employees can initiate quality improvements on their own.

Xerox gives its workers what the company calls "line of sight" training, in which employees familiarize themselves with how their job fits into upstream and downstream activities. The training helps empowered employees make better decisions that support other workers and contribute to the organization's goals.[40]

Power. Many of today's most competitive companies are giving workers the power to influence work procedures and organizational direction through quality circles and self-directed teams. At Prudential Insurance Company's Northeastern Group Operations, teams made up of clerical, processing, technical, and quality control specialists are empowered to approve claims of a certain type or for a certain customer up to a dollar amount representing 95 percent of all claim submissions. Another team decided employees could save the company money by processing claims from home. Workers, free to set their own hours, are setting new records for productivity.[41]

Rewards. Two of the ways in which organizations can reward employees financially based on company performance are through profit sharing and employee stock ownership plans (ESOPs). At W. L. Gore & Associates, makers of Gore-Tex, compensation takes three forms—salary, profit sharing, and an associates stock ownership program.[42] At Reflexite Corporation, a growing and profitable technology-based business, employees own 59 percent of the company's stock.

Empowerment Applications

Many of today's organizations are implementing empowerment programs, but they are empowering workers to varying degrees. At some companies, empowerment means encouraging employee input while managers maintain final authority for decisions; at others it means giving front-line workers almost complete power to make decisions and exercise initiative and imagination.[43] At Nordstrom, a department store chain, for example, employees are given the following guidelines: "Rule No. 1: Use your good judgment in all situations. There will be no additional rules."[44]

Exhibit 12.4 shows a continuum of empowerment, from a situation where front-line workers have no discretion (for example, a traditional assembly line), to full empowerment, where workers actively participate in determining organizational strategy. Current methods of empowering workers fall along this continuum. When employees are fully empowered, they are given decision making authority and control over how they do their own jobs, as well as the power to influence and change such areas as organizational goals, structures, and reward systems. An example is when self-directed teams are given the power to hire, discipline, and dismiss team members and to set compensation rates. Few organizations have moved to this level of empowerment. One that has is W. L. Gore and Associates. The company, which operates with no titles, hierarchy, or any of the conventional structures associated with a company of its size, has remained highly successful and profitable under this empowered system for more than 30 years. The culture emphasizes teamwork, mutual support, freedom, motivation, independent effort, and commitment to the total organization rather than to narrow jobs or departments.[45]

Empowerment programs are difficult to implement in established organizations because they destroy hierarchies and upset the familiar balance of power. A study of *Fortune* 1000 companies found that the empowerment practices that have diffused most widely are those that redistribute power and authority the least; for example, quality circles and other types of participation groups, and job enrichment and redesign.[46] Managers may have difficulty giving up power and authority, and while workers like the increased freedom, they may balk at the added responsibility that freedom brings. Most organizations begin with

Exhibit 12.4 *The Empowerment Continuum*

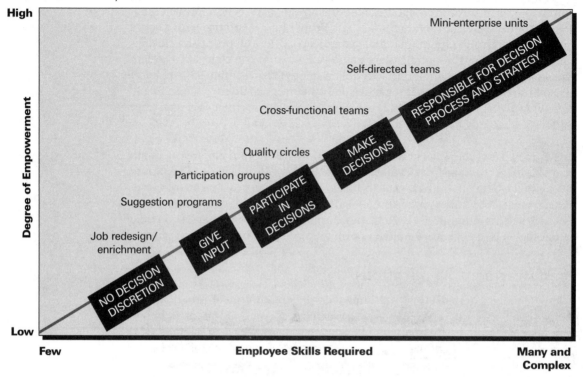

Source: Based on Robert C. Ford and Myron D. Fottler, "Empowerment: A Matter of Degree," *Academy of Management Executive,* Vol. 9, No. 3 (1995): 21–31; Lawrence Holpp, "Applied Empowerment," *Training* (February 1994): 39–44; and David P. McCaffrey, Sue R. Faerman, and David W. Hart, "The Appeal and Difficulties of Participative Systems," *Organization Science,* Vol. 6, No. 6 (November–December 1995): 603–27.

small steps and gradually increase employee empowerment. For example, at Recyclights, a small Minneapolis-based company that recycles fluorescent lights, CEO Keith Thorndyke first gave employees control of their own tasks. As employee skills grew and they developed a greater interest in how their jobs fit into the total picture, Thorndyke recognized that workers also wanted to help shape corporate goals rather than having a plan handed down to them as a finished package.[47]

The trend toward empowering lower-level workers is likely to grow, with more companies moving up the continuum of empowerment shown in Exhibit 12.4. Whether an organization starts with job redesign or moves immediately to self-directed teams, there are steps managers can take to smoothly implement empowerment programs.

The Empowerment Process

When managers decide that delegation of power is important, the process can be accomplished in three stages. The first stage is to diagnose conditions within the organization that cause powerlessness for subordinates. The second stage is to engage in empowerment practices that will increase power at lower levels. Stage three involves feedback to employees that reinforces their success and feelings of effectiveness.

The first stage of diagnosis means looking carefully at organizational and job design elements at the middle and lower levels that reduce power. Recall from Exhibit 12.2 that such factors as too many rules, little task variety, being stuck in a remote location, rewards for routine output rather than innovation, and no opportunity for participating in task forces all reduce power. By analyzing these factors within organizations, the necessary changes for empowerment can be identified.

In stage two of empowerment, the old factors that generate powerlessness are changed, and employees are given access to the elements described in the previous section: information; knowledge and skills; power to make decisions; and rewards based on company performance. This stage usually starts with a clear goal or vision, from the top, publicly stated. Top managers make clear their desire for empowerment, and they articulate clear organizational goals. Employees no longer need to walk in step, but they should all head in the same direction. Next is widespread communication and information sharing. Employees must understand what's going on, otherwise they will not use power.

Employees must also be educated in the knowledge and skills they need to contribute to meeting organizational performance goals. In addition, a systematic change in structure is needed to increase employee power. This means jobs will be given more variety, rules will be withdrawn, high-level approvals will no longer be needed, physical locations can be consolidated, levels of the hierarchy can be eliminated, and employees can participate in teams and task forces as they see fit. These structural changes provide the basis for enlarged jobs and enlarged decision making. With clarity on overall company direction and goals, complete information, and a structure that provides latitude, employees can make decisions that use their power to enact task accomplishment.

At Hampton Inns, for example, employees are empowered to do whatever is necessary to honor the company's "100% Satisfaction Guarantee." They are given comprehensive ongoing training so that they understand the mission and rationale behind the guarantee and have the knowledge to make effective decisions that meet organizational goals.[48]

In the third stage, which is feedback, employees learn how they are doing. Many companies place new emphasis on pay for performance, so employees' success is immediately rewarded. Career advancement is also encouraged as another way to reward excellence. At each Hampton Inn, managers set aside discretionary bonuses to be given to employees who go above and beyond the call of duty. The company also has a nationwide awards program to recognize workers who raise the standards of customer service to a higher level. Positive feedback reinforces employee feelings of self-efficacy, so that they become comfortable and prosper under empowerment.

The organization that empowers employees will look and act differently, with major changes in structure, information sharing, and decision making responsibility.

HORIZONTAL POWER

Horizontal power pertains to relationships across departments. All vice presidents are usually at the same level on the organization chart. Does this mean each department has the same amount of power? No. Horizontal power is not defined by the formal hierarchy or the organization chart. Each department makes a unique contribution to organizational success. Some departments will have greater say and will achieve their desired outcomes, while others will not. For example, Charles Perrow surveyed managers in several industrial firms.[49] He bluntly asked, "Which department has the most power?" among four major departments: production, sales and marketing, research and development, and finance and accounting. Partial survey results are given in Exhibit 12.5. In most firms, sales had the greatest power. In a few firms, production was also quite powerful. On average, the sales and production departments were more powerful than R&D and finance, although substantial variation existed. Differences in the amount of horizontal power clearly occurred in those firms.

Horizontal power is difficult to measure because power differences are not defined on the organization chart. However, some initial explanations for departmental power differences, such as those shown in Exhibit 12.5, have been found. The theoretical concept that explains relative power is called strategic contingencies.[50]

Strategic Contingencies

Strategic contingencies are events and activities both inside and outside an organization that are essential for attaining organizational goals. Departments involved with strategic contingencies for the organization tend to have greater power. Departmental activities are important when they provide strategic value

Exhibit 12.5 *Ratings of Power among Departments in Industrial Firms*

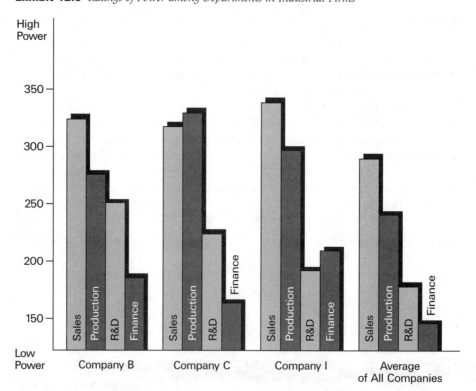

Source: Charles Perrow, "Departmental Power and Perspective in Industrial Firms," Mayer N. Zald, ed., *Power in Organizations* (Nashville, Tenn.: Vanderbilt University Press, 1970), 64.

by solving problems or crises for the organization. For example, if an organization faces an intense threat from lawsuits and regulations, the legal department will gain power and influence over organizational decisions because it copes with such a threat. If product innovation is the key strategic issue, the power of R&D can be expected to be high.

The strategic contingency approach to power is similar to the resource dependence model described in Chapter 3. Recall that organizations try to reduce dependency on the external environment. The strategic contingency approach to power suggests that the departments most responsible for dealing with key resource issues and dependencies in the environment will become most powerful.

Power Sources

Jeffrey Pfeffer and Gerald Salancik, among others, have been instrumental in conducting research on the strategic contingency theory.[51] Their findings indicate that a department rated as powerful may possess one or more of the characteristics illustrated in Exhibit 12.6.[52] In some organizations these five **power sources** overlap, but each provides a useful way to evaluate sources of horizontal power.

Dependency. Interdepartmental dependency is a key element underlying relative power. Power is derived from having something someone else wants. The power of department A over department B is greater when B depends upon A.[53]

Exhibit 12.6 *Strategic Contingencies that Influence Horizontal Power among Departments*

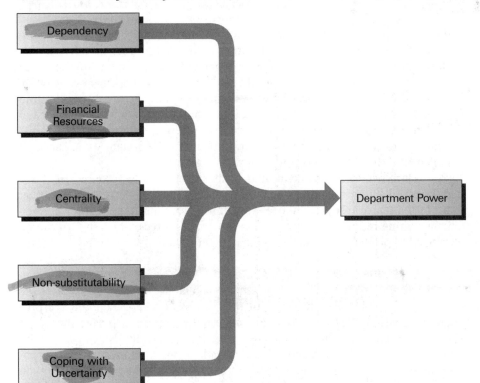

Many dependencies exist in organizations. Materials, information, and resources may flow between departments in one direction, such as in the case of sequential task interdependence (Chapter 4). In such cases, the department receiving resources is in a lower power position than the department providing them. The number and strength of dependencies are also important. When seven or eight departments must come for help to the engineering department, for example, engineering is in a strong power position. In contrast, a department that depends upon many other departments is in a low power position.

In a cigarette factory, one might expect that the production department would be more powerful than the maintenance department, but this was not the case in a cigarette plant near Paris.[54] The production of cigarettes was a routine process. The machinery was automated and production jobs were small in scope. Production workers were not highly skilled and were paid on a piece-rate basis to encourage high production. On the other hand, the maintenance department required skilled workers. These workers were responsible for the repair of automated machinery, which was a complex task. They had many years of experience. Maintenance was a craft because vital knowledge to fix machines was stored in the minds of maintenance personnel.

Dependency between the two groups was caused by unpredictable assembly line breakdowns. Managers could not remove the breakdown problem; consequently, maintenance was the vital cog in the production process. Maintenance workers had the knowledge and ability to fix the machines, so production managers became dependent upon them. The reason for this dependence was that maintenance managers had control over a strategic contingency—they had the knowledge and ability to prevent or resolve work stoppages.

Financial Resources. There's a new golden rule in the business world: "The person with the gold makes the rules."[55] Control over various kinds of resources, and particularly financial resources, is an important source of power in organizations. Money can be converted into other kinds of resources that are needed by other departments. Money generates dependency; departments that provide financial resources have something other departments want. Departments that generate income for an organization have greater power. The survey of industrial firms reported in Exhibit 12.5 showed sales as the most powerful unit in most of those firms. Sales had power because salespeople find customers and sell the product, thereby removing an important problem for the organization. The sales department ensures the inflow of money.

Power accrues to departments that bring in or provide resources that are highly valued by an organization. Power enables those departments to obtain more of the scarce resources allocated within the organization. "Power derived from acquiring resources is used to obtain more resources, which in turn can be employed to produce more power—the rich get richer."[56]

Centrality. **Centrality** reflects a department's role in the primary activity of an organization.[57] One measure of centrality is the extent to which the work of the department affects the final output of the organization. For example, the production department is more central and usually has more power than staff groups (assuming no other critical contingencies). Centrality is associated with power because it reflects the contribution made to the organization. The corporate finance department of an investment bank generally has more power than the stock research department. At Morgan Stanley Group, research analysts say they've been pressured to alter negative research reports on the stocks of the firm's corporate clients. "We were held accountable to corporate finance," a former Morgan Stanley analyst said, "playing the game the way corporate finance dictated."[58] By contrast, in the manufacturing firms described in Exhibit 12.5, finance tends to be low in power. When the finance department has the limited task of recording money and expenditures, it is not responsible for obtaining critical resources or for producing the products of the organization.

Nonsubstitutability. Power is also determined by **nonsubstitutability**, which means that a department's function cannot be performed by other readily available resources. Nonsubstitutability increases power. If an employee cannot be easily replaced, his or her power is greater. If an organization has no alternative sources of skill and information, a department's power will be greater. This can be the case when management uses outside consultants. Consultants might be used as substitutes for staff people to reduce the power of staff groups.

The impact of substitutability on power was studied for programmers in computer departments.[59] When computers were first introduced, programming was a rare and specialized occupation. People had to be highly qualified to enter the profession. Programmers controlled the use of organizational computers because they alone possessed the knowledge to program them. Over a period of about ten years, computer programming became a more common activity. People could be substituted easily, and the power of programming departments dropped.

Today, however, the power of computer programming departments has increased again, as organizations battle the "Millennium Problem." Most large corporations use computer systems that were programmed 30 years ago to deal only in two digit dates, which will convert the year 2000 into 00, throwing the entire system out of whack. The complex conversion process has to be done manually, and programmers with the skills to handle the conversion are highly prized.

Coping with Uncertainty. The chapters on environment and decision making described how elements in the environment can change swiftly and can be unpredictable and complex. In the face of uncertainty, little information is available to managers on appropriate courses of action. Departments that cope with this uncertainty will increase their power.[60] Just the presence of uncertainty does not provide power, but reducing the uncertainty on behalf of other departments will. When market research personnel accurately predict changes in demand for new products, they gain power and prestige because they have reduced a critical uncertainty. Forecasting is only one technique for **coping with uncertainty**. Sometimes uncertainty can be reduced by taking quick and appropriate action after an unpredictable event occurs.

Three techniques departments can use to cope with critical uncertainties are (1) obtaining prior information, (2) prevention, and (3) absorption.[61] *Obtaining prior information* means a department can reduce an organization's uncertainty by forecasting an event. Departments increase their power through *prevention* by predicting and forestalling negative events. *Absorption* occurs when a department takes action after an event to reduce its negative consequences.

Horizontal power relationships in organizations change as strategic contingencies change. For example, in recent years, a few unions have increased their power by involving themselves in companies' strategic contingencies. In addition to the more well-known activities of work stoppages and strikes, these unions have become involved in pressuring companies' banks and creditors, challenging applications for financing and industrial revenue bonds, and using boycotts of products, banks, and health insurance companies. Unions have gone so far as to embarrass directors and executives by picketing their homes, opposing management in proxy battles, and communicating directly with stockholders.[62] These activities create new uncertainties and strategic issues for an organization, which can be reduced with the union's cooperation—thereby increasing union influence.

POLITICAL PROCESSES IN ORGANIZATIONS

Politics, like power, is intangible and difficult to measure. It is hidden from view and difficult to observe in a systematic way. The remainder of this chapter explores more fully what political behavior is, when it should be used, and some political tactics that may be effective.

Definition

Power has been described as the available force or potential for achieving desired outcomes. *Politics* is the use of power to influence decisions in order to achieve those outcomes. The exercise of power and influence has led to two ways to define politics—as self-serving behavior or as a natural organizational decision process. The first definition emphasizes that politics is self-serving and involves activities that are not sanctioned by the organization.[63]

In this view, politics involves deception and dishonesty for purposes of individual self-interest and leads to conflict and disharmony within the work environment. This dark view of politics is widely held by laypeople. Recent studies have shown that workers who perceive this kind of political activity at work within their companies often have related feelings of anxiety and job dissatisfaction. Studies also support the belief that inappropriate use of politics is related to low employee morale, inferior organizational performance, and poor decision making.[64]

While politics can be used in a negative, self-serving way, the appropriate use of political behavior can serve organizational goals.[65] The second view sees politics as a natural organizational process for resolving differences among organizational interest groups.[66] Politics is the process of bargaining and negotiation that is used to overcome conflicts and differences of opinion. In this view, politics is very similar to the coalition-building decision processes defined in Chapter 11 on decision making.

The organization theory perspective views politics as described in the second definition—as a normal decision-making process. Politics is simply the activity through which power is exercised in the resolution of conflicts and uncertainty. Politics is neutral and is not necessarily harmful to the organization. The formal definition of organizational politics is as follows: **Organizational politics** involves activities to acquire, develop, and use power and other resources to obtain the preferred outcome when there is uncertainty or disagreement about choices.[67]

Political behavior can be either a positive or a negative force. Politics is the use of power to get things accomplished—good things as well as bad. Uncertainty and conflict are natural and inevitable, and politics is the mechanism for reaching agreement. Politics includes informal discussions that enable participants to arrive at consensus and make decisions that otherwise might be stalemated or unsolvable.

One reason for a negative view of politics is that political behavior is compared with more rational procedures in organizations. Rational procedures are considered by many managers to be more objective and reliable and to lead to better decisions than political behavior. Rational approaches are effective, but only in certain situations. Both rational and political processes are normally used in organizations.

Rational Choice Versus Political Behavior

Rational Model. The **rational model** of organization is an outgrowth of the rational approach to decision making described in Chapter 11. It describes a number of activities beyond decision making, as summarized in Exhibit 12.7. Behavior in the rational organization is not random or accidental. Goals are clear and choices are made in a logical way. When a decision is needed, the goal is defined, alternatives are identified, and the choice with the highest probability of achieving the desired outcome is selected. The rational model of organization is also characterized by extensive, reliable information systems, central power, a norm of optimization, uniform values across groups, little conflict, and an efficiency orientation.[68]

Political Model. The opposite view of organizational processes within organizations is the **political model**, outlined in Exhibit 12.7. This model assumes organizations are made up of coalitions that disagree about goals and have poor information about alternatives. The political model defines the organization as made up of groups that have separate interests, goals, and values. Disagreement and conflict are normal, so power and influence are needed to reach decisions. Groups will engage in the push and pull of debate to decide goals and to reach decisions. Decisions are disorderly. Information is ambiguous and incomplete.

Exhibit 12.7 *Rational Versus Political Models of Organization*

Organizational Characteristic	Rational Model	Political Model
Goals, preference	Consistent across participants	Inconsistent, pluralistic within the organization
Power and control	Centralized	Decentralized, shifting coalitions and interest groups
Decision process	Orderly, logical, rational	Disorderly, characterized by push and pull of interests
Rules and norms	Norm of optimization	Free play of market forces; conflict is legitimate and expected
Information	Extensive, systematic, accurate	Ambiguous; information used and withheld strategically
Beliefs about cause-effect relationships	Known, at least to a probability estimate	Disagreements about causes and effects
Decisions	Based on outcome-maximizing choice	Result of bargaining and interplay among interests
Ideology	Efficiency and effectiveness	Struggle, conflict, winners and losers

Source: Based on Jeffrey Pfeffer, *Power in Organizations* (Marshfield, Mass.: Pitman, 1981), 31.

Bargaining and conflict are the norm. The political model applies to organizations that strive for democracy and participation in decision making by empowering workers. Purely rational procedures do not work in democratic organizations.

Mixed Model. In many organizations neither the rational model nor the political model characterizes things fully, but each will be observed some of the time. This might be called a **mixed model**. One model may dominate, depending on organizational environment and context. The important thing is that both models apply to organizational processes. Managers may strive to adopt rational processes, but it is wishful thinking to assume an organization can be run without politics. Bargaining and negotiation should not be avoided for fear they are improper. The political model is an effective mechanism for reaching decisions under conditions of uncertainty and disagreement.

The rational model applies best to organizations in stable environments with well-understood technologies. It is inadequate when there is uncertainty and conflict.

USING POWER AND POLITICAL INFLUENCE

One theme in this chapter has been that power in organizations is not primarily a phenomenon of the individual. It is related to the resources departments command, the role departments play in an organization, and the environmental contingencies with which departments cope. Position and responsibility more than personality and style determine a manager's influence on outcomes in the organization.

Power is used through individual political behavior, however. Individual managers seek agreement about a strategy to achieve their departments' desired outcomes. They negotiate decisions and adopt tactics that enable them to acquire and use power.

Thus, to fully understand the use of power within organizations, it is important to look at both structural components and individual behavior.[69] While the power base comes from larger organizational forms and processes, the political use of power involves individual-level activities. This section briefly summarizes tactics managers can use to increase the power base of their departments and political tactics they can use to achieve desired outcomes. These tactics are summarized in Exhibit 12.8.

Exhibit 12.8
Power and Political Tactics in Organizations

Tactics for Increasing the Power Base	Political Tactics for Using Power
1. Enter areas of high uncertainty	1. Build coalitions
2. Create dependencies	2. Expand networks
3. Provide resources	3. Control decision premises
4. Satisfy strategic contingencies	4. Enhance legitimacy and expertise
	5. Make preferences explicit, but keep power implicit

Tactics for Increasing the Power Base

Four **tactics for increasing the power base** are discussed in the following paragraphs:

Enter Areas of High Uncertainty. One source of departmental power is to cope with critical uncertainties.[70] If department managers can identify key uncertainties and take steps to remove those uncertainties, the department's power base will be enhanced. Uncertainties could arise from stoppages on an assembly line, from the required quality of a new product, or from the inability to predict a demand for new services. Once an uncertainty is identified, the department can take action to cope with it. By their very nature, uncertain tasks will not be solved immediately. Trial-and-error will be needed, which is to the advantage of the department. The trial-and-error process provides experience and expertise that cannot easily be duplicated by other departments.

Create Dependencies. Dependencies are another source of power.[71] When the organization depends upon a department for information, materials, knowledge, or skills, that department will hold power over the others. This power can be increased by incurring obligations. Doing additional work that helps out other departments will obligate the other departments to respond at a future date. The power accumulated by creating a dependency can be used to resolve future disagreements in the department's favor. An equally effective and related strategy is to reduce dependency on other departments by acquiring necessary information or skills. For example, data processing departments have created dependencies in many health care organizations because of the enormous amount of paperwork. Doing paperwork fast and efficiently has created a dependency, giving data processing more power.

Provide Resources. Resources are always important to organizational survival. Departments that accumulate resources and provide them to an organization in the form of money, information, or facilities will be powerful. For example, marketing departments are powerful in industrial firms because they bring in financial resources.

Satisfy Strategic Contingencies. The theory of strategic contingencies says that some elements in the external environment and within the organization are especially important for organizational success. A contingency could be a critical event, a task for which there are no substitutes, or a central task that is interdependent with many others in the organization. An analysis of the organization and its changing environment will reveal strategic contingencies. To the extent that contingencies are new or are not being satisfied, there is room for a department to move into those critical areas and increase its importance and power.

In summary, the allocation of power in an organization is not random. Power is the result of organizational processes that can be understood and predicted. The abilities to reduce uncertainty, increase dependency on one's own department, obtain resources, and cope with strategic contingencies will all enhance a department's power. Once power is available, the next challenge is to use it to attain helpful outcomes.

Political Tactics for Using Power

The use of power in organizations requires both skill and willingness. Many decisions are made through political processes because rational decision processes do not fit. Uncertainty or disagreement is too high. There are five major political **tactics for using power** to influence decision outcomes.

Build Coalitions. Coalition building means taking the time to talk with other managers to sway them to one's point of view.[72] Most important decisions are made outside formal meetings. Managers discuss issues with each other and reach agreements on a one-to-one basis. Effective managers are those who huddle, meeting in groups of twos and threes to resolve key issues.[73] An important aspect of coalition building is to build good relationships. Good interpersonal relationships are built on friendship, trust, and respect. Reliability and the motivation to work with others rather than exploit others are part of coalition building.[74]

Expand Networks. Networks can be expanded (1) by reaching out to establish contact with additional managers and (2) by coopting dissenters. The first approach is to build new alliances through the hiring, transfer, and promotion process. Placing in key positions people who are sympathetic to the outcomes of the department can help achieve departmental goals.[75] On the other hand, the second approach, cooptation, is the act of bringing a dissenter into one's network. One example of cooptation involved a university committee whose membership was based on promotion and tenure. Several female professors who were critical of the tenure and promotion process were appointed to the committee. Once a part of the administrative process, they could see the administrative point of view and learned that the administrators were not as evil as they suspected. Cooptation effectively brought them into the administrative network.[76]

Control Decision Premises. To control decision premises means to constrain the boundaries of a decision. One technique is to choose or limit information provided to other managers. A common method is simply to put a department's best foot forward, such as selectively presenting favorable criteria. A variety of statistics can be assembled to support the departmental point of view. A university department that is growing rapidly and has a large number of students can make claims for additional resources by emphasizing its growth and large size. Such objective criteria do not always work, but they are a valuable step.

Decision premises can be further influenced by limiting the decision process. Decisions can be influenced by the items put on an agenda for an important meeting or even by the sequence in which items are discussed.[77] Items discussed last, when time is short and people want to leave, will receive less attention than those discussed early. Calling attention to specific problems and suggesting alternatives also will affect outcomes. Stressing a specific problem to get it—rather than problems not relevant to one's department—on the agenda is an example of agenda setting.

Enhance Legitimacy and Expertise. Managers can exert the greatest influence in areas in which they have recognized legitimacy and expertise. If a request is within the task domain of a department and is consistent with the department's vested interest, other departments will tend to comply. Members can also identify external consultants or other experts within the organization to support their cause.[78] For example, a financial vice president in a large retail firm wanted to fire the director of human resource management. She hired a consultant to evaluate the human resource management projects undertaken to date. A negative report from the consultant provided sufficient legitimacy to fire the director, who was replaced with a director loyal to the financial vice president.

Make Preferences Explicit, but Keep Power Implicit. If managers do not ask, they seldom receive. Political activity is effective only when goals and needs are made explicit so the organization can respond. Managers should bargain aggressively and be persuasive. An assertive proposal may be accepted because other managers have no better alternatives. Moreover, an explicit proposal will often receive favorable treatment because other alternatives are ambiguous and less well defined. Effective political behavior requires sufficient forcefulness and risk taking to at least try to achieve desired outcomes.

The use of power, however, should not be obvious.[79] If one formally draws upon his or her power base in a meeting by saying, "My department has more power, so the rest of you have to do it my way," the power will be diminished. Power works best when it is used quietly. To call attention to power is to lose it. People know who has power. There is substantial agreement on which departments are more powerful. Explicit claims to power are not necessary and can even harm the department's cause.

When using any of the preceding tactics, recall that most people feel self-serving behavior hurts rather than helps an organization. If managers are perceived to be throwing their weight around or are perceived to be after things that are self-serving rather than beneficial to the organization, they will lose respect. On the other hand, managers must recognize the relational and political aspect of their work. It is not sufficient to be rational and technically competent. Politics is a way to reach agreement. When managers ignore political tactics, they may find themselves failing without understanding why.

SUMMARY OF KEY ISSUES

This chapter presented two views of organization. One view, covered only briefly, is the rational model of organization. This view assumes that organizations have specific goals and that problems can be logically solved. The other view, discussed throughout most of the chapter, is based upon a power and political model of organization. This view assumes the goals of an organization are not specific or agreed upon. Organizational departments have different values and interests, so managers come into conflict. Decisions are made on the basis of power and political influence. Bargaining, negotiation, persuasion, and coalition building decide outcomes.

The most important idea from this chapter is the reality of power and political processes in organizations. Differences in departmental tasks and responsibilities inevitably lead to differences in power and influence. Power differences determine decision outcomes. Uncertainty and disagreement lead to political behavior. Understanding sources of power and how to use politics to achieve outcomes for the organization are requirements for effective management.

Many managers prefer the rational model of decision making. This model is clean and objective. Rational thinking is effective when decision factors are sharply specified because of manager agreement and good information. Political processes, however, should not be ignored. Political decision processes are used in situations of uncertainty, disagreement, and poor information. Decisions are reached through the clash of values and preferences, and by the influence of dominant departments.

Other important ideas in this chapter pertain to power in organizations. The traditional view of vertical power, with power centralized at the top, still applies to most organizations. However, as today's organizations face increasing global competition and environmental uncertainty, top managers are finding that empowering lower-level employees helps their organizations run leaner and more profitably, fight off competition, and move rapidly into new markets.

Research into horizontal power processes has uncovered characteristics that make some departments more powerful than others. Such factors as dependency, resources, and the removal of strategic contingencies determine the influence of departments. Political strategies, such as coalition building, expanded networks, and control of decision premises, help departments achieve desired outcomes. Organizations can be more effective when managers appreciate the realities of power and politics.

Finally, despite its widespread use in organizations, many people distrust political behavior. They fear political behavior may be used for selfish ends that benefit the individual but not the organization. If politics is used for personal gain, other managers will become suspicious and will withdraw their support. Politics will be accepted when it is used to achieve the legitimate goal of a department or an organization.

Discussion Questions

1. If an organization decides to empower lower-level workers, are future decisions more likely to be made using the rational or political model of organization? Discuss.
2. Explain how control over decision premises gives power to a person.
3. In Exhibit 12.5, research and development has greater power in company B than in the other firms. Discuss possible strategic contingencies that give R&D greater power in this firm.
4. If you are a lower-level employee in an organization, how might you increase your power base?
5. Some positions in an organization are practically powerless. Why would this be? How could those positions be redesigned to have greater power?
6. State University X receives 90 percent of its financial resources from the state and is overcrowded with students. It is trying to pass regulations to limit student enrollment. Private University Y receives 90 percent of its income from student tuition and has barely enough students to make ends meet. It is actively recruiting students for next year. In which university will students have greater power? What implications will this have for professors and administrators? Discuss.
7. Do you believe it is possible to increase the total amount of power in an organization by delegating power to employees? Explain.
8. The engineering college at a major university brings in three times as many government research dollars as does the rest of the university combined. Engineering appears wealthy and has many professors on full-time research

status. Yet, when internal research funds are allocated, engineering gets a larger share of the money, even though it already has substantial external research funds. Why would this happen?

9. Which model—rational, political, or mixed—would be used in each of the following decision situations: quality-control testing in a production department, resource allocation in an executive suite, and deciding which division will be in charge of a recently built plant?

Notes

1. Thomas A. Stewart, "Get with the *New* Power Game," *Fortune*, 13 January 1997, 58–62.

2. Examples are Michael Korda, *Power: How to Get It, How To Use It* (New York: Random House, 1975), and Robert J. Ringer, *Winning through Intimidation* (Los Angeles: Los Angeles Book Publishing, 1973).

3. John R. P. French, Jr., and Bertram Raven, "The Bases of Social Power," *Group Dynamics*, in D. Cartwright and A. E. Sander, eds. (Evanston, Ill.: Row Peterson, 1960), 607–23.

4. Ran Lachman, "Power from What? A Reexamination of Its Relationships with Structural Conditions," *Administrative Science Quarterly* 34 (1989): 231–51; Daniel J. Brass, "Being in the Right Place: A Structural Analysis of Individual Influence in an Organization," *Administrative Science Quarterly* 29 (1984): 518–39.

5. Robert A. Dahl, "The Concept of Power," *Behavioral Science* 2 (1957): 201–15.

6. W. Graham Astley and Paramijit S. Sachdeva, "Structural Sources of Intraorganizational Power: A Theoretical Synthesis," *Academy of Management Review* 9 (1984): 104–13; Abraham Kaplan, "Power in Perspective," in Robert L. Kahn and Elise Boulding, eds., *Power and Conflict in Organizations* (London: Tavistock, 1964), 11–32.

7. Gerald R. Salancik and Jeffrey Pfeffer, "The Bases and Use of Power in Organizational Decision-Making: The Case of the University," *Administrative Science Quarterly* 19 (1974): 453–73.

8. Richard M. Emerson, "Power-Dependence Relations," *American Sociological Review* 27 (1962): 31–41.

9. Rosabeth Moss Kanter, "Power Failure in Management Circuits," *Harvard Business Review* (July–August 1979): 65–75.

10. Bro Uttal, "Behind the Fall of Steve Jobs," *Fortune*, 5 August 1985, 20–24; Deborah C. Weise, "Steve Jobs versus Apple: What Caused the Final Split," *Business Week*, 30 September 1985, 48.

11. A. J. Grimes, "Authority, Power, Influence, and Social Control: A Theoretical Synthesis," *Academy of Management Review* 3 (1978): 724–35.

12. Astley and Sachdeva, "Structural Sources of Intraorganizational Power."

13. Jeffrey Pfeffer, "The Micropolitics of Organizations," in Marshall W. Meyer, et al., *Environments and Organizations* (San Francisco: Jossey-Bass, 1978): 29–50.

14. Jeffrey Pfeffer, *Managing with Power: Politics and Influence in Organizations* (Boston: Harvard Business School Press, 1992).

15. Robert L. Peabody, Perceptions of Organizational Authority," *Administrative Science Quarterly* 6 (1962): 479.

16. Sydney Finkelstein, "Power in Top Management Teams: Dimensions, Measurement, and Validation," *Academy of Management Journal* 35 (1992): 505–38.

17. Jeffrey Pfeffer, *Power in Organizations* (Marshfield, Mass.: Pitman, 1981).

18. Erik W. Larson and Jonathan B. King, "The Systemic Distortion of Information: An Ongoing Challenge to Management," *Organizational Dynamics*, Vol. 24, No. 3, Winter 1996, 49–61; Thomas H. Davenport, Robert G. Eccles, and Lawrence Prusak, "Information

Politics," *Sloan Management Review* (Fall 1992): 53–65.

19. Andrew M. Pettigrew, *The Politics of Organizational Decision-Making* (London: Tavistock, 1973).

20. Astley and Sachdeva, *Structural Sources of Intra-organizational Power*; Noel M. Tichy and Charles Fombrun, "Network Analysis in Organizational Settings," *Human Relations* 32 (1979): 923–65.

21. Steven Lipin, "Golub Solidifies Hold at American Express, Begins to Change Firm," *The Wall Street Journal*, 30 June 1993, A1.

22. Kanter, "Power Failure in Management Circuits."

23. Ibid., 70

24. David C. Wilson and Graham K. Kenny, "Managerially Perceived Influence over Intradepartmental Decisions," *Journal of Manage-ment Studies* 22 (1985): 155–73; Warren Keith Schilit, "An Examination of Individual Differences as Moderators of Upward Influence Activity in Strategic Decisions," *Human Relations* 39 (1986): 933–53.

25. David Mechanic, "Source of Power in Lower Participants in Complex Organizations," *Administrative Science Quarterly* 7 (1962): 349–64.

26. Peter Moroz and Brian H. Kleiner, "Playing Hardball in Business Organizations," *IM*, January/February 1994, 9–11 .

27. Richard T. Mowday, "The Exercise of Upward Influence in Organizations," *Administrative Science Quarterly* 23 (1978): 137–56.

28. Warren K. Schilit and Edwin A. Locke, "A Study of Upward Influence in Organizations," *Administrative Science Quarterly* 27 (1982): 304–16.

29. Richard S. Blackburn, "Lower Participant Power: Toward a Conceptual Integration," *Academy of Management Review* 6 (1981): 127–31.

30. Edwin P. Hollander and Lynn R. Offermann, "Power and Leadership in Organizations," *American Psychologist* 45 (February 1990): 179–89.

31. Thomas A. Stewart, "New Ways to Exercise Power," *Fortune*, 6 November 1989, 52–64; Thomas A. Stewart, "CEOs See Clout Shifting," *Fortune*, 6 November 1989, 66.

32. Frank Shipper and Charles C. Manz, "Employee Self-Management without Formally Designated Teams:

An Alternative Road to Empowerment," *Organizational Dynamics* (Winter 1992): 48–61; Bob Filipczak, "Ericsson General Electric: The Evolution of Empowerment," *Training* (September 1993): 21–27.

33. David E. Bowen and Edward E. Lawler III, "Empowering Service Employees," *Sloan Management Review* (Summer 1995): 73–84.

34. Ibid., and "Southwest Airlines' Herb Kelleher: Unorthodoxy at Work," an interview with William G. Lee, *Management Review* (January 1995): 9–12 .

35. Arnold S. Tannenbaum and Robert S. Cook, "Organizational Control: A Review of Studies Employing the Control Graph Method," in Cornelius J. Lamners and David J. Hickson, eds. *Organizations Alike and Unlike* (Boston: Rutledge and Keegan Paul, 1980), 183–210.

36. Stewart, "New Ways to Exercise Power."

37. David P. McCaffrey, Sue R. Faerman, and David W. Hart, "The Appeal and Difficulties of Participative Systems," *Organization Science*, Vol. 6, No. 6 (November–December 1995): 603–27.

38. Jay A. Conger and Rabindra N. Kanungo, "The Empowerment Process: Integrating Theory and Practice," *Academy of Management Review* 13 (1988): 471–82.

39. David E. Bowen and Edward E. Lawler III, "Empowering Service Employees," *Sloan Management Review* (Summer 1995): 73–84.

40. Gordon Brockhouse, "Can This Marriage Succeed?" *Canadian Business*, October 1992, 128–35; Bowen and Lawler, "Empowering Service Employees."

41. Peter C. Fleming, "Empowerment Strengthens the Rock," *Management Review* (December 1991): 34–37.

42. Shipper and Manz, "An Alternative Road to Empowerment."

43. Robert C. Ford and Myron D. Fottler, "Empowerment: A Matter of Degree," *Academy of Management Executive*, Vol. 9, No. 3 (1995): 21–31.

44. Jeffrey Pfeffer, "Producing Sustainable Competitive Advantage Through the Effective Management of People," *Academy of Management Executive*, Vol. 9, No. 1 (1995): 55–69.

45. Robert C. Ford and Myron D. Fottler, "Empowerment: A Matter of Degree."

46. David P. McCaffrey, Sue R. Faerman, and David W. Hart, "The Appeal and Difficulties of Participative Systems," *Organization Science*, Vol. 6, No. 6 (November–December 1995): 603–27.

47. Michael Barrier, "The Changing Face of Leadership," *Nation's Business*, January 1995, 41–42.

48. Jules Sowder, "The 100% Satisfaction Guarantee: Ensuring Quality at Hampton Inn," *National Productivity Review* (Spring 1996): 53–66.

49. Charles Perrow, "Departmental Power and Perspective in Industrial Firms," in Mayer N. Zald, ed., *Power in Organizations* (Nashville, Tenn.: Vanderbilt University Press, 1970), 59–89.

50. D. J. Hickson, C. R. Hinings, C. A. Lee, R. E. Schneck, and J. M. Pennings, "A Strategic Contingencies Theory of Intraorganizational Power," *Administrative Science Quarterly* 16 (1971): 216–29; Gerald R. Salancik and Jeffrey Pfeffer, "Who Gets Power—and How They Hold onto It: A Strategic-Contingency Model of Power," *Organizational Dynamics* (Winter 1977): 3–21.

51. Pfeffer, *Managing with Power*; Salancik and Pfeffer, "Who Gets Power"; C. R. Hinings, D. J. Hickson, J. M. Pennings, and R. E. Schneck, "Structural Conditions of Intraorganizational Power," *Administrative Science Quarterly* 19 (1974): 22–44.

52. Carol Stoak Saunders, "The Strategic Contingencies Theory of Power: Multiple Perspectives," *Journal of Management Studies* 27 (1990): 1–18; Warren Boeker, "The Development and Institutionalization of Sub-Unit Power in Organizations," *Administrative Science Quarterly* 34 (1989): 388–510; Irit Cohen and Ran Lachman, "The Generality of the Strategic Contingencies Approach to Sub-Unit Power," *Organizational Studies* 9 (1988): 371–91.

53. Emerson, "Power-Dependence Relations."

54. Michel Crozier, *The Bureaucratic Phenomenon* (Chicago: University of Chicago Press, 1964).

55. Pfeffer, *Managing with Power*.

56. Salancik and Pfeffer, "Bases and Use of Power in Organizational Decision-Making," 470.

57. Hickson, et al., "Strategic Contingencies Theory."

58. Michael Siconolfi, "At Morgan Stanley, Analysts Were Urged to Soften Harsh Views," *The Wall Street Journal*, 14 July 1992, A1.

59. Pettigrew, *Politics of Organizational Decision-Making*.

60. Hickson, et al., "Strategic Contingencies Theory."

61. Ibid.

62. Aaron Bernstein, "The Unions Are Learning to Hit Where it Hurts," *Business Week*, 17 March 1986, 112–14; and James Worsham, "Labor Comes Alive," *Nation's Business*, February 1996, 16–24.

63. Gerald R. Ferris and K. Michele Kacmar, "Perceptions of Organizational Politics," *Journal of Management* 18 (1992): 93–116; Parmod Kumar and Rehana Ghadially, "Organizational Politics and its Effects on Members of Organizations," *Human Relations* 42 (1989): 305–14; Donald J. Vredenburgh and John G. Maurer, "A Process Framework of Organizational Politics," *Human Relations* 37 (1984): 47–66; Gerald R. Ferris, Dwight D. Frink, Maria Carmen Galang, Jing Zhou, Michele Kacmar, and Jack L. Howard, "Perceptions of Organizational Politics: Prediction, Stress-Related Implications, and Outcomes," *Human Relations*, Vol. 49, No. 2 (1996): 233–66.

64. Ferris, et. al., "Perceptions of Organizational Politics: Prediction, Stress-Related Implications, and Outcomes"; John J. Voyer, "Coercive Organiza-tional Politics and Organizational Outcomes: An Interpretive Study," *Organization Science*, Vol. 5, No. 1 (February 1994): 72–85; and James W. Dean, Jr., and Mark P. Sharfman, "Does Decision Process Matter? A Study of Strategic Decision-Making Effectiveness," *Academy of Management Journal*, Vol. 39, No. 2 (1996): 368–96.

65. Pfeffer, *Managing with Power*; Moroz and Kleiner, "Playing Hardball in Business Organizations."

66. Amos Drory and Tsilia Romm, "The Definition of Organizational Politics: A Review," *Human Relations* 43 (1990): 1133–54; Vredenburgh and Maurer, "A Process Framework of Organizational Politics."

67. Pfeffer, *Power in Organizations*, 70.

68. Ibid.

69. Daniel J. Brass and Marlene E. Burkhardt, "Potential Power and Power Use: An Investigation of Structure and Behavior," *Academy of Management Journal* 38 (1993): 441–70.

70. Hickson, et al., "A Strategic Contingencies Theory."

71. Pfeffer, *Power in Organizations*.

72. Ibid.

73. V. Dallas Merrell, *Huddling: The Informal Way to Management Success* (New York: AMACON, 1979).

74. Vredenburgh and Maurer, "A Process Framework of Organizational Politics."

75. Ibid.

76. Pfeffer, *Power in Organizations*.

77. Ibid.

78. Ibid.

79. Kanter, "Power Failure in Management Circuits"; Pfeffer, *Power in Organizations*.

chapter thirteen

Interdepartmental Relations and Conflict

While reading this chapter, think about your answers to the following questions:

- What behavioral changes take place when people are in a conflict situation?

- What are the contextual and organizational factors that lead to interdepartmental conflict, and what qualities of interdepartmental relationships influence the frequency and intensity of that conflict?

- What are the benefits from interdepartmental cooperation and the losses from conflict?

- What are some techniques organizations use to reduce or manage conflict between departments?

anagers regularly deal with decisions about how to get the most out of employees, enhance job satisfaction and team identification, and realize high organizational performance. One question is whether conflict or collaboration should be encouraged. Will people be more highly motivated when they are urged to cooperate with one another or when they compete?

The notion of conflict has appeared in previous chapters. In Chapter 6, we talked about horizontal linkages, such as teams and task forces, that encourage coordination among functional departments. Chapter 7 examined the trend in today's globally competitive companies toward flatter, more horizontal structures that emphasize cooperation rather than competition among employees in self-directed teams. In Chapter 11 on decision making, coalition building was proposed as one way to resolve disagreements among departments. Chapter 12 examined power and political processes for managing competing claims on scarce resources. The very nature of organizations invites conflict, because organizations are composed of departmental groupings that have diverse and conflicting interests.

PURPOSE OF THIS CHAPTER

This chapter examines the nature and resolution of conflict more closely. Organizational conflict comes in many forms. Departments differ in goals, work activities, and prestige, and their members differ in age, education, and experience. The seeds of conflict are sown in these differences. Conflict has to be effectively managed or an organization may fail completely to achieve its goals.

In the first sections of this chapter, intergroup conflict is defined, and the consequences of conflict are identified. Then the causes of interdepartmental conflict in organizations are analyzed, followed by a detailed discussion of techniques for preventing and reducing conflict.

WHAT IS INTERGROUP CONFLICT?

Intergroup conflict requires three ingredients: group identification, observable group differences, and frustration. First, employees have to perceive themselves as part of an identifiable group or department.[1] Second, there has to be an observable group difference of some form. Groups may be located on different floors of the building, members may have gone to different schools, or members may work in different departments. The ability to identify oneself as a part of one group and to observe differences in comparison with other groups is necessary for conflict.[2]

The third ingredient is frustration. Frustration means that if one group achieves its goal, the other will not; it will be blocked. Frustration need not be severe and only needs to be anticipated to set off intergroup conflict. Intergroup conflict will appear when one group tries to advance its position in relation to other groups. **Intergroup conflict** can be defined as the behavior that occurs between organizational groups when participants identify with one group and perceive that other groups may block their group's goal achievement or expectations.[3] Conflict means that groups clash directly, that they are in fundamental opposition. Conflict is similar to competition but more severe. **Competition** means rivalry between groups in the pursuit of a common prize, while *conflict* presumes direct interference with goal achievement. Intergroup conflict within organizations can occur in both horizontal and vertical directions.

Horizontal Conflict

As shown in Exhibit 13.1, **horizontal conflict** occurs between groups or departments at the same level in the hierarchy.[4] Production may have a dispute with quality control because new quality procedures reduce production efficiency. The sales department may disagree with finance about credit policies that make it difficult to win new customers. Marketing and R&D may fight over the design for a new product. Horizontal coordination of some sort is needed to reduce conflict and achieve collaboration.

Vertical Conflict

Conflict also arises vertically between hierarchical levels.[5] **Vertical conflict** arises over issues of control, power, goals, and wages and benefits. A typical source of vertical conflict is between headquarters executives and regional plants or franchises. For example, one study found conflict between a local television station and its New York headquarters. As another example, franchise owners for Taco Bell, Burger King, and KFC are in conflict with headquarters because of the

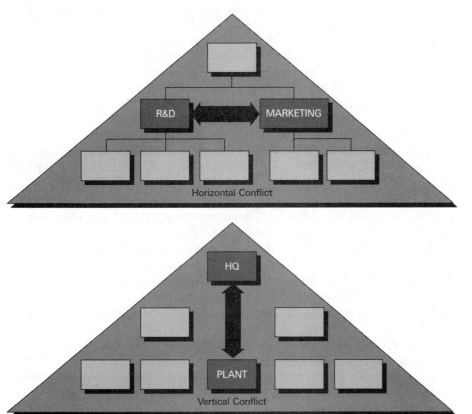

Exhibit 13.1
Types of Intergroup Conflict

rapid increase of company-owned stores, often in neighborhoods where they compete directly with franchisees. Some franchisees have gone so far as to take headquarters to court over this issue.[6] Vertical conflict can occur among any levels of the hierarchy, such as between crew leaders and supervisors.

THE NATURE OF INTERGROUP CONFLICT

Intergroup conflict in both vertical and horizontal directions has been studied in a variety of settings. Experimenters and consultants have been able to observe conflict and to test methods for reducing or resolving conflict. This research has provided several insights into the behavioral dynamics that occur within and between groups.

At one time, the U.S. air-traffic controllers union became embroiled in a conflict with the Federal Aviation Administration (FAA). The mismanagement of that intergroup conflict was a disaster for the air-traffic controllers.

In the early 1980s, 12,000 air-traffic controllers joined together in a strike against the federal government, demanding higher pay and better working conditions. The controllers were supremely confident, dedicated to their cause, and certain they would win.

One month later, the controllers' strike seemed to symbolize a suicide march rather than a courageous mission, and a year later, the Professional Air Traffic Controllers Organization (PATCO) was dead. Most of its members were fired from their government jobs. The union was found by the courts to have broken the law by striking against the government. It was decertified.

What happened to bring about such a dramatic shift in the prospects of PATCO union members? Why did PATCO leaders miscalculate so badly? Union members badly overestimated their importance to air travel and their worth to the government. Members genuinely believed the government could not operate the nation's air transport system without the controllers. They also believed that their enormous demands were justified. However, while controllers probably do endure more stress than ordinary government workers, they were more highly paid than other workers and also had job security. An average salary of $33,000 didn't seem that low to outsiders.

Several other reasons for PATCO's failure also surfaced. One was extreme internal cohesiveness. When the government issued an ultimatum with the backing of the full power of the presidency and the federal government, PATCO didn't flinch. Instead of compromising, PATCO members pulled together to stick it out. The emotional commitment to union solidarity became more important than the logical rationale for the strike.

Moreover, PATCO members didn't listen. They refused to believe President Ronald Reagan, who insisted that federal strikes were illegal and would be broken regardless of cost. Drew Lewis, secretary of transportation, said that if a strike were called, the strikers would be dismissed and there would be no amnesty. PATCO didn't gain the support of other unions, such as the Airline Pilots Association or the International Machinist's Union. They were overconfident to the point of believing they could shut down the airline system by themselves.

The Professional Air Traffic Controllers Organization made several blunders and miscalculations, with tragic human and financial costs. The union members lost their jobs as air-traffic controllers, and the union itself was dead at the tender age of thirteen.[7]

Types of Changes

The **behavioral changes** that took place among PATCO officials and union members during the strike are similar to changes that take place in most conflict situations. The types of changes frequently observed during intergroup conflict are as follows:[8]

1. People strongly identify with a group when members share a common mission or value. Members think of their group as separate and distinct from other groups. They develop pride and show signs of the "we" feelings that characterize an in-group. This in-group identification was very visible among members of PATCO.

2. The presence of another group invites comparison between "we" and "they." Members prefer the in-group to the out-group. The "they" for PATCO members was the Federal Aviation Administration.

3. If a group perceives itself in intense conflict with another group, its members become more closely knit and cohesive. Members pull together to present a solid front to defeat the other group. A group in conflict tends to become more formal and accepting of autocratic leader behavior. This strong internal cohesiveness was clearly visible among members of PATCO.

4. Group members tend to see some other groups as the enemy rather than as a neutral object. PATCO perceived the FAA and the Department of Transportation as adversaries, and members displayed negative sentiments toward them.

5. Group members tend to experience a "superiority complex." They overestimate their own strengths and achievements and underestimate the strength and achievements of other groups. This certainly took place in PATCO. Overconfidence in their ability and strengths was the biggest mistake PATCO members made.

6. Communication between competing groups will decrease. If such communication does take place, it tends to be characterized by negative statements and hostility. Members of one group do not listen or give credibility to statements by the other group. PATCO, for example, did not fully assimilate the statements made by President Reagan and Transportation Secretary Lewis.

7. When one group loses in a conflict, members lose cohesion. Group members experience increased tension and conflict among themselves and look for a scapegoat to blame for the group's failure. After the failed strike, PATCO members blamed one another and their leaders for the strike's failure and their loss of jobs.

8. Intergroup conflict and associated changes in perception and hostility are not the result of neurotic tendencies on the part of group members. These processes are natural and occur when group members are normal, healthy, and well-adjusted.

These behavioral outcomes of intergroup conflict research were vividly displayed in PATCO. They also can be observed in other organizations. Members of one high school or college often believe their school is superior to a rival school. Employees in one plant perceive themselves as making a greater contribution to the organization than do employees in other plants. Once these perceptions are understood, they can be managed as a natural part of intergroup dynamics.

Model of Intergroup Conflict

Exhibit 13.2 illustrates a **model of intergroup conflict**. The circles toward the left of the model are the organizational and intergroup factors that set the stage for intergroup conflict. An intergroup situation typically leads to conflict when a specific incident or frustration triggers a dispute. The circles at the top indicate the responses managers can make to control emergent conflict.

As discussed in Chapter 3, a number of factors contribute to differentiation among departments within an organization. Departments pursue different goals and cope with different elements of the external environment, and employees develop behaviors and attitudes that will lead to success in their specific department. For example, a research and development department is characterized by a long-time horizon, while a sales department is focused on short-term results. Physical separation also contributes to differentiation.

A conflict at Apple Computer between the Apple II and Macintosh groups reflects the model in Exhibit 13.2. Organizational factors that led to the conflict were physical separation of the two groups and different goals. The trigger for conflict was an annual meeting in which senior executives devoted most of the program to Macintosh products and ignored Apple II's innovations, which were the backbone of the company at that time. The consequence for Apple was poor morale and decreased performance in the Apple II division. Management responded by paying more attention to Apple II and by changing conditions so the Apple II group would not be physically removed from the rest of the organization.

Exhibit 13.2 *Model of Intergroup Conflict in Organizations*

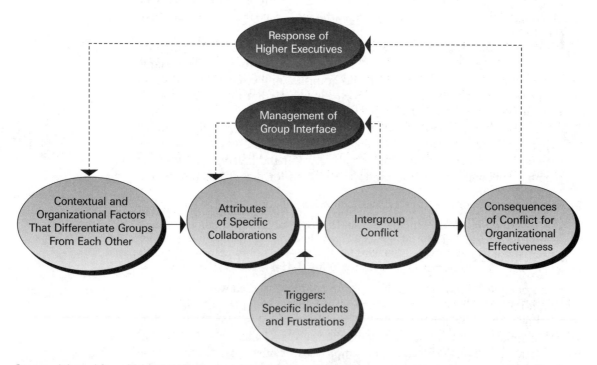

Source: Adapted from Richard E. Walton and John E. Dutton, "The Management of Interdepartmental Conflict," *Administrative Science Quarterly* 14 (1969): 73–84; and Louis R. Pondy, "Organizational Conflict: Concepts and Models," *Administrative Science Quarterly* 12 (1967): 296–320.

Differentiation also occurs between lower-level workers and management. Workers often do not feel involved in the organization, feel powerless and alienated, and perceive that management doesn't care about their needs. For example, triggered by pilot frustration over on-the-job fatigue, a conflict is brewing between pilots and airline executives concerning pilots' rest time. Some pilots fly as many as 16 hours in a row with as little as 8 hours of free time between flights. The pilot's union has enlisted the help of the National Transportation Safety Board and the Federal Aviation Administration to impose stronger rest rules. Airline executives, already facing constant cost pressure, stringently oppose the new rules, which would translate directly into economic and lifestyle benefits for the pilots.[9]

INTERDEPARTMENTAL CONFLICT

Much of the work in organization theory has been concerned with interdepartmental conflict. In this section, we will explore some of the causes of conflict as well as techniques for managing conflict between departments.

Contextual and Organizational Factors

The potential for interdepartmental conflict exists in any situation in which separate departments are created, members have an opportunity to compare themselves with other groups, and the goals and values of respective groups appear mutually exclusive. Several of the topics covered in previous chapters explain why organizational groups are in conflict with one another. Five of these topics are reviewed here.

Environment. Recall from Chapter 3 that departments are established to interact with major domains in the external environment. As the uncertainty and complexity of the environment increase, greater differences in skills, attitudes, power, and operative goals develop among departments. Each department is tailored to fit its environmental domain and, thus, is differentiated from other organizational groups. Moreover, increased competition, both domestically and internationally, has led to demands for lower prices, improved quality, and better service. These demands translate into more intense goal pressures within an organization and, hence, greater conflict among departments.

Size. As organizations increase in size, subdivision into a larger number of departments takes place. Members of departments begin to think of themselves as separate, and they erect walls between themselves and other departments. Employees feel isolated from other people in the organization. The lengthening hierarchy also heightens power and resource differences among departments.

Technology. Technology determines task allocation among departments as well as interdependence among departments. Groups that have interdependent tasks interact more often and must share resources. Interdependence creates frequent situations that lead to conflict.

Goals. The overall goals of an organization are broken down into operative goals that guide each department. Operative goals pursued by marketing, accounting, legal, and human resources departments often seem mutually exclusive. The accomplishment of operative goals by one department may block goal accomplishment by other departments and, hence, cause conflict. Goals of innovation also often lead to conflict because change requires coordination across departments. Innovation goals cause more conflict than do goals of internal efficiency.

Structure. Organization structure reflects the division of labor as well as the systems to facilitate coordination and control. It defines departmental groupings and, hence, employee loyalty to the defined groups. The choice of a divisional structure, for example, means divisions may be placed in competition for resources from headquarters, and headquarters may devise pay incentives based on competition among divisions.

Attributes of Interdepartmental Relationships

Environment, size, technology, goals, and structure are elements of the organizational context that can lead to conflict between departments. These contextual dimensions determine the specific organizational characteristics that generate conflict, as illustrated in Exhibit 13.3. The organizational context translates into eight attributes of interdepartmental relationships that influence the frequency, extent, and intensity of conflict between departments. These eight **sources of interdepartmental conflict** are operative goal incompatibility, differentiation, task interdependence, resource scarcity, power distribution, uncertainty, international context, and reward system.

Operative Goal Incompatibility. Goal incompatibility is probably the greatest cause of interdepartmental conflict in organizations.[10] The operative goals of each department reflect the specific objectives members are trying to achieve. The achievement of one department's goal often interferes with another department's goals. University police, for example, have a goal of providing a safe and secure campus. They can achieve their goal by locking all buildings on evenings and weekends and not distributing keys. Without easy access to buildings, however, progress toward the science department's research goals will proceed slowly. On the other hand, if scientists come and go at all hours and security is

Exhibit 13.3
Sources of Interdepartmental Conflict

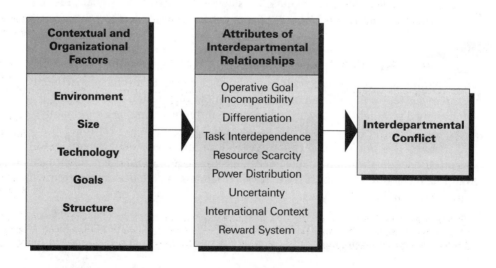

Contextual and Organizational Factors	Attributes of Interdepartmental Relationships	Interdepartmental Conflict
Environment	Operative Goal Incompatibility	
Size	Differentiation	
Technology	Task Interdependence	
Goals	Resource Scarcity	
Structure	Power Distribution	
	Uncertainty	
	International Context	
	Reward System	

ignored, police goals for security will not be met. Goal incompatibility throws the departments into conflict with each other.

The potential for conflict is perhaps greater between marketing and manufacturing than between other departments because the goals of these two departments are frequently at odds. Exhibit 13.4 shows examples of goal conflict between typical marketing and manufacturing departments. Marketing strives to increase the breadth of the product line to meet customer tastes for variety. A broad product line means short production runs, so manufacturing has to bear higher costs.[11] Other areas of goal conflict are quality, cost control, and new products. Goal incompatibility exists among departments in most organizations.

Differentiation. Differentiation was defined in Chapter 3 as "the differences in cognitive and emotional orientations among managers in different functional departments." Functional specialization requires people with specific education, skills, attitudes, and time horizons. For example, people may join a sales department because they have ability and aptitude consistent with sales work. After becoming members of the sales department, they are influenced by departmental norms and values.

Departments or divisions within an organization often differ in values, attitudes, and standards of behavior, and these cultural differences lead to conflicts.[12] Consider an encounter between a sales manager and an R&D scientist about a new product:

> *The sales manager may be outgoing and concerned with maintaining a warm, friendly relationship with the scientist. He may be put off because the scientist seems withdrawn and disinclined to talk about anything other than the problems in which he is interested. He may also be annoyed that the scientist seems*

Exhibit 13.4 *Marketing-Manufacturing Areas of Potential Goal Conflict*

Goal Conflict	MARKETING *versus* Operative goal is customer satisfaction	MANUFACTURING Operative goal is production efficiency
Conflict Area	*Typical Comment*	*Typical Comment*
1. Breadth of product line	"Our customers demand variety."	"The product line is too broad—all we get are short, uneconomical runs."
2. New product introduction	"New products are our lifeblood."	"Unnecessary design changes are prohibitively expensive."
3. Production scheduling	"We need faster response. Our lead times are too long."	"We need realistic customer commitments that don't change like wind direction."
4. Physical distribution	"Why don't we ever have the right merchandise in inventory?"	"We can't afford to keep huge inventories."
5. Quality	"Why can't we have reasonable quality at low cost?"	"Why must we always have options that are too expensive and offer little customer utility?

Source: Based on Benson S. Shapiro, "Can Marketing and Manufacturing Coexist?" *Harvard Business Review* 55 (September–October 1977): 104–14; and Victoria L. Crittenden, Lorraine R. Gardiner, and Antonie Stam, "Reducing Conflict Between Marketing and Manufacturing," *Industrial Marketing Management* 22 (1993): 299–309.

to have such freedom in choosing what he will work on. Furthermore, the scientist is probably often late for appointments, which, from the salesman's point of view, is no way to run a business. The scientist, for his part, may feel uncomfortable because the salesman seems to be pressing for immediate answers to technical questions that will take a long time to investigate. All the discomforts are concrete manifestations of the relatively wide differences between these two men in respect to their working and thinking styles. . . .[13]

Cultural differences can be particularly acute in the case of mergers or acquisitions. Employees in the acquired company may have completely different work styles and attitudes, and a "we against them" attitude can develop. One reason for the failure of many mergers is that although managers can integrate financial and production technologies, they have difficulty integrating the unwritten norms and values that have an even greater impact on company success.[14]

Task Interdependence. Task interdependence refers to the dependence of one unit on another for materials, resources, or information. As described in Chapter 4 on technology, pooled interdependence means little interaction; sequential interdependence means the output of one department goes to the next department; and reciprocal interdependence means departments mutually exchange materials and information.[15]

Generally, as interdependence increases, the potential for conflict increases.[16] In the case of pooled interdependence, units have little need to interact. Conflict is at a minimum. Sequential and reciprocal interdependence require employees to spend time coordinating and sharing information. Employees must communicate frequently, and differences in goals or attitudes will surface. Conflict is especially likely to occur when agreement is not reached about the coordination of services to each other. Greater interdependence means departments often exert pressure for a fast response because departmental work has to wait on other departments.[17]

Resource Scarcity. Another major source of conflict involves competition between groups for what members perceive as limited resources.[18] Organizations have limited money, physical facilities, staff resources, and human resources to share among departments. In their desire to achieve goals, groups want to increase their resources. This throws them into conflict. Managers may develop strategies, such as inflating budget requirements or working behind the scenes, to obtain a desired level of resources. Resources also symbolize power and influence within an organization. The ability to obtain resources enhances prestige. Departments typically believe they have a legitimate claim on additional resources. However, exercising that claim results in conflict. For example, in almost every organization, conflict occurs during the annual budget exercise, often creating the political activities described in Chapter 12.

Power Distribution. As explained in the previous chapter, power differences evolve even when departments are at the same level on the organization chart. Some departments provide a more valuable service or reduce critical uncertainties for the organization. For example, sometimes a conflict builds up between sales and marketing departments because of power differences. Over the past decade, the role of marketing has expanded into the realm of strategic planning, which means more involvement in analyzing the competition with senior management.

Sales, meanwhile, focuses on customer needs. Marketing's growing influence has elevated the conflict with sales departments in some companies to a battle for dominance. Power differences often provide a basis for conflict, especially when actual working relationships do not reflect perceived power.[19]

Uncertainty. Another factor for predicting interdepartmental conflict is the uncertainty and change experienced by organizational departments. When activities are predictable, departments know where they stand. They can rely on rules or previous decisions to resolve disputes that arise. When factors in the environment are rapidly changing or when problems arise that are poorly understood, departments may have to renegotiate their respective tasks.[20] Managers have to sort out how new problems should be handled. The boundaries of a department's territory or jurisdiction become indistinct. Members may reach out to take on more responsibility, only to find other groups feel invaded. In a study of hospital purchasing decisions, managers reported significantly higher levels of conflict when purchases were nonroutine than when purchases were routine.[21] Generally, as uncertainty about departmental relationships increases, conflict can be expected to increase.

International Context. The increasing importance of the international sector of the business environment has created another source of conflict within organizations. In companies operating globally, cultural differences provide a breeding ground for conflict among organizational units. Indeed, some companies are finding that cultural differences provide more potential for conflict than any other single factor. Research done by Geert Hofstede on IBM employees in 40 countries discovered that mindset and cultural values on issues such as individualism vs. collectivism strongly influence organizational and employee relationships and vary widely among cultures.[22] IBM itself discovered just how widely they vary when it attempted an ambitious team project, known as Triad, with Siemens AG of Germany and Japan's Toshiba Corporation. The cross-cultural team approach was expected to generate creative leaps and lead to dazzling discoveries, but culture got in the way.

Siemens scientists were shocked to find Toshiba colleagues closing their eyes and seeming to sleep during meetings, a common practice in Japan. The Japanese, accustomed to working in large, informal groups, found it almost painful to be forced to schedule meetings in small, individual offices. Employees of IBM complained that the Germans plan too much and that the Japanese, who like to constantly review ideas, wouldn't make a decision. Because German and Japanese workers sometimes found it difficult to communicate their ideas clearly in English, they began talking among themselves in their native languages. Suspicions began to circulate that some researchers were withholding information, and conflicts among the three groups grew. Although Triad continues to work through cultural differences, results of the project have been disappointing.[23]

Reward System. The reward system governs the degree to which subgroups cooperate or conflict with one another.[24] An experiment with student groups illustrates how incentives influence conflict.[25] In one-half of the groups, called cooperative groups, each student's grade was the grade given for the group's project. All students in those groups, regardless of individual contribution, received the same grade. In the remaining groups, called competitive groups, students were rewarded on the basis of their personal contribution to the group project. Each student was graded individually and could receive a high or low grade regardless of the overall group score.

The outcome of these incentives on conflict was significant. When the incentive system rewarded members for accomplishing the group goal (cooperative groups), coordination among members was better, communication among members was better, productivity was greater, and the quality of the group product was better. When individuals were graded according to their personal contributions to the group (competitive groups), they communicated less with each other and were more frequently in conflict. Members tried to protect themselves and to succeed at the expense of others in the group. The quality of the group project and productivity were lower.

Incentives and rewards have similar impact on conflict between organizational departments. When departmental managers are rewarded for achieving overall organization goals rather than departmental goals, cooperation among departments is greater.[26] Bechtel, for example, provides a bonus system to division managers based upon the achievement of Bechtel's profit goals. Regardless of how well a manager's division does, the manager isn't rewarded unless the corporation performs well. This incentive system motivates division managers to cooperate with each other. If departments are rewarded only for departmental performance, managers are motivated to excel at the expense of the rest of the organization.

THE COOPERATIVE MODEL OF ORGANIZATION

The preceding section looked at several causes and examples of interdepartmental conflict. The very nature of an organization, with goal incompatibility, task interdependence, scarce resources, and power differences, invites conflict. Conflict is natural and inevitable.

Research suggests that when conflict is focused on substantive organizational rather than personal issues, it can be beneficial because it helps organization members clarify objectives, expectations, and behaviors, and make better decisions about how to achieve organizational goals.[27] Top managers dealing with complex, nonprogrammed decisions, for example, make better choices when they discuss rather than ignore conflicting points of view. When conflict in teams is suppressed rather than acknowledged, a problem known as "groupthink" may emerge, in which team members are reluctant to disagree with one another and poor decisions are made for the sake of consensus and group harmony.[28]

However, whereas in the past managers often encouraged conflict and competition, the emerging view is that cooperation is the best way to achieve high performance. The new trends in management we have discussed in previous chapters—including clan control, high-involvement corporate cultures, time-based competition, and self-directed teams—assume employee cooperation is a good thing. This means successful organizations must find healthy ways to confront and resolve conflict. Managers champion a **cooperative model** of organization, meaning they foster cooperation and don't stimulate competition or conflict, which work against the achievement of overall company goals.

Groups in conflict develop mistrust of one another and pay more attention to beating their rivals than to performing their tasks. When that happens, the stronger party begins to feel invincible. Competition can sometimes have a healthy effect, but carried to an extreme, it can lead to long-term losses and a detrimental impact on the entire organization.

If an organization achieves an ideal of no conflict, it is probably in trouble. Conflict is a sign of an active, ongoing, forceful organization. However, conflict becomes a problem when there is too much and when it is used for motivational purposes. Exhibit 13.5 summarizes several benefits from cooperation and losses from conflict.

Benefits From Cooperation

The new viewpoint about cooperation proposes that internal competition is bad for organizations. The Vince Lombardi philosophy, "Winning isn't everything. It's the only thing," may do more harm than good within companies. One expert argues the ideal amount of competition between departments is zero—none at all.[29] Managers should discourage even informal competition, designing work to encourage cooperation. The reason is that competition prevents the free exchange of ideas, resources, and skills. Competition and conflict should be with other companies. Employees should identify with the entire organization as one team.

To achieve the cooperative state, for example, managers can design bonuses and incentive systems to enhance cooperation. Incentives should never be designed as prizes that only one department can win, because no department will help any other department. The result will be ill will and declining productivity. Incentives should be designed so that any department that reaches a certain goal is eligible for the bonus.[30]

The **benefits from cooperation** are discussed in the following paragraphs.

Productive Task Focus. Departmental employees do not become preoccupied with achieving their own goals. Instead, they are able to focus on the overall goals of the organization. For example, research in employment agencies found that when interviewers worked cooperatively to fill positions, they filled significantly more jobs than did interviewers in an agency that competed fiercely to fill job openings. The sharing of information about candidates and job openings far outweighed the intense effort generated by competition. A study of managers in an engineering firm and a utility company found that a goal of cooperation was associated with more cooperative assistance, exchange of resources and information, and more progress on tasks.[31]

Employee Cohesion and Satisfaction. Under conditions of cooperation, "we-feelings" and in-group identification occur for employees throughout the organization. Members are attracted to the organization as a whole, not just the group, and receive satisfaction from both memberships. Members across departments cooperate with each other and link the achievement of departmental tasks to

Benefits from Cooperation	Losses from Conflict
1. Productive task focus	1. Diversion of energy
2. Cohesion and satisfaction	2. Altered judgment
3. Goal attainment	3. Loser effects
4. Innovation and adaptation	4. Poor coordination

Exhibit 13.5
Organizational Benefits from Cooperation and Losses from Conflict

organizational goals. One study of twenty organizational units found strong social ties between groups in low-conflict organizations and an image of order and meaning about the organization. High-conflict organizations were seen as chaotic by employees, who had only weak ties to other groups.[32] Other research suggests conflict creates stress that often produces negative results. While some employees may seem to work hard under competition, they are less satisfied and are less likely to worry about company goals. A study of supervisors found that supervisors who engendered competitiveness were seen as less effective and as managing less effective departments. Supervisors rated high were able to engender a cooperative orientation. Employees simply enjoyed the cooperative arrangement more. Their jobs were more satisfying, partly because they achieved more.

Organizational Goal Attainment. Under the cooperative model, the organization is able to achieve overall goals because energy is not wasted on interdepartmental rivalries. Competition and conflict are created toward other organizations, not toward other departments within the organization. Moderate competition and conflict against other organizations stimulate participants to work hard.[33] Cohesion results in an enjoyable work atmosphere. The intensity of an athletic team achieving its goal is an example of benefits of competition against other organizations. Cooperation does not mean complacency, which can be as big a problem as internal conflict. An organization can prosper and achieve its overall goals when subgroups are doing their tasks well and cooperating with one another.

Innovation and Adaptation. Cooperation encourages creativity and innovation, helping organizations develop new technologies, products, and services quickly. As discussed in Chapter 8, when technical, marketing, and production people are sharing information and ideas and working simultaneously on projects, companies are able to speed new products to market for time-based competition. In addition, cooperation among departments is essential for companies to keep pace in today's rapidly changing, competitive environment. When employees are obsessed with their own departments' tasks and with defeating other departments, innovation is stifled, and organizations are not poised to change and grow with the environment. Today's most successful companies are pushing cooperation to the limit.

Losses From Conflict

When conflict is too strong or is not managed appropriately, several negative consequences for organizations may arise. These **losses from conflict** include diversion of energy, altered judgment, loser effects, and poor coordination.

Diversion of Energy. One serious consequence of conflict is the diversion of a department's time and effort toward winning a conflict rather than toward achieving organizational goals.[34] When the most important outcome becomes defeating other departments, no holds barred, resources are wasted. In extreme cases, sabotage, secrecy, and even illegal activities occur. At the Centers for Disease Control AIDS laboratory, for example, the important battle against this disease was slowed when a noted virologist actually ordered another scientist's experiments to be thrown away because of conflicts among departments about the type of research the lab should be conducting.[35]

Altered Judgment. One finding from intergroup research is that judgment and perceptions become less accurate when conflict becomes more intense. The over-confidence and unrealistic expectations of PATCO members discussed earlier is an example. Moreover, when a group makes a mistake, it may blame perceived opponents within the organization rather than acknowledge its own shortcomings. People involved in conflict also have a poor understanding of ideas offered by competitors.[36]

Loser Effects. Another unfortunate aspect of intense interdepartmental conflict is that someone usually loses. The losing department undergoes substantial change. Losers may deny or distort the reality of losing. They may withdraw. They often seek scapegoats, perhaps even members or leaders in their own department. Dissension replaces cohesion. Losers generally tend toward low cooperation and low concern for the needs and interests of other department members.[37]

Poor Coordination. The final problem with conflict is the emphasis given to achieving departmental goals. Departmental goals serve to energize employees, but these goals should not become an all-consuming priority. Departmental goals must be integrated with the goals of the organization. Under intense conflict, coordination does not happen. Collaboration across groups decreases. Groups have less contact, and they are not sympathetic to other points of view. Under intense conflict, achieving departmental goals and defeating the enemy take priority. There is no room for compromise.[38]

TECHNIQUES FOR MANAGING CONFLICT AMONG GROUPS

The ideal situation for most organizations is to have only moderate intergroup *competition* and *conflict*. Managers should not let conflict get so great that losses from conflict occur. To the extent possible, they should strive to stimulate cooperation to encourage productive task focus and organizational goal attainment.

Changes in Attitude and Behavior

Reducing extant conflict is often a challenge. When conflict has been too great, participants may actively dislike each other and may not want to change. The target of conflict management techniques can be either the *behavior* or the *attitude* of group members.[39] By changing behavior, open conflict is reduced or eliminated, but departmental members may still dislike people in other departments. A change in behavior makes the conflict less visible, or keeps the groups separated. A change in attitude is deeper and takes longer. A new attitude is difficult to achieve and requires a positive change in perceptions and feelings about other departments. A change in attitude is the basis for a true cooperative organization.

    The techniques available for managing conflict are arranged along a scale in Exhibit 13.6. Techniques near the top of the scale, such as formal authority, will change behavior but not attitudes. Techniques near the bottom of the scale, such as rotating group members or providing intergroup training, are designed to bring about positive change in cooperative attitudes between groups.

Exhibit 13.6

*Strategies for
Managing Conflict
among Groups*

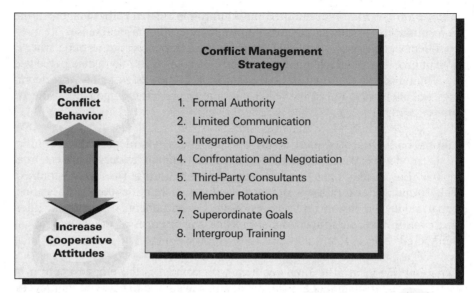

Source: Adapted from Eric H. Neilsen, "Understanding and Managing Conflict," in Jay W.
Lorsch and Paul R. Lawrence, eds., *Managing Group and Intergroup Relations*
(Homewood, Ill.: Irwin and Dorsey, 1972), 329–43.

Formal Authority. Formal authority means senior management invokes rules, regulations, and legitimate authority to resolve or suppress a conflict. For example, the advertising and sales departments may disagree about advertising strategy. The sales force may want a strategy based on direct mail while advertising prefers to use radio and television. This type of conflict can be resolved by passing it to the marketing vice president, who uses legitimate authority to resolve the conflict.

   At Continental Airlines, top managers used formal authority to force cooperation between marketing and operations when the departments disagreed over flight scheduling. Cooperation between the two units dramatically improved Continental's on-time performance, moving the airline from near the bottom of the U.S. Department of Transportation ranking to the top.[40] The disadvantage of this technique is that it does not change attitudes toward cooperation and may treat only the immediate problem. The formal authority method is effective in the short run when members cannot agree on a solution to a specific conflict.[41]

Limited Communication. Encouraging some communication among conflicting departments prevents the development of misperceptions about the abilities, skills, and traits of other departments. When departments are in severe conflict, controlled interaction can be used to resolve the conflict. Often the interaction can be focused on issues about which the departments have a common goal. A common goal means the departments must talk and cooperate, at least for the achievement of that goal. For example, Datapoint Corporation experiences frequent conflict between the research and development and manufacturing divisions. Since senior managers in these divisions are located in the same city, a forum was devised for them to resolve differences. "Summit meetings" were created where managers could bring their disagreements for discussion and resolution. A dispute about R&D security in a new building was resolved in this fashion. This technique may make a small impact on attitude change.[42]

Integration Devices. As described in Chapter 6, teams, task forces, and project managers who span the boundaries between departments can be used as integration devices. Bringing together representatives from conflicting departments in joint problem-solving teams is an effective way to reduce conflict because the representatives learn to understand each other's points of view.[43] Sometimes a full-time integrator is assigned to achieve cooperation and collaboration by meeting with members of the respective departments and exchanging information. The integrator has to understand each group's problems and must be able to move both groups toward a solution that is mutually acceptable.[44]

As an outgrowth of teams and task forces, many organizations today are restructuring into permanent multidisciplinary self-directed work teams focused on horizontal process rather than function. Chapter 7 describes these self-directed teams, which eliminate old boundaries between departments by bringing together employees from several functions, such as design, engineering, production, sales, supply, and finance. Teams and task forces reduce conflict and enhance cooperation because they integrate people from different departments.

An old-line insurance company, Aid Association for Lutherans, reorganized into teams to try to reduce misunderstanding among departments that led to delays in processing claims or inquiries. Each team now has specialists who can handle any of the 167 tasks required for policyholder sales and service. Misunderstandings that once led to interdepartmental conflict are now worked out quickly within the teams, and procedures that once took almost a month are now completed in just five days.[45]

Confrontation and Negotiation. **Confrontation** occurs when parties in conflict directly engage one another and try to work out their differences. **Negotiation** is the bargaining process that often occurs during confrontation and that enables the parties to systematically reach a solution. These techniques bring appointed representatives from the departments together to work out a serious dispute.

Confrontation and negotiation involve some risk. There is no guarantee that discussions will focus on a conflict or that emotions will not get out of hand. However, if members are able to resolve the conflict on the basis of face-to-face discussions, they will find new respect for each other, and future collaboration becomes easier. The beginnings of relatively permanent attitude change are possible through direct negotiation.

For example, one technique used by companies is to have each department head meet face-to-face once a month with each of the other department heads and list what he or she expects from that department. After discussion and negotiation, department heads sign off on their commitments to perform the services on the list. The regular contact develops managers' skills as well as their desire to work out conflicts and solve problems among themselves.[46]

Confrontation is successful when managers engage in a "win-win" strategy. Win-win means both departments adopt a positive attitude and strive to resolve the conflict in a way that will benefit each other.[47] If the negotiations deteriorate into a strictly win-lose strategy (each group wants to defeat the other), the confrontation will be ineffective. Top management can urge group members to work toward mutually acceptable outcomes. The differences between win-win and win-lose strategies of negotiation are shown in Exhibit 13.7. With a win-win strategy—which includes defining the problem as mutual, communicating openly, and avoiding threats—understanding can be changed while the dispute is resolved.

Exhibit 13.7
Negotiating Strategies

Win-Win Strategy	Win-Lose Strategy
1. Define the conflict as a mutual problem	1. Define the conflict as a win-lose situation
2. Pursue joint outcomes	2. Pursue own group's outcomes
3. Find creative agreements that satisfy both groups	3. Force the other group into submission
4. Use open, honest, and accurate communication of group's needs, goals, and proposals	4. Use deceitful, inaccurate, and misleading communication of group's needs, goals, and proposals
5. Avoid threats (to reduce the other's defensiveness)	5. Use threats (to force submission)
6. Communicate flexibility of position	6. Communicate high commitment (rigidity) regarding one's position

Source: Adapted from David W. Johnson and Frank P. Johnson, *Joining Together: Group Theory and Group Skills* (Englewood Cliffs, N.J.: Prentice-Hall, 1975), 182–83.

Third-Party Consultants. When conflict is intense and enduring, and department members are suspicious and uncooperative, a third-party consultant can be brought in from outside the organization to meet with representatives from both departments. Such consultants should be experts on human behavior, and their advice and actions must be valued by both groups. Third-party consultants can make great progress toward building cooperative attitudes and reducing conflict.[48]

Sometimes called "workplace mediation," the use of third-party consultants is growing as companies recognize the costs of intense workplace conflict. The Saskatchewan Research Council makes regular use of outside counselors. According to Jonathan France of the human resources department, "When we've got a squeaky wheel, we prefer to oil it than to replace it."[49]

Typical activities of third-party consultants are as follows:

- Reestablish broken communication lines between groups.
- Act as interpreter so that messages between groups are correctly understood and are not distorted by preconceived biases.
- Challenge and bring into the open the stereotyping done by one group or the other. Exposing stereotypes often leads to their dissolution.
- Bring into awareness the positive acts and intentions of the other group. This forces a cognitive reassessment of one group's stance toward the other group.
- Define, focus, and resolve the specific source of conflict.

With negative emotions removed, a cooperative attitude can be established and nurtured to replace the previous conflict.[50]

Member Rotation. Rotation means individuals from one department can be asked to work in another department on a temporary or permanent basis. The advantage is that individuals become submerged in the values, attitudes, problems, and goals of the other department. In addition, they can explain the problems and goals of their original department to their new colleagues. This enables a frank, accurate exchange of views and information. Rotation works slowly to reduce conflict but is very effective for changing the underlying attitudes and perceptions that promote conflict.[51]

Shared Mission and Superordinate Goals. Another strategy is for top management to create a shared mission and establish superordinate goals that require cooperation among departments.[52] As discussed in Chapter 10, organizations with strong, adaptive cultures, where employees share a larger vision for their company, are more likely to have a united, cooperative work force. Recent studies have shown that when employees from different departments see that their goals are linked together, they will openly share resources and information.[53] To be effective, superordinate goals must be substantial, and employees must be granted the time to work cooperatively toward those goals. The reward system can also be redesigned to encourage the pursuit of the superordinate goals rather than departmental subgoals.

Perhaps the most powerful superordinate goal is company survival. If an organization is about to fail and jobs will be lost, groups forget their differences and try to save the organization. The goal of survival has improved relationships between groups in meat-packing plants and auto supply firms that have been about to go out of business.

Intergroup Training. A strong intervention to reduce conflict is intergroup training. This technique has been developed by such psychologists as Robert Blake, Jane Mouton, and Richard Walton.[54] When other techniques fail to reduce conflict to an appropriate level or do not fit the organization in question, special training of group members may be required. This training requires that department members attend an outside workshop away from day-to-day work problems. The training workshop may last several days, and various activities will take place. This technique is expensive, but it has the potential for developing a company-wide cooperative attitude.

Intergroup training is similar to the OD approach described in Chapter 8 on innovation and change. The steps typically associated with an intergroup training session are as follows:

1. The conflicting groups are brought into a training setting with the stated goal of exploring mutual perceptions and relationships.
2. The conflicting groups are then separated, and each group is invited to discuss and make a list of its perceptions of itself and the other group.
3. In the presence of both groups, group representatives publicly share the perceptions of self and other that the groups have generated, while the groups are obligated to remain silent. The objective is simply to report to the other group as accurately as possible the images that each group has developed in private.
4. Before any exchange takes place, the groups return to private sessions to digest and analyze what they have heard; there is great likelihood that the representatives' reports have revealed to each group discrepancies between its self-image and the image the other group holds of it.
5. In public session, again working through representatives, each group shares with the other what discrepancies it has uncovered and the possible reasons for them, focusing on actual, observable behavior.
6. Following this mutual exposure, a more open exploration is permitted between the two groups on the now-shared goal of identifying further reasons for perceptual distortions.
7. A joint exploration is then conducted of how to manage future relations in such a way as to encourage cooperation between groups.[55]

Intergroup training sessions can be quite demanding for everyone involved. It is fairly easy to have conflicting groups list perceptions and identify discrepancies. But exploring their differences face-to-face and agreeing to change is more difficult. However, if handled correctly, these sessions can help department employees understand each other much better and lead to improved attitudes and better working relationships for years to come.

SUMMARY OF KEY ISSUES

This chapter contains several ideas that complement the topics of power and decision making in the two previous chapters. The most important idea is that intergroup conflict is a natural outcome of organizing. Intergroup conflict can occur in both horizontal and vertical directions. Much of the work in organization theory has been concerned with conflict between departments.

Differences in goals, backgrounds, and tasks are necessary for departmental excellence. These differences throw groups into conflict. Some conflict is healthy and should be directed toward successful outcomes for everyone. Understanding the role of organizational conflict and the importance of achieving appropriate levels of conflict are important lessons from this chapter.

The most recent thinking suggests managers should encourage cooperation within the organization. Conflict and competition should be directed toward other organizations. This approach increases cohesion, satisfaction, and performance for the organization as a whole. Severe conflict among departments can lead to disregard and dislike for other groups, and perceiving them as inferior or as the enemy; hence, cooperation will decrease. Organizations can manage conflict with techniques such as member rotation or intergroup training. Some organizations are pushing cooperation even further by establishing permanent cross-functional work teams that virtually eliminate boundaries between departments.

Discussion Questions

1. Define *intergroup conflict*. How does this definition compare with that of competition? What is vertical as opposed to horizontal conflict?
2. Briefly describe how differences in tasks, personal background, and training lead to conflict between groups. How does task interdependence lead to conflict between groups?
3. What impact does conflict have on people within conflicting groups?
4 Discuss the organizational losses from interdepartmental conflict.
5. Intergroup training is located at a higher level on the scale of conflict-resolution techniques than is member rotation. What does this mean in terms of the impact the two techniques have on behavior versus attitudes? Can you think of situations in which rotation might have greater impact on attitudes than would intergroup training? Discuss.
6. Do you believe cooperation will stimulate higher performance than competition among departments? Discuss.
7. Discuss why some conflict is considered beneficial to organizations.

Notes

1. Clayton T. Alderfer and Ken K. Smith, "Studying Intergroup Relations Imbedded in Organizations," *Administrative Science Quarterly* 27 (1982): 35–65.

2. Muzafer Sherif, "Experiments in Group Conflict," *Scientific American* 195 (1956): 54–58; Edgar H. Schein, *Organizational Psychology*, 3d ed. (Englewood Cliffs, NJ.: Prentice-Hall, 1980).

3. M. Ascalur Rahin, "A Strategy for Managing Conflict in Complex Organizations," *Human Relations* 38 (1985): 81–89; Kenneth Thomas, "Conflict and Conflict Management," in M. D. Dunnette, ed., *Handbook of Industrial and Organizational Psychology* (Chicago: Rand McNally, 1976); Stuart M. Schmidt and Thomas A. Kochan, "Conflict: Toward Conceptual Clarity," *Administrative Science Quarterly* 13 (1972): 359–70.

4. L. David Brown, "Managing Conflict among Groups," in David A. Kolb, Irwin M. Rubin, and James M. McIntyre, eds., *Organizational Psychology: A Book of Readings* (Englewood Cliffs, NJ.: Prentice-Hall, 1979), 377–89.

5. Brown, "Managing Conflict among Groups."

6. Amy Barrett, "Indigestion at Taco Bell," *Business Week*, 14 December 1994, 66–67; Susan V. Lourenco and John C. Glidewell, "A Dialectical Analysis of Organizational Conflict," *Administrative Science Quarterly* 20 (1975): 489–508.

7. Harry Bernstein, "Union Misjudged Government," *Houston Chronicle*, 4 September 1981, copyright © Los Angeles Times—Washington Post News Service; Paul Galloway, "Negotiating Consultant Says Air Controllers Can't Win Strike," *Houston Chronicle*, 25 August 1981, copyright © Chicago Sun-Times; Susan B. Garland, "Air-Traffic Controllers: Getting Organized Again," *Business Week*, 18 May 1987, 52.

8. These conclusions are summarized from Sherif, "Experiments in Group Conflict"; M. Sherif, O. J. Harvey, B. J. White, W. R. Hood, and C. W. Sherif, *Intergroup Conflict and Cooperation* (Norman, Okla.: University of Oklahoma Books Exchange, 1961); M. Sherif and C. W. Sherif, *Social Psychology* (New York: Harper & Row, 1969); and Schein, *Organizational Psychology*.

9. Andy Pasztor, "An Air-Safety Battle Brews over the Issue of Pilots' Rest Time," *The Wall Street Journal*, 1 July 1996, A1.

10. Thomas A. Kochan, George P. Huber, and L. L. Cummings, "Determinants of Intraorganizational Conflict in Collective Bargaining in the Public Sector," *Administrative Science Quarterly* 20 (1975): 10–23.

11. Victoria L. Crittenden, Lorraine R. Gardiner, and Antonie Stam, "Reducing Conflict between Marketing and Manufacturing," *Industrial Marketing Management* 22 (1993): 299–309; Benson S. Shapiro, "Can Marketing and Manufacturing Coexist?" *Harvard Business Review* 55 (September–October 1977): 104–14.

12. Eric H. Neilsen, "Understanding and Managing Intergroup Conflict," in Jay W. Lorsch and Paul R. Lawrence, eds., *Managing Group and Intergroup Relations* (Homewood, Ill.: Irwin and Dorsey, 1972), 329–43; Richard E. Walton and John M. Dutton, "The Management of Interdepartmental Conflict: A Model and Review," *Administrative Science Quarterly* 14 (1969): 73–84.

13. Jay W. Lorsch, "Introduction to the Structural Design of Organizations," in Gene W. Dalton, Paul R. Lawrence, and Jay W. Lorsch, eds., *Organization Structure and Design* (Homewood, Ill.: Irwin and Dorsey, 1970), 5.

14. Morty Lefkoe, "Why So Many Mergers Fail," *Fortune*, 20 June 1987, 113–14; Afsaneh Nahavandi and Ali R. Malekzadeh, "Acculturation in Mergers and Acquisitions," *Academy of Management Review*, Vol. 13, 1988, 79–90.

15. James D. Thompson, *Organizations in Action* (New York: McGraw-Hill, 1967), 54–56.

16. Walton and Dutton, "Management of Interdepartmental Conflict."

17. Joseph McCann and Jay R. Galbraith, "Interdepartmental Relationships," in Paul C. Nystrom and William H. Starbuck, eds., *Handbook of Organizational Design*, Vol. 2 (New York: Oxford University Press, 1981), 60–82.

18. Roderick M. Cramer, "Intergroup Relations and Organizational Dilemmas: The Role of Categorization Processes," in L. L. Cummings and Barry M. Staw, eds., *Research in Organizational Behavior*, Vol. 13 (New York: JAI Press, 1991), 191–228; Neilsen, "Understanding and Managing Intergroup Conflict"; Louis R. Pondy, "Organizational Conflict: Concepts

and Models," *Administrative Science Quarterly* 12 (1968): 296–320.

19. Richard Devine, Overcoming Sibling Rivalry between Sales and Marketing," *Management Review*, (June 1989): 36–40; John A. Seiler, "Diagnosing Interdepartmental Conflict," *Harvard Business Review* 41 (September–October 1963): 121–32.

20. Walton and Dutton, "Management of Inter-departmental Conflict"; Pondy, "Organizational Conflict"; Kenneth W. Thomas and Louis R. Pondy, "Toward an 'Intent' Model of Conflict Management among Principal Parties," *Human Relations* 30 (1977): 1089–1102.

21. Daniel S. Cochran and Donald D. White, "Intraorganizational Conflict in the Hospital Purchasing Decision Making Process," *Academy of Management Journal* 24 (1981): 324–32.

22. Geert Hofstede, "The Interaction between National and Organizational Value Systems," *Journal of Management Studies*, Vol. 22 (1985): 347–57; and Geert Hofstede, "The Cultural Relativity of the Quality of Life Concept," *Academy of Management Review*, Vol. 9 (1984): 389–98.

23. E. S. Browning, "Computer Chip Project Brings Rivals Together, but the Cultures Clash," *The Wall Street Journal*, 3 May 1994, A1.

24. Walton and Dutton, "Management of Interdepartmental Conflict."

25. Morton Deutsch, "The Effects of Cooperation and Competition upon Group Process," in Dorwin Cartwright and Alvin Zander, eds., *Group Dynamics* (New York: Harper & Row, 1968), 461–82.

26. Gordon Cliff, "Managing Organizational Conflict," *Management Review* (May 1987): 51–53.

27. Allen C. Amason, "Distinguishing the Effects of Functional and Dysfunctional Conflict on Strategic Decision Making: Resolving a Paradox for Top Management Teams," *Academy of Management Journal*, Vol. 39, No. 1 (1996): 123–48; Karen A. Jehn, "A Multimethod Examination of the Benefits and Detriments of Intragroup Conflict," *Administrative Science Quarterly*, Vol. 40, June 1995, 256–82; and Allen C. Amason, Kenneth R. Thompson, Wayne A. Hochwarter, and Allison W. Harrison, "Conflict: An Important Dimension in Successful Management Teams," *Organizational Dynamics*, Vol. 24, No. 2 (Autumn 1995): 20–55.

28. Amason, et. al., "Conflict: An Important Dimension in Successful Management Teams."

29. Alfie Kohn, "No Contest," *Inc.*, November 1987, 145–48.

30. Alfie Kohn, *No Contest: The Case against Competition* (Boston: Houghton Mifflin, 1986).

31. Dean Tjosvold, "Cooperative and Competitive Interdependence: Collaboration between Departments to Serve Customers," *Group and Organizational Studies* 13 (1988): 274–89.

32. Reed E. Nelson, "The Strength of Strong Ties: Social Networks and Intergroup Conflict in Organizations," *Academy of Management Journal* 32 (1989): 377–401.

33. Joe Kelly, "Make Conflict Work for You," *Harvard Business Review* 48 (July–August 1970) 103–13; Stephen P. Robbins, *Managing Organizational Conflict: A Nontraditional Approach* (Englewood Cliffs, N.J.: Prentice-Hall, 1980).

34. Seiler, "Diagnosing Interdepartment Conflict."

35. Jonathan Kwitny, "At CDC's AIDS Lab: Egos, Power, Politics, and Lost Experiments," *The Wall Street Journal*, 12 December 1986, A1.

36. Blake and Mouton, "Reactions to Intergroup Competition."

37. Schein, *Organizational Psychology*; Blake and Mouton, "Reactions to Intergroup Competition," 174–75.

38. Pondy, "Organizational Conflict."

39. Neilsen, "Understanding and Managing Intergroup Conflict."

40. Scott McCartney, "How to Make an Airline Run on Schedule," *The Wall Street Journal*, 22 December 1995, B1.

41. Pondy, "Organizational Conflict."

42. Neilsen, "Understanding and Managing Intergroup Conflict."

43. Robert R. Blake and Jane S. Mouton, "Overcoming Group Warfare," *Harvard Business Review* (November–December 1984): 98–108.

44. Blake and Mouton, Overcoming Group Warfare"; Paul R. Lawrence and Jay W. Lorsch, "New Management Job: The Integrator," *Harvard Business Review* 45 (November–December 1967): 142–51.

45. John Hoerr, "Work Teams Can Rev Up Paper Pushers, Too," *Business Week*, 28 November 1988, 64–72.

46. Wilson Harrell, "Inspire Action—What Really Motivates Your People to Excel?" *Success*, September 1995, 100.

47. Robert R. Blake, Herbert A. Shepard, and Jane S. Mouton, *Managing Intergroup Conflict in Industry* (Houston: Gulf Publishing, 1964).

48. Leonard Greenhalgh, "Managing Conflict," *Sloan Management Review* 27 (Summer 1986): 45–51.

49. Tamsen Tillson, " War in the Work Zone," *Canadian Business*, September 1995, 40–42.

50. Thomas, "Conflict and Conflict Management."

51. Neilsen, "Understanding and Managing Intergroup Conflict"; Joseph McCann and Jay R. Galbraith, "Interdepartmental Relations."

52. Nielsen, "Understanding and Managing Intergroup Conflict"; McCann and Galbraith, "Interdepartmental Relations"; Sherif et al., *Intergroup Conflict and Cooperation.*

53. Dean Tjosvold, Valerie Dann, and Choy Wong, "Managing Conflict between Departments to Serve Customers," *Human Relations* 45 (1992): 1035–54.

54. Robert R. Blake and Jane S. Mouton, "Overcoming Group Warfare"; Schein, *Organizational Psychology*; Blake, Shepard, and Mouton, *Managing Intergroup Conflict in Industry*; Richard E. Walton, *Interpersonal Peacemaking: Confrontation and Third-Party Consultations* (Reading, Mass.: Addison-Wesley, 1969).

55. Mark S. Plovnick, Ronald E. Fry, and W. Warner Burke, *Organizational Development* (Boston: Little, Brown, 1982), 89–93; Schein, *Organizational Psychology*, 177–78, reprinted by permission of Prentice-Hall, Inc.

part five

Strategy and Structure for the Future

5

14

chapter fourteen

Interorganizational Relationships

While reading this chapter, think about your answers to the following questions:

- Why are relationships among organizations becoming less adversarial and more cooperative, and what impact does this have on management?

- What is meant by an organizational ecosystem?

- What are the major differences between the resource dependence perspective and the collaborative network perspective?

- What is the population ecology perspective, and how do the concepts of variation, selection, retention, and the struggle for existence apply to organizations?

① - "web" metaphor

② - Types of IOR's
    - tool
    * (Oliver, 1990 (6))

③ - Models of IOR
    - pop ecol (TD)
    * (Baler-Zammuto)

④ Culture (cognitive)
    * (Chatton - John)
    1994

Many organizations are rethinking how to cope with a chaotic and turbulent environment. Chapter 13 described how to reduce boundaries and increase cooperation within companies. A more recent trend is to reduce boundaries and increase collaboration *between* organizations to survive in a wildly changing environment.

For example, Chrysler Corporation and its supplier companies long treated each other with distrust and suspicion. Chrysler selected parts suppliers strictly on their ability to build components at the lowest possible cost and exploited suppliers by pitting one against the other. Then Chrysler hit bottom with a fourth quarter loss of $664 million in 1989. New car development was running $1 billion over budget, and the company was in dire financial straits. From this crisis, Chrysler's senior executives asked whether a new kind of relationship with suppliers could be created. They wanted a more personal, collaborative relationship in which both parties shared in risks and rewards to create value jointly. Chrysler managed to transform the contentious supplier relationships by virtually eliminating supplier bidding. Trusted, capable suppliers were brought onto Chrysler's car design development teams early. Suppliers used their own engineers to design components for new cars and made substantial investments to meet Chrysler's needs more efficiently. In return Chrysler gave suppliers long-term contracts and recognized the need for suppliers to make a fair profit. The transformation of supplier relationships from an adversarial game to one of cooperation and trust has boosted Chrysler to the lead in the U.S. auto industry. Its return on investment outstrips those of its rivals, and it is now considered one of the most innovative and well-managed companies in the world.[1]

In today's new economy, webs of organizations are emerging. A large company like Wal-Mart develops a special relationship with a supplier such as Procter & Gamble that eliminates go-betweens by sharing complete information and reducing the costs of salespersons and distributors. You can see the results of interorganizational collaboration when a movie such as *The Hunchback of Notre Dame* is launched. Prior to seeing the movie, you may read a cover story in *People* magazine, see a preview clip on a television program such as *Entertainment Tonight*, find action toys being given away at a fast food franchise, and notice retail stores loaded with movie-related merchandise. For the movie *The Lion King*, coordinated action among companies yielded $200 million in addition to box-office and video profits. In the new economy, organizations think of themselves as teams that create value jointly rather than as autonomous companies that are in competition with all others.

PURPOSE OF THIS CHAPTER

This chapter explores the most recent trend in organizing, which is the increasingly dense web of relationships among organizations. Companies have always been dependent on other organizations for supplies, materials, and information. The question is how these relationships are managed. At one time a large, powerful company like General Motors would have tightened the screws on small suppliers. Today a company can choose to develop positive, trusting relationships like Chrysler did. Or, a large company like General Motors may find it difficult to adapt to the environment and create a new organizational form, such as Saturn, to operate with a different structure and culture. The notion of horizontal relationships described in Chapter 7, and the understanding of environmental uncertainty discussed in Chapter 3, are leading to the next stage of organizational evolution, which is horizontal relationships *across* organizations. Organizations can choose to build relationships in many ways, such as appointing preferred suppliers, establishing agreements, business partnering, or investigating joint ventures or even mergers and acquisitions.

Interorganizational research has yielded perspectives such as resource dependence, networks, and population ecology. The sum of these ideas can be daunting, because it means managers no longer can rest in the safety of managing a single organization. They have to figure out how to manage a whole set of interorganizational relationships, which is a great deal more challenging and complex.

ORGANIZATIONAL ECOSYSTEMS

Interorganizational relationships are the relatively enduring resource transactions, flows, and linkages that occur among two or more organizations.[2] Traditionally, these transactions and relationships have been seen as a necessary evil to obtain what an organization needs. The presumption has been that the world is composed of distinct businesses that thrive on autonomy and compete for supremacy. A company may be forced into interorganizational relationships depending on its needs and the stability of the environment.

A new view described by James Moore argues that organizations are now evolving into business ecosystems. An **organizational ecosystem** is a system formed by the interaction of a community of organizations and their environment. An ecosystem cuts across traditional industry lines. A company can create its own ecosystem. Microsoft travels in four major industries: consumer electronics, information, communications, and personal computers. Its ecosystem also includes hundreds of suppliers, including Hewlett Packard and Intel, and millions of customers across many markets.[3] Traditional boundaries are dissolving. Circuit City uses its expertise gained selling televisions and stereos to sell used cars. Shell Oil is the largest seller of packaged sausages in the Scandinavian countries. Wal-Mart created an ecosystem based on well known brands and low prices in rural and small-town markets. Today, Wal-Mart cannot be categorized simply as a retailer. It is also a wholesaler, a logistics company, and an information services company. Wal-Mart, like other business ecosystems, develops relationships with hundreds of organizations cutting across traditional business boundaries.

Is Competition Dead?

No company can go it alone under a constant onslaught of international competitors, changing technology, and new regulations. Thus, competition, which assumes a distinct company competing for survival and supremacy with other stand-alone businesses, no longer exists. In that sense competition is dead. But a new form of competition is in fact intensifying.[4]

For one thing, companies now need to co-evolve with others in the ecosystem so that everyone gets stronger. Consider the wolf and the caribou. Wolves cull weaker caribou, which strengthens the herd. A strong herd means that wolves must become stronger themselves. With co-evolution, the whole system becomes stronger. In the same way, companies co-evolve through discussion with each other, shared visions, alliances, and managing complex relationships, as we saw between Chrysler and its suppliers in the opening case. As another example, AT&T, America Online, Microsoft, and Netscape developed a set of overlapping alliances to provide Internet services.

In today's world, conflict and cooperation exist at the same time. In New York City, Time Warner refused to carry Fox's 24-hour news channel on its New York City cable systems. The two companies engaged in all-out war that included court lawsuits and front page headlines. But this all-out conflict masked a simple fact: the two companies can't live without each other. Fox and Time Warner are wedded to one another in separate business deals around the world. They will never let the local competition in New York upset their larger interdependence on a global scale. Mutual dependencies and partnerships have become a fact of life in business ecosystems. Companies no longer operate autonomously or with a single voice. A senior executive at DreamWorks sued Disney, but that hasn't stopped Disney's ABC network from acquiring television shows from DreamWorks. Companies today may use their strength to win conflicts and negotiations, but ultimately cooperation carries the day.[5]

The Changing Role of Management

Within business ecosystems managers learn to move beyond traditional responsibilities of corporate strategy and designing hierarchical structures and control systems. If a top manager looks down to enforce order and uniformity, the company is missing opportunities for new and evolving external relationships.[6] In this new world, managers think about horizontal processes rather than vertical structures. Important initiatives are not just top down, they cut across the boundaries separating organizational units. Moreover, horizontal relationships now include linkages with suppliers and customers, who become part of the team.

Business leaders can learn to lead economic co-evolution. Managers learn to see and appreciate the rich environment of opportunities that grow from cooperative relationships with other contributors to the ecosystem. Rather than trying to force suppliers into low prices or customers into high prices, managers strive to strengthen the larger system evolving around them, finding ways to understand this big picture and how to contribute.

This is a broader leadership role than ever before. For example, the CEO of Advanced Circuit Technologies in Nashua, New Hampshire, formed a coalition of ten electronic firms to jointly package and market noncompeting products. This coalition even adopted a single name: Electronic Packaging Team. Members can still conduct their own business, but they now bid on projects larger than they could deliver individually and call upon the other partners for elements they can't do themselves. The coalition landed a job with Compaq Computer Corp. to design and build a specialized computer board that none of the companies could have handled alone.[7]

Interorganizational Perspectives

Understanding this larger organizational ecosystem is one of the most exciting areas of organization theory. The models and perspectives for understanding interorganizational relationships ultimately help managers change their role from top down management to horizontal management across organizations.

There are three different approaches to understanding interorganizational relationships. By understanding these perspectives, managers can assess their environment and adopt strategies to suit their needs. The first perspective is called the resource dependence theory, which was briefly described in Chapter 3. It describes rational ways organizations interact with one another to reduce dependence on the environment. The second perspective is about collaborative networks, wherein organizations allow themselves to become dependent on other organizations to increase value and productivity for both. The third perspective, population ecology, presents a different view of how organizations survive in a changing environment. Population ecology examines how new organizations fill niches left open by established organizations, and how a rich variety of new organizational forms benefit society. These approaches to the study of interorganizational relationships will be described in the remainder of this chapter.

RESOURCE DEPENDENCE

Resource dependence represents the traditional view of relationships between organizations. As described in Chapter 3, the **resource dependence** theory argues that organizations try to minimize their dependence on other organizations for the supply of important resources, and try to influence the environment to make resources available.[8] When threatened by greater dependence, organizations will assert control over external resources to minimize that dependence. The resource dependence theory argues that organizations do not want to become vulnerable to other organizations because of negative effects on performance.

The amount of dependence on a resource is based on two factors. First is the importance of the resource to the firm, and second is how much discretion or monopoly power those who control a resource have over its allocation and use.[9] For example, a Wisconsin manufacturer made scientific instruments with internal electronics. It acquired parts from a supplier that provided adequate quality at the lowest price. The supplier was not involved in the manufacturer's product design, but was able to provide industry standard capacitors at fifty cents each. As industry standards changed, other suppliers of the capacitor switched to other products, and in one year the cost of the capacitor increased to $2 each. The Wisconsin firm had no choice but to pay the higher price. Within 18 months, the price of the capacitor increased to $10 each, and then the supplier discontinued production altogether. Without capacitors, production came to a halt for six months. The scientific instruments manufacturer allowed itself to become dependent on a single supplier and had made no plans for redesign to use substitute capacitors or to develop new suppliers. A single supplier had sufficient power to increase prices beyond reason and to almost put the Wisconsin firm out of business.[10]

Organizations aware of resource dependence tend to develop strategies to reduce their dependence on the environment, and learn how to use their power differences.

Resource Strategies

When organizations feel resource or supply constraints, the resource dependence perspective says they maneuver to maintain their autonomy through a variety of strategies, several of which were described in Chapter 3. One strategy is to adapt to or alter the interdependent relationships. This could mean purchasing ownership in suppliers, or developing long-term contracts or joint ventures to lock in necessary resources, or building relationships in other ways. For example, interlocking directorships occur when boards of directors include members of the boards of supplier companies. Organizations may join trade associations to coordinate their needs, sign trade agreements, or merge with another firm to guarantee resource and material supplies. Some organizations may take political action, such as lobbying for new regulations or deregulation, favorable taxation, tariffs, or subsidies, or push for new standards that make resource acquisition easier. Organizations operating under the resource dependence philosophy will do whatever is needed to avoid excessive dependence on the environment to maintain control of resources and hence reduce uncertainty.

Power Strategies

In the resource dependence theory, large, independent companies have power over small suppliers. For example, power in consumer products has shifted from vendors such as Rubbermaid and Procter & Gamble to the big discount retail chains such as Wal-Mart and Kmart. In manufacturing, giants like General Electric and Ford can account for 10–50 percent of many suppliers' revenue, giving the large company enormous power. When one company has power over another, it can ask suppliers to absorb more costs, ship more efficiently, and provide more services than ever before, often without a price increase. For example, Rubbermaid Inc. derives about 15 percent of its revenues from Wal-Mart. When Rubbermaid's raw material costs increased, Wal-Mart would not accept a higher price. Wal-Mart also offered more shelf space to Rubbermaid's competitors. As a result, Rubbermaid's earnings dropped 30 percent and it closed nine facilities. In manufacturing, a company like General Motors can use its power to tighten the screws on suppliers. It can force suppliers into competition with one another for low prices, and then drop vendors, virtually putting them out of business. General Electric called in 300 suppliers to its appliance division and told them they must slash costs by 10 percent. Often the suppliers have no alternative but to go along, and those who fail may go out of business.[11]

The resource power of large companies means that small companies must be lean and nimble and not count on price competition alone. A small supplier should not depend on a large company as a sole customer, because it can be put out of business if its product goes out of style or if the customer changes its mind. When Totes Inc. created a new product called slipper socks, the company sold $14 million a year largely through Kmart and Wal-Mart. But within two years, both discount retailers found suppliers that made knockoff slipper socks for 25 percent less, and they turned to these new suppliers. Totes had to be ready for this eventuality, developing new products and finding alternative ways to distribute products to consumers. Being on the receiving end of a power imbalance means building relationships with other customers, innovating constantly, and perhaps joining forces with other small suppliers.[12]

COLLABORATIVE NETWORKS

North American companies typically have worked alone, competing with each other, believing in the tradition of individualism and self-reliance. But today, thanks to an uncertain international environment, a realignment in corporate relationships is taking place. The **collaborative network** perspective is an emerging alternative to resource dependence theory. Companies join together to become more competitive and to share scarce resources. As a new wave of technology based on digital communications builds, for example, computer manufacturers, local phone companies, cable television operators, cellular phone companies, and even water and gas utilities have been teaming up.[13] As companies move into their own uncharted territory, they are also racing into alliances as a way to share risks and cash in on rewards. In many cases companies are learning to work closely together. Consider the following examples:

- AT&T, the world's largest telecommunications company, is reaching out everywhere these days, dropping its traditional do-it-from-scratch approach to team up with such major, established companies as Viacom Inc. as well as small pioneering companies, ensconcing itself in almost every corner of the rapidly changing communications industry.[14]
- Many big companies, such as Motorola, Sony, Time Warner, IBM, and Kodak are joining forces with smaller firms to obtain innovative new technologies and markets. Small, pioneering companies get the benefit of the larger firm's financing and marketing capabilities.[15]
- Canada's garment manufacturers and retailers have formed high-level strategic partnerships. Electronic reordering as products are sold helps retailers display the right products at the right times, and gives Canadian manufacturers a competitive speed and flexibility advantage over low-cost factories in other parts of the world.[16]
- With corporate research budgets under pressure, the hottest R&D trend is collaboration. Companies are figuring out how to fruitfully connect with outside experts in other companies, consortiums, universities, and government labs. With technology more complex, no single company can do it all. Siemens, IBM, and Toshiba are teaming up to develop a new memory chip. General Motors, Ford, and Chrysler have formed 12 research consortiums on such topics as electric-vehicle batteries and better crash dummies.[17]

Why all this interest in interorganizational collaboration? Major reasons are the sharing of risks when entering new markets, the ability to mount expensive new programs and reduce costs, and to enhance organizational profiles in selected industries or technologies. Cooperation is a prerequisite for greater innovation, problem solving, and performance.[18] In addition, partnerships are a major avenue for entering global markets, with both large and small firms developing partnerships overseas and in North America.

From Adversaries to Partners

Cooperation and teamwork are replacing once-bitter rivalries among suppliers, customers, and competitors. In North America, collaboration among organizations initially occurred in not-for-profit social service and mental health organizations, where public interest was involved. Community organizations collaborated to achieve greater effectiveness for each party and better utilize scarce resources.[19] With the push from international competitors and international examples, hard-nosed American managers are shifting to a new partnership paradigm on which to base their relationships.

Consider the example of Digital Equipment Corporation. When chief executive Robert Palmer took over, Digital was in horrible shape. One of Palmer's strategies was to build alliances with previous enemies, such as Microsoft. Palmer expected to announce an alliance with MCI Communications Corporation and Microsoft to provide products and services to companies needing internal networking systems. As Palmer said, "The model that existed in the 1970s and that we carried on too long in the 1980s was that you do everything yourself. Don't share technology, don't cooperate with other companies. Get all the benefit by being the do-all, be-all, end-all yourself. That model doesn't work in the 1990s."[20]

A summary of this change in mindset appears in Exhibit 14.1. More companies are changing from a traditional adversarial mindset to a partnership orientation. More and more evidence from studies of General Electric, Corning, Amoco, and Whirlpool indicate that partnering allows reduced costs and increased value for both parties in a predatory world economy.[21] The new model is based on trust and the ability of partners to develop equitable solutions to conflicts that inevitably arise. In the new orientation, people try to add value to both sides and believe in high commitment rather than suspicion and competition. Companies work toward equitable profits for both sides rather than just for their own benefit. The new model is characterized by lots of shared information, including electronic linkages for automatic ordering and face-to-face discussions to provide corrective feedback and solve problems. Sometimes people from other companies are on site to enable very close coordination. Partners are involved in each other's product design and production and invest for the long term. It's not unusual for business partners to help each other outside whatever is specified in the contract.[22]

For example, AMP, a manufacturer of electronic and electrical connectors, was contacted by a customer about a broken connector that posed serious problems. It wasn't even AMP's connector, but the vice president and his sales manager went to a warehouse on a weekend and found replacement parts to get the customer back on line. They provided the service with no charge as a way to enhance the relationship. Indeed, this kind of teamwork treats partner companies almost like departments of one's own company.[23]

Companies like Whirlpool Corporation use suppliers to design new products. The design work for the gas burner system for a new Whirlpool gas range was done by supplier Eaton Corporation. In this new view of partnerships, dependence on another company is seen to reduce rather than increase risks. Greater value can be achieved by both parties. By being imbedded in a system of interorganizational relationships, everyone does better by helping each other. This is a far cry from the belief that organizations do best by being autonomous and independent. A sales representative may have a desk on the customer's factory floor and may have access to information systems and the research lab.[24] Coordination in this type of relationship may be so intimate that it's hard to tell one organization from another.

An example of how partnership can boost both parties involves Empire Equipment Company, a New York manufacturer that wanted to reduce

Exhibit 14.1 *Changing Characteristics of Interorganizational Relationships*

	Traditional Orientation: Adversarial	**New Orientation: Partnership**
Relationships	Suspicion, competition, at arm's length	Trust, mutual added value, high commitment
Profit goals	Price, efficiency, for self only	Equity, fair dealing, profits for all
Information sharing	Limited information interchange and feedback	Electronic linkages to share key information, problem feedback and discussion
Conflict management	Legal resolution of conflict	Mechanisms for close coordination, people on site
Involvement	Minimal involvement and up-front investment	Extensive involvement in partner's product design and production
Contract terms	Short-term contracts	Long-term contracts
Contract specification	Limits the business relationship	Business assistance beyond the contract

Source: Based on Jeffrey H. Dyer, "How Chrysler Created an American Keiretsu," *Harvard Business Review*, July–August 1996, 42–56; Myron Magnet, "The New Golden Rule of Business," *Fortune*, 21 February 1994, 60–64; and Peter Grittner, "Four Elements of Successful Sourcing Strategies," *Management Review*, October 1996, 41–45.

procurement costs of filters, an important but expensive component. Based on a commitment from Empire that the supplier would be a partner in the strategy and share in any cost-saving measures that emerged, the supplier agreed to cooperate with a study to examine these costs. An Empire team of experts and managers toured the supplier's operation and tracked each step of the production process. It became obvious that the direct-manufacturing costs were only about 30 percent of the total product costs. The remaining costs were from the indirect functions of marketing, developing, engineering, testing, packaging, and shipping. After meeting with engineering staff, production managers, quality inspectors, and other personnel, the team determined that much of this indirect cost was attributable to two factors: erratic and inefficient ordering patterns, and excessive and redundant post-production specifications for quality measurement and testing. By making long-term volume commitments, improving forecasting, coordinating order size, and altering quality specifications, the team was able to reduce costs by 46 percent.[25] Empire achieved savings for itself and additional value for its supplier by becoming intimately involved in the supplier's production with the attitude of fair dealing and mutual added value.

POPULATION ECOLOGY

This section introduces a different perspective on relationships between organizations. The **population ecology** perspective differs from the other perspectives because it focuses on organizational diversity and adaptation within a population of organizations.[26] A **population** is a set of organizations engaged in similar activities with similar patterns of resource utilization and outcomes. Organizations within a population compete for similar resources or similar customers, such as financial institutions in the Seattle area.

Within a population, the question asked by ecology researchers concerns the large number and variation of organizations in society. Why are new organizational forms that create such diversity constantly appearing? Their answer is that individual organizational adaptation is severely limited compared to the changes demanded by the environment. Innovation and change in a population of organizations takes place by the birth of new forms and kinds of organizations more so than by the reform and change of existing organizations. Indeed, organizational forms are considered relatively stable, and the good of a whole society is served by the development of new forms of organization through entrepreneurial initiatives. New organizations meet the new needs of society more so than established organizations that are slow to change.[27]

What does this theory mean in practical terms? It means that large established organizations often become dinosaurs. Sears, GM, and IBM are so large that adaptation to a rapidly changing environment becomes nearly impossible. Hence new organizational forms that fit the current environment, such as Toyota, Wal-Mart, and Microsoft, will emerge to fill a new niche and over time take away business from established companies.

Why do established organizations have such a hard time adapting to a rapidly changing environment? Michael Hannan and John Freeman, originators of the population ecology model of organization, argue that there are many limitations on the ability of organizations to change. The limitations come from heavy investment in plant, equipment and specialized personnel, limited information, established viewpoints of decision makers, the organization's own successful history that justifies current procedures, and the difficulty of changing corporate culture. True transformation is a rare and unlikely event in the face of all these barriers.[28]

At this very moment new organizations are appearing in the used car industry. One example is CarMax, which provides huge lots with fixed-price cars that take the pain out of shopping. CarMax and similar companies make traditional used car dealers look like dinosaurs. Another recent change is the development of corporate universities within large companies like Motorola and Fedex. There are more than 1,000 corporate universities, compared to just 200 a few years ago. One reason they've developed so fast is that companies can't get desired services from established universities, which are too stuck in traditional ways of thinking and teaching. A third example is the steel industry, which two decades ago was dominated by a few huge firms. Then a new organizational form called the minimill emerged, led by companies such as Nucor. These minimills created highly efficient steel production methods and are taking business away from the giants.[29]

According to the population ecology view, the changing environment determines which organizations in a population survive or fail. The assumption is that individual organizations suffer from structural inertia and find it difficult to adapt to environmental changes. Thus, when rapid change occurs, old organizations are likely to decline or fail, and new organizations emerge that are better suited to the needs of the environment.

Currently, huge AT&T is working hard to renew itself in the rapidly changing telecommunications world. A part of this strategy is the appointment of a new chief executive who will replace long-time CEO Robert Allen. AT&T analysts say this change is long overdue, because the many restructurings and downsizings initiated by Allen have not produced effective results. Based on the history of telephone companies, population ecology researchers would say that successful change is unlikely.[30] For example, in the early 1900s when the telephone industry was new, over 400 telephone companies existed in Pennsylvania alone. Most used magneto technology, which means each telephone carried its own battery. A major innovation was a common battery—a power source located within the central office used for voice transmission among all telephones connected there. This was a powerful innovation, but most phone companies failed to adapt. Thus, as the common battery became more popular, the magneto-based companies went out of business.[31] Over the years consolidation occurred until only a few phone companies are left, and now AT&T, the dominant long distance carrier, may be in the twilight of its dominance.

The population ecology model is developed from theories of natural selection in biology, and the terms *evolution* and *selection* are used to refer to the underlying behavioral processes. Theories of biological evolution try to explain why certain life forms appear and survive while others perish. Such theories suggest the forms that survive are typically best fitted to the immediate environment.

Forbes magazine recently reported a study of American businesses over 70 years, from 1917 to 1987. Baldwin Locomotive, Studebaker, and Lehigh Coal & Navigation were among 78 percent of the top 100 companies in 1917 that did not survive to see 1987. Of the 22 that remained in the top 100, only 11 did so under their original names. The environment of the 1940s and 1950s was suitable to Woolworth, but new organizational forms like Wal-Mart and Kmart became dominant in the 1980s. In 1917, most of the top 100 companies were huge steel and mining industrial organizations, which were replaced by high-technology companies such as IBM and Merck.[32] Two companies that seemed to prosper over a long period were Ford and General Motors, but they are now being threatened by world changes in the automobile industry. No company is immune to the processes of social change. From just 1979 to 1989, 187 of the companies on the *Fortune* 500 list ceased to exist as independent companies. Some were acquired, some merged, and some were liquidated.[33]

Organizational Form and Niche

The population ecology model is concerned with organizational forms. **Organizational form** is an organization's specific technology, structure, products, goals, and personnel, which can be selected or rejected by the environment. Each new organization tries to find a **niche** (a domain of unique environmental resources and needs) sufficient to support it. The niche is usually small in the early stages of an organization, but may increase in size over time if the organization is successful. If a niche is not available, the organization will decline and may perish.

From the viewpoint of a single firm, luck, chance, and randomness play important parts in survival. New products and ideas are continually being proposed by both entrepreneurs and large organizations. Whether these ideas and organizational forms survive or fail is often a matter of chance—whether external circumstances happen to support them. A woman who started a small electrical contracting business in a rapidly growing Florida community would have an excellent chance of success. If the same woman were to start the same business in a declining community elsewhere in the United States, the chance of success would be far less. Success or failure of a single firm thus is predicted by the characteristics of the environment as much as by the skills or strategies used by the organization.

Process of Change

The population ecology model assumes that new organizations are always appearing in the population. Thus, organization populations are continually undergoing change. The process of change in the population is defined by three principles that occur in stages: **variation**, **selection**, and **retention**. These stages are summarized in Exhibit 14.2.

Variation. New organizational forms continually appear in a population of organizations. They are initiated by entrepreneurs, established with venture capital by large corporations, or set up by a government seeking to provide new services. Some forms may be conceived to cope with a perceived need in the external environment. In your own neighborhood, for example, a new restaurant may be started to meet a perceived need. In recent years, a large number of new firms have been initiated to develop computer software, to provide consulting and other services to large corporations, and to develop new kinds of toys. Other new organizations produce a traditional product such as steel, but do it using minimal technology and new management techniques that make the new steel companies far more able to survive. Organizational variations are analogous to mutations in biology, and they add to the scope and complexity of organizational forms in the environment.

Selection. Some variations will suit the external environment better than others. Some prove beneficial and thus are able to find a niche and acquire the resources from the environment necessary to survive. Other variations fail to meet the needs of the environment and perish. When there is insufficient demand for a firm's product and when insufficient resources are available to the organization, that organization will be "selected out." Only a few variations are "selected in" by the environment and survive over the long term.

Retention. Retention is the preservation and institutionalization of selected organizational forms. Certain technologies, products, and services are highly valued by the environment. The retained organizational form may become a dominant part of the environment. Many forms of organizations have been institutionalized, such as government, schools, churches, and automobile manufacturers. McDonald's, which owns a huge share of the fast-food market and provides the first job for many teenagers, has become institutionalized in American life.

Institutionalized organizations like McDonald's seem to be relatively permanent features in the population of organizations, but they are not permanent in the long run. The environment is always changing, and, if the dominant organizational forms do not adapt to external change, they will gradually diminish and be replaced by other organizations. Already, Taco Bell has been drawing in McDonald's customers because the Mexican fast-food chain kept lowering prices while McDonald's consistently raised them. Unless it adapts, McDonald's might no longer be price-competitive in the fast-food market.[34]

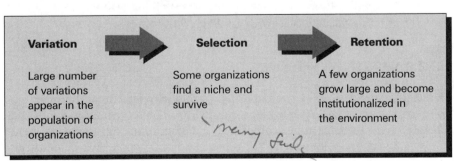

Exhibit 14.2
Elements in the Population Ecology Model of Organizations

From the population ecology perspective, the environment is the important determinant of organizational success or failure. The organization must meet an environmental need, or it will be selected out. The process of variation, selection, and retention leads to the establishment of new organizational forms in a population of organizations.

Strategies for Survival

is just possible in pop. ecol. ?

Another principle that underlies the population ecology model is the **struggle for existence**, or competition. Organizations and populations of organizations are engaged in a competitive struggle over resources, and each organizational form is fighting to survive. The struggle is most intense among new organizations, and both the birth and survival frequencies of new organizations are related to factors in the larger environment. Factors such as size of urban area, percentage of immigrants, political turbulence, industry growth rate, and environmental variability have influenced the launching and survival of newspapers, telecommunication firms, railroads, government agencies, labor unions, and even voluntary organizations.[35]

In the population ecology perspective, **generalist** and **specialist** strategies distinguish organizational forms in the struggle for survival. Organizations with a wide niche or domain, that is, those that offer a broad range of products or services or that serve a broad market, are generalists. Organizations that provide a narrow range of goods or services or that serve a narrower market are specialists.

In the natural environment, a specialist form of flora and fauna evolved in protective isolation in places like Hawaii, where the nearest body of land is 2,000 miles away. The flora and fauna are heavily protected. In contrast, a place like Costa Rica, which experienced wave after wave of external influences, developed a generalist set of flora and fauna that has better resilience and flexibility for adapting to a broad range of circumstances.

A corporate example of a specialist is Olmec Corporation, a New York-based toy manufacturer that markets more than 60 African-American and Hispanic dolls. Mattel, on the other hand, is a generalist, marketing a broad range of toys, including a Disney line, Barbie, and many other dolls of various ages and ethnic features.[36]

Specialists are generally more competitive than generalists in the narrow area in which their domains overlap. However, the breadth of the generalist's domain serves to protect it somewhat from environmental changes. Though demand may decrease for some of the generalist's products or services, it usually increases for others at the same time. In addition, because of the diversity of products, services, and customers, generalists are able to reallocate resources internally to adapt to a changing environment, whereas specialists are not. However, because specialists are often smaller companies, they can sometimes move faster and be more flexible in adapting to a changing environment.[37]

SUMMARY OF KEY ISSUES

This chapter has been about the important evolution in interorganizational relationships. At one time organizations considered themselves autonomous and separate, trying to outdo other companies. Today more organizations see themselves as a part of an ecosystem. The organization may span several industries, and will be anchored in a dense web of relationships with other companies. In this ecosystem, collaboration is as important as competition. Indeed, organizations may compete and collaborate at the same time, depending on locations and issues. In this business ecosystem, the role of management is changing to include the development of horizontal relationships with other organizations.

Three perspectives have been developed to explain relationships among organizations. The resource dependence perspective is the most traditional, arguing that organizations try to avoid excessive dependence on other organizations. In this view, organizations devote considerable effort to controlling the environment to assure ample resources while maintaining independence. Moreover, powerful organizations will exploit the dependence of small companies. The collaborative network perspective is an emerging alternative. Organizations welcome collaboration and interdependence with other organizations to enhance value for both. Many executives are changing mindsets away from autonomy toward collaboration, often with previous corporate enemies. The new mindset emphasizes trust, fair dealing, and profit goals for all parties in a relationship.

The population ecology perspective explains why organizational diversity continuously increases with the appearance of new organizations filling niches left open by established companies. This perspective says that large companies cannot adapt to meet a changing environment, hence new companies emerge with the appropriate forms and skills to serve new needs. Through the process of variation, selection, and retention, some organizations will survive and grow while others perish. Companies may adopt a generalist or specialist strategy to survive in the population of organizations.

Each of these perspectives is valid. They represent different lenses through which the world of interorganizational relationships can be viewed. Organizations experience a competitive struggle for autonomy, they can thrive through collaborative relationships with others, and the slowness to adapt provides openings for new organizations to flourish. The important thing is for managers to be aware of interorganizational relationships and to consciously manage them.

Discussion Questions

1. The concept of business ecosystems implies that organizations are more interdependent than ever before. From personal experience, do you agree? Explain.
2. How do you feel about the prospect of becoming a manager and having to manage a set of relationships with other companies, rather than just managing your own company? Discuss.
3. Assume you are the manager of a small firm that is dependent on a large manufacturing customer that uses the resource dependence perspective. Put yourself in the position of the small firm, and describe what actions you would take to survive and succeed. What actions would you take from the perspective of the large firm?
4. Many managers today were trained under assumptions of adversarial relationships with other companies. Do you think operating as adversaries is easier or more difficult than operating as partners with other companies? Discuss.
5. Discuss how the adversarial versus partnership orientations work among students in class. Is there a sense of competition for grades? Is it possible to develop true partnerships in which your work depends upon others? Discuss.

6. The population ecology perspective argues that it is healthy for society to have new organizations emerging and old organizations dying as the environment changes. Do you agree? Why would European countries pass laws to sustain traditional organizations and inhibit the emergence of new ones?

7. How might the process of variation, selection, and retention explain innovations that take place within an organization? Explain.

Notes

1. Jeffrey H. Dyer, "How Chrysler Created an American Keiretsu," *Harvard Business Review*, July–August 1996, 42–56, and James Bennett, "Detroit Struggles to Learn Another Lesson From Japan," *The New York Times*, 19 June 1994, F5.

2. Christine Oliver, "Determinants of Interorganizational Relationships: Integration and Future Directions," *Academy of Management Review*, Vol. 15 (1990): 241–65.

3. James Moore, *The Death of Competition: Leadership and Strategy in the Age of Business Ecosystems* (New York: HarperCollins, 1996).

4. James Moore, "The Death of Competition," *Fortune*, 15 April 1996, 142–44.

5. Elizabeth Jensen and Eben Shapiro, "Time Warner's Fight with News Corp. Belies Mutual Dependence," *The Wall Street Journal*, 28 October 1996, A1, A6.

6. Sumantra Ghoshal and Christopher A. Bartlett, "Changing the Role of Top Management: Beyond Structure and Process," *Harvard Business Review*, January–February 1995, 86–96.

7. Jessica Lipnack and Jeffrey Stamps, "One Plus One Equals Three," *Small Business Reports*, August 1993; 49–58.

8. J. Pfeffer and G. R. Salancik, *The External Control of Organizations: A Resource Dependence Perspective*, (New York: Harper & Row, 1978).

9. Derek S. Pugh and David J. Hickson, *Writers on Organizations*, 5th ed. (Sage, 1996).

10. Peter Grittner, "Four Elements of Successful Sourcing Strategies," *Management Review* (October 1996): 41–45.

11. This discussion is based on Matthew Schifrin, "The Big Squeeze," *Forbes*, 11 March 1996, 45–46; Wendy Zellner with Marti Benedetti, "CLOUT!" *Business Week*, 21 December 1992, 62–73; Kevin Kelly and Zachary Schiller with James B. Treece, "Cut Costs or Else," *Business Week*, 22 March 1993, 28–29; Lee Berton, "Push From Above," *The Wall Street Journal*, 23 May 1996, R24.

12. Ibid.

13. Kathy Rebello with Richard Brandt, Peter Coy, and Mark Lewyn, "Your Digital Future," *Business Week*, 7 September 1992, 56–64.

14. Edmund L. Andrews, "AT&T Reaches Out (and Grabs Everyone)," *The New York Times*, 8 August 1993, Section 3, 1, 6.

15. Rebello, et. al. "Your Digital Future"; Mark Lander with Bart Ziegler and Ronald Grover, "Time Warner's Techie at the Top," *Business Week*, 10 May 1993, 60–63.

16. Mark Stevenson, "Virtual Mergers," *Canadian Business*, September 1993, 20–26.

17. Peter Coy with Neil Gross, Silvia Sansoni, and Kevin Kelly, "What's the Word in the Lab? Collaborate," *Business Week*, 27 June 1994, 78–80.

18. Christine Oliver, "Determinants of Interorganizational Relationships: Integration and Future Directions," *Academy of Management Review*, 15 (1990): 241–65; Ken G. Smith, Stephen J. Carroll, and Susan J. Ashford, "Intra- and Interorganizational Cooperation: Toward a Research Agenda," *Academy of Management Journal* 38 (1995) 7–23; Timothy M. Stearns, Alan N. Hoffman, and Jan B. Heide, "Performance of Commercial Television Stations as

an Outcome of Interorganizational Linkages and Environmental Conditions," *Academy of Management Journal* 30 (1987): 71–90; Keith G. Provan, "Technology and Interorganizational Activity as Predictors of Client Referrals," *Academy of Management Journal* 27 (1984): 811–29; David A. Whetten and Thomas K. Kueng, "The Instrumental Value of Interorganizational Relations: Antecedents and Consequences of Linkage Formation," *Academy of Management Journal* 22 (1979): 325–44.

19. Keith G. Provan and H. Brinton Milward, "A Preliminary Theory of Interorganizational Network Effectiveness: A Comparative of Four Community Mental Health Systems," *Administrative Science Quarterly*, 40 (1995): 1–33.

20. Audrey Choi, "Digital's New Attitude Toward Old Enemies Puts It Back in Game," *The Wall Street Journal*, 9 April 1996, A1, A10.

21. Myron Magnet, "The New Golden Rule of Business," *Fortune*, 21 February 1994, 60–64; Peter Grittner, "Four Elements of Successful Sourcing Strategies."

22. Peter Smith Ring and Andrew H. Van de Ven, "Developmental Processes of Corporate Interorganizational Relationships," *Academy of Management Review*, 19 (1994): 90–118; Dyer, "How Chrysler Created an American Keiretsu"; Magnet, "The New Golden Rule of Business"; Grittner, "Four Elements of Successful Sourcing Strategies."

23. Magnet, "The New Golden Rule of Business"; and Grittner, "Four Elements of Successful Sourcing Strategies."

24. Fred R. Blekley, "Some Companies Let Suppliers Work on Site and Even Place Orders," *The Wall Street Journal*, 13 January 1995, A1, A6.

25. Peter Grittner, "Four Elements of Successful Sourcing Strategies," *Management Review* (October 1996): 42.

26. This section draws from Joel A. C. Baum, "Organizational Ecology," in Stewart R. Clegg, Cynthia Hardy, and Walter R. Nord, eds., *Handbook of Organization Studies* (Thousand Oaks: Sage, 1996); Jitendra V. Singh, *Organizational Evolution: New Directions* (Newbury Park, Calif.: Sage, 1990); Howard Aldrich, Bill McKelvey, and Dave Ulrich, "Design Strategy from the Population Perspective," *Journal of Management* 10 (1984): 67–86; Aldrich, *Organizations and Environments;* Michael Hannan and John Freeman, "The Population Ecology of Organizations," *American Journal of Sociology* 82 (1977): 929–64; Dave Ulrich, "The Population Perspective: Review, Critique, and Relevance," *Human Relations* 40 (1987): 137–52; Jitenda V. Singh and Charles J. Lumsden, "Theory and Research in Organizational Ecology," *Annual Review of Sociology* 16 (1990): 161–95; Howard E. Aldrich, "Understanding, Not Integration: Vital Signs from Three Perspectives on Organizations," in Michael Reed and Michael D. Hughes, eds., *Rethinking Organizations: New Directories in Organizational Theory and Analysis* (London: Sage: forthcoming); Jitendra M Singh, David J. Tucker, and Robert J. House, "Organizational Legitimacy and the Liability of Newness," *Administrative Science Quarterly* 31 (1986): 171–93; Douglas R. Wholey and Jack W. Brittain, "Organizational Ecology: Findings and Implications," *Academy of Management Review* 11 (1986): 513–33.

27. Derek S. Pugh and David J. Hickson, *Writers on Organizations;* Lex Donaldson, *American Anti-Management Theories of Organization* (Cambridge University Press, 1995).

28. Michael T. Hannan and John Freeman, "The Population Ecology of Organizations."

29. Stephen Baker, "The Minimill that Acts Like a Biggie," *Business Week*, 30 September 1996, 100–04, and Thomas Moore, "The Corporate University: Transforming Management Education," Presentation in August, 1996. Thomas Moore is the Dean of the Arthur D. Little University.

30. John J. Keller, "A Telecom Novice is Handed Challenge of Remaking AT&T," *The Wall Street Journal*, 24 October 1996, Al, A6.

31. William P. Barnett, "The Organizational Ecology of a Technology System," *Administrative Science Quarterly*, 35 (1990): 31–60.

32. Peter Newcomb, "No One is Safe," *Forbes*, 13 July 1987, 121; "It's Tough Up There," *Forbes*, 13 July 1987, 145–60.

33. Stewart Feldman, "Here One Decade, Gone the Next," *Management Review* (November 1990): 5–6.

34. Patricia Sellers, "Pepsi Keeps on Going after No. 1," *Fortune*, 11 March 1991, 61–70.

35. David J. Tucker, Jitendra V. Singh, and Agnes G. Meinhard, "Organizational Form, Population Dynamics, and Institutional Change: The Founding Patterns of Voluntary Organizations," *Academy of Management Journal* 33 (1990): 151–78; Glenn R. Carroll and Michael T. Hannan, "Density Delay in the Evolution of Organizational Populations: A Model and Five Empirical Tests," *Administrative Science Quarterly* 34 (1989): 411–30; Jacques Delacroix and Glenn R. Carroll, "Organizational Foundings: An Ecological Study of the Newspaper Industries of Argentina and Ireland," *Administrative Science Quarterly* 28 (1983): 274–91; Johannes M. Pennings, "Organizational Birth Frequencies: An Empirical Investigation," *Administrative Science Quarterly* 27 (1982):120–44; David Marple, "Technological Innovation and Organizational Survival: A Population Ecology Study of Nineteenth-Century American Railroads," *Sociological Quarterly* 23 (1982): 107–16; Thomas G. Rundall and John O. McClain, "Environmental Selection and Physician Supply," *American Journal of Sociology* 87 (1982): 1090–1112.

36. Maria Mallory with Stephanie Anderson Forest, "Waking Up to a Major Market," *Business Week*, 23 March 1992, 70–73.

37. Arthur G. Bedeian and Raymond F. Zammuto, *Organizations: Theory and Design* (Orlando, Fla.; Dryden Press, 1991); Richard L. Hall, *Organizations: Structure, Process and Outcomes* (Englewood Cliffs, N.J.: Prentice–Hall, 1991).

15

chapter fifteen

Toward the Learning Organization

While reading this chapter, think about your answers to the following questions:

- What are five basic organization configurations, and how do strategy, structure, technology, environment, size, and other characteristics fit together within each for organizational effectiveness?

- What seven forces must organizations manage to ensure effectiveness?

- Why do today's managers need to create learning capability and build learning organizations?

- What six characteristics are present in a learning organization?

- What occurs during the three stages of a corporate transformation?

For hundreds of years, the Kalahari Bushmen were nomadic hunters and foragers in the harsh, unpredictable Southern African desert. The Bushmen developed the skills to find water during a drought, to live on reptiles and plants in the absence of game, and to fashion bows and arrows from limited sources. They traveled in bands bound together by ties of kinship and friendship. Their mobility and few possessions enabled Bushmen to switch easily to more successful bands, in this way capitalizing on success wherever it was found over a wide geographical area. The flexible band system was enhanced by values of equality, sharing, and gift giving. A hunter's kill would be used to feed neighbors, who would later reciprocate. Gift giving meant that useful artifacts and utensils were widely shared. Hunting camps had grass huts facing the center of a circle where the cooking hearths were hubs of continuous discussion and social exchanges. The Bushmen also bonded through a deep culture of shared mythology, stories, and dances.

Enter civilization. In recent years, exposure to material wealth has fostered a transformation. Bushmen now accumulate possessions, which hamper mobility, forcing a life-style shift from foraging to farming. A new community structure has evolved, with families living in separate, permanent huts. Entrances are located for privacy, and hearths have been moved inside. Survival skills have deteriorated, with bows and arrows produced only for curio shops. Without sharing and communication, a hierarchy of authority—the chief—is used to resolve disputes. Tension and conflicts have increased, and the tribe's ability to handle drought and disaster today is nonexistent. No longer are there shared stories and mythology that bind the tribespeople into a community.[1]

The emerging herder-farmer society resembles a bureaucracy that excels in a stable, safe environment, leaving the participants vulnerable to sudden environmental changes. The hunter-forager society resembles today's entrepreneurial and learning organization, based on little hierarchy, equality of rewards, shared culture, and a flowing, adaptable structure designed to seize opportunities and handle crises.

Many organizations in industrialized societies have evolved toward bureaucratic forms, as discussed in Chapter 5. And in the face of complex, shifting environments, these organizations no longer work. The hunter-forager society of the Kalahari Bushmen is a metaphor for the learning organization that many companies want to become. Can a bureaucratic herder-farmer society be transformed backward to a skilled, flowing, adaptable hunter-forager society? How can traditional organization structures be transformed into fluid, learning systems?

PURPOSE OF THIS CHAPTER

The previous chapter described how today's companies respond to increasing uncertainty and instability through interorganizational collaboration. The purpose of this chapter is to examine another way companies cope with and adapt to rapid changes, by increasing their own ability to learn and change. The chapter integrates materials from previous chapters about organization design to describe the coming generation of learning organizations. The first section describes how structure, technology, strategy, and other characteristics fit together for organizational effectiveness and identifies the key issues each organization must resolve. The second section describes the learning organization, which resembles the original bands of Kalahari Bushmen. The final sections briefly examine the process of corporate transformation and the role of organizational leadership in transforming from a traditional to a learning organization.

ORGANIZATIONAL DESIGN CONFIGURATIONS

In this section, we will integrate concepts from earlier chapters. A key task for top leaders is to decide on goals and strategy, and then to design the organizational form appropriate for the strategy. By fitting the pieces together into the right configuration, an organization can maintain a high level of effectiveness.

Strategy Formulation and Implementation

The starting point for defining organizational configuration is **strategy**, which is the current set of plans, decisions, and objectives that have been adopted to achieve the organization's goals. **Strategy formulation** includes the activities that lead to establishment of a firm's overall goals and mission and the development of a specific strategic plan as described in Chapter 2.[2] For example, a firm might formulate a strategy of differentiation, low-cost leadership, or focus. **Strategy implementation** is the use of managerial and organizational tools to direct and allocate resources to accomplish strategic objectives.[3] It is the administration and execution of the strategic plan. The concepts of organization design are especially relevant for implementation. The direction and allocation of resources are accomplished with the tools of organization structure, control systems, culture, technology, and human resources.

Organizational Form and Design

Organizational form and design are the ultimate expression of strategy implementation. Each chapter of this book has dealt with some aspect of design. Top leaders must design the organization so all parts fit together into a coherent whole to achieve the organization's strategy and purpose.

A framework proposed by Henry Mintzberg[4] suggests that every organization has five parts, as illustrated in Exhibit 15.1. Top management is located at the top of the organization. Middle management is at the intermediate levels, and the technical core includes the people who do the basic work of the organization. The technical support staff are the engineers, researchers, and analysts who are responsible for the formal planning and control of the technical core. The administrative support staff provide indirect services and include clerical, maintenance, and mail room employees. The five parts of the organization may vary in size and importance depending upon the overall environment, strategy, and technology.

Mintzberg proposed that these five organizational parts could fit together in five basic configurations, in which environment, goals, power, structure, formalization, technology, and size hang together in identifiable clusters. This framework defines key organizational variables and tells managers the appropriate configuration for specific environments and strategies.

Exhibit 15.1

*The Five Basic Parts
of an Organization*

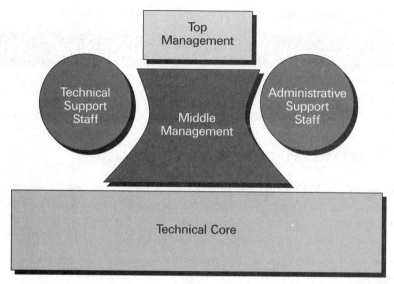

Source: Based on Henry Mintzberg, *The Structure of Organizations* (Englewood Cliffs, N.J.: Prentice-Hall, 1979) 215–97; and Henry Mintzberg, "Organization Design: Fashion or Fit?" *Harvard Business Review* 59 (January–February 1981): 103–16.

The **five organization configurations** proposed by Mintzberg are entrepreneurial structure, machine bureaucracy, professional bureaucracy, divisional form, and "adhocracy."[5] A brief description of each configuration follows. Specific organizational characteristics associated with the appropriate configuration for strategy implementation are summarized in Exhibit 15.2.

Entrepreneurial Structure. The organization with an **entrepreneurial structure** is typically a new, small company in the first stage of the organizational life cycle, described in Chapter 5. The organization consists of a top manager and workers in the technical core. Only a few support staff are required. There is little specialization or formalization. Coordination and control come from the top. The founder has the power and creates the culture. Employees have little discretion, although work procedures are typically informal. This organization is suited to a dynamic environment. It can maneuver quickly and compete successfully with larger, less adaptable organizations. Adaptability is required to establish its market. The organization is not powerful and is vulnerable to sudden changes. Unless it is adaptable, it will fail.

Machine Bureaucracy. **Machine bureaucracy** describes the bureaucratic organization, also discussed in Chapter 5. This organization is very large, and the technology is routine, often oriented to mass production. Extensive specialization and formalization are present, and key decisions are made at the top. The environment is simple and stable because this organization is not adaptable. The machine bureaucracy is distinguished by large technical and administrative support staffs. Technical support staffs, including engineers, market researchers, financial analysts, and systems analysts are used to scrutinize, routinize, and formalize work in other parts of the organization. The technical support staff is the dominant group in the organization. Machine bureaucracies are often criticized for lack of control by lower employees, lack of innovation, a weak culture, and an alienated work force, but they are suited to large size, a stable environment, and the goal of efficiency.

Exhibit 15.2 *Dimensions of Five Organizational Types*

Dimension	Entrepreneurial Structure	Machine Bureaucracy	Professional Bureaucracy	Divisional Form	Adhocracy
Strategy and goals:	Growth, survival	Defender; efficiency	Analyzer; effectiveness	Portfolio; profit	Prospector; innovation
Age and size:	Typically young and small	Typically old and large	Varies	Typically old and very large	Typically young
Technology:	Simple	Machines but not automated	Service	Divisible, like machine bureaucracy	Very sophisticated, often automated
Environment:	Simple and dynamic, sometimes hostile	Simple and stable	Complex and stable	Relatively simple and stable; diversified markets	Complex and dynamic
Formalization:	Little	Much	Little	Within divisions	Little
Structure:	Functional	Functional	Functional or product	Product, hybrid	Functional and product (matrix)
Coordination:	Direct supervision	Vertical linkage	Horizontal linkage	Headquarters (HQ) staff	Mutual adjustment
Control:	Clan	Bureaucratic	Clan and bureaucratic	Market and bureaucratic	Clan
Culture:	Developing	Weak	Strong	Subcultures	Strong
Technical support staff:	None	Many	Few	Many at HQ for performance control	Few and within project work
Administrative support staff:	Few	Many	Many to support professionals	Split between HQ and divisions	Many but within project work
Key part of organization:	Top management	Technical staff	Production core	Middle management	Support staff and technical core

Source: Adapted and modified from Henry Mintzberg, *The Structuring of Organizations: A Synthesis of the Research* (Englewood Cliffs, N.J.: Prentice-Hall, 1979), 466–71.

Professional Bureaucracy. The distinguishing feature of a **professional bureaucracy** is that the production core is composed of professionals, as in hospitals, universities, and consulting firms. While the organization is bureaucratized, people within the production core have autonomy. Long training and experience encourage clan control and a strong culture, thereby reducing the need for bureaucratic control structures. These organizations often provide services rather than tangible products, and they exist in complex environments. Most of the power rests with the professionals in the production core. Technical support groups are small or nonexistent, but a large administrative support staff is needed to handle the organization's routine administrative affairs.

Divisional Form. Organizations with a **divisional form** are typically large and are subdivided into product or market groups, as discussed in Chapter 6 on designing organization structures. There are few liaison devices for coordination between divisions, and the divisional emphasis is on market control using profit and loss statements. The divisional form can be quite formalized within divisions because technologies are often routine. The environment for any division will tend to be simple and stable, although the total organization may serve diverse markets. Many large corporations, such as General Motors, Procter & Gamble, Ford, and Westinghouse, are divisional organizations. Each division is somewhat autonomous, with its own subculture. Centralization exists within divisions, and a headquarters staff may retain some functions, such as planning and research.

Adhocracy. An **adhocracy** develops to survive in a complex, dynamic environment. The adhocracy resembles the global matrix or transnational structure described in Chapter 7. The technology is sophisticated, as in the aerospace and electronic industries. Adhocracies are typically young or middle-aged and quite large but need to be adaptable. A team-based structure typically emerges with many horizontal linkages and empowered employees. Both technical support staff and the production core have authority over key production elements. The organization has an elaborate division of labor but is not formalized. Employee professionalism is high, cultural values are strong, and clan control is stressed. With decentralization, people at any level may be involved in decision making. The adhocracy is almost the opposite of the machine bureaucracy in terms of structure, power relationships, and environment.

The point of the five configurations is that top management can design an organization to achieve harmony and fit among key elements. For example, a machine bureaucracy is appropriate for a strategy of efficiency in a stable environment; but to impose a machine bureaucracy in a hostile and dynamic environment is a mistake. Managers can implement strategy by designing the correct structural configuration to fit the situation.

The Effective Organization

An additional idea proposed by Mintzberg is that for an organization to be effective, it must manage the interplay of seven basic forces.[6] The organization's form can be designed to help manage this interplay as illustrated in Exhibit 15.3.

The first force is **direction**, which is the sense of vision, goals, and mission for the organization. (Chapter 2 described how managers set a strategic direction for the organization by establishing a mission and goals.) The entrepreneurial form best typifies a single organizational direction and common purpose.

The next force is **efficiency**, which is the need to minimize costs and increase benefits. The best known structure for efficiency is the machine bureaucracy because it focuses on rationalization and standardization.

The third force, **proficiency**, means carrying out tasks with a high level of knowledge and skill. Proficiency is the advantage of the professional bureaucracy, which uses highly trained professionals to achieve excellence.

Recall from Chapter 2 that managers can also develop internal organization characteristics of strategic orientation, top management, organization design, and corporate culture that contribute to excellence.

The fourth force, **innovation**, discussed in detail in Chapter 8, refers to the organization's need to develop new products and services to adapt to a changing external environment. The adhocracy form of organization is best for meeting the need for innovation and change.

The fifth force in Exhibit 15.3 is **concentration**, which means focusing organizational efforts on particular markets. As we learned in Chapter 6, divisional organizations achieve the advantage of concentration by focusing activities on specific products or markets.

Two additional forces within the pentagon of Exhibit 15.3 are cooperation/culture and conflict/politics. Cooperation is the result of common culture values and reflects the need for harmony and cooperation among a diverse set of people. (Chapter 10 described how leaders can build strong, adaptive corporate cultures, while Chapter 13 examined the emerging view that cooperation, not competition

Exhibit 15.3 *A System of Forces and Forms in Organizations*

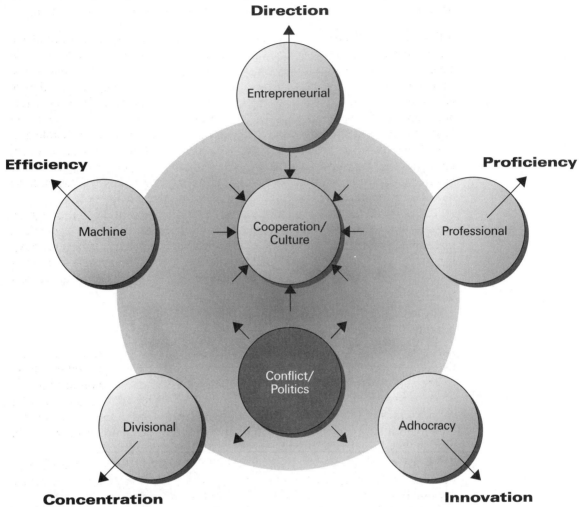

or conflict, is the best way to achieve high performance). Conflict can cause negative politics (discussed in Chapter 12) and a splitting apart of individuals and departments because of the need for individual success and recognition.

An important purpose of organizational form is to enable an organization to achieve the right balance among the seven forces. An effective organization such as 3M stresses innovation, while an organization such as Wal-Mart stresses efficiency and proficiency in its design. A conglomeration such as Hanson Industries stresses concentration; Southwest Airlines succeeds by creating a strong culture based on participation and cooperation.

Each organization has to find out what works. It cannot maximize all needs simultaneously. By understanding these forces and designing the right structure to achieve strategic outcomes, leaders can create effective organizations. This is a continual leadership process, because a configuration may work for a period of time and then need to be reorganized to achieve a new period of harmony and effectiveness.[7] Ultimately, organizational form will fit the needs of formulated strategy and the environment.

THE LEARNING ORGANIZATION

The field of management is undergoing a worldwide, fundamental shift. This shift was described in Chapter 1 as a transition from a modern to a postmodern organization paradigm. Many companies are transforming away from traditional, hierarchical management toward full participation by every employee. The shift is also reflected in new organizational forms, such as the network organization, virtual corporation, and horizontal organization described in Chapter 7. The remainder of this chapter focuses on the newest way of thinking about organizations brought about by this paradigm shift.

The management shift has been prompted by two accelerating trends. The first is the increasing rate of change brought by global competition. Organizations must adapt faster and be able to do more things well. The second trend is a fundamental change in organizational technologies. Traditional organizations were designed to manage machine-based technologies, with a primary need for stable and efficient use of physical resources, such as in mass production. However, new organizations are knowledge-based, which means they are designed to handle ideas and information, with each employee becoming an expert in one or several conceptual tasks. Rather than striving for efficiency, each employee in knowledge-based companies must continuously learn and be able to identify and solve problems in his or her domain of activity.[8]

In this new world order, the responsibility of management is to create organizational learning capability. In many industries, the ability to learn and change faster than competitors may be the only sustainable competitive advantage. Hence, many companies are redesigning themselves toward something called the learning organization.

Managers began thinking about the concept of learning organization after the publication of Peter Senge's book, *The Fifth Discipline: The Art and Practice of Learning Organizations*, in which Senge describes the kinds of changes managers need to undergo to help their organizations adapt to an increasingly chaotic world.[9] His original concepts about how managers build learning capability have evolved to include characteristics of the organization itself.

There is no single model of learning organization. The learning organization is an attitude or philosophy about what an organization is and the role of employees. The notion of the learning organization may replace any of the designs described in Exhibit 15.2. The learning organization is a paradigm shift to a new way of thinking about organizations.

In the **learning organization**, everyone is engaged in identifying and solving problems, enabling the organization to continuously experiment, improve, and increase its capability. The essential value of the learning organization is problem solving, in contrast to the traditional organization that was designed for efficiency. In the learning organization, employees engage in problem identification, which means understanding customer needs. Employees also solve problems, which means putting things together in unique ways to meet customer needs. The organization in this way adds value by defining new needs and solving them, which is accomplished more often with ideas and information than with physical products. When physical products are produced, ideas and information still provide the competitive advantage because products are changing to meet new and challenging needs in the environment.[10]

Learning Capability

Consider three traditional ways of gaining competitive advantage through financial, marketing, and technological capabilities, as illustrated in Exhibit 15.4.[11] These traditional sources of competitive advantage are taught in most business schools. Financial capability pertains to financial efficiencies as reflected in wise investment decisions and a profitable return to investors. Marketing capability pertains to building the right products, establishing a close relationship with customers, and effectively marketing products and services. Technology capability refers to technical innovation, research and development, new products, and up-to-date production technologies.

But in a world that is shifting from machines to ideas, these traditional capabilities now require organizational learning capability, also illustrated in Exhibit l5.4. The learning component of competitive advantage refers to the ability to advance financial, marketing, and technological capabilities to a higher level by disengaging employees from traditional notions of efficiency and engaging them in active problem solving that helps the organization change. The more learning capability is increased, the more adaptable and successful the organization.

Learning capability is not about learning the principles of accounting or marketing. It means enhancing the organization's and each person's capacity to do things they were not able to do previously. This is knowledge acquired not from textbooks and past experience but from actually engaging in independent action, experimenting, and using trial and error. Experimentation extends from an accounting clerk trying a new software program to the organization's strategy to always modify and update products to meet changing customer needs. Increasing knowledge is not something stored intellectually or in computers; it reflects

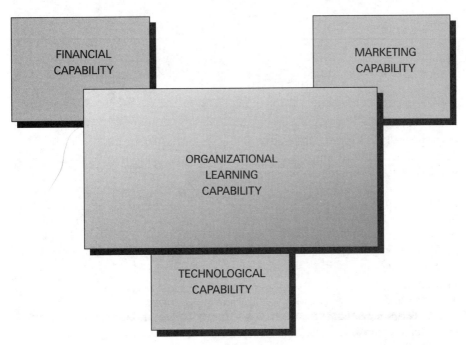

Exhibit 15.4

Organizational Learning Capability Is a Critical Source of Competitive Advantage

Source: Adapted from Dave Ulrich and Dale Lake, "Organizational Capability: Creating Competitive Advantage," *Academy of Management Executive* 5, No. 1 (1991): 77. Used by permission.

expanding know-how, similar to the increase in capability gained from learning to ride a bike or paint a portrait.[12]

Although the learning organization cannot be precisely defined, it is an extension of the concepts described in this book and is typically associated with certain characteristics. Exhibit 15.5 indicates how the learning organization goes beyond both the traditional hierarchy and the horizontal organization described in Chapters 6 and 7. In the traditional hierarchy, top management was responsible for directing organizational strategy and took responsibility for thinking and acting. Employees were simply factors of efficient production to be assigned to routine tasks that did not change. The breakthrough of the horizontal organization is that employees are empowered to think and act to design work methods on behalf of the organization. Although top managers still provide the primary strategic direction, employees have greater latitude in executing this direction and can sometimes identify and anticipate customer needs.

The further breakthrough of the learning organization is that employees contribute to strategic direction to an extent not before achieved. Employees identify needs so that strategy emerges from the accumulated activities of employee teams

Exhibit 15.5 *Evolution of the Learning Organization*

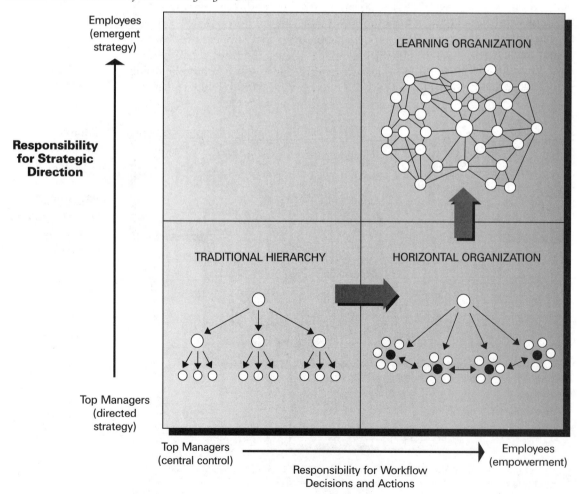

serving customers.[13] The strategy emerges within the overall vision of the organization's future that all employees share, so innovations and improvements by respective teams add to the organizational whole. The learning organization resembles a web in which different parts of the organization are adapting and changing independently while at the same time contributing to the company mission.

In addition to increased employee responsibility over both organizational means and ends, the shift to a learning organization philosophy is associated with mindful leadership, a strong culture, shared information, empowered employees, emergent strategy, and horizontal structure. These characteristics of the learning organization are illustrated in Exhibit 15.6, and each is described as follows.

Mindful Leadership

The learning organization starts in the minds of the organization's leaders. The learning organization requires mindful leadership—people who understand it and can help other people succeed. Leaders in a learning organization have three distinct roles.

Design the Social Architecture. The social architecture pertains to behind-the-scenes behavior and attitudes. The first task of organization design is to develop the governing ideas of purpose, mission, and core values by which employees will be guided. The mindful leader defines the foundation of purpose and core values. Second, new policies, strategies, and structures that support the learning organization are designed and put into place. These structures reinforce new behavior. Third, leaders design effective learning processes. Creating learning processes and ensuring they are improved and understood requires leader initiative. With these design actions, the learning organization idea can take hold.[14]

Create a Shared Vision. The shared vision is a picture of an ideal future for the organization. This may be created by the leader or by employee discussion, but

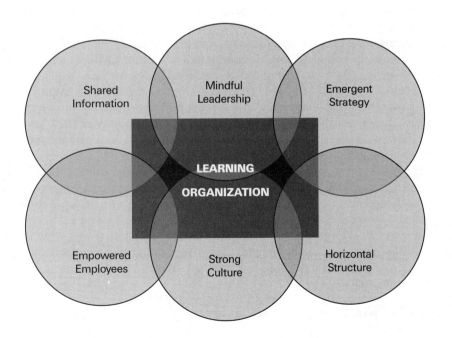

Exhibit 15.6
Interacting Elements in a Learning Organization

the company vision must be widely understood and imprinted throughout the organization. This vision represents desired long-term outcomes, hence employees are free to identify and solve immediate problems on their own that help achieve the vision. However, without a shared vision that provides harmony and unity of mind, employee actions will not add to the whole. Without a strong vision, employees may fragment and move in different directions.

Servant Leadership. Learning organizations are built by servant leaders who devote themselves to others and to the organization's vision. The image of a leader as a single actor who builds an organization by himself or herself is not appropriate for the learning organization. Leaders give away power, ideas, and information. The learning organization requires leaders who devote themselves to the organization. Indeed, many people become leaders who serve others and the organization.[15] One example of a servant leader is George Sztykiel, chairman of Spartan Motors. Spartan builds chassis for fire trucks and motor homes. Sztykiel's attitude is reflected in his statements to new employees: "Welcome. We think this is a good corporation. It is run on the same principles that a family is, because we think that's the most effective way human beings have managed to get along." Sztykiel also said, "I am not the boss. I am the number one servant of this corporation." At Spartan, everyone has equal opportunity, and all share in the gains of continuous learning.[16]

Empowered Employees

The learning organization uses empowerment to an extraordinary degree. The process of empowerment was described in Chapter 12. In the learning organization, cross-functional teams become the basic unit. People work together to identify needs and solve problems. In the learning organization, leaders know that people are born with curiosity and experience joy in learning, so they strive to develop this intrinsic motivation and curiosity, which can lead to improved performance. When Monsanto's chemical and nylon plant in Pensacola, Florida, gave teams the responsibility and authority for hiring, purchasing, and job assignments, the plant experienced increases in both profitability and safety.[17]

Learning organizations invest heavily in training, providing abundant learning opportunities for everyone.[18] For example, at Foldcraft, a manufacturer of institutional seating in Kenyon, Minnesota, president Chuck Mayhew teaches a six-hour class in the basics of business. Working with groups of 30–35 employees at a time, Mayhew first focuses on employees' personal finances and gradually leads workers into a discussion of Foldcraft's financial statements. The class ends with Mayhew talking individually with workers about their specific jobs and how they impact the company's profitability.[19]

Training workers to understand the business and giving them the power to make decisions based on what they know helps to create a sense of ownership and pride among employees. At Springfield Remanufacturing Corporation, 30 percent of each job is learning. People are expected to think and act as owners of their part of the business, because real owners need not be told what to do. They can figure it out for themselves. Employees are given the knowledge and information needed to make a decision and are trusted to act in the best interest of the company.[20]

AES Corporation, a Connecticut power producer, pushes empowerment to a remarkable level to create a sense of ownership and a climate of trust among workers. Not only do teams of workers make virtually all operational decisions, but an ad hoc team of coal handlers and maintenance workers actually manages a $33 million investment fund for AES. The team has consistently matched, and once bettered, the returns of its corporate counterparts.[21] The learning organization increases individual responsibility for achieving the company's vision, allowing workers to be intellectually excited and engaged in the struggles and successes that come from difficult challenges.

Emergent Strategy

Business strategy emerges bottom up as well as top down. Since many employees are in touch with customers, suppliers, and new technologies, they identify needs and solutions. Customer needs may result in new products that define the company's strategy. Employees at the top and the bottom develop sensitive antennae for technological and market change. They look at what customers ask for, and they look at what the customer may need tomorrow. Hundreds, perhaps thousands of people are in touch with the environment, providing much data about external needs. This information accumulates into the strategy. For example, Nucor Steel developed a strategy of low-cost production that reflects the vision of CEO Ken Iverson, who heard about and took a $270 million chance on new technology for a thin-slab minimill. But employees helped acquire the new technology and found new products and processes that used it. The result was astonishing, with Nucor producing a ton of sheet steel in forty-five man-minutes versus three man-hours for big steelmakers.[22]

Strategy also emerges from a network of partnerships with suppliers, customers, and even competitors. As discussed in Chapter 14, organizations develop partnerships—sometimes with legal contracts, sometimes with informal agreements—that share information and create emerging strategies. The learning organization does not act autonomously. Information from partners provides data to the organization about new strategic needs and directions.[23] More companies are evolving into alliances, joint ventures, and electronic linkages, which were discussed in Chapters 7 and 9. Organizations become collaborators rather than competitors, experimenting to find the best way to learn and adapt.

Some companies, such as Chevron, Andersen Windows, and Springfield Remanufacturing, encourage a free exchange of information with other organizations, allowing teams to regularly visit and observe their "best practices." These leading-edge companies believe that a mutual sharing of good ideas is the best way to keep their organizations competitive.[24] Strategy in the learning organization can emerge from anywhere.

Strong Culture

What does the culture of a learning organization look like? Corporate cultures were described in Chapter 10, and the learning organization reflects those values and more. To really become a learning organization, a company must have the following values:

1. The whole is more valuable than the part, and boundaries are minimized.[25] The learning organization stresses the company as a whole system. Only by employee understanding of the overall vision and desire to improve the whole will the learning organization succeed. The culture also reduces

boundaries, as Jack Welch is trying to do at General Electric. Welch clearly recognized the importance of culture when he told a group of employees: "A company can boost productivity by restructuring, removing bureaucracy, and downsizing, but it cannot sustain high productivity without cultural change."[26] Welch wants to create a culture of "boundarylessness," and is striving to break down barriers between departments, divisions, and external organizations. Removing boundaries enables the free flow of people, ideas, and information that allows coordinated action to innovate and adapt to an uncertain and changing environment. Reducing boundaries also means more partnerships with suppliers, customers, and competitors.

2. The culture also values a sense of community and compassion and caring for one another.[27] People like to belong to something, and the learning organization becomes a place for creating a web of relationships that nurtures and develops each person within the community. People learn and experiment as part of a team and as part of a larger community.

   Activities that create differences among people are discarded. At Intel Corporation, everyone, including CEO Andrew Grove, has a small, open cubicle. This open environment, which is increasingly being used at companies like Aluminum Company of America, Procter & Gamble, and Hewlett-Packard, reflects the dissolution of old hierarchies and the emphasis on interaction and cooperation.[28] The learning organization also discards status symbols such as executive dining rooms and reserved parking spots. Caring, egalitarian cultures provide the secure climate for experimentation, frequent mistakes, and failures that enable learning.

Shared Information

The learning organization is flooded with information. To identify needs and solve problems, people have to be aware of what's going on. Formal data about budgets, profits, and departmental expenses are available to everyone. Each person is free to exchange information with anyone in the company. In the move toward information- and idea-based organizations, information sharing reaches extraordinary levels. Like the oil in a car's engine, information is not allowed to get low. Managers believe too much information sharing is better than too little. Employees can pick what they need for their tasks.

The president of Quad/Graphics is hooked via e-mail to 6,500 employees. He receives and answers approximately 60 messages a day.[29] Emery Olcott, president and CEO of Canberra Industries, Inc., prefers to communicate in person with employees, particularly when the company is facing difficult issues such as downsizing or relocation.[30]

The learning organization also encourages widespread communication among all employees; ideas are shared throughout the organization and may be implemented anywhere. At the Danish company Oticon, all incoming mail is scanned into a computer and, with few exceptions, anyone can access anyone else's mail. The same applies to financial documents.[31]

Employees at Springfield Remanufacturing meet in group sessions where department heads go over all production and financial figures, encouraging questions. Employees also have access to daily printouts from cost accounting that detail every job in the plant.[32] The days of managers hoarding information to make decisions are long gone in learning organizations.

Horizontal Structure

In the learning organization, the formal vertical structure that created distance between managers and workers is disbanded. So too are pay and budget systems that pit individual against individual and department against department. As described in Chapter 7, teams are the fundamental structure in a horizontal organization. People work together along a production process to create an output for a customer. Teams of employees produce the product or service, and they deal with the customer, making changes and improvements as they go along. In learning companies, bosses are practically eliminated, with team members taking responsibility for training, safety, scheduling vacations, purchases, and decisions about work and pay.

Boundaries between departments are reduced or eliminated. In addition, boundaries between organizations become more diffuse. As discussed in the previous chapter, companies are collaborating in unprecedented ways. The network organization and the emerging virtual organization, also described in Chapter 7, consist of groups of companies that join together to attain certain goals or exploit specific opportunities. These new structures provide the flexibility needed to adapt to rapidly changing competitive conditions.

Incentive systems are also changed in the learning organization. Studies have shown a connection between pay systems and worker commitment and performance.[33] And, as we learned in Chapter 13, incentive systems can dramatically affect whether employees cooperate or compete with one another. The learning organization encourages a cooperative model to keep employees learning and growing. Solar Press, Inc. went through a series of pay system transformations to find an incentive system that encourages growth and learning of employees. The initial system gave a bonus to each employee without regard to company performance or employee learning. A new system awarded production bonuses by team. This increased productivity but also pitted teams against one another and became an administrative nightmare. The final system gives profit-sharing bonuses to everyone in the company based on company performance. This system emphasizes teamwork and interdepartmental coordination.[34]

At Springfield Remanufacturing, workers get 10 percent bonuses when company goals are met. Springfield further enhances learning by paying $500 for each new idea adopted; one employee made a quick $7,500 and appreciated being rewarded for thinking and acting.[35] Some companies are moving to a system called pay for knowledge, which gives workers a raise for each new task learned.

ORGANIZATIONAL TRANSFORMATION AND LEADERSHIP

Almost every organization today is struggling to adapt to rapid social and economic changes, and many are incorporating elements of the learning organization, moving toward greater information sharing, empowering employees, and changing corporate cultures and structures to be more flexible and adaptive. Yet, the process of transforming from a traditional organization to a learning organization is not easy and organizations sometimes have to go through crises to break out of old ways of doing things and begin developing learning capability. This section will discuss the process of transformation, which is typically completed in three stages under the guidance of a transformational leader.

Corporate Transformations

As the head of one large U.S. corporation said: "The tragedy of top management . . . is that it is so much more reassuring to stay as you are, even though you know the result will be certain failure, than to try to make a fundamental change when you cannot be certain that the effort will succeed."[36] The process of organizational change is complex and messy, and many top managers stick with the known because of fear of the unknown. For organizations to transform, there often has to be intense pressure to improve, or even a threat to the company's very survival. More organizations are facing such a threat today than ever before because of complex and rapid changes, as we have discussed throughout this book. Today's organizations must confront the "chaos of constant change" to survive the whirlwind.[37]

The transformation of a company typically involves three phases.[38] The first is **crisis**, in which managers realize that the company is now or will soon be uncompetitive unless changes are made. In this stage, managers often downsize the work force, cut out several layers of management, and lower production costs. The old mold is broken. Moving through the crisis involves simplification by reducing functions and product lines. Costs are reduced by instituting controls and lowering expenses. Assets may be sold and some units may be relocated or shut down. Also during this period the problems are analyzed by leaders to plan the subsequent turnaround. Leaders also create a new vision about what the organization can become in the future.

The second phase is to **reinvest** organizational capability. Now that the firm's competitive scope has been simplified, expenses are under control, and size has been reduced, the organization stabilizes. Top leaders will mobilize commitment to the new vision, using the symbolic management techniques described in Chapter 10. Organization structure and corporate culture will be changed to reflect the new mission and goals. Leaders will invest in new equipment to enhance technological capability and in new marketing and financial programs to improve sales and show a profit. The most important focus of this phase, however, is investing in human factors and organizational capability by implementing a shared mind-set, empowering workers, and creating a capacity for change, continuous learning, and future growth.

The final phase is **rebuilding**, wherein the organization begins to grow. The focus shifts away from efficiency toward innovation and branching out for growth. New cultural values and behavior patterns have become institutionalized so that the organization can continue to adapt and change.[39] Leaders may reposition products or decrease prices to penetrate new markets or may add new product lines. Organizational expansion becomes the priority, with new people hired and support functions such as research and development and human resource management increased.

Each company undergoes transformation in its own way, but some aspects of these three stages are typically present.

Transformational Leadership

Leadership is perhaps the most widely studied topic in the organization sciences. What kind of people can lead an organization through major changes? One type of leadership that has a substantial impact on organizations is transformational leadership.

Transformational leaders are characterized by the ability to bring about change, innovation, and entrepreneurship. Transformational leaders motivate followers to not just follow them personally but to believe in the vision of corporate transformation, to recognize the need for revitalization, to sign on for the new vision, and to help institutionalize a new organizational process.[40]

Throughout previous chapters, we have discussed the need for large-scale changes in organizations—whether to implement a new corporate culture or self-managed team structure, grow to a new stage in the life cycle, or expand internationally. A massive administrative change involves a fundamental transformation of mission, structure, and the political and cultural systems of an organization to provide a new level of organizational capability.[41] In a situation of crisis or rapid change, a transformational leader should emerge who can impose major changes on the organization. To do so, the transformational leader must successfully achieve the following three activities.[42]

Creation of a new vision. The vision of a desired future state will articulate that the organization must break free of previous patterns and that old structures, processes, and activities are no longer useful. The leader must be able to spread the vision throughout the organization.

At AT&T, a new strategic vision was articulated under the leadership of CEO Robert Allen. Following the breakup of AT&T in 1984, the company quickly lost market share and was a dinosaur on the brink of extinction when Allen was hired. He spent time and energy spreading his new vision throughout the organization, seeing his primary goal as "helping our people learn how to win again."[43] Although leaders must involve managers and employees throughout the organization through task forces or other mechanisms, they alone are ultimately responsible for initiating a new vision.

Mobilization of Commitment. Widespread acceptance of the new mission and vision is critical. At General Motors, Roger Smith took nine hundred top executives on a five-day retreat to discuss his vision and gain their commitment. At Siemens Rolm, a U.S. telecommunications business owned by Siemens AG of Germany, 600 managers attended a three-day institute and then went back and mobilized commitment to the new vision in their own units.[44] Large-scale, discontinuous change requires special commitment, or it will be resisted as inconsistent with traditional organizational goals and activities.

Institutionalization of Change. The new practices, actions, and values must be permanently adopted. This means major resources must be devoted to training programs, retreats, and employee gatherings to implement the new organizational style. Changes may involve the technical, financial, and marketing systems as well as administrative structures and control systems. A long time period, perhaps several years, may be required for the leader to bring about full implementation. The transformational leader must be persistent to move the organization toward a new way of doing and thinking. The new system may alter power and status and revise interaction patterns. New executives may be hired who display values and behaviors appropriate for the new order of things. The new system is then institutionalized and made permanent.

SUMMARY OF KEY ISSUES

This chapter covered several topics concerning organizational forms relevant to the future, the trend toward learning organizations, and organizational transformation and leadership. Top leaders are responsible for the organization's design configuration. They decide on strategy formulation and then implement strategy by selecting organizational structure and form. Five forms described in the chapter are entrepreneurial, professional bureaucracy, adhocracy, divisional form, and machine bureaucracy. The selection of the configurations among these forms helps managers deal with basic forces, such as efficiency, direction, and innovation.

The paradigm shift occurring in the field of management has resulted in the learning organization. Enhanced learning capability is associated with mindful leadership, empowered people, emergent strategy, strong culture, shared information, and horizontal structure. Changing from a traditional to a learning organization is complex and organizations may have to go through crises to break out of old ways of doing things. The process of organizational transformation typically involves the three stages of crisis, reinvestment, and rebuilding. The process is often led by a transformational leader who creates a new vision for the organization, mobilizes commitment to the vision, and institutionalizes new practices, behaviors, and values.

Discussion Questions

1. Do you agree that creating organizational learning capability is more important for competitive advantage than is creating financial, marketing, or technological capability? Explain.
2. How do the five organizational forms proposed by Mintzberg help an organization deal with the system of seven primary forces?
3. What do you think of the concept of the learning organization? Which aspects seem least realistic? Would you like to work in one?
4. What might managers do during the rebuilding stage of transformation to prevent the problems of the past? Discuss.
5. Why are cultural values of minimal boundaries and compassion and caring important to a learning organization? Discuss.

Notes

1. David K. Hurst, "Cautionary Tales from the Kalahari: How Hunters Become Herders (and May Have Trouble Changing Back Again)," *Academy of Management Executive* 3, No. 5 (1991): 74–86.

2. Milton Leontiades, "The Confusing Words of Business Policy," *Academy of Management Review* 7 (1982): 45–48.

3. Lawrence G. Hrebiniak and William F. Joyce, *Implementing Strategy* (New, York: Macmillan, 1984).

4. Henry Mintzberg, *The Structure of Organizations* (Englewood Cliffs, N. J.: Prentice-Hall, 1979), 215–97; idem, "Organization Design: Fashion or Fit?" *Harvard Business Review* 59 (January–February 1981): 103–16.

5. Mintzberg, *The Structure of Organizations;* idem, "Organization Design."

6. Based on Henry Mintzberg, "The Effective Organization: Forces and Forms," *Sloan Management Review* (Winter 1991): 54–67.

7. Danny Miller, "Organizational Configurations: Cohesion, Change, and Prediction," *Human Relations* 43 (1990): 771–89.

8. Peter M. Senge, "Transforming the Practice of Management," *Human Resource Development Quarterly* 4 (Spring 1993): 5–32.

9. Peter Senge, *The Fifth Discipline: The Art and Practice of Learning Organizations* (New York: Doubleday/Currency, 1990).

10. Robert B. Reich, "The Real Economy," *Atlantic Monthly*, February 1991, 35–52.

11. Dave Ulrich and Dale Lake, "Organizational Capability: Creating Competitive Advantage," *Academy of Management Executive* 5, No. 1 (1991): 77–92.

12. Senge, "Transforming the Practice of Management."

13. Ken Peattie, "Strategic Planning: Its Role in Organizational Politics," *Long Range Planning* 26, No. 3 (1993): 10–17.

14. Peter M. Senge, "The Leader's New Work: Building Learning Organizations," *Sloan Management Review* (Fall 1990): 7–23.

15. Ibid.

16. Edward O. Welles, "The Shape of Things to Come," *Inc.* February 1992, 66–74.

17. Jeffrey Pfeffer, "Producing Sustainable Competitive Advantage through the Effective Management of People," *Academy of Management Executive*, Vol. 9, No. 1 (1995) 55–72.

18. Lucien Rhodes with Patricia Amend, "The Turnaround," *Inc.*, August 1986, 42–48.

19. John Case, "The Open Book Revolution," *Inc.*, June 1995, 26–43.

20. Jack Stack, "The Great Game of Business," *Inc.*, June 1992, 53–66.

21. Alex Markels, "A Power Producer Is Intent on Giving Power to Its People."

22. Myron Magnet, "Meet the New Revolutionaries," *Fortune*, 24 February 1992, 94–101.

23. Marc S. Gerstein and Robert B. Shaw, "Organizational Architectures for the Twenty-First Century," in David A. Nadler, Marc S. Gerstein, Robert B. Shaw, and associates, eds., *Organizational Architecture: Designs for Changing Organizations* (San Francisco: Jossey-Bass, 1992), 263–74.

24. Justin Martin, "Are You as Good as You Think You Are?" *Fortune*, 30 September 1996, 142–52; John A. Byrne, "Management Meccas," *Business Week*, 18 September 1995, 122–34.

25. Mary Anne Devanna and Noel Tichy, "Creating the Competitive Organization of the 21st Century: The Boundaryless Corporation," *Human Resource Management* 29 (Winter 1990): 455–71; Fred Kofman and Peter M. Senge, "Communities of Commitment: The Heart of Learning Organizations," *Organizational Dynamics* (Autumn 1993): 4–23.

26. Sumantra Ghoshal and Christopher A. Bartlett, "Rebuilding Behavioral Context: A Blueprint for Corporate Renewal," *Sloan Management Review* (Winter 1996): 23–36.

27. Kofman and Senge, "Communities of Commitment."

28. Joan O'C. Hamilton, Stephen Baker, and Bill Vlasic, "The New Workplace," *Business Week*, 29 April 1996, 106–17.

29. "Interview with Harry V. Quadracci," *Business Ethics* (May–June 1993): 19–21.

30. Ronald Recardo, Kathleen Molloy, and James Pellegrino, "How the Learning Organization Manages Change," *National Productivity Review* (Winter 1995/96): 7–13.

31. Oren Harari, "Open the Doors, Tell the Truth," *Management Review* (January 1995): 33–35.

32. Rhodes with Amend, "The Turnaround."

33. Stephen Wood, "High Commitment Management and Payment Systems," *Journal of Management Studies*, Vol. 33, No. 1 (January 1996) 53–77.

34. Bruce G. Posner, "If at First You Don't Succeed," *Inc.*, May 1989, 132–34.

35. Rhodes with Amend, "The Turnaround."

36. Ghoshal and Bartlett, "Rebuilding Behavioral Context: A Blueprint for Corporate Renewal."

37. Tom Broersma, "In Search of the Future," *Training and Development*, January 1995, 38–43.

38. Brian Dumaine, "The New Turnaround Champs," *Fortune*, 16 July 1990, 36–44; John M. Stopford and Charles Baden-Fuller, "Corporate Rejuvenation," *Journal of Management Studies* 27 (1990): 399–415; Richard C. Hoffman, "Strategies for Corporate Turnarounds: What Do We Know about Them?" *Journal of General Management* 14 (Spring 1989): 46–66.

39. Barbara Blumenthal and Philippe Haspeslagh, "Toward a Definition of Corporate Transformation," *Sloan Management Review* (Spring 1994): 101–06.

40. Robert J. House and Jitendra V. Singh, "Organizational Behavioral: Some New Directions for I/O Psychology," *Annual Review of Psychology* 38 (1987): 669–718; Bernard M. Bass, *Bass & Stogdill's Handbook of Leadership: Theory, Research, and Managerial Applications*, 3d ed. (New York: Free Press, 1990); Joseph Seltzer and Bernard M. Bass, "Transformational Leadership: Beyond Initiation and Consideration," *Journal of Management* 16 (1990): 693–703.

41. Noel M. Tichy and Mary Anne Devanna, *The Transformational Leader* (New York: John Wiley, 1986).

42. Noel M. Tichy and David O. Ulrich, "The Leadership Challenge—A Call for the Transformational Leader," *Sloan Management Review* 26 (Fall 1984): 59–64.

43. Ghoshal and Bartlett, "Rebuilding Behavioral Context."

44. Gillian Flynn, "On Track to a Comeback," *Personnel Journal* (February 1996): 58–69.

Glossary

adaptability/entrepreneurial culture a culture characterized by strategic focus on the external environment through flexibility and change to meet customer needs.

adhocracy a sophisticated organization that typically uses teams and is designed to survive in a complex, dynamic environment.

administrative principles a closed systems management perspective that focuses on the total organization and grows from the insights of practitioners.

advanced information technology microprocessors and other computer-related information-transmitting devices and systems that have enabled organizations to revolutionize their operations and increase productivity.

ambidextrous approach a characteristic of an organization that can behave both in an organic and a mechanistic way.

analyzability a dimension of technology in which work activities can be reduced to mechanical steps and participants can follow an objective, computational procedure to solve problems.

authority a force for achieving desired outcomes that is prescribed by the formal hierarchy and reporting relationships.

behavioral changes alterations in behavior that occur during intergroup conflict.

benchmarking a process whereby companies find out how others do something better than they do and then try to imitate or improve on it.

benefits from cooperation positive consequences of cooperation, including productive task focus, employee cohesion and satisfaction, organizational goal attainment, and innovation and adaptation.

boundary-spanning roles activities that link and coordinate an organization with key elements in the external environment.

bounded rationality perspective how decisions are made when time is limited, a large number of internal and external factors affect a decision, and the problem is ill-defined.

buffering roles activities that absorb uncertainty from the environment.

bureaucracy an organizational framework marked by rules and procedures, specialization and division of labor, hierarchy of authority, technically qualified personnel, separate position and incumbent, and written communications and records.

bureaucratic control the use of rules, policies, hierarchy of authority, written documentation, standardization, and other bureaucratic mechanisms to standardize behavior and assess performance.

bureaucratic culture a culture that has an internal focus and a consistency orientation for a stable environment.

Carnegie model organizational decision making involving many managers and a final choice based on a coalition among those managers.

centrality a trait of a department whose role is in the primary activity of an organization.

centralization refers to the level of hierarchy with authority to make decisions.

change process the way in which changes occur in an organization.

charismatic authority based in devotion to the exemplary character or the heroism of an individual and the order defined by him or her.

clan control the use of social characteristics, such as corporate culture, shared values, commitment, traditions, and beliefs, to control behavior.

clan culture a culture that focuses primarily on the involvement and participation of the organization's members and on rapidly changing expectations from the external environment.

coalition an alliance among several managers who agree through bargaining about organizational goals and problem priorities.

collaborative network an emerging perspective whereby organizations allow themselves to become dependent on other organizations to increase value and productivity for all.

collectivity stage the life cycle phase in which an organization has strong leadership and begins to develop clear goals and direction.

competition rivalry between groups in the pursuit of a common prize.

complexity refers to the number of levels in a hierarchy and the number of departments or jobs.

computer integrated manufacturing computer systems that link together manufacturing components, such as robots, machines, product design, and engineering analysis.

confrontation when parties in conflict directly engage one another and try to work out their differences.

consortia groups of firms that venture into new products and technologies together.

contextual dimensions traits that characterize the whole organization, including its size, technology, environment, and goals.

contingency a theory meaning one thing depends on other things; the organization's situation dictates the correct management approach.

contingency control model a model that describes contingencies associated with market, bureaucratic, and clan control.

continuous process production a completely mechanized manufacturing process in which there is no starting or stopping.

cooperative model model of organization in which managers foster cooperation rather than competition and find healthy ways to confront and resolve conflict.

cooptation occurs when leaders from important sectors in the environment are made part of an organization.

coping with uncertainty a source of power for a department that reduces uncertainty for other departments by obtaining prior information, prevention, and absorption.

craft technology technology characterized by a fairly stable stream of activities but in which the conversion process is not analyzable or well understood.

creative departments organizational departments that initiate change, such as research and development, engineering, design, and systems analysis.

crisis the first of three phases in the transformation and turnaround of an organization suffering from decline in which managers downsize the work force and lower production costs.

cultural strength the degree of agreement among members of an organization about the importance of specific values.

culture the set of values, guiding beliefs, understandings, and ways of thinking that is shared by members of an organization and is taught to new members as correct.

data the input of a communication channel.

decision learning a process of recognizing and admitting mistakes that allows managers and organizations to acquire the experience and knowledge to perform more effectively in the future.

decision premises constraining frames of reference and guidelines placed by top managers on decisions made at lower levels.

decision support system a system that enables managers at all levels of the organization to retrieve, manipulate, and display information from integrated data bases for making specific decisions.

departmental grouping structure in which employees share a common supervisor and resources, are jointly responsible for performance, and tend to identify and collaborate with each other.

differentiation the cognitive and emotional differences among managers in various functional departments of an organization and formal structure differences among these departments.

differentiation strategy a strategy in which organizations attempt to distinguish their products or services from others in the industry.

direct interlock occurs when a member of the board of directors of one company sits on the board of another.

divisional form large organizations that are subdivided into product or market groups.

divisional grouping grouping in which people are organized according to what the organization produces.

divisional structure structuring the organization according to individual products, services, product groups, major projects, or profit centers; also called product structure or strategic business units.

domain an organization's chosen environmental field of action.

domestic stage first stage of international development in which a company is domestically oriented while managers are aware of the global environment.

dual-core approach an organizational change perspective that identifies the unique processes associated with administrative change compared to those associated with technical change.

dynamic network a structure in which a free market style replaces the traditional vertical hierarchy.

effectiveness the degree to which an organization realizes its goals.

efficiency the amount of resources used to produce a unit of output.

elaboration stage the organizational life cycle phase in which the red tape crisis is resolved through the development of a new sense of teamwork and collaboration.

electronic data interchange the linking of organizations through computers for the transmission of data without human interference.

empowerment power sharing; the delegation of power or authority to subordinates.

engineering technology technology in which there is substantial variety in the tasks performed, but the activities are usually handled on the basis of established formulas, procedures, and techniques.

entrepreneurial stage the life cycle phase in which an organization is born and its emphasis is on creating a product and surviving in the marketplace.

entrepreneurial structure typically, a new, small entrepreneurial company consisting of a top manager and workers in the technical core.

escalating commitment persisting in a course of action when it is failing; occurs because managers block or distort negative information and because consistency and persistence are valued in contemporary society.

ethical dilemma when each alternative choice or behavior seems undesirable because of a potentially negative ethical consequence.

ethics the code of moral principles and values that governs the behavior of a person or group with respect to what is right or wrong.

ethics committee a group of executives appointed to oversee company ethics.

ethics ombudsperson a single manager who serves as the corporate conscience.

executive information systems interactive systems that help top managers monitor and control organizational operations by processing and presenting data in usable form.

external adaptation how an organization meets goals and deals with outsiders.

five organizational configurations these are entrepreneurial structure, machine bureaucracy, professional bureaucracy, divisional form, and adhocracy.

focus strategy a strategy in which an organization concentrates on a specific regional market or buyer group.

formalization stage the phase in an organization's life cycle involving the installation and use of rules, procedures, and control systems.

formalization the degree to which an organization has rules, procedures, and written documentation.

functional matrix a structure in which functional bosses have primary authority and product or project managers simply coordinate product activities.

functional grouping placing employees together who perform similar functions or work processes or who bring similar knowledge and skills to bear.

functional structure the grouping of activities by common function.

general environment includes those sectors that may not directly affect the daily operations of a firm but will indirectly influence it.

generalist an organization with a wide niche or domain.

geographic grouping organizing resources to serve customers or clients in a particular geographic area.

global company a company that no longer thinks of itself as having a home country.

global geographic structure a form in which an organization divides its operations into world regions, each of which reports to the CEO.

global matrix structure a form of horizontal linkage in an international organization in which both product and functional structures (horizontal and vertical) are implemented simultaneously.

global product structure a form in which product divisions take responsibility for global operations in their specific product areas.

global stage the stage of international development in which the company transcends any one country.

global teams work groups made up of multinational members whose activities span multiple countries; also called transnational teams.

globalization strategy the standardization of product design and advertising strategy throughout the world.

goal approach an approach to organizational effectiveness that is concerned with output and whether the organization achieves its output goals.

groupware programs that enable employees on a computer network to interact with one another through their PCs.

heroes organizational members who serve as models or ideals for serving cultural norms and values.

high tech technology-based information systems.

high touch face-to-face discussion.

high-velocity environments industries in which competitive and technological change is so extreme that market data is either unavailable or obsolete, strategic windows open and shut quickly, and the cost of a decision error is company failure.

horizontal conflict behavior that occurs between groups or departments at the same level in the hierarchy.

horizontal corporation a structure in which vertical hierarchy and departmental boundaries are virtually eliminated.

horizontal linkage the amount of communication and coordination that occurs horizontally across organizational departments.

horizontal linkage model a model of the three components of organizational design needed to achieve new product innovation: departmental specialization, boundary spanning, and horizontal linkages.

hybrid structure a structure that combines characteristics of both product and function or geography.

idea champions organizational members who provide the time and energy to make things happen; sometimes called "advocates," "intrapreneurs," and "change agents."

incremental change a series of continual progressions that maintain an organization's general equilibrium and often affect only one organizational part.

incremental decision process model describes the structured sequence of activities undertaken from the discovery of a problem to its solution.

indirect interlock occurs when a director of one company and a director of another are both directors of a third company.

information that which alters or reinforces understanding.

information ambiguity a situation in which issues cannot be objectively analyzed and understood and additional data cannot be gathered that will resolve the issues.

information amount the volume of data about organizational activities that is gathered and interpreted by organization participants.

information richness the information carrying capacity of data.

institutional perspective an emerging view that holds that under high uncertainty, organizations imitate others in the same institutional environment.

integration the quality of collaboration between departments of an organization.

integrator a position or department created solely to coordinate several departments.

intensive technology a variety of products or services provided in combination to a client.

interdependence the extent to which departments depend on each other for resources or materials to accomplish their tasks.

intergroup conflict behavior that occurs between organizational groups when participants identify with one group and perceive that other groups may block their group's goal achievement or expectations.

interlocking directorate a formal linkage that occurs when a member of the board of directors of one company sits on the board of another company.

internal integration a state in which organization members develop a collective identity and know how to work together effectively.

internal process approach an approach that looks at internal activities and assesses effectiveness by indicators of internal health and efficiency.

international division a division that is equal in status to other major departments within a company and has its own hierarchy to handle business in various countries.

international stage the second stage of international development, in which the company takes exports seriously and begins to think multidomestically.

interorganization relationships the relatively enduring resource transactions, flows, and linkages that occur among two or more organizations.

intranet a private, internal network that uses the infrastructure and standards of the Internet but is cordoned off from the public with the use of software programs known as *firewalls*.

intuitive decision making the use of experience and judgment rather than sequential logic or explicit reasoning to solve a problem.

joint venture a separate entity for sharing development and production costs and penetrating new markets that is created with two or more active firms as sponsors.

language slogans, sayings, metaphors, or other expressions that convey a special meaning to employees.

large-batch production a manufacturing process characterized by long production runs of standardized parts.

learning organization an organization in which everyone is engaged in identifying and solving problems, enabling the organization to continuously experiment, improve, and increase its capability.

legends stories of events based in history that may have been embellished with fictional details.

level of analysis in systems theory, the subsystem on which the primary focus is placed; four levels of analysis normally characterize organizations.

liaison role a person located in one department who is responsible for communicating and achieving coordination with another department.

life cycle a perspective on organizational growth and change that suggests organizations are born, grow older, and eventually die.

long-linked technology the combination within one organization of successive stages of production, with each stage using as its inputs the production of the preceding stage.

losses from conflict negative consequences of conflict for organizations, including diversion of energy, altered judgment, loser effects, and poor coordination.

low-cost leadership a strategy that tries to increase market share by emphasizing low cost compared to competitors.

machine bureaucracy a very large organization in which the technology is routine and often oriented to mass production.

management champion a manager who acts as a supporter and sponsor of a technical champion to shield and promote an idea within the organization.

management control systems the formalized routines, reports, and procedures that use information to maintain or alter patterns in organizational activity.

management information system a system that generally contains comprehensive data about all transactions within an organization.

management science approach organizational decision making that is the analog to the rational approach by individual managers.

market control occurs when price competition is used to evaluate the output and productivity of an organization.

matrix bosses department heads and program directors who have complete control over their subordinates.

matrix structure a strong form of horizontal linkage in which both product and functional structures (horizontal and vertical) are implemented simultaneously.

mechanistic an organization system marked by rules, procedures, a clear hierarchy of authority, and centralized decision making.

mediating technology the provision of products or services that mediate or link clients from the external environment and allow each department to work independently.

meso theory a new approach to organization studies that integrates both micro and macro levels of analysis.

mission the organization's reasons for its existence.

mission culture a culture that places emphasis on a clear vision of the organization's purpose and on the achievement of specific goals.

mixed model a description of an organization that displays both rational and political model characteristics.

model of intergroup conflict a graphic representation of the organizational and intergroup factors that set the stage for intergroup conflict, the triggers that set off a dispute, and the responses managers can make to control emergent conflict.

multidomestic company a company that deals with competitive issues in each country independent of other countries.

multidomestic strategy competition in each country is handled independently of competition in other countries.

multifocused grouping a structure in which an organization embraces structural grouping alternatives simultaneously.

multinational stage the stage of international development in which a company has marketing and production facilities in many countries and more than one-third of its sales outside its home country.

myths stories that are consistent with the values and beliefs of the organization but are not supported by facts.

negotiation the bargaining process that often occurs during confrontation and enables the parties to systematically reach a solution.

networking linking computers within or between organizations.

niche a domain of unique environmental resources and needs.

nonprogrammed decisions novel and poorly defined, these are used when no procedure exists for solving the problem.

nonroutine technology technology in which there is high task variety and the conversion process is not analyzable or well understood.

nonsubstitutability a trait of a department whose function cannot be performed by other readily available resources.

official goals the formally stated definition of business scope and outcomes the organization is trying to achieve; another term for **mission**.

operational control a short-term control cycle that includes the four stages of setting targets, measuring performance, comparing performance against standards, and feedback.

operative goals descriptions of the ends sought through the actual operating procedures of the organization; these explain what the organization is trying to accomplish.

organic an organization system marked by free-flowing, adaptive processes, an unclear hierarchy of authority, and decentralized decision making.

organization theory a macro approach to organizations that analyzes the whole organization as a unit.

organizational behavior a micro approach to organizations that focuses on the individuals within organizations as the relevant units of analysis.

organizational change the adoption of a new idea or behavior by an organization.

organizational decision making the organizational process of identifying and solving problems.

organizational development a behavioral science field devoted to improving performance through trust, open confrontation of problems, employee empowerment and participation, the design of meaningful work, cooperation between groups, and the full use of human potential.

organizational ecosystem a system formed by the interaction of a community of organizations and their environment, usually cutting across traditional industry lines.

organizational environment all elements that exist outside the boundary of the organization and have the potential to affect all or part of the organization.

organizational form an organization's specific technology, structure, products, goals, and personnel.

organizational goal a desired state of affairs that the organization attempts to reach.

organizational innovation the adoption of an idea or behavior that is new to an organization's industry, market, or general environment.

organizational politics activities to acquire, develop, and use power and other resources to obtain one's preferred outcome when there is uncertainty or disagreement about choices.

organizations social entities that are goal-directed, deliberately structured activity systems linked to the external environment.

paradigm a shared mind-set that represents a fundamental way of thinking, perceiving, and understanding the world.

Parkinson's law a view that holds that work expands to fill the time available for its completion.

people and culture changes changes in the values, attitudes, expectations, beliefs, abilities, and behavior of employees.

personnel ratios the proportions of administrative, clerical, and professional support staff.

political model a definition of an organization as being made up of groups that have separate interests, goals, and values in which power and influence are needed to reach decisions.

political tactics for using power these include: build coalitions, expand networks, control decision premises, enhance legitimacy and expertise, and make preferences explicit while keeping power implicit.

pooled interdependence the lowest form of interdependence among departments in which work does not flow between units.

population a set of organizations engaged in similar activities with similar patterns of resource utilization and outcomes.

population ecology model a perspective in which the focus is on organizational diversity and adaptation within a community or population of organizations.

power sources there are five sources of horizontal power in organizations: dependency, financial resources, centrality, nonsubstitutability, and the ability to cope with uncertainty.

power the ability of one person or department in an organization to influence others to bring about desired outcomes.

problem identification the decision-making stage in which information about environmental and organizational conditions is monitored to determine if performance is satisfactory and to diagnose the cause of shortcomings.

problem solution the decision-making stage in which alternative courses of action are considered and one alternative is selected and implemented.

problemistic search occurs when managers look around in the immediate environment for a solution to resolve a problem quickly.

product and service changes changes in an organization's product or service outputs.

professional bureaucracy an organization in which the production core is composed of professionals.

programmed decisions repetitive and well-defined procedures that exist for resolving problems.

project matrix a structure in which the project or product manager has primary responsibility, and functional managers simply assign technical personnel to projects and provide advisory expertise.

quality circles groups of six to twelve volunteer workers who meet to analyze and solve problems.

radical change a breaking of the frame of reference for an organization, often creating a new equilibrium because the entire organization is transformed.

rational approach a process of decision making that stresses the need for systematic analysis of a problem followed by choice and implementation in a logical sequence.

rational model a description of an organization characterized by a rational approach to decision making, extensive and reliable information systems, central power, a norm of optimization, uniform values across groups, little conflict, and an efficiency orientation.

rational-legal authority based on employees' beliefs in the legality of rules and the right of those in authority to issue commands.

reasons organizations grow growth occurs because it is an organizational goal; it is necessary to attract and keep quality managers; or it is necessary to maintain economic health.

rebuilding the final phase in turnaround and recovery in which the organization begins to grow, moving away from efficiency toward innovation.

reciprocal interdependence the highest level of interdependence in which the output of one operation is the input of a second, and the output of the second operation is the input of the first (for example, a hospital).

reengineering a cross-functional initiative involving the radical redesign of business processes to bring about simultaneous changes in organization structure, culture, and information technology and produce dramatic performance improvements.

reinvest the turnaround and recovery phase in which the organization stabilizes, and its structure and culture are changed to reflect its new mission and goals.

resource dependence means that organizations depend on the environment but strive to acquire control over resources to minimize their dependence.

retention the preservation and institutionalization of selected organizational forms.

rites and ceremonies the elaborate, planned activities that make up a special event and often are conducted for the benefit of an audience.

routine technology technology characterized by little task variety and the use of objective, computational procedures.

rule of law that which arises from a set of codified principles and regulations that describe how people are required to act, are generally accepted in society, and are enforceable in the courts.

satisficing the acceptance by organizations of a satisfactory rather than a maximum level of performance.

scientific management a classical approach that claims decisions about organization and job design should be based on precise, scientific procedures.

sectors subdivisions of the external environment that contain similar elements.

selection the process by which organizational variations are determined to fit the external environment; variations that fail to fit the needs of the environment are "selected out" and fail.

self-directed team a group of workers with different skills who rotate jobs and assume managerial responsibilities as they produce an entire product or service.

sequential interdependence a serial form of interdependence in which the output of one operation becomes the input to another operation.

service technology technology characterized by simultaneous production and consumption, customized output, customer participation, intangible output, and being labor intensive.

simple-complex dimension the number and dissimilarity of external elements relevant to an organization's operations.

small-batch production a manufacturing process, often custom work, that is not highly mechanized and relies heavily on the human operator.

social responsibility management's obligation to make choices and take action so that the organization contributes to the welfare and interest of society as well as itself.

sources of interdepartmental conflict eight factors that generate conflict, including operative goal incompatibility, differentiation, task interdependence, resource scarcity, power distribution, uncertainty, international context, and reward system.

specialist an organization that has a narrow range of goods or services or serves a narrow market.

stable-unstable dimension the state of an organization's environmental elements.

stakeholder any group within or outside an organization that has a stake in the organization's performance.

stakeholder approach also called the constituency approach, this perspective assesses the satisfaction of stakeholders as an indicator of the organization's performance.

stories narratives based on true events that are frequently shared among organizational employees and told to new employees to inform them about an organization.

strategic contingencies events and activities inside and outside an organization that are essential for attaining organizational goals.

strategic control the overall evaluation of the strategic plan, organizational activities, and results that provides information for future action.

strategy a plan for interacting with the competitive environment to achieve organizational goals.

strategy and structure changes changes in the administrative domain of an organization, including structure, policies, reward systems, labor relations, coordination devices, management information control systems, and accounting and budgeting.

strategy formulation the activities that lead to the establishment of an organization's overall goals and mission and the development of a specific strategic plan.

strategy implementation the use of managerial and organizational tools to direct and allocate resources to accomplish strategic objectives.

strategy the current set of plans, decisions, and objectives that have been adopted to achieve the organization's goals.

structural dimensions descriptions of the internal characteristics of an organization indicating whether stability or flexibility is the dominant organizational value.

structure the formal reporting relationships, groupings, and systems of an organization.

struggle for existence a principle of the population ecology model that holds that organizations are engaged in a competitive struggle for resources and fighting to survive.

switching structures an organization creates an organic structure when such a structure is needed for the initiation of new ideas.

symbol something that represents another thing.

symptoms of structural deficiency signs of the organizational structure being out of alignment, including delayed or poor-quality decision making, failure to respond innovatively to environmental changes, and too much conflict.

system resource approach an organizational perspective that assesses effectiveness by observing the beginning of the process and evaluating whether the organization effectively obtains resources necessary for high performance.

tactics for increasing the power base these include: enter areas of high uncertainty, create dependencies, provide resources, and satisfy strategic contingencies.

task environment sectors with which the organization interacts directly and that have a direct effect on the organization's ability to achieve its goals.

task force a temporary committee composed of representatives from each department affected by a problem.

team building activities that promote the idea that people who work together can work together as a team.

teams permanent task forces often used in conjunction with a full-time integrator.

technical complexity the extent of mechanization in the manufacturing process.

technical or product champion a person who generates or adopts and develops an idea for a technological innovation and is devoted to it, even to the extent of risking position or prestige.

technology changes changes in an organization's production process, including its knowledge and skills base, that enable distinctive competence.

technology the tools, techniques, and actions used to transform organizational inputs into outputs.

top leader the head of both functional and product command structures in a matrix.

total quality management an organizational approach in which workers, not managers, are handed the responsibility for achieving standards of quality.

traditional authority based in the belief in traditions and the legitimacy of the status of people exercising authority through those traditions.

transformational leadership the ability of leaders to motivate followers to not just follow them personally but to believe in the vision of organizational transformation, to recognize the need for revitalization, to commit to the new vision, and to help institutionalize a new organizational process.

transaction processing systems automation of the organization's routine, day-to-day business transactions.

transnational model a form of horizontal organization that has multiple centers, subsidiary managers who initiate strategy and innovations for the company as a whole, and unity and coordination achieved through corporate culture and shared vision and values.

two-boss employees employees who must maintain effective relationships with both department heads and program directors in a matrix structure.

uncertainty occurs when decision makers do not have sufficient information about environmental factors and have a difficult time predicting external changes.

value based leadership a relationship between a leader and followers that is based on strongly shared values that are advocated and acted upon by the leader.

variation appearance of new organizational forms in response to the needs of the external environment; analogous to mutations in biology.

variety in terms of tasks, the frequency of unexpected and novel events that occur in the conversion process.

venture teams a technique to foster creativity within organizations in which a small team is set up as its own company to pursue innovations.

vertical conflict behavior between groups that arises over issues of control, power, goals, and wages and benefits.

vertical information system the periodic reports, written information, and computer-based communications distributed to managers.

vertical linkages communication and coordination activities connecting the top and bottom of an organization.

whistle-blowing employee disclosure of illegal, immoral, or illegitimate practices on the part of the organization.

work flow automation a form of advanced information technology in which documents are automatically sent to the correct location for processing.

work flow redesign reengineering work processes to fit new information technology.

Name Index

A

Ackerman, Linda S. 139n25, 140
Adams, Dennis A. 214n18
Adices, Ichak 112n41
Adler, Nancy J. 162n28, 163
Adler, Paul S. 78n17, 80, 80n25, 81, 90n48, 189n21
Ahmad, Mohamed Ibrahim 55n27
Aiken, Michael 86n37, 108n24, 186n10, 207n3
Akers, John 3
Akinnusi, David M. 197n49
Alderfer, Clayton T. 298n1
Aldrich, Howard E. 8n23, 51n15, 330n26
Alexander, Keith 191n31
Alexander, Suzanne 47n3
Alfie, Kohn 309n29, n30
Allaire, Paul 139
Allen, Robert 355
Altier, William J. 127n14
Amason, Allen C. 308n27, n28
Amburgey, Terry L. 123n4
Amelio, Gilbert 115
Amend, Patricia 350n18, 352n32, 353n35
Anderson, Paul A. 253n12
Andrews, Edmund L. 328n14
Applegate, Lynda M. 94n59, n61
Archer, Earnest R. 251n9
Argote, Linda 73n2, 87n43, 91n49
Argyris, Chris 39 40n48
Arnold, Bill 235
Arnold, William W. 29n10
Arnst, Catherine 5n4
Arogyaswamy, Bernard 236n19
Asch, David 217n31, 218
Ashford, Susan J. 328n18
Astley, W. Graham 271n6, 109n30, 272n12, 274n20
Atkin, Robert A. 63n50
Aubin, Jean 256n28, n29
Austin, Nancy K. 235n16

B

Babcock, Judith A. 61n43
Bacharach, Samuel B. 207n3
Badaracco, Joseph L. Jr. 241n30
Baden-Fuller, Charles 354n38
Bailetti, Antonio J. 191n31
Baker, Edward 256n28
Baker, Octave V. 7n18
Baker, Stephen 103n9, 106n16
Baker, Stephen 331n29
Baker, Stephen 352n28
Barker, James R. 223n50
Barnett, William P. 332n31
Barnevik, Percy 105
Barney, Jay B. 60n39
Barrett, Amy 300n6
Barrett, Paul. M. 111n37
Barrier, Michael 280n47
Bartholomew, Doug 215n22
Bartimo, Jim 211n11
Bartlett, Christopher A. 6n11, 146n30, 171n47, n48, 173, 325n6, 352n26, 354n36, 355n43
Bartz, Carol 197
Bass, Bernard M. 355n40
Baum, J. Robert 254n15
Baum, Joel A. C. 330n26
Bazerman, Max H. 63n50
Beard, Donald W. 52n17
Beatty, Richard W. 36n39
Becker, Selwyn 107n20, 109n32
Beckhard, Richard 39, 40n48
Bedeian, Arthur G. 334n37
Beer, Michael 199n57
Behling, Orlando 254n15
Bell, Cecil H. Jr. 200n61
Bell, Gerald D. 87n40
Benedetti, Marti 327n11, n12
Benjamin, Robert I. 216n26
Bennett, Amanda 14n30
Bennett, James 323n1
Bennis, Warren G. 39, 40n48
Bergquist, William 15n31, 33
Bernstein, Aaron 286n62
Bernstein, Harry 300n7
Berry, Jonathan 58n5, 239n22
Berton, Lee 327n11, n12
Beyer, Janice M. 232n5, 234, 234n12
Birnbaum, Jeffrey H. 64n57
Bissett, M. J. 210n9
Black, Jill E. 159n17, 160
Blackburn, Richard S. 277n29
Blai, Boris 251n9
Blake, Robert R. 311n36, 313n43, n44, n47, 315, 315n54
Blau, Judith R. 189n22
Blau, Peter M. 87n40, 108n27, 109n30
Bleakley, Fred R. 49n7, 329n24
Blenkhorn, David L. 38n45
Blevins, Randy 191
Blowers, E. A. 109n31
Bluedorn, Allen C. 51n15, 107n20
Blumenthal, Barbara 354n39
Boeker, Warren 283n52
Boje, David M. 15n32
Boland M. 109n30
Boland W. 109n30
Booth, Patricia 6n10
Borys, Bryan 62n45, n49
Boudreau, John W. 214n17
Boulding, Elise 271n6
Bounds, Gregory M. 235n14
Bourgeois, L. J. III 263n43
Bowen, David E. 81n28,. 82, 83n32, 277n33, 278n34, n39, n40
Bradley, Allen 64
Bradshaw, Patricia J. 108n26
Brandt, Richard 103n9, 106n16, 328n13, n15
Brass, Daniel J. 271n4, 288n69
Bratton, William 26
Bremmer, Brian 62n46 50n9 51n13
Bridges, William 7n16
Brimelow, Peter 109n28
Brinkerhoff, Derick 41n55
Brittain, Jack W. 330n26
Brockhouse, Gordon 278n40
Brockner, Joel 264n48
Broderick, Renae 214n17
Broersma, Tom 354n37
Bronikowski, Karne 194n39
Brooks, Geoffrey R. 184
Brown, Andrew D. 232n3
Brown, David L. 299n4, n5
Brown, Donna 162n26
Brown, John 112n40

367

Hinings, C. R. 11n27, 112n40, 282n50, 283n51
Hitt, Michael A. 10n26, 32, 36n34, 239n22
Hochwarter, Wayne A. 308n27, n28
Hodder, James E. 256n27
Hoerr, John 313n45
Hof, Robert D. 103n9, 106n16,115n45, 152n2, 191n31, 194n39, 249n1
Hoffman, Alan N. 328n18
Hoffman, Richard C. 354n38
Hofstede, Geert 307n22
Holbek, Jonny 58
Holdaway, E. A. 109n31
Hollander, Edwin P. 277n30
Holpp, Lawrence 280
Holstein, William J. 152n1, 163n30
Holusha, John 79n20
Hood. W. R. 301n8
Hooijberg, R. 237n21, 238
Hooper, Laurence 4n3
Hori, Shintaro 109
Hoskisson, Robert E. 10n26, 32, 239n22
Hosmer, LaRue Tone 240, 240n25, n28
House, Robert J. 18n35, 241n31, 330n26, 355n40
Howard, Jack L. 286n63
Howell, Jane M. 190n26
Hrebiniak, Lawrence G. 25n3, 86n38, 341n3
Hsu, Cheng-Kuang 108n22, n25
Huber, George P. 92n50, 93n53, n54, n55, n56, 102n5, 304n10
Hughes, Michael D. 330n26
Hull, Frank 87n40
Hurst, David K. 340n1
Huseman, Richard C. 92n52
Hussein, Saddam 258
Huxley, Stephen J. 256n27

I

Iacocca, Lee 126, 127n9
Imparato, Nicholas 6n9, 15n31
Indik, B.P. 109n30
Ingols, Cynthia 190n23
Ireland, R. Duane 10n26, 32 36n34, 239n22
Irving, Richard H. 222n45
Issack, Thomas F. 254n16
Ito, Jack K. 91n49
Ivancevich, John M. 5n7

J

Jackson, Susan E, 254n19
Jacob, Rahul 29n11, 135n20
James, Jene G. 243n40
James, T. F. 109n31
Janis, Irving L. 253n13, 254
Jarman, Beth 112n43, 115n46
Jarvenpaa, Sirkka L. 158n13
Javetski, Bill 5n8

Javidan, Mansour 59n38
Jehn, Karen A. 308n27, n28
Jelernter, Carey Quan 239n23
Jelinek, Mariann 197n50
Jemison, David B. 55n27 62n45, n49
Jennings, Daniel F. 190n25
Jensen, Elizabeth 325n5
Jobs, Steven 113, 271
Johansen, Robert 164n37, 165n40
Johne, Axel 192n32
Johnson, Clark 28
Johnson, David W. 314
Johnson, Frank P. 314
Johnston, Marsha 7n20
Jones, Althea 78n14
Jones, Patricia 28
Jorgensen, Mark 243
Joyce, William F. 341n3
Jurkovich, Ray 52n17

K

Kacmar, K. Michele 286n63
Kahaner, Larry 28
Kahn, Robert L. 271n6
Kalathur, Suresh 216n24
Kanter, Rosabeth Moss 41n55, 190n23, n24, 271n9, 275, 275n22, 276n23, 291n79
Kanungo, Rabindra N. 278n38
Kaplan, Abraham 271n6
Kaplan, Robert S. 35n31, 36n39, 220n41
Kasarda, John D. 109n29
Keating, David E. 156n6
Keisler, Sara 93n53
Kekre, Sunder 216n24
Kelleher, Herb 231, 278n34
Keller, John J. 47n1, 331n30
Keller, Robert T. 88n45
Kelly, Joe 310n33
Kelly, Kevin 7n14, 61n41, 164n36, 327n11, n12, 328n17
Kennedy, Allan A. 233n7
Kenny, Graham K. 276n24
Keon, Thomas L. 108n22
Kerwin, Kathleen 128n15, 191n31
Kessler, Eric H. 188n16
Kets de Vries, Manfred F.R. 170n46
Kiechel, Walter III, 6n13, 127n14
Killman, Ralph H. 188n16
Kim, Linsu 188n14
Kimberly, John R. 107n20, 112n41, 115n44, 195n43
King, Jonathan B. 273n18
Kirkpatrick, David, 4n3
Kirsch, Laurie J. 223n49
Kleiner, Brian H. 276n26
Kline S. M. 86n38
Koberg, Christine 52n16
Koch, James V. 35n30
Kochan, Thomas A. 298n3, 304n10
Koenig, Richard 91, 91n49

Kofman, Fred 351n25, 352n27
Kolb, David A. 299n4
Kolodny, Harvey 92n50
Konrad, Walecia 47n4
Korda, Michael 270n2
Koslow, Linda 252
Kotter, John P. 7n16, 25n2, 61n44, 64n54, 181n2, 182, 233n6, 237, 236n20, 251
Kramer, Barry 107n18
Kroc, Ray 186
Kueng, Thomas K. 328n18
Kumar, Parmod 286n63
Kupfer, Andrew 50n8, 51n12
Kurschner, Dale 8n22
Kwitny, Jonathan 310n35

L

Labich, Kenneth 34n26, 215n19
Lachman, Ran 271n4, 283n52
Lake, Dale 347, 347n11
Lamners, Cornelius J. 278n35
Land, George 112n43, 115n46
Landler, Mark 135n22, 196n48, 328n15
Lang, James R. 63n51
Langley, Ann 255n23
Larson, Erik W. 147n33, 209n6, 273n18
Lavin, Douglas 47n1
Lawler, Edward E. III 83n32, 158n11, 277n33, 278n34, n39, n40
Lawrence, Paul R. 56, 56n31, n32, 57, 57n34, 128n16, 142n27, n31, 305n12, 306n13, 312, 313n44
Leatt, Peggy 88n44
Leavitt, Harold J. 256n26, n30
Leblebici, Huseyin 61n40
Lee, C. A. 282n50
Lee, Mark C. S. 214n18
Lee, William G. 231n1, 278n34
Lefkoe, Morty 306n14
Lei, David 79n21, n23, 80n26, 163n31, 164n32-n34
Leidner, Dorothy E. 214n16
Leifer, Richard 189n18, 223n48, n49
Lengel, Robert H. 87n43, 125, 208n5, 212n14, n15
Leontiades, Milton 341n2
Lesly, Elizabeth 27n4, 264n49
Levine, David I. 189n21
Lewin, Arie Y. 14n29, 26
Lewis, Virginia L. 112n41
Lewyn, Mark 328n13, n15
Lieber, Ronald B. 193n33
Likert, Rensis 39, 40n48
Lindblom, Charles 249n4
Lindgren, Bob 127n12, 160n19
Lingle, John H. 35n32
Lioukas, Spyros 109n30
Lipin, Steven 274n21
Lipnack, Jessica 325n7
Lippitt, G. L. 116

Subject Index

Reading for Real

Teach Students to
Read with Power,
Intention, and Joy in
K–3 Classrooms

Kathy Collins

Stenhouse Publishers
Portland, Maine

Stenhouse Publishers

www.stenhouse.com

Copyright © 2008 by Kathy Collins

Library of Congress Cataloging-in-Publication Data

Collins, Kathy, 1964-
  Reading for real : teach students to read with power, intention, and joy in K–3 classrooms / Kathy Collins.
      p. cm.
  Includes bibliographical references and index.
  ISBN 978-1-57110-703-9 (alk. paper)
  1. Reading (Elementary) 2. Study skills. I. Title.
  LB1573.C535 2008
  372.4—dc22
                      2008011559
Cover and interior design by Designboy Creative Group
Cover and interior photographs by Gelfand-Piper Photography

Manufactured in the United States of America on acid-free, recycled paper
14 13 12 11 10 09 08 9 8 7 6 5 4 3 2

For Ian, Owen, and Theo,
the members of my favorite club

Contents

Acknowledgments

When I was a graduate student, I worked full time at what was then called the Teachers College Writing Project, first as a receptionist and then as an assistant to founding director Lucy Calkins. Upon graduation from my master's program, I planned to leave behind the expense of New York City to begin my teaching life and school loan repayments. It was at that time that the Writing Project became the Teachers College Reading and Writing Project (TCRWP) when it received a substantial grant to study the teaching of reading.

Lucy asked if I would stay on at the Project as a research assistant on the reading grant. The focus of my research, she said, would be in the primary grades. Most of my time would be spent gathering information in classrooms as I worked alongside teachers and students, and then sharing the information, data, and observations in various study groups and think tanks. By taking this job, I would work very closely with Lucy Calkins, Randy Bomer, then codirector of the Project, and Kate Montgomery, the upper-grade research assistant at that time. Although I had been longing for years to have my own classroom, I took the position without hesitation. After all, as Jacqui Getz told me at the time, "You'd be crazy not to!"

So this is the point where my acknowledgments begin, because this is the time when an image of reading clubs began to take shape at the Project. I start by thanking Lucy Calkins for offering me the job that changed my life in so many ways. Lucy nudged, pushed, and often forced me up a very steep learning curve. I continue to make my way up, and Lucy still throws me a rope, offers me a boost, and challenges me to keep on moving. I will always be professionally and personally grateful to Lucy for all the ways she's supported and encouraged me through the years and changes.

I want to thank Randy Bomer for schoolin' me with kindness when I was in over my head. Gosh, I'm still in over my head on many occasions, and I am grateful that I can still rely on Randy Bomer to offer wisdom, advice, a few laughs, and great dinner company. I want to thank Kate Montgomery, my upper-grade research partner on the grant. She didn't know it, but I tried in vain to "mind meld" with her when we were research assistants together.

I remember an image of reading clubs in primary classrooms first being discussed in one of our weekly very early morning meetings. Much of the conversation was based on the great work and powerful ideas of so many educators with whom we studied. Lydia Bellino, Laurie Pessah, Liz Phillips, Shirley McPhillips, and Mimi Aronson were in on reading clubs from the beginning, working closely with the teachers in their schools and opening up classrooms so that we could spend lots of time watching teachers and students as they made their way through cycles of reading clubs. Lydia, Laurie, Liz, Shirley, and Mimi helped us keep our vision for reading clubs tethered to the real needs and strengths of teachers and students.

There were many classrooms in which I observed, but there were three teachers with whom I spent most of my time. I want to thank Hannah Schneewind, Susana Gonzalez-Condell, and Tricia Lyons for letting me spend hours and hours in their wonderful classrooms. Their exquisite teaching and professional generosity has made a lasting impact on so many of us.

There were many other teachers who opened their classrooms as well. I want to thank Renée Dinnerstein, Alice Ressner, Jacqi McGarry, Bill Fulbrecht and Phyllis Allen, and Connie Norgren at PS 321 in Brooklyn as well as the late Ronnie Ranere and Karen Khan at the Bronx New School for opening their primary classrooms to my eyes, ears, and notebook on many occasions.

I also had the good fortune to spend some time in the upper-grade classrooms of Kathleen Tolan, Donna Santman, Katherine Bomer, Kathy Doyle, and Terry Moore. In these upper-grade rooms, it was so easy to recognize the power and imagine the potential of book talks, and to see how conversations about characters, themes, and stories could change the thinking of individuals and the affect the tone and identity of a community of learners. We primary teachers learned so much about supporting talk in our classrooms by acknowledging the possibilities that were so evident in upper-grade classrooms. These educators, and so many others, including Cheryl Tyler, Mary Ann Colbert, Amanda Hartman, Stephanie Parsons, Leah Mermelstein, Teresa Caccavale, Ginny Lockwood-Zisa, Barbara Pinto, Lisa Ripperger, and Shanna Schwartz, have contributed so much to my understanding of the power of reading clubs.

I owe a debt of gratitude to Kathleen Tolan, Laurie Pessah, and the incredible group of primary grades staff developers and office staff with whom I worked at the TCRWP. I've missed your company in so many ways over the last few years, and our conversations echo throughout this book. I want to thank the members of all of the study groups, literacy coaching groups, leadership groups, and think tanks that I've been a part of over the years. I've been very fortunate to have studied alongside hundreds of deeply committed and hardworking educators who've braved traffic and after-school hunger to make their way up to Teachers College for frequent meetings, sometimes in dank basement rooms. I want to thank the educators who attended the Reading Think Tank retreats over the years for spending time to talk and think, almost exclusively, about the teaching of reading.

Dozens and dozens of literacy educators from other learning communities from around the world have spent time making presentations and participating in study groups with the TCRWP community during school years and at summer institutes. We've learned so much in your company and from your books and articles, and I thank you.

I also must thank past and present educators and authors in the field of literacy education who continually feed us with the big ideas, the minute details, and the sparks of inspiration to teach in a way that lets us match our practice to our beliefs.

I am grateful for my students and colleagues at PS 321 in Brooklyn as well as the teachers and students of many other schools around the country, who have invited me to think with them. Thanks for allowing teaching and learning to be a work in progress and for being patient with imperfection.

Pat Johnson, Rebecca Applebaum, and Anna Jaross took time from their busy lives to read the next-to-finished manuscript, and I'm grateful for their wise feedback and advice. They solved problems I couldn't, appreciated things I didn't, and were instrumental in my push to finish. I also want to thank Mary Baldwin and Brenda Augusta for reading an early draft and encouraging me to keep on going on this project when I had my doubts.

Thank you to Danielle Dehm, principal, and Claire Noonan, school-based literacy queen, at the Victor Primary School in Victor, New York, for allowing me to take pictures in their school. It was a pleasure to spend time in the wonderful classrooms of Ryan Charno, Christie Cambio, Amanda Phillips, Katie Tribula, and Maureen Unterborn. Thanks also to Julie Gelfand of Gelfand-Piper Photography for taking the photographs.

I am very grateful to Philippa Stratton for being such a supportive editor and cheerleader, sounding board and gentle task master. Philippa knows just what kind of feedback I need to keep myself going, and she administers it in perfect doses. Thanks also to Erin Trainer for reeling me in as I flailed wildly near the finish. Thanks to Robin Miura, Jay Kilburn, and Sean McGee for making it all look so good. In fact, thanks to everyone at Stenhouse who kept a straight face whenever I said the book was "coming along."

I want to thank Ayse, Chuck, and Otto Gilbert for inviting me to write in their beautiful home and for kindly letting me come and go as needed. Their home was the place where I wrote most of this book and where I acquired a taste for strong tea and Cuban music. I am thankful to Maleia Grabinski for taking terrific care of Theo a couple of mornings a week so I could squeeze in a few more hours of writing time.

I also want to say thank you to my parents, Carol and George Collins, as well as my brothers, George and Tom, my in-laws Lanie and Hugh Fleischer, and the Herzog and Niemuth families for checking in, cheering me on, and resisting the impulse to ask, "Aren't you finished yet?"

Finally, I owe so very much to my home team, Ian, Owen, and Theo Fleischer, for all of their support, encouragement, love, and good humor... and for being so snuggly, inside and out.

Introduction

For a couple of years before I launched my first cycle of reading clubs in my own classroom, I had the privilege of working as a research assistant to Lucy Calkins, founding director of the Teachers College Reading and Writing Project (TCRWP), and Randy Bomer, then codirector of the Project. A major part of my job was to spend lots of time in some of the most wonderful classrooms across the boroughs of New York City and in Tenafly, New Jersey. I watched closely as teachers launched reading workshops in their classrooms. I sat beside hundreds of students, listening to them read and talk about their books with each other. I watched young readers as they chose texts, handled challenges, and responded to what they were reading. I observed and transcribed dozens and dozens of mini-lessons, small-group strategy lessons, and reading conferences led by teachers who were, and are still, my icons of teaching virtue.

In those days, the Project was fine-tuning its version of the reading workshop. We were operating under the influence of work and research by literacy educators from all over the world. We were putting our ideas to the test within the classrooms of many generous teachers. We were meeting in frequent study groups and think tanks and spending weekends together at retreats in order to figure out the characteristics of a powerful reading workshop, one that would have a profound effect on our students' abilities to decode print, make meaning, and develop long-lasting positive relationships with reading. During many of our study sessions and discussions, we spent a lot of time thinking about ways to add more authentic and beneficial reading opportunities to classroom reading time.

You see, there was a concern that young students were spending quite a bit of their reading time doing activities other than actually reading. We found that instead of reading books that they could, in fact, read, they were spending more time doing tasks such as the following: writing responses to stock questions about assigned texts; completing worksheets on which they were to color all the objects that had a short *e* sound; listening to books on tape; making mobiles, hats, puppets, and other crafts based on stories that had been read aloud to them; and so on. Although one can argue that some of these tasks are closely connected with and helpful to students' reading development, there was widespread concern that these activities were taking up too much of the precious time that students could spend actually reading, thinking, and talking about books they read themselves.

We also worried that students viewed the act of reading as simply a means to an end. For many children, the reward or purpose of reading was not in the reading itself, but rather in the follow-up activity, the opportunity to make a puppet at the end of the story, the time to circle all the words ending with *th* in the worksheet packet, or the chance to use the sacred felt-tip markers to draw an alternate ending, for example. For these kids, the purpose of reading was to do the work that followed, and the work that followed was always initiated or assigned by the teacher. We wondered if our students were learning that the reason they were reading in school was to complete some sort of task or to answer someone else's questions.

Sure, many students enjoy these tasks and activities. I know I sure did when I was little. There were not many things that I liked more than the scent of slightly damp worksheets that came right off the ditto machine. While it's true that children may enjoy many of these tasks, there are certainly a number of kids in any class who hold a different view. They're the ones who say aloud, or at least think quietly to themselves, "Ugh, I have to write a report on this book after I finish it?" or "I don't want to draw a new cover for this book because I can't draw elephants with lips." For those children, the act of reading carried with it a low-grade tension because of their anticipation of the dreaded tasks that usually followed.

We thought long and hard about how to ensure that the structures and teaching methods we used during reading workshop were research based and featured the most effective teaching practices. We wanted reading workshops to be characterized by high expectations and great results. Yet we also strived to create reading workshops in which there were opportunities for teachers to implicitly and explicitly show their students that reading offers its own rewards. We wanted students to experience real-life motivations for reading. We wanted to teach them that people read for many different purposes: for pleasure, for escape, for the sake of getting lost in a story, for finding information and gaining knowledge, and for so many other reasons that probably don't have anything to do with puppets, written response, or other externally assigned follow-up activities. We also held on tight to a vision of a reading workshop in which children are joyful, playful, and purposeful with texts. We wanted to "give children opportunities to construct their own responses" (Clay 1998, 190) to their reading. We wanted reading workshops in which our students both learn to read and love to read.

Our vision for reading workshops and our observations of children who were highly engaged with their reading were the catalysts behind implementing reading clubs at various times of the year in primary-grade classrooms. This is the idea I want to share with you in this book.

Reading clubs arose out of a deep commitment to helping each of our students develop a resourcefulness in using strategies to read the words and understand the texts, a flexible and confident reading identity, and a sense of joy, playfulness, enthusiasm, and intention toward their reading.

I hope you'll see the many ways in which reading clubs provide opportunities for students to orchestrate all the reading strategies they know in order to do purposeful, self-directed, and joyful reading that is full of intention and investment. I will share stories of children talking with depth and excitement about things they wonder, what they've noticed, and what they are thinking about texts. I'll show you how reading clubs can be a stable bridge that spans the reading our kids do in school and the reading we hope they do throughout their lives.

In Part I, I provide a rationale for and a vision of reading clubs as they're implemented in hundreds of classrooms around the country. I will help you envision reading clubs by sharing stories of the reading, talking, and thinking that takes place. I pull back the curtain so you can see the nuts and bolts and the behind-the-scenes work. In Part II, I offer suggestions for instruction and tips for setting up successful reading partnerships that will support students in any kind of reading club. In Part III, I describe different kinds of reading clubs in detail and offer tried-and-true ideas for planning instruction and for dealing with challenges that may arise. When you finish this book, it is my hope of hopes that you will be inspired to launch reading clubs in your own classroom.

A Behind–the–Scenes View of Reading Clubs

Some of you may know that for many years the Teachers College Reading and Writing Project community used the term reading centers *instead of* reading clubs *to describe the structure I've written about in this book. Over a dozen years ago when teachers such as Hannah Schneewind, Susana Gonzalez, and Tricia Lyons were pioneering this work in their classrooms, the name* reading centers *stuck for some reason, although those of us involved were never quite satisfied calling this structure* reading centers. *As the work of the TCRWP expanded well beyond New York City and the tristate area, it became more evident that the name* reading centers *was problematic.*

The term was confusing because people tend to have deeply ingrained ideas about centers, whether the term conjures up the image of literacy centers or word study centers, pretend-play centers or math centers. When we taught workshops and institutes for teachers, we would have to begin our sessions about reading centers by essentially asking teachers to let us redefine what they already knew about them. That wasn't easy. It was obvious that the term centers *was already taken.*

In addition to being unclear, the name reading centers *was also a bit misleading because it didn't quite capture the essence of what went on between children and their texts when they got together in what we're now calling* reading clubs.

In Part I, I introduce reading clubs by showing you what they are and how they work, offering some behind-the-scenes insights and providing a view of what reading clubs look and sound like. For those of you who like to dive right in or are familiar with reading clubs and interested in getting into the specifics of instruction, you might decide to go straight to Part II—and that would be okay with me.

A Rationale for Reading Clubs

Every free moment they had, Alex and Sulima would head straight for the tank that housed their classroom's new arrival, the Yet-to-Be-Named turtle. They were like sideline play-by-play announcers narrating the turtle's every move, which tended to involve very little narrating and lots of waiting. As days passed and the turtle remained mostly stock-still and hidden, Alex and Sulima began to worry. They hunted through the classroom library, gathering books containing turtle information. They asked their teacher, Susana Gonzalez, if they could put their book collection in a basket next to the turtle tank. They rifled through the texts to find pictures of turtles that looked like theirs, and they read those sections of the books to find information that would help them energize their turtle, or at least diagnose the problem.

Unfortunately, after a couple of days, Alex and Sulima realized they were not satisfied with the information the books offered. Their teacher told them that if the books didn't help, they could think of other ways to find the information they needed. Alex and Sulima decided to write a letter to the Bronx Zoo containing their questions about turtle care and about how to determine turtle gender. They included a drawing of their turtle, labeling its different parts because they noticed such diagrams in many of the turtle books they had read.

Every morning, in the classroom I shared with Jessica Borg Weinberger, Emily and Jordan would huddle over a children's yoga book as they waited for the morning meeting to begin. They would mimic poses from the yoga book, and they'd make up their own new poses, complete with yogalike names such as the Flying Bird or the Stretching Cat. After a few days, other children began to join them in this corner of the classroom meeting area for a kind of yoga study. Max brought in one of his mom's yoga books from home, and the group compared poses between the grown-up book and the kids' yoga book. They used sticky notes to mark cool poses and jotted notations on them rating the level of difficulty (super easy, so-so, and super hard). They asked if they could have time to teach the other kids some of the cool poses that they discovered in the books. "It'll be good for us," Emily assured me. "Yeah, Max's mom told him that if you do yoga, you won't get stressed out," Jordan added.

These vignettes from real classrooms are examples of kids' organic, adult-free interactions with books and with each other. Both of these anecdotes, and any others like them they bring to mind from your own classroom, tell the story of children who are highly engaged and purposeful with texts. Their concerns and interests affect their reading, and their reading affects their lives. We treasure these moments and often tell others about them, but they do leave us with questions: What are the conditions that lead to this sort of highly engaged, childlike play/work, and what are the characteristics of it? Can we formalize and then replicate this kid-initiated, joyful, authentic reading in order to extend the learning opportunities it affords to all of the students in our classrooms?

The children in these stories didn't really know it, but we could say they were participating in self-made reading clubs. The term *reading clubs* may very well suggest many different things to teachers. The reading clubs described in this book were created to provide opportunities for students to orchestrate all of their reading skills and strategies for authentic reading purposes and to develop the kinds of reading habits that will likely encourage a lifelong relationship to reading. The reading clubs I describe are a formal structure giving students time to read and talk about books with a high level of engagement, purpose, and joy, much like the way Alex, Sulima, Max, Jordan, Emily, and their classmates approached reading.

So, What Do Reading Clubs Look Like?

Here is a simple, bare-bones description of reading clubs: a reading club is a couple of kids reading and talking about a small collection of books that go together in some way. During a cycle of reading clubs, partners choose a reading club of interest that contains books they can read, and they determine their own purposes and plans (with a healthy dose of teacher support and instruction, of course, especially during the first couple of reading club cycles).

Whenever I try to explain reading clubs, the idea of a group of musicians getting together to jam comes to mind. When I imagine musicians getting together in a garage or basement or living room somewhere, I picture one of them sharing a new piece of music that she's been working on lately. As others join in to offer their musical contributions, the original little groove is adjusted, revised, or moved in new directions as a result of the musical improvisation and collaboration. The whole process is energetic and joyful, exuberant perhaps, and there is a feeling among the musicians that they are making something important and new.

Reading clubs are a kind of reading jam session. Readers, usually working in partnerships, get together with a basket of books in which they are interested. They read, then stop and talk back and forth to find clarity, exchange thoughts, and grow ideas. Just like a musical jam session, there is improvisation in reading clubs—the book talks may cause the readers to revise, alter, or move their thinking in new directions. The readers are engaged because they're reading and talking to serve their own purposes, to satisfy their own interests, and to meet their own goals. There is a growing sense of agency (Johnston 2004), a habit of exploration, and a feeling of exuberance shared by reading club participants. (For a detailed explanation of reading partnerships, see Chapter 5.)

We can imagine that during a nonfiction study in a kindergarten reading workshop, the teacher launches a cycle of nonfiction reading clubs. Malika and Jeremy decide to study dolphins in their reading club because they want to look for information about how dolphins raise their young. Their club basket contains a couple of books at Levels C and D (Fountas and Pinnell 1996), which they can read conventionally. The other books are too hard for them to read with accuracy, fluency, and comprehension, but there are detailed photographs and illustrations for them to study closely. For a week or so, Malika and Jeremy read texts about dolphins, grow ideas from the illustrations and photographs, and talk about what they're learning and what they're wondering. They use their background knowledge to help situate the new information they're acquiring, and they use a variety of strategies, skills, and nonfiction reading habits to make sense of the information. In a second-grade class down the hall, the teacher has launched character reading clubs to support the study of characters in texts in an effort to strengthen students' abilities to infer as they read. Sara and Natasha want to become experts about Poppleton. Sara says she likes Poppleton because she's "into" pigs, and Natasha agrees to study Poppleton because the Poppleton books are her favorite chapter books. They gather several books into a basket for their Poppleton club. They spend their time reading and talking about the texts and share their ideas about Poppleton. They both agree that Poppleton "acts crazy sometimes." They make a plan (with a bit of teacher nudging) to reread the books in order to figure out why Poppleton sometimes acts this way. Natasha suggests that they each read a different book, put sticky notes on the parts where Poppleton acts crazy, and then get back together to talk. They read by themselves for a bit, and when they get together again, they talk about the parts of the books they've noted. Time runs out, so they jot their plan for the next day on the to-do list they keep in their reading club basket. Natasha writes, "Keep talking about why Poppleton acts crazy."

Then, in June, during a whole-class study called Readers Set Goals and Make Plans for Reaching Them, first graders Hans and Stephanie gather books that they want to practice reading aloud. Their mothers will soon have babies, and Hans and Stephanie share the goal of reading aloud to their new baby siblings. They gather books that they think babies will like, and they spend their reading club time reading these books aloud in their best voices. Stephanie brings in a couple of stuffed animals so that she and Hans can practice reading books while holding a "baby" on their laps. At the end of the week, Hans asks the teacher if he and Stephanie can go to the pre-K class and read to some of those little kids for practice.

In reading clubs, our students orchestrate all of the knowledge and strategies they've accumulated for reading and talking about texts in order to think deeply about topics or texts of interest. Often in reading clubs, the students' collaboration as readers, thinkers, and talkers results in their desire do something or make something out of their new expertise or knowledge, whether it's reading aloud *Goodnight Moon* in their best storyteller voice because they've determined that book is the best first book ever for newborn babies, or whether it's making a big book of dolphin information for the nonfiction section of the school library. These projects tend not to be assigned, so the inspiration for them most often arises naturally from the children's own interests and the conversations they've had around their reading. Keeping these classroom stories in mind, I think it may be helpful now to list some defining reading club characteristics:

A reading club is simply a basket of books that have been gathered together because the texts relate to each other in some way; a reading club is not a particular place in the classroom, nor does it involve a particular activity or task, other than reading and talking about texts.

In the classroom examples above, the teachers launch reading clubs during particular parts of the curriculum. The "club" is actually two to four students who meet with a basket of books over the course of a week or so. So, during a nonfiction study, for example, a teacher may pull together texts for several different reading club baskets, such as Whales Club, Mummies Club, Ants Club, and so on. Her students may invent and put together some other club baskets based on their interests as well, such as Ferocious Dinosaur Club, Dogs and Cats Club, Human Body Club, and so on. During any cycle of reading clubs, the options students can choose from are typically based on student input and interests as well as the appropriate texts and materials that are available.

During a cycle of reading clubs, the reading partners choose a club in which they are interested and work with those texts for about a week or so. Depending on their interest level and the progress they've made, the partners may or may not decide to switch clubs for the next week in the cycle. There is more information below and throughout the following chapters about pulling together texts for reading clubs and procedures for launching them.

Reading clubs are not a daily structure in the reading workshop. They are implemented at certain times of the year, usually for two to four weeks at a time. In other words, reading clubs are an intermittent part of a balanced literacy program.

In the course of a school year, a teacher might implement only five or six reading club cycles, and usually these cycles last from two to four weeks. This means that there may be only ten to fifteen weeks of reading clubs spread throughout the whole school year.

Many teachers tend to implement their first cycle of reading clubs at some point in the fall, but most of the reading club cycles tend to occur in the winter and spring, when students are quite familiar with the procedures and expectations for reading workshop, and for working and talking with a partner. There is more information about these issues in the chapters that follow.

Let's imagine it's February, and our class is engaged in a three-week cycle of reading clubs that support and enhance our nonfiction reading unit. Talia and Max, two similar kinds of readers, choose the Birds Club in Week 1 because they want to learn more about birds. The next week of the cycle, they decide to focus specifically on pigeons because Max discovered there's a pigeon family living under his neighbor's air conditioner. He watches the pigeons from his bedroom window and tells Talia he wants to learn more about them. To create a new basket of texts to support their pigeon focus, Max and Talia skim their bird books and put sticky notes on the pigeon sections for easy access, and they relabel their club basket "Pigeon Research."

About a week and a half later, the class begins the third week of the nonfiction reading club cycle. Talia and Max decide to go in a whole different direction, mostly because Talia feels like it's her turn to choose. She's tired of studying birds, she tells Max, and so they choose the Human Body reading club. During these weeks of the cycle of nonfiction reading clubs, Max, Talia, and all of the other students are orchestrating strategies to read with power, using what they know about nonfiction reading to help them grow ideas about their topics, and learning the valuable lessons that you can read to learn about things you are interested in and that you can talk about your reading with a buddy.

In reading clubs, students tend to be matched with a partner who is at a very similar reading level and who has some similar interests, and, together, the partnership chooses which reading club they'll work in.

In reading clubs, students usually work with a partner who shares a similar reading level. Together, the students select a reading club that interests them and that contains the kinds of books they can read with accuracy, fluency, and comprehension. The partners make plans for the work they will do together, although the teacher offers guidance and suggestions, especially at first.

During reading club time, the partners may read a text together and talk about it, or they may decide to read texts separately and then get back together to talk about their texts. The partners may jot notes or use graphic organizers to keep track of their thinking, their ideas, and their work. There is much more information about instruction to support reading partnerships throughout the book, especially in Chapters 4 and 5.

Sometimes two sets of partners may select the same reading club basket. For this situation to work, there needs to be enough texts in the reading club basket for both partnerships to stay engaged. Usually, especially in kindergarten and first grade, the two partnerships tend to work separately, but they may end up talking together to share information, to clear up confusion, or to get ideas from each other. I've found that it's easier for older children to collaborate successfully across partnerships within a reading club than it is for our youngest readers, although this largely depends on the particular students involved and the support offered by the teacher.

The books in the reading club that the partners choose are at or very near the partners' independent reading level.

Students "need lots of books they can read right at their finger tips" (Allington 2001, 68), because in order to become stronger readers, students need to have as much time as possible with texts they can read with high levels of accuracy, fluency, and comprehension. What that means for reading clubs is that it's essential that most of the books in the reading club basket are at an accessible reading level for the partners working in the club.

Although we want students to choose their own reading clubs, sometimes we may need to guide them toward reading clubs containing books they can read well. As Sharon Taberski says, "We need to match children with books that are appropriate for their stage of reading" (2000, 63). During a character study one year, I remember having to gently direct Deanna and Reina away from the Junie B. Jones Club and toward the character study clubs that contained books written at levels they could read conventionally, with accuracy, fluency, and comprehension. Although they were disappointed at first, I explained to them that in order to do their best work and have the most fun, they needed to choose a club that had books they could read together. I briefly (and enthusiastically) introduced them to the characters in a couple of reading club baskets that were closer to their reading level.

While it's true that for the vast majority of reading club work, it's essential that students can read the books in the club with high levels of accuracy, fluency, and comprehension, there may be exceptions. In nonfiction reading clubs, there might be a book or two in the basket that would not be characterized as a just-right book (Routman 2003, 93). For example, the partners working in the Whale Club might find mostly accessible texts in their basket, but there also might be a book or two that the partners aren't able to read conventionally, such as a Dorling Kindersley book containing fascinating photographs and a grown-up layout. In situations like this, which usually happen during nonfiction clubs, we can teach students to be resourceful, using their prior knowledge and strategies to study illustrations and photographs to further their understanding of their topic.

In Appendix A, I offer suggestions for the kinds of texts that are found in a comprehensive classroom library and necessary for students to participate in reading clubs that capture their interests, pique their curiosity, and appeal to their ability and potential as readers.

Partners read and talk about the texts in their reading clubs, and then they share ideas, ponder questions, celebrate discoveries, develop theories, and so on.

In a reading club session, a visitor to the classroom would likely observe a high level of engagement in a variety of work. Visitors would observe partners talking about their books, or reading their books, or jotting ideas, questions, or thoughts on a variety of media—sticky notes, graphic organizers, and so on. Although there is no set recipe for how students have to approach their work in reading clubs, the teacher models things they can do during reading workshop mini-lessons and conferences, as well as during read-aloud time.

Although the students in each reading club might be working toward different purposes, there are typical ways they tend to approach their work together. In many cases, the partners might begin by reading a text in the basket by themselves and then talking about their texts with each other. Sometimes they might decide to read a text or portion of a text together, depending on the type of text and their purpose. In many classrooms, partners keep a folder in their reading club basket that contains their notes, plans, and other artifacts of their work.

In many clubs, just like in real life, the students might have an initial purpose in mind for their reading. ("Let's read and find out information about how dolphins take care of their babies.") In other clubs, also like real life, the students' areas of interest and lines of inquiry arise after they've read some of the texts. ("I've noticed that Poppleton sometimes acts crazy. Let's reread to figure out why.")

📖 *The work that students do in their reading clubs enables them to become experts about their topics and increases their comfort and familiarity with different kinds of texts and reading strategies.*

During a cycle of reading clubs, the whole class works in similar kinds of reading clubs that are connected by an overarching theme, purpose, or genre, although partnerships tend to choose a specific reading club based on their own interests, and also on the accessibility of the texts in the club. Students grow more familiar with different types of texts, different approaches to reading a text, and different purposes for rereading. They become more proficient at integrating reading strategies with authentic reading purposes and habits, which is one of our main goals as we implement reading clubs.

One of the primary intentions students have in reading clubs is to gain some sort of expertise about the topic of study. After all, partners choose a club of interest and are presented the opportunity to read multiple texts on a topic and talk about their ideas and wonderings with a partner. In many classrooms, the teacher tells students that careful readers often find ways to share their new learning or new ideas by doing something, making something, or presenting the information somehow. In reading clubs, the teacher tends not to assign specific culminating projects or tasks. Instead, she supports, encourages, guides, and sometimes even collaborates on the students' own plans for projects or actions. In Chapter 6, there is information about projects and celebrations.

📖 *During reading clubs, the teacher confers with reading club partners. The teacher actively supports and extends students' work by teaching them helpful strategies or by offering ideas for how to push their thinking further.*

During reading clubs, the teacher moves about the room conferring with partnerships in the same way as he or she would confer anytime during the reading workshop (Calkins 2001). The instruction offered during reading club conferences tends to teach reading strategies and habits of proficient readers. During conferences, the teacher may also help students make plans for their work, and she might show them a way they can keep track of their thinking and talking. The teacher may also support the partner conversations in order to nudge the talk and ideas to a higher level. There are several examples of reading club conferences in the upcoming chapters.

When engaged in a cycle of reading clubs, there is still time in the day devoted to independent reading. Reading clubs do not replace independent reading.

It's essential that students have as much time as possible to read books with fluency, accuracy, and comprehension, so my colleagues and I at the Teachers College Reading and Writing Project have figured out some options for fitting in reading clubs in addition to time for independent reading. These options are described in Chapter 2.

*   *   *

As you can see, the reading clubs described in this book differ from other structures that teachers typically implement to support reading instruction. Reading clubs are different from literacy centers or literacy work stations in which students are working on mostly teacher-initiated literacy tasks around the classroom while the teacher is conducting guided reading groups or alternative versions of small-group instruction. In reading clubs, students are reading and talking about books they *can* read, with their own intentions front and center while the teacher confers with them.

Reading clubs are different from what some teachers call "center time," during which groups of children across the room are engaged in a variety of work and play, from building with blocks to making art, from science investigations to math explorations, and much more. Reading clubs are centered on reading and talking about books and topics of interest.

Reading clubs as described in this book are not quite the same thing as literature circles or book clubs either, although they certainly have elements in common with these structures. In most versions of book clubs or literature circles, a group of students tends to read one book and talk about it, and then they move on to another text, which may or may not be connected in some way to the text they've just read.

It's important to say that the other structures I mentioned above, literacy centers, work stations, center time, literature circles, and book clubs, offer valuable support and important experiences for readers. My intention here is to simply add another idea to the vast collection of approaches and structures for teaching reading in ways that matter to our students' reading lives, as well as to their reading scores.

Why Add Reading Clubs to Everything i Already Do?

Implementing reading clubs at various times in the year is worth our while because they are a powerful component of a balanced literacy framework and offer unique opportunities for both teachers and students. For one thing, when we confer with our students during reading clubs, we are able to draw upon our real-life reading experiences to support and extend their work. In *By Different Paths to Common Outcomes*, Marie Clay writes about the power of personalizing our instruction and suggests that "instruction needs to meet an individual learner on a personal level whenever learning is challenging" (1998, 31). In reading clubs, our students are reading in ways that are closely related to the ways that proficient and enthusiastic readers approach their reading. Because we can connect with our students in profound and genuine ways as readers, our teaching can become more personal.

During reading clubs, we become more than our students' instructors, evaluators, timekeepers, or behavior managers. We become their reading mentors. I've heard Dr. Richard Allington talk of how critical it is for students to have relationships with richly literate adults, and through the structure of reading clubs, we are able to develop more intimate and rich reading relationships with the students in our classes. In reading clubs, it feels so natural to share joys and struggles, habits and helpful hints around literacy. I have come to see how much easier it is to connect our more experienced reading lives to our students' nascent reading lives when they are engaged in reading clubs.

There is yet another compelling reason to have cycles of reading clubs interspersed throughout the year: reading clubs provide opportunities for students to solidify their newly acquired reading skills and strategies by applying them in real-life "readerly" ways. What I deeply appreciate about reading clubs is that the work young readers do in them is very similar to the work that proficient, joyful readers do in real life: We do things like read a slew of books in a row by an author we have fallen in love with. We find books about building stone walls and compare the techniques they describe as we plan our own building project. We gather and swap books and magazines for brides and compare notes on the ideas in them with a friend who is planning a wedding at the same time. We follow a new interest in a genre and read science fiction for a few weeks straight. We use all we know about reading, all the strategies we've ever used and all the prior knowledge that we can apply, to understand the text in front of us.

How Are Reading Clubs Like Real-Life Reading?

At this point, it may be helpful to examine how the experience of students who are participating in a classroom reading club might mirror a particular real-life reading experience (see Figure 1.1). By laying these stories side by side, it is my intention to show how the work and purposes of reading clubs in school are very similar to the kinds of reading that many of us do in real life.

Figure 1.1	
Real Life Reading Club	**Classroom Reading Club**
Planning a Trip to Alaska	*Becoming an Expert On Insects*
Aaron, Ken, and Scott are going to Alaska over the summer. The first cycle of their "reading club" work is to create an itinerary. They cull through travel books to decide where they want to go in Alaska. They talk to people who've lived and traveled in Alaska to get recommendations. They compare and contrast information from different travel books and blogs to help them create an itinerary. After they decide where they're going, the work in their "reading club" changes a bit. Ken reads about Alaskan history and Native cultures; Aaron reads about Alaskan hiking and outdoor activities and looks into what they need to pack; Scott researches digital cameras because he wants to buy a great one for the trip. Aaron, Ken, and Scott talk about the information they've collected, and they trade texts back and forth. They start to pay attention to stories about Alaska in the newspaper and on the news, and Scott records a televised documentary about Alaska so they can watch it together. As their trip approaches, they begin looking at weather reports online, and they pack and repack their bags accordingly. All this reading and talking results in a fun-filled Alaskan adventure with no bear mishaps or camping disasters and lots and lots of beautiful pictures.	Dito and Margot are reading partners who decide to study insects in their nonfiction reading club. Their teacher has put together a basket of several books on insects that are at their reading level, and Dito and Margot decide to add another book to the collection because the photographs are so gory and fascinating! They talk about what kinds of things they want to learn about insects and make a plan for which books they'll start reading. After a day or two of reading and talking about lots of insects, Dito and Margot decide that they really want to learn more about ants because they believe that ants have a fascinating life, in comparison with other insects. They decide to reread the books in their club for information specific to ants, and they put sticky notes on the ant pages. Dito and Margot talk a lot about ant colonies and study the ant colony illustrations because that's what interests them most at this point. Dito asks his mom for an ant farm, and Margot and other kids try to build an ant colony in the block area of the classroom. One day during recess, Dito notices ants at the edge of the playground, and he runs to get Margot so they can do some ant research. They find two orange pylons and use them to block the area so kids won't stomp on the ants by accident.

The two scenarios in Figure 1.1, the real-life adult "reading club" and the in-school first-grade reading club, share some characteristics. First, for a period of time (either days or weeks), the readers are reading and talking about several texts that are related in some way. In these cases, the texts are connected by topic—for Aaron, Ken, and Scott, most all of the texts they are reading are about Alaska, and for Dito and Margot, the texts they focus on are about insects in general, and then ants specifically.

In both of these reading clubs, the readers' lives were affected by their reading. Aaron, Ken, and Scott read to help them make informed decisions and wise purchases for their trip to Alaska. Dito and Margot read to discover more about insects, a subject of interest to them. Their growing knowledge resulted in Dito's plans to raise ants in an ant farm and in Margot's plans to recruit friends to build a supersized model ant colony in the block area of the classroom. They both felt empowered enough to declare themselves ant researchers and to create a safe haven for ants on the playground.

Dito and Margot are learning very early on in their reading lives that a powerful chain reaction can begin with the words on a page. This is a priceless reading lesson, one that is more likely to create lifelong readers than any of our strategy or skill lessons. Of course, strategy and skill instruction is important because we need to teach our students to read well and to read with power. But we also need to teach them to value reading, to see how reading can feed their lives and fuel their hopes. These are the lessons that will keep our students reading with interest and enthusiasm well beyond their forty weeks in our classrooms, and these are the lessons they can learn in reading clubs.

How Reading Clubs Fit into the Day and Across the Year

I can easily recall the last few weeks of that summer before I began my first year of teaching. Let me just say that they were not restful or relaxing, nor were they restorative. I would wake up in the middle of the night, sweaty with terror. I had a recurring dream that it was the first day of school, but my classroom wasn't ready when my students arrived. In the typical version of this nightmare, I was usually dressed in running shorts and a ratty, old Yankees T-shirt with my hair pulled back into a messy ponytail while the children and their families arrived, all shiny and clean. I was moving tables and chairs from this spot to that spot, and I continually wiped my sweaty brow with my grimy forearm as I greeted my students. There's more to it, but I'll spare you. Let me just say it was horrifying and involved mice. I'd wake up looking like the figure in Edvard Munch's painting, *The Scream*. Show me the research that says dreams tend to last for only a few seconds. This one, I'm sure, lasted for hours.

The daytime version of this nightmare was a nagging worry about how I could possibly fill a whole day for first graders. You see, I had no experience with primary grades at that point. The first day of first grade would be the first time I spent a full day with students that young. My student-teaching experience took place in a high school for new arrivals to the United States. Consequently, I could fill forty-five minutes for teenage English language learners, but planning for a whole day for five- and six-year-olds—yikes!

When I drafted plans for that first day of school, I realized the actual challenge was not filling up the day. Instead the challenge was filling the time in worthwhile, meaningful ways until the three o'clock dismissal. I'd stretch things out, add a million little activities to the day, but no matter what I did, I struggled to get to three o'clock in a way that seemed to matter. I was worried.

Phew. Once school began, I quickly realized what a needless worry that was. As anyone who has taught for a minute would know, concerns about filling the day very quickly turn into struggles to fit in everything. Since that first year of teaching, my questions about scheduling the day have evolved from "How am I supposed to fill a whole day?" to "How do I fit everything in?" to "What is worth fitting in?" After all, as Lucy Calkins often reminds us, choosing to include something in our daily schedule is, by necessity, a choice to reject something else (2001).

Year in and year out, I've chosen to make reading clubs an important part of literacy instruction in my classroom. I value reading clubs, not just because they provide a structure in which students get the chance to orchestrate all they know about reading well, but also because reading clubs are one of the only structures that enables my students to apply what they've learned about reading in ways that closely resemble the reading people do in real life, outside the boundaries of school grounds and beyond the confines of class assignments. I believe that any chance we get to cut away at the imaginary paper wall that separates in-class reading and real-life reading is worth every minute of time it takes.

The structure of reading clubs has inherent characteristics that make it easy to implement in any classroom, whether or not you have an ongoing reading workshop (although it certainly helps to have an ongoing reading workshop); whether or not you are a kindergarten teacher, a third-grade teacher, or a teacher of any grade, really; whether or not your students are proficient readers or emergent readers; whether or not you are a very experienced teacher or a brand-new teacher; whether you live in a warm climate or not; whether you have vanity license plates or not; whether you wear your keys on a lanyard or not... I could keep going, but I'll stop to say that reading clubs are easy to implement in any classroom because they are flexible in two essential ways:

1. There's a variety of kinds of reading clubs to meet the needs of your students and your curriculum.

2. Reading clubs are easy to fit into a day and to schedule across the year.

Variety in Kind: The Wide World of Reading Clubs

There are many different reading clubs that we may implement in our classrooms, and this gives us plenty of flexibility and choice from year to year. In order to make wise decisions about what cycles of reading clubs to launch given the many options we have, it's essential to consider our students' strengths, needs, and interests, as well as the demands of the curriculum. In the following section, I describe three broad categories of reading clubs: genre-based reading clubs; reading power reading clubs; and healthy habits reading clubs. Specific kinds of reading clubs within these categories and ideas for instruction will be elaborated upon in Chapters 7 through 9.

Genre-Based Reading Clubs

In many of our classrooms, we spend time throughout the year engaged in genre studies during reading workshop. After all, when we consider the characteristics of well-rounded or avid readers, it's most likely the case that they read a variety of genres with proficiency and interest. Of course, an avid reader may have a genre of choice, yet he is likely to be versatile enough to read and enjoy other genres.

In the classroom, many of our students "lock in" to particular genres. Many teachers notice that once students are able to read chapter books, they rarely look at anything else. Picture books might seem too babyish compared to text-dense chapter books; poetry might seem insubstantial compared to the number of pages in a chapter book, and nonfiction might not hold a child's interest as much as a character from the chapter book series they are reading at a particular moment in time.

Of course, we don't want to rip a genre of choice from a child's hands and say, "You will read poetry, and you will enjoy it. Got it?" What we do want our students to know is that there is a wide range of genres in the world of text, and it's important that they know how to deal with them. We could also tell them if they enjoy reading chapter books that have a main character who is a boy their age, they can also find pleasure in reading *Nathaniel Talking*, a book of poems by Eloise Greenfield, for example.

Some typical genres that teachers most often study in their classrooms through the structure of reading groups are the following:

· nonfiction

· poetry

· fairy tales/folktales

· mystery books

· concept books

· biographies

In Chapter 7, I'll provide more information about launching and planning genre-based reading clubs.

Reading Power Reading Clubs

I call another category of reading clubs "reading power reading clubs." I willingly acknowledge this is a clumsy and vague title, and if I had time and $500,000 in prize money to offer, I'd be tempted to launch a nationwide contest to name this category. For now, anyway, "reading power reading clubs" will do because it does act as a unifying term for the kinds of reading club cycles that I have put together in this category. Each of the cycles of these reading clubs may be quite different from one another, yet they do share a big characteristic: they're designed so that students use all of their reading skills to dig into their texts and to read and talk about their books with greater focus and deeper comprehension.

Within the upper-grade reading curriculum developed at the Teachers College Reading and Writing Project, this kind of reading has been called "close-in reading." The reading clubs in this category provide instruction to teach even our youngest readers how to read in a close-in way so that they can move beyond surface-level comprehension, retelling, and plot summaries.

The following are some examples of reading club cycles that are part of this category:

· Readers care about the characters in their books (character clubs).

· Readers notice, talk about, and think about themes in their books (theme-based reading clubs).

· Readers find series they love (series book clubs).

· Readers have authors they love (author study clubs).

The reading clubs in this category will be discussed in more detail in Chapter 8.

Healthy Reading Habits Reading Clubs

The reading clubs that are part of this category are designed specifically to help students transfer all they know about reading to the reading they do when they are outside of our classrooms. The objective in these reading clubs is to teach students how to be active readers who create and maintain their own vibrant, unique reading lives, rather than passive readers who rely on class assignments and reading homework to keep their reading lives going.

These are the reading clubs that I envision to be part of this category:

· Readers set their goals to become stronger at reading (reading goals clubs).

· Readers invent their own reading projects that affect their lives (reading project clubs).

This category of reading clubs differs from the other two categories in one fundamental way, which also makes them a bit more challenging when planning instruction. These reading clubs are not whole-class studies in the same way that genre-based reading clubs and reading power reading clubs are.

In other words, during these healthy habits reading clubs, each set of partners might be doing very different kinds of reading work. One year, during reading goals clubs, I had four students who wanted to learn more about particular topics, four students who wanted to become experts about the body of work of particular authors, two students who wanted to put together their own anthologies of poetry, four students who wanted to read all the books in particular series, two students who wanted to make their own Top Ten Lists of Favorite Books for Six-Year-Olds, and so on. The thing that unifies these healthy habits reading clubs is that all of the students are working on getting better at something as readers, even though their purposes and work may be very diverse from one partnership to the next. The challenge for teachers, then, is to develop plans for whole-class instruction that will matter to everyone.

Compare this with a nonfiction reading club cycle, for example, in which all the students are reading and thinking and talking about nonfiction texts. The teacher plans whole-class lessons to support everyone's work in nonfiction even though each set of partnerships might be studying a different nonfiction topic. Similarly, during a character study reading club cycle, all of the students have selected a character about whom they will become a sort of expert. Again, during a character study, the teacher will teach everyone how careful readers get to know their characters well, and so on, even though the students are all getting to know a different character (who lives in books at the students' just-right reading levels). During these reading clubs, all of the partnerships are engaged in similar kinds of work, even though the details of their club topic may be different from one another. We call these whole-class studies because all of the reading clubs are connected by an overarching whole-class topic, such as nonfiction, character study, thematic study, fairy tales, and so on.

Over the years, I've tended to save the healthy habits clubs for the end of the year in order to capitalize on my students' greater capacity for independent work. In Chapter 9, I'll offer details about how to plan for and what to teach in these healthy habits reading clubs.

Reasons to Use a Variety of Reading Clubs

As a final note about the variety of kinds of reading clubs, I would like to suggest that over the course of a school year, it makes sense to launch at least one cycle of reading clubs from each of the three categories. There are a couple of reasons I make this suggestion. First, each of the three categories offers different experiences for our students: the genre-based reading clubs expose them to genres they may or may not pick up on their own; the reading power clubs teach students ways to dig into their texts to deepen their understanding; and the healthy habits clubs allow students to have quite a bit of ownership over their reading. Second, for teachers, the experience of launching one cycle of reading clubs within a particular category makes launching any cycle of reading clubs within that category much easier, because there are similarities in the ways we approach reading clubs within a specific category.

The Importance of Flexibility

Every year, I launched a cycle of poetry reading clubs in the spring. I chose to do this based on my own interest in poetry, my students' enthusiasm for writing poetry, and my school's annual Poetry Month. One year, however, instead of launching poetry clubs as I usually did, I chose, at almost the last moment, to launch a cycle of author study reading clubs instead.

The idea to toss aside my plans for poetry reading clubs developed as I noticed how fixated my students were on particular authors during interactive read-aloud time. They wanted me to read aloud (and then reread) every text written by Ezra Jack Keats, Kevin Henkes, and Mem Fox, to name a few. If a new book came out by one of their favorite authors, my students begged me to read it aloud to them. When I would finish reading the new book, it was like my students had just finished a sublime meal. There was a brief moment where they sat quietly. They seemed blissfully sated, as if they were savoring a veritable feast provided by their beloved author.

One time, Julie brought in a wizened copy of *Pet Show* by Ezra Jack Keats that she found at a stoop sale. (A stoop sale is a Park Slope, Brooklyn, version of a garage sale or yard sale.) With much fanfare, Julie showed the book to everyone. It was such a celebrated discovery that you would have thought she had dug up the intact teeth and jawbones of a Tyrannosaurus Rex right there in our Brooklyn neighborhood. My students asked—no, actually, they demanded—that I put aside our chapter book for that day and instead read aloud *Pet Show* during read-aloud time. I resisted slightly (just to have a little teacher fun), but I was privately enchanted by their persistence. At that point, I decided I would find a way to capitalize on my students' passion for Ezra Jack Keats by launching a whole-class author study and a cycle of author study reading clubs instead of the poetry study that I had originally planned to do. So, this was a year that I chose to put aside poetry reading clubs in order to fit in a cycle of author study reading clubs. I share this story to show the flexibility we have and the ability to be very responsive to the idiosyncrasies of each class due to the wide variety of reading clubs from which we can choose. The chapters in Part III offer detailed suggestions about how to launch a variety of reading clubs.

Flexibility in Scheduling: Almost Any Time of the Year is the Right Time for Reading Clubs

Within the large community of teachers who regularly implement reading clubs in their classrooms, I know at least a dozen different ways teachers have scheduled them throughout the year. In my own classroom, I've tended to spread out reading clubs across the year in the way illustrated by Figure 2.1.

Figure 2.1		
Time of Year	**What Kind of Reading Club Cycle?**	**How Long Did the Cycle Last?**
Mid-October	Concept books/ABC books	Two Weeks-ish*
February-ish	Nonfiction	Three Weeks-ish
March-ish	Character	Two Weeks-ish
April–May-ish	Poetry or author study	Two Weeks-ish
June	Reading projects/reading goals	One to Two Weeks
* As you know, -ish represents approximation and variation based on each year's idiosyncrasies.		

Reading clubs are flexible because they can be condensed into a brief two-week cycle or stretched out into a four-week cycle. How long they last depends on a variety of factors, including the curricular unit in which we implement them and our students' strengths, needs, and interests as readers. In my classroom, a cycle of nonfiction reading clubs typically lasted about four weeks, which tended to be the longest cycle of any kind of reading clubs. My students always exhibited incredible energy for nonfiction reading, and there were many different ways that I could approach nonfiction clubs. In contrast, whenever my class engaged in author study clubs, they tended to last no longer than two weeks.

Although Figure 2.1 shows how I typically scheduled reading clubs in my classroom across the school year, I think it's important to say that I would not hesitate to vary the kinds of clubs and the timing of them from year to year, depending on the students in my class. For example, if I had a class full of strong first-grade readers who were able to read books at high levels, I might implement character reading clubs earlier in the school year, perhaps in December, because my students would be reading books with a bit more character development, presumably. I would then consider doing a series books reading club cycle in March. During these series books reading clubs, I would guide my reading club partnerships toward series books at a level that is just right for them or slightly higher, especially if I scaffold their reading by providing a book introduction (Fountas and Pinnell 1996) and an introduction to the series itself.

If I had many students who were struggling readers, I could schedule a reading club cycle called Getting Stronger as Readers in place of, or in addition to, the other reading clubs listed in the chart. During this type of reading club cycle, my students would be part of clubs designed to work on what is challenging them most as readers, such as a Reading Like a Storyteller club to work on fluency or a Building Reading Stamina and Focus club for those students who are beginning to read longer books that tend to have more characters and multiple story lines, or a Super Word-Solvers club for those students who need more work with word-solving strategies.

It's important to make clear that if I had many students who were struggling as readers, these reading clubs would not be their only source of support or guidance. In conjunction with the Getting Stronger as Readers clubs, I would, of course, meet with my students in guided reading groups and provide strategy lessons. I would utilize everything at my disposal, including shared reading, interactive writing, one-to-one conferences, small-group instruction, and so on, to offer them the instruction they need to grow stronger as readers.

Ease in Daily Implementation: Fitting in Reading Clubs

One of the most advantageous characteristics of reading clubs is we can easily fit them into the day without having to move or cut out other components of balanced literacy or other content areas. I tended to tuck cycles of reading clubs into the reading workshop by temporarily replacing existing partner reading time with reading club time.

In order to accommodate a cycle of reading clubs, I altered the typical format for my reading workshop. I tried different things with varying success, and I've found that it's easiest and works best to temporarily replace regular partner reading with reading clubs. This isn't an enormous change to the routine or flow of the reading workshop. Figure 2.2 shows a few options for how teachers might rearrange their reading workshop when they are engaged in a cycle of reading clubs.

Figure 2.2

A Typical Reading Workshop (with no reading clubs in place)	A Reading Workshop During a Cycle of Reading Clubs: Option A	A Reading Workshop During a Cycle of Reading Clubs: Option B
Mini-lesson 5–10 minutes *Independent reading time* Also known as private reading time; students read individually while the teacher confers with individuals or instructs small groups of readers. *Mid-workshop instruction* 1 minute or so during which the teacher calls for students' attention and offers strategy support, reminders, encouragement, etc. *Partner reading time* Students meet with partners to read and talk about books while the teacher confers with partnerships or instructs small groups of readers. *Teaching share time* 5 minutes or less	*Mini-lesson that supports reading club work* 5–10 minutes *Reading clubs* The students work with reading club partners while teacher confers with partnerships; students may read together or read independently and then meet to talk about texts. *Teaching share time* Five minutes or less spent sharing student work from reading clubs. *Individual reading time* Also known as private reading time; students read individually while the teacher confers with individuals or instructs small groups of readers.	*Abbreviated mini-lesson* This lasts a few minutes at most and is meant mostly to rally students to have a successful and focused reading time. *Individual reading time* Also known as private reading time; students read individually while the teacher confers with individuals or instructs small groups of readers. *Mini-lesson that supports reading club work* 5–10 minutes *Reading clubs* The students work with reading club partners while the teacher confers with partnerships; students may read together or read independently and then meet to talk about texts. *Teaching share time* 5 minutes or less spent sharing student work from reading clubs

There are other options in addition to those shown in Figure 2.2, including the choice to split the reading workshop into two distinct parts that occur separately in the day. In this case, one portion of reading workshop is composed of a mini-lesson and independent reading time during which the teacher confers as students read their just-right books. This tends to happen in the morning. Then, usually in the afternoon, the reading club portion of the workshop occurs. It begins with a mini-lesson to support reading club work and is followed by reading clubs and share time.

No matter how reading clubs are scheduled in the day, one thing that all of the options have in common is that students still have independent reading time with their just-right books. Maximizing the amount of time students spend reading these books is essential and nonnegotiable; private reading time when students are reading their just-right books as the teacher confers with individuals or small groups happens every single day, even when cycles of reading clubs are occurring. It's worth repeating that we try to make sure that even during reading club cycles, our young readers are spending as much time as possible reading books that are just right for them.

When Is the Right Time for Reading Clubs?

Because reading clubs are not an ongoing, daily structure throughout the school year, I consider reading clubs as more of a seasonal offering. Teachers tend to implement them strategically at different points of the school year on an as-needed or as-desired basis. When you plan the times of the year when you'll launch a cycle of reading clubs, there are some helpful things that you'll want to consider:

Reading clubs fit well into various studies.

There are a variety of reasons for scheduling reading clubs at particular times in the year. Reading clubs can enhance or complement the reading, thinking, and talking work that students do in certain studies or units.

As I look across the year of teaching reading, I want to think about the studies that seem to be a natural match for a cycle of reading clubs, specifically the studies in which reading clubs can enhance the work students do. When planning for a nonfiction reading study, for example, I always include reading clubs in my plans. During a nonfiction study, I want to make sure that I not only teach my students the strategies they need to read nonfiction well, but also teach them about the pathways that nonfiction readers take in order to become experts about topics of interest. I rely on nonfiction reading clubs to provide my students with authentic purposes to read nonfiction texts and opportunities to talk about what they've learned, what they wonder, and what they think about the topic. Actually, this rationale for implementing reading clubs during a nonfiction study holds true for most any genre-based unit of study, whether it's nonfiction or biography, poetry or mystery books, and so on. For many studies, I find that implementing reading clubs provides students with an opportunity to read texts of interest for authentic, self-directed purposes, using all the skills and strategies they're learning about reading and book talks.

Reading clubs can also complement the work that we're doing in particular studies by offering balance to the study's content. When we spend time in the reading workshop emphasizing print strategies or the "in one's mind" work of reading, I find that putting reading clubs into our workshop helps my students remember to talk and grow ideas about their books in addition to figuring out the words.

Typically at some point during October, when I tend to spend a lot of time teaching my students strategies to figure out words in mini-lessons, during shared reading, and so on, I would notice that highly engaged book talks seemed to fade out of view. My students were focusing closely on figuring out the words in their books, sometimes to the exclusion of having big thoughts about the stories. At this time, it was helpful to put a cycle of reading clubs into place. I would usually launch a reading club cycle that focused on alphabet books, or ABC books, as my students called them. It's true that most of my first graders would know the alphabet and letter/sound relationships by this time, but my objective here wasn't alphabet recitation or letter/sound practice. My intent was to get my students talking well and excitedly about books again, and ABC books offer lots of talk and big idea potential.

My students would spend time figuring out characteristics of the genre of ABC books, making comparisons among books, reading the words and using all the clues the illustrations, book theme, and context offer when the words are tricky. In this case, the ABC reading clubs complemented the work my students were doing during a particular study in reading workshop.

Reading clubs energize the reading workshop and the other components of a balanced literacy framework.

Another reason I would decide to schedule reading clubs at particular times of the year was because they have a rejuvenating effect on our students' approach to their reading. We have to admit that there are times of the year when, at best, our students go through the motions of the reading routines in our classrooms—or when, at worst, the routines fall apart.

It helps enormously that the work readers do in reading clubs tends to be purpose driven. In other words, students aren't reading just-right books simply because it's "what they do" during reading. In reading clubs, the partners read books that have been gathered because they connect in some way, and the students themselves figure out the work they want to do with them. For example, during our ABC book clubs, some of the plans my students made included the following:

· figuring out the trick of ABC books (i.e., trying to find all of the items on the page that start with the letter of that page)

· comparing and contrasting ABC book structure (i.e., noticing that some books used only uppercase letters, some used both upper- and lowercase, some put X, Y, Z on the same page, etc.)

· categorizing different kinds of ABC books (i.e., piles of ABC books that give information, ABC books that have animals, ABC books with tricks in them, etc.)

· studying wordless ABC books (i.e., trying to figure out what the words on each page would be and putting sticky notes on the pages with their ideas)

· singing the ABC song while reading the texts and tracing the letters with their fingers

Because students make their own plans and invent their own purposes for their reading work (sometimes with a teacher's gentle nudging, of course), there is a high level of engagement during reading clubs. Many teachers notice that after a cycle of reading clubs, the reading workshop is revitalized because students transfer the energy and sense of purpose they experienced in reading clubs into the other reading opportunities we provide our students.

Reading clubs strengthen and deepen students' book talks.

Reading clubs are perfect antidotes to low-energy, low-motivation downturns during partner reading time in the reading workshop. There are times of the year, usually after the first few months of school, when we observe and confer with reading partners, and it seems as if students are merely cooperating but not collaborating much to grow ideas about their books. You may notice this when you kneel down to listen in to reading partners' conversations, and the talk follows the same pattern day after day. You'll hear things like, "Retell your book first, and then

I'll retell mine," or "Show me the most important part of your book, and I'll show you mine," or "Let's read this together and then talk about it," or even "Show me the part that made you think that." It's not that these are bad ways of talking, but after the first month or two of school these ways of working together might be just a kids' version of "the same ol' same ol'." It's these times when a cycle of reading clubs can add a little fuel injection to the partner work.

The very nature of reading clubs helps students talk well (or better) about books. During a cycle of reading clubs, the partners dig into books that go together in some way, so there are many connections and comparisons they can make across books. These connections and comparisons offer a concrete base from which students can develop theories, ponder questions, and grow new ideas.

In reading clubs, the books are all connected in some way, so the reading partners can make plans for their reading and thinking work that often continues for days. For example, during a cycle of character study reading clubs, the partnership trying to get to know Poppleton might decide to reread several of the books to figure out whether or not Cherry Sue is really Poppleton's best friend. As they reread, they make a plan to focus on Poppleton's friendships, and they are energized whenever they find evidence that helps them answer their question about whether or not Poppleton and Cherry Sue are best buddies. Across the room, another partnership is reading Biscuit books to find evidence to prove their idea that Biscuit is a good puppy. At the next table over in the Junie B. Jones Club, the partners decide to compare the causes of Junie's trouble across books to see whether there is a pattern of behavior. In reading clubs, the partners can set purposes for their reading more easily, because the books go together in some way.

In contrast, during regular reading partner time when reading clubs are not in place, partners meet daily and bring their independent reading books together. The books in their independent reading baggies will tend to connect in just one way: they will all be at or near the same level. Other than that, the books may not have much in common at all. For instance, Kadeem and Jonathan were partners, and their combined books had a range of topics, so their talks tended to be more book specific and brief, rather than idea based and deep. Now, this is not to say that regular reading partners can't have strong book talks. I'm simply suggesting that the nature of reading clubs offers support mechanisms that enable students to talk well about books. Just the fact that the books in a reading club go together in some way serves to support and scaffold students' conversations. For these reasons, many teachers use a cycle of reading clubs to ratchet up the books talks, and then when the students resume regular partner reading after the reading club cycle has ended, they will have set higher standards for themselves with regard to book talks within partnerships.

Of course, reading clubs alone can't spark powerful conversations. Teaching students to talk well about books is an all-day, everyday enterprise. We model good conversations, teaching the form (etiquette) and the content of strong talk across the day, during interactive read-aloud and shared reading, through formal and informal conversations with students in the morning, after lunch, at recess, and so on. In Chapter 5, I offer some ideas for supporting talk for reading club partnerships.

Final Thoughts on Fitting Reading Clubs into the Classroom

My hope is that this chapter showed that reading clubs are easily integrated into a reading curriculum. Reading clubs are not an ongoing, daily part of reading workshop, and teachers often plan to do four or five cycles of reading clubs per school year in coordination with particular parts of the curriculum. If a cycle of reading clubs usually lasts for two or three weeks, that's about fifteen weeks of the school year at most. Rest assured, you can still teach math if you're also adding reading clubs to your literacy instruction. Reading clubs are an incredibly malleable structure that provides opportunities for our students to apply the reading, thinking, and talking skills and strategies they are learning in ways that closely match the reading work that proficient and avid readers do with text outside of the classroom. For more information about the details of implementing reading clubs, please check the study guide materials in Appendix I.

Focusing on
Reading Club Fundamentals

I'm writing this book in the loft of a beautiful house. The walls are full of artwork, and the large windows are full of views of the Chugach Mountains and the big, dramatic Alaskan sky. On most days as I write, my mouth waters from the scent of spice-rich desserts or artisan breads baking in the kitchen below. In many ways, this is my dream home. Okay, so it's not my home!

Ayse Gilbert, a family friend, invited me to use space in her home to write. This is a good thing, because I can't work at my own house, what with mounds of laundry growing in baskets, piles of bills and to-do lists pointing their fingers at me, phone calls to return . . . oh, yeah, and a three-year-old and a five-year-old. So it is with great pleasure that I show up at the Gilberts' home a few mornings a week for a few hours at a time. I make some tea and then sit myself down to write and stare.

Ayse is known around town as an amazing cook. Sometimes, if she's in the kitchen when I'm brewing my tea, I'll ask her a question about cooking. The other day we talked about immersion blenders. I confided that one of my well-worn excuses for not cooking often is that I don't have the right gadgets. Truth be told, one of my secret pleasures is to lie in bed thumbing through a Williams-Sonoma catalog and thinking, "If only I had that Dutch oven, in Sonoma green, preferably, I would definitely make a savory stew," or "Until I have one of those deluxe angled potato ricers, I will not dare to make mashed potatoes!"

As we talked about kitchen gadgets and essential kitchen tools, Ayse told me to open a drawer in the cabinet behind me. I opened it to find only about four gadgets in it. "Now, look in the drawer below," she said. Again, less than a half-dozen cooking tools. She said that she regularly uses only a handful of tools when she cooks, whether it's a meal for her family or a fund-raiser dinner for seventy-five people. The humbling lesson I learned from Ayse that day is that it's not necessary to have every cooking gadget under the sun, even if they look so cool and necessary and come in beautiful colors. Although, after our talk, I realized I must get a Microplane grater (with a cool design) because it can be used in many ways: to zest the skin of a lemon for a fruit tart, to grate Parmesan cheese over a dish of pasta, or to shave dark chocolate onto the top of a fancy birthday cake.

This idea that the most impressive and efficient cooks often rely on just a handful of essential, multiuse kitchen tools resonated because I could see a clear connection with teaching. As a teacher, there are certain kinds of instruction that are essential and multipurpose and serve as vital tools in a teacher's repertoire for reading clubs.

In the chapters of Part II, I share ideas for multiuse instruction helpful in whatever kind of reading clubs you plan to cook up in your classroom.

Effective Teaching Practices for Reading Clubs

It's one thing to set a schedule for implementing reading clubs at points during a yearlong reading curriculum, but it's quite another to make plans for the daily instruction that occurs within a cycle of reading clubs, especially when each cycle of reading clubs involves quite different texts, talk, skills, and habits. To make planning easier and to keep priorities for reading clubs in the foreground, it's helpful to first consider some of the background that all kinds of reading clubs have in common. First, we want to make sure that we're teaching with the best practices for instruction in mind so that we can most effectively support our students. Second, we want to consider the skills, strategies, and habits for reading and for talking about texts that our students will need in order to do their best work.

We Rely on the Best Practices for Teaching

The teaching we do in reading clubs adheres to what are widely considered to be some of the best practices in reading instruction:

- teach skills, strategies, and habits through demonstration and modeling
- maximize students' time with books they can read with high levels of fluency, accuracy, comprehension, and interest
- provide time for students to have self-initiated and self-maintained talks about books
- balance whole-class, small-group, and one-to-one instruction

We Teach Through Demonstration and Modeling

"Children learn from what is demonstrated to them, from what they see others doing" (Smith 1988, 55). During whole-class mini-lessons, small-group instruction, and conferences with partnerships, there are built-in opportunities to model what we want to see our students doing on their own. Additionally, "explicit modeling and gradual release of responsibility can be applied to whole-class teaching, small-group teaching, or individual interactions" (Johnson 2006, 9).

In a mini-lesson, we tend to state the teaching point and then say, "Let me show you what that looks like," before demonstrating exactly what we want to see our students doing (Calkins 2001). We can use this demonstration technique in any format, whether we're teaching the whole group, a small group, or working with a partnership during a reading conference.

Demonstration teaching is different than narrating what we want our students to do. Compare the two excerpts, shown in Figure 3.1, from a mini-lesson during a cycle of fairy tale reading clubs in a kindergarten class. These excerpts are intended to teach the children to study the illustrations to help them figure out the characters' thoughts and feelings. One is an example of demonstration teaching, and the other is an example of narration.

Figure 3.1	
Teaching with Demonstration	**Teaching with Narration**
So, today I want to teach you that careful readers really study the pictures of the characters to figure out what the characters might be thinking and feeling. Watch me while I do this: I'm going to read the picture in this version of Cinderella because I want to figure out what she might be feeling in this part. Watch me. (The teacher thinks aloud, actually using the strategy in real time the way the students could use it, too.) Hmm, Cinderella isn't smiling here. Her face looks sad, so I'm wondering if she's sad. Hmm, look at her shoulders. They're slumped down. I think she's really bummed out because this is the part where she thinks she won't get to go to the ball. She looks like she's sad and probably really disappointed. Okay, so readers, did you notice how I really studied the picture of Cinderella to get more information about how she might be feeling in this part? I looked really closely at her face to see her expression. I looked really closely at her body to see if her gestures gave me information. When I did this, did you see how I was able to say, "I think Cinderella looks sad, and she's probably disappointed too that she couldn't go to the ball"?	So, today I want to teach you that careful readers really study the pictures of the characters to figure out what the characters might be thinking and feeling. When you look at the characters in the pictures, look at their faces really closely to see what the facial expression is. Look at this illustration of Cinderella. See her face? Look at the body gestures too. Look at Cinderella's shoulders all slumped over. Sometimes gestures, like slumped shoulders, can tell us stuff. Turn and tell your partner what you think Cinderella is feeling in this picture. (Kids turn and talk about illustration.) Okay, so remember to look at the pictures closely, study the characters' faces and their body language because that will help you figure out how they might be feeling or what they might be thinking.

Although these are excerpts from a mini-lesson taught to the whole class, the demonstration teaching here could easily be replicated during a strategy lesson for a small group of children or within a reading conference with a pair of partners. Some characteristics of demonstration teaching include the following:

· The teacher does what he wants his students to do or uses the strategy he wants the student to control; he uses materials in the demonstration that are similar to the materials the students use.

· The teacher thinks aloud about what she's doing as she demonstrates.

· The teacher shows students what to do/how to do something; she doesn't simply tell them or list directions for the task.

· A phrase that cues a demonstration might be something like, "Watch me as I try this," or something more specific like, "I'm going to read this page. Watch how I try several strategies to figure out a tricky word that I'll encounter."

The next part of the sample mini-lesson excerpt would be to provide students with opportunities for guided practice, or active engagement, right there in the middle of the mini-lesson. Having students try the strategy in the moment that follows the demonstration portion of the lesson enables the teacher to do a quick assessment to see who gets it and who might need more support. It also provides students an experience with the skill or strategy in the moment because they may or may not need to use that particular strategy in their own work that day, or for many days for that matter (Calkins 2006).

We Keep the Level of Texts in Mind and Match Students to Books They Can Read

One spring, during a cycle of reading clubs in our unit of study on characters, my instructional plans had to account for several very strong first-grade readers as well as those children in my class who were struggling. The types of character clubs available for students to choose from acknowledged the range of readers in my classroom. I had two sets of partners who chose to read Judy Moody books. At the other end of the continuum of readers, my students chose among the Mrs. Wishy-Washy Club, Biscuit Club, and the Moms Club. This Moms Club didn't have a true character like the other clubs because I took lower-level texts that had moms in the stories and gathered them into a basket. The students studied the moms in these books in much the same way that the other students studied their characters. One of my big goals is to have enough satisfying reading club options so that all of my students, from the strongest to the most struggling, participate in reading clubs in which they can read the books with comfort and interest. And when they encounter text difficulties, they are likely to "own" the strategies that will help them overcome the challenges.

As important as it is to make sure that students can read most of the books in their reading clubs, there also may be compelling reasons to allow students to have a difficult, yet high-interest, text as part of their reading club basket. As I mentioned earlier, I tend to let my students keep a higher difficulty, high-interest text or two in their reading club basket during nonfiction reading clubs.

One year during a nonfiction study, Jonah and John gathered books about outer space for their nonfiction reading club. They found several books that were at their just-right reading level for nonfiction, but they also wanted to include an eyewitness-type of book on space that had amazing photographs and an engaging layout. Although they wouldn't be able to read the text conventionally, I did view the book as worthwhile because they could "read" and interpret the photographs, illustrations, and other graphics, as well as use the text features to find information.

In fact, John and Jonah did just that. They would look between photographs of the planets in the different books and make up theories about why some of the planets are so colorful and why some are "pretty boring looking." They used the index to find the sections about asteroids and comets, and so on. Although they weren't using their print strategies in this text to read with accuracy, I would still argue that Jonah and John were doing resourceful, purposeful, and very worthwhile work as they moved between this book and the others, reading the texts, studying photographs and illustrations, and making connections and comparisons.

The idea of making sure that reading club baskets are filled with mostly books the students can comfortably read leads us to consider another aspect of reading clubs: the partnerships. I think it makes sense that during reading clubs the partnerships are mostly ability based (Collins 2004). If our partners share similar reading levels and their reading club basket contains texts that are just right for them, then both partners have equal access to the texts in the reading club, and neither partner becomes dominant by virtue of having more of the reading power. There is more information about reading club partnerships in Chapter 5.

We Provide Opportunities for Student-Initiated Talks About Books

"Children of all ages, preschool to high school, need frequent opportunities to formulate their thoughts in spoken language... Children need to ask their questions, to explain things to other children, to negotiate meanings between themselves and other children, and between themselves and adults" (Clay 1998, 28). In order for our students to talk well about books with each other, we need to provide ongoing modeling of good conversational habits, and we need to hold the belief that even our youngest students can and will be invested in book talks that they initiate on their own. This sense of trust is critical because without it, we'll tend to hover over their book talks by assigning talk topics, and we'll continue to worry that without our presence, our students won't have high-quality conversations about books.

During reading clubs, students tend to have a purpose in mind as they read, and these purposes often drive the talk between partners. Even though the whole class might be engaged in nonfiction reading clubs, each partnership is engaged in their own nonfiction reading club topic (although sometimes two or three partnerships may be part of the same reading club). For this reason, it is a necessity that the students' talk arises from their own work together rather than in response to a whole-group prompt. For example, during an author study, each reading club partnership is becoming an expert about a particular author, but each might have a different focus for their thinking and talking about their particular author. It would be virtually impossible for a teacher to direct or prompt or mandate the content of everyone's talk by saying something like, "Readers, today your job is to talk about where you think your author got his or her ideas." Of course, we can teach them that this is a possibility for their talk about an author because, after all, if we think of adult readers, we know that people often talk about where an author may have gotten his or her ideas for a text.

What teachers can do to support reading club talk is to teach students the characteristics of strong conversations throughout the day and to teach students a repertoire of things readers can talk about, without mandating what they must talk about. There is more information about how to support students' talk in Chapters 5 and 6.

We Balance Large-Group, Small-Group, and One-to-One Instruction

During reading clubs, we have several ways to convey strategy and skill instruction. We teach students in whole-class mini-lessons, in small-group settings, and during reading conferences with partnerships. Typically, a reading club session begins with a whole-group mini-lesson (Calkins 2001). We try to keep this as brief as possible so that students get maximum reading time, but also because there is no way that a whole-class lesson can ever be perfectly gauged for the immediate needs of every reader in the classroom. Even so, a mini-lesson is an efficient way to transmit information, and for both instructional and community purposes, it's worth our while to gather our students for a brief mini-lesson before sending them off to their own independent reading work.

After the mini-lesson, our students will go off to places around the room with their reading club partners to read and talk about their books. During that time, the teacher offers instruction to students in a couple of ways: through reading conferences with partnerships or through small-group instruction, usually in the form of guided reading or strategy lessons.

Maximizing the Impact of Instruction

Although our conferences, mini-lessons, small-group instruction, and teaching share time for reading clubs are very similar in structure and tone to our conferences, mini-lessons, small-group instruction, and teaching share time at other times of the day, there are some things to consider that will maximize their impact for students' reading club work.

Whole-Class Mini-Lessons

No matter what my teaching emphasis is during cycles of reading clubs, I have found that it's very helpful to teach mini-lessons as if I were participating in a reading club myself. Many of us have found that when we demonstrate skills and strategies using texts from one of the actual reading club baskets during mini-lessons, we provide our students with demonstrations that are closely connected to the work they will do in their own clubs.

There are a couple of things worth considering when choosing which reading club basket you'll use as your demonstration club for mini-lessons. One year, during a nonfiction reading club cycle, I selected the Ants Research Club for demonstration because Reina and Deanna, two of my most challenged readers, had chosen to be in the Ants Research Club that week. By modeling strategies with texts from their reading club, I offered them more support and helped to jump-start their work together. Also, while I demonstrated from the Ants Research Club during mini-lessons, I noticed an extra benefit that I hadn't originally considered. Over the course of the week, as I used the texts from their basket for teaching demonstrations, I was, in effect, giving Reina and Deanna book introductions (Fountas and Pinnell 1996). Then when Deanna and Reina went to their reading club after the mini-lesson, they would often begin by replicating the work I demonstrated, which helped them get started right away and stay focused.

On the other hand, you may decide to select a neutral club, one that no students are working in, to be your demonstration club. When we demonstrate from a reading club basket that no partnerships have chosen for the current week, that reading club basket becomes a more appealing option for the next week. In some ways, it's as if we're offering previews and doing publicity for the books in that basket. Also, in the case of nonfiction, your students can easily become experts about two topics when you pick a neutral club: the topic they've chosen to study in their own club and the one you've chosen to use as your demonstration club for mini-lessons.

Reading Conferences During Reading Clubs

After the mini-lesson, my students leave the whole-class meeting area to go to their reading club spot. After giving them a quick moment to settle in, I move around the room to conduct reading conferences with partnerships (Anderson 2000, Calkins 2001, Goldberg and Serravallo 2007). We use reading conferences to offer precise instruction that's fine-tuned to an individual's or a partnership's needs. This direct instruction is efficient teaching that will have immediate and long-lasting effects on young readers.

Conferences are often characterized as instruction delivered in a personal, intimate way, yet we can also use the details of our conferences with a particular partnership in ways that serve the good of the whole community of readers. For example, after a conference with Herbert and Ryan, I quietly asked the other partners working at their table to stop for a moment and gather round. "Hey, readers, I'm sorry to interrupt you, but I just had to share the great work that Herbert and Ryan were doing today because I think it would be helpful for everyone. As they read one of their poems, they decided to… " This only takes a minute or so, but it's an efficient way to spread the reading wealth. Kathleen Tolan, TCRWP deputy director for reading, calls these "table conferences," and their power to quickly disseminate important information is great.

In a reading club variation on a typical conference, I often add a "By the way, another thing… " sort of reading tip at the end of a conference. I remember one conference with Bruce and Molly in which I taught them a strategy for reading poetry with feeling and fluency. At the end of the conference, I tagged on another bit of teaching, although this was about a reading habit or purpose, not a reading strategy. I said, "You know, now that you guys are working on reading with a voice that really shows the feelings you get from a poem, you might consider doing what some poetry lovers do—you could find a poem that means so much to you and memorize it so that it always stays with you." Although we do want our conferences to be fine-tuned, clear, and brief, it makes sense during reading clubs to tuck in some ideas about reading habits and reading options that the students may not have thought about themselves.

Small-Group Instruction in the Form of Strategy Lessons

During a session of reading clubs, we can also convene small groups of children for strategy lessons (Calkins 2001). I would tend to gather a small group after I'd had a chance to confer with two or three partnerships first. There are two reasons I would confer around the room before settling in for small-group instruction: first, by conferring with partners in different places in the room, I can make my presence felt, which serves as a not-so-subtle management strategy; and second, I've found that when I gather the small group first, right after the mini-lesson, I tend to spend too much time with that group, which means that I lose conferring time. I acknowledge that this problem is particular to people like me who have trouble keeping things tight and quick.

So imagine that we've just conferred with a couple of partnerships and now we're pulling together a group of six readers for a strategy lesson. In a strategy lesson, we meet with children who have similar reading needs to teach them a strategy that will be useful to them (Calkins 2001).

Now imagine that we're in a cycle of reading clubs in which our students are becoming experts on characters (and learning how to infer, determine importance, synthesize information, and use text evidence to support ideas, by the way). We may decide to gather the six strongest readers for a strategy lesson about how to read dialogue well because it reveals lots of information about a character's thoughts, feelings, and motivations. We decide to teach them about this because we notice that the texts in their reading clubs have long dialogue passages, and we've observed the students whipping through the dialogue without considering what it tells them about the characters.

Perhaps on another day, we decide to pull together two sets of partners who are struggling because they need more support to monitor for meaning when they get to tricky parts of their books. Then at the end of Week 2 of character study reading clubs, we notice that several partnerships continue to collect bits information about their characters. They are listing tidbits about their characters, and it looks like their goal is simply to accumulate as many little tidbits as possible. My intention in this strategy lesson would be to teach them how to take information they gather about characters and analyze it a bit in order to get a deeper sense of their characters. I would teach them to extend their thinking by saying, "I notice that my character _____, and it makes me think that _____." Rather than have separate conferences to teach this strategy, we save time by gathering the partnerships together for a strategy lesson.

Share Time After Reading Clubs as Whole-Class Instruction

When we gather students together for share time at the end of reading clubs, we have a captive audience and a fertile moment for instruction. The work the students have just done in reading clubs is fresh, and they haven't necessarily switched their mental gears toward the next thing on the schedule, unless it's lunch or recess. During the share time that follows reading clubs, I usually ask students to bring their reading club baskets to the meeting area and sit near their partners. We can use this precious time together in several ways.

We can spend the five or so minutes of share time modeling a strategy for the whole class that we just taught someone to use during a reading club conference. After we model the strategy, we can give our students a minute or two to try it themselves, right there in the meeting area. We can share a snippet of a strong partner conversation we heard in an effort to lift the level of everyone's conversations. We can get the students to name what they noticed about the conversation that made it go so well, and then we might even offer them an opportunity to try to use the particular conversation technique.

Perhaps we notice some dysfunctional things occurring in reading clubs. We can use share time to patch up the problems. We might remind students how partners make plans together, model how planning might sound, and then give students a few minutes, right there in share time, to make a plan for the next day. We can pass out index cards so they can jot down their plan to have for tomorrow.

Share time offers valuable opportunities to extend, fine-tune, or even fix our teaching. A wonderful resource about maximizing the potential of share time is *Don't Forget to Share: The Crucial Last Step in the Writing Workshop* by Leah Mermelstein (2007).

Opportunities for Reading Club Instruction Throughout the Day

Besides the period of time we devote to reading clubs in a day, we can also find other times to support our students' reading club work. We can use the other components of balanced literacy as well as the teachable moments that often arise outside of our literacy work.

Anytime our students are aligned in partnerships, whether they are line partners, seat partners, math partners, field trip partners, or any other kind of partner, we offer support and instruction for how to cooperate well with others and for how to deal with difficulty in partnerships. I often share the story of how Sereena took a deep breath as she approached me upon arrival one morning. "Ms. Collins," she said, "I've got to talk to you about my partner." She told me that she didn't want to hold hands with Edward, her seat partner, who was also her line partner whenever we left the classroom. She told me, in a stage whisper, that Edward picked his nose and didn't wash his hands. "It makes me feel sort of sick when I have to hold his hand," she said, obviously relieved to get this off her chest.

Sereena's concerns were far removed from a reading club partnership issue (although Edward's reading club partner would also benefit from any nose-picking intervention), but I tried to deal with this particular situation in a way that could be generalized for any kind of issue one might have with a partner. I told Sereena that I was glad she brought this up so she could let her partner know something was bothering her. "It's important that when you have a problem or a concern with someone that you let that person know right away so that the problem can get solved and so that both of you will be happier," I said. Then I suggested that instead of breaking up the partnership over this hygiene issue, we could talk to Edward with kindness and discretion and tell him that he needs to deal with his nose-picking habit differently. "What should we say?" I asked Sereena. She suggested three things: he could use a tissue, he could wash his hands, or, better yet, he could stop picking altogether because it's gross. During the morning meeting that day, without offering the gory details of the situation, I told the class how Sereena and Edward worked out a problem by talking about it with each other, and if anyone else wanted help with resolving partner problems, they could go to either of them for advice. These "teachable moments" tend to arise unexpectedly, and we have to be on our toes to harness their power in ways that will help our students.

Our balanced literacy components also offer opportunities to support reading clubs at other times in the day, but we can more easily plan for these. For example, if my class is spending two weeks in author study reading clubs, I could spend those two weeks of read-aloud time engaged in an author study as well. One year during author study reading clubs, I spent a week reading aloud several books by Donald Crews. The conversations we had, the strategies we used, and the plans we made for our Donald Crews study became helpful models for the work the students could do in their partnerships during reading clubs. Likewise, during shared reading, we can model the strategies we think will be particularly helpful for our students during reading clubs, and we can use texts that are similar to the ones our students are reading in their clubs.

In a school day, there are so many things to do, so much to cover, and so little time for everything. It's necessary that we become resourceful and look for teaching opportunities in the big and small, scheduled and unscheduled, formal and informal moments each day and use the best practices we know in any of these teachable moments.

Supporting Students to Do Their Best Work

When we sit down to plan for reading clubs, we may have a strong sense of how to teach because we're keeping our ideas about the best practices for instruction in mind. The challenge then becomes deciding what to teach. Whenever we plan any cycle of reading clubs, we'll want to include the skills, strategies, and habits our students need to read the texts well, and we'll want to include instruction for helping our students have strong conversations about their texts.

We consider the skills, strategies, and habits our students need in order to read with proficiency, purpose, and engagement.

When I plan for the work my students will do in reading clubs, I always begin by considering what real-life readers would do and what habits of mind they need to use if they were doing a similar kind of reading. For example, when I plan for what I want my students to learn during character study reading clubs, I always begin by considering what I and other proficient readers might do when we think about the characters in our texts.

I think about the times when I've felt keenly attached to characters in a book. When I read *Random Family* by Adrian LeBlanc I couldn't get the characters out of my mind. I carried Coco and her kids with me all the time, and I couldn't wait until the next moment I would have a chance to read. My emotions about Coco ran wide and deep—I was charmed by her, mad at her, thrilled for her, scared for her, worried for her, and so on. I would gossip about Coco with Amanda Hartman, a colleague at the Project who had just read the book. I remember reading large chunks of the book with a low-grade anxiety because I was so concerned for Coco and her kids.

So how might this experience with the characters in a heart-wrenching, adult-themed book inform my teaching to students who would be reading about characters like Mrs. Wishy-Washy, Biscuit, Judy Moody, or Horrible Harry? Well, to start, I could share what it's like to get to know a character. I could show them strategies readers use to learn as much as they can about their characters, which is an ideal time to teach them about inferring. I could teach my kids that careful readers tend to react to their characters because when we really get to know our characters, what they say and do can surprise us, anger us, frustrate us, inspire us, and make us laugh, cry, or simply smile. I can demonstrate how careful readers talk back to our characters as we read when we hear our minds say things like, "Awww, don't do that," or "Hey, that was a brave thing to say," or "There you go again, being so mischievous," in response to the characters in our books. These are all the things that we do when we care about book characters, and these are certainly things that our young readers can learn to do as well.

So, as we make plans for specific reading club cycles, a wise way to begin is by asking ourselves, "What are the characteristics of proficient reading for these types of texts or for this type of reading?" For instance, if our students are reading books by the same author in an author study, we can name several things we do when we read books by an author we love. If our students are going to be in poetry reading clubs, we can list the skills, strategies, and habits of avid poetry readers.

In short, as you plan instruction for reading clubs:

· think about your own reading experiences with the types of texts and the kind of work that will be present in the reading clubs.

· ask other readers about their experiences, habits, and challenges with the types of texts and kinds of work that your students will likely encounter in the reading clubs.

· consider the real-life habits of mind, skills, and strategies your readers will need to read the texts in their clubs well.

We consider the characteristics of strong conversations and plan instruction accordingly.

Because reading clubs offer a wonderful opportunity to strengthen our students' abilities to have high-quality, highly literate conversations about texts, it's important that we begin with an idea of what great talk would sound like within a particular kind of reading club while also keeping in mind the characteristics of strong conversations in general. With regard to conversations in general, we hope to see our reading club partnerships developing the ability to discuss an idea for a while in their conversations, to make room for both partners' voices and ideas, to use text evidence to support their ideas, to stay focused on the texts and ideas that arise in their reading club, and to have strategies for fixing the conversation when it lags or breaks down altogether.

We can model all of this on a daily basis during our interactive read-aloud conversations so our students have an image of what a great conversation can sound like. Of course, the degrees to which students are able to do any of these things independently will likely be different from one grade to the next and from one partnership to the next. As we confer with reading club partners, we always look for ways to teach, support, and then extend their conversation skills.

In addition to the general conversation skills we want to teach, we can also hold high expectations for the content of reading club talk as we acknowledge that we might talk differently about different types of texts. When our students are reading poetry, for example, we might expect to hear more about author's craft than we would expect of students in series book clubs. This is not to say that kids in series book reading clubs would never discuss author's craft, but we can imagine other content that would be as or more compelling, such as characters' tendencies, plot similarities and differences, and so on.

In short, as you think about supporting talk in reading clubs:

· plan instruction to support ambitious yet reasonable expectations for your students' conversations, and consider a continuum for growth across the year.

· imagine content for conversation you'd expect to hear within the particular reading club cycle (i.e., How might kids discussing poetry talk differently than kids in a Martin Luther King, Jr., biography club? How might a conversation in a nonfiction club on snails be different than a conversation in a character club on Toot and Puddle?).

· consider the habits, skills, and strategies conversationalists need to listen intently, talk clearly, and think deeply.

When we begin our planning for reading clubs by thinking about how we can do our best work and what our students need to learn in order to do their best work, we are reaching for high goals and setting ambitious standards for both our students and ourselves.

Instruction That Supports Readers in Any Kind of Reading Club

No matter the cycle of reading clubs, we want to help our students learn ways to make plans for their work together, follow through on their plans with comprehension and focus, and then wrap up their reading clubs having gained insight and having grown ideas from their work together. In this chapter, I suggest ways to approach instruction on these matters for any cycle of reading clubs.

Helping Students Plan Well in Reading Clubs

One of the main questions teachers have about reading clubs conveys a concern with student engagement. They ask, "How do I know what my students are doing? I can only confer with a few partnerships during a reading club session, so I'm left wondering about the other kids. How can I be sure they are on task and doing good work?" This is an enormous question that isn't just a reading club question. What about during math, when we gather a few students to offer extra support? How can we be sure the rest of the students are staying on task? Well, in the case of math, there are a couple things we can do. We can ask them to turn in work for evaluation at the end of the period, or we can be clear about exactly what the assignment is and how many problems they have to figure out during that period and then check to see that they completed the task.

In reading clubs, it's not practical (or advisable) to have students turn in an assignment each day, because then they'd be spending more time writing than reading and talking about their ideas. We also can't assign them exactly what they have to do on a particular day, because each of the reading club partnerships is working in a slightly different way. For example, during a cycle of kindergarten ABC reading clubs, Eric and Malik are rereading the pictures in *From A to Z* to see if they missed any items connected to the featured letter on each page, whereas Dominick and Chelsea are singing the ABC song as they turn the pages in their ABC books. The rest of the partnerships are probably working in different ways than these, so to assign one task for every partnership will derail students from reading and talking in ways that meet their own purposes or fulfill their own interests.

Rather than designing a "one-size-fits-all" type of assignment or creating individual assignments for each partnership in an effort to make sure our students are staying on task, it seems to me that the real task is to teach our students strategies so they can stay focused and keep their reading, thinking, and talking work going well through each reading club session and across the week. If our students have plans and purposes for their work, they are more likely to stay focused. We can teach our students how to make wise plans, and also teach them strategies for sticking with their plans and ways to revise them if necessary. In other words, we want to teach them how to launch their own work and how to proceed once they've gotten it started. Figure 4.1 contains a list of some teaching ideas to support students in planning and maintaining their work across time.

Figure 4.1

Supporting Our Students with Planning for Their Reading Club Work

Big Idea for Planning	What a Reader Can Do	Strategies for Doing It
Readers plan for how to begin their work together.	Readers make a plan for which books they will read first. *(Making a plan for which text to read first encourages students to examine the texts they've got in their club rather than jumping right in to read with no real sense of intention.)*	· Readers can survey books by skimming and scanning to see which text makes sense to read first. · Readers can survey the books by skimming through them and then deciding to read the books that seem easier at first. This can help them to warm up to their topic/subject. · Readers in series book clubs may want to survey the books to see if there's an order in which the books are meant to be read. For example, does the series have a Book One?
	Readers make a plan for how they'll read the books in their reading club. *(Deciding how they'll read the books in their club helps to ensure that both partners are engaged during reading club time. Each partner has a task.)*	· Partners can decide if they want to both read one book together (which works well if the text is a picture book, a highly illustrated nonfiction text, or an easy text.) · Partners may decide to each read a different text and then get together to talk about what they've learned, noticed, etc. · Partners may decide to read for a certain length of time and then stop to talk. · Partners may assign a focus to their reading, such as "Let's read our books and collect all the information we can about hermit crabs."

Figure 4.1 *(continued)*

Big Idea for Planning	What a Reader Can Do	Strategies for Doing It
Readers plan for how to begin their work together. *(continued)*	Readers may begin by sharing what they already know about the topic/author/genre/etc. even before they begin reading the texts in their reading club. (*Airing their prior knowledge can help make the reading easier because partners are likely to share some vocabulary and concepts that they might encounter in their texts.*)	· Readers can share prior knowledge about their topic in order to warm up to the vocabulary and concepts they will encounter in the texts. · Readers might make a list of things they already know (or think they know) about their topic.
Readers can set goals for their learning.	Readers consider what they want to learn about, think about, or what they might be wondering about before they get started. These are their learning goals. (*This can help give students an initial direction for their work.*)	· Partners can talk about what they hope to learn in their reading club. (*For example, "I want to learn how sharks can go without sleep."*) · Partners can share things they wonder about. (*For example, "I wonder why Ezra Jack Keats always writes stories about Peter?"*) · Partners can write these things down to help remind them of their learning goals.
	Readers may add new goals or change their goals. (*In the middle of a reading club cycle, it can be helpful to ask students to check to see if they need to adjust their goals or plans. This helps keep their work from getting stale.*)	· Partners talk often to make sure they are still working together on reaching a learning goal. · If partners figure out something that they were wondering about, they might say to each other, "So what do we want to think about next?"

Figure 4.1 *(continued)*		
Big Idea for Planning	**What a Reader Can Do**	**Strategies for Doing It**
Readers can set goals for their learning. *(continued)*	Readers may have quantity goals to help them stay on the job. *(For some partnerships, it may help their focus if they make concrete plans.)*	· Partners can decide how much they want to read in a particular reading club session before they get together to talk. · Partners may decide they want to figure out a certain number of things. *(For example, "Let's try to find at least five things that Cynthia Rylant teaches us about Poppleton in this book.")* · Readers can write down their plans for how much, how long, etc.
Readers have ways to solve conflicts or problems that occur in their reading club.	Partners can compromise. *(This is essential partnership teaching, and it's often revisited throughout the year.)*	· Partners can take turns reading, jotting, writing, talking, etc. · Partners might need to take a short break from their work together so that they can think of a solution to their problem.
	Readers have ways to avoid a dead end in their reading clubs. *(Sometimes about halfway through the club cycle, students might feel "done," so it helps to teach them ways to add a spark to their work.)*	· Readers can reread texts or parts of texts to find things they hadn't noticed or thought about the first time they read the text. · Readers can reimagine their plans for their work by looking at what they've done so far and thinking about what they'd still like to do. · Readers might add another text to their club. · Readers can decide what they want to make of their learning and how they could present it to others. · Partners can check in with other partnerships to see what they're working on because that might provide new ideas.
Readers can jot notes about their plans and goals.	Readers can keep track of what they're working on.	· Readers can make to-do lists and keep them in their reading club basket. · Readers can use T-charts in different ways. *(For example, What we think we know/What we want to know; What we notice in the text/ What we think about it; and so on.)*

Helping Students Grow Ideas in Their Reading Clubs

One of the things I love best about reading clubs is that they provide time for students to linger with the same texts over a stretch of days. Because these texts are all connected in some way, our students are also steeping themselves in a particular topic, subject, or line of thinking for these days. I've found that this time spent in one "place" enables students not only to name and mention the things they find in texts, but also to have thoughts and theories about things they find in texts.

In a kindergarten class, a dozen pairs of children were scattered about the room with their reading club baskets nearby. Each of their reading club baskets contained a copy of *From A to Z*, a book the students knew well because their teacher had read it out loud to them a couple of times, and two other ABC books that the students had chosen themselves for their reading club basket. Some of the partnerships also had little letter books, texts that featured just one letter throughout and a picture on each page of an object beginning with the featured letter.

In this classroom, the teacher was concerned that the students were just making statements to each other rather than having actual conversations about their texts. She shared an example of one partnership where the children were simply calling out the objects on their pages. Although they were taking turns and staying focused, two positive things, the teacher was concerned that they, and others like them, rarely seemed to cross paths in conversation. She really wanted to move students toward talking with each other, not at each other. During conferring time on this day, we decided to do a little research. Our intention was to collect snippets of partner conversations in order to get a kind of baseline for the way they were talking. We felt that studying the students' talk would enable us to come up with ideas to help partners grow ideas together rather than just make statements to each other.

Sasha and Rashad were reading texts from their ABC book club basket. Here's a brief snippet of how their talk went:

Sasha is holding a book on her lap, and Rashad is looking at it with her. Sasha is flipping through the pages.

Sasha: S, this is my page. My name has two S's in it.

Rashad:	My name has R. Where's the R page?
Sasha:	S S S. *(turns the page)* T T T. U U U. VVV. WWW. XXX... *(She turns the pages and just says the name of the letter, three times for some reason.)*
Rashad:	There's a xylophone. Look, a xylophone. That's like that other book. *(Rashad looks around distractedly trying to find another book.)* Wait.
Sasha:	No, let's go. What's next? *(She turns the page.)* YYY.

At this point, I couldn't help myself. I said something, breaking my silent researcher stance. "Hey, guys. May I stop you for a second? I noticed that you're reading the pages so well, calling out the letters that you see. That's one thing ABC book readers do a lot. But I heard Rashad say something that he noticed. On the X page, here, he noticed the xylophone picture and said that another book had a xylophone on the X page, too. Did I get that right, Rashad?" He nodded and showed us the xylophone page in the other book.

"So, what do you guys think about that? What's your idea about that, about how the X pages in different books can have the same picture?" I asked

Sasha said, "Maybe they like xylophones or something."

Rashad said, "Yeah, they like to draw xylophones, and X is for xylophones, too. Look, xylophone's on our alphabet chart, too! (He points at the horizontal ABC chart that borders the top of the chalkboard.) "A xylophone!"

"Yeah, I knew that," Sasha said, sounding a bit blasé.

"When readers notice something about their books like you guys did, they sometimes take a moment to get an idea about what they noticed. Take a moment, you two. What are you thinking about your discovery... another X and another xylophone! What ideas do you have about it? Why might there be so many X pages that use xylophones?" (I didn't know exactly where we were going with this, but I wanted them to stay a bit longer with this noticing.)

Sasha said, "Xylophones are good for X pages because they have an X at the beginning."

"Maybe they can't think of other things for X," Rashad said.

Sasha replied, "Let's find more xylophones. Let's look at these books, too."

Rashad said, "We can also ask other kids if they have xylophones in their books, too."

In reflecting on this snippet of partner work, I realized that I assumed the role of the nudger in order to help the students have an interactive conversation. I kept trying to get Sasha and Rashad to say more when they made statements of observation. Posing questions such as, "What are you thinking about that?" or "What is your idea about that?" to both people in the partnerships may have a few beneficial effects. Nudging questions like these (and others) can:

- help students say more about a topic.
- help students stay longer with a topic or line of inquiry.
- help students interact more with each other, especially in cases when Partner B offers her thoughts about Partner A's observation.
- move partners toward other purposes and plans as they investigate their ideas.

When we support our students in developing the habit of saying more about what they notice, wonder, and question, we are on our way to helping them grow ideas and determine further purpose for their work. Instead of conversations that are characterized by partners taking turns to make statements that do not intersect in any way, we can help them to pearl their statements for the ideas behind them by teaching our students to say more about what they are thinking. When we do this, we're supporting our students' engagement in what Richard Allington calls "thoughtful literacy." He writes that thoughtful literacy is going "beyond the ability to read, remember, and recite on demand." In other words, teaching our students strategies for growing ideas about what they are reading provides opportunities for them to use more sophisticated thinking strategies such as analysis, evaluation, and synthesis (Allington 2001, 93).

The chart in Figure 4.2 details some things we can teach our students to help them grow ideas, rather than just make statements.

Figure 4.2		
Teaching Ideas to Help Students Grow Ideas About Their Reading Club Topic		
Big Idea for Growing Ideas About a Topic	**What a Reader Can Do**	**Strategies for Doing It**
Readers can stay with an idea that they get from the words and pictures in texts and think more about it until it feels finished.	Readers often notice or wonder about things when they read, and they can add their thoughts to what they notice or wonder. *(Teaching students to add their thinking to what they notice or wonder about a text can help them move into deeper terrain than staying on the surface of the text.)*	· Readers can say things like, "I notice that... and it makes me think..." *(For example, a child might say, "I notice that the dad is cooking on all the pages, and it makes me think that this dad is a chef/that dads can cook too/ that this author wants us to know that dads can cook, and it doesn't have to be just moms.")* · Readers can say things like, "I'm wondering why... My idea about that is... " *(For example, "I'm wondering why Poppleton just doesn't tell Cherry Sue that he doesn't want to keep eating with her. My idea about that is that Poppleton might not want to hurt her feelings, and sometimes it's hard to say things if we think we'll hurt someone's feelings.")* · Readers can get in the habit of adding their thoughts to the statements they make about their books by saying things like, "I'm thinking that... " or "My idea about that is..." or "I think the reason is... ," etc.

Figure 4.2 *(continued)*

Big Idea for Growing Ideas About a Topic	What a Reader Can Do	Strategies for Doing It
Readers can stay with an idea that they get from the words and pictures in texts and think more about it until it feels finished. *(continued)*	Partners can help each other say more. *(It's important to find ways to engage both partners, the one who's talking about the text at the moment and the one who is listening.)*	· The listening partner can say, "Say more about that." · The listening partner can ask, "What does that make you think?" · The listening partner can say, "Show me the part you're talking about and let's say more about it."
	Partners can take one idea and keep it afloat for a while. *(Providing students with simple ways of growing their conversation stamina is essential for helping them to grow ideas that go deeper than a surface level of understanding.)*	· The listening partner can add to what his or her partner said. · The listening partner can have a different thought and share that. · The partners can ask each other, "Is there anything else you want to say about that?" · Partners can remind each other to stay with the idea by saying something like, "Let's get back to the subject we were just talking about."
Readers grow ideas by accumulating their thinking across texts.	Readers keep other texts they know in mind as they read.	· Sometimes readers make connections between books and say something like, "This reminds me of… because… " · Sometimes readers may keep the other reading club books out while they read one of the texts so they can easily move between books. · Readers can put sticky notes in books when they read something that feels compelling. Then it will be easy to find later.

Figure 4.2 *(continued)*

Big Idea for Growing Ideas About a Topic	What a Reader Can Do	Strategies for Doing It
Readers grow ideas by accumulating their thinking across texts. *(continued)*	Readers can compare and contrast texts. *(Noticing similarities and differences among texts that are connected in some way—by topic, character, genre, etc.—and then thinking about the significance of those similarities and differences can be a stepping-stone to the skills of critical reading and evaluation of text.)*	· Readers notice when one book says something different than another book, and they can reread the parts to think about why there is different information in the texts. · Readers notice when several texts have the same information, and they can think about why the author(s) say(s) the same thing across books. *(For example, "I noticed that almost every Nate the Great book says that he likes pancakes. I think it's because the author is trying to give us information so we can get to know Nate, in case you haven't read any other books about him.")*
	Readers can put ideas from texts in their own words and keep these ideas in mind as they read other texts. *(Synthesizing texts can be difficult for our youngest readers, but we can help them get started with this sophisticated strategy by encouraging them to pause after finishing a book to gather their ideas about it.)*	· When readers finish a book or a part of a book, they can take a moment to gather their ideas and thoughts about the text by saying something like, "This taught me that... " or "This made me think about... " or "The thing that sticks with me from this book is... "

Figure 4.2 *(continued)*		
Big Idea for Growing Ideas About a Topic	**What a Reader Can Do**	**Strategies for Doing It**
Readers can invent a system or method to keep track of their thinking and help them grow ideas.	Readers can use sticky notes, graphic organizers, and simple note-taking methods as artifacts to keep track of their ideas across time in their reading club. *(This is essential partnership teaching, and it's often revisited and built upon throughout the year.)*	· Partners might jot down their big ideas that they've talked about to keep track of them. · Partners can look back at the artifacts that show what they thought about throughout the week of reading clubs to see how their ideas have grown or changed or both.

Supporting Reading Comprehension in Reading Clubs

Each cycle of reading clubs has its own set of comprehension issues that are worth our instructional energies. For example, we know that character studies are perfect opportunities to spotlight the skill of inferring and that poetry studies offer a perfect venue to teach students how to envision texts in ways that support their understanding of them. So it makes sense that in these reading club cycles a teacher would spend some days offering strategies to help his students infer or envision well in order to understand their texts better.

Although each reading club might have particular comprehension skills and strategies that are well worth teaching during mini-lessons and modeling during read-aloud time, it's also important to keep in mind that more generalized instruction to support comprehension is always worth our time. After all, students who are engaged in a character study or a poetry study need to orchestrate lots of comprehension strategies, not just inferring or envisioning, in order to understand their texts as best they can.

When we confer with partnerships during any cycle of reading clubs, we'll want to watch and listen for how we can support students' comprehension in ways that will help them no matter the book or the setting in which they are reading. Some of the particular ways we can support our students' overall comprehension is to help them monitor for meaning, from the word level to the whole-text level, to show them how to tell when their comprehension has broken down, and to teach them ways to reboot their comprehension when it does break down. The chart in Figure 4.3 offers some ideas for promoting thoughtful literacy and dealing with some general reading comprehension issues we might observe during any kind of reading club cycle.

Figure 4.3		
Ideas for Teaching Comprehension Within Reading Clubs		
Big Idea for Comprehension	**What a Reader Can Do**	**Strategies for Doing It**
Readers can get ready to read in ways that will make their reading easier.	Readers can think about what they already know about the topic. *(Teaching students to begin by activating prior knowledge or gathering their thoughts about a topic can offer support because it can bring to the forefront specific vocabulary and concepts they might encounter in their texts.)*	· Before a reader reads about something, he can make his task easier by getting ready. He can think and talk about what he already knows about the topic. *(For example, on the first day of reading clubs, the partners might begin by saying, "Let's see. We're going to be studying beetles. Let's talk about what we think we already know about them.")* · Partners can jot down a list of things they already know and then share them with each other. *(By sharing the wealth of their knowledge, they are widening their combined prior knowledge in ways that might make reading easier and text more comprehensible.)* · Readers can think about things they already know for sure, things they think they know, and things they wonder about their topic. *(Sometimes young readers will be mistaken about what they think they know for sure about a topic. For example, Sean says, "Spiders are beetles," with an air of authority, and he may not be able to revise this idea, even in the face of text that contradicts it. It makes sense to introduce the idea of uncertainty by helping students make "I think that… " statements in addition to "I know that… " statements.)*

Figure 4.3 (continued)

Big Idea for Comprehension	What a Reader Can Do	Strategies for Doing It
Readers can get ready to read in ways that will make their reading easier. (continued)	Readers can think about what they already know about the genre and how books in the genre might go. (When proficient readers sit down with a text, they have a framework in mind for what they expect to see based on what they know about the genre. For example, nonfiction readers approach their texts differently than mystery readers based on what they know about how these genres tend to go.)	· Readers can skim the text to figure out how it goes and then make a plan for how to read it. (For example, as partners skim a nonfiction book on beetles, they might find particular sections of interest and plan to read those. Partners who are in series book clubs might try to figure out if any of the texts are meant to be read first by looking closely at the book covers, the blurbs on the back, and so on.)
	Readers can skim and scan texts to figure out an order for reading them. (Sometimes in a reading club basket, there are texts that may be more complex than others, and when students begin with the easier texts, they are warming themselves up to read the texts that are more difficult.)	· Readers can look for the book that seems to be the easiest and begin by reading that one because this helps them get solid with their topic. · Readers can try to identify which book makes sense to read first. (For example, readers can check to see if the series has a Book One, a book that they've read themselves or had read to them before, etc.) · Readers can skim and scan through texts to determine a range of difficulty. They can find books that have lots of picture support, books that have helpful features that make reading easier, etc.

Figure 4.3 *(continued)*

Big Idea for Comprehension	What a Reader Can Do	Strategies for Doing It
Readers have strategies to understand their reading.	Readers can retell what happened in their texts.	· Partners can retell what just happened in their books to help each other understand the stories. · Partners can retell parts of their books to themselves to make sure they've understood what has happened.
	Readers can put the text into their own words.	· Readers can read a chunk of text and then state what happened or what they've learned using their own words, not the author's words. · Readers can jot ideas in their own words on sticky notes to help them keep track of their thinking.
	Readers can talk with others about what they're learning/thinking as they read, using text evidence to support their ideas.	· Partners can make plans to read chunks of text and then get together to share what they are thinking and learning. · Partners can check in with each other as they read. · Partners can ask each other to show the part of the book where they got a particular idea.
Readers have strategies to help them deal with confusing parts of their books.	Readers notice when they are confused or when they don't understand something they've read.	· When it's hard to retell to yourself or to another person what happened in a part of the story, it may have been confusing. · Readers notice when they've been daydreaming while they are reading because that means they may not have understood that part of the text. · When it's difficult to picture what's going on in a text, it might mean that part is tricky to understand. · When a reader realizes she doesn't understand, she thinks about the best way to fix it.

Figure 4.3 *(continued)*

Big Idea for Comprehension	What a Reader Can Do	Strategies for Doing It
Readers have strategies to help them deal with confusing parts of their books. *(continued)*	Readers have strategies to deal with confusing parts.	· Readers can reread confusing parts and try to make a picture in their mind. · Readers can read aloud the confusing parts. · Readers can ask someone to help them understand the confusing parts. · Readers can use text features such as headings and illustrations to help them understand confusing parts.
Readers have strategies to figure out unfamiliar vocabulary.	Readers can figure out what an unfamiliar word or expression means.	· When readers encounter a word or expression they've never seen before, they can read back and read on to figure out what it might mean. · Readers can look closely at the word or expression and think of a more familiar synonym that would work in its place. · Readers can check in a dictionary or ask someone else to help them.
	Readers try to "own" new words and expressions.	· When readers encounter new words or expressions, they can use the new vocabulary in their speaking and writing so that the word becomes part of their repertoire.

The teaching ideas included in these charts support readers in any cycle of reading clubs. The strategies listed can be taught during mini-lessons for the whole class if many students need that particular kind of instruction and during partner conferences or small-group instruction if the strategy pertains to less than half of the students.

Random Acts of Teaching Kindness

In many reading club cycles across the years, I've found there are certain lines of instruction I often will follow that don't fall into any of the broad categories described above. They offer students strategies and support for any kind of reading club, although in many cases, the instruction detailed in Figure 4.4 is more likely to take place during partner conferences rather than during whole-class mini-lessons.

Figure 4.4		
Big Idea for Supporting Readers	**What a Reader Can Do**	**Strategies for Doing It**
Readers have a variety of purposes for rereading.	Readers can go back and reread to help them understand their texts.	· When readers say, "Huh?" or find that they can't picture what they're reading, they go back and reread to fill in the blurry parts. · When readers get to the end of a chunk of text and have trouble saying what it was about, they can reread to figure it out.
	Readers reread to verify information or to cross-check information between books.	· Readers can reread to double-check their information. · Readers can reread a chunk in Book A if they find some different information in Book B.
	Readers can reread to find text evidence to support their ideas.	· Partners can ask each other to reread parts of their books to find support for their ideas. · When readers get an idea about a character, for example, they can reread parts of the book to look for more evidence to support the idea.
	Readers can reread to rethink the text and/or their ideas.	· Readers have a purpose or reason for rereading, and it usually involves rethinking.

Figure 4.4 *(continued)*		
Big Idea for Supporting Readers	**What a Reader Can Do**	**Strategies for Doing It**
Readers find that their reading can affect their lives in some way.	Readers share what they've been thinking and learning.	· Readers can think to themselves, "What is it about this that I think other people would want to know?" · Readers can figure out the best way to share information (orally, in writing, drawing, role playing, etc.).
	Readers can be inspired to do something or to make something based on what they've read and what they thought about their reading.	· Readers can ask themselves, "How does this make me want to live my life differently?" · Readers can ask themselves, "What have I learned from this study?" or "What new thinking have I done because of the reading and conversations I've had?" · Readers can ask themselves, "What can I write, make, or do to share my knowledge and new ideas with others?"

Final Thoughts About Multiuse Teaching

The teaching ideas included in the charts in this chapter are meant to be shapeless enough that they can be sculpted to fit any cycle of reading clubs, yet substantial enough that they make an impact on students' work. These teaching ideas are also meant to be used on an as-needed basis. In other words, they may not be essential instruction for every cycle of reading clubs.

In your first couple of reading club cycles, for example, you may find it necessary to spend time leading whole-class lessons to teach your students how to plan well for their reading club work. After your students have been through a couple of reading club cycles, it's reasonable to hope that your students won't need as much support to plan for their work. What was once whole-class instruction on planning might turn into teaching during reading conferences for a couple of partnerships that need support.

Creating the Conditions for Reading Partners to Talk Well About Texts

Today as I write, I'm in Kaladi Brothers coffee shop wearing my brand-new noise reduction headphones. Normally, I'm one who thrives on environmental noise when I write. I especially like to eavesdrop on nearby conversations, but today the conversations around me are not so interesting. The intermittent sucking sound of the espresso machine and the musical choices the baristas have made are more distracting than usual. So here I sit, in near silence, looking a little like an air traffic controller. The only thing I can hear is myself swallowing and clearing my throat.

Maybe it's the caffeine, but as I sit here soundproofed, I'm having visions of myself as a first- and second-grade reader. This sense of silence and being lost in my own noise reminds me of what my reading life was like in elementary school. These words come to mind: solitary, detached, and disconnected.

I don't remember talking about anything I read in school, not with the teacher and certainly not with another student. Well, actually, I did talk to the teacher when she would ask me questions about the story in our round-robin reading group. I'm sure they were comprehension questions, not that I remember any of them. I don't remember ever picking a book to read in school, with the exception of choices made during my class's weekly trip to the school library. Any of the books I read in class were chosen for me by my teacher. Consequently, I never felt attached to my reading in school. I was doing it because it was assigned to me, and I was a teacher pleaser.

What a difference I see in my students and in your students when I'm lucky enough to visit your classrooms. Our children don't read in isolation. During our daily interactive read-aloud time, we read aloud a variety of texts to our students and then support their growing conversational abilities by modeling characteristics of proficient, engaged reading and high-quality book talks. For many of us, our students have reading partners with whom they read and think and talk about their books. They have regular opportunities for self-initiated book talks, and they learn how to maintain conversations and grow ideas. Our students read and think about texts in the company of others, and they're so much stronger for it.

In this chapter, I offer suggestions for maximizing the power of reading partnerships in general, with the specific intention to help you strengthen the work students do in their reading clubs. It's important to remember that the benefits of strong reading partnerships extend way beyond the boundaries of reading clubs and into the realm of any kind of interaction or conversation.

A Rationale for Making Reading Partnerships

Those of us who have regular partner reading time in our literacy block have come to see that successful reading partnerships "provide a motivating format and critical practice for students as they learn to think and talk about books" (Daley 2005, 7). Yet, once when I was doing a full-day workshop for teachers on launching reading partnerships in K–2 classrooms, a participant asked me what she should say if her principal questioned her about partnerships. "It's a little noisy, she'll tell me," said the teacher. "She will want to know the point of putting kids into partnerships."

Whenever I had presented workshops about reading partnerships in the past, I was so naive that it never occurred to me that reading partnerships in K–2 classrooms would need to be defended or rationalized. After all, everywhere in my teaching and staff development communities, we've seen how reading partnerships yield many benefits for young readers. This teacher's question left me with some homework, which was to pull together a rationale for reading partnerships for those who might not see their power and for those teachers who may be reluctant to fit them in:

Reading partnerships help to build children's stamina for attending to texts.

Early in the year during reading workshop in K–2 classrooms, our students don't have the reading stamina to stay focused on their texts for extended stretches of private reading time. When we provide time for students to meet with a reading partner, most often following private reading time, we are extending their time spent reading in a delightfully underhanded way, while also providing opportunities to talk about their texts.

Reading partnerships offer more time for children to read just-right books.

According to Dr. Richard Allington, readers need to spend as much time as possible reading books that are at their reading level, books that they can read without struggle (Allington 2001). When we add time for reading partnerships to our reading workshop, we are also providing more time for students to read just-right books. It's quite efficient, really—reading partnerships help to increase reading stamina for just-right books. Nice.

Partnerships provide opportunities for rereading and rethinking texts.

In reading clubs, partners select a reading club basket for their work during a week or so. Over the course of that week, they'll have opportunities to read and reread their books both by themselves and with their partners. They'll learn to read these texts with increasing fluency, and they'll talk about the books in deeper ways, because they're getting to know them well. Of course, some students might resist rereading, and if that's the case, we'll want to frame rereading as "rethinking," and teach students about different purposes for and benefits they'll get from "rethinking" their texts.

Reading partnerships support children's growing listening comprehension and expressive language abilities.

When students work with partners, they can stretch their oral language abilities because working with a partner during reading time calls upon a different register and mode of discourse than playing with a friend at recess or talking to a buddy in the lunchroom. Through partnerships, we can teach our students strategies for improving their listening comprehension as well as strategies for making themselves clear to others.

Reading partnerships provide time to talk about books in authentic ways.

When students talk about books in ways that matter to them, their investment in their reading increases. According to Gretchen Owocki, "Partner reading promotes thoughtful exploration of book content" (2003, 106). In reading partnerships, there is no teacher-mandate about what kids talk about, nor is there a whole-class guiding question that they must address during partner time. Instead, if you were to walk around a classroom during reading partner time, you'd hear students talking about a variety of things, such as what they notice and wonder about, ideas they've come up with about the character or the information, connections they make between the text and something else, and so on. Some partners would be role-playing scenes together and other partners would be taking on the role of detectives, trying to find clues about their characters.

Reading partnerships give children opportunities to solve problems and resolve conflicts independent of the teacher.

Part of our instruction for partnerships is to teach students strategies to solve problems that they encounter with their partners. In any partnership, there's likely to be struggles, and we can provide students with the tools that will help them fix most problems. Many of us have found that this ability and willingness to problem-solve independently carries over into other parts of the day, whenever students have a hard time with one another.

Reading partners provide each other a cheerleader, coach, and helper when the teacher is working with other readers.

During partner reading time, students have a built-in companion for dealing with reading challenges. Instead of calling out for the teacher when encountering difficulty or stopping work altogether while waiting on the teacher to come by, students in partnerships offer each other support with challenges. This has several positive effects on the community. For one thing, because reading partners can help each other, the teacher is able to focus more on the reading conference at hand instead of dealing with the potential distraction caused by students who are waiting for help. Also, the students grow to rely on each other and become a supportive community.

Now, imagine that you find yourself at a Friday evening cocktail party or a Sunday morning brunch. The host tells a group of people you've just met that you're an elementary school teacher. You hear "oohs" and "ahhs" and the inevitable, "Isn't that cute?" And just as you're about to take a bite of some tiny finger food or pour maple syrup onto your Belgian waffle, a parent of a first grader corners you and says, "You're a teacher? Good. I have a question. What's the point of reading partnerships? My kid has one in her class. I never had a reading partner, and I learned to read… " Well, my friend, you are now armed with several handy-dandy reasons why reading partnerships are beneficial to young readers. Now, please enjoy the party or the brunch because you'll have to leave soon to do some lesson-planning for the week ahead.

Successful Reading Partnerships

Over the years within the Teachers College Reading and Writing Project community, teachers have approached reading partnerships in a wide variety of ways; some that worked rather well and others that might have been problematic for some reason. As we've gathered in study groups to talk about partner reading, we've come to realize that teacher-assigned, long-term, ability-based reading partnerships tend to work most successfully.

It's certainly worth noting, however, that every classroom has its own special chemistry and is filled with a variety of student needs and strengths. So even though

I am convinced of the effectiveness of long-term, ability-based reading partnerships because of my own positive experiences with them, I believe that teachers are best served when they create reading partnerships based on the needs and strengths of the kids in their own classrooms.

Why Ability–Based Partnerships?

One of our objectives in reading workshop is to maximize the amount of time that our students are reading and thinking and talking about just-right books, which are books they can read with high levels of accuracy, fluency, and comprehension. Research shows that maximizing the time our students spend reading just-right books is essential to their reading development (Allington 2001). So, if during independent reading time, Felix is reading books at Fountas and Pinnell Level F, it makes sense that he meets with a reading club partner who is also reading books at or very near that level. Both Felix and his partner will spend more time with books that will help them become stronger readers.

I used to think that precisely matching students' reading levels was the priority when assigning ability-based partnerships, but I've come to soften that stance a bit. For one thing, there's research suggesting that students can benefit from reading with someone who is a bit stronger as a reader than they are (Owocki 2007).

Although I would hesitate to create reading club partnerships where one reader is considerably stronger than the other, I've seen instances where a slight difference in levels can benefit both students. For example, Jennifer, a reader of Level F books, was partnered successfully with Andrea, a reader of Level H, during a cycle of nonfiction reading clubs. Jennifer was an ambitious reader who was on the verge of surging ahead. By partnering with Andrea, she was prepped for reading texts at a higher level. As for Andrea, she was content to read and talk about any book, even those that would be considered "easy reads" for her. These easy reads gave Andrea plentiful opportunities to improve her fluency. There was another perk to this partnership: Andrea and Jennifer enjoyed each other and had fun reading together! Although attitudes about enjoyment and levels of fun aren't assessed in high-stakes tests, I would argue vigorously that they are essential characteristics of reading workshop and reading partnerships.

If I were to match students who read at different levels because I thought it would benefit those individual readers, I would make sure that their just-right reading levels were not much more than a level or two apart. I would tend not to match a reader such as Eliza, a proficient reader of books like Magic Tree House series, with Morgan, a proficient reader of books like the Biscuit series, during a cycle of series book reading clubs, for example. It just seems that even though Morgan and Eliza might be the best of friends and the partnership would work socially, I suspect that it would be less successful with regard to benefiting the children as readers. After all, Morgan would have very limited access as a reader if they chose the Magic Tree House Club, which would suit Eliza. On the other hand, Eliza may very well have little patience spending much time in the Biscuit Series club, which would fit Morgan's needs as a reader.

Why Long-Term Partnerships?

We've found that long-term partnerships work very well for young readers and are very good for teachers. When students are paired for a stretch of time, which typically means months, they are more likely to invest in developing conversations further, solving problems together, and offering support for each other. If partners are switched and rearranged often, we've noticed that it's difficult for the readers to develop a rhythm for working together. Consequently, when teachers switch partnerships often, the instruction is often overly focused on partnership management issues.

For teachers, the decision to assign partnerships that will last for months at a time alleviates the work of reconfiguring partnerships every week or two. This can be a labor-intensive process, and it's usually fraught with second-guessing and mismatched pairs. I recommend saving yourself the trouble and going for longer-term partnerships (in class, that is; I would not be so bold or misguided as to make a recommendation for your personal life).

Assigning long-term reading partnerships isn't easily done in the beginning of the year. In many cases, second- and third-grade teachers assign long-term partnerships after two or three weeks of school, whereas first-grade teachers might take three or four weeks to create their partnerships. For kindergarten, most teachers decide to wait until a number of students can read conventionally before assigning long-term partnerships. Prior to this shift toward conventional reading, kindergarten teachers might gradually increase the time spent with the same partner, going from a couple of days to a couple of weeks or so.

Before creating the long-term reading partnerships, it's necessary to observe students' interpersonal dynamics and assess students as readers to determine their just-right reading levels. Even though my main criterion for assigning partners is closely matching students' reading levels, I also consider the social world of my class and my students' interpersonal needs. After all, it's my desire to create partnerships that are built to last!

How long should partnerships last? Weeks, months, the whole year? In my class, I tended to assign reading partnerships in early October (during the fourth week of school), and it was my intention to keep them together until after the holiday break. When we returned to school in January after the holiday break, I would spend time that first week back assessing my students, and I might decide to reconfigure several partnerships while leaving some to continue working together. Before that point in the year, I would only change partnerships if one partner's reading level surged far ahead of the other's.

Now for a cautionary tale: It's only fair to reveal that I vividly remember years when long-term partnerships in my class were a struggle for the students and for me. These were years when the social chemistry in my class was either volatile or vulnerable, in spite of all my best intentions. These were the years when there were several students who were hard to partner, for any number of reasons. I made the error of stubbornly refusing to reconfigure partnerships because I was committed to long-term partnerships. In this case, I was paying more attention to how I thought it was supposed to go than to the special characteristics of students right in front of me.

In retrospect, I would have handled things differently by considering the students' needs. There are several things I could have done. For instance, I could have changed partners each month or every two weeks so kids wouldn't be mired in difficult situations for long stretches at a time. In a worst case scenario, I could have had three days a week of partner time instead of daily partner time as a way to alleviate the pressure for both my class and myself. Oooh, if only I had it to do over again... but that's another story altogether, isn't it?

What Do Partnerships Need to Be Successful?

The most successful partnerships share some characteristics, regardless of the partners' reading levels and temperaments. Successful partnerships tend to be flexible. They know a number of ways of working together, and they can get past interpersonal difficulties quickly. Successful partnerships are invested and purposeful in their work. These are some of the more obvious characteristics of high-functioning partnerships, but underneath these things, there is plenty of necessary instruction. Here are some ideas for teaching that will support partnerships in doing their best reading, thinking, and talking anytime they work together:

Partnerships need time each day to read together and to talk about what they've read.

Like anything else, partner work improves with practice. At first, we might hear stilted conversations between partners that rarely go deeper than retelling or talking about their favorite parts. As they gain more experience through daily time together, their partner conversations will improve and the partnerships will work more and more smoothly together.

Partners need to have strong images of partnership etiquette.

In many classes, the first week or so of partnership instruction is characterized by etiquette lessons, ranging from the important idea that you look at your partner while she's talking to you to courteous ways to help a partner who is stuck on a word. This partnership etiquette can be modeled and expected throughout the day, whether students are standing near their line partners, sitting next to their seat partners, talking with their writing partners, and so on.

Partners need strategies to solve problems and conflicts with invitations to invent their own strategies.

It's inevitable that partners will encounter difficulties with each other and with their work, some partners more than others. I've heard it all, from Emma's issues with being dominated in her partnership to Sereena's personal hygiene concerns about her chronic nose-picking partner. Just like any good couples' counselor, we want to give our young reading partners strategies to deal with their difficulties and invite them to invent their own ways of solving conflicts in their partnerships based on what they know about getting along well with people in the real world.

Partners need a variety of ways to work together with invitations to invent their own ways.

It's very helpful to model ways that partners might work together. For example, we suggest that partners who are reading books that are between Fountas and Pinnell levels A–G or so will want to hold the book in the middle and figure out how they'll read it together. For chapter book readers, we have to teach a variety of ways they can approach their partnerships. When students have many possibilities for what they can do in their partnerships, their work together is less likely to get stale or feel rote.

Partners need to have a repertoire of things readers might talk about with invitations to invent their own.

Once partners know how to work well together, we want to support them in having strong book talks. Part of this instruction is teaching them about the characteristics of good conversations in general as well as the qualities of good book talks. We can model these things during the interactive read-aloud time. It's important that we avoid mandating what partners need to talk about together. For example, if we teach our students that readers sometimes talk about the parts of the book that really stuck with them, we would say, "This is one thing you and your partner might talk about today," rather than, "Today when you meet with your partner, you'll want to talk about the part of the book that mattered to you." Mandating the content of their conversations is dangerous because this makes their conversations teacher-directed rather than authentic responses to their texts.

Reading partners need to have a sense of purpose with invitations to invent.

There are several approaches we can have when teaching students about having purposes for their work. Some purposes can be about the way they will work together ("How about if we read your book first and then talk about it, and we can read my book next?"), and some might be about the content for their talk ("How about if we talk about our characters? Mine did something so weird that I want to tell you about."). We also want to teach them to always consider the Golden Purpose of Reading Partnerships: reading partnerships can help readers understand their stories better and grow ideas about books, reading, and life.

Reading partners need to have opportunities to reflect and set goals.

I've found it so helpful to give partnerships time to reflect on their work together. For the first few weeks of partnerships, we might take a moment to reflect on partner work at the end of the week. We can provide guiding questions for partners to consider, such as, "What went well in your partnership this week?" or "What do you and your partner want to try next week?" We can ask students to reflect orally or in writing, depending on their needs and strengths and our intentions.

Once our students understand the community expectations for reading partner work, we can help them to hold themselves accountable for working well together in a way that supports their reading, thinking, and talking. Every few months, my students would create or revise reading partnership contracts with each other. They used this time to determine their priorities and goals for working successfully together. Appendix B provides an example of a basic, bare-bones reading partnership contract.

The Details of Partnership Instruction

One of the most predictable things about reading partnerships is that we tend to expend a lot of instructional energy on launching them at the beginning of the year. Then, after a month or two, any time we could spend on instruction for partnerships tends to give way to all the other reading instruction that our students need. This isn't necessarily a problem for our young readers, but it is a problem for partnerships. There is a consequence of not focusing on partnerships in our teaching in an ongoing way. Many of us have noticed that by December or January, the daily partnerships may become sort of robotic or unenthusiastic. The honeymoon is over. When this happens, it's time to spice things up! This requires attention to partnerships to see what they need to become stronger and more joyful, and then a commitment to devoting some instructional time to supporting them.

How Do We Fit in Partnership Instruction?

This is one of the most frequent questions I've been asked when I've presented workshops on reading partnerships. With all we've got to teach young readers about *reading*, it may seem daunting to find places to fit in partnership instruction. It's important to consider the various structures during reading workshop that we have for teaching our students. We have whole-class mini-lessons, small-group instruction, midworkshop teaching, conferences, and share time during which we can support the work of our classroom partnerships.

One suggestion for fitting in partnership instruction across the year (and not just during the first month or so) is to devote about three whole-class mini-lessons during each study to support the work of reading partnerships. In other words, as we plan instruction for upcoming units of study, it helps to devote a few mini-lessons to instruction that would benefit partnerships and strengthen their work together. So, as I plan studies for reading, I'd want to spend some time observing partnerships at all levels to see what they need to know to help them work more cooperatively and what they need to know that will help their books talks become stronger. Then I can plan a few mini-lessons during each study that would have a positive effect on the partnerships' work.

I've known teachers who've spent several consecutive share sessions at the end of reading workshop working on improving the work of partnerships. For example, if a teacher notices that many partners seem to be stuck in a habit of retelling books together, she might pose an inquiry question like this to her students: "You know what I've noticed? Many of you meet with your partners and immediately retell your books. It's like you've gotten into this habit of retelling, and the thing about getting into a habit is that it can be hard to break. Habits can also make something feel sort of ho hum instead of fun and interesting. But you know what? There are things we can do to move past a habit. One thing that can help is to consider other things you could do, to try some new things. Right now, talk with your partner about some other things you can do together besides retelling." As students turn and talk, the teacher listens in and soon reconvenes the class. "So, readers, you guys named several different things, like acting out a scene from the story to rereading a book like a detective. This week, we are going to be the kinds of partners that try different things besides retelling. We're going to try to move past that habit and do some new things." For the rest of the week during share time, this class would spend time talking about and demonstrating other ways of working with a partner, besides retelling, that they tried during partner reading time.

Obviously, there are plentiful teaching moments to support partnerships within reading workshop, but we also have opportunities to strengthen partnerships during all of the balanced literacy components, as well as during the different subjects we teach throughout the day.

Supporting Partnerships Across the Year

Once we commit to providing instruction for partnerships all year long, we can envision what we might teach. After all, we hope that the content for September partnership instruction will be quite different from April instruction, no matter what grade we teach.

It has helped me to think about a three-phase partnership curriculum that is flexible enough to account for the differences among the grades and general enough to be adapted for different grades. I call this curriculum the Three Cs of Partnership Instruction, and I used to be very proud of that. I never had the opportunity to capitalize on alliteration before. I'm over it now.

Anyway, the phases of instruction are cooperation, conversation, and collaboration.

Cooperation

For many teachers, the first focus of instruction for partnerships is teaching students strategies for working well together—cooperation strategies, one might say. With regard to teaching students about talking with a partner, a teacher would support his students in basic conversation etiquette during this phase. In a kindergarten, this phase of instruction might last weeks longer than in a first grade, for example, and a third-grade teacher might only need to spend a week or so in this phase if his students have had plenty of prior experience working with reading partners.

Of course, the content of instruction on cooperation would also be different in a kindergarten and a third-grade classroom. For instance, a teacher might spend considerable time teaching his kindergartners how to sit side by side and hold a book in the middle so both partners can see it, whereas a third-grade teacher might teach her students how to help each other understand what's going on in each of their chapter books.

The table in Figure 5.1 details some of the objectives for this phase and the possibilitites for instruction that a teacher might pursue.

Figure 5.1	
Cooperation: Getting Partnerships and Book Talks off the Ground	
Partnership Curriculum: *Cooperation Within Partnerships*	**Conversation Curriculum:** *Cooperation in Conversations*
· Students will understand the expectations for partner reading time. · Students will have a repertoire of ways to work together. · Students will have a repertoire of ways to solve problems in their partnerships. · Students will begin to self-manage their partnerships. · Students will notice characteristics of positive cooperation across the day and apply them to their reading partnerships.	· Students will understand how to be an active listener. · Students will understand how to be a helpful speaker. · Students will use courteous conversation behaviors. · Students will know a variety of things they could talk about with partners. · Students will begin to pay attention to conversations across the day and in their lives.

Conversation

This is the second phase of a possible partnership curriculum, and it's the one that is likely to be the longest phase, especially in kindergarten and first-grade class-rooms. For older students who have had years of experience with reading partners, this may not be a time-consuming part of the curriculum. In these classrooms, teachers might spend less whole-class instruction in this phase and do more of this teaching in small groups or during partner conversations. In any classroom, the read-aloud with accountable talk is an invaluable component for helping students grow stronger at talking about books. In general, this is the phase during which we teach students how to have good conversations in general and good book talks in particular (see Figure 5.2).

Collaboration

Our ultimate hope for book talks is that they enable students to grow new ideas and new ways of thinking about texts. We also hope that a result of regular book talks is that our students' comprehension habitually plumbs beneath the literal,

Figure 5.2	

Conversation: Improving Talk and Levels of Engagement During Partner Time

Partnership Curriculum: *Talking Well with a Partner*	Conversation Curriculum: *Having Strong Conversations*
· Students will think toward partnerships as they read independently. · Students will have something to say to their partners. · Partners will make plans for their work together. · Partners will have strategies to stay focused in their book talks. · Partners will be able to resolve differences with civility.	· Students will talk about their books with others. · Students will have a variety of things to talk about with each other. · Students will nurture their conversations by speaking clearly and listening intently. · Students will have a variety of ways to start conversations. · Students will have a variety of ways to maintain conversations. · Students will incorporate the qualities of great conversations and strong book talks into their partnerships.

surface level of understanding characters, stories, and themes. In *Knee to Knee, Eye to Eye: Circling in on Comprehension*, Ardith Cole says, "The easiest way to get a conversation going is to create an environment that honors wondering" (2003, 23), and when readers wonder together about texts, characters, and themes, they grow ideas about these things and their conversation is more likely to be collaborative in nature.

Randy Bomer, formerly a TCRWP colleague, once said that collaboration has happened when people's ideas have changed in some way as a result of a conversation or a series of conversations. Recently, I had dinner with three friends who were enthusiastically supporting one presidential candidate while I was firmly supporting another. My friends were working hard on me, trying to get me to change my mind about who I was supporting. This conversation had several elements of collaboration, although nobody changed their mind. For one thing, as a result of this conversation, I learned things that I hadn't known before, so my thinking was broadened. My friends told me things about their candidate that made me appreciate and like their candidate more, even though the new information didn't make me want to change my position. By vocally defending my views about my candidate in the face of alternative viewpoints, I was inadvertently solidifying my position and strengthening my view. Although this conversation didn't result in the kind of collaboration where any of us changed our minds, we each walked away with new understandings, ideas to consider, and a strengthened position, at least in my case.

In the world of the classroom, evidence of collaboration can often be more subtle and fleeting. Children tend not to reflect on conversations in the same way I did in my example, so they don't often even realize they've collaborated in their partnerships. Unfortunately we are likely to miss dozens of examples of collaborative moments because we're off conferring with other partnerships.

It may be helpful here to include an example of kid collaboration that I observed so that we have a shared vision of how it can sound. I was working in a second-grade classroom listening to a partnership talk about Junie B. Jones. Devin and Zoe were partners in the Junie B. Jones club during a character study. The day before, they each had finished reading a Junie B. Jones book, and they were planning to swap books. In the meantime, they had begun a conversation about their opinion that Junie B. Jones was really a brat even though she was funny sometimes. On the day I observed, they were continuing that conversation. Zoe said, "I agree that she's a brat, but she can also be sort of nice sometimes, like in this part... " Zoe showed Devin the part she was referring to and gave a quick overview of what Junie did that was nice.

"Yeah, that was nice, but even bratty people can be nice sometimes," Devin said.

"Yeah, that's like my sister!" Zoe said, and the girls laughed. "She's so bratty to me, but sometimes she does really nice stuff like let me play with her when her friends are over."

"Sometimes I'm bratty to my little brother 'cause he's so annoying, but mostly I'm nice. Am I nice?" Devin asked.

"You're nice," Zoe assured her. "I guess sometimes nice people can be bratty... "

"And bratty people can be nice, right?" Devin said. "Maybe people can be nice *and* bratty sometimes."

"Yeah, nobody's perfect," Zoe said.

This conversation evolved from what seemed like a statement of fact: Junie B. Jones is a brat. Through their talk together, Zoe and Devin made some connections between real life and the life of Junie B. Jones, and their statement of fact became more nuanced, more sophisticated. They went from labeling Junie as an absolute brat to finding some ambiguity when they realized that she is nice sometimes. Then they connected this with real life—the dual nature of people. Finally, they settled on the thought that nobody is perfect—themselves, their siblings, and Junie B. included. That is an example of kid collaboration.

In order for this collaboration to occur, Devin and Zoe had to be not only invested in their texts, but also invested in their conversation. They certainly were, because they carried its content from one day to the next. They also had to have the conversational stamina to stay with one topic for a while, until it felt exhausted.

Even though Zoe and Devin weaved in personal connections, they didn't stray too far away from the book talk, which can be a common issue when young readers make personal connections. They easily can get carried out of the world of the book to the world of the connection itself.

Figure 5.3 gives examples of some things we can consider to increase the possibilities for collaboration among partners during their conversations.

Figure 5.3	
Collaboration: Growing Ideas in Partnerships and Book Talks	
Partnership Curriculum: *Working Toward New Ideas*	**Conversation Curriculum:** *Growing New Ideas in Conversations*
· Students will stick with a topic of conversation. · Students will disagree with civility. · Students will make plans together for their reading, set purposes for their reading, and make goals for their reading. · Students will be more curious about and interested in each other's thinking. · Students may jot notes as they read to get ready for partner time. · Students will read with their partner in mind, and they'll be able to imagine parts of texts that will be of interest to their partners.	· Students will talk about their books and develop theories about stories, characters, genre, etc. · Students will grow ideas. · Students will express opinions and support them with evidence from the texts. · Students' conversations will be characterized by longer focus on individual topics or ideas. · Students will use a variety of comprehension and conversation strategies.

I think about the students I've taught and the ones you've taught. They are not reading in silence with only the sound of their own thoughts running through their heads. They are reading with company, talking about books with their teachers and with each other. They are initiating conversations, sharing ideas and opinions, expressing emotions, and admitting confusion. Because they choose their own books, they are realizing their own tastes and interests, pursuing their own goals and determining their own purposes, and they are learning what's hard and what's possible as a reader. They are so much more engaged as readers and tuned in to other readers and thinkers around them. So much of this is due to the wonderful work and play they experience within their reading partnerships.

Assessments and Projects:

How Have Reading Clubs Changed Us as Readers, Thinkers, and Talkers?

Assessment is an ongoing process during any study, not simply an end-product of a study. During a cycle of reading clubs, we constantly observe and assess our students as they read and talk about books to determine both the skills and strategies they are using effectively and what they are ready to learn to do. When we assess our students while they are in the act of reading and talking about texts and then turn the information and analysis from our assessments into whole-class, small-group, and one-to-one instruction, we are much more likely to make an immediate and long-term impact on our students' reading, thinking, and talking.

During a cycle of reading clubs, we'll cast a wide net of assessment. We'll assess and observe our students prior to launching the clubs to help us plan fine-tuned instruction. We'll assess while our students are engaged in reading club work to monitor the progress they're making and the struggles they're facing and to keep our instruction responsive to their strengths and needs. We'll assess after they've finished the reading club cycle to find how they have grown and changed as readers, thinkers, and talkers.

Assessment Prior to a Cycle of Reading Clubs

As we approach a study or unit in reading in which we plan to launch reading clubs, it's helpful to begin by determining what our students already know about the kinds of texts that will be part of their reading clubs and what their level of experience is with reading, talking, and thinking about these types of texts. When we begin a cycle of reading clubs with this information on hand, we are able to more closely match our instruction to our students' needs. This pre-assessment can happen in several different ways:

We can observe and take notes on what our students do and say as we let them explore the kinds of texts they'll soon encounter in reading clubs.

For a few days before we launch reading clubs, we tend to let our students explore the kinds of texts they'll encounter in their reading clubs during partner reading time. We can pay close attention to what they do and say about these texts in order to figure out how to angle our teaching for the reading club cycle. As my students explore the kinds of texts they'll soon be reading in reading clubs, I want to note the following sorts of things:

- comments they make about the texts (which can reveal their preconceptions, prior knowledge, what catches their interest in the texts, etc.)

- how students approach and navigate the texts (which can reveal their familiarity with a variety of text structures)

- attitudes they exhibit about the texts (which can reveal their interest level, reading habits, etc.)

For example, prior to a nonfiction study as my students were exploring nonfiction texts during partner reading, if I heard several students say nonfiction was boring or if they seemed resistant to put down their chapter books to read nonfiction, I'd want to be sure to find nonfiction of interest to them for reading clubs. If, prior to a cycle of poetry clubs, many of my students struggle to read unfamiliar poems because there is a lack of helpful picture support, I will be sure to gather poetry books that have stronger picture support and poetry books with easier poetry, and I will be sure to make poetry booklets full of the poems we've learned in class over the course of the year.

We can use what we know about our readers as they read their just-right books to help us plan reading strategy instruction during reading clubs.

If many of my students are reading texts with considerable picture support during reading time, I'll want to make sure that the books in the reading clubs also offer lots of picture support. If many students still need support in reading with fluency and phrasing as we approach a character study reading club cycle, I might decide to guide them into character clubs with books that are slightly easier than their just-right reading level, so they can work on both reading with improved fluency and reading with a deeper understanding of characters.

In general, I'll want to make sure that the levels of texts in the reading club baskets reflect the readers' abilities. I'll want to think about the decoding and comprehension skills and strategies readers need at different levels because it's important to incorporate that into my instruction.

We can use our read-aloud time to model proficient reading of the kinds of texts students will have in their reading club baskets and provide opportunities for conversations about the texts to determine the kinds of talk support our students will need.

A week or two before launching a reading club cycle, many teachers use read-aloud time to warm students up to the reading, thinking, and talking they'll soon be doing in their reading clubs. During these read-aloud sessions, we can model how proficient readers read the sorts of texts they'll soon encounter in their reading clubs. We can listen for clues to students' attitudes and ideas about the kinds of texts we're reading. We can provide opportunities for some whole-class conversations to help us figure out strategies we could teach.

Perhaps we notice that our students have a hard time sticking with a topic in conversation. This suggests that we might plan to teach them that readers stick to a topic for a while in a book talk. We can prompt our students to turn and talk to their partners about the read-aloud text to see how comfortable they are using the strategies they'll use often in their reading clubs. If character reading clubs are coming up, I could plan to observe students' comfort with inferring because I know that's something I plan to teach them to do well during the reading club cycle. So, as I read *Koala Lou* by Mem Fox, I could say something like, "Readers, turn and talk to your partner. Tell each other what you think Koala Lou must be feeling right now." As they talk to each other, I could scoot around, listening in to get a sense of their ability to make inferences.

Most often, we conduct pre-assessment for reading clubs informally and gather information through conversations with and observations of readers. Figure 6.1 presents some guiding questions we might consider.

Figure 6.1	
Questions to Consider for Pre-assessment	**How Might We Get This Information?**
What do my students already know about the kinds of texts they'll encounter in their reading clubs?	· Put out baskets of books that will likely be in reading clubs and let students explore them. Listen for prior knowledge that they are bringing to their work ("Oh, let's check the index to see if there's information about that."), including their understandings and misunderstandings about the genre or type of text ("We can start reading right here in the middle to find the information we want. We don't have to start on the first page in these kinds of books."). · Compile a chart of students' notions about the kinds of books or the kinds of work they'll be doing soon (i.e., What do we know now about poetry? What can help us get to know our characters well? What are some special features of nonfiction texts?).

Figure 6.1 *(continued)*	
Questions to Consider for Pre-assessment	**How Might We Get This Information?**
What are my students' attitudes toward and prior experiences with the kinds of texts they'll encounter in their reading clubs?	· Conduct informal interviews with questions such as "What do you think about poetry?" or "Who is one of your favorite characters in books?" or "What kinds of nonfiction books do you like to read?" · Prior to the beginning of clubs, read aloud and talk about a text that would fit with the reading club cycle and note students' opinions, attitudes, ideas, etc.
What are my students' abilities with regard to the skills and strategies that are most necessary to read the texts they'll encounter in their reading clubs?	· Consider the skills and strategies that students will need to read and talk about the texts in the upcoming reading club cycle, and take a couple of days to monitor students' proficiency using these skills and strategies as they read their just-right books. · In read-aloud time, prompt students to use the strategies you plan to teach during reading clubs. Listen to a range of readers to get a sense of their comfort with the strategies. · Check to see that the reading levels of the books that will be part of reading clubs largely reflect the reading levels of your students.

In-the-Moment Assessment: Assessing in the Midst of a Reading Club Cycle

Have you ever sat alongside a child during a reading conference and wondered, "What the heck am I going to teach right now?" Perhaps the child is reading a high-level text with accuracy, fluency, and comprehension, and it's hard to discern any reading vulnerabilities she has. Or maybe you're working with a child who has so many needs that it's difficult to figure out where to go first. Or maybe your principal is observing you, and your mind simply goes blank.

In those moments when I'm mentally scrambling to decide what to teach, I fantasize about having a Magic Eight Ball to shake that will tell me exactly what to do.

I imagine saying to the child, "Just a second, Jeremy. Let me check something," as I turn ever so slightly away to give the Magic Eight Ball a quick, covert jiggle while silently mouthing the question, "What should I teach this child?" Of course, I know what the Magic Eight Ball is going to say, because it always says the same thing: "The answer you're looking for is right in front of you." Thanks. Maybe I should get reading conference tarot cards.

During reading clubs, our ongoing observations and assessments while students are in the act of reading and talking about their books may give us lots of questions (and the occasional moments of instructional paralysis), but they can also help us answer several questions that reveal both what our students have learned and what we can plan to teach.

In the midst of a reading club cycle, I'll want to watch my students' use of strategies and their proficiency with various reading skills, both to plan instruction for the upcoming weeks of reading clubs as well as to plan instruction beyond the cycle of reading clubs. The information I gather during reading clubs is also useful as I plan for small-group instruction and the work we'll do in the other balanced literacy components. These are some broad categories of information I tend to look for as I watch students during reading clubs:

- In general, what are they doing well and what do they need to learn to do with regard to print strategies, fluency, and comprehension strategies?
- In particular, what are they doing well and what do they need to do better with regard to the content of our reading club study?
- What are their book talk strengths and struggles?

For different cycles of reading clubs, I've used a variety of assessment sheets. Appendix C provides a general, all-purpose assessment sheet form that would work for any kind of reading club. Figure 6.2 shows a portion of an in-progress sample of this sheet. The students' names go in the left-hand column along with the books or topic they're working with. I put partners' names one above the other. In the top row, I jot the skills and strategies for reading and for book talks that are taught during the reading club cycle. I carry these assessment sheets on my note-taking clipboard and quickly fill in the boxes depending on what I see (or don't see) my students doing. I either make notes on these assessment sheets while I'm conferring, or else I add notations on this sheet by cross-checking with my conferring notes. I can use this sheet to assess students' use of these strategies during both reading clubs time and during independent reading workshop.

In the boxes next to the students' names, I always jot the dates of conferences as well as notes about strategy use or nonuse. I also indicate whether I observed the student using the strategy independently (without prompting or instruction) or whether the student needed a little nudging to use the strategy. If a child needs a lot of extra support, I usually highlight the box. If many boxes are highlighted for a particular child, I would develop an instructional plan to offer extra support to the student, and I'd consider how the other components of balanced literacy could help. If many boxes are highlighted for a particular strategy, indicating that many students still need extra support, I would decide whether or not to offer more whole-class instruction on the strategy or whether I should pull together small groups to teach the strategy.

Figure 6.2

Sample Assessment Sheet for Use During Reading Clubs

Reading Club Cycle _____ *Character Reading Clubs* _____   Start Date: _____

Students' Names	Target Skills and Strategies		
	Knows, uses char. names in retelling and/or in talks about the story	Makes inferences about main character	Cross-checks to figure out tricky words
Leni (Biscuit)	3/4/08 Yes	3/5/08 Needs support to infer traits	
Crystal (Biscuit)	3/4/08 Yes	3/5/08 "B is playful because he always plays"	
Michael (Horrible Harry)	3/6/08 Yes	3/6/08 "HH trouble-maker…" (used HH's actions as text. ev.)	
Alex (Horrible Harry)		3/6/08 HH tries to make kids laugh (uses actions+dial. as text. ev.)	

I tend to gather this information during reading conferences and small-group instruction. Yet sometimes in the midst of a cycle of reading clubs, I may have a specific skill or strategy that I'd like to assess. In this case, I'll set up a slightly more formal opportunity for assessment. For example, during a poetry study I usually spend a stretch of time teaching strategies for reading with fluency and prosody. To assess this skill specifically, I might set up an opportunity for each of my students to demonstrate their skill. One year, I asked each of my students to select a poem they knew pretty well and liked a lot, and I made them a copy of the poems. Over the course of a few days, I met with all of the students in a one-on-one setting and asked them each to read aloud the poem they chose. Twice they read the poem aloud, and I assessed their fluency. After the students read aloud their poem, we had a brief conversation about why they chose that particular poem. This gave me some insights into their ideas, attitudes, and tastes in poetry.

Another way of assessing in the midst of a reading club cycle is to examine the artifacts of the students' work. My students kept work folders in their reading club basket that held any kind of note taking, writing, or idea organizing they did in their reading club. For example, during nonfiction reading clubs, I spend some time teaching my students to synthesize and summarize text by jotting their thoughts on sticky notes as they read or on a note-taking sheet, such as an information web. I would tell my students that I'll be looking through their reading club work folders after school. "I'm going to look at your sticky notes or information webs because I want to see how it's going when you jot summarizing and synthesizing notes," I would say. This will give me information about who needs more support in the form of a conference or small-group instruction (if there are several children with similar needs) as well as information about students who are able to synthesize well and are ready to move on to other instruction. There are examples of note-taking sheets in Appendix D.

Finally, besides looking for information on how students are integrating the skills and strategies I've been teaching them for reading and talking about books, I'll also want to observe my students' attitudes about, engagement with, and knowledge of the texts in the reading clubs. I'll look for evidence that they are comfortable in negotiating the special characteristics of the texts and the work they are doing, that they have strategies to deal with difficulty, and that they can determine purposes and make plans for reading texts with a partner.

Assessment at the End of a Reading Club Cycle

It's rather simple, actually. At the end of the reading club cycle, you'll want to devote two days to administering a multiple-choice test to see what your students can do as readers. On these test days, they'll need number 2 pencils, a nutritious breakfast, and a sign on your door that says "QUIET — TESTING" in all capital letters. No, I'm just kidding. Maybe this is not really funny. Maybe it's not the time for joking about high-stakes testing in the early grades. Sorry.

Let me start this again: Because one of the defining characteristics of reading clubs is that they provide opportunities for our students to read in authentic ways, with the same kinds of purposes, plans, and intentions that proficient, avid readers often have, it makes sense that any end-of-reading-clubs assessment is also as authentic as possible.

If reading clubs enable students to become experts about a topic, an author, a series, and so on, we can ask students to demonstrate their expertise by giving them opportunities to present something, to make something, or to write something that shows others what they've learned or how they've changed as readers. There are many ways to do this. Here are some suggestions:

Self-Reflections

At the end of a reading club cycle, we can give the students opportunities to reflect on the ways they've grown as readers in general or how they've become experts on their reading club topic in particular. This can be done several ways. Depending on our students' writing abilities and stamina, we can give them opportunities to complete written reflections of the work they did or the knowledge they acquired in the reading club cycle.

These self-reflections can be responses to our questions. Many teachers create reflection sheets with questions that ask students to consider particular aspects of their work in the reading club. After students have had several reading club experiences as well as some opportunities to reflect on their work, teachers are less apt to ask prompting questions on the reflections and instead offer open-ended questions for the student to reflect as he or she sees fit. There are several examples of reflection sheets in Appendix E.

Oral Presentations

After students have worked in a reading club for a week or at the end of a whole cycle of reading clubs, teachers often provide time on the last day for the students to share their thinking and learning with others in the form of an oral presentation. These presentations usually occur in partnership-to-partnership or small-group settings.

In these configurations, partners meet with other partners and share what they've learned, what they did as readers, and what their partnership did particularly well. The teacher might prompt specific talking points by saying things like, "Make sure you tell the other partnership about the new information you learned about your topic," or "Talk about the character you got to know in your club in a way that gives the other partnership a real sense of your character's personality." Other times, the teacher may leave these oral presentations more open-ended. As the partners share with each other, the teacher might scurry around so she can listen in to what many of them are saying.

Reading Club Projects

At the end of a cycle of reading clubs, many teachers give students a chance to make a project that reflects what they know and how they've changed as readers, thinkers, and talkers. Marie Clay says, "A teacher's call for a child to construct a response, whatever form that response takes, requires the child to relate, link, remember, call up, relearn, monitor, problem-solve, and all those other powerful mental activities that help children and adults adapt and create new solutions (Clay 1998, 190). In the best-case scenario, the students would decide for themselves how best to share their learning. During a fairy tale/folktale study, then, in one classroom, many things might occur. For example, Anna and Sophia acted out their favorite scene from *Rumplestiltskin*, the fairy tale they studied, while Louis and Charlotte acted out a scene from one of the versions of *Little Red Riding Hood*. All the dramatists used props and costumes. John and Jonah decided they wanted to write another version of *Three Billy Goats Gruff*, using John Scieszka as their mentor. Several other partnerships decided to rank the versions of the fairy tale they studied using a variety of criteria, depending on their fairy tale. The Cinderella partners, for example, ranked the versions of *Cinderella* according to the nastiness factor of the stepmother and stepsisters. Joseph and Morgan practiced reading aloud one of the shorter versions of their fairy tale because they wanted to read it to the principal.

There are a couple of challenges when students work on projects at the end of a reading club cycle. First, it's difficult to find time for students to work on them. In my experience, I've offered partner reading time for a few days at the end of the reading club cycle for my students to work on their projects together. I've also let them work on their projects during our choice time, if they chose to do so. Many partnerships would do some of the work at home as well.

Second, some partnerships may not be as inspired as others to turn their reading club work into some sort of "thing." If this is the case, we can, of course, gently nudge them toward some sort of work. We might suggest some things they could do and let them choose which one they are most interested in, or we can give them time to research the other partnerships to see what they are doing. That might ignite some inspiration. If it's simply the case that Adrian and Emily are at a loss for what to do with *The Three Bears*, we can have a book talk with them as a way to find out what they've learned, what they're thinking about, and what meaning they've constructed after reading several versions.

Some teachers create whole-class projects based on the work students have done in their reading clubs. One year, for example, as a culminating project for our work in nonfiction reading clubs, my students all contributed a page of facts to our class Big Book Insect Anthology. Each student chose a piece of new information they learned about their insect and designed a page for our big book that presented the fact. They used the features of nonfiction in their pages, and then we all worked together to figure out how to organize the information. The students came up with book sections such as "Insects That Sting," "Insects That Don't Bother People," "Beetles," and so on. A small group of students divided labor to create a table of contents, an index, and a book cover, complete with a back cover blurb.

In another class, after the students studied characters in their reading clubs, the whole class wrote character riddles that they posted on the bulletin board outside of their classroom. Some of the riddles included, "I'm a pig. I like baths and the library. Who am I?" and "I'm an adventurous girl. I tell fibs sometimes, but I'm a good friend anyway. Who am I?" For homework, each child thought of three riddles they could ask about their character, and they met with their partner to decide which one they would publish on the bulletin board. The rest of the riddles that weren't published on the bulletin board were written on little pieces of paper, and the class had a new game: Guess the Character! They kept the riddles in a jar, and a few students created a game board with a spinner to go along with it.

When we decide that our students will make, do, write, or present some sort of culminating project after their reading club work, it's important that we allow them to create and execute their own self-initiated projects as often as possible.

Final Thoughts

It's important to remember that what our students have learned or have been exposed to during our instruction doesn't always appear in their repertoire of reading skills, strategies, and habits immediately. The evidence of learning may take some time to rise to the surface, because the student may still be in the midst of processing and controlling it. Don't despair! Here are some ways to track learning long after the cycle of reading clubs is over:

· Look for evidence of new habits and attitudes in students' independent reading that they've carried away from the reading club cycle.

· Watch how students think and talk about texts with their partners once the reading club is finished.

· Provide opportunities in read-aloud for students to think and talk about texts in the ways they did during reading club cycles.

You may find yourself excited and surprised by the new skills and habits your readers show long after they've completed their reading clubs.

Zooming In: Planning Instruction for Specific Kinds of Reading Clubs

I'll never forget one August several years ago when Stephanie Parsons, my friend and colleague at PS 321, reported to school with a brand-new plan book. This plan book was unlike anything I had seen before. Many teachers, myself included, share a general dissatisfaction with commercially produced plan books. The ones that are sold in teacher supply stores never seem to match the demands we have for them. There's not enough space to write plans, or the space to write plans is not organized as we would like. Many plan books seem to be produced with secondary school teachers' needs in mind as they contain several pages dedicated to class lists and grading grids. And sometimes, it is the simple (yet superficial) fact that most mass-produced plan books aren't aesthetically pleasing. Yes, unappealing fonts and bland color schemes can be a deal-breaker.

Stephanie decided to take matters into her own hands. She designed a plan book that fit her needs and that was custom-made to her own tastes and specifications. She published it herself at the local independently owned copy shop. Was I jealous! I mean impressed. Okay, jealous and impressed. Stephanie's plan book was a sight to behold. You could even say it glowed.

It's important that the tools we use in our classrooms to do our jobs well are in alignment with our teaching personalities, our organizational styles, and our belief systems. For these reasons, I think it can be frustrating when we feel we don't have any other choice but to use a particular tool that doesn't quite suit our needs.

That said, I'm about to humbly share one of the tools I've used for reading clubs, my planning guide. My reason for including this is not to suggest that this is the planning guide that must be used in order for your clubs to be successful, but rather to make the point that all kinds of reading clubs have certain planning considerations in common. I use this planning guide for any kind of reading club because it includes all the elements I need to consider so that my plans for reading clubs are thorough and responsible. Even though the details and content of nonfiction reading clubs and independent project reading clubs are quite different, the major considerations that underlie planning for them are quite similar, and these considerations are reflected in this planning guide.

In the chapters that follow, I will use my planning guide as a framework for presenting ideas about various kinds of reading clubs. Of course, you'll want to design your own planning guide to meet your idiosyncratic teaching needs, your particular organizational style, and your deeply felt font preferences. Appendix F provides a blank version of my planning guide form and Appendix G provides several example planning guides for a variety of reading clubs.

Reading Club Planning Guide

Reading Club Cycle: _____   Dates: _____

Readers' needs:
I think about the issues and interests, needs and strengths of the readers in my class. I want this to be the starting point for my reading club planning. I might list several things that I want to work on with small groups of students, as well as any whole-class concerns I might have.

Featured skills and strategies that I will teach:
In this section, I try to think about the demands the particular cycle of reading clubs might put on my students. For example, if I'm going to launch mystery book reading clubs, I know my students will have to develop their abilities for reading with an eye for detail and nuance. I know they'll need support in accumulating the story across pages. In other words, I try to figure out some "survival strategies" students will need to read the texts in the particular kind of reading club cycle I'm planning to implement. These featured skills and strategies will also include instruction that helps my students talk well about texts.

Real-life purposes, habits, and goals readers might have:
If we're trying to launch reading clubs that enable students to do the kind of reading that real readers do outside the boundaries of a classroom, it's essential to think about the real-life habits, purposes, and goals that readers have and find ways to include these things in our instruction.

Getting ready for reading clubs:
I list the things I need to do to get my students and my classroom ready for the reading club cycle that is imminent. This may include changes to the classroom library, plans for familiarizing students with the kinds of texts they'll soon be reading and the kinds of conversations they'll soon be having, and considering the kinds of note taking students may do within their reading clubs.

Teaching emphasis for reading clubs, Week 1:
I tend to plan to build upon the skill set my readers already have as word-solvers and meaning-makers and also to teach my students some survival strategies for reading the texts in their reading clubs. I also make plans for instruction about partner work, talking well about texts, and so on.

Teaching emphasis for reading clubs, Week 2:
Weeks 2 and 3 are flexibly planned in advance, and I watch my students carefully during the first week of reading clubs in order to determine an appropriate direction to take my students during Weeks 2 and 3. In the chapters that follow, I will share specific ideas for different kinds of reading clubs.

Teaching emphasis for reading clubs, Week 3 (optional):
Week 3 (or even Week 4) tends to be an optional extension of the reading club cycle. If my students are highly engaged in their work, if there are curricular reasons to extend the reading clubs, I will. If we start a third week of reading clubs, we may reconfigure the reading club baskets into different categories.

Assessment:
I want to use authentic assessments that provide information about my students' reading and talking skills, as well as how they've changed as a result of their reading club work.

Possible project/celebration/outcome of reading clubs:
For many cycles of clubs, ideas for projects and celebrations arise organically based on students' interests and the direction of their work. This may be hard to plan in advance.

What's Your Genre?
Genre-Based Reading Clubs

We were nearing the end of our book club meeting, and so it was time to decide what we would read next. It was Ellen's turn to bring the selection of books from which we'd choose. Ellen is on my Top Ten List of Well-Read Friends, so I was eager to see the choices she would offer. As she pulled some books from her bag, she told us that she wanted to do something different this time. Ellen said she chose books in genres that we hadn't yet read in our book club, and according to her informal research, the books she brought were said to be highly regarded in their particular genres.

After explaining her plan, she handed out the books to the group. We flipped through them, skimmed some pages, read the blurbs, and made comments to each other as we passed the books around. As usual, we took a vote to select the next book we'd all read, and characteristic of this particular book club, there was a considerable amount of influence peddling, voter intimidation, and quid pro quo in the air.

Although I don't remember all of the titles or genres Ellen brought, I do remember that we ended up reading *Something Wicked This Way Comes* by Ray Bradbury. It wasn't only a choice for a particular title, it was also a choice for a particular genre. And it wasn't my choice. By a long shot.

A few days later, I went to the local independent bookstore to buy *Something Wicked This Way Comes*. The knowledgeable clerk directed me to an unfamiliar area in the store. I had never set foot in this section before, not even to take a shortcut to the café! As I moved along the aisle, I felt as if I were on another planet as a reader. I was a little disoriented and a bit hesitant. For a moment, I even forgot my purpose for being there, although maybe I'm being a little melodramatic in my recollection. In any case, when I found the Ray Bradbury book I had to buy, it looked and felt different than my usual choices.

You see, I'm a creature of habit as a reader... not that there's anything wrong with that. I go to the same sections of the bookstore time after time, and the majority of my reading life occurs within the comfortable confines of a few preferred genres. *Is* there anything wrong with that? After all, there are good habits and bad habits, and I would think that having almost any kind of reading habit is probably a good sort of habit to have. In this case, however, my book club assignment made me know that being a creature of habit as a reader had limited my reading life.

I quickly realized that my habits had also limited my reading abilities once I began to read *Something Wicked This Way Comes*. This book was my first venture into the genre of sci-fi/fantasy, and I had to work really hard just to understand the story. I had trouble suspending disbelief when I needed to, and I struggled unsuccessfully to cozy up to the characters, which is something I typically do as a reader. Frequently, I found myself rereading, especially those parts where strange, supernatural things happened. As a reader, I was breaking a sweat.

As you might imagine, I didn't participate much at the book club meeting that followed. I nodded here and there while filling up on snacks, but I was really more content to listen to my friends' conversation. A few people in our book club are experienced readers of books like this, and they did most of the talking. They helped me see and appreciate aspects of the text, the genre, and the author's craft that I hadn't noticed much in the midst of reading the book myself. They clarified the story as well, which I found helpful.

Although I haven't returned to that genre since, it was an important experience for me to read a text outside of my typical reading territory. I became aware of some of my limitations as a reader while also stretching myself to grow. I opened a door to a new genre and took a look around, even though I was admittedly eager to return to the comfort of my usual genres and bookstore aisles. And once again, for the zillionth time, I was reminded of the enormous benefits of talking about books with others.

Although it's absolutely fine (and probably most typical) to have text genres that we tend to read most of all, I would also say that venturing outside of our comfort books is an empowering experience. It's also an experience that we are wise to provide to our youngest readers.

Before delving into the details of planning instruction for genre-based reading clubs, it's important to state that although we may plan to spotlight the genre of nonfiction in February, for example, I am not suggesting that we limit our students' interactions with nonfiction texts to only that time. Throughout the school year and throughout the day, we want our young readers to read, think, and talk about a wide variety of texts within many different genres. So it's important to select texts from a variety of genres for interactive read-aloud time and shared reading across the year. Also, it's wise to have a variety of genres represented in the portion of our library that is leveled according to text difficulty so that our students have opportunities to select just-right texts in different genres for their independent reading time all year long. After all, if we consider the most proficient, engaged readers we know, it's likely that they navigate the worlds of several different genres each day.

On a related note, if we plan to spotlight nonfiction texts in February reading clubs, for example, that wouldn't mean our students would be "done" with nonfiction for the year after that study is complete. Instead, we would encourage them to continue to select just-right nonfiction texts of interest for their independent reading, and we would still read aloud a variety of nonfiction texts even after the nonfiction study is finished.

It makes a lot of sense for our students to explore a mix of genres while they are still developing their reading palates. Our students bring a wide variety of tastes, interests, and life experiences to our classrooms, and it's important that they realize there is a wide world of texts available that will appeal to their passions and sensibilities, and interests and tastes, not only to their reading levels.

Planning Instruction for Genre-Based Reading Clubs

After making the decision about the genres you want to study closely with your students, it's time to plan the details for how your genre-based reading clubs will go. No matter the genre, there are some typical ways that I tend to approach the work the class will do within a genre study. In this chapter, I hope to clearly describe a pathway for genre-based reading clubs using poetry as the example genre and using the planning guide for reading clubs (see Appendix F) as a framework.

What are the featured reading skills and strategies that I will teach during this reading club cycle?

When we teach children how to read texts within a genre well, we'll want to consider the skills and strategies they'll need to read the words, to understand the texts, and to have thoughts about what they've read. Often I've chosen a couple of reading or talking skills to focus on during a reading club cycle, and I try to select skills and strategies that seem to be essential for negotiating the particular genre my students are learning to read well. I like to think of these as survival skills and strategies.

In the case of poetry, I would say that predicting is a skill that a poetry reader might use occasionally, but being able to envision, to create mental images from the words in poetry, seems to me to be one of the essential survival skills for reading poetry. Because most poetry doesn't come with comprehensive illustrations, if it's even illustrated at all, it's crucial that poetry readers make their own rich pictures in their minds as they read. Also, because exquisite and precise words and imagery are characteristics of poetry and much of the craft work involved in writing poetry, I would say that poets invite us—no, they rely upon us—to richly envision as we read their poems.

In one of my favorite books about teaching poetry, *For the Good of the Earth and Sun*, Georgia Heard quotes poet Stanley Kunitz, who says, "Above all, poetry is intended for the ear. It must be felt to be understood, and before it can be felt, it must be heard" (Heard 1989, 8). If poetry is meant to be read aloud, it's easy to argue that fluency, particularly with respect to prosody, is an important skill that avid readers of poetry need to have in their reading repertoire. With this in mind, I would make sure to plan instruction that teaches young readers how to make mental pictures and read with fluency in a poetry study. If I were launching reading clubs for a poetry study in third or fourth grade, I might very well pick other strategies to focus on during whole-class instruction, such as interpretation. After determining the survival strategies I would teach students to use with particular genres, I would also make sure that I observe my students closely as they read the particular genre during our study and offer instruction on any other strategies they might need.

Although it's helpful to consider what I've called the "survival strategies" for particular genres and make instructional plans to teach them to young readers, it's worth emphasizing that we don't want our students to be "one-trick ponies" with regard to strategy use. By this I mean we want to be careful that our students don't rely heavily on a particular strategy or two at the exclusion of the other thinking work necessary to read with deepening comprehension. A proficient reader is able to orchestrate lots of strategies for figuring out words and making meaning, so even though we may highlight a particular strategy in a sequence of mini-lessons, we always would want to offer our students instruction so that they become the kinds of readers who easily use a variety of strategies to figure out words and to understand what they are reading. Our brief, whole-class mini-lessons over a few days may focus on the strategy of making mental images, but we would want to make sure that our reading conferences and small-group instruction support students to become the kinds of readers who are flexible and automatic with a variety of strategies.

Extending to Other Genres: Helping Yourself Plan Instruction for Focus Skills and Strategies

1. Read a variety of texts in the genre and pay attention to the reading skills and strategies you most often use to negotiate the text, to deal with difficulty, and to understand what you're reading.

2. Gather a sample of children's texts (across a range of difficulty levels) in the genre you're about to study together. Look through the texts and think about the skills and strategies your students are likely to need in order to read these texts with fluency, accuracy, and understanding.

3. Notice any special qualities, text structures, or other characteristics of the genre, and include those in your list of items to consider teaching during mini-lessons, conferences, and small-group instruction.

4. Appendix H offers specific ideas for skill and strategy instruction in other genres.

What are some purposes, habits, and goals that readers of the genre might have?

It's important that we move beyond planning genre studies for the purpose of "covering" genre to planning genre studies for the purpose of broadening the scope and possibilities for our children's reading, thinking, and talking. When we keep in mind the fact that we're teaching students to read for a lifetime, it makes sense to teach our students about the power of developing good habits, having a sense of purpose, and determining goals for themselves and their reading. We'll also want to find ways to tuck in examples of the joy and passion characteristic of avid readers of the particular genres we intend to study as we make our curricular plans.

If we imagine implementing a poetry study in our classroom, the following is a list of possible habits, purposes, and goals for reading poetry that we may want to include in our instruction.

Readers of poetry may:

· read poetry aloud

· read poetry to soothe and comfort themselves

· read poetry to appreciate beautiful language and unique imagery

· read poetry to help them better understand life and world events

· read poetry because it evokes emotions such as sadness, hilarity, joy, anger, surprise, confusion, and so on

· have favorite poets

· have favorite poems that they reread and keep in special places like wallets, notebooks, picture frames, refrigerator doors, and so on

- have themes they particularly like (nature, love, politics, fear, etc.) and look for poems about these themes
- think of other people when they read poetry ("My best friend would love this poem"; "This poem sounds like so-and-so"; etc.)
- buy poetry books for special occasions and give poems as gifts to others
- have favorite lines from poems
- memorize favorite poems
- read poetry to inspire writing poetry

We may decide that some of these habits or goals are worth mentioning in our instruction, and then we can teach strategies to help students acquire a particular habit or meet a personal goal. I think it's worth a few mini-lessons to teach kids that poetry is meant to be read aloud and there are things we pay attention to in order to read it aloud well. We notice white space, line breaks, and punctuation; we consider the tone and theme of the poem and try to make our voices reflect them; we can practice reading poems aloud and notice their rhythm; and so on. The beauty of this instruction is that it isn't limited to poetry studies. This teaching can help kids with reading aloud well in any genre or situation.

Other items on this list of habits, goals, and purposes could be taught on a smaller scale, such as during reading conferences or small-group work within a poetry study. We can also use our share sessions at the end of reading club time each day to teach our students about good habits, real purposes, and personal goals that avid readers of poetry, or any other genre, might have.

Extending to Other Genres: Helping Yourself Plan Instruction About Reading Habits and Goals

1. Read the genre yourself (or reflect on a time when you read the genre in the past) and think about your purposes, habits, and goals. You might also talk to others who are well-read in the genre and ask them about these things.

2. Think about the outcomes that may occur when reading in the genre. For example, a nonfiction reader might be reading about a particular topic to help her understand something better. A reader of poetry might be trying to

find the perfect poem to post on his website. A reader of Eleanor Roosevelt biographies may be trying to find inspiration and strength for her own life and actions.

3. Appendix H offers specific ideas for habits and goals instruction for other genres.

Getting Ready for Reading Clubs

In order to get our students ready for the work they'll do in reading clubs, there are a few important things to consider before you kick off your genre-based clubs. It's enormously helpful to provide time for students to develop a sense of the characteristics, the look, the sound, and the typical structures of the genre before they dive into their reading club work. We'll want to make sure to reorganize the classroom library so that it supports the genre study, and we'll want to think about how we'll get the genre-based books into our students' hands.

Surrounding Ourselves in the Genre

Right before the official start of the genre-based reading club cycle, it's worth the time to spend a week or more preparing students and whetting their appetites for the upcoming genre study by reading aloud texts in the genre and providing opportunities for students to explore the genre on their own.

During the week or so preceding genre-based reading clubs, I would take some time during our morning meeting to ask my students what they already know about the particular genre we'll soon be studying. I would take notes and put their ideas on a chart so that as we progress through the actual study, they'll be able to see how their ideas about the genre have changed and grown. Often, some of their ideas will end up being revised or dropped altogether. One year, several students argued that poetry always rhymes, and I put that on the "What We Know About Poetry" chart. Of course, soon into the study, that idea was quickly discarded.

In *Reading & Writing Informational Text in the Primary Grades* (2003), Nell Duke and V. Susan Bennett-Armistead suggest the importance of exposing children to the diversity of texts within genre categories. In the days before and throughout our poetry reading clubs, for example, I'll likely read aloud poetry as much as possible both during our formal interactive read-aloud time and in any other moments in the day when I can tuck it in. I'll read aloud many different kinds of poems, from silly poems to serious poems; from poems that speak to current events in the world to poems that address important topics in our classroom; from information-poetic texts (Duke and Bennett-Armistead 2003) to limericks; from several poems by one particular author to several poems on the same topic by a variety of authors.

During shared reading, I'll use poems as the text we read and think about together. I'll ask my students to talk about what they notice, and I'll invite them to read the poems along with me so we can practice using our poetry-reading voices. I'll ask students to close their eyes and let the words wash over them. I'll ask them what they are picturing as I read the poem. We'll talk about any number of other things, too, that pique the children's interest in poetry.

As we surround ourselves with poetry during some of the components of balanced literacy, I also invite my students to assume the roles of poetry finders so that they bring in examples of poetry from real life. Some kids might bring in books of poetry they have at home, while others might bring in things like greeting cards and found poetry. Some might share stories of discovering poems in unexpected places, such as in the subway or on a poster in the doctor's office. Others may debate whether or not songs are really poems set to music.

I know many teachers who create a spot in the classroom for children to bring in the texts they've found and other artifacts of the genre they'll soon be studying. The items become a collection rich with possibilities. Children can sort through the collection and notice different kinds of texts that are characteristic of a single genre. With regard to poetry, children may also begin to notice and name different categories of the genre; for example, poems that rhyme, poems by kids, and so on. After discovering the rich variety of poetry, "Students begin to know what different kinds of poetry sound like, and they come to their own understanding of what makes a poem a poem" (Heard 1989, 3).

For homework, we can assign our students to have conversations about the genre with prompts such as these: "Ask someone at home if they have a favorite poem from childhood"; "Ask someone at home to tell you all they know about poetry"; "Read this poem with someone at home and ask them 'What do you think?'"

I also try to notice and make public the times when students' oral language approximates the genre in some way. For example, as we were just beginning a nonfiction reading study, Michael came into school one morning telling anyone within earshot, "I learned some amazing things about snakes on the TV show I watched last night. First, I learned that some of them can eat whole rats, if they're hungry, that is, and second, I learned that there are some snakes that can jump!" I told Michael that the way he explained his snake facts sounded a lot like a nonfiction book. "Michael, you said those facts like you are an authority on snakes. I can imagine what you'd write in a nonfiction book about snakes." I pretended that I had a book in my hands and began acting as if I were reading it, a technique many of us have learned from Natalie Louis, the coauthor with Lucy Calkins of *Writing for Readers: Teaching Skills and Strategies* (2003). I looked over the imaginary cover and "read" it aloud, "Amazing Information About Snakes by Michael." I turned the imaginary pages and read, "Are you interested in learning about snakes? Then this book has information for you!" I turned an imaginary page and read, "First, did you know that snakes can eat whole rats at one time, if they're hungry, that is!" Then I turned another imaginary page and read, "'Second, did you know that some snakes can jump?' Gee, Michael, you're talking like a nonfiction author."

One of my favorite examples of a student's oral language matching a genre occurred when Julian took off his Yankees hat and his curls sprang to life one spring morning. Stephanie yelled, "Julian, your hair is hyper!" What an image her words created, right in the midst of our poetry study! I immediately cut a big square of butcher paper and wrote, "We Speak Like Poets!" on the top. During our morning meeting, I told my class about Stephanie's comment (after asking Julian's permission), and I wrote it on a sticky note, which I placed on the chart. When I hear students say things that seem to match the genre we are about to study (or another genre altogether), I try to acknowledge it in the moment or jot it down in my notes for use at a later time. I also invite students to be on the lookout for when their talk sounds like text.

This work of collecting artifacts and morsels of oral language is more than an exercise in accumulating examples to make a pretty classroom display of the genre. When artifacts of the genre are gathered, students can compare and contrast the examples and begin to develop their own ideas and theories about genre boundaries, characteristics, and definitions.

How might we surround ourselves in the genre before the official launch of our genre-based reading clubs?

- read aloud a variety of texts or excerpts from texts in the genre
- use texts from the genre for shared reading
- notice and make public oral language that sounds like the genre

- encourage students to be "genre detectives" and invite them to bring in their findings
- assign conversation topics about the genre for homework

Reconfiguring the Classroom Library to Support the Genre Study

It's important that the classroom library changes throughout the year to reflect the studies that you and your students are doing. With regard to a genre-based reading club cycle, you'll want to make sure texts in the genre are featured prominently. Throughout the year, I tend to have several baskets full of texts from different genres. I would label these baskets simply Books of Poetry, ABC Books, or Nonfiction, for example. Then, in addition to these general baskets, I put together a few baskets of books that are more specific, such as Poems About Food, Poetry by Eloise Greenfield, Books About the Human Body, or Bird Books. These baskets might be considered to be subsets of the genre, and eventually in reading club cycles, partners will select one of these subsets for their club. My students are also encouraged to invent subsets of the genres themselves to add to the classroom library.

So, as I get ready for a poetry study, I make a couple of general poetry baskets that are filled with a variety of poetry books, laminated poems that we've learned together throughout the year in shared reading, and some student-authored poetry. I'll also make several more specific poetry baskets. For example, I've often made a basket labeled "Poetry About Families," which contains anthologies of family poems, as well as individual published poems about families that I've either laminated or put into plastic sheet protectors. Other subset baskets I've made in advance have included Poetry About Animals, Poems by Langston Hughes, or Silly Poems. Usually students will gather some poetry texts together to create other subset baskets that may eventually become reading club baskets.

One morning Anna and Sarah approached me with a pile of six poetry books with several sticky notes peeking over the edges of the pages. They told me that each of the books had some poems about rain. "Can we make a 'Rainy Poems' basket?" they asked. I found an empty basket and gave them an index card to design the label, and—voilà—we had a rainy poems basket in our library. As you might imagine, every year these more specific baskets in the genre change for a variety of reasons. They depend heavily on the new texts in the genre that I have acquired and on my students' interests and discoveries.

Getting Books into Students' Hands

Besides reading aloud texts in the genre to the class, it's also a good idea to give reading partners two to three days to get their hands on books to informally explore the genre they will soon be studying. In my class, I framed these as discovery days. I would tell my students that soon they would become experts about reading poetry, but first I wanted to give them time to warm up to poetry books by getting to know what was available in our classroom.

During these discovery days preceding the actual launch of clubs, I gather my students in the meeting area right after independent reading time. "Readers," I begin, "we've got baskets of poetry books that are full of wonderful stuff. I put these on each table, so you and your partner can explore poetry books together, and your partnership work for the next few days will be to see what kinds of things you discover about poetry. As you and your partner flip through the books, you'll want to make sure you're doing a lot of noticing about how the books go, what's inside them, and what you're thinking about poetry itself. I bet you'll even find some jewels in the books, poems that you treasure for one reason or another. During share time, we'll talk about your discoveries."

There are great benefits when we give students a few days to get their own hands on texts in the genre. First, they can see for themselves the wide world of the genre. For poetry, students will see that there are books in which all the poems are by one poet (like *Nathaniel Talking* by Eloise Greenfield), books containing poems by many different authors (such as *Songs of Myself: An Anthology of Poems and Art* edited by Georgia Heard), and books in which all the poems are about a particular theme or topic (such as *Spectacular Science: A Book of Poems* by Lee Bennett Hopkins).

Familiarizing themselves with different ways that books within a genre are organized or structured is important work for readers. When we know different ways the texts are structured, we can make purposeful book choices. For example, if we want to read poems about baby brothers, we might go to a book of poetry by a poet who has written a poem or two about siblings. In this case, we'd want to use the table of contents or index to locate the exact poems we have in mind. On the other hand, we can choose an anthology of family poems and read in a more "beginning to end" manner. We can also talk about purposes and intentions for reading when students discover that many different types of poetry books exist.

Students will also discover some text conventions that are particular to the genre of study. In a poetry study, my students have noticed that often books of poetry have tables of contents and indexes. Some have found that there are different kinds of indexes, such as those alphabetized by poem title, by author, or by poems' first lines. Students have talked about how poems usually have only a little picture to go with them. While hoping they discover the text features typical to particular genres, I also want to teach my students how to use these features in ways that help them as readers.

Another benefit of letting students muck about in the genre before taking off into reading clubs is that they get ideas for what kinds of reading clubs might interest them. For example, Emma and Taylor noticed that their tabletop basket had two books of poetry about kids' lives, *Meet Danitra Brown* by Nikki Grimes and *Nathaniel Talking* by Eloise Greenfield. They asked if they could make a Kids' Lives poetry basket, and then they went around to the other tables during partner reading time asking if students had any poetry that they might borrow for their Kids' Lives basket.

One tip to consider during these several days of playing around in the genre: No matter what sort of discovery kids make, it helps to ask them to think about how this discovery will affect their reading life. For example, after a couple of days, Daniel and Alexis declared that they didn't like poetry.

"Hmmm. That's a big thing to say. Can you say why you don't like it?" I asked.

Daniel started by complaining that poetry books don't have good pictures.

"What do you mean? Can you show me?" I asked.

"Look here, the pictures are little," said Alexis.

"Yeah, and some poems don't even have pictures," added Daniel.

"Oh, I see. So you guys think this is a problem. Why?" I asked.

"I like pictures," Daniel said.

"Say more."

"Well, pictures help you figure things out when you're reading," Alexis said. "I like them."

"You know, I agree with you. They are fun to look at, and they are helpful, too. So I'm wondering about something. Are you saying that because poetry doesn't have lots of good pictures, it's harder to read the poems?" I asked.

"Yeah," Alexis said as Daniel nodded in agreement.

"I think you guys discovered one of the challenges in reading poetry. You have to make the pictures in your minds because there might not be a great picture that goes along with a poem. You'll have to be the kind of readers who work really hard to read the words, make sense of the poems, and make pictures in your minds. The great thing is that we'll all learn to do that well."

When students make any kind of text or genre observation, I always try to follow up with questions and comments like the following:

- How does that affect you as you're reading this?
- How will that help you/challenge you as a reader?
- What does that make you think?
- Why do you think it's like that?
- Say more about that.

It's Reading Club Time!

Your students have had several days to explore books and texts in the genre and you've likely had several whole-class conversations about what they've noticed. Now it's their time to make decisions about what and how they'll read in the genre. Imagine now that it's time to begin our first official week of genre-based reading clubs.

Let's imagine that we're going to start the first week of reading clubs on a Monday. I tend to let my partnerships select their reading clubs on the Friday before in order to build anticipation and excitement. Also, when the clubs are settled on Friday, it lets us hit the ground running on Monday.

So, on the Friday before, I gather my students into a circle in the meeting area with the reading club baskets in the middle. I "introduce" the club baskets to the class in an attempt to generate enthusiasm for them. I show off some of the texts in the baskets, and I have students close their eyes and imagine the possibilities for what they might do in a particular club. For example, after I introduce the Silly Poems basket and show some of the texts it contains, I might say something like, "Okay, close your eyes. Think about being in this club next week. Imagine what you and your partner might do. Maybe you'll read poems aloud together. Maybe you'll discover the poem that makes you laugh the hardest. Maybe you'll figure out how poets make poems silly. Maybe you'll invent something totally different... "

If some students had created a reading club basket on their own, I would let them introduce that basket to the class. When Anna and Sarah made the Rainy Poems basket, Anna introduced it by telling their classmates something like, "Me and Sarah were noticing that there were lots of poems about rain and rainy weather, and we asked Ms. Collins if we could make a basket, and she said we could; so we put all the poems in the basket and made this label for it with an umbrella and a puddle. Sarah made the puddle. I made the umbrella. All these lines are supposed to be rain." I nudged her to say more about what was in the basket. "Oh, there's lots of poems about rain and stuff. Some of them are short, and some are long, and some are funny, and some of them are about puddles, and there's the Langston Hughes poem that we learned." I then told the students that if anyone found any kind of poem that would fit into any of our reading club baskets, please bring it into class for us to share.

After we spend less than ten minutes in a circle together having a sort of meet and greet with the reading club baskets, I put the baskets on tables around the room. The reading partners take about five minutes to walk around together and shop for the reading club they'll participate in during the following week. It's usually the case that many partnerships already know which club they want to sign up for, while other children need some guidance or nudging. I tend to pay extra close attention to the students who struggle as readers because I want to make sure they are selecting a reading club that contains texts that would be accessible for them with respect to reading level. Sometimes I've had to redirect (or strong-arm, unfortunately) students toward clubs that may not be their first choice in order to make sure they will be in a club containing texts that they can, in fact, read. I tend to stack the deck of a couple of reading clubs with easier or familiar texts so that there are always a couple of options for kids who struggle as readers.

As students shop for their reading clubs, I post a sign-up chart on the chalkboard (see Figure 7.1). Once they decide on their club and check it with me, they sign their names on the chart under the name of the reading club. In my experience, I've found that usually no more than two partnerships work successfully out of one club basket, and that only really works if there are enough texts to sustain the work of two partnerships.

It's important to note that many of my second- and third-grade colleagues have had success with foursomes working together in one reading club. Again, there needs to be enough books for four students to be engaged, and the four students need to be able to work cooperatively and collaboratively as they make plans for their work and have conversations about their discoveries and ideas.

Figure 7.1		
Reading Club Sign-Up Chart		
Poetry Reading Clubs		
Rainy Poems	Arnold Adoff Poetry	Kids' Life Poems
Poems About School	Silly Poems	Poems About Bedtime
Space Poems	Shape Poems	Karla Kuskin Poems

Once the partnerships all select and sign up for a reading club for the following week, we gather back in a circle at the meeting area to figure out where in the room each reading club will meet. This is a small but helpful thing to do in advance because it eliminates the time some kids might spend arguing over who gets to work in the warmth and light of the sunbeam that shines on the carpet only during reading time. Having a predetermined work place also enables all of the partners to get started quickly instead of walking around the room in search of a place to work. They know just where to take their reading club basket, so they can get started right away. Now that the students have chosen the club they want to work in for the next week or so, let's turn our attention to instruction.

One of the things I love about reading clubs is that there isn't one ideal-not-to-be-missed pathway to take in one's teaching. Some may consider this the gift of reading clubs while others may view this as the curse. Because your students' individual strengths and needs as readers, thinkers, and talkers are inevitably different from my students' strength and needs, I hesitate to lay out a precise plan because it's impossible to create something that would be appropriate for every teacher.

There is no way that the details of my daily teaching during poetry reading clubs (or any reading clubs for that matter) would be ideal in your classroom.

Even so, we can acknowledge that there are elements in our teaching that we'd likely have in common: we'll teach our students what they need as readers, in general; we'll teach our students what they need as readers of the genre, in particular; and we'll support our students as they learn how to think and talk in meaningful ways about texts. We can easily get teaching ideas for reading clubs from several dependable sources:

- from what we learn about our students' strengths and needs as readers during independent reading time with just-right books
- from what we learned by observing and listening to our students' conversations and comments when we surrounded them in the genre in the previous days or week
- from what we know about the genre itself and the skills, strategies, and habits necessary to read the genre with success and joy

Although the specific teaching points may differ from one class to another, my colleagues at the Teachers College Reading and Writing Project and I have realized that there can be a predictable rhythm for how the weeks that comprise a cycle of genre-based reading clubs may go:

- Week 1: Let's learn how to read and talk about poetry (or any genre/topic) with power. (This first week is often devoted to teaching skills and strategies that will help students read and talk about the texts in the genre with success.)
- Week 2: Let's learn to read, think, and talk across our texts and grow ideas from them. (Some students may want to stay in the same club for this second week, but I tend to let my students switch to a new club.)
- Week 3: Let's read, think, and talk about poetry (or any genre/topic) to grow new ideas and to develop theories. (This week is often optional. The reading club baskets tend to be reconfigured in more sophisticated categories.)

It's important to note here that each week of reading clubs as described above may last more than five days, depending on your students' needs and interests. (I use the term *week* loosely.)

Week 1: Let's Learn How to Read and Talk About Poetry (or Any Genre/Topic) with Power

The very first week or so of a reading club cycle is often the time when we support our students by teaching (or reinforcing) the skills and strategies they'll need to read, think, and talk about the genre well. For example, if making mental pictures and reading with fluency are two of the survival skills we believe our young readers need to use in order to read poetry well, we can plan to concentrate on teaching strategies for envisioning and reading with fluency during that first week or so.

We may also want to find ways to share habits and eccentricities that readers of the genre might have. For example, one year I told my students about a friend who has a collection of poems that inspire her in much the same way that each of the New York Yankees players has his own inspiring song that blasts from the stadium's PA system when he's up to bat. As a possibility for their reading club work, I suggested that they look for poems that inspire them in some way. "As you're reading poems and thinking about them, notice if you find any poems that get you pumped up, poems that make you think, poems that give you a strong feeling, poems that make you remember something important, and so on. You could begin your own collection of inspiring poems."

We'll also consider teaching our students about the different text features and text structures they may encounter in the genre they'll be reading. In the case of poetry, there are different ways books of poetry are set up or structured, and it helps readers to be aware of the structures so they can easily find what they are looking for in a book.

When we have expectations once we know how a text is set up, we are able to read it efficiently and with purpose. For example, if a student is looking for a poem about sharks within an anthology of sea life poetry, she will know to search the table of contents or the index to look for a shark poem.

If there are text features particular to the specific genre we're studying, we'd want to show students how to use those features to help them read the texts with more power. For instance, books of poetry often have illustrations that accompany the poems. We can teach students that, like pictures in storybooks, these illustrations may tell the story of the poem, but more likely, these illustrations may reflect a small part or the big idea or theme of the poem. We can teach them strategies for how to "read" and think about these illustrations in order to gain a better understanding of the poem.

Also, during this first week of genre-based reading clubs, we might have to support the students in their work in partnerships by reminding them of strategies for working and talking well together. This teaching may be a sort of touch-up instruction that I've found to be necessary at different points throughout the year. Your students might need some extra support for many aspects of partnerships, from working cooperatively with a partner to building book talk stamina. You might want to spend a bit of time helping partners set purposes and then make plans for their work. See Figure 7.2 for some teaching possibilities in Week 1 of a poetry reading club cycle.

Figure 7.2

Week 1 Teaching ideas for Poetry Reading Clubs

Reading poetry with fluency
Why is fluency important for reading poetry? What can help me read a poem with fluency?
using meaning of poem, using tone of poem, listening for rhythm in poems, and reading them with rhythm; using line breaks, punctuation, white space to help fluency; rereading to deepen understanding, which will help us read it well; picking up the pace of reading; etc.

Envisioning
Why is it essential to make pictures in your mind when reading poetry?
using the words, images to make pictures; finding lines or words that evoke strong images; dealing with difficulty when envisioning; using the image the poem evokes to understand the poem better; making connections to the image

Talking about poetry
What might poetry readers talk about together?
finding parts that matter; discussing what you think the poet is trying to make you think, feel, and/or understand; making connections/comparisons between poems; naming the craft in a poem; discussing opinions about poets and poems

Word-solving and meaning-making
How do readers of poetry figure out tricky parts?
strategies for making meaning of unfamiliar words or phrases; using envisioning to figure out tricky parts; strategies for figuring out multisyllabic words; strategies for understanding unfamiliar vocabulary or syntax

Support for working in partnerships
How can we do our best work together while enjoying ourselves?
strategies for working well together; strategies for talking well with partners; strategies for making plans

Disclaimer: This is meant to offer suggestions and possibilities, not to lay out a replicable curriculum.

As the first week of genre-based reading clubs draws to a close, you may want to give your reading partners some time to reflect on how their reading club went for the week. Perhaps you will give your students a reflection sheet to complete (see Appendix E for a couple of examples), or you may decide to ask them to talk to each other in reflection.

You'll also want your students to choose their reading clubs for the upcoming week. Some of your partnerships might choose to stay in the same reading club. I would let that happen if I felt that the partners had a compelling reason, such as unfinished work or passionate interest in the reading club. Most often, I've found that students are ready to switch to another reading club after the first week of the cycle.

Extending to Other Genres: Helping Yourself Plan Instruction for Week 1 of Genre-Based Reading Clubs

It's important to develop plans for any kind of genre-based reading clubs by first considering what the readers in your class need most. If you have many readers who are still largely working on becoming resourceful word solvers, you'll want to incorporate word-solving instruction into your plans for reading clubs. On the other hand, if the majority of your students are fairly proficient at word-solving in their just-right books, you might want to plan instruction that supports them in other ways, perhaps working with them on fluency or comprehension.

It's helpful to consider whether or not there are any "survival strategies" that readers need to use to navigate the particular genre with power. For example, one might argue that for our youngest nonfiction readers, an ability to study the illustrations and photographs and state ideas about them seems essential, especially if the text's difficulty level is beyond their comfort zone. For older nonfiction readers, being able to synthesize what they've read would be an important skill to acquire.

You may decide that you want to use your reading club cycle to improve your students' abilities to talk about texts with others. If this is the case, it will be helpful to study your students' partner conversations prior to the launch of reading clubs. You'll want to identify what instruction they need to help them have conversations characterized by more depth, more stamina, or more exchanges of ideas.

Weeks 2 and 3: Let's Learn to Read with Power, Think with Depth, and Talk with Stamina Across Our Texts

By the time the first week of reading clubs comes to a close, you will have lots of data to draw upon as you plan instruction for the second, third, and occasionally fourth weeks of reading clubs. During the first week of clubs, you will have observed your students reading texts in the genre, and you may have noticed areas in which they need more instructional support. You will have listened to and participated in many partner conversations about the texts in reading clubs, so you will likely have ideas for what to teach that will lift the level of partner work and partner talk.

For the second week of the reading club cycle, you may decide that it makes sense to revisit some of the teaching points you made during the first week, especially if you aren't convinced (or have no evidence to suggest) that your students integrated that first week's instruction into their reading work.

When we decide to revisit some of the strategies for reading, thinking, and talking about texts that were covered in the first week, we often find that the repetition and extra practice with strategies help our students to read texts in the genre with strength and to talk to partners about texts with ease. The repetition also gives students more time and opportunities to digest the instruction.

Sometimes we may hesitate to revisit teaching points in the name of moving on, getting ahead, and maintaining pace, but often the repetition and extra time is necessary. It's helpful to know that our students typically choose new clubs for Week 2, so they will have a different set of texts with which to apply the strategies you're revisiting. The opportunity to use these skills and strategies across books (and across reading clubs) helps young readers "own" the skills and strategies.

On the other hand you may decide, based on your observations and data, that your students are ready to push ahead. If this is the case, it's worthwhile to plan instruction that will deepen students' reading skills as well as their abilities to think and talk about the texts in their reading clubs. During any genre study, the second and third weeks of reading clubs can take shape in many ways, depending on what makes sense for your students.

In the case of a poetry genre study, there are several different ways I've angled instruction for the second and third weeks. I tend to select an angle for the second week that will enable my students to think and talk across different texts in the genre, and then I choose a different focus for the third week. My intention for the third week is that it has a sort of "advanced course of study" feeling. The following list is a sample of some of the ways in which I've approached the second and third weeks of a poetry study. It's important to state that this list is not exhaustive nor chronological, and the items in this list can be generalized for use in any genre study, not just poetry.

- Poems (or any other kind of topic or genre) make us think and feel.

- Readers notice similarities and differences among texts and grow ideas about what they notice.

- Readers can have great conversations about poetry (or any texts in other genres).

- Readers develop a taste for poetry (or any other genre).

Although I've included this list of potential teaching ideas, I want to be clear that I am not suggesting that these are the only ways, or even the best ways, to angle reading clubs in every classroom. By sharing several different approaches I've taken during Weeks 2 and 3, I hope to show that my planning for reading clubs is flexible from year to year and depends largely on what each class can already do and what they need to learn to do.

Poems make us think and feel.

I've chosen this focus for instruction mostly during Week 2 when I've noticed during Week 1 that my students tended to read through poems as if they were eating potato chips, one right after the other. Perhaps this is because poems tend to be short texts and books of poetry usually contain lots of poems. I suspect that students rush from poem to poem because they may feel like they have lots of poems to get through, which is likely to be very similar to the way they approach a bag of potato chips. If it seems like my students are simply stuffing themselves with poetry, trying to read as many poems as they can, rather than taking time to savor them or have thoughts about them, I would want to plan instruction that will show them how to linger more with poetry, like avid readers of poetry do, and how to slow down enough to pay attention to the thoughts and feelings they get from poems.

Besides the fact that lingering with poems is a habit of avid poetry readers, the time spent slowing down with a text offers additional benefits. If students are staying with a text longer, they're apt to have more to say about it. As a result, they're likely to spend more time talking about the text, so their conversation stamina grows while their conversation content deepens.

If I choose this angle for Week 2, I could imagine spending instructional time on several fronts. I could revisit the idea that readers have thoughts as they read (which I've certainly covered in previous studies) and teach them strategies that will help them attend to, or catch, their thoughts. I could teach them to notice places where they have reactions to poems, and I could model a variety of kinds of reactions and responses that poetry readers might have, such as emotional reactions ("This makes me sad/mad/happy/etc."), connections ("This poem is really similar to that one." or "This poem makes me think about my dad because... "), and questions ("What does the poet mean in this part?" or "Why did Eloise Greenfield write so many poems about a boy named Nathaniel?").

The following is a list of possible teaching points for mini-lessons, conferences, small-group instruction, and share time that could lead our students to be the kind of poetry readers who linger, who think and feel, and who are affected by poems.

- Readers of poetry read in a thoughtful way, trying to really "taste" the poem and understand it well. Strategies for slowing down include: rereading it a couple of times; reading it once, thinking or talking about first impressions, and then reading it again, noticing different thoughts and impressions.

- After reading a poem once, reread it, this time making your voice match the tone and feeling of the poem.

- When we read poetry, we pay attention to the feelings it gives us. (We may think it's silly, sad, funny, thoughtful, happy, confusing, etc.) Then we reread it to find the exact parts that made the feelings strong.

- We notice when a poem reminds us of something in our own lives, and we think about how the poem is like or unlike what we know from our own lives.

- When we read poems, we want to get a clear picture in our minds, and we can find parts of the poem that make a clear picture for us.

- When there are parts in a poem that aren't so clear, we can reread them, trying to get a picture in our minds. We can share those parts with our partners and try to figure them out together.

- When we realize that a poem made us feel a certain way, we can reread it to try to figure out what the poet did as a writer to make us feel that way.

Readers notice similarities and differences among texts and grow ideas about what they notice.

Another direction I've taken my students, usually during the second week of reading clubs, is to teach them how to look across texts in the reading club basket and to think about the ways they are similar and different. When readers make these sorts of discoveries, they develop theories about both genre boundaries ("Poems have line breaks that make them look different than other kinds of things") and genre variations ("Some poets use line breaks to make a shape, but other poets use line breaks more to help us read the poem better"). When they carefully read and study several texts in a genre, they begin to deepen their understanding about the genre.

Comparing and contrasting poems can be done in a rather surface-level way, such as when Anthony told his partner, "These poems about rain are different because this one is mostly about umbrellas and this one is mostly about puddles," or when Marissa remarked to her partner, "These three poems about rain all have sound effects in them." We can teach our students to go beneath the surface in their comparisons when we teach them simply to say more about what they've noticed.

One way to do this is to teach them to add on to their noticing statement by saying, "and I think this is because... " For example, Anthony might say, "These two poems are about rain, but this one is about umbrellas and this one is about puddles. I think this is because you can write different poems about something. Maybe this poet forgot his umbrella or something so he wanted to write about it."

"Yeah, and this poet maybe liked to stomp in puddles when he was little," Anthony's partner might add.

Another way to support students as they compare and contrast texts is to teach them that they can sort and categorize the texts in their clubs. For example, in their Poems About Families Club, Jackson and Maleia decided to find the poems that are about sisters and brothers. They put sticky notes in their books to mark the sibling poems. They had marked about ten sibling poems with sticky notes, and then I suggested they go back and reread these poems more closely, looking for ways they may connect and differ. Jackson and Maleia realized that several poems were about times when siblings do not get along, and they named these "Poems About Brothers and Sisters Who Have Trouble." Another category they named was "Poems About Being a Little Brother or Sister." This rereading, sorting, and recategorizing of texts naturally lead students to think more deeply about the texts' meaning, message, and themes.

The following is a list of possible teaching points for mini-lessons, conferences, small-group instruction, and share time that could lead our students to be the kind of poetry readers who bring all they've read to any text they are reading now. This will help them make meaningful connections so they can better understand the texts, the genre, and themselves.

· Readers carry memories of poems they've read before as they read new poems, and they often say to themselves, "This poem reminds me of this other poem, because... "

· Readers can put a couple of poems side by side and read them over and over to figure out the ways they are alike or different.

· When readers notice the ways poems are alike or different, they name the similarities or differences and then tell what this makes them think.

· Readers of poetry may notice a variety of ways that poems are similar or different, such as their angle on a topic (poems about bears, for example, one about bear cubs and the other about hibernation), their tone (a silly poem about homework and an anguished poem about homework), their craft (a rhyming poem about tulips and a poem about tulips that compares them to soldiers), and so on.

Readers can have great conversations about poetry.

If I believed that my students were able and inclined to respond and react to the texts in their reading clubs without a lot of extra instruction, and if I saw evidence that they were comparing and contrasting texts, I might choose to focus my instruction on helping them talk well with others about texts in whichever genre we were studying. The beauty of this angle of instruction is that it explicitly supports our students' conversations, and it implicitly boosts our students' reading awareness. After all, in order to have a conversation about a text, it's essential to have had thoughts about the text and to have thoughts about what's being said during the conversation. It's necessary to be a wide-awake reader, thinker, and talker.

When planning instruction to help strengthen the conversation, I can work on two fronts—the content of the conversation and the format of the conversation. With regard to content, I want to teach my students to talk about things that matter to them, to pursue their ideas in the company of others, and to value input from others. With regard to format, I may want to teach my students to have conversations that are characterized by civility, growing stamina, and strategies for solving conversation problems, such as reviving dying conversations and avoiding conversational dead ends.

Here is a short list of possible teaching points for mini-lessons, conferences, small-group instruction, and share time that could help our readers talk about poetry (or texts in any other genre) with more depth and stamina.

- Readers can jot notes on sticky notes as they read to help them remember what they want to talk about with a partner.

- Readers can make plans for conversations.

- Readers in conversation make sure both voices are heard and offer each other invitations by saying things like, "What do you think?" or "I'd like to hear your ideas about this."

- Readers in conversation make sure they understand each other and can ask each other to clarify, to give more details, or to restate their ideas when necessary.

- Readers of poetry talk about a wide range of things, such as what they notice, what they wonder, what they think their poems are about, etc. (This is not likely to be brand-new instruction. Students will be familiar with this idea from previous instruction about talk.)

When I reflect on the many cycles of genre-based reading clubs I launched in my classroom, I could offer a ballpark estimate and say that these cycles tended to last for a bit more than two weeks. Nonfiction reading clubs were the exception in that they tended to last about four weeks, which was longer than any other kind of reading clubs. It's important to say that the length of time reading clubs would last was dependent on several factors, such as curricular obligations, students' needs and interests, and enthusiasm for the unit of study.

Even though the genre-based reading club cycle ends and you may turn off the spotlight on a particular genre, that doesn't mean that the genre itself disappears from the classroom. As stated earlier, I would, as much as possible, continue to include texts of the genre we just studied for interactive read-aloud, shared reading, and content-area studies. I would also make it easy for students to continue to choose the genre for their independent reading time by including leveled texts from the genre in the leveled library book baskets.

It's also worth noting that I've even repeated a cycle of a whole-class genre study within one school year. One February, we studied nonfiction via reading clubs on insects (to support our life science inquiry on insects), and then in May, we put the spotlight on nonfiction again in another cycle of reading clubs. The students' work was stronger in May than in February, and they noticed the difference themselves.

Teaching our students to feel familiar and comfortable within the boundaries of a variety of genres expands their reading and talking repertoire, and it increases their confidence in both reading and talking about a wide range of texts. As Lucy Calkins says, the reading club is the part of our literacy work that especially "embodies our commitment to a literacy of thoughtfulness" (Calkins 2001, 322).

Reading Power
Reading Clubs

About a year ago, a friend asked me for advice about air travel with young children. You see, since we've been living in Alaska, I've traveled back and forth from Anchorage to New York on many occasions with my young sons, so I've earned some mama points, and my kids have earned some frequent flier miles! There are not many areas in which I could or would offer parenting advice, but air travel with young, energetic, diapered children is one of them.

At the time of my friend's inquiry, I thought about my most recent trip with my kids in tow, when Owen was three and a half and Theo was not quite two years old. "I bring lots of books," I said. "Owen reads almost the whole time, which is great because then I can concentrate on keeping Theo out of the cockpit."

My friend, whose children are the same age as mine, had a look of panic on her face.

"Oh, I'm just kidding," I said trying to reassure her. "Theo never went for the cockpit. Not with all the air marshals they've got on board these days," I said, thinking I was sort of funny.

"No, that's not what freaked me out," my friend said. "It's just that... well, are you saying Owen can read?"

Then I realized what had happened, what had caused my friend to look so panicked. When I told her that Owen reads almost the whole time on the airplane, she immediately pictured my three-and-a-half-year-old reading conventionally. Reading the print. Decoding the text. This, I assured her, was not the case.

Sure, there are some children who are able to read conventionally at that young age, but Owen wasn't one of them. Even so, I considered him a reader, and I naturally called his interactions with books "reading" although he wasn't reading the words yet.

We early childhood teachers call lots of things that our students do with texts "reading," and rightly so. When our youngest students gather around a favorite picture book and debate the motives of the main character, they may not be reading each of the words in the text, but they are reading the pictures and supporting their ideas based on the meaning they've made of the story. When a group of children act out a scene from *Pippi Longstocking* during choice time and pretend they are Pippi, Annika, Tommy, and Mr. Nilsson, we would call that reading response. When we're on a field trip and one of our students spots a sign of a cigarette with a big red slash through it and blurts out to everyone, "Hey, no smoking here," we are likely to reply, "Oh, thank you for reading that sign to us. Good thing none of us smokes."

Our view, as early childhood teachers, of what constitutes reading and who is a reader is much more wide-angled than the views of most other people (I'm thinking nonteachers), who tend to define a reader as one who can read the words. Within young children's early approximations, their energetic engagement with texts, and their fearless capacity for sharing their thoughts about stories, we early childhood teachers see the small, yet foundational, building blocks of a reading life. We see reading as a much richer and more multilayered enterprise than simply decoding the words on the page.

So, on the long flight from Anchorage to anywhere, when Owen, and now Theo, take turns sitting in the window seat looking at book after book, asking questions, noticing details, and offering ideas about them, I call that reading. If I were to interrupt Owen or Theo in the middle of a book, they'd say something like, "Mom, just let me finish this part about the Gulper eel," even though they were not attending to the print at all. They look like they're reading, they talk about books like they've read them, and they're attracted to all kinds of texts, from the Sunday comics to auto advertisements, from picture books about insects to chapter books about a young girl growing up on the prairie. I'm not suggesting that they are precocious or that this is unique. I would say that Owen, Theo, and many, many, many children like them have reading power, even though they may not be reading the words yet. These children are, in the words of Frank Smith, members of the "literacy club" even before they are "able to read or write a single word for themselves" (Smith 1988, 2).

Unfortunately, I've noticed that often after students begin to decode proficiently and with accuracy, they may temporarily cast aside all the little extras of their reading lives. Children who once had lots to say about books become readers who don't want to look up from the page to share a thought. Children who once lingered over pictures in their books no longer have the patience or desire to study illustrations, especially once they enter the world of chapter books. Children who once were free-range readers, enjoying a wide variety of books, become locked into levels, fearful of venturing beyond the boundaries of a colored dot in the upper right-hand corner of their texts.

Simultaneously, our wide-angled view of reading power tends to narrow as children progress from grade to grade. There's a conventional wisdom within schools that reading power is quantifiable and must be characterized by high reading levels, test scores, reading rates, and a solid reading résumé, but this is a limited view of reading power. Some of the most powerful readers I've encountered are the youngest ones who don't yet have percentiles and ratings attached to their reading. These young readers work so hard to understand the pictures and the words as we read to them, and they stop us frequently for clarification or to offer comments about the story; they have favorites they want to read over and over again, and to them, books and other texts are often associated with warmly connected moments with loved ones and characterized by joyful engagement. I'd like to suggest that we acknowledge and celebrate our broad ideas of what constitutes reading power and teach with them in mind.

In this chapter, I'll describe a few different kinds of reading clubs that serve to refuel and replenish young readers' power and reignite the spark for reading that in some cases goes dormant once reading becomes solely about getting the words right. The clubs in this chapter provide a wonderful balance between getting the words right and digging into the story, between thinking hard about texts and having fun all the while.

Character Study Reading Clubs: Getting to Know Our Characters Well to Better Understand Our Books and Ourselves

We are born studying characters. Research suggests that the faces and voices of primary caregivers are the first sights and sounds that attract and hold babies' attention. Research also tells us that infants can detect their caregivers' moods by watching their facial expressions and gestures and listening to the tone of their voices. Getting to know the main characters in their lives is an important way that babies make sense of their surroundings and develop expectations about their world.

Likewise, when our young students study the characters in their books, they are learning a powerful tool for understanding the world of the text. Over and over my colleagues and I have seen that when our youngest readers' attend to the characters in their books, their level of comprehension and engagement increases. Their conversations become richer. Perhaps this is true because the characters in a story offer concrete and often visual footholds that students can step on to steady themselves as they climb their way through the twists and turns of a story. When we teach our children strategies for getting to know their characters, purposes for understanding characters, and ways to use what they know about their characters to better understand their stories, they become the kind of readers who pay close attention as they read and have thoughts that lead to substantive conversations.

Like any cycle of reading clubs, a character study can follow many different pathways, depending on one's students and the kinds of books they read. In the following section, I will follow the planning guide format to outline some ways that colleagues and I have approached character study reading clubs.

Featured Skills and Strategies to Teach in a Character Study

During a reading club cycle in which students are learning how to get to know the characters in their books, there are several different skills and strategies that will help them do this work well. Typically, during a character study, I've tended to shine a spotlight on the reading skill of inferring, while also teaching students to sharpen the habit of mind of moving from simply noticing and naming to growing ideas about what they've noticed. During many character studies, I've also spent time teaching my students about the importance of using evidence from the text to support their ideas, because this helps to keep the conversations tethered to the books. Although these are the survival skills I've tended to highlight during a character study, it's important to note that I would make adjustments as necessary to meet the needs of particular classes and individual students.

It's worth noting again that even though I may select a couple of survival skills to highlight during mini-lessons in a cycle of reading clubs, I continue to use my reading conference time and small-group work sessions to support students with their particular word-solving and meaning-making needs as well as teaching them to use the survival strategies with a growing ease and automaticity.

Inferring: What's Really Going On?

When readers attend to their characters' facial expressions, tone, words, and actions in both the illustrations and the words of the text, they need to infer in order to understand the characters' thoughts, feelings, and motivations. In addition to attending to what the text offers via illustrations and words, we also want to teach readers to use prior knowledge, purposeful rereading, and conversations to help them infer and interpret texts (Miller 2002).

The ability to infer well and in ways that help a reader understand the story better can be a difficult skill to teach, because the inferences readers make are usually based on "off the page" information that requires readers to align their prior knowledge with what's going on in the text. "Inferring involves using personal knowledge and experience to construct meanings that are not explicitly stated in the text" (Owocki 2003, 45). Many people refer to inferring as "reading between the lines" or "having thoughts about parts of the story that the author doesn't tell us directly." Both of those ways of describing inferring seem easier for adults and older students to understand, and in my experience, these sorts of abstract images and words to describe inferring have been lost on my young students. For many reasons, a character study is a perfect time to put a spotlight on the skill of inferring because it brings the lofty, abstract aspect of inferring back down to earth and into the able hands of Mrs. Wishy-Washy, Poppleton, Horrible Harry, and many other beloved book friends.

In character studies, I've joined some colleagues in making the skill of inferring a bit more concrete by framing students' work as that of "character detectives." I'll say something like, "Readers, when you're trying to learn as much about a character as you can, you need to be like a character detective. You'll want to be resourceful and look for clues that will help you figure out more details about the characters' thoughts and feelings." We can teach students to attend to the character's external qualities, such how the character looks and dresses, where and how the character lives, and so on. We can remind them to pay attention to the character's facial expressions to figure out what the character might be thinking or how the character might be feeling. We can teach students to keep track of the character's actions, words, and tone to figure out the character's mood, personality, and motivation. We can teach them to watch the character across pages in order to notice any changes that occur in the character's behavior, attitudes, and relationships.

From Noticing and Naming to Growing Ideas About Characters

One fall when my class was riding the bus on our way to the Staten Island Children's Museum, a few students noticed that the sky ahead was very ominous looking. "Look, the sky is so dark," Michael said. "Yeah, it looks like night over there," added his seat partner, Sam. They were silent as they both looked out the window. I turned around and said, "You noticed something about the sky. What does it make you think?"

"There might be a storm over there," Michael said. Sam said that it was probably raining hard. "Good thing that we'll be inside the museum," Sam added. We all agreed that we were glad our field trip would be an indoors adventure. This simple interaction is illustrative of the move from simply noticing something toward having a relevant thought or idea about what's been noticed.

In *Choice Words*, Peter Johnston suggests that when students notice, "instruction can begin with a joint focus of attention because the children are already attending" (Johnston 2004, 18). When our students say things and share observations about their characters, we want to nudge them toward having ideas about the things they've noticed. We can teach them to move beyond noticing and naming toward having an idea by asking them to extend their thoughts through questions like, "And what does that make you think?" or "What are your ideas about that?"

Angelica and Michael were studying the character of Biscuit in their club. Angelica said, "Biscuit likes to play." Michael and I looked at each other, and I whispered into his ear, "Ask Angelica this: What does that make you think?" Michael looked at Angelica and said, "What does that make you think?"

Angelica said, "Well, I think Biscuit likes to play because he's a puppy, and puppies like to play, so I think he's a regular puppy." Angelica and I then looked at Michael when he said, "We got a puppy once, and my mom said that playing is how puppies learn about stuff." Again, I whispered into the partnership, this time to Angelica, and said, "Ask Michael this: What does that make you think?" She did, and Michael replied, "Maybe Biscuit is learning about stuff, like mud and balls and stuff. Even though he's playing, he's also learning new stuff. Maybe that's why the girl didn't get mad at him for getting muddy."

At first, when we ask our students, "What does that make you think?" after they make noticing types of comments, they may simply repeat their original statement because they are not used to being nudged for more. It helps enormously to make this interaction a classroom habit, holding our students accountable for having ideas about what they notice throughout the day and across content areas. After all, posing the simple question, "What does that make you think?" can push anyone to move past the act of noticing and naming and into the territory below surface-level thoughts about the story, where we have deeper ideas about the text.

Using Text Evidence to Support Ideas

Any reading club cycle is ideal for teaching or reminding our students to state or show evidence from the text that supports their ideas. For children who are reading early-level books, this might mean they learn to turn the page to show their partners the details in pictures that support their ideas. Dito and Jennifer were talking about the character in the book *I Am*. On each page there's an illustration of the little girl engaged in an activity with a line of text that reads something like, "I am jumping./I am running./I am climbing." and so on. Dito told Jennifer that he thought this girl was lonely. With my prompt, Jennifer said, "Show me the parts that make you think that." Dito went on to turn the pages and say, "See, here she's jumping by her own self. Here she's climbing by her own self." Dito was about to turn the page in his effort to prove his point beyond a reasonable doubt when Jennifer told him to stop. "I notice something,'" she said. "Go back to the jumping page." Dito thumbed back to that page.

"I don't think the girl is lonely," Jennifer said. "She's got a dog, and the dog is playing with her on each page. See? The dog is jumping right here." Then Jennifer turned the pages to prove her point that the girl did have some companionship and that she wasn't lonely at all. I left Dito and Jennifer in the midst of a discussion about whether the dog counted as a friend or not. If Dito hadn't used text evidence to support his idea, Jennifer would have never grown her idea, and this conversation likely would not have occurred.

Likewise, for readers of chapter books and other higher-level text, we can teach them to use text evidence to support their ideas, although it's not quite as easy as turning the pages and pointing to illustrations. When partners study a character in a chapter book, they'll need to figure out a plan for keeping track of their ideas about their characters. In some cases, we might teach students to jot ideas on sticky notes and leave them on pages that offer evidence. In other cases, we might show students how to use a T-chart to compile evidence, with the left-side column containing the theory about the character (i.e., Junie B. Jones is a nice kid) and the right side listing parts or pages of the story to support that point.

It feels important to say that although I've shared three ideas for skill/strategy instruction during a reading club character study, I want to be clear that any actual instructional decisions I make from year to year depend largely and mostly on the strengths and needs of the students in that particular class.

Real-Life Purposes, Habits, and Goals Readers Might Have in a Character Study

If we think about our own relationships to memorable characters in the books we've read, we would probably have a range of responses and connections to these characters. We might be attracted to and repelled by characters in those books, and it's often the case that our relationships to characters are one of the most important aspects of reading that keep us returning to a book once we've started it. We just have to find out what happens!

Sometimes our relationships with characters have a life beyond the book pages. There are certain characters that stay with us, for a wide variety of reasons, even when we put the book down. These characters may become a sort of guardian angel on our shoulder who shows up in our life at trying times, reminding us to avoid certain situations, substances, and people, perhaps. On the other hand, other compelling characters may be the rebel on our shoulder nudging us to go for it, to take a chance, to have some fun.

Other characters who stick with us may offer us a model of how to live our lives. I've learned that Atticus Finch is one of those characters for many people, myself included. In less lofty terms, when I was about ten years old, Harriet the Spy inspired me to carry around a notebook and hide in depths of a nearby furniture store warehouse recording observations and transcribing conversations (yes, even curse words!) between the warehouse workers.

Here is a list of ideas about different habits, purposes, and goals we might consider teaching our students during a cycle of character study reading clubs:

- Readers can have feelings for a character in their books.

  "I really like Biscuit because..." or "I don't like the rat because he's..." "I admire Charlotte because she's..."

- Readers may develop a personal connection to their character.

  "I'm like Poppleton because..." or "I would do the same thing as Opal because..."

- Readers may feel personal distance from their character.

  "I would never do what Pippi did in school because..." or "I don't like Anna Maria because sometimes she's mean to the others."

- Readers think about their character even when they aren't reading their books.

  "This reminds me of when Jim felt bad about not being able to read." or "I can't stop thinking about Elmer. I'm so worried he'll get caught."

- Readers make plans to get back to their reading because they can't wait to see what happens to their characters.

  "I can't wait to finish my book to see if she finds her special necklace." or "I can't get Shiloh out of my mind..."

· Readers choose books sometimes because of the characters.

"I like reading about girl characters." "I like characters who have amazing adventures." "I like characters who are animals."

· Readers learn lessons from their characters.

"The most important thing I've learned from Charlotte is…" "Mrs. Frizzle shows us how important it is to have fun when you're working hard."

· Characters can change how readers think about things, people, and so on.

"I used to not like spiders at all, but now I see Charlotte in every spider web." or "Ruby, the Copy Cat, showed me that people who copy aren't always annoying. Sometimes they just want to be like someone else."

· Readers can be inspired by their characters.

"I want to keep a notebook just like Amelia did." or "If I hear someone getting teased, I want to be just like Pippi and tell them to stop it."

· Readers recommend characters to others.

"Oh, if you like to read Junie B. Jones books, I bet you'll like Judy Moody."

Getting Ready for Character Study Reading Clubs

For a couple of weeks leading up to the launch of character study reading clubs, it makes a lot of sense to facilitate discussions during read-aloud time that are focused on the characters of the texts. We can begin to familiarize our students with the idea of main character, secondary characters, and even terms like *protagonist* and *antagonist*, if we choose to do so. If we're reading a chapter book, we can follow the main character across chapters, noticing with students if the character's life or feelings change in any way. We can ask students to consider the reasons they think the change occurred.

One year in Hannah Schneewind's first-grade class at PS 321, she and her students collected a list, a long vertical list, of characters they knew well from all they had read until that point of the year. The list, if I remember correctly, ran about eight feet long. Some of the characters were minor figures in their books, whereas others they listed were the books' stars. I made one of these lists in my class one year, and my students and I sorted and categorized the characters on the list. For example, we put a black box around the names of characters who were the main characters in their books, and we put a star by the names of the characters who were in more than one book. Some kids went through the list and put check marks by characters they wish were actually in our class, and others went through the list to find characters they thought could be their friends. When we read *The Biggest House in the World* by Leo Lionni, Harshel and Sela debated whether the snail's shell itself was a character.

Before launching character study reading clubs, you might consider taking a week or so to get ready by using the power of read-aloud time to focus on characters, by setting up students to have conversations about characters for homework, and by changing the classroom library in ways that will support your character study and character reading clubs. Here are some ideas:

- Focus read-aloud conversations on the characters in the text for a week or two before the character study reading club cycle begins. This will help in a couple of ways: it will expose students to some of the upcoming content of the character study, and it will offer a model of substantive conversations about characters.

- For homework, assign conversations about characters. Ask students to talk to grown-ups in their families about characters they loved when they were little. Sometimes it helps if you open it up to characters in any setting, not just in children's literature. Some parents might name Bobby and Cindy from the Brady Bunch, while others might name Betsy and Tacy from the Betsy-Tacy books. Some parents may have been Encyclopedia Brown fans while others might have loved Clifford. One year, I had a parent who told his child that his favorite characters were the Heat Miser and the Freeze Miser from *The Year Without a Santa Claus.*

- As always, it helps to change the classroom library to support the study and the work the students will be doing. For a cycle of character reading clubs, it helps to gather some texts that feature characters into specific character baskets. It's important to gather character baskets that take into consideration the range of reading levels in the class. It is also wise to make a basket or two that has a mix of characters in them, such as a Characters Who Have Pets basket or Girl Characters baskets, and so on.

It's Reading Club Time!

Typically, I would devote time for students to study two characters during a character club cycle, which means that a character study reading club cycle tends to last for almost three weeks. Occasionally, I've added an extra week to character clubs either because my students were highly engaged in the work of getting to know their characters well or because I felt that another week would help them internalize and control the skills and strategies they were learning to use. The chart in Figure 8.1 shows some of the approaches I took in my character reading clubs:

Figure 8.1

Big Idea for Readers During Character Study Reading Clubs	Specific Strategies for Readers
Readers are character detectives, looking for clues in their books to help them get to know their characters.	· Readers pay close attention to the way a character looks by examining the illustrations or making mental pictures when the author offers descriptions. · Readers notice the character's facial expressions and body language in illustrations and as explained in the text because that can tell us how a character might be feeling. · Readers think about the character's words and actions to figure out what the character is like, what his or her motivations and feelings are, and so on. · Readers use text evidence to support their ideas about the characters.
Readers make connections with characters, and this helps them understand the character better.	· Characters may remind us of ourselves or people we know, and we can use that connection to think: What does this tell me about the character? (*For example, "This character is bossy like my big sister, always bossing everyone around. My mom says my big sister is bossy because she takes after my dad, so maybe that's why this character is so bossy too. I'm going to reread to see if that's the reason."*) · Characters may get into situations that remind us of our own lives or experiences, and we can use this knowledge from our own lives to imagine what the character might be feeling or thinking. · Characters from one book might remind us of other characters we know. We can compare and contrast two characters in order to get to know a character better.
Readers notice if the character changes in some way.	· Readers get to know their character, so it's easier to notice times when the character does something that's "out of character." · Readers pay attention to the problems a character has and watches how the character deals with problems. This can tell a reader a lot about his character. · Readers pay attention to the part of the book where a character changes because it's usually an important part of the story.

Figure 8.1 *(continued)*	
Big Idea for Readers During Character Study Reading Clubs	**Specific Strategies for Readers**
Readers pay attention to the relationships the character has because they can tell us more about the character.	· Readers notice how the character relates to others in the story because this tells the reader more about the character. · Readers sometimes think about whether they would want this character as a friend/relative by watching how the character relates to others in the book.
Readers can pay close attention to the secondary characters and notice how they affect the main character and the story action.	· Sometimes readers find the secondary characters interesting, and they follow one of them through a story, attending to how the secondary character affects the story and the main character.
Readers can grow ideas about the character in their books.	· Whenever readers notice something about a character, they can say, "I notice that ABC, and it makes me think XYZ." (*For example, "I notice that Poppleton sometimes explodes at his friends, like when he squirted Cherry Sue and when he yelled at Fillmore about the pills in the cake. This makes me think that he's got a temper, sort of."*) · Readers notice when things happen over and over to a character, and they think about the reasons why because it might tell a lot about that character. (*For example, "I notice that Laura Ingalls gets mad at Mary a lot, and it makes me wonder if she's sort of jealous. I'm going to reread the parts where Laura gets mad to see what causes it."*)
Readers can learn from their characters.	· Readers can learn how to deal with challenges by paying close attention to the ways their characters handle problems. · If readers admire the character in their book, they can think about ways they can emulate the character in their real lives. · When a character has difficulty, a reader can think of advice to offer or think of ways she could help the character. · Readers notice the kinds of characters that grab their attention and can look for other books with those types of characters. (*For example, "I like mischievous kids like Junie B. Jones, so next I'm going to read Pippi or Horrible Harry."*)

As always, there are so many other possibilities and directions that one could take in any reading club. Your decisions will be based, of course, on your students' strengths, needs, and interests. I've included a sample planning guide for author study reading clubs in Appendix G.

Series Books Reading Clubs

Do you remember the debate several years ago about the Goosebumps books? On one side, parents and educators were celebrating the fact that kids, boys especially, were voraciously reading the Goosebumps books with interest and enthusiasm. On the other side, there were parents and educators who were worried that the books weren't high-quality children's literature. They were concerned that Goosebumps offered the same benefits to young readers as Twinkies offer to young eaters.

Then, right down the middle, there were those who agreed that while the books weren't exactly highbrow children's literature, they did in fact have some value and were unlikely to ruin a young reader's reading life. No matter where you fell on that issue that divided a teaching nation (surely a bit melodramatic), I think we can all agree that there are several benefits when young readers find a series of books that they love.

Reading texts in a series is comforting and empowering for young readers. As they move from book to book within a series, their confidence grows because they're familiar with the lay of the land in the texts. As the reader begins each successive book in a series, she brings more and more schema to her reading. She is familiar with the world of the text because she's gotten to know the characters, the settings, and the way the stories tend to go.

When young readers fall for a series of books, we can breathe a sigh of relief, especially if those books are at the child's just-right reading level. We can trust that while the reader is engaged in the series, she is reading books that will help her grow stronger as a reader. Usually most of the texts within a book series tend to be close to the same reading level, but occasionally a series may contain some titles that are harder than others. Because many of the characters and conventions within a series are consistent from one book to the next, the slight increase in text difficulty in one of the titles may be more easily handled by readers than if they were dealing with the same sort of difficulty in a book that was not part of a familiar series.

Many teachers find that a series book study is a perfect way to give readers a boost into the next reading level, if they are ready. Let's say that Clarissa and DeMane are reading texts at their current just-right level with fluency, accuracy, and comprehension. You determine they're ready for a boost into a higher level. You plan to conduct a couple of guided reading lessons featuring a Nate the Great book, which is a series in the next higher level. You introduce the book well and offer support for some of the challenges they may encounter in *Nate the Great* during the guided reading book introduction and as you coach them while they are reading during the guided reading session (Fountas and Pinnell 1996).

When you follow up with DeMane and Clarissa, you suggest they select the Nate the Great series for the upcoming series books reading club cycle, which will begin in a couple of days. All of this seems to offer a very safe and well-supported entry into a higher level. Clarissa and DeMane have had the benefit of a guided reading lesson to get them started in the series. They have the support of each other during the reading club cycle. They'll be able to talk about the books, which will serve to support their comprehension.

It's worth noting an interesting thing about a series book study: it has elements of both an author study and a character study. After all, Frog and Toad are wonderful characters to study, Frog and Toad books work well as a series book study, and those books could easily be part of an Arnold Lobel basket during an author study. Many teachers have rightly asked, "What's the difference between these reading clubs, then, if they are all based on the same texts?" The difference is in our teaching focus and the reading work that students will do within each of these kinds of reading clubs.

Before I offer ideas for instruction within a series books reading club cycle, I want to share these observations:

- A series book study may not be a great choice for most kindergarten students, unless many of them in a classroom are able to read texts at levels found in a series. On the other hand, I know some kindergarten teachers who have launched series books reading clubs in which students selected from options like PM Starters Series, Sunshine Books Series, and so on.

- Series book studies seem to make sense at times when many students are ready to move up to the next level or need to strengthen their control of skills and strategies by reading within their current level for a bit more time.

- Many teachers launch a couple of cycles of series books reading clubs at different points in the year. I know second- and third-grade teachers who launch a series book study in the early fall, once they've determined their students' reading levels, and then they conduct another series book study later in the spring. Often the instruction is very similar in the two different series book studies, but in the springtime, students are likely to be reading higher-level series than they did in the fall.

Featured Skills and Strategies I Might Teach in a Series Book Study

As always, the skills and strategies I would teach in series books reading clubs are largely dependent on what my students can do and what they need to do to read with more fluency, accuracy, and comprehension. Even so, when the whole class is gathered around series books for a short period of time, there are skills and strategies we can teach to help them effectively negotiate series book reading. The skills and strategies I might teach within a series book study are things like accumulating the story across pages and chapters, summarizing text, making and using connections across books, determining importance, and reading with stamina and focus. Depending on my students' needs, some of these strategies, like reading with stamina and focus, would be taught during whole-class mini-lessons because they would be useful to most all of the readers. Other strategies might be taught in small-group settings, especially if there are only a handful of partners who need the particular support.

Real-Life Purposes, Habits, and Goals Readers Might Have in a Series Book Study

Last winter, some friends loaned my husband and me a DVD box set of the first season of a particular television show, which shall remain nameless. Ian and I had never watched this show when it aired in prime time, although we had heard lots of favorable buzz about it. We were curious, but skeptical. I hadn't been hooked on a TV show since a former roommate and I would look forward to *Melrose Place* every week. (I can't believe I'm revealing that to you.) Anyway, one long, dark winter night, we put in the DVD of this weekly television show just to watch an episode or two, but in spite of myself, I got hooked. Ian and I stayed up until 2:30 in the morning watching one episode after another, not to mention all of the deleted scenes. The next night, same thing. It was the weekend, we rationalized. We'd go cold turkey on school nights. Even though we weren't watching during the week, I couldn't get the show out of my mind. I looked forward to the next opportunity we'd have to pop in the DVD. The following weekend, when we got through every episode from that first season, I felt a huge letdown. It was 1:00 in the morning, and I wanted more.

I'm sure we can all imagine a series we've gotten hooked on, whether it is a series of books, a television series, or a movie that has several sequels. Whatever the medium, people who are hooked on a series share many similar purposes, habits, and goals, and these are things we can share with our students during a series books reading club cycle.

- Readers get hooked on a series because the characters are compelling to them for some reason, which they can state. *("I really, really like Tooter Pepperday books because she reminds me of my best friend." "I love to read Pippi Longstocking books because she does such crazy things. I want to see what she'll do next.")*

- Readers get hooked on a series because the stories are appealing to them for some reason, which they can state. *("I love to read Magic School Bus books because they have a silly story, but they also give lots of information about stuff.")*

- Readers get hooked on a series because they love to talk about it with other people. *("Me and my friend are reading Harry Potter books right now. Even though we saw the movies, we like to talk about the parts of the books that are different than the movies.")*

- Readers look forward to reading more books in the series because they want to see what happens next. *("I want to read the next Little House book because I want to know how the move turns out for Laura's family.")*

- Readers use what they know from one book in the series to help them understand what's going on in another book in the series. *("I think that the setting of Magic Tree House books can make them tricky. I know that sometimes I might need to ask somebody about the hard words and the stuff that I don't know about.")*

- Readers look forward to the next book in the series and are eager to read it. *("Guess what my brother told me? J. K. Rowling is writing another Harry Potter book! I thought she was done. I can't wait!" or "We've read Henry and Mudge Books 1 to 4. I wonder if anyone has Book 5 that we could borrow. We want to stay in order.")*

- Readers have favorite titles within the series and compare and contrast the story lines among the books. *("My favorite Poppleton book is the first one because each of the stories introduced us to his friends. One of the Poppleton stories I didn't really like was the one when Poppleton went to buy a coat from Zacko. I didn't like how mean Zacko was to Poppleton.")*

- Readers recommend series books to other people they think will be interested. *("I know you love Junie B. Jones books. I think you'll like Tooter Pepperday, too, 'cause she's sort of like Junie." Or "You might like Clifford books if you like Curious George. They are both animals who have lots of adventures," or "Captain Underpants books are so funny. I bet you'd love them.")*

Getting Ready for Series Books Reading Clubs

Just like for any cycle of reading clubs, I would want to spend a week or so before the official launch of the clubs to scaffold my students to get them ready for the work they'll soon be doing independently. I'd find ways to expose my students to the kinds of texts they'll soon encounter, and I'd model proficient reading and strong conversations using these same kinds of texts during read-aloud time.

During read-aloud time for a week or so prior to a series books reading club cycle, I would select a couple of titles from a series to read to my students. I would model the habits and strategies of a proficient series book reader, and I would facilitate the kinds of quality conversations about the texts that I want my students to have in their reading club partnerships. I would select a series for the read-aloud during this time that is similar in level to the kind of series that the bulk of my students could read. I would also want to choose two or three titles from the series that I could get through in a week or two.

On the first day, I might gather my students for read-aloud and say something like, "You know, we will soon have series book clubs so we can become experts about a series or two of books, and I thought that it would be great to choose a series to read during read-aloud for the next week or so. I gathered titles from these two series. Let's think about which one we'd like to read." I would then offer a quick synopsis of the two series, and I'd pass out books for students to look through. We'd have a brief discussion about which series to read together and then make the choice, perhaps by voting if necessary.

Once we chose the series, I'd model how a series book reader figures out which book to read first. "You know, some series have an actual first book that it's important to start with because it introduces you to the characters and because the next books build upon the story. It's like Harry Potter books. I guess you could read the fourth one first, but then you might not know all the history and details of the characters as well as if you had started with the first one in the series. Then on the other hand, some series, like Frog and Toad, are the kind of series where it doesn't matter really which book you start first. Let's figure out what makes sense for our series. Sometimes there's a clue on the cover; like it might say 'Book One' or something like that."

As I read the books in the series aloud, I would model good habits, such as making connections from one of the texts to the other, using my schema from the first book to help me get quickly into the second book, and so on. I would also have my students turn and talk about the story in partnerships at various points as I read aloud. If, for instance, I think aloud as I read to model what it sounds like to concisely summarize a part of the story, I would use the next turn-and-talk prompt to give my students practice summarizing. I could say something like, "Phew... a lot just happened in this part. Turn and talk with your partner and try to summarize together what just happened." We would have several whole-class conversations about the texts as well in which I acted less as a content contributor to the conversation and more as a host/facilitator. After the whole-class talk, I could take a few minutes to name the helpful conversation moves I noticed the students making as they talked. I could say something like, "I noticed you guys really were talking a lot about the idea of whether Horrible Harry is really bad or not. I love when that happens in a conversation, when we find something that we stick with for a while. Lots of voices were heard, and we checked back with the book several times to make sure we were being accurate about what happened. That was a strong part of our conversation, I think. I'm looking forward to thinking about this more in the next Horrible Harry book." (At some point in the year, after students have had lots of experience with whole-class conversations, I give them the responsibility to reflect on what they think went well in a conversation.)

Besides using read-aloud time to expose my students to series book reading before the official launch of our study, I also would want to get some books in their hands for independent reading. This means that we'd have to reconfigure some classroom library baskets into series book baskets. For example, I'd go through our Level J baskets and pull out the Frog and Toad books and put them into a designated Frog and Toad basket. We'd make series baskets for the range of readers in the classroom. For our students who read books at the earliest levels, this means that we might have to gather books like Mrs. Wishy-Washy books and put them into a basket called Mrs. Wishy-Washy Series.

Once we made series book baskets at a variety of levels, I'd strongly suggest that everyone shop for one or two titles from a series that they can read well during independent reading workshop. This means that during the week before we officially launch series book clubs, the students have a chance to explore a series first.

We can also use homework to open up dialogue about reading between our students and their families. In anticipation of a series book study, we could assign homework like the following: "Ask someone at home if they ever had a series of books they loved to read when they were little. If the person did have a series he or she loved, ask, 'Can you tell me what that was like?'"

There is another consideration in preparation for launching this cycle of reading clubs that I want to share. Before a cycle of series book clubs begins, I try to have a very specific plan in mind for each of the partnerships. I figure out which partnerships I will nudge forward into a series of books that are at a higher level than what they are reading now. I realize that I will have to do some preparatory work with them, such as guided reading or strategy lessons (Calkins 2001) to support them in the higher-level texts, so I'll make plans for doing so. For other partnerships, I may decide to have them choose a series that's composed of texts in their current just-right reading level. I'll make this decision for partnerships who need to spend more time strengthening their reading in a particular level.

It's Reading Club Time!

The series book club baskets are set, and my students have chosen the series they will be reading for the next week or two. For children in series with books higher than Level L or M, it makes sense if they stay in the same series for about two weeks so they have time to read at least a couple of the texts in the series and have substantial conversations about them. The readers who are reading books at levels lower than L will most likely choose a series for one week and then choose another series for the next week. Figure 8.2 shows some possible approaches to use during series books reading clubs. Appendix G provides a sample planning guide for series books reading clubs.

Figure 8.2	
Big Idea for Readers During Series Books Reading Clubs	**Specific Strategies for Readers**
Readers figure out how to approach their series.	· Readers use all the information available on series book covers to see if that helps them decide which book to read first and next and next. · Readers can skim the books in a series to figure out which one they want to start with, especially if the author hasn't written them to be read in a specific order. · Partners decide if they want to read the same title at the same time or if they want to each read a different title and then talk about the books. · When partners decide to read different titles, they can trade the books with each other after they're finished. This is helpful for the conversation because then both partners know the same books well. · Readers try to figure out if their books are "to be continued" from one book to the next, or if each book is its own separate story.

Figure 8.2 *(continued)*	
Big Idea for Readers During Series Books Reading Clubs	**Specific Strategies for Readers**
Readers figure out what's important in a book and keep that in mind as they read (*determining importance and accumulating the text across pages and chapters*).	· Readers can retell what happened in a part of the book or within a chapter and then say, "The important part of this is... " · Readers can review the events in the chapter and think about what are the important parts to keep in mind. · Readers can jot the ideas and events they think are important on sticky notes. · As readers meet new characters in their texts, they try to name the relationship the new character has to the main characters, and they determine whether this is a character to hold in their minds or whether he or she is a fleeting character, one who just passes through the story.
Readers use what they know from the first book in the series to help them understand the next book. Readers make connections between books in a series.	· Readers keep in mind what they learned about the characters in the first book when they encounter the same characters again in the next books. · Readers notice similarities between books in a series and say things like, "This is similar to what happened in that other book. In both books, she got into an argument with a classmate." · Readers use what they know from the previous books they've read in order to make good predictions about the characters and the events in the book they are currently reading. · Readers notice when characters change across books in a series because they've gotten to know the characters really well.
Readers read with increasing stamina and focus.	· When readers realize they don't know what's going on in the story, they may have lost focus or concentration. It helps to go back and reread. · When readers have pictures in their minds of the story and characters, they can stay focused more easily. · When a reader puts down a book on one day and picks it up on the next day, it helps to retell to oneself what happened in the last section read. · Readers can flip back through the book and skim some parts to refresh their memory about what has happened so far. · Readers have ways to deal with noise distractions. They can politely ask someone to be quieter, or they can read with their hands over their ears.

Author Study

One summer, years before we had children or iPods, my husband and I drove across the country listening to the CDs from the big, black simulated leather CD case we lugged along. We made a car trip rule that whoever was driving was also the DJ because it was in our best interest to keep the driver awake and happy. So it was on a desolate stretch of highway in the middle of some big state when Ian slept and I drove, awake and happy, as I binged on all of my Wilco and U2 CDs, one after another, for hours.

I had never before listened to the music of U2 in such a concentrated way. After a while, I began to notice recurring images and metaphors in the lyrics. I soon stopped singing along and got lost in thought. In several songs, I noticed that love is equated to a temple and there is the image of crawling toward something. I realized that love is never easy and breezy in U2 songs. I began to wonder about the songs' meanings. I wondered why they used the image of crawling and the word *temple* so often. It's not exactly a rhyme generator—temple, bemple, simple, pimple, dimple. I wondered why love was so hard for U2. After all, wasn't Bono happily married to his high school sweetheart? I wondered where they got the ideas for their songs. I noticed themes within and across albums. I wondered and wondered about these things as I drove and listened. I think I may have woken Ian up to tell him my U2 epiphanies. How fun for him. In retrospect, we could say I was deeply engaged in a kind of audio author study.

My U2 study has much in common with an author study that would take place in a classroom. In our classes, we gather several texts by an author, we read and reread them in a concentrated period of time, we make connections among the texts, we wonder about and question things we notice, and we talk about our thinking.

Author studies are important because the realization that one can have a favorite author is a significant milestone for a reader. Having favorite authors is a characteristic that's typical of avid, passionate readers. Having favorite authors or authors whose work one knows well is empowering because it allows a reader to be more selective. When readers have a sense of their preferences, they also have a reading identity they can cultivate. I want my students to have tastes as readers, especially in knowing what they love and what they like. This self-knowledge will help them become independent and discerning readers who can easily maintain a reading life, mostly because they can find things they like to read. With regard to favorite authors, I hope my students know they can pursue and think about the work of authors they love. I want to teach them the real-life ways that avid readers read, think, and talk across texts by their favorite authors. In Appendix G, I've included a planning guide with suggestions for author study reading clubs.

Building Healthy
Reading Habits

Although I'm wary of the trend to impose business models and corporate mind-sets on the very human and interpersonal work between students and teachers, I have to admit there is one big lesson we educators can learn from big business. That lesson is to "hook 'em while they're young!"

A marketing objective for companies is to create lifelong, loyal consumers. Research shows that from a young age, we develop brand loyalty. In many cases, the brands we grew up using tend to be the brands we seek out as adults. Companies capitalize on this by directly marketing to children. If we read the business section of any newspaper over the course of a week, there's likely to be an article or two about how companies are spending billions of advertising and marketing dollars in their attempts to capture younger and younger consumers.

We teachers are not likely to have billions of dollars on hand (sigh) or a product to sell, but with respect to literacy, we, too, want to hook 'em while they're young. Frank Smith writes that "our strongest affiliations are to the clubs we join first" and that's why it's critical that our students are immediate and enthusiastic members of the Literacy Club (Smith 1988, 6). We want our students to develop the habit of making reading a big part of their lives as soon as possible. We want them to value the experience and reap the benefits of reading so that they're more likely to live text-filled lives outside of the classroom. It is our hope of hopes that the students we teach will walk out of our classrooms at the end of the year with visions of summer reading plans and the understanding that reading can be an integral and pleasurable part of their lives outside of school.

In this chapter I'll describe a couple of reading club cycles meant to give students the tools necessary (or, at the very least, an experience with the tools necessary) to build their own self-sustaining reading lives. These reading clubs, Setting Goals to Become Stronger Readers and Inventing Our Own Reading Projects, give students the pleasure of setting their own goals and imagining their own projects in ways that ingrain habits of mind about reading as well as provide a sense of agency as readers (Johnston 2004). The combination of developing good habits, growing a sense of agency, and experiencing pleasure as readers is more likely to enable us to hook 'em while they're young.

The two kinds of healthy habits reading clubs I will discuss in this chapter have a lot in common with each other, and in some cases, teachers have merged them into one cycle of reading clubs called Readers Set Goals and Invent Their Own Projects. I'll weave details about both kinds of clubs throughout the various sections of this chapter, so you can decide for yourself if it makes sense to separate them into two distinct cycles of clubs or if you'd prefer to combine them into one longer reading club cycle.

When is the Right Time for Healthy Habits Clubs?

I've found that the Setting Reading Goals Clubs and Inventing Reading Projects Clubs are wonderful as back-to-back, year-end units of study, each taking about two weeks or so. They seem to fit best at the end of the year because by then our students have increased stamina for reading and can work more independently during reading workshop than they could have earlier in the year. Also, by June our students are equipped with a vast repertoire of strategies to figure out words and the meaning of their texts, and they know a variety of ways to work and talk with partners. Through the course of the year in reading workshop, it's likely that most of the students have developed a sense of purpose for their work during reading time, which is very important for successful healthy habits reading clubs.

Another benefit of ending the year with these reading clubs is that they provide a perfect segue into our students' summer reading lives. The work our students do in these reading clubs offers a dress rehearsal of sorts for how they might lead their reading lives over the summer, when they are typically left to their own devices. In these reading clubs, our students either set their own goals or imagine meaningful projects around reading, and they learn how to make and revise plans for their work. These clubs call upon young readers to develop a sense of responsibility and ownership for their reading, and they teach students that they have the power to determine their own purposes, intentions, projects, and goals as readers.

Although there are many reasons to implement these reading clubs during the final month or so of the school year, I have known teachers who have launched them at other times of the year, as well. For example, a third-grade teacher might decide that the last couple of weeks of school in December, right before the holiday break, is an opportune time to give his students the experience of planning their own reading projects to help them get ready for reading during the school vacation. Some second- and third-grade teachers choose to launch Setting Reading Goals Clubs in early January, right after the break. This cycle of reading clubs coincides nicely with the spirit of the New Year, resolutions and fresh starts, setting goals, making plans, and then doing the work to reach them.

What Are the Featured Reading Skills, Strategies, and Habits i Will Teach During These Reading Clubs?

One of the challenges of these kinds of reading clubs is determining what exactly to teach. Because there is no unifying whole-class study going on that connects all the clubs, it can be difficult to figure out an instructional thread that will make sense for everybody. During poetry reading clubs, everyone is reading and talking about poetry, so teaching students to envision as they read is a very sensible thing to teach. All of the readers will need to use this strategy. During author study reading clubs, everyone has chosen an author whose work they want to get to know well, so teaching students how to make connections between books in order to understand the stories better is one possible idea for whole-class instruction. In most reading club cycles, when the partnerships are doing the same sort of work with similar texts (albeit with different levels of texts), it's not as difficult to figure out a string of mini-lessons that will be pertinent to most all of the readers.

In healthy habits reading clubs, however, everyone has chosen a reading goal to meet or a reading project to work on, but the projects or goals may be quite different from one partnership to another. There might be a wide variety of clubs that reflect the different goals and projects of the readers in the room. Here is a sample of the clubs students created in one cycle of Setting Reading Goals clubs in my classroom:

Reading Like a Storyteller Club

The underlying work in this club was improving reading fluency. Two children invented this club to achieve their goal of becoming stronger at reading aloud because they would soon have baby siblings in their lives. I also gently encouraged two other children to participate in this club because they needed to work on reading with more fluency.

My First Chapter Book Club

The two children who invented this reading club were newcomers to the world of chapter books having very little picture support. One partner chose a Horrible Harry book, and the other chose a Junie B. Jones book. They wanted to work on making their own pictures in their minds as they read these books. Over the course of the week, they offered each other support by talking about their books together, summarizing the parts, or sketching parts where they got strong images in their minds.

Funny Books Club

In this club, two kids pulled together a basket of several books that they said were really funny. With my nudges, they reread the books to figure out what made them so funny. Over the course of the week, they read and reread several books to find others that met their funny criteria and made them laugh out loud. They ended up making a version of a top ten list of funny books that they wanted to duplicate for everyone in the class.

Author Club

Two sets of partners wanted to work in this reading club. One partnership chose to focus on Kevin Henkes books because they loved the characters in them. They decided to pick some scenes to act out, using the little bits of speech text that Henkes included as part of the illustrations. The other partnership chose to study different authors and then report their discoveries to each other. One partner decided to study Tomie dePaola books, while his partner read Ezra Jack Keats.

What is the teaching, then, that we might focus on in mini-lessons during the healthy reading habits clubs if all the partnerships have different purposes? If we're trying to plan instruction that will be immediately useful to as many students as possible, it seems to make sense to use this time to support good work habits and strong reading habits. I've spent time in both the reading projects clubs and reading goals clubs teaching my students strategies for making plans and sticking to them; staying focused on a project or goal; note taking to record thoughts, plans, new ideas, and progress; talking with partners to offer support and to check in; and so on.

The teaching points and strategy instruction in these mini-lessons serve to keep the students afloat as they work on meeting their goals or finishing their projects for reading, but really the teaching and learning during these reading club cycles can easily cross content-area boundaries. For example, during a Reading Projects cycle of clubs, we could teach our students that people get ready for their projects by making a list of what they need and then gathering the materials. This advice and instruction makes sense for anyone working on any project: for the child whose reading project is to read everything he can about snakes because he wants to be able to have a strong argument for getting one as a pet and for the child who is planning to paint a self-portrait for her dad's birthday. This advice makes sense for the newlyweds about to host their first Thanksgiving dinner and the friends who are going to trek through Nepal in six months. What we teach our students about planning, maintaining, and completing projects and goals can be transferred to any kind of work, in or out of school, from art projects, to writing for an audience, to planning a dinner party for six, to researching the human genome.

It's important to remember that we can use reading conferences and small-group instruction to offer more precise support for readers in these healthy habits clubs. One day, I approached Joelle and Henry, who were the founding (and only) members of the Teeth Research Club. They decided they wanted to study human teeth because they each lost one and both now had a wiggler on deck. They'd gathered several nonfiction texts about the human body as well as *Arthur's Loose Tooth* in their basket. I stopped short of their work space for a moment to observe them. Joelle and Henry were sitting quietly and looking at different books. They seemed to be racing through the texts, flipping pages quickly, in what looked to be an effort to just get through them. Every once in a while, Henry blurted out a fact about the human body to Joelle, who didn't seem very interested.

"How's it going?" I asked (Anderson 2000). This kind of open-ended question doesn't pass judgment on the work they're doing, nor does it lock them into a yes or no response like if I asked them, "Are you guys reading about the human body?" Also, questions like "How's it going?" or "What are you thinking about as you look through that?" or "What are you thinking about so far?" presume that the child is engaged and purposeful. I tend to begin conferences with an open-ended question or comment because I know that sometimes children have intentions that I just didn't realize during my quick observation.

"We're reading our books," Joelle responded without looking up.

"Hmm, I can see that. It seems like you're looking for something in particular the way you're both flipping through the pages so fast. Either that or you're trying to get through the books so fast."

"Ms. Collins, did you know that blood in your body isn't red? Did you know that? It's bluish-purplish," Henry said.

"Oooh, that's gross," Joelle blurted out.

"Guys, I want to check in with you for a second. Your project is to study teeth, and your planning card says you want to find out more information about teeth. How's that going?"

"Well, we're doing that," Joelle said.

"How so?" I asked.

"We're looking through the pages for teeth information," replied Henry.

"You know, I want to remind you of something that will help you find the information you're looking for more quickly. You can check the index and the table of contents in your books to see exactly where the teeth pages are. Watch me. Hmmm, I want to find out stuff about teeth. Let's see, where is T in this index? Oh, here it is. I'm looking for teeth. [I slid my finger down the T entries in the index.] Oh, here it is, "teeth." Wow, it looks like there are a few pages on teeth. Let's check out page 43. 43. 43. [I said this as I flipped for the page.] Look, this whole page is about teeth. Let me put a sticky note on this page to save it. Did you guys see what I did? I looked for teeth information by using the index to find the information quickly. You guys can do that, too. Look in your books to see if there's an index or table of contents, and then use it to find the information you're looking for. Go ahead."

I watched as Joelle and Henry did this. "Hey, look, Henry. There are some teeth pages in my book. Give me a sticky note!" Joelle said.

In this conference, I made a choice to remind Joelle and Henry about using the index to find information more quickly and efficiently. There were other things I could have taught. For example, I could have helped them make a focused plan for their work if they didn't have one. I could have taught them to begin by thinking together about what they wanted to know about teeth or what they wondered about teeth so that they could begin to create a framework for their research together. If they had made a plan already, I could have given them a strategy to stick with it. I could have taught them to make a to-do list that they could check off when they got things done. If I had several other partnerships whose projects involved studying a topic of interest like Joelle and Henry and their teeth research, I could gather them together for small-group instruction in the form of a five-minute strategy lesson to teach them what I just taught Joelle and Henry.

Getting Ready for Healthy Habits Reading Clubs

Getting ready for healthy habits reading clubs is a little different from preparing for other kinds of clubs. For one thing, we don't have to change our classroom library very much to support these clubs. In healthy habits reading clubs, each partnership is likely to be working on unique projects or goals, so it's virtually impossible to change the library around to support everyone's work. This stands in contrast to nonfiction reading clubs, for example, when we feature the nonfiction texts by putting them in the limelight to increase their visibility and accessibility. In healthy habits reading clubs, each partnership might very well be doing work that is different from anyone else's. There's no way that we can switch around the library and spotlight certain texts in a way that will reflect each partnership's intentions and meet each of their needs equally well.

So instead of reconfiguring the library to support these clubs, we might spend a little time making sure our students are aware of what the classroom library offers so that they'll be able to find what they need. It's helpful to offer a mini-tour during a morning meeting or two, to show them the kinds of texts that are available.

It also helps to add more tools to the library, such as different size sticky notes; bookmarks and page clips; various note-taking sheets such as planning sheets, blank webs, and T-charts; or to-do lists with check-off boxes. For these reading clubs, I've also always provided open-ended note-taking sheets for students to write self-reflections.

Many of our students may not yet be familiar with the act of setting their own goals and working to reach them, nor have many of our students had the experience of working on a project they invented themselves. Most of the work they do in school tends to be assigned and paced by an adult, especially in the younger grades.

Helping our students make good choices for goals and projects can be one of the most challenging aspects of these reading clubs. For this reason, it's worth the time to have a few good, substantive conversations with our students about setting goals and planning projects in general, and then about reading goals and reading projects specifically.

When I think about the kinds of goals or projects that I would like to see my students choose, my hope is that they meet these criteria:

· The project or goal is helpful and beneficial to the reader.

· The project or goal is meaningful for the reader.

· The project or goal is realistic and possible to finish or achieve.

In an ideal world, our students would choose goals or projects that meet these criteria. Our classrooms, however, are in the reality-based world, so it's more realistic that we'll have several students like Charles, who says his reading goal is to count how many times he sees the word *underpants* in his chapter book, or readers like Brittany, who tells you her project is to read all of the Harry Potter books, even though it will likely be years before she can read those with accuracy, fluency, and comprehension. For many children, we'll need to have conferences during which we nudge them toward another goal or project based on what we know about their reading strengths and needs and their life interests and passions. We want to support them in choosing a goal or project that will have more of a positive long-term (or even shorter-term) effect on their reading lives than counting how many times they find a particular word or struggling through high-status texts. I've found that having several whole-class conversations about goal-setting and project-planning helps children envision more fruitful intentions.

We can approach these conversations about reading projects or goal-setting by talking about projects and goals in general. One year, I shared the story of a beading project. I told my students that when I was in third grade, one of my classmates made a necklace out of love beads. I thought her necklace was so beautiful, and I wanted to make one just like it. For my birthday, I asked for and received a love bead kit. "You know what, you guys? At that moment, when I opened that present, I gave myself a project to make love bead jewelry."

"Every day after school I would set up my love bead kit at the kitchen table, and I worked on my project. I made a necklace for myself, but I didn't stop there. I made some bracelets for my mom and my grandma, and when I was running out of love beads, I made little rings for my friends. I loved making those things, and it was so fun to give them as presents. You know what I learned about projects from this? I learned that it's so important to pick a project that means a lot to you and that you'll enjoy working on for a while. Right now, think about yourself. Have you ever worked on something for several days like I worked on love bead jewelry? Do you remember ever giving yourself a project to do?"

After a bit of time, I asked the students to talk in partnerships about their projects. Many kids had something to share, and there was a wide range of projects. Students talked together about things like building snow forts after the big blizzard; making model cars with an older brother; setting up a dollhouse; cleaning out a bedroom to find a beloved Susan B. Anthony coin; and so on.

After sharing some brief details of the projects that kids had experienced, we tried to determine the characteristics of the ones they loved the most. The next day, we had a discussion about how we sometimes abandon projects or lose interest in them and talked about strategies for avoiding those problems.

Quickly, we moved from talking about goal-setting and project-planning in general to imagining reading goals and projects, specifically. We brainstormed and listed possibilities at first, and then students began to think about what kinds of goals or projects would suit them as readers. I emphasized the criteria of finding a project or setting a goal that would help them get stronger at reading, that would be meaningful to them, and that would be realistic to finish within a couple of weeks.

For these kinds of reading clubs, I tend to spend a week or so having these sorts of conversations with the whole class and with individual students who might need extra support to make wise choices. During private reading time for a week or two prior to launching the clubs, I confer with students about their reading strengths and needs, as well as their interests. In some cases, I would suggest possible projects and goals for particular students who I believed needed more guidance in making a selection that would meet the criteria listed earlier.

It's Reading Club Time!

Once your students have decided on their reading goal or project, our work for whole-class instruction is to teach lessons that help keep students engaged and focused. During conferences and small-group instruction, we can attend to the particular details of a partnership's specific projects and goals.

In any reading club cycle, it's extremely helpful to model during mini-lessons as if you and the class are partners in a reading club. During a concept book study in a kindergarten, that might mean that all of the teaching points and demonstrations are done using materials from the Counting Books club, for example, as you pretend that you and the students are working together in that club. During whole-class instruction for healthy habits clubs, it helps to do the same thing, to model and demonstrate strategies as if you and the students are working together on a goal or a project. One year, the "project" I was working on during mini-lessons was putting together a poetry anthology for our student teacher, who had just wrapped up her work with our class. She was planning to be with us again on the last day of school to say good-bye, so I told my students that I wanted to make a poetry anthology for her so she'd always remember our class. I taught all the mini-lessons for a week or two from the point of view of a reader working on this project.

Figure 9.1 presents some of the areas I've tended to cover during mini-lessons in a cycle of healthy habits clubs.

Figure 9.1	
Big Idea for Readers During Healthy Habits Reading Clubs	**Specific Strategies for Readers**
Readers get ready to work on their project or goal by thinking about what they need to do their work.	· Readers envision the work they'll do and make a list of things they'll need to do it. · Readers gather the materials they need and keep them in one place so they are accessible. · Readers have a vision for what they want to happen with their goal or project, and they try to think of the steps it will take to meet the goal or finish the project.
Readers make plans for their work.	· Readers can jot their plans on a to-do list or on a planning card and check them off when they finish them. · Readers sometimes get stuck at a point in their project or goal, and they can ask their partner to help them get through the hard part. · Readers can share their plans with others to help get more ideas.

The Transition to Summer and Beyond

With our support and guidance during the healthy habits reading clubs, our students have the opportunity to imagine, plan, and execute a purpose-driven reading experience for themselves. Now, it's crucial to help them transfer this process to their reading lives outside of the classroom. With summer looming ahead (presuming that it's the end of the year), we can help our students make summer reading plans using what they've learned during healthy habits reading clubs.

In my class, the homework assignments for reading at the end of the year are designed to help students make summer reading plans and to remind them to transfer what they've learned as readers in school to reading anytime, any place. So we make (nonbinding) contracts for summer plans, we create support networks for each other, and we imagine staying in touch as readers, although I may not and cannot hold students accountable for meeting the expectations set forth in the summer reading contracts they create. Perhaps the things they said they'd do in their contracts won't happen exactly as they planned, but at these young ages, it's valuable to have a vision of a rich summer reading life full of books and reading friends.

Some of the most important ideas I hope they carry from the classroom to their lives outside of school follow.

Readers Get Better at Reading by Reading — Reading a Lot

Students need to read over the summer to avoid summer reading loss (Allington 2001). For many students, teachers need to help their families make plans that will support their children's summer reading. Teachers can recommend appropriate titles and share ways that families can get books into their kids' hands. Schools can set up schoolwide expectations for reading over the summer and develop systemic ways to support families who need help. Some schools partner with the public library to make sure all students have a library card, and they collaborate on summer reading programs and book recommendations. Some schools open the school library over the summer for a few hours a few days a week so children can borrow books. In other schools, teachers organize and write grant proposals for money to buy books for their students (Allington 2001).

Readers Are Resourceful

Avid readers are scrappy about their reading. Many times when they find themselves idle, they can't help but search for something to read, whether it's flipping through a tabloid while standing in a long supermarket line, squinting to read the fine print in the ads that surround them on the subway, studying the nutritional information on the cereal box at breakfast, or making a sidelong glance at the text message the person next to us is typing away on the bus ride home.

Readers are also resourceful in the face of difficulty. Whether it's a tricky word or a confusing part of a book, readers work to make sense of what they're reading. If the text is simply too hard and the reader feels some tension and too much confusion, the resourceful reader will put the text down because she knows she'll be able to find something that is a better fit.

Reading Is Social

Avid readers talk about what they've read. They tell their friends about what they are reading, they recommend books to others, and they read with people in mind. Readers listen to book recommendations, and they often read texts they've heard about from others. Readers have reading buddies with whom they trade books and have similar reading sensibilities; they join book clubs in which they talk and learn about books with readers who may or may not be like them; they attend book talks presented by authors while sitting alongside strangers with whom they share a connection—a reading connection.

Readers Have Evolving Tastes and Identities

Readers know what they like, but they are open to new possibilities with regard to authors, themes, genres, and kinds of texts. They know that the more reading experiences they have, the more powerfully they'll be able to read. Readers know that it might just take one text or one recommendation for their reading identity to change. The reader who only reads mysteries becomes the reader who loves mysteries and poetry after her friend sends her a book of poetry for her birthday. Avid readers are responsive, open, and welcoming to new texts and to other readers.

Wait—Who Is This Avid Reader?

If I were asked to state my Ultimate Goals as a Teacher of Reading, I wouldn't think of year-end benchmarks and report card rubrics. Instead, to answer this very important question, I would do what my friend Donna Santman, author of *Shades of Meaning* (2005), suggests. I would think about my students well beyond the year they spend in my classroom. In fact, I would project twenty years ahead and imagine my hopes for my students' ongoing relationships to books and literacy at that point in their lives.

With this in mind, I would answer the question by saying that I want to teach my students to read with passion. I want them to become active, engaged, fervent readers who live their lives as if they *need* to read. I want my students to love to read and to share their reading with others. I want my students to be avid, highly engaged readers for the rest of their lives.

When I think of avid readers, I don't have a portrait of one in mind. Instead, I picture something more like a slideshow or a collage of snapshots showing many different kinds of readers. When I think about the characteristics of avid readers, I tend not to think about what they read. I think about *how* they read. I am more interested in their habits, their level of engagement with text, and their reading quirks and idiosyncrasies. It doesn't matter whether they read highfalutin Henry James sorts of text with sentences that last for pages and words that require a dictionary, or whether they read things like the latest best-selling self-help book on curing the paralyzing fear of velvet furniture. The author, the text, and the genre being read are merely details and not the most important, nor the most revealing, characteristics of an avid reader.

When I envision an avid reader, I imagine someone who figuratively leans into the book she's reading. She has reactions to the story, like when she reads on the subway and inadvertently attracts attention as she says out loud, "Oh, no you didn't!" in response to a character's actions. An avid reader feels for the characters in his books, like when he gets an anticipatory feeling of dread in the pit of his stomach as he begins the chapter in which the protagonist finally heads home to deal with his father's wrath. He has thoughts in and around the text and sees implications for and connections with his life and the world in whatever he's reading. Avid readers read with a pulse. An avid, engaged reader is someone who can't help but have a rich, highly engaged reading life because her life, her interests, and her reading are tightly woven together.

It might be helpful to take a moment to think of a time in your life when you were carried away by your reading. How did it feel? What were the circumstances? Was anyone else involved? How did this moment or period live on to affect your life or change your thinking? Can you replicate this experience for the students in your classroom?

Goodness gracious. We have a lot of good work to do.

Final Thoughts

I harbor a dark secret that I must reveal. As a teacher who has worked almost exclusively with students and teachers of kindergarten, first-, and second-grade classrooms, I admit that I've had my share of upper-grade envy. Don't get the wrong idea—it's not that I don't love the primary grades. I *do* love teaching little kids, wiggly-toothed and eager, kids like Rubin who come back from the cafeteria after lunch oblivious to the feel or smell of the food on their faces; kids like Esther who beg their moms to go to school on days when they've got a fever, a body rash, and an imminent need for a bathroom; kids like Miranda who tell you over and over that you're the best teacher they've ever had (not to mention the only teacher they've ever had). I love kids like Jordan who can probably name the date and time when he read his first chapter book. It was such a momentous occasion that if I project into the future, I can picture Jordan as a college student rolling up a sleeve to receive his first tattoo—the smiling faces of Frog and Toad inside a heart.

For our young learners, going to school and learning to read are so new and exciting, and our little ones are thrilling to watch as the puzzle pieces begin to fall into place. Yes, yes, this is all true. Even so, sometimes, just sometimes, I can't help but wonder what it would be like to teach older students. I have fantasized about having more sophisticated book talks. I have longed to venture deeply into issues and characters, characters that are a bit more developed than, say, Little Bear or Biscuit. I have wanted, just once, to read aloud a book that contained a little adolescent angst or a story about an orphan who survived in the untamed wilderness with just a bungee cord, a trusty mutt, a paper clip, and a crusty loaf of bread. Sometimes I've longed to read and talk about something a bit more juicy than Henry's dog Mudge slobbering all over that prissy cousin Annie!

I've felt green with upper-grade envy because I held a very naive perception. I thought teaching reading just *had* to be easier for upper-grade teachers than it was for primary-grade teachers. It just seemed less mysterious and daunting to teach reading to kids who could read the words already. I believed upper-grade teachers were at a distinct advantage because they have lots more in common with the kind of reading work their students are doing than we primary teachers have in common with the work our young students are doing.

Several years ago I was part of a book club that read *Corelli's Mandolin* by Louis de Bernières. Although I've forgotten much of what happened in the book, I do remember having to work hard to hold on to the story as I read it. It was set on the Greek island of Cephalonia during World War II, and it was written with a European perspective on the war. I had very little prior knowledge or schema to call upon—the setting, culture, history, and point of view were unfamiliar to me, and the movie hadn't been released at that point.

My experience reading *Corelli's Mandolin* is likely to be quite similar to the difficulty that Nora, a fifth grader, might encounter as she reads *Catherine, Called Birdy*, a book set in medieval times. I could imagine conferring with Nora and saying something like, "Look, Nora, I know what it's like to read a book with an unfamiliar setting and time period. In fact, that's just what's happening to me now with the book I'm reading. Let me show you a strategy I use to help me understand what's going on." I could quickly forge a connection with Nora because she and I are dealing with the same challenges as readers. Using our reading connection and my own reading experience, I could teach her a helpful reading strategy.

Teachers of primary-grade students, on the other hand, usually have to dig into our memories and turn on our imaginations in order to relate to what many of our children are going through as they take those early steps as readers. Let's tell the truth now: we're either big fakers or great actors, depending on how you look at it, when we pretend we're making miscues as we read *The Hungry Giant* aloud to our students during shared reading in our attempts to demonstrate a particular decoding strategy.

In spite of my misguided belief that the grass is greener in the other grades, I'm happy to report that through the years I've gotten over my upper-grade envy. One thing that helped was implementing reading clubs into my reading workshop at various points throughout the year. I realized that reading clubs enabled me to make connections to my young readers in much the same ways that upper-grade teachers connect to their students. It is during reading clubs that my young students' reading most closely resembles real-life reading and allows them to integrate all they know about reading the words, understanding the text, and setting purposes for reading in order to develop the kinds of positive reading habits that will last a lifetime.

When my young readers participate in reading clubs at different times throughout the year, they are doing an early childhood version of the reading, thinking, and talking work characteristic of book clubs. It's during reading clubs that my students set their own purposes and have their own intentions for their reading, which are often very similar to the purposes and intentions that you or I might have for our reading. Reading clubs offer us a bridge between the teaching of skills and strategies to readers and the modeling of a highly engaged, purposeful reading life. Reading clubs also help us connect the reading our students must do in school to the reading we hope they choose to do once they are outside of our classrooms.

Appendixes

Appendix A: Ingredients for a Comprehensive K–3 Classroom Library

A Comprehensive K–3 Classroom Library Contains:

Baskets of leveled books that represent the range of learners

Some recommend that about 40–50 percent of the books in a classroom library are leveled and that the level is clearly indicated so students can easily find a variety of books that are just right for them as readers.

Baskets of books representing various genres

These baskets tend to be large and contain a variety of kinds of texts within a particular genre. Some examples: nonfiction, poetry, mysteries, biographies, wordless picture books, ABC books, graphic novels, etc.; whatever types of texts that are of interest and appropriate for the readers in the class.

Baskets of books gathered around topics

These baskets change throughout the year, depending on students' interests, class studies, the season, etc. Some examples: sharks, dinosaurs, Halloween books, books about school, books about Martin Luther King, Jr., books about families that have babies, etc.

Baskets of books featuring individual authors

The featured authors change throughout the year. Early in the school year, it's helpful to feature authors the students know well from the previous year. Some examples: Ezra Jack Keats, Mem Fox, Donald Crews, Dav Pilkey, Cynthia Rylant, Arnold Lobel, Authors We Know Well, etc.

Baskets of books arranged by series or character

Some titles within different series are found in the leveled baskets, but others might be housed in their own baskets dedicated to the particular series. Some examples: Magic Tree House, Magic School Bus, Horrible Harry, Frog and Toad, Poppleton, Judy Moody, Cam Jansen, Biscuit, Mrs. Wishy-Washy.

Baskets of books that support the work of the current unit of study

During any unit of study or cycle of reading clubs, the texts that best support the study take center stage in the classroom library. They should be easy for students to find. An example: during a poetry study, there might be baskets such as Poetry by Arnold Adoff, Poems About Nature, Silly Poems, Shape Poems.

Baskets of texts other than books

It's important to acknowledge the wide variety of texts and kinds of reading by including them in the classroom library. Some examples are: Sunday comics, maps, greeting cards, material from the Internet, songs we've learned, laminated puzzles and word jumbles from the kids' pages found in most newspapers, etc.

Baskets of "kids' picks"

These baskets contain categories of books the students imagine and then gather and label (e.g., Books We Love from Home, Favorite Books from Kindergarten, Top 10 Funniest Stories, Rain Poetry, Characters with Pets).

Baskets of shared reading texts and emergent storybooks

Some examples: copies of Mrs. Wishy-Washy, The Hungry Giant, poems, and other texts learned during shared reading.

Basket of books the teacher has read aloud

These baskets hold the books the teacher has read aloud—picture books and chapter books—and it helps to clean them out every month or so.

Baskets containing materials and tools readers need

These baskets contain sticky notes, bookmarks, pencils, graphic organizers the students know how to use, strategy tools, index cards, etc.

Other Classroom Library Considerations

Location—Where is the library in the classroom? Are book baskets found only in the library, or are some baskets spread around the classroom (for example, art books in the art area)?

Changes—How does the library change to reflect the work, time of year, etc.?

Design—Is the library visually appealing and well organized so that readers can find books?

Access—How do students borrow and return books? When are students able to borrow books? Is there informal time when students may browse?

Appendix B: Partnership Contract

At different points in the year, with some level of fanfare and an air of "official business," I ask my students to sign partnership contracts. These are "official" classroom documents. I make a copy of the contracts for the partnerships to file in their work folders, and I keep the originals in my files. Occasionally before the partnerships get together to work in their reading clubs, I'll ask them to take out their contracts, read them together, and then talk about what they are doing well and whether there are areas in which they still need work. I usually keep the contracts open-ended in that I let the students determine for themselves what they need to work on together. Here is one version of the contract.

Our Reading Partnership Contract

Date: _____

We will try our best to work well together to help each other become stronger readers, thinkers, and talkers.

Here is a list of things we will do as partners that will help us do our best work together:

1. _____

   _____

2. _____

   _____

3. _____

   _____

4. _____

   _____

Partner signatures: _____ and _____

Appendix G: Assessment Sheet

Sample Assessment Sheet for Use During Reading Clubs			
Reading Club Cycle _____		Start Date: _____	
	Target Skills and Strategies *(Fill in skills and strategies taught during this reading club cycle.)*		
Students' Names			

Appendix D: Reading Club Note-Taking Sheets

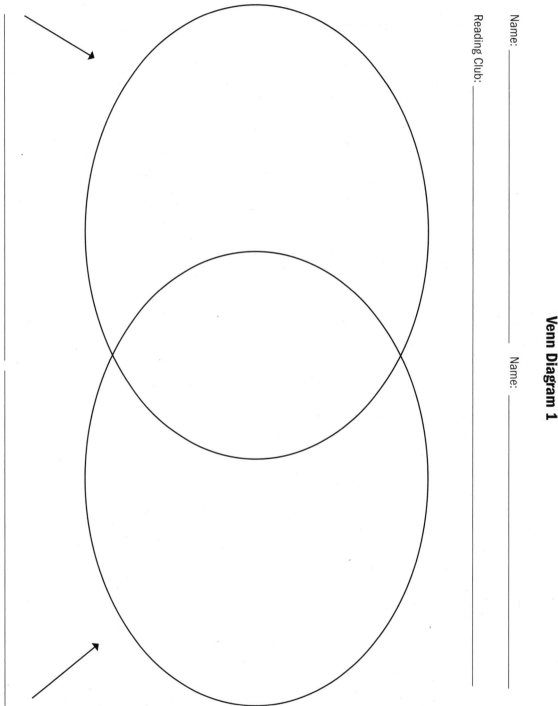

Name: _____   Name: _____

Reading Club: _____

Venn Diagram 1

Name: _____   Name: _____

Reading Club: _____

Venn Diagram 2

Comparing & Contrasting Versions of a Fairy Tale/Folk Tale

Name: _____   Name: _____

Our Reading Club: _____

New Information Web
"Hey, I didn't know that!"

Information:

~~~~~~~~~~~~~~~~~~~~~~~~~~~

I'm thinking…

Information:

~~~~~~~~~~~~~~~~~~~~~~~~~~~

I'm thinking…

Information:

~~~~~~~~~~~~~~~~~~~~~~~~~~~

I'm thinking…

OUR TOPIC

Information:

~~~~~~~~~~~~~~~~~~~~~~~~~~~

I'm thinking…

Information:

~~~~~~~~~~~~~~~~~~~~~~~~~~~

I'm thinking…

Information:

~~~~~~~~~~~~~~~~~~~~~~~~~~~

I'm thinking…

Name: _____   Name: _____

Our Reading Club: _____

Collecting Information Web

OUR TOPIC

Questions & Wonderings: _____

_____

_____

Name: _____   Name: _____

Our Reading Club: _____

T-Chart for Growing Ideas	
What we noticed, learned, and found in the text:	What it makes us think, wonder, and question:

Name: _____   Name: _____

Our Reading Club: _____

What we learned about our character from the book:	Page #	What this information makes us think about our character:
Title: _____		

Name: _____   Name: _____

Our Reading Club: _____

To-Do List

☐ _____

☐ _____

☐ _____

☐ _____

☐ _____

☐ _____

☐ _____

Name: _____   Name: _____

Our Reading Club: _____

First Day	**Last Day**

Our first thoughts, expectations, beliefs, and ideas:

What have we learned? How have we changed? What's new for us?

Reading, thinking, and talking together...

Appendix E: Reading Club Reflection Sheets

These two reflection sheets focus on how well the partners worked together. I usually give students reflection sheets at the end of a week during a cycle of reading clubs. The partners talk with each other first about the inquiries on the reflection sheet, and then they respond. A variation could be to ask students to respond to these questions orally during reflection conferences, or by drawing rather than writing their responses.

Reading Club Reflection Sheet

How did your partnership go this week?

Partners' Names: _____ and _____ Date: _____

Your reading club:

What did you and your partner do well this week in reading clubs?

What do you and your partner need to work on in order to make your partnership stronger?

What advice would you give to other partners?

Do you have any questions or wonderings about working with a partner?

(We can change the items in the checklist to reflect the specific teaching and learning that occurs within a cycle of reading clubs.)

Reading Club Reflection Sheet

How did your partnership go?

Partners' Names: _____ and _____ Date: _____

Your reading club:

Put an X in the boxes of the things that went well for you and your partner this week:

☐ We stayed focused on our work.   ☐ We took turns talking.
☐ We listened to each other.   ☐ We took turns making plans and choosing books.
☐ We peacefully and quickly solved any problems.   ☐ _____

What is something that you and your partner want to get better at next week?

This type of reflection sheet asks students to reflect on the content of their work within the cycle of reading clubs. The one below is for a nonfiction cycle, but it can be easily adapted for any kind of reading club.

Reading Club Reflection

Nonfiction Reading Clubs

Partners' Names: _____ and _____

Reading Club: _____

Why did you select this reading club?

Share some of your new learning about your topic:

Share some of your lingering questions about your topic:

What's next?

This type of reflection sheet asks students to reflect on the reading work they did within the cycle of reading clubs. The one below is for a character club cycle, but it can be easily adapted for any kind of reading club.

Reading Club Reflection

Character Study Club

Partners' Names: _____ and _____

Reading Club: _____

What did you do as a reader to help you get to know your character?

We worked on growing ideas about our characters by paying attention to what they do, what they say, how they look, and how the other characters respond to them. Share some of the work you and your partner did to grow ideas about your character:

What did we notice about our character?	What ideas did we grow about our character from the things we noticed?
Example: *1) Shelly runs all the time to school, to her classroom, to her mom's arms. 2) Shelly likes to play tag at recess. 3) Shelly wears sneakers in every picture. 4) Shelly gets yelled at by her mom and her teacher and the crossing guard for running around all the time.*	Example: *We think Shelly has a lot of energy because she's always running around. We feel bad for her a little because she keeps getting in trouble, but she's not trying to be bad. We think she just can't help it, and maybe someday she'll be a famous athlete.*
Your turn:	Your turn:

What did you learn to do as a reader in your reading club that will be helpful for anytime you're reading?

Appendix F: Reading Club Planning Guide

Reading Club Planning Guide

Reading Club Cycle: _____   **Dates:** _____

Readers' needs:

Featured skills and strategies that I will teach:

Real-life purposes, habits, and goals readers might have:

Getting ready for reading clubs:

Teaching emphasis for reading clubs, Week 1:

Teaching emphasis for reading clubs, Week 2:

Teaching emphasis for reading clubs, Week 3 (optional):

Assessment:

Possible project/celebration/outcome of reading clubs:

Appendix G: Sample Planning Guides for Reading Clubs

Sample Character Study Planning Guide

Reading Club Planning Guide

Reading Club Cycle: *"Readers Get to Know Their Characters Well"*

Dates: _____

Readers' needs:

Baskets of character reading clubs for all readers (levels C/D to level M), work folders, sticky notes, note-taking sheets, T charts?

Rebecca, Gregory, Samantha—more support with cross-checking (esp. for meaning)

Eliza, Rohan, Sean, Gabby—likely to pick high-level text; support with multiple story lines

Sabrina, Theria, Alex, Daniel, Julia G.—help moving past retelling to other kinds of book talk

Featured skills and strategies that I will teach:

· *identifying characters (main character, secondary characters, naming characters' relationships to one another)*

· *inferring to identify character traits and character motivations: using all the information we've got: our schema; attending to characters' actions, dialogue, appearance, facial expressions, gestures, etc.*

· *growing theories about character motivation (Why would she do or say that? How would you have handled that? Given what you know about the character, were those actions/words in character or out of character?)*

· *thinking deeper about characters by moving from noticing/naming to growing an idea (You noticed... What does that make you think? Given what you noticed, what ideas do you have about that?)*

· *connecting to characters—personal connections with characters (I'm like that. My brother is such a different kind of big brother...)*

· *Vocab work: expanding the way we express ideas, thoughts, noticings about characters—moving beyond "nice"*

Real-life purposes, habits, and goals readers might have:

Readers fall for their characters.

Readers get to know their characters.

Readers think about the characters even when they aren't reading the book.

Readers can learn about life and people by getting to know the characters in their books.

Getting ready for reading clubs:

· *create a whole-class list of favorite characters on a chart*

· *Read-aloud time: read two or three books featuring the same main character over the course of the week, whole class talks about character, model inferring to get to know character, etc.*

· *Shared reading: "Aunt Lavinia" by Eloise Greenfield (or other poem with a "character")*

· *Homework: name characters they've loved from books we've read; talk to grown-ups at home about characters they loved when they were little; poem "Aunt Lavinia" on homework, ask someone at home what they learned about Aunt Lavinia*

· *create character baskets across levels, feature them prominently in library, design labels in choice time*

· *give students a couple of days to talk about the characters in their book baggies in their partnerships as practice before they select a character club*

Teaching emphasis for reading clubs Week 1:

Readers have strategies to get to know characters well.

· *identify characters (main, secondary, name character relationships, select one to really get to know)*

· *infer what a character thinks by listening to words, paying attention to actions, looking at appearance, facial expressions, gestures*

· *use text evidence to support ideas*

· *study our character across books (notice habits, consistent traits, surprises, changes, etc.)*

· *study our character's relationships to other characters*

Teaching emphasis for reading clubs Week 2: *(Students may pick different characters or stay with the same character from Week 1.)*

When we study characters, we can understand why they say things and act the way they do.

(It might be necessary to repeat some teaching from the first week, based on what students are doing as readers, thinkers, and talkers.)

· *We can connect to our character to help us understand him or her better (Am I like this character? Am I different from this character? Do I know anyone like this character? How does my connection help me think about this character?)*

· *We can grow theories about why the character does and says things (My character said/did this. I think the reason is...)*

· *We can notice if and when the character changes within a book or across books and try to figure out what or who caused the change.*

· *We can focus on the different relationships our characters have and think about what they teach us about our character.*

Teaching emphasis for reading clubs Week 3 (optional): *(What is the energy like for character clubs? Is a third week necessary, helpful, and/or requested by students? If it is called for, will the instruction revisit previously taught strategies, will it focus on talking about texts, or will there be a new direction of study altogether?)*

We can put together baskets of books with different characters and think lots about the connections between them. Some basket reconfigurations might be: characters who are bullies; characters who are detectives; characters who are quirky; characters who are girls; characters who are pigs; characters who are pets; characters who are teachers; characters who are funny; etc.

· *Different characters can have similar characteristics. How are different characters alike?*
· *We can compare different characters and think about what motivates them, how they react to things, and how they relate to the other characters in their stories.*
· *We can grow ideas about why authors make certain choices about characters. (e.g., Why are bullies often bigger than other kids? Why do detectives always have a best friend who helps them?)*
· *We can think about what our character teaches us about life, about kids, etc.*

Assessment:

· *Conference conversations about characters—ask probing questions to find out students' ability to infer, grow ideas (i.e., as students read, say, "What are you thinking about that?" or "What does that make you think about the character?")*
· *Examine work folders, look at T charts, sticky notes, etc., to determine use of skills, strategies, etc.*
· *Toward end of character study, ask students to freewrite about their character, sharing all they've learned and all they wonder about.*

Possible project/celebration/outcome of reading clubs: *(As much as possible, it's beneficial to let students develop ideas for projects instead of having a project imposed on them. The following is a list of ideas I've gathered from teachers.)*

· *Come to school as your favorite character—look and act like a character you've gotten to know.*
· *Write character riddles for the bulletin board.*
· *Design a pretend web page for your favorite character.*
· *Act out a scene that best represents your character.*
· *Write a guessing game about your character that features three facts about the character (e.g., I am a pig who loves to read, etc.)*
· *Introduce your character to someone else, either in writing, drawing, role playing, etc.)*

Sample Series Book Study Planning Guide

Reading Club Planning Guide

Reading Club Cycle: *"Readers Find a Series That They Enjoy and Read Several Books"*

Dates: _____

Readers' needs:

Baskets of series books reading clubs for all readers, work folders, sticky notes, note-taking sheets, T charts?

Iliamna, Randy, and Shelby—put together Brand-New Readers series (Levels B/C)

Quentin, Lilly, Frances, and Drake—introduce series at Level L via guided reading for a couple of days before launching series book study

Featured skills and strategies that I will teach:

· *identifying characters (main character, secondary characters, naming characters' relationships to one another)*

· *inferring to identify character traits and character motivations: using all the information we've got: our schema; attending to characters' actions, dialogue, appearance, facial expressions, gestures, etc.*

· *using schema acquired after reading first book in the series to read more books in series*

· *making connections, noticing differences between texts in a series (i.e., how characters change, plot conventions, etc.)*

· *accumulating text across chapters—determining importance; carrying info. from one chapter into the next and next*

· *summarizing story from the chapter level to the whole-book level*

Real-life purposes, habits, and goals readers might have:

Readers find a series that they enjoy and read several books in the series.

Readers get to know their characters in the series and notice when the characters grow, change, or act out of character.

Readers get familiar with a series' plot tendencies, author's craft, settings, etc., and keep this information in mind from one book to the next.

Readers try to find other series that they love.

Readers can name why they love a particular series and use what they know about themselves as readers to select another series.

Getting ready for reading clubs:

· *create a whole-class list of series books that are found in the classroom*

· *Read-aloud time: read a couple of books from a series over the course of the week, whole class talks about the series, model strategies for understanding the story, accumulating the story across a whole book*

· *Shared reading: pull dialogue exchanges from a familiar book to study dialogue (reading with fluency, reading with expression, strategies for figuring out who's talking, etc.)*

· *Homework: name series they know or love; talk to grown-ups at home about series they loved when they were little*

· *create series book baskets across levels, feature them prominently in library, design labels in choice time*

Teaching emphasis for reading clubs Week 1:

Readers have strategies that help them get into a series.

· *We can identify characters (main, secondary, name character relationships, select one to really get to know).*

· *We can infer what a character thinks by listening to words, paying attention to actions, looking at appearance, facial expressions, gestures.*

· *We use text evidence to support our ideas.*

· *We strategically choose the order in which we'll read the books (i.e., Is there a Book 1? If not, how does a reader choose which book in the series to start with?)*

· *We reread books, or parts of books, to deepen our understanding, to clear up confusion, etc.*

Teaching emphasis for reading clubs Week 2: *(Students may pick a different series or stay in the same series book club from Week 1.)*

When we read a series of books, we may see patterns in the stories, in the characters, in the way the books are written. (It might be necessary to repeat some teaching from the first week, based on what students are doing as readers, thinkers, and talkers.)

· *We can make connections between books—finding aspects that are similar and things that are different.*

· *We can notice if and when the character changes within a book or across books and try to figure out what or who caused the change.*

· *We can focus on the different relationships our characters have and think about what they teach us about our character.*

· *We can follow the stories across different books in the series to see if the author follows a similar pattern from book to book.*

· *We can find the problem and solution in the book, if there is one, and then look across texts to see if the author has particular issues he or she tends to write about in the series.*

Teaching Emphasis for Reading Clubs Week 3 (optional): *(What is the energy like for series book clubs? Is a third week necessary, helpful, and/or requested by students? If it is called for, will the instruction revisit previously taught strategies, will it focus on talking about texts, or will there be a new direction of study altogether?)*

We can put together baskets of books with books from different series and think lots about the connections between them. Some basket reconfigurations might be: series books that have mysteries; series books set in school; series that are funny; etc. The topics for many of these reconfigurations might possibly overlap with reading clubs about characters or authors (e.g., series books with strong girl characters; series books about detectives; series books by Cynthia Rylant; etc.)

· *We can compare different series and think about how they are similar and different.*

· *We can read different series to figure out our preferences and favorites.*

· *We can think about what our character teaches us about life, about kids, etc.*

Assessment:

· *Conference conversations about a series of books—ask probing questions to find out students' sense of the series, to determine how they are approaching a series (e.g., as students read, ask "What have you noticed about your series so far?" or "Why did you choose to read that book in the series first? How did reading that book help you with this book so far?")*

· *Examine work folders, look at T charts, sticky notes, etc., to determine use of skills, strategies, etc.*

· *Toward the end of series book study, ask students to freewrite about their series, describing what they know about it or how it has helped them as a reader, etc.*

Possible project/celebration/outcome of reading clubs: *(As much as possible, it's beneficial to let students develop ideas for projects instead of having a project imposed on them. The following is a list of ideas I've gathered from teachers.)*

· *Introduce your series to someone else (perhaps orally, in writing, or by drawing, for example).*

· *Rank the books in your series.*

· *Make a trail guide to your series (i.e., which book to start with, little tips that will help readers, blurbs for the books, etc.)*

· *Design a pretend web page for your series.*

· *Act out a memorable scene from a series.*

· *Write a guessing game about your series that features three facts (e.g., I am a pig who loves to read; etc.)*

Sample Author Study Planning Guide

Reading Club Planning Guide

Reading Club Cycle: *"Readers Have Favorite Authors and Read Their Texts"*

Dates: _____

Readers' needs:

Baskets of author study reading clubs for all readers (levels C/D to level M), work folders, sticky notes, note-taking sheets

Rebecca, Gregory, Samantha—more support with cross-checking (esp. for meaning)

Eliza, Rohan, Sean, Gabby—likely to pick high-level text; support with multiple story lines

Sabrina, Theria, Alex, Daniel, Julia G.—help moving past retelling to other kinds of book talk

Featured skills and strategies that I will teach:

- *making connections across books by an author (similarities, differences in characters, settings, themes, tone, writing style, etc.)*
- *comparing books by an author*
- *developing theories or ideas about an author based on his/her work*
- *using text evidence to support ideas*

Real-life purposes, habits, and goals readers might have:

Readers have authors they love and read anything they can by their favorite authors.

Readers compare books by an author and grow ideas about the author.

Readers have lots of reasons why particular authors are their favorites—genre, craft of writing, topic choice, types of characters, themes, etc.

Readers look for information about favorite authors.

Getting ready for reading clubs:

- *create a whole-class list of favorite authors*
- *Read-aloud time: read a few books by the same author across a week, lead whole-group conversations about the author, texts, etc., that will serve as models for partner talk*
- *Shared reading: compare/contrast a couple of texts by the same author within a week*
- *Homework: name authors they've loved from books we've read; talk to grown-ups at home about authors they loved when they were little*
- *create author baskets across levels, feature them prominently in library, design labels in choice time*
- *give students a couple of days to talk about what they think of the authors in their book baggies during their partner reading time as practice before they select an author study reading club*

Teaching emphasis for reading clubs Week 1:

When we read different texts by an author, we notice things the author often does as he or she writes.

· *notice similarities and differences across books*

· *learn information about author from blurb, Internet, etc.*

· *use information about author to think about choices he/she makes in her books*

· *reread books by an author to try to pick a favorite*

Teaching emphasis for reading clubs Week 2: *(Students may pick different authors or stay with the same author from Week 1.)*

When we study an author, we think about reasons why the author writes certain things in certain ways. (It might be necessary to repeat some teaching from the first week, based on what students are doing as readers, thinkers, and talkers.)

· *We can notice the copyright date of the books and think about how the author's work has changed over time.*

· *We can grow theories about where the author got his/her ideas based on all we know about an author.*

· *We can name and appreciate special qualities and talents of our favorite author.*

· *We can notice if and when the author changed across books and try to figure out what or who caused the change.*

· *We can grow ideas about what the author might want us to learn, to think about, to wonder about as we read his/her books.*

Teaching emphasis for reading clubs Week 3 (optional): *(What is the energy like for author clubs? Is a third week necessary, helpful, and/or requested by students? If it is called for, will the instruction revisit previously taught strategies, will it focus on talking about texts, or will there be a new direction of study altogether?)*

We can put together baskets of books with different authors who share something in common and think lots about the connections between them. (Some basket reconfigurations might be: authors who write about friendships; authors who write about their memories; authors who write about their childhood; authors who teach us lessons; authors who use lots of details; authors who are illustrators too; authors who write in different genres; authors who write funny books; etc.)

· *Different characters can have similar characteristics. How are different characters alike?*

· *We can compare different characters and think about what motivates them, how they react to things, and how they relate to the other characters in their stories.*

· *We can grow ideas about why authors make certain choices about characters (e.g., Why are bullies often bigger than other kids? Why do detectives always have a best friend who helps them?)*

Assessment:

· *Conference conversations about authors—ask probing questions to find out students' thoughts and ideas about the author they've chosen (e.g., What have you noticed about your author so far? What does that make you think? As you've read several books by your author, what are you thinking? Is there a special characteristic you could name about your author?)*

· *Examine work folders, look at T charts, sticky notes, etc., to determine use of skills, strategies, etc.*

· *Toward end of author study, ask students to freewrite about their author, sharing all they've learned and all they wonder about.*

Possible project/celebration/outcome of reading clubs: *(As much as possible, it's beneficial to let students develop ideas for projects instead of having a project imposed on them. The following is a list of things various students have chosen to do that I've gathered from teachers.)*

· *Top 3 or Top 5 lists: students rank and rate the books by their favorite author based on self-chosen criteria*

· *Author Promotions: students write "ads" for their author, "If you like books about mischievous kids, you'll love books by _____.")*

· *Book Reviews: students study the genre of book reviews and write one about a text or texts by their favorite author*

· *Guide to Favorite Authors: whole class puts together a guidebook about authors they've studied and perhaps present it to school library*

Appendix H: Focuses for Learning in Genre-Based Reading Clubs

---

Genre-Based Reading Clubs

What reading skills, strategies, habits, and goals
might we highlight in genre-based reading clubs?

Strategies and Skills for Reading Nonfiction Texts
- Readers know how to use the features of nonfiction to help them understand the information.
- Readers of nonfiction often have a purpose in mind as they read, such as information they are looking for or questions they want answered.
- Readers of nonfiction have strategies to help themselves read and understand tricky words and unfamiliar vocabulary.
- Readers of nonfiction can determine importance as they read.
- Readers of nonfiction can synthesize the text they've read and put it into their own words.
- Readers of nonfiction know how to take notes as they read.
- Readers of nonfiction accumulate information on topics.
- Readers of nonfiction compare and contrast information between books.
- Readers of nonfiction can become experts about their topics by having thoughts about the information they are learning.

Habits, Purposes, and Goals
Nonfiction readers may:
- have a new topic of interest that they want to learn about
- have a topic of interest that they want to learn more about
- read nonfiction to become experts about a particular topic
- read nonfiction to better understand something important to their lives
- read many kinds of texts on a particular topic
- learn lots of new vocabulary and concepts from their reading
- do something, make something, act in some way based on their reading
- like the feeling of learning new things as they read

Strategies and Skills for Reading Mysteries
· Readers of mystery books pay close attention to details in the text as they read.
· Readers of mystery books notice setting and pay close attention to what the characters do and say.
· Readers of mystery books look for clues to solve the mystery as they read.
· Readers of mystery books determine importance as they read to help them avoid following red herring clues.
· Readers of mystery books use text evidence to support their ideas.
· Readers of mystery books envision the sights and sounds of the story as they read to help them notice clues.
· Readers of mystery books make sensible predictions and abandon predictions if new evidence suggests they were wrong.

Habits, Purposes, and Goals
Readers of mysteries:
· pay close attention to the characters, settings, and plot
· reread parts of their books to find clues
· pay attention to the big events of the story but also notice details
· can retell parts of their books
· learn how to read mysteries well as they learn how mysteries tend to go
· make and revise predictions as they read through their books
· make mental pictures as they read
· understand the conventions of mysteries (clues, red herrings, resolution, etc.)
· might like stories with suspense
· might like stories in which there is something to solve

Strategies and Skills for Reading Concept Books
(i.e., ABC Books, Number Books, Opposites Books, Shape Books, Color Books, etc.)
· Readers of concept books have expectations for how their particular type of book tends to go (sense of genre).
· Readers of concept books can use their knowledge about the concepts to help them read (activating schema).
· Readers of concept books can compare and contrast books (making connections).
· Readers of concept books can learn new things and get new ideas from their books (synthesizing text, determining importance).
· Readers of concept books can predict what might be next as they turn the pages (predicting).

Habits, Purposes, and Goals
Concept book readers may:
· read a kind of concept book to learn more about the concept (alphabet, numbers, etc.)
· make predictions as they read
· like to read concept books because they know things about the concept featured in the book
· find favorite concept books
· talk with others about what they notice in concept books
· get stronger at reading concept books after reading a few of them
· learn how concept books go
· learn new things about the concept they are studying

Strategies and Skills for Reading Fairy Tales/Folktales

· Readers of fairy tales and folktales (FT/FTs) notice similarities and differences among different fairy tales/folk tales.
· Readers of FT/FTs are familiar with the conventions of FT/FTs, and this helps them predict how the story might go.
· Readers of FT/FTs get to know the characters well.
· Readers of FT/FTs compare and contrast different versions of the same FT/FT.
· Readers of FT/FTs pay attention to the problem and how it's solved.
· Readers of FT/FTs read the dialogue exchanges with expression and fluency because they know the characters well.

Habits, Purposes, and Goals
Readers of fairy tales and folktales:

· have favorite ones
· like to explore different versions of the stories
· like to retell their stories because they know them so well
· like to act out parts of their stories sometimes
· reread their favorite ones over and over
· might like stories set in bygone days
· might like stories that are not realistic or that have some sort of magical things happening

Appendix Í: Study Group Materials

The following items are included as possible professional study materials for teachers to use during or after reading this book.

A Girlfriends' Guide to Reading Clubs

(The title of this section comes with apologies to the real Girlfriends' Guides to a variety of topics, which you can find in your local independent bookstore. I also apologize to the boy-friends in the teaching profession who might be reading this, my husband included. I trust you know you're welcome here.)

When we try new things or want to learn about something, we often consult a text on the subject. In many cases, however, it's conversations about the task or topic that are immediately and perfectly helpful. For example, take panty hose. Imagine that the only authority on panty hose you have is the text on the package in which they came. You'd have washing instructions, the ubiquitous size grid, the name of the color, and information about the type of panty hose—opaque, control top, sandalfoot, sheer, and so on.

Do any packages tell you how to deal with the trauma of getting a run in your panty hose when you only have minutes left to get out the door for the big event you've been looking forward to for months? No, reading the package won't help with that. That's when you call your mom or your friend while trying to sound like you're not in a panic. Like some all-knowing character from the movies, they'll calmly tell you about the Clear Nail Polish Trick, and voilà, your problem is solved immediately and with empathy. The text on the package of panty hose didn't do that.

This does connect to reading clubs, believe it or not: Over the last couple of years, I've made dozens of presentations to teachers brand new to the idea of reading clubs and to teachers familiar with reading clubs, and I'm always interested in the questions teachers ask each other during the breaks and at the end of our sessions together as well as the responses they offer.

So, in this section, I'm going to share some of the typical questions that I've overheard and the answers I've collected from listening to teachers helping each other, hence this is the Girlfriend's Guide to Reading Clubs.

If my principal and some district administrators come into my classroom during reading clubs, and they ask me to tell them the pedagogical rationale for why my students are in reading clubs, what can I say?

Well, the first thing I want to say is that you're lucky. You're lucky because by asking you what you're doing, your principal acknowledges your professionalism and ability to figure out and talk about your instruction. Second, you're lucky because these visitors didn't just stop by your class, take a look around, and make huge assumptions about your teaching without ever talking to you about it. Instead, they bothered to ask you, dear teacher, about the events in your classroom. Here's hoping it wasn't a major interruption. Now, back to your question. There are several things you might consider telling your visitors.

- Reading clubs provide opportunities for students to orchestrate all of the reading work they've done so far. They are using the skills and strategies they've learned in authentic, self-directed ways. Reading clubs also provide opportunities to spotlight particular comprehension strategies as needed.

- Cycles of reading clubs rejuvenate the reading workshop and the reading work our students are doing. It's sort of like cross-training. The students get a different way of working together for a short amount of time and can therefore work different reading, thinking, and talking muscles. Then when a cycle of reading clubs is over, the students will bring their new power to their independent reading, thinking, and talking.

- Reading clubs reenergize partner work and book talks, because the books in reading clubs are connected in some way. This enables students to notice similarities and differences among the books, and it gives students lots of things to talk about. Almost always, this comparing/contrasting talk gives students an idea, theory, or thought they want to explore together.

- Reading clubs provide a bridge between school reading and real-life reading. What students do in reading clubs is very closely related to the work that real-life avid readers do. Reading club partners make plans for their reading, set goals, talk about what they've read and what they think about it, and accumulate knowledge about the topic.

Question to consider: What else could you say in support of reading clubs?

My student teacher is interviewing me for a paper, and she asked me to explain reading clubs. What is a concise way to define and describe reading clubs and the kinds of work students do in them?

A reading club is not a place in the room, nor is it a particular activity. A reading club is a couple of kids who meet to read and talk about books that connect in some way. Often one or two partnerships work within a reading club, and the reading club basket contains between four and eight books, depending on the club topic, the level at which readers are reading, and their plans for their work. The partners will read and reread the books in the club, talking about what they notice, what they're thinking, and what questions they have. They'll likely develop some ideas about ways to pursue their reading club topic, and they'll make plans for the kinds of work they want to do.

Question to consider: What other information would be helpful to tell the student teacher?

My friend is a teacher at another school who is interested in launching reading clubs in her classroom. She has a few really practical questions: What's in the reading club basket? How are students partnered for reading clubs?

Reading club baskets contain books or other texts that pertain to the topic of the reading club. In the old days, we used to fill the baskets up with as many books on the topic as we had (or borrowed). For example, one year, the kids who were studying Cynthia Rylant during a cycle of author study clubs had nearly twenty books in their basket, and I kept adding more. Once, during nonfiction reading clubs, I went to the public library and borrowed all the books on snails for the snails reading club. The partners were overwhelmed each time they faced their club basket filled to the top with books. Most of the work they did that week was to simply try to get through the books.

At one of our study group meetings at the Teachers College Reading and Writing Project, we talked about the problem presented when there are too many books in reading clubs. We realized that the students try hard just to get through all of the books, and it is overwhelming to them. They don't talk much about their reading because they just try to get it all read! After naming the problem and describing its characteristics, we decided that it makes more sense to begin with fewer books in a reading club basket. The priority is to first include texts that are just right for the partnership, and then maybe a title or two that would be considered high interest.

During cycles of reading clubs, students tend to provide each other with books. There is a real community-sharing component. During poetry clubs one year, Julia brought in a poetry anthology from home that contained several Langston Hughes poems. She put sticky notes on the pages with the Hughes poems and lent it to the students in the Langston Hughes club. It often happens that students will notice that a book they have in their independent book bin relates to another reading club in the classroom, and they generously lend the book to the club. I invite this to happen, and we celebrate when it does.

In addition to books, it's important that students have all the reading supplies they need in their reading club so they are not spending precious reading club time looking for index cards, or sticky notes, or a sharpened pencil. Here are some items that I've tended to include in each of the reading club baskets:

· A folder (either a pocket folder or a manila folder) for each of the partnerships in the club so they can "file" the work they are doing in their clubs. The folders might contain note-taking sheets, planning sheets, sticky notes they've accumulated, to-do lists, etc.

· Sticky notes, index cards, pencils, bookmarks, etc.

· A variety of blank, yet formatted, note-taking sheets, often in the form of a graphic organizer. Students decide which graphic organizer best holds their work. We had blank T-charts, a blank Venn diagram (with a decent-size inner, overlapping section), a blank web, and so on. My students learned how to use these note-taking sheets during other times of the day, such as during science time, so I didn't have to do much teaching about them during reading club time. If I were to add a sheet that was unfamiliar to them, I would demonstrate how to use it during a mini-lesson or model how to use it during read-aloud time.

There are several ways that teachers have arranged partnerships for reading clubs. In many classrooms, students work with their usual reading partners during reading club cycles. This eliminates the labor and time needed to reassign partnerships. Also, because the reading partners are at or very near the same reading level, it's easier to ensure that the reading club books will be appropriate for each of the partners.

That said, there are some reasons why teachers may switch up the partners during reading club cycles. One year, during a nonfiction reading club cycle on insects (which also supported our science unit), my students signed up for the insect topics they were most interested in studying. From their expressions of interest, I assigned partners with similar reading levels as much as possible. If seven students wanted to study butterflies, I would assign the ability-based partners and then see if the extra student wanted to pick another topic. If his heart were set on butterflies, I might try to enlist another student at or near his level to join him in the butterfly study.

This brings us to the question of how students end up in particular reading clubs. I try to let my students feel that they've chosen the club as much as possible, but sometimes I have to guide students to particular clubs, without much kicking and screaming, I hope. This is especially and unfortunately the case mostly with struggling readers. For example, during a character study reading club cycle, Sam wanted desperately to be in the Horrible Harry club because his best friend, Michael, said that was the club he wanted to pick. Horrible Harry books were much too difficult for Sam, so I had to try to entice him into another character club. I said something like, "Sam, I know you are really excited about Horrible Harry, but I think that another character club might fit you better as a reader. I have an idea though. You can take a Horrible Harry book home to read with a grown-up, and you and the grown-up can be in a Horrible Harry club together. That way, you'll get to know the Horrible Harry books, and I bet you and Michael can have some fun talks about Harry. But for your reading club in class, you need to pick a character that lives in books that are just right for you. Let's see. Hmmm. What about Titch? He's a kid that has some fun stuff going on... Take a look at Titch. I think you'd like to get to know him." Sam agreed (albeit reluctantly) to join Nicole in the Titch club, but in the end, they enjoyed their work together while reading books that were just right for them.

So, girlfriends, boyfriends, and significant others, I hope this section answered some questions about reading clubs.

Reflecting on Our Personal Experiences in the Reading Clubs in Our Lives

One of the most helpful ways to envision reading clubs in our classrooms is to think about times in your life when you've read as if you were in your own reading club. (It's important to differentiate a reading club from a book club—participants in a book club typically read one book at a time and then meet to talk about that book.)

I've included a few actual real-life reading club scenarios that teachers have shared with me to help you think about the times in your life when you were in a reading club, whether you knew it or not.

Reading Club Scenario 1

The *New York Times Book Review* just came out with a list the top twenty-five novels of the last twenty-five years. You decide to create a little project for yourself. Over the next year (or ten), you plan to read each of the books on the list that you haven't read yet. You ask your best friend to do this with you so that you have someone with whom you can talk about the books. Another goal that arises from this project is to create your own list of top twenty-five favorite books, which requires that you reread lots of old favorites.

Reading Club Scenario 2

Your cousin is getting married, and he's asked you to select a poem to read aloud during the ceremony. You're a little excited and intimidated because you want to pick the *perfect* poem for the occasion and for the couple. You spend a few evenings at an independent bookstore reading through poetry books trying to find the perfect poem. You find three poems that seem like they'd be great, so you enlist the help of another friend to help you decide which one to read during the ceremony. You and your friend read the poems and talk about the couple, trying to decide which poem connects best with their personalities and interests, as well as with the tone of the wedding.

Reading Club Scenario 3

You're in line at the supermarket, and one of the tabloid headlines screams, "Surprising Secret Plans of Brad and Angelina." Oh my goodness! You grab a copy of the tabloid and move over to a longer checkout line so you have time to read about these secret plans. You have to know. The person ahead of you wants a price check on several things, so you have even more time to pick up another tabloid with a teaser that reads, "Brad and Angelina Struggling to Make It Work!" Well, you must read that. After all, it's important to be well-rounded, right? You compare the articles and realize that they contradict each other over and over again. You notice that none of the quotes are attributed to either Brad or Angelina and instead come from "a close friend of the couple," or "a family member." You realize you don't care much about the secret plans anymore, and you turn to a photo essay titled, "Celebrities' Trendiest Kids." Your groceries are getting scanned by this point, and you decide to buy the magazine for a friend because her child wears the same cool shoes as Gwyneth Paltrow's son.

Reading Club Scenario 4

You're at a barbecue, and all of a sudden there's a heated discussion about gas prices, oil exploration in the Arctic National Wildlife Refuge (ANWR), and alternative energy policy. You don't say much, although you're instinctively against oil drilling in the ANWR. You hesitate to participate in the discussion because you feel like you don't have any factual information to support your opinions. You hear lots of contradictory information, so you decide to wade through the issue to solidify your stand. You Google "ANWR" and find gazillions of items to explore on both sides of the issue.

Reading Club Scenario 5

You love to read spy thrillers and are excited that a new one by your favorite author is coming out at the end of the month. In the meantime, you reread an earlier book by this author to get yourself primed to read the new one, and you set your TiVo to record her interview on *Larry King Live*. You call your best friend to tell her about the new book, and you decide that you'll both read it right away.

Reading Club Scenario 6

You read an interview with the author of a newly published historical fiction title, and you decided to buy it, even though you rarely read historical fiction. The author sounded really interesting, and the book sounded great. The book is set during World War I. When you're finished reading it, you realize that you'd like to learn more about this period of history, so you ask your friend, who is a history buff, to recommend a title of a good nonfiction book about that time period.

I suspect that most of you can make a connection with at least one of these scenarios, even if the details of your own personal reading club are considerably different. These real-life reading club scenarios have a few characteristics in common whether the reader is skimming tabloids or reading historical nonfiction:

· In a span of time, the reader reads at least a couple of texts that are connected in some way. They may be connected in a variety of ways, such as by topic, by genre, by author, by readers' purpose, and so on.

· In each of these scenarios, there is a social component in, around, and behind the reading work. The readers talk about their texts with others, choose their texts based on the recommendations of others, or have other people in their mind while they're reading.

· The reading in these reading club scenarios tends to result in some sort of action or project, a new understanding, or an intention to explore something new or different. The reading affects the readers' lives in some way.

I invite you to think about times in your life when you've been in a reading club. Here are some guiding questions that you might consider to help you think about your reading club and its possible implications for your teaching:

1. Why did you start this reading club in your life? How did it all begin? What were the circumstances and your intentions?

2. What were some of the things you did while you were in the reading club? How did you gather texts? What was the social aspect of this work? Who did you talk to, who did you think about, and how did they affect your reading?

3. What was the outcome of the reading club? How did it affect or change your life? What happened next?

4. What can you bring from your personal experience into your instruction?

References

Allington, Richard L. 2001. *What Really Matters for Struggling Readers: Designing Research-Based Programs*. New York: Longman.

Anderson, Carl. 2000. *How's It Going? A Practical Guide to Conferring with Student Writers*. Portsmouth, NH: Heinemann.

Calkins, Lucy. 2001. *The Art of Teaching Reading*. New York: Longman.

Calkins, Lucy, and Natalie Louis. 2003. "Writing for Readers: Teaching Skills and Strategies." In *Units of Study in Primary Writing: A Yearlong Curriculum*, ed. Lucy Calkins. Portsmouth, NH: Heinemann.

Calkins, Lucy, with Marjorie Martinelli. 2006. "Launching the Writing Workshop." In *Units of Study for Teaching Writing in Grades 3–5*, ed. Lucy Calkins. Portsmouth, NH: Heinemann.

Clay, Marie M. 1998. *By Different Paths to Common Outcomes*. Portland, ME: Stenhouse.

Cole, Ardith D. 2003. *Knee to Knee, Eye to Eye: Circling in on Comprehension*. Portsmouth, NH: Heinemann

Collins, Kathy. 2004. *Growing Readers: Units of Study in the Primary Classroom*. Portland, ME: Stenhouse.

Daley, Allyson. 2005. *Partner Reading: A Way to Help All Readers Grow*. New York: Scholastic.

Duke, Nell, and V. Susan Bennett-Armistead. 2003. *Reading & Writing Informational Text in the Primary Grades*. New York: Scholastic.

Fountas, I., and G. Pinnell. 1996. *Guided Reading: Good First Teaching for All Children*. Portsmouth, NH: Heinemann.

Goldberg, G., and J. Serravallo. 2007. *Conferring with Readers: Supporting Each Student's Growth and Independence*. Portsmouth, NH: Heinemann.

Heard, Georgia. 1989. *For the Good of the Earth and Sun: Teaching Poetry*. Portsmouth, NH: Heinemann.

Johnson, Pat. 2006. *One Child at a Time: Making the Most of Your Time with Struggling Readers, K–6*. Portland, ME: Stenhouse.

Johnston, Peter H. 2004. *Choice Words: How Our Language Affects Children's Learning*. Portland, ME: Stenhouse.

Mermelstein, Leah. 2007. *Don't Forget to Share: The Crucial Last Step in the Writing Workshop*. Portsmouth, NH: Heinemann.

Miller, Debbie. 2002. *Reading with Meaning: Teaching Comprehension in the Primary Grades*. Portland, ME: Stenhouse.

Owocki, Gretchen. 2003. *Comprehension: Strategic Instruction for K–3 Students*. Portsmouth, NH: Heinemann.

Owocki, Gretchen. 2007. *Literate Days: Reading and Writing with Preschool and Primary Children*. Portsmouth, NH: Heinemann.

Pierce, Kathryn Mitchell, and Carol J. Gilles. 1993. *Cycles of Meaning: Exploring the Potential of Talk in Learning Communities*. Portsmouth, NH: Heinemann.

Routman, Regie. 2003. *Reading Essentials: The Specifics You Need to Teach Reading Well*. Portsmouth, NH: Heinemann.

Santman, Donna. 2005. *Shades of Meaning: Comprehension and Interpretation in Middle School*. Portsmouth, NH: Heinemann.

Smith, Frank. 1988. *Joining the Literacy Club: Further Essays into Education*. Portsmouth, NH: Heinemann.

Taberski, Sharon. 2000. *On Solid Ground: Strategies for Teaching Reading K–3*. Portsmouth, NH: Heinemann.

index

Page numbers followed by an *f* indicate figures.

A

B

C